# A Jockey's Life

Also by Dick Francis

*Break In*
*Proof*
*The Danger*
*Banker*
*Twice Shy*
*Reflex*
*Whip Hand*
*Trial Run*
*Risk*
*In the Frame*
*High Stakes*
*Knockdown*
*Slayride*
*Smokescreen*
*Bonecrack*
*Rat Race*
*Enquiry*
*Forfeit*
*The Sport of Queens*
*Blood Sport*
*Flying Finish*
*Odds Against*
*Dead Cert*
*For Kicks*
*Nerve*

# A Jockey's Life
## The Biography of Lester Piggott

Dick Francis

G. P. Putnam's Sons / New York

G. P. Putnam's Sons
*Publishers Since 1838*
200 Madison Avenue
New York, NY 10016



Set in Lasercomp Sabon

Library of Congress Cataloging-in-Publication Data

Francis, Dick.
A jockey's life.

Includes index.
1. Piggott, Lester, 1935– . 2. Jockeys—Great
Britain—Biography. I. Title.
SF336.P5F73 1986 798.4'0092'4 [B] 86-9467

Printed in the United States of America
1 2 3 4 5 6 7 8 9 10

# Contents

# Author's Note

The Appendices to this book are the work of Dorothy Laird, who for her own pleasure kept records of Lester's wins (and those of other jockeys) for very many years.

I am most grateful to her for offering me the use of them as they have proved invaluable throughout. She also willingly searched for obscure details whenever I asked, and checked all my facts and read the proofs.

Dorothy Laird is the distinguished author of authorised biographies of the Queen (*How the Queen Reigns*) and of Queen Elizabeth the Queen Mother. Her next authorised biography will be of Princess Anne. She has written also a deeply researched history of Ascot racecourse.

There is no bibliography for this book as it has been written from prime sources.

I read only a 36-page booklet by Charles Fawcus, 'The Classic 28', finding it very helpful with chronology.

## List of Illustrations

# A Jockey's Life

# Introduction

The trouble with being a genius is that to yourself you are not. You are you, a familiar identity, understood. Genius is perceived by others, but not from the inside out.

To Lester, being Lester is normal. A prosaic fact of existence. Nothing to get steamed up about. To everyone else, the idea of being Lester is incredible.

Genius is something beyond ability, beyond talent, beyond learning. Genius is the plus factor which turns admiration to a lump in the throat and leaves you wondering why your own feet are forever stuck in treacle.

To watch Lester switch a horse to the outside, set it running and take it to the post with a length in hand, to see the inward smile with which he acknowledged his mastery privately to himself, this was to see in action the same sort of total professional understanding that has moved every other creative or interpretive genius since history began.

There is a tendency to revere most those manifestations of genius which leave visible objects to posterity, like buildings, paintings, inventions, books. In all bygone ages, other achievements have had to rely for immortality on a combination of factual records and convincing eye-witness reports, and genius which expressed itself physically - voice, personality, muscular skill - had largely to be taken on trust. The Electronic Age of the twentieth century has changed all that, and performers have come into their own at last.

Electronics arrived too late to give substance to the legend of

Fred Archer, and came barely adequately in time to do justice to Gordon Richards, but they have done Lester Piggott proud. The films of his races are there for ever and, although we now may take this for granted, just think how fascinating it would have been had *we* been able to see a screening of Diomed winning the 1780 Derby.

With so much of Lester's life on permanent record, with video tapes by the thousand and newspaper clippings by the ton, one might expect the world to know him well.

Except by sight, it does not.

Few of the electronic-age heroes have remained so private while living in so public a context. Few have retreated so successfully from self-exposure, parrying every exploring thrust with a wrinkled forehead, a half grin, and long, long, non-speaking pauses. In the public side of his life, Lester seldom explains, seldom defends himself, never blames others, never bursts out in temperamental rages. Lester's public life, to an extraordinary extent, goes on privately inside his own head.

Everyone journeys through character as well as time. The person one becomes depends on the person one has been, and no one is static from birth to death. Like everyone else, Lester grew and changed and adjusted, living the common voyage across experience to maturity. No one should look upon a man at fifty as being the same as he was at seventeen, although all too often they do. Lester's life is not just a tally of dazzling achievements but also the story of the development of an exceptional man.

# Origins

Bonfires blazed coast to coast the night Lester was born. Bright coloured stars filled the sky and every schoolchild in Britain knew the date. The fifth of November, 1935. Fireworks in honour of Guy Fawkes, who failed to blow up the Houses of Parliament on the same day in 1605.

Not that his parents cared much about gunpowder, treason and plot, or the fun and bangs going on all around. Iris and Keith Piggott were in Wantage Hospital in Berkshire, one exhausted but both relieved at the safe arrival of their first – and only – child. They already supposed that as he was a boy he would become a jockey. The seeds of his destiny were so thickly sown, the road ahead so clearly marked, that on the day of his birth the only real question was how far and how well he would travel.

The passing of a family skill from one generation to the next is common in many trades, and it seems to occur more routinely the more the job invades normal family life. Racing, for those earning a living by it, is a total commitment, the almost exact opposite of the general norm. The job is there from dawn to bedtime, public holidays definitely included: and it is fair to say that no one does it who doesn't like it.

In both Iris's and Keith's families, the involvement with racing was absolute and of long duration. Iris was a Rickaby, a name stretching back into the mists of Turf history. Her great-grandfather, Fred, trained the winner of the Derby in 1855, a colt named Wild Dayrell. Her father, another Fred, won the Oaks as a jockey in 1896 on the filly Canterbury Pilgrim, the One Thousand Guineas in 1891 and a host of other races besides. Her brother, Fred, won the One Thousand Guineas four times and died during the First World War in his mid-twenties. Her brother's son Bill Rickaby was in the leading ranks of jockeys from after the Second World War until his retirement in 1968.

Iris herself was a jockey of no mean achievement and would undoubtedly have won a great many more races had they been regularly open to women. In her day, there was only one race, the ancient and venerable Newmarket Town Plate, still held once a year over four and a half miles of Newmarket Heath. Men ride against women, all being amateurs, and the prize is traditionally a pound of sausages and a bottle of champagne. Iris won the race twice, and once finished second. (The girl who beat her, and who was her greatest contemporary rival, was Eileen Joel who, as Mrs John Rogerson, became one of the best-loved owners in British racing.)

In Keith Piggott's family, the racing tradition had been repeatedly passed down through the female line. In the thoroughbred Stud Book, the dam's influence is acknowledged to be as persistent as the sire's, and what's good for horses seems to hold true enough also for humans.

There was also through several generations a steady tie with one place, the training stables at Danebury, near Stockbridge in Hampshire. As far as can be reliably traced, the Piggott family's racing ancestry started in earnest with a certain 'Old John' Day, who farmed and trained at Danebury in the late eighteenth century. He had many sons, nearly all of whom were engaged in racing. One, Sam, won the Derby three times – on Gustavus, 1821; Priam, 1830; and Pyrrhus the First in 1846. The time-span alone proves the durability of his talent.

Another, William, distinguished himself by being warned-off for nobbling a horse trained by his father, and it must be admitted that the Days of Danebury were, for several decades, a red hot source of scandalous results and huge betting coups which were considered excessive even in their own immoderate times.

But skill spurted through them all. A third brother, John – known as John Day II – amassed Classics like picking raspberries.

He won sixteen altogether, but no Derbys. The Oaks and the One Thousand Guineas fell to him five times each which suggests that he was extra good with fillies, and he also won the Two Thousand Guineas four times and the St Leger twice.

John Day II took out a training licence while still a regular jockey, and prepared Pyrrhus the First for the Derby, won by his brother Sam. For years he trained at Danebury, but in later life moved to Findon, near Worthing in Sussex, a village with a racing tradition as strong as Lambourn's. (A hundred years after him, the same Downs saw the emergence of chart-topper Ryan Price.)

A third brother, also confusingly called John, and known as John Day III, turned his attention exclusively to training. He took over Danebury when John Day II moved out, although his own successes there seem to have been moderate. He did, however, produce one jewel in the shape of a daughter, Kate. She, not surprisingly, did as many trainers' daughters do, and married the stable jockey. She also had the good sense to pick a remarkably good jockey, Tom Cannon, who might have been champion for the best part of his long career had it not been for his staggering contemporary rival, Fred Archer. Tom Cannon, Fred Archer and a third great jockey, George Fordham, struck sparks off each other all over Britain from about 1870 to Archer's death in 1886, in displays of jockeyship which have probably never been surpassed.

All three were endowed with endless physical energy, travelling hundreds of miles by train and horse in pursuit of winners. Fred Archer several times rode more than 200 winners in a season, a feat seldom achieved even now with cars and aeroplanes. Archer was champion for thirteen years and Fordham for fourteen. Tom Cannon himself rode 1,544 winners, including the Two Thousand Guineas four times, the Oaks four times, the One Thousand Guineas three times, the St Leger once, and the Derby once, on Shotover in 1882.

It is easy enough always, as each generation becomes 'modern' and as history recedes, to denigrate the achievements of earlier men, to think of their successes as somehow second rate because they were not scored within living memory. But Archer, Fordham and Cannon were, according to all who saw and evaluated them through piercingly knowledgeable eyes, the equal of anything racing will ever produce.

Cannon, of the three, had the smallest frame and the gentlest nature, and relied for success more on judgment of pace and delicacy of touch than on sheer brute force. He too took out a trainer's licence while still actively engaged as a jockey, and became the master of Danebury. In 1888 he sent Playfair from there to Aintree to win the Grand National.

Tom Cannon and Kate Day produced three sons and a daughter, and all three boys became jockeys. The eldest, Mornington (Morny), was six times champion and the second, Kempton, won the Derby in 1904 on St Amant. The third, Tom, made less impression in the saddle and set up as a trainer at Compton in Berkshire. Their sister, Margaret, did as her mother before her, and married one of her father's stable jockeys.

Margaret Cannon's husband came from an ancestry of farmers who rode to hounds and as amateur jockeys, but who were not in the mainstream of Flat racing tradition. By the time of the marriage, financial disaster had overtaken her prospective father-in-law who had lost his farm and livelihood through an outbreak of foot-and-mouth disease and had taken instead to pub-keeping as the landlord of the Crown Hotel at Nantwich in Cheshire. Margaret Cannon married the elder of his sons, an ex-apprentice to her father at Danebury. His name was Ernie Piggott.

Ernie Piggott grew into a tall stylish man with a strong, good-looking, intelligent face and prowess to match. In his earlier years, he rode as much in France and Belgium as in England, but increasing weight meant he had to turn to steeplechasing instead of the Flat. Only after he won the 1912 Grand National on Jerry M did he settle finally in England.

His illustrious career included two more Grand National wins, both on Poethlyn – one, the war-time substitute at Gatwick in 1918, the second back at Aintree the following year – and he was champion jump jockey three times.

Ernie Piggott and Margaret Cannon had two sons, Victor and Keith. Both rode as jump jockeys between the two world wars, with Keith probably having the greater success. Small and immensely sturdy, he took more than five hundred winners past the post, including the Champion Hurdle winner African Sister in 1939.

Keith, born in 1904, was apprenticed on the Flat to a trainer called Bert Lines in Newmarket, and afterwards transferred to Frank Barling. His new boss sent Grand Parade to win the 1919 Derby, and also took ten of the twenty-four races at one Royal Ascot meeting, a record so far unbroken. Keith, then growing heavier, returned to his father Ernie and rode jumpers both for him and trainers like Tom Coulthwaite who trained the Grand National winners, Eremon, Jenkinstown and Grakle; Keith would have been on Grakle but for breaking his thigh and being laid up for a year. In later life came compensation in the shape of Ayala whom he trained to win the National in 1963.

All this lay ahead, however, when in a union universally considered appropriate, Keith Piggott married Iris Rickaby on 16 September, 1929.

# Childhood

With such a heredity, the boy resulting from the confluence of these families would have to have been blind, retarded or limbless *not* to have been a jockey; and he was none of these things. He did have one quite severe physical defect, invisible and unsuspected, but it would have taken more than that to stop him.

They called him Lester Keith. Keith, of course, after his father, and Lester after Iris's brother Frederick Lester Rickaby who was killed at the end of the First World War. He in turn had been named after the American jockey Lester Reiff, who rode in Britain at the turn of the century.

Iris Rickaby Piggott took her child back to the square, modern, red-bricked house where she and Keith lived in the village of Letcombe Regis in Berkshire. Keith was at the height of his career. His father, Ernie, was quietly training a few horses just down the road, and his uncle Charlie (Ernie's brother) was saddling a stream of them for Keith to ride from his stable by Cheltenham racecourse. There were enough successes to make life sweet, and no tragedies bad enough to sour it.

Lester's childhood, as far as his family went, was rooted in a secure, caring, hardworking background. He describes his childhood as having been happy; which is to say not that he was in any way pampered, but that he received exactly the sort and amount of affection which suited him best. From his mother, he got no-nonsense love and a great deal of worldly level-headed advice. From his father, instruction from an early age in the finer points of horsemanship and an intense and lasting father–son devotion.

What the parents had to work on was raw material imbued with talent, tenacity and intelligence, and if their imprint still shows on the finished article, one can hardly say they did a bad job.

The infant Lester was variously described as a sweet little boy and a proper little devil, which sounds totally normal. His most irritating habit as a toddler was to sit on the floor with his back to people and not answer when he was spoken to. He frequently didn't do what he was told, and he didn't like strangers.

At quite a young age he had an operation for adenoids, as it was considered that they were blocking the back of his nose and hindering his speech. Not a great deal was made of his excessively nasal intonation as, in fact, his father spoke in much the same way, though to a lesser extent. Nor was much weight given to the fact that he spoke seldom because, when he did speak, his command of words was suitable for his age. Out with the adenoids, it was thought, and hey presto.

Out came the adenoids and Lester went on precisely as before. After a while, when he was about four, a further and more radical adenoid operation was carried out, this time removing tonsils as well. And it was after this that the specialist treating him asked Iris and Keith to go and see him, and to bring their son. They went and talked in his consulting room, with Lester playing quietly on the floor.

'I think,' said the ear-nose-and-throat man, 'that your son is deaf.'

The parents were astounded and disbelieving. 'He can't be,' they said. 'He hears what we say. He answers us.'

'He hears a little,' they were told, 'but he's very bright, and he lip-reads.'

Iris and Keith still didn't believe him.

'I'll show you,' the doctor said. He got Lester to stand at his knee, and asked him a simple question. Lester answered without hesitation.

'He's not deaf,' Keith asserted.

The doctor shook his head, picked up a large sheet of paper and held it in front of his mouth so that Lester could see only his eyes looking over the top. He asked Lester another question, just as simple. Lester gave no sign at all of having heard. The doctor put down the paper and asked the same question again. Lester answered at once.

This demonstration, once or twice repeated with exactly the same results, reluctantly convinced the Piggotts. They cast their minds back and found explanations for so much behaviour that they had considered just 'Lester's way'. The refusal to answer when he had his back to people: he didn't know they wanted an answer unless he saw them speak. The impedimented speech: he didn't know how words *ought* to sound. He didn't obey ... when he couldn't hear the instructions; and the withdrawal from strangers was because he found their lips difficult to read.

'And it explained,' Keith said, 'a habit he had of going right up close to the wireless and pressing his ear against it. He did it often ... but we never thought it was because he couldn't hear properly.'

Tests were made. Lester's ears proved to be receptive to low-frequency sounds but progressively insensitive higher up the scale. He has the sort of hearing which lets in whispers and blots out screams. He was fitted with a hearing aid, but he wouldn't wear it. He simply took it off and left it lying about, and all efforts to persuade him ended in failure. Lester, said his mother resignedly, never did what he didn't want to. He continued to lip-read and to speak indistinctly and seemed perfectly happy with things as they were.

Lester's ability to lip-read grew like an extra sense at such an early age that not only his parents but countless others afterwards didn't realise he couldn't hear much of what they said. He says himself that it's no disadvantage as if he is bored with a conversation he doesn't have to listen, and there's no doubt that his habit of switching off goes right back to birth.

It is still no use expecting a Piggott answer if you speak to the back of his head. No use looking too far away from him while you speak. He hears chiefly with his eyes, prefers to talk to one person at a time, and has a tendency to look uncomprehending for long periods at receptions. On the other hand, when everything is quiet at night he can hear distant sounds, like owls hooting and trains running on rails three miles away; and he can hear quite well on the telephone, even on ordinary receivers not fitted with a volume-booster switch like his own at home.

Lester himself is inclined to think his deafness resulted from falling on his head off a pony when he was six. He was knocked unconscious and suffered from concussion, and he believes – wrongly – that this made him deaf. It's probable he thinks so because it must have been at about this time that he came to realise that his hearing was different from that of everyone else.

The difficulty with hearing and the fact of his being an only child combined powerfully from the start to turn him inwards to himself. Add to this natural isolation a focus of interest, and you have all the ingredients of super-single-mindedness. He saw horses all around him: they were his father's job, his mother's interest, his family's tradition. The barrier of deafness kept most of the rest of the world away as if in the misty distance. The active young mind fed and filled and grew on talk of racing, and nothing much else seemed as real or as important.

It wouldn't have been enough, of course, without one other decisive gift: the bonus that he was born with the build and balance of a natural athlete. As a child, his face was rounded and chubby and his body that of any normal boy. He was slight but not tiny for his age, nor in any obvious way physically remarkable, but he was endowed nonetheless with innate economy and grace of movement. He could run faster than any others of his age that he came across, and developed an early skill at any game he tried to play. At school, the retired soldier in charge of physical education, Sergeant-Major Glaser, spotted this flair when Lester was at least as young as seven, and encouraged him to run and to play cricket. When Lester was eleven, Glaser told him he could earn his living at any sport he cared to choose.

Lester clearly remembers this first coach, but the old talent scout was fighting a losing battle: every day after school, Lester's single desire was to get on his bicycle and pedal home to the only really important activity in life, riding horses.

The first school he attended was King Alfred's in Wantage, a sturdy old building on the side of the town nearest Letcombe Regis. Home and school were about two miles of leafy lanes apart with no main roads to cross, so that as soon as he could manage it, before he was six, he took himself to and from by bike. Even allowing for the fact that more was expected from war-time children by way of physical effort, it is evident that

Lester's incredible stamina dated from a very early age. The road from Letcombe to Wantage is by no means flat.

As might be expected, he did not excel academically. Quite probably he might have done if he had been inclined that way, but his whole cast of mind, apart from his difficulty in hearing the masters, was against it. He did enough school work to keep himself out of trouble and out of bottom place in class, and it is clear that his lack of academic progress was due to lack of interest, not of intellect. What he did want to learn, he learned fast and thoroughly, and first of all he wanted to read.

He read everything to do with racing. Not a word of 'Dickens and books like that'. Nothing in the mainstream of the national literary heritage. Nothing about history, art, music or philosophy. Everything about racing. And literally everything he could lay his hands on, from ancient books of memoirs to the stop-press in the evening papers.

His own antecedent, William Day, wrote two fascinating books of revelation about the early Victorian racing scene which make the modern Turf look like an antiseptic nursery school. Those, and books like George Lambton's immortal *Men and Horses I Have Known* were what Lester devoured instead of Noddy. The habit of reading, once acquired, is impossible to shake off. Lester reckons he has now read almost every book ever published on the subject of racing, and finds reading his chief relaxation.

Next after reading, he wanted to learn about figures. Not just twice-times-two, and certainly not cube roots and the square on the hypotenuse. He was not even inclined towards the mathematics of betting, in the way of the baby who was taught to count by his bookmaker father – 'One, six-to-four, two . . .'

Lester's figures were those to be found in the delicate salmon-pink pages of the *Financial Times*. Lester's 'Pink 'Un' told him the winners on the Stock Market and summed up the prospects of fast movers in minerals and shipping. Lester by the age of thirteen knew his way round the *Financial Times* as familiarly as round *Comic Cuts*.

Iris remembers a day when the bank manager came to call and tried to find a certain report he wished to discuss. Lester watched him turning the closely-printed pages unsuccessfully and began fidgetting with impatience. Finally, unable to stand the sight any longer, he snatched the paper out of the bank manager's hands and turned immediately to the page required.

'He was quite small,' Iris says. 'The bank manager was astonished.'

Lester's interest in finance has been called everything from 'shrewd' to 'too mean to give you a dirty look'. Under every stone on the Turf there are stories of how Lester avoids paying for anything if he can inveigle someone else into doing it, stories all trying to prove that, compared with Lester, Scrooge was a non-starter. Lester never pays, they say. Lester is always missing at hand-in-pocket time. Lester gives you things, and then asks for the money.

Lester, on the other hand, is demonstrably not a miser, because his parsimoniousness does not begin at home. He lives well, dresses well, and spends a lot of money on things he likes, and he always has. Towards his own family he is open-handedly generous, and when among long-time friends pays his share as a matter of course.

According to Iris, his closeness as far as other people are concerned is her fault. 'I detest spongers,' she said. 'When Lester was a young child, I knew so many jockeys who earned a lot and had nothing to show for it when they retired. There was one who lived at Cheltenham who had a beautiful house and everything of the best, but he didn't take care of his money. There were always hangers-on, letting him pay for everything. He ended up with nothing. No house, no money ... taking any odd-job, and when he was old, practically begging. I saw him once outside a racecourse, walking up and down in sandwich boards. It made me so angry. And there were others. One of them earned thousands and thousands, but he had no sense. He thought he ought always to pay for everyone because he earned more than they did. He would have five or six so-called friends with him most of the time, and he would pay all their hotel bills and so on ... They just took all they could get out of him and never suggested he should save for when he had to stop riding. So then, when he did stop, he hadn't put a great deal away. He'd earned enough to be comfortably off for the rest of his life but he'd wasted it all on bloodsuckers who deserted him at once, as soon as his money dried up. Well, I suppose Lester heard me talking about this a great deal, and certainly I did warn him over and over again not to let people take advantage of him, not to lavish his money on people who were only out for what they could get. I told him to save for being well-off when he was older. And I suppose that perhaps I did rather too good a job.'

Her ever persisting passion on this subject entirely explains Lester's evasiveness with cash. She gave him as a little boy not just casual advice on the subject once or twice, but fierce and often reiterated cautionary tales about the poverty awaiting victims of spongers.

Lester grew up with a determination not to be 'done' that has lasted all his life and is as much an automatic part of his psychological make-up as looking before crossing the road. The people who have to pay up small sums after Lester has walked away think of each such act as a deliberate meanness directed towards them personally. They're wrong: Lester walks away from paying out of deep-seated subconscious mental habit. It doesn't seem mean to him, but merely normal and prudent.

Occasionally he does play it awarely as a game, grinning fiendishly as he manoeuvres someone else into coughing up for the taxi. Occasionally, on the other hand, he will pay up cheerfully when outmanoeuvred by someone else; cheerfully, that is, when it is quite clear to both Lester and opponent that a game has been played.

Back in his childhood, though, it was no game. He learned that a fool and his money were soon parted, and he didn't mean to be a fool.

Life for all wartime children tended to be austere, and it is significant that at the start of hostilities Lester was two months short of four. From then until he was nearly ten, during his most impressionable years, he heard phrases like 'make a sacrifice', 'do without', and 'there isn't any' used as regular everyday speech. Half the children in his class at school were refugees, evacuated from London. He saw no lighted windows after dark. He lived in a world where treats were rare, new clothes scarce, and petrol for pleasure not allowed. He saw no bananas, lemons or pineapples. Sweets were rationed to four ounces a week, and there was no ice cream. Everyone lived on a boring and restricted diet and put up with it more or less cheerfully. Lester, therefore, passed his childhood without lavish food and without resenting its absence, a basic training which was to stand him in very good stead.

Of all the deprivations of his young years, he compensated as an adult for only one, developing a passion for ice cream. Any ice cream stall near the exit gate of a racecourse acted on him later like a magnet, and on a hot day, tired after riding, he couldn't resist this appeal. Give him ice cream anywhere anytime, and he disposes of it fast. 'Mad for it,' he says. 'And I know it puts on weight, because I've weighed myself before and after eating it, and a plateful puts on a whole pound. American ice cream is best. They have forty-two varieties in those Howard Johnson restaurants.'

In most respects, his life followed a normal pattern. His parents took him most years for a holiday at the seaside to places like Selsey in Sussex and Devon, during which he acquired another lasting interest, swimming.

To offset his aloneness at home, his mother occasionally asked other children to tea. Lester was usually pleased enough at the prospect of having others to play with, but halfway through the visit he would get bored and disappear, leaving his mother to do the entertaining. Walking away from boredom is something he has done all his life.

He had few toys, from his own choice, and was not possessive of them. He was a naturally tidy child, highly organised and punctual. If he said he would do a thing at a certain time, he did it; and except when circumstances prevent it, he maintains this habit to this day. He was strong and healthy. He caught a few colds but cannot remember having had measles or other infectious diseases. He disliked the school food ('potatoes and milk and muck like that') and didn't eat it, which helped to keep him light. And one of his chief childish pleasures was stealing apples.

A wholesome, well-regulated childhood in a straightforwardly sensible home. Sturdy foundations for a skyscraper.

It was during the war years that his father taught him to ride. He had no other teacher, then or ever, except his own eyes, and hardly needed one, as the teacher he did have was patient, persistent and expert, and obviously did a good job.

Keith at that time had rented a stable in Letcombe Regis from a man called Grimey Whitelaw, and was training a few horses on his own account. Racing continued on a small scale throughout the war, mostly with the object of maintaining the thoroughbred blood lines. The Derby was run at Newmarket, which was safer from bombs than Epsom, and a restricted number of other meetings, both Flat and National Hunt, took place. Keith rode in as few as ten races a year, a lean time to be a jockey, and although Lester went with him three or four times, he remembers seeing Keith race only once. It was at Windsor in 1944, when Lester was eight. 'One of those doodle-bugs came over just before the race started . . . we were all lying on the ground, but it went over and came down towards London.' The flying bomb made an impression, but not the actual race.

From Lester's point of view, Keith was a kind teacher, insistent but not impatient. 'He used to tell me all the time. Anything I did wrong, he used to put me right.'

Although he had ridden various other children's ponies from the age of two, the first he himself called his own was Brandy, a half-tamed creature from the New Forest who made an indelible impression on the whole family. Keith and Lester set off from Letcombe with a car and trailer to fetch it from Fulke Walwyn who had a stable at East Ilsley, about ten miles away. Fulke had agreed to lease the pony to Keith for a fiver, but wouldn't sell it.

On the outward journey, Lester suddenly saw the empty trailer *passing* the car in which he sat beside his father, and they both watched, mesmerised, while it ran on ahead into a ditch. There it stuck, damaged and too heavy for them to shift, but rather than go home without Brandy, they drove on to East Ilsley and sent for a motor horsebox. The one which arrived had room for six full-grown racehorses, and it went solemnly to Letcombe containing one thirteen-hands pony.

Brandy proved to be the least suitable children's pony in riding history. 'It was wild. It was fast, but it was wild. It put the old man on his back two or three times. It really used to have a go. It used to run away with me all over the place. Disappear.'

Brandy took off regularly with Lester and pulled up miles

away across the Downs when at last it got tired. Its speed was so great that it was an attraction at informal war-time amusements. 'They used to get Freddie Fox, Gordon Richards and the old man – all those sort of jockeys – for past-and-present races. Brandy and the old man used to win all the time. Go like hell.'

It says a good deal for the son's balance and the father's courage that the young Lester was let loose on this unpredictable bolter long before he had the strength to control it, but there is little doubt that Brandy adjusted Lester to racing speeds while most children of his age were on the leading-rein.

One day when Keith and Lester were on one of their regular long rides over the Downs, two single-engined aeroplanes collided overhead. Although they were fighter aircraft, it was an accident, as both were American from a nearby training base. Keith and Lester reined-in and saw pieces of aeroplane falling not far away, and Lester set off instantly to take a closer look. When Keith caught him up, Lester had stopped and was peering concentratedly down at something on the ground. To his horror, Keith saw that it was the body of one of the pilots.

Before Keith could take any action, his son spoke. 'He's dead,' he said.

No hysterics, no tears, no visible emotion. Just a calm statement of something he understood, although he had not seen a dead person before. He was seven at the time.

Keith and Lester rode home matter-of-factly and Keith and Iris waited for their son to have nightmares when the shock of what he'd seen hit his imagination. Nothing happened. Nothing at all. Lester never referred to the pilot again and nor did his parents, for fear of stirring up horrors, and after a while they were not sure that he even remembered. From a very early age, and certainly by this time, Lester's mind accepted reality prosaically, and his reaction to everything, good or bad, was filtered through an inner damping process. The cool head he took to racing was already in full command on the day he saw a man fall out of the sky and looked at his dead face with dispassionate interest instead of fright.

Although by the age of eight or nine Lester could ride like an angel, he still couldn't get up on a pony without help, owing mostly to his small size but partly to a surprising inability to jump up. This made him doubly keen never to fall off away from help, but also posed problems when it came to gymkhanas.

Owing to war-time restrictions on crowds and a general shortage of petrol, the only available shows were the sort of local gymkhanas run by the Pony Club and the Red Cross, and young Lester, already eager to race, wasn't going to miss them. He used to ride to nearby gymkhanas alone on his pony, compete in every event he could, and ride home again. His chief complaint was that he couldn't go in for anything such as obstacle races, which involved dismounting and getting up again without help.

'I didn't win at gymkhanas to begin with, but as time went on, I did. One of the last few gymkhanas I rode in was at Faringdon, and I rode the pony from Lambourn to Faringdon and won a few things and rode home again.'

Lambourn to Faringdon is ten miles, and Lester was eleven.

Before he was ten, he was beginning to ride the racehorses in Keith's stable. None of his relations was surprised and no one made a fuss of it or told him how extraordinarily advanced he was in ability. Even Keith and Iris, though expecting him to be good, didn't quite realise what they had on their hands. However brilliant any child may be, he still has a long way to go, and it was probably what Lester couldn't yet do which filled their thoughts, not what he could. In any case, both of them also, like most horse-racing families, were down-to-earth in approach and despised airs and graces. Achievements from Lester were more often greeted by a parental 'yes, but next time ...', rather than 'Well done.'

Keith, for all his kindness, was firm and exacting. 'He was pretty strict. He didn't stand any nonsense, you know.' He insisted on Lester riding every possible day, knowing that no one, whatever their natural talent, ever achieved greatness without constant and dedicated practice.

The end of the war brought little let up in the general picture of countrywide austerity, but it did at least allow the resumption of racing. Keith turned exclusively to training and bought a larger stable at Lambourn, and the family moved there when Lester was eleven.

The house with its twin gables stood high off the road on a bank in the centre of the Berkshire village, with the stable yard immediately behind it. Life re-established itself fairly smoothly but, owing to the transport problem, Lester (no longer able to cycle to school because it was now too far) became a weekly boarder at King Alfred's. This unpopular arrangement lasted until Christmas 1947 when Lester left King Alfred's and went instead to a tiny private school in Upper Lambourn. There, the one lady teacher, Miss Amy Westdrake, took ten or twelve pupils and gave individual attention. Lester travelled to and fro again on his bicycle, two miles each way.

In the spring of 1948, aged twelve, he followed a course entirely normal for the sons of racehorse trainers, and became legally apprenticed to his father.

# Apprenticeship

The difference from that day to the next was almost unnoticeable. Lester had been riding out with the string of racehorses at morning exercise for some two years, and merely continued to do so. The new school allowed more flexible hours than King Alfred's, but he was already accustomed to them. He worked as usual in the stables every minute available, standing on a bucket to groom the parts of a horse he couldn't reach from the ground. Nothing external changed, but internally Lester took a giant mental stride towards maturity. He had been looking forward to being apprenticed, and felt that the real part of his life was just beginning. It excited him. He waited with a sense of dawn breaking for his first professional race.

It came on 7 April 1948, in the Easter school holidays, when Keith without any apparent trepidation put his shrimp-sized son onto a racing saddle for the first time, in an apprentice race at Salisbury. The horse, The Chase, was a three-year-old filly which Lester had regularly ridden in gallops at home. The new jockey knew his mount, he knew how to pace himself over the distance, he was unexcitable by temperament and unlikely to lose his head. Other boys had started even younger – his own great-grandfather Tom Cannon at nine, Stanley Wootton and many others at ten and eleven. To Lester himself, twelve seemed pretty old. As usual in the Piggott family, no one made any fuss.

The Chase went well enough on that first occasion though without troubling the judge, and Keith gave Lester sporadic practice through the summer. There were five more races at places like Bath, Kempton Park and Worcester, three of them on The Chase again, and two on another horse, Secret Code. At Chepstow on 31 July, in the last of those races, Secret Code finished second.

Came the summer school holidays, and The Chase was due to run at Haydock on Wednesday, 18 August. Lester was to be in the saddle for a tough appearance against seasoned jockeys, as it was not an event for apprentices only. The race was a seller (the winner to be sold for auction afterwards), and one of the other entries was Prompt Corner, a horse formerly trained by Keith, which had been sold three months previously. Its new trainer was Ginger Dennistoun who was never averse to winning his races by off-course strategy if he could get the chance.

He said to Keith Piggott, 'It's no good us taking both of the horses up to Haydock. We might as well work them both at home and take the best one.' So the horses were galloped together. Dennistoun brought Prompt Corner to Keith's gallops and Sam Wragg rode it, finishing perhaps half a length in front of Lester on The Chase.

'You won't go now, will you?' Dennistoun said to Keith, but before Keith could answer the twelve-year-old Lester said quickly, 'You didn't take the 7-lb allowance into consideration.'

The horses were both carrying the weight they would have in the race, but as Lester was an apprentice he could have claimed 7 lb less, and if he had carried 7 lb less, he would have won. So Keith said he would send The Chase to Haydock, and that didn't please Ginger Dennistoun very much.

Bill Rickaby, Lester's cousin, was engaged to ride Prompt Corner at Haydock, but on the day of the race he couldn't get to the course because of bad weather. An on-the-spot replacement jockey would have to be found.

Ginger Dennistoun, also having trouble in reaching the course, found out where the Piggotts were staying, and telephoned Keith to say he didn't think he could get there, and he wouldn't be having a 'go' with Prompt Corner. Eventually, however, he arrived and engaged Davy Jones to ride. At that point, he instructed the jockey to win if he could, but at the last minute he changed his mind again and told him not to as there had been no time to arrange suitable bets.

Lester says, laughing, 'Prompt Corner finished second to me and it could have won. Davy was just behind me, hauling on his reins and yelling, "Go on, *go on*." And I rode my first winner. But if Davy had been trying, he'd have beaten me. What a carry on, eh?'

The face which the winning jockey took into the unsaddling enclosure betrayed none of those thoughts. He stood 4 ft 6 ins in his racing boots and weighed less than five stone, and although he was a child he already knew what not to say in public, a lesson some adults never learn in all their lives.

The pressmen, routinely interviewing the winning trainer – Keith – found that Lester was only twelve; and suffering as so often happens from a dearth of rivetting subject matter, they fell on this fact with enthusiasm. Lester, from his very first win, was news.

As for Lester himself, he and Keith drove home contentedly in the horsebox to Lambourn, and Lester went to bed. It was after all, as he pointed out, past his normal bedtime. What else would you expect him to do?

Quite.

The fact that Lester went quietly off to bed sums up perfectly the professionalism of his family. Wild celebrations with screams and kisses would be unthinkable. A job of work had been successfully completed and life would go on as before. That the local paper had sent a photographer to record his triumphal return was just one of those things. The photographer took a picture of Lester going upstairs to bed, carrying (naturally) his own bag.

Life, of course, never went on quite as before. More photographers arrived, some of them from the Press Association and Reuters, whose pictures travel far. Lester was photographed on and off horses, with and without parents, bicycling, boxing, reading, playing draughts, sitting in armchairs, perching on fences, chewing bits of straw. Lester-fever got into full swing right at the beginning, and never stopped.

Iris went on record as saying, 'He's just an ordinary boy.'

It is difficult for any mother of a sensible child to realise that her son is *not* ordinary, but her action was at once illuminating, the shape of things to come, and the buttress of the levelheadedness which has saved Lester always from complacency. Iris probably feared more than was necessary that too much publicity would turn his head; but she knew all about the destructive effects of adulation, and she didn't intend Lester to be spoiled by success.

The Press, in consequence, came to regard her as a dragon, an obstacle always in their way, a suffocating influence. 'Always there, mothering him at the races,' they complained: and Iris said, 'How did they expect Lester to *get* to the races? He'd been leading apprentice for three years before he was old enough to drive. Keith couldn't leave the yard six days a week, chauffering our son. Someone had to, though, so I did it. The Press never seemed to realise that that was why I was always there waiting to take Lester home.'

To take him safely home, out of the reach of temptations, corruptions, and hangers-on. Lester himself took his fame phlegmatically, felt no need to skip out of his mother's care, and had no intention at all of losing his way. After the excitements of the first win, he rode in nineteen more races during the summer holidays and the autumn, but The Chase had left his father's yard, sold in the auction after the Haydock selling-race win, and there were no more signals of the future to come.

Many of the horses he rode in this early time were owned by Betty Lavington, who had some of her many horses with Keith. Her father, Wilfred Harvey, had horses (including Ascot Gold Cup winner Supertello) with Jack Waugh at Chilton, and in due course her daughter, in the way that racing families intertwine, married Newmarket trainer John Winter, brother of champion National Hunt jockey/trainer Fred.

Betty Lavington saw Lester's potential from the start, and it was she, owner of The Chase, who gave him his first ride and his first winner.

The following year, 1949, was for a long while unproductive. Lester, always a realist, tailored his expectations to match the actual present, and says he wasn't in that year particularly keen or ambitious. Neither did he feel frustrated nor disappointed, but accepted life as it came. This pragmatic attitude, already well developed by thirteen, is at the very root of his character and has been the bedrock of a stability impervious to storms. Lester sees things as they are: a gift not given to most.

On 7 April, at Bath he set out to ride a mare called Betsy for his father. It was a wet and windy day and the filly wasn't keen to go down to the start. Practical Keith flapped his macintosh behind her to get her going, whereupon she kicked up her heels and bolted, young Lester hanging on for dear life, but unable to stop.

At the end of the chute at Bath, where the 6-furlong races start from, there is a high brick wall. Betsy headed straight for it at a full gallop. Lester's solution to imminent annihilation was to yank her head round towards the rails, a manoeuvre so successful that she somersaulted over the top and landed in a heap on the other side. Neither horse nor rider were more than shaken, but they took no part in the actual race: the saddle's girths were broken.

It was over a year from his first win to his second, although he had, in between, ridden in a large number of races. Press interest was not exactly sleeping but no longer at fever pitch, and Lester acquired a good deal of experience without anyone commenting or expecting too much. This invaluable groundwork flowered again on Saturday, 20 August when he won the apprentices' handicap race at Newbury on Forest Glade, trained by his father. There were no stop-go shennanigans on this occasion and also less public acclaim, but on his next winner, Secret Code, at Bath on 1 September, he started favourite. Both of these horses were owned by Betty Lavington: she gave Lester not only his first winner, but his second and third also.

Two further successes followed, one in September, one in October, and then on 28 October, he rode Flurry for Frank Hartigan in a selling handicap at Thirsk. There was no photo-finish in those days. 'I didn't win the race,' Lester says in amusement. 'The judge gave it to me. It was a short race, five furlongs, and we were spread all across the course. Fred Hunter was on the rails and I was in the centre, and he was half a length in front at the post. The judge didn't see him, I suppose.'

They all count. That was official win number five, and with one more in November Lester finished the 1949 season with 6 wins from his 120 rides.

At about this point, the Berkshire school inspectors began to try to put a stop to the budding career. During the Second World War the school leaving age had been raised from fourteen to fifteen, although the first year the ordinance came into actual effect was 1947. This was a shade too soon for Lester as Berkshire County Council, once the law had been changed, set out in his case especially to enforce the new regulations strictly.

Under the old rules, Lester, fourteen on 5 November 1949, would have been free after that to do as he pleased. Under the new, his days were supposed to be spent sitting behind a desk.

As well try to stop bamboo shoots growing. Lester needed racing as racing needed Lester. If Lester had to be in school by law, in school he would be – but not during the times when he was wanted on a racecourse. Accordingly, for the summer and autumn terms of 1950 Lester's timetable was as follows:

Six thirty am, rise and ride out at exercise on one of his father's string. Have breakfast, bicycle to school at approximately eight and have lessons for half of the morning. Go home, be driven to the races, ride in races, be driven home. Eat. Cycle back to school for more lessons. Cycle home, go to bed. Same most days, Monday to Friday.

His devoted teachers, Miss Amy Westdrake, and her sister Mrs Lunn, saw to it that his total daily hours of schooling were what the law required, unstintingly working for him early and late while in addition teaching their more normal pupils during normal school hours. Their belief in Lester was unbounded and most effectively expressed.

Berkshire County Council didn't exactly give up. They tried to obtain a ruling that no person under fifteen should be allowed to go anywhere where gambling was taking place. Although they didn't say so, the move was a direct attempt not only to stop Lester from riding in so many races at fourteen, but to stop him from going to the racetrack altogether. Perhaps they truly thought he might be better off in a schoolroom, but one wonders. In any case, the ruling was not passed, and Lester pursued his long legal and arduous days dutifully to the discontent of almost everyone.

Lester, incidentally, never passed an official school examination. He failed the examination for transferring from the lower school at King Alfred's in Wantage, to the upper, and at Miss Westdrake's school he sat for no School Certificate (as it was then) or any other paper qualification. His intelligence in life terms was (and is) colossal. In the presence of such unstoppable natural gifts, a formal education was in his case irrelevant.

Since 1950, of course, it has been made impossible for anyone to start Flat racing so young. Not only is the school leaving age at least sixteen, but the minimum age for apprenticeship to any trade is now also sixteen. Lester was lucky. Boys nowadays have no chance of developing racing skills while their bodies are pliable and light. Lester himself might never have been able to Flat-race at all if he hadn't been allowed to start until sixteen, because by then he was too heavy for the ultra-light weights carried in apprentice races.

By the opening of the 1950 season, Lester was known as 'a useful boy' and was put up regularly by a widening pool of trainers around the Lambourn area: Fred Templeman, Frank Hartigan, 'Atty' Persse, and Frank and Ken Cundell in particular.

Possibly because at fourteen he was developing in straightforward physical strength, the winners began coming at regular and diminishing intervals: one in April, three in May, three in June, six in July.

By 1 August, two significant things had happened, though they had been gradual developments, not dates to put fingers on. First, the whole professional racing world had come to realise that this slightly over-publicised kid really did have genuine skill and promise, and second, and probably infinitely more importantly, a positive hunger for winning had grown in Lester himself. He was coming to understand what he could do, and from that very knowledge grew zest, enthusiasm, determination, dedication and perseverance. Genius gets nowhere much without those qualities, and with their growth during the summer of 1950 the genius dormant in Lester Piggott germinated and thrust upward into the sun.

It wasn't the securest of plants at that stage and there were tribulations ahead, but its arrival, if not universally welcomed, was undeniable, unmistakable, and a gust of new wind through an ageing scene.

A bunch of by then middle-aged jockeys had dominated racing since the early thirties, among them Charlie Smirke, Charlie Elliott, Ken Gethin, Eph Smith, Tommy Weston, Rae Johnstone, Michael Beary, Billy Nevett, Dick Perryman and, above all, that great gentleman Gordon Richards. They had monopolised racing throughout the war while the limited programme had been kept going in order to maintain the blood lines and the breeding industry, and they were cosily established as a more or less exclusive group. Younger brothers like Doug Smith were making progress but, on the whole, apprentices had had few opportunities for six or seven years, which meant there were few established jockeys in their twenties.

Lester and the Mercer brothers, Manny and Joe, were the vanguard of the new teen-aged generation which swept into the vacuum and rearranged the status quo. Lester remembers that none of the old guard was antagonistic but that Charlie Elliott alone positively helped him with advice.

'They were all close,' he says. 'They'd all known each other a long time. They used to bet all the time [jockeys are not allowed to, according to the regulations] and they would fiddle about discussing their chances and putting their money on, and then sometimes going out and beating the horse they'd backed! Racing was run for them really. Down at the start, one particular starter would line everyone up [there were no stalls then] and ask Gordon Richards if he was ready. "Ready, Gordon?" And if Gordon nodded, the race would start. They were all on good-pals terms with the Stewards, too. I called Eph Smith a four-letter word one day after he'd tried to unbalance me in a race and he trotted straight off to the Stewards to complain. The jockeys aren't so close a group nowadays. There's not so much betting, but in those days there was a bookie's runner in and out of the changing room all the time.'

Berkshire County Council would have had a fit.

The fourteen-year-old Lester, already in many respects exceedingly adult, didn't and couldn't join the established group. It is probable that they tolerated him willingly, though, because from 1 August onwards in 1950 he became a top-rank money spinner for them, winning thirty-nine races in eleven weeks and finishing as leading apprentice.

That season, aged fourteen, he rode in 404 races and won 52 of them. He finished with more winners than many established jockeys, such as Ken Gethin and Joe Sime, and was beaten by only ten of the great names, headed of course by Gordon Richards, who scored 201, followed by Doug Smith and Harry Carr.

This great burgeoning summer ended, however, on a sour note. Lester was reported to the Stewards for dangerous riding in a race at Newbury, and on the following Wednesday stood before them at an enquiry in Newmarket (*see* page 51). It was the day of the Cambridgeshire; 25 October. The Stewards gave Lester a three weeks' suspension which, in effect, meant the rest of the season, but allowed the ban to start from the following day so that he should be able to ride in the Cambridgeshire as planned.

Lester rode Zina, a three-year-old filly, on whom he had won convincingly at Newbury only seven days earlier. Trained by Frank Cundell, she again ran a great race, flashing across the line with two others, Kelling and Valdesco. The horses were spread out across Newmarket's wide Rowley Mile course, where the angle of the finish can be deceptive. Both Lester and Frank Cundell thought that Zina had won, and Lester rode confidently into the winner's enclosure. The other two jockeys, Doug Smith and Ken Gethin, accepted that this was right, and took second and third unsaddling places without question.

The photograph of the very close finish stunned everybody. Kelling, not Zina, had passed the post first, his nose stretching out like an arrow. The official distances were a neck and a head. Lester's day, Lester's year, ended disconsolately. The pictures of him taken that afternoon show a downcast semi-child with rounded cheeks and a faint air of bewilderment at the speed and thoroughness with which his triumphant progress had gone wrong.

Flat jockeys wore at that time no protective helmets under their silk caps, and the silk caps did nothing at all for anyone's appearance. Full grown men looked stunted in them. On Lester, in photographs, they ballooned his face unbecomingly: but that was how caps were worn then, and one had to put up with the results. There's no doubt that modern crash helmets do more for a jockey than simply shield his skull.

Lester turned fifteen, went for a skiing holiday, rode his father's horses at exercise and waited for spring.

The new season started off about as discouragingly as the old had ended, as within ten days of resuming Lester broke his collar-bone and was out of action until mid-April (*see* page 87). He walked to keep fit and came back with confidence, riding winners steadily week by week. One of the first of these was Zucchero, considered by Lester still to be one of the best horses he ever rode.

Zucchero (Italian for sugar) was trained at Compton in Berkshire during his three-year-old season by Ken Cundell, who had been steadily engaging Lester from very early on. Lester consequently partnered Zucchero in a preliminary race at Hurst Park and then in the Blue Riband Derby Trial Stakes at the Epsom Spring Meeting on 26 April, winning the latter not unexpectedly at 7–1. That race, and the Great Metropolitan on the same course two days before, were the first 'big' races Lester had won: not the biggest in prize money, but definitely in prestige.

Zucchero, dark and devilish, was a difficult horse to manage and train. After an unsuccessful two-year-old season, he was acquired by bookmaker George Rolls and sent to Ken Cundell who knew his new charge had kinks about starting in races. *If* he would start, he could fly. Ken's solution was to go down to the start himself and hold his horse's head, pointing him in the right direction and not letting go until the tapes went up. (This was, of course, in the days before stalls.) Ken would practically throw Zucchero forwards into the contest, and most often these tactics worked. Starters were tolerant of awkward horses and allowed such manoeuvres; perhaps in later years the brilliant Zucchero, if he couldn't have been persuaded into a stall at all, would never have won a race.

His next run after the Blue Riband Trial was in the Derby itself. Lester at fifteen was the youngest jockey in the field but saw no reason on that account to be nervous. Ken Cundell in his morning coat met him at the start and held Zucchero's head as usual. Came the 'off', the tapes flew up, and Zucchero took two firm paces backwards. Ken Cundell pointed to the way ahead despairingly, Lester kicked and urged frantically, and

Zucchero finally and reluctantly set off on the journey that but for his pigheadedness could have put him in the starriest record books. He finished well back in the ruck, never being able to make up the ground lost.

At the time I (Dick Francis) was also riding regularly for Ken Cundell but on his jumpers, and I saw a good deal of Zucchero, saddling him up and giving Lester a leg up in the parade ring once or twice while Ken went down to the distant starts.

After the Derby, the wayward animal won two not very important races six days apart, at Windsor and Sandown Park, and only eight days later lined up for the King George VI and Queen Elizabeth Festival of Britain Stakes at Ascot, towards the end of July. Lester thought these three races were too close together and that the stamina needed for the 'King George' might have been squandered at Sandown: but Zucchero wouldn't work well at home and Ken couldn't get him to gallop properly except in races. Zucchero went to the start at Ascot and again stuck his toes in. Even then, starting well last, he flew through the field to finish a scant three-quarters of a length behind the winner, Supreme Court, and a further six lengths in front of the third horse, Tantiemme, who was a dual winner of the Prix de l'Arc de Triomphe.

This disappointment was slightly mitigated by the fact that a few days earlier, at Sandown, Lester had won the Eclipse Stakes, by then his biggest win by far in either prize money or prestige; and he had done it on a chance ride, the French horse Mystery IX, proving conclusively that his talent was international and of serious proportions.

The 1951 season, which had brought fifteen-year-old Lester his first ride in the Derby, his first big-race wins and his first star-quality mounts, ended dramatically and prematurely for him in August at Lingfield, where he broke his leg (*see* page 89). Despite this rotten disaster, he maintained his position as leading apprentice, with a total of 51 victories from 432 rides.

The fall terminated not only his riding but also his earning capacity for the year.

The payment of apprentices' racing fees is distinctive in that half goes to the apprentice and half to his master. This arrangement, set up in the mists of time, is based on the premise that the master is teaching the apprentice his job, and deserves a reward. Some trainers make a much better job of training their apprentices than others, notably in the past Stanley Wootton, Frenchie Nicholson and Sam Armstrong. Those like Frenchie, who among others taught Paul Cook and Pat Eddery, really worked hard at making successful careers for their boys, and in cases like those the apprenticeship system worked at its best. In later years, Reg Hollinshead has kept up the tradition, producing jockeys such as Walter Swinburn and Paul Eddery.

Keith Piggott was demonstrably a good school-master to his own son, but he also produced the Forte twins, Dominic and John, nephews of Charles Forte, the hotelier tycoon. Keith was a good teacher of apprentices, down to earth, practical and hard-working. Although entitled by the system to take half of Lester's earnings for himself, he didn't. He banked it all for his son, and also gave him, at twelve, thirteen and fourteen, pocket money of five shillings a week (approximately £3 now). This wasn't any act of principle. Lester simply didn't want more. He seldom spent the whole of it, and saved the rest. Apart from that, he left his finances to his father during his apprenticeship and concentrated on winning.

It was the intensity of his concentration allied to his relative inexperience which caused recurring accusations of rough riding. He'd been taught, for instance, that to go round on the inside rail was the shortest way, and that the shortest way was best. There, accordingly, was where he tried to race. Then, with a horse full of running, he would find himself boxed in. He would know, often enough, that he was expected to win, and he knew he had to quicken: and he would take any opening, however small, however non-existent, to force his way through.

He was scolded, fined and suspended for aggression but, as he says in later years, 'It was anxiety, really. I thought if I went back and said I couldn't win the race because I couldn't get out, no one would like it. As you get older, you don't get in those positions where you've got to push your way out. Of course, you've got to make mistakes sometimes, but as you get older you can see what's going to happen from the time the gates open, and you get into a place where you're not going to be shut in or tied up. But all this takes time. That's what it really boils down to. At the beginning, when you're young, you just don't think about what you're going to do until you're doing it.'

The authorities and some of the Press might censure those early misjudgments, but the romantic British public took Lester to their hearts, liking his fierce determination and certain he would bring their bets home if he could.

He started his last season of apprenticeship as a national mini-hero, and he let no one down.

By March 1952 his leg had solidly mended, he was sixteen, and he had grown. He was no longer a lightweight jockey. He could ride at only a little under eight stone, and people were predicting that he'd never fulfil his promise, that he would never be champion jockey because he would be too big.

Lester shrugged all that off and got on with the job.

During the winter, he had been engaged to ride as first jockey for the flour magnate, J. V. Rank, for the coming season, an enormous promotion in professional standing, but J. V. Rank died suddenly early in the year, before any of his horses ran. Mrs Rank kept them on for a while but gradually sold them. Lester thus only temporarily came into the full enjoyment of his first top appointment, but the kudos of having been *engaged* for it, while still an apprentice, clung to him like gold dust.

One of the Rank horses, Gay Time, provided some of the peaks of a busy year. Trained by Noel Cannon at Druid's Lodge near Stonehenge, Gay Time won for the first time that season at nearby Salisbury, and next time out ran in the Derby.

The big race that year was won by Tulyar, ridden by Charlie Smirke. Lester's account of the event is as follows: 'There were a lot of runners that year, as many as there had ever been, and I couldn't lay up to begin with. They went very fast and Gay Time wasn't a very fast horse. I got into a lot of trouble and I was a long way behind coming into the straight. I switched to the outside then and got a good run, and it looked like I would win. Charlie Smirke was in front. He had had to go to the front a bit soon on Tulyar, and by the end the horse was tired and beginning to pull himself up, and he came off the rails towards me, hanging to the right. He impeded me. I finished second. If it had been now, I'd have got the race on an objection, but there were no head-on cameras in those days. At the time, I was sure I would have won if it hadn't been for being hampered, but as it happens, Tulyar always beat Gay Time afterwards, like when they met in the King George.'

Lester didn't lodge an objection to Tulyar, not because he wasn't convinced of the justice of his case, but because Gay Time fell over when he was pulling up. He lost his footing on the road the horses had to cross at that point, and pitched Lester off. Gay Time, then loose, gave himself a gay old time eluding capture, ending a good distance away in some woods. Lester couldn't even weigh in until his saddle was brought back to the weighing room, and by then it was understood that it was too late for him to object.

After Gay Time had lost again to Tulyar in the King George VI and Queen Elizabeth Stakes, Mrs Rank sold him to the Queen, in whose colours he won at Goodwood and finished fifth in the St Leger, ridden by Gordon Richards.

Lester himself could do little wrong. The winners came fluently, his score steadily mounting. In the end-of-year statistics, he was taken off the apprentices' table and given full jockey status for his 79 wins from a huge pool of 620 rides.

1953 was depressingly different.

Lester's apprenticeship officially ended in February of that year, and he could reasonably have looked forward to a smooth continuation of his starry career. Life however turns on its favourites sometimes and Lester went oddly off form.

'It happens to a lot of boys,' he says. 'They're good while they're young. Then they go off. They grow. That's what it was like with me. It had all been too easy. I hadn't worried much, it had all just come.'

He thought his instinctive touch had left him, that his best days were gone. His wins-to-rides ratio had fallen to fewer than one in ten. He felt heavy. He was seventeen and a good deal taller. The differences he felt in himself, the ending of a comparatively carefree era of unforced success, and the anxieties which took its place, most probably were all the result of the natural physical, mental and psychological developments of his body. The mid-teens, the upheaval years of hormone change from boy to man, are enough to cope with on their own. Because of his ecstatically acclaimed career, of which perhaps at that time too much was euphorically expected, puberty and the onset of manhood had to be quietly managed in public. A good many infant prodigies fade entirely under that sort of strain.

Lester took things calmly and rode competently enough and with competitiveness, but without the old easy inspiration. No one reproached him, least of all his parents, but neither did anyone give him much advice. He saw eventually that his future depended on himself: that he would have to sort himself out and build his own road ahead.

Everyone, including himself, had taken it for granted that when he grew too heavy for the Flat he would turn to jumping and follow in his father's and grandfather's distinguished wake. Keith had been tough, tireless and consistently successful. Ernie, Keith's father, had been champion jump jockey several times both in England and in France. Lester was expected to inherit the great tradition. Since Keith Piggott trained jumpers in addition to Flat racers, his son accepted that he would henceforth ride them, but less with enthusiasm than resignation.

During the 1953 Flat season his only winners of any consequence were the Royal Vase at Royal Ascot on Absolve, and two good races on Zucchero (by now trained by Bill Payne), the Coronation Cup at Epsom in June and the Rose of York Stakes at York in August. All the rest were for prizes of under £1,000. His Derby mount, Prince Charlemagne, finished 15th. He rode 41 winners in all, scarcely more than half his previous year's total.

Troubled and increasingly heavy, he approached his first winter of jump racing with a lonely and slowly growing determination to put himself back into top Flat-racing shape for 1954. Physical shape, mental shape, all the way.

He asked his mother to give him less to eat.

# Jumping

Keith and Iris had never regulated Lester's diet, but had given him what he wanted to eat; and considering he was a normally growing boy, they were wise. He had never, in any case, eaten greedily or wanted a great deal. When he asked to be given less, Iris as usual did as he said. Lester, all along the line, was lucky in his parents.

By his eighteenth birthday he was approaching what proved to be his final height of five feet seven and a half inches, although no one could be sure of it at the time as some young men are still growing at twenty. He had inherited a light frame, but even so the expected weight of a male of that build and age would be over nine stone, and that seemed to be the weight his body was trying to achieve.

For a full-time Flat race jockey, a body weight of nine stone was nearly impossible: most Flat horses in Lester's early days carried seven stone something or eight stone something. Nine and over was the top of the handicap, with comparatively few in that bracket.

For a jump jockey, however, nine stone is light. On jumpers, Lester would be back where he started, able to ride absolutely everything from the weight point of view. He was accustomed to the jumpers in his father's stable, and that Keith could train them successfully is without doubt: he produced Ayala to win the Grand National in 1963.

Keith's jumpers ten years earlier were mainly selling platers or moderately good old horses, and looking at it squarely, this was not the material his son needed. But then Lester had made his way upwards before from the springboard of Keith's runners, and the elder Piggott philosophically believed he might do so again.

Keith had taught Lester how to ride over jumps as part of his general education, and Lester had had a good deal of practice on the schooling grounds at home. Accordingly, in his normal calm way, he went out to race over hurdles for the first time on 27 November 1953. The place was Kempton Park; the horse, Tangle, trained by Bill Payne. Tangle set off well, made a couple of jumping errors early on and finished second to last. No one could feel any excitement.

After a pause, Bill Payne, who had produced many a Lester winner on the Flat, offered him a chance on Eldoret in a handicap hurdle at Wincanton on Boxing Day. Eldoret, incidentally, had presented apprentice Joe Mercer with his first win – on the Flat – a year earlier at Bath, and Lester himself had ridden him to victory on the Flat in 1950. Lester therefore accepted the jumping ride with gratitude, started favourite, rode a well-planned race and won by five lengths with plenty in hand.

His next win, on 2 January 1954 at Newbury, was again for Bill Payne: he made all the running on Stranger, and beat this book's author into third place. I took my revenge at Sandown two weeks later, on 15 January, when Lester again partnered Stranger and I was on Deal Park, trained by Peter Cazalet, for whose stable I regularly rode. Stranger started at 7–4, Deal Park at 9–4; first and second favourites. Stranger led for most of the way, but Deal Park passed him on the approach to the second last hurdle and won after a strong contest up the hill, both horses finishing very tired.

Lester has photographs of *himself* leading the field of fourteen, with Deal Park in the background. *I* have a photograph of Deal Park leading Stranger over the last hurdle (*see* no. 6). There am I, looking determined and slightly apprehensive, with my mount getting awkwardly into his stride, followed by an equally determined little demon bunched over his horse's withers, not giving up for a second, although I'd already passed him. For young Lester, no race was lost until the winning post was reached.

The fact that Lester's photographs and mine show alternative versions of the same event do not, incidentally, reflect our ignoble vanities: the photo agencies used to send free to jockeys whatever pictures they thought would please the jockeys most!

For five weeks or so Lester rode no more hurdle races but came back with a flourish at Ludlow on Strokes and Deux Points, scoring a double for his father.

A week later he was back in the winner's spot on Corola Pride at Worcester, with Mull Sack lined up for the first race at the Cheltenham Festival the next day.

Lester had never ridden at Cheltenham; so Keith, in his thorough and no-nonsense way, insisted that he should walk the course.

They stopped at Cheltenham on the way back from Worcester and set off on the nearly two-mile grassy hike. Lester went without much enthusiasm ('and it was dark by the time we got round!'), but the next afternoon, putting the lesson to good use, he duly won on Mull Sack.

With his overall score then standing at six, Lester was engaged to ride in the Triumph Hurdle, run in those days at Hurst Park but later transferred to Cheltenham. He rode Prince Charlemagne, his partner from the 1953 Derby, who was setting out in a hurdle race for the first time, aiming high at the N.H. event considered the crown for four-year-olds.

Prince Charlemagne might not have had quite enough class for the Derby, but he was nonetheless a very good horse. His trainer, Tommy Carey, wanted to have a bet on him in the Triumph Hurdle and, needing to know his state of readiness, took him to Kempton Park a week before the Triumph to gallop in a training session over the course after the day's racing had ended. (Many trainers follow this practice. It gives their horses a taste of racecourse experience, and racecourses themselves in general offer a better surface and better-built jumps than the gallops back home.)

Lester rode Prince Charlemagne alongside two other very good horses trained by two other trainers, Bob Read and Stanley Wootton, and went easily all the way round until he reached the last hurdle. Prince Charlemagne flattened it, went through it without jumping, but despite this setback, finished upsides and level with his companions.

Tommy Carey beamed with pleasure and went away to put

his money on with confidence for the Triumph. Unknown to the other trainers, unknown to any but Lester, he had packed Lester's weight-cloth with lead and had sent his horse out to gallop carrying a colossal 13 st. If Prince Charlemagne could carry 13 st and finish level with the horses so far considered the best of the year's four-year-old hurdlers, what could he not do with the 10 st 10 lb he was allotted in the Triumph?

Lester with a straight face went out to demonstrate, and Prince Charlemagne gave an exact repeat performance, going easily throughout the race and making a total mess of the last hurdle. The trainer's bet might have come nastily unstuck right there, but Prince Charlemagne recovered and produced enough Derby-class speed to regain and keep the lead. He had started favourite at 11–4, having opened at 5–1; and Tommy Carey cheerfully pocketed his extensive winnings.

Prince Charlemagne that day beat a field of eleven other horses, *eight* of which had won the last time out, with two others second. It has to be, in hindsight, one of the most remarkable Triumphs.

Lester had a fall later in the day. Jump racing is a great leveller.

He rode a couple more winners for his father, ending his first jumping season with 9 wins, 3 seconds and 4 thirds from 25 rides. Considering his obvious ability and his light (for jumping) weight, the National Hunt world had beaten a remarkably subdued path to his door.

Lester enjoyed jump racing to a certain extent, but it was only in that first season that he made any real effort to advance into a jumping career. He does, all the same, acknowledge a debt to his N.H. experience. Jumping toughens you up, he says. It did him good. He saw the other side of racing and grew in understanding. The people he rode against were bigger, stronger and earthier men, full of jokes. He found jump jockeys easy to get on with, and says: 'They always were much more of a sporting lot. But at that time, there were one or two you wouldn't want to go up on the inside of. Like Bryan Marshall. You wouldn't want to poke up on his inside going into a hurdle. You'd get flattened. They were entitled to do it. Nowadays, they probably wouldn't be doing it so much. You never see a jumping jockey put another fellow in trouble if he can help it, do you? If you're going into a jump and you want a bit of room, they'll give it to you. They're not going to *do* you, and put you on the floor or through the wing; that's where they're so fair.'

He thinks that compared with racing over jumps, the Flat is easy. Conversely, he also says that one needs to be fitter to ride on the Flat.

This apparent contradiction is borne out by all jockeys who have tried both. The fact is that in a jumping race, although the distance covered is almost always longer, the jockey's body frequently changes position, the spine straightening as the horse lands over the jumps. In a Flat race, the crouch over the withers is constant, with the head tipped back to see the way ahead. The strain on all muscles is definitely more when they can't bend or stretch, particularly in races as long as a mile and a half, like the Derby. Because of the crouch, it is also harder to breathe; in a short Flat race, a jump jockey hardened to three miles or more over fences can get out of breath. In a Flat race, too, one usually has to ride harder for longer approaching the winning post, and can finish exhausted.

Lester took the usual tumbles in his jump races. 'Bound to happen. Law of averages.' He emerged more or less unscathed, although one day at Newbury he cracked his shoulder blade. 'My own fault. I fell off,' he says laconically.

In his third season he rode Rich Bloom for Walter Nightingall, winning in October, but coming to grief next time out.

'I rode Rich Bloom again at Kempton on Boxing Day, and he fell. There's that hurdle just round the bend, past the stands, and he galloped straight through it. He wasn't a good jumper. He probably hadn't been schooled enough. Some horses feel like that, as if they've never been steadied at home. They tend to grab at the hurdles. I had an easy fall really. There were quite a few runners and they galloped all over me, and one put his foot right on my face. Cut all over. Before that happened I could have got up and got out of the way. But you don't, do you? You're usually better staying on the ground.' He tells the story with tolerance: many worse things happened on the Flat (*see* chapters beginning on pp. 87 and 153).

The statistics of his sporadic jumping history tell their own tale. After the first season in 1953–54, he rode only 1 winner from 15 rides in 1954–55. In 1955–56, he rode in no N.H. races at all; 1956–57 saw 6 wins (including Rich Bloom) from only 9 rides. In 1957–58 he rode 2 wins from 3 rides, and in 1958–59, 2 from 2.

After that, he stopped. He never closed the door with finality on jumping but simply drifted away from it through being offered more and more opportunities to ride flat races abroad during the winter. No one tried to stop him because of the danger.

Four of his later wins (out of four rides) were for Pierre Raymond, the innovative hairdresser who was one of the originators of the 'swinging' sixties. Pierre Raymond bought his most prolific winner, Royal Task, from Keith, and became a good friend of all the Piggotts. It was in his colours that the Keith Piggott-trained Ayala won the Grand National, but with Pat Buckley, not Lester, on board.

Lester might have done more National Hunt racing if he had been offered top-class horses, but those top horses were in stables where jockeys like Fred Winter, Dave Dick, Tim Molony and that fellow Dick Francis had first claim. Besides, Lester rode only in hurdle races, and not at all over the bigger fences, and there were the established hurdles specialists, Harry Sprague, Ken Mullins and Johnny Gilbert in his way.

Fourteen of Lester's grand total of 20 jumping winners were trained by his father. One might say that he never got a full chance to show what he could do, though from my memories of him he had all the physical and mental equipment to get to the top if his heart had been in it. His record of 20 wins from a total of 54 rides can be called spectacular, but he did very definitely prefer to ride on the Flat, and jumping was to him always second best.

# The Shape of the Racing Year

Within this book, the names of many races constantly recur, and I thought it might be helpful for anyone not closely involved in the sport if I set out here the regular shape of a Flat-race jockey's season. The list is selective, geared to Lester's experiences; several big races have been omitted.

I've given the races the titles they're best known by, leaving out in most cases the names of the present sponsors. Races initiated by sponsors, such as the Waterford Crystal Mile, are the exceptions. The King George VI and Queen Elizabeth Stakes at Ascot was called The King George VI and Queen Elizabeth Festival of Britain Stakes for that one Festival year only, 1951, and became the King George VI and Queen Elizabeth Diamond Stakes when de Beers started sponsoring it.

The Flat season opens on a Thursday in the second half of March and closes in the first half of November. Dates of all races vary a little from year to year. This table includes the main Irish races and a few French races also, as to Lester they were a normal part of the calendar.

The races starred * are commonly regarded as preparation for the classics. In the Age column, c = colts, f = fillies, g = geldings.

Here goes.

| *Month* | *Racecourse* | *Race* | *Age of contestants* | *Distance in furlongs* |
|---|---|---|---|---|
| April | Ascot until 1978, Salisbury thereafter | One Thousand Guineas Trial* | 3-yr-old f | 7 |
| April | | Two Thousand Guineas Trial* | 3-yr-old c | 7 |
| April | Newbury | Fred Darling Stakes* | 3-yr-old f | 7 |
| April | Newbury | Greenham Stakes* | 3-yr-old c & g | 7 |
| April | Newbury | Spring Cup | 4-yr-olds & upwards | 8 |
| April | Newmarket | Craven Stakes* | 3-yr-old c & g | 8 |
| April | Newmarket | Free Handicap* | 3-yr-olds | 7 |
| April | Sandown | Esher Cup* | 3-yr-olds | 8 |
| April | Sandown | Classic Trial* | 3-yr-old c & g | 10 |
| April | Epsom | Great Metropolitan Handicap | 4-yr-olds & upwards | 12 (originally 18) |
| April | Epsom | Princess Elizabeth Stakes* | 3-yr-old f | 8 |
| April | Epsom | Blue Riband Stakes* | 3-yr-old c & g | 8 |
| April/ May | Newmarket | One Thousand Guineas | 3-yr-old f | 8 |
| April/ May | Newmarket | Two Thousand Guineas | 3-yr-old c & f | 8 |
| April/ May | Newmarket | Jockey Club Stakes | 4-yr-olds & upwards | 12 |
| May | Chester | Chester Vase* | 3-yr-old c & f | 12 |
| May | Chester | Chester Cup | 4-yr-olds & upwards | 18 |
| May | Lingfield | Oaks Trial Stakes* | 3-yr-old f | 12 |
| May | Lingfield | Derby Trial Stakes* | 3-yr-old c & f | 12 |
| May | The Curragh | Irish One Thousand Guineas | 3-yr-old f | 8 |
| May | The Curragh | Irish Two Thousand Guineas | 3-yr-old c & f | 8 |
| May | York | Dante Stakes* | 3-yr-old c & f | 10 |
| May | York | Yorkshire Cup | 4-yr-olds & upwards | 14 |
| May | Longchamp | Prix Lupin | 3-yr-old c & f | 10 |
| May/ June | Epsom | The Derby | 3-yr-old c & f | 12 |
| May/ June | Epsom | Coronation Cup | 4-yr-old & upwards c & f | 12 |
| May/ June | Epsom | The Oaks | 3-yr-old f | 12 |
| June | Chantilly | French Derby (Prix du Jockey Club) | 3-yr-old c & f | 12 |
| June | Chantilly | French Oaks (Prix de Diane) | 3-yr-old f | 10 |
| June | Royal Ascot | Gold Cup* | 3-yr-old & upwards c & f | 20 |
| June | Royal Ascot | King Edward VII Stakes | 3-yr-old c & g | 12 |
| Late June | Longchamp | Grand Prix de Paris | 3-yr-old c & f | 15 |
| Early July | The Curragh | Irish Derby | 3-yr-old c & f | 12 |
| July | Sandown | Eclipse Stakes | 3-yr-old & upwards c & f | 10 |
| July | Newmarket | Princess of Wales Stakes | 3-yr-olds & upwards | 12 |
| July | The Curragh | Irish Oaks | 3-yr-old f | 12 |
| July | Ascot | King George VI and Queen Elizabeth Stakes | 3-yr-old & upwards c & f | 12 |
| July | Goodwood | Sussex Stakes | 3-yr-old & upwards c & f | 8 |
| July | Goodwood | Goodwood Cup | 3-yr-olds & upwards | 21 |
| August | Newbury | Geoffrey Freer Stakes | 3-yr-olds & upwards | 13 |
| August | York | Yorkshire Oaks | 3-yr-old f | 12 |

* From 1986, 3-yr-old & upwards c & g, 4-yr-old and upwards f.

| *Month* | *Racecourse* | *Race* | *Age of contestants* | *Distance in furlongs* |
|---|---|---|---|---|
| August | York | Benson & Hedges Gold Cup† | 3-yr-old & upwards c & f | 10 |
| August | York | Ebor Handicap | 3-yr-olds & upwards | 14 |
| August | York | Great Voltigeur Stakes | 3-yr-old c | 12 |
| August | York | William Hill Sprint (formerly Nunthorpe Stakes) | 2-yr-olds & upwards | 5 |
| August | Goodwood | Waterford Crystal Mile | 3-yr-olds & upwards | 8 |
| Sept. | Doncaster | St Leger | 3-yr-old c & f | 14 |
| Sept. | Ascot | Queen Elizabeth II Stakes | 3-yr-olds & upwards | 8 |
| Sept. | Ascot | Royal Lodge Stakes | 2-yr-olds | 8 |
| Oct. | Newmarket | Cheveley Park Stakes | 2-yr-old f | 6 |
| Oct. | Newmarket | Middle Park Stakes | 2-yr-old c & f | 6 |
| Oct. | Newmarket | Cambridgeshire Handicap | 3-yr-olds & upwards | 9 |
| Oct. | Longchamp | Prix de l'Arc de Triomphe | 3-yr-old & upwards c & f | 12 |
| Oct. | Longchamp | Prix de l'Abbaye de Longchamp | 2-yr-old & upwards c & f | 5 |
| Oct. | Longchamp | Grand Criterium | 2-yr-old c & f | 8 |
| Oct. | Newmarket | Dewhurst Stakes | 2-yr-old c & f | 7 |
| Oct. | Newmarket | Champion Stakes | 3-yr-old & upwards c & f | 10 |
| Oct. | Newmarket | Cesarewitch Handicap | 3-yr-olds & upwards | 18 |
| Oct. | Doncaster | William Hill Futurity (formerly Observer Gold Cup) | 2-yr-old c & f | 8 |
| Oct. | Doncaster | November Handicap | 3-yr-olds & upwards | 12 |

† Benson & Hedges sponsored this race for the last time in 1985.

# Never Say Die

Lester came to the 1954 Flat season in a determined frame of mind, but it was not until May that the winners began to flow freely. By then he had shed the winter pounds and survived the hiccup of a short suspension for 'crossing' when finishing second on Loll (disqualified) during the Epsom Spring Meeting.

Robert Sterling Clark, an American owner of immense wealth and prestige, had arranged in an informal way for Lester to ride for the season on some of the horses he had in training in England. One of those horses was an only moderately promising three-year-old which nevertheless had been entered more or less at birth for the Derby.

Never Say Die would not have been trained in England at all had Sterling Clark not quarrelled with the American racing authorities some years before and transferred his horses to Europe in a huff. The American racing authorities had barred him from running in certain races a horse which had some Arabian blood in its make up (a faintly hypocritical decision, or at least one of questionable logic, when one remembers that all thoroughbreds now racing are descended from three original stallions imported into England from the Middle East, one of which was the Darley *Arabian*.) Whatever the rights or wrongs, Sterling Clark sent his horses to three English trainers, one of them being Joe Lawson, who had moved his stables from Manton in Wiltshire to Newmarket after the war.

Joe Lawson, seventy-three by the time he trained his one and only Derby winner, had been a jockey himself and then head-lad to Alec Taylor, whose yard he took over in 1928. A year later Lawson won his first classic with Pennycomequick for the late Lord Astor, and by 1954 his tally was the Oaks three times, the Two Thousand Guineas four times and the One Thousand Guineas three times. One of the Oaks and one of the One Thousand Guineas had been for Sterling Clark in 1939, with the great filly, Galatea II. In addition, Joe Lawson had had five or six runners placed in the Derby, and was known as a trainer of proven skill and staying power.

Robert Sterling Clark in 1954 was himself seventy-eight, and it is interesting that the veteran owner and trainer put up the then youngest ever jockey to win the big race.

Never Say Die was foaled in America, after his dam, Singing Grass, had been sent to England to be covered by Nasrullah, third in the 1943 Derby. Sterling Clark, stud owner himself, was intensely interested in breeding his own winners. Singing Grass was out of his brood-mare Boreale, who was out of another of his mares, Galaday II; and Galaday II was the dam of Galatea II. Never Say Die was, accordingly, the result of much thought and planning, but by June 1954 had never come truly up to expectations.

He had won once without tremendous distinction as a two-year-old, not ridden by Lester. Lester rode him for the first time at the 1954 Liverpool Spring Meeting (this meeting, which culminates in the Grand National, consisted of both Flat and jumping races at that time). It was surprisingly early in the season for the appearance of a Derby prospect, but Joe Lawson wanted to get going. Joe Lawson was the only person who steadfastly believed in the colt.

Lester rode with enthusiasm but was disappointed to finish in second place six lengths behind the winner. The horse that beat him, however, was a good one of Jack Jarvis's, and the race, the Union Jack Stakes, was, at one mile, perhaps too short. Excuses were easy to find.

Next time out, less easy. Lester rode Never Say Die in the Free Handicap at Newmarket, and the horse ran badly. This time it was only seven furlongs, but the distance couldn't altogether account for the depressing performance.

Towards the end of May, Joe Lawson, still with undiminished

faith, ran Never Say Die again at Newmarket. Lester, with better prospects in races on the same day at Bath (which won) asked to be excused, and Manny Mercer was engaged in his place. The colt ran a stop-go-stop sort of race to finish third, and again no one but Joe Lawson saw any breathtaking promise.

At that point a grand mix-up nearly caused the horse to be scratched from the Derby. Joe Lawson told Sterling Clark's racing manager, Gerald McElligot, who oversaw all the Clark horses in England, that the horse hadn't run well because it was hanging badly. McElligot interpreted this as 'hanging to the right', and wrote to Sterling Clark to tell him it was no use trying for the Derby because it was on a left-hand track. Sterling Clark had already, in resignation, agreed to scratch when Joe Lawson found out. In horror, he said he had been misunderstood; the horse hung to the *left*. Very well, said Sterling Clark, let the horse take whatever chance he had: which privately he thought small enough.

He himself made no plans to come to England to see the race. He had booked himself into a health farm for the Epsom week and Joe Lawson couldn't persuade him to postpone that visit.

The trainer's next worry was to find a jockey. He knew Lester had been disappointed in the two early races, and he felt he might not be mentally committed to the utmost. Lawson wanted a jockey filled with his own faith. He asked Manny Mercer who had ridden Never Say Die at Newmarket: he asked Charlie Smirke and at least one other, but all were engaged for other horses, and none, it would be fair to say, would have chosen to change.

Joe Lawson asked Lester, Lester said yes. Still, on his side, without expectation, still without excitement.

Lester, however, then did some thinking of his own, and he thought chiefly of the problems inbuilt in the good-looking chestnut colt. Never Say Die was to some extent an intelligent horse, quiet to ride, but he did hang very definitely to the left. He was a heavy horse in front, with a heavy head. He used to get hold of his bridle on the left side and lie on it, and over a period of time he had got one-sided. Joe Lawson's solution to the problem had been to use an American noseband (a band of fluffy sheepskin designed to keep the horse's attention in front of his eyes) and to add various pieces to the bit, so that the horse's mouth was full of metal devices to correct the left-handed bias.

Lester came to the conclusion that at Epsom the left-handedness would be a positive asset, and he asked Joe Lawson to leave all the corrective additions at home. Lester said he would like to ride the horse in a plain ordinary bridle. Never Say Die had never raced before in a plain bridle. It says a good deal for Joe Lawson's instinctive trust in Lester's abilities that he agreed to let the young jockey have his way.

Lester's limp enthusiasm all the same persisted until he actually saw Never Say Die in the parade ring before the race, when it was quite clear to him that the colt had improved enormously during the past two or three weeks. Joe Lawson said the horse had done a very good gallop a few days earlier, and that he himself was strongly confident. Lester went down to the post with rekindled hope and every intention of winning.

The public were less impressed. During the near-scratching scare, the ante-post price had drifted right out to 200–1. By the start, Never Say Die stood at 33–1, in no way popularly fancied. Sterling Clark, on his distant health farm, gave the Derby no more than a fleeting thought.

Lester knew from the 1-mile Liverpool race that his mount had a bit of early speed and would be able to take a good place in the race from the beginning, so he aimed when the tapes went up to take up fifth or sixth position, which he easily achieved. The horse was going really comfortably all the way from then on, lying fourth, fifth or sixth for the first mile.

Coming round Tattenham Corner the order was: Rowston Manor, joint favourite; Landau, the Queen's runner; Darius, the Two Thousand Guineas winner, which finished third; Blue Sail, ridden by the American star jockey, Johnny Longden; and Never Say Die, prominent because of the long white blaze down his chestnut nose. These were followed by Elopement, who had beaten Never Say Die at Newmarket, then Narrator and Arabian Night, which eventually ran on into second place.

There was little bunching, plenty of room for everybody. Lester brought Never Say Die to a wide outside position and made a long smooth accelerating run to the winning post, easily passing everything on the way. The official distances were two lengths between first and second, and a neck between second and third. Behind, strung out in an amazingly long procession, the other runners came in at six- and seven-length intervals, with almost a furlong between first and last.

Lester says of Never Say Die: 'He won easily. He came away well in the straight, and one of the things he did do was stay. He finished really well. He won quite comfortably really.'

The crowd cheered him, even those who hadn't backed him. The lad who did the horse, Alfred Vase, led his charge proudly into the winner's enclosure, the owner being far away in a state of shocked astonishment in his clinic.

Joe Lawson was ecstatic.

Lester, in his contained way, was driven quietly home by his father, and at his usual time went to bed.

The flavour of Lester's tremendous triumph lasted a scant two weeks. Never Say Die was to run in the King Edward VII Stakes at Royal Ascot and Lester of course was to ride. He thought Never Say Die might be good enough to win, but there were two contra-indications. First, Arabian Night, second in the Derby at level weights, would at Ascot carry 8 lb less than Never Say Die; and second, more importantly, Ascot is a right-hand track.

Lester's own words on the subject of Never Say Die's left-handedness: 'He was perfectly all right on a left-handed course, but if you were going the other way he was inclined to come out. There are certain horses that don't go one way at all. You run them one way and they're useless, and the other way they're champions. You try to tell people it makes all that difference and they don't believe you, but it's a fact.'

Whatever his misgivings, Lester gave his mount the best chance he could, and in doing so became involved in a triple bumping incident which led to one of the most controversial suspensions in racing. Never Say Die did not and could not win the right-handed King Edward VII Stakes. He finished fourth: and because of the bumping, Lester was called in front of the Stewards, who withdrew his licence and banished him from racing. (*See* pp. 52–5.)

Without Lester, Never Say Die ran next time out in the St

Leger, and won easily. The St Leger, run at Doncaster, is a left-handed race.

Lester generously told Charlie Smirke, who was taking his place, how the awkward horse could best be ridden. Charlie Smirke gratefully took the advice and made a trouble-free and triumphant passage.

Never Say Die never ran again after the St Leger, and for the most chivalrous of reasons. Sterling Clark decided that he himself would win no more prize money that season so that the Queen might head the winning owners' list for the first time. There were only a few hundred pounds between them; he would bow out and leave her precarious lead safe.

He left Never Say Die at stud in England where the best of his progeny was Larkspur who won the 1962 Derby, and a filly, Never Too Late II. She was trained in France but came to England in 1960 to win both the One Thousand Guineas and the Oaks, sire and daughter between them thus taking four of the five English classics.

In the long history of the Derby, Never Say Die might not be considered one of the greatest of winners; but on his day, and going his own sweet left-handed way, he was as good as ever Joe Lawson thought him.

# Suspensions: Part I

'When you're young, if you really want to win races, you'll do anything to get there first. You see it happen all the time with kids. They get in a bad position and they've just got to get out.'

That is the voice of the mature Lester. Young Lester at fourteen had skill, determination and courage above all. What he lacked was experience.

Time is the gift of experience. Time to think in advance, time to see what's going on around, time to be cool. Every jockey finds that his first races pass in a flash, but by the time he's ridden several hundred, there's all the time in the world.

By the spring of 1950, fourteen-year-old Lester was ready to do 'anything' to win races. At the Lincoln Spring Meeting, he was 'severely cautioned' about his riding, and at Hurst Park at Whitsun he was not merely cautioned but suspended for the rest of the meeting. (Such a suspension usually meant for a period of one day.)

At Kempton Park in July, he was cautioned for crossing and suspended for the rest of the meeting (one day), and in August at Worcester the same thing happened, except that he was also fined 20 sovereigns for boring.

His actual sins were to push forward through too-small gaps, bumping the horses on each side, and to cross too closely in front of other horses, impeding their progress. All of these first suspensions were the result of his dash and his wish to please: the anxiety not to disappoint all those whose hopes rode with him.

The consequence of his injudicious exits from tight corners was the growth of a syndrome which followed him all his career: if Piggott was in any way involved in a bumping incident, then it was automatically Piggott's fault. A factor apparently overlooked was that older jockeys, sensing Lester's fast approach between them, deliberately narrowed any gap to shut him off, and by leaving it too late effectively caused the bumping themselves. Lester became a handy universal scapegoat: the other jockeys grew to know they wouldn't be blamed.

'I did deserve some of the suspensions,' Lester says, 'but in some of them I was hard done by. In everything, if you do a few things wrong, you're the first to get the blame each time.'

He thinks those suspensions he felt he had earned probably did him good: but if continual trouble finally taught him he had to be careful, it offered no advice on *how* to smother a surge of race-winning instinct in the heat of the moment.

The British racing public, along with the trainers Lester rode for, perceived with crystal clarity that his youthful rough riding wasn't the result of ill nature or outbursts of temper or downright villainy. The British racing public continued to cheer him with hoarse throats and the trainers forgave him the lost races and signed him up for the instant of his return.

Lester himself took the suspensions, well earned or less earned, in equal silence, never letting his feelings get further than a frown. He was already, at fourteen, adept at damping down his miseries and keeping them in control: disasters didn't destroy him then or at any time after.

By October 1950, his dual reputation was in full swing. To the public he could do little wrong. To the Stewards he could do little right. When Lester rode too enthusiastically on Barnacle at Newbury, the thunderclouds were already gathered above him, waiting for an opportunity to burst. The Newbury Stewards reported Lester to the Jockey Club for 'boring and crossing'. Lester himself can't remember anything particular happening, but the Jockey Club Stewards upheld the local stewards' judgment (which they normally do) and suspended Lester for three weeks, which meant for the rest of the season.

The main recurring official reason for most of Lester's suspensions, all his career, was that he rode with 'disregard for the safety of other jockeys'. It is worth pointing out that while this might be a strong opinion, it was not born out in fact. In no Piggott 'incident' was anyone ever hurt. No horses fell, no riders were ever unseated.

'You could understand the fury,' Lester said, 'if I had killed someone. But no one was even bruised.'

As happened over and over again later, after one big bang of authoritarian anger, a quiet period ensued. In 1951, Lester didn't come before any stewards for any reason. By 1952, things livened up slightly with a one-meeting suspension for 'crossing' at Goodwood. In 1953, the same thing happened at the Eclipse meeting at Sandown, and in October that year Lester was fined 25 sovereigns and suspended for the rest of the Warwick meeting for lining up in the wrong position! (No stalls in those days.)

At the Epsom Spring Meeting in 1954, Lester rode Loll for Michael Pope. The horse finished second but was disqualified for crossing. Lester's explanation that the horse had swerved unexpectedly and not by his (Lester's) intention was discounted and Lester was suspended for the rest of the meeting.

At Royal Ascot that year, Loll ran again with a different jockey and swerved in exactly the same way. The jockey wasn't suspended: he wasn't even asked for an explanation.

By Derby day, 1954, Lester's tally of suspensions was:

1950 – four one- or two-day suspensions, and one of three weeks

1951 – no suspensions

1952 – one single-meeting suspension

1953 – two single-meeting suspensions (one for lining up wrongly)

1954 – suspension on Loll at Epsom.

In considering Lester's longest and worst suspension, it is important first to reconstruct what actually happened to him and Never Say Die in the King Edward VII Stakes at Royal Ascot in June 1954.

The incident which caused all the trouble took place at the point where the horses come round the last bend into the straight, a distance of some two and a half furlongs, or a third of a mile, from the winning post.

All bends, but that bend at Ascot particularly, tend to throw horses slightly wide as they gallop round at a speed nearing forty miles an hour, the hooves having to find extra purchase on the turf in the same way as a car's tyres grip round a bend in the road.

One doesn't have to rely on spoken opinions or memories for what occurred because the sequence of events was captured on a British Paramount newsreel film. Frame by frame, it speaks for itself.

Sir Gordon Richards, riding Rashleigh, came round the bend with two other horses between him and the rails. The horses were Garter, ridden by Bill Rickaby, next to Sir Gordon, and Dragon Fly, ridden by Doug Smith, next to the rails. Rashleigh was thrown a little wide by being on the outside of three coming round the bend, as also in his turn was Garter. Gaps opened between the horses.

All jockeys know that gaps open up in this configuration. Experienced jockeys are ready for them, waiting to take advantage and go through, for this is often the opportunity one looks for in starting what one hopes may be a winning run.

Lester, racing behind the trio on Never Say Die, saw the fairly large gap which had opened between Garter and Dragon Fly, and advanced into it. There were now four horses more or less side by side with Sir Gordon on Rashleigh on the outside.

If Rashleigh had run straight from that point nothing would have happened, but Gordon was already working to correct his outward swing and to stop Lester's advance, and was pulling Rashleigh in again towards the rails. Garter couldn't get back to his former position because Never Say Die was now in it, and he was severely squeezed between Never Say Die and Rashleigh. Rashleigh came right across onto him and a good deal of hard bumping occurred over the next few strides. Never Say Die, with his heavy head and bias to the left, was banging against Garter from the inside, with Gordon on the outside pulling to the right. Garter it was, therefore, who was on the receiving end from both.

The mêlée straightened itself out with Gordon pulling his horse out again a shade to get away from contact with Garter, and from that point all four horses ran straight for more than the final two furlongs. It is as well to note that the four horses involved were not in the lead when they came round the bend: Blue Prince II and Arabian Night were both in front.

In the last stages of the race, there was another upheaval. Arabian Night, comfortably leading, suddenly swerved, then crashed against the rails and bounced off, severely impeding Blue Prince II and a horse called Tarjoman which had come forward to challenge. Rashleigh, with Gordon working hard, went past the mix up to win, with Tarjoman second and Blue Prince II third. Arabian Night, at a standstill, finished nowhere. Never Say Die, with every chance if he had had enough speed, finished fourth.

The Ascot Stewards raised an objection against Gordon Richards for the earlier incident, and called in all the jockeys concerned. No investigation was held into the Arabian Night bumping, although many present, including some of the Press, thought that this was what the official enquiry was about.

The Stewards did not at that point have the newsreel film to consult, and there were, of course, in those days no camera-patrol films, giving a head-on view. They had to rely on their own impressions, seen through binoculars from six hundred yards away, and on what the jockeys told them. Their own impression had been that Rashleigh had caused the bumping through pulling over towards the rails. The newsreel film shows all of Rashleigh's side from head to tail, clearly at an angle to the rails and the track. The Stewards' first impression was correct.

When they heard that Lester had compounded the trouble by taking Never Say Die forward and by not being able to control his mount's heavy left-swinging head, they removed the blame from Gordon altogether and transferred it entirely to Lester.

Bill Rickaby, who rode Garter, is Lester's cousin. It's not known whether this fact made any difference one way or another. It is known, however, that Lord Rosebery, owner of Garter, was extremely annoyed by what had occurred, and it was possibly he who suggested the enquiry.

The Ascot Stewards suspended Lester for the rest of the meeting and reported him to the Stewards of the Jockey Club. And that, in the opinion of the bulk of the racing world and certainly the crowd that day at Ascot would have been more than enough.

They had seen Rashleigh cross towards the rails with their own eyes, and whatever else had happened, that cross *must* have contributed to the bumps.

At the enquiry held at Ascot before racing the following day, the three Jockey Club Stewards (different from the four Ascot Stewards) upheld the Ascot Stewards' opinion that the bumping had been solely caused by Never Say Die, and that Lester should not have moved forward into the gap which had opened between Garter and Dragon Fly. Gordon's account, that Rashleigh had been turned sideways by Never Say Die's forcing Garter against his rump, was accepted.

The Jockey Club Stewards' enquiry lasted barely twenty minutes.

They took Lester's licence away completely and actually without setting a time limit on the sentence, though it was suggested that he could apply to return at the end of six months. The severity of the sentence was received with consternation by most of the racing people and with outrage by the general public who wrote to the newspapers in unprecedented numbers to complain.

The Stewards, perhaps taken aback by the furore and by several critical attacks upon themselves, made a highly unusual statement to defend themselves. Lester, they said, had relied on the good nature of other jockeys to open up and let him through. Even if this had been true, the sentence shouldn't have been six months' banishment, but in fact it wasn't true. Sufficient gap *had* opened up, before Gordon pulled Rashleigh across to retrieve his former position.

It is instructive to reflect what would have happened if the two jockeys had been on each other's mounts.

It is certain that if Lester had crossed on Rashleigh, the Ascot Stewards would have brought him in on an objection, because they did in fact in the first instance object to Gordon for that reason. Gordon, a brilliant jockey, would very likely on Never Say Die have moved forward legitimately into the opened gap: it is after all the way to win races. After the collisions, would Gordon, riding a horse notorious for its left-hand bias, have lost his licence for six months? Would he even have been censured for bumping against Garter? He might instead have been treated with understanding, even if not with sympathy.

Lester, for crossing, would have been suspended. For how long, is anyone's guess.

At the distance of thirty years, it seems incredible that a few seconds of bumping, so far from the winning post, affecting the outcome of the race not at all and doing no damage to any man or any horse, should have been considered serious enough for the sort of swingeing sentence usually reserved for dishonesty.

Given that the sentence was out of all proportion to what was at most a misjudgment, and on the part of *two* jockeys, not one, the short question arises: why?

The Stewards said they were taking into consideration Lester's eight previous suspensions (but one or two of those were in themselves suspect). The snowball effect, the blame-Piggott syndrome, had gathered the fury of an avalanche.

The forces at work were varied, and at least one of them was rooted deep in the origins of organised racing. The owners in distant times put their own servants onto their horses as jockeys, so for generations all jockeys were considered to be servants: and they were servants not in the friendly atmosphere of today, but in the much more severe 'upstairs-downstairs' era.

Lester was not a servant. In his own home, he was the son of the master of the house, son of a man who owned his own stables and employed his own staff. Lester hadn't been taught and hadn't imagined that others might consider him in the category of a servant because he was a jockey. The social upheavals of the Second World War were still bubbling away in 1954, but a total change of attitude had not yet happened among many of the older generation. The more senior of those acting as Stewards at race meetings, it would be fair to say, were happier with the behaviour patterns of twenty or more years earlier.

Lester, young but serious in mind, felt no natural subservience to Stewards and tried to explain things to them, person to person, adult to adult. They brushed his explanations aside and seemed to be irritated by what they judged his lack of proper respect.

'It's different now,' he says. 'The next generation, they listen. You go in now and you explain what happened, and the Stewards will listen and understand, and most often they take no action because they can see what it was like.'

Lester at eighteen was self employed, independent and well on track to the top. He had just won the Derby to universal acclaim, with the word 'genius' shyly and self-consciously appearing in journalists' columns. The myth of Lester was growing, and on its own would not go away.

It is a curious fact that Lester's most savage suspensions often followed closely upon his most dazzling achievements: as if the one provoked the other. There's a streak in human nature which reacts to the spectacle of immense success with an urge to destroy it. Lester was of the forceful new world, busy usurping the old; Lester had just won a spectacular victory: Lester was ripe for being slapped down.

It's certain that if any such normal feelings coloured either the Ascot or the Jockey Club Stewards' judgment during the Never Say Die enquiry, they were not aware of them. They did honestly believe that their findings were impartial. They were men of honour.

On the other hand, the second jockey involved was the very one for whom they had nothing but the warmest regard. Twenty-six years champion jockey, winner at last of the Derby on Pinza in 1953 after years of trying, and recently knighted, Sir Gordon Richards was probably the most-liked man in racing. Everyone, including the Stewards, admired and respected him and hastened to smooth his path. Everyone deferred to him in a way they have done to no man since, and they were right to do so, as he was and is one of the nicest men ever to set foot on the Turf.

When Sir Gordon Richards retired from his later career as a trainer, the Jockey Club made him an honorary member, an honour not bestowed on a professional jockey before or since.

The Ascot Stewards would of course have censured Gordon for his riding of Rashleigh had they thought he deserved it but, subconsciously, they must have been relieved to decide that they wouldn't have to.

At the Jockey Club enquiry, the Stewards not only took away Lester's licence but they stipulated also that he must leave his father and go to work for a different trainer. They were of the opinion that Keith had encouraged Lester in his 'disregard of the safety of other jockeys'.

The truth was not that Keith had actively encouraged Lester but that back in 1950 he hadn't told him that what he was doing was wrong.

Lester's thoughts, thirty-five years on: 'Probably it would have been better if once or twice he'd said I was wrong when I cut in or cut somebody off . . . if he'd said well, it's not worth doing something like that. But it's difficult. You can't do two things – do your best to win all the time and be careful all the time. It doesn't work out.'

Keith was another of the subterranean forces which set off the avalanche, and not because of urging Lester to ride roughly, which he didn't, but because of his uncomplicated pride in his son's achievements. His beaming face, it would seem, was taken to be approval of Lester's strong riding; therefore Keith, too, should be punished.

There was among the older generation a real sense of loss for the past and a clinging to the pleasant concept of amateurism, to playing the game for its own sake, to losing gracefully.

Lester had no intention of losing, gracefully or otherwise. The game, for Lester, was winning.

Such an attitude was considered unsportsmanlike. It was fine to win races, so the thinking went, but one must not be seen to be trying too hard. No matter that such an expectation was unrealistic – an over-polite jockey who lost a race from an excess of good manners would be roundly cursed and replaced – it was all the same strongly held. Harold Larwood and Douglas Jardine, who had won back the Ashes with bodyline bowling, were still in semi-disgrace.

In racing, Sir Gordon Richards was seen as the *parfit gentil* knight, winning presumably from grace and magic, not from all sorts of effort. Lester's modest demeanour in victory gained him no points at all. The powers-that-were correctly sensed that he had no respect for the myth of amateurism, and they resented his rejection of it.

From all these causes, a full-blown allergy had developed. Every time Lester was in any way involved in a fracas, official irritation against him took a larger step forward than the occurrence itself warranted. By 1954, the merest rumour of his involvement was producing automatic hostility, with steam coming down nostrils and the urge to squash erupting like a rash.

It took a very long time for this allergy to subside. In a later enquiry, for instance, Geoff Lewis was severely cautioned for giving evidence in Lester's favour and saying a collision had not been Lester's fault.

So in 1954 the avalanche of buried, unrecognised and unconsidered feelings rolled down the hill in civilised tones and did its brutal work. The unjust sentence was delivered.

Lester left home and went to Newmarket, stunned but again mostly silent, to work in the yard of Jack Jarvis. Jack Jarvis taught Lester none of the better ways he was supposedly there to learn, as the trainer was ill in bed most of the time and almost never left the house. Lester's cousin, Bill Rickaby, was Jack Jarvis's stable jockey, and Lester lived in Newmarket with his mother's sister and her husband, Mr and Mrs Fred Lane. This, the family thought, would most sympathetically and safely see Lester through his banishment from home.

Lester's terse opinion of the sentence was quoted at the time to be 'unfair and ridiculous', (which can't have pleased his judges) and he has not changed his opinion since. Time has rubbed out the bitterness, but it was then, he says, that he really saw the world as it was.

What subsequently went on behind the scenes cannot be known, but suddenly towards the end of September the Stewards told Lester to reapply for his licence. The ban had lasted a week over three months.

During that time, Sir Gordon Richards had had a heavy fall and decided to retire, leaving trainer Noel Murless without the jockey whose services he had rejoiced in for very many years. A successor had to be found, and found soon. When Gordon retired, there were two full months left of the season. Owners who had horses trained by Noel Murless at that time included the Queen, Prince Aly Khan and Sir Victor Sassoon. It is certain that Noel wouldn't have engaged any jockey who was not acceptable to those owners and, equally, he wanted the best he could get. Immediately Lester was told he could have back his licence, Noel invited him to be his stable jockey.

The step from depression to exhilaration was dramatic.

Lester's licence was restored on 28 September, and the very next day he was back with a winner; and such was the fervour of the public's disgust with his suspension that the prolonged cheering of uninhibited affection practically lifted the roof off Newmarket's stands. Other wins followed on 1 and 2 October, and on 6 October at York, he won his first race for Noel Murless, on Evening Trial, owned by Sir Victor Sassoon.

Soon after, Lester rode and won for one of his Ascot judges. Bygones were all of a sudden definitely bygones. The allergy, well and truly scratched, had subsided. The road ahead again shone bright.

The successful come-back all the same exacted its price.

In the limbo of indefinite suspension at Jack Jarvis's, working as a stable-lad and not knowing at what point he should be fit for racing, Lester was unprepared for the suddenness of the reprieve. His weight through the months of banishment had edged upwards towards nine stone, and he was faced with the daunting task of losing one of these stones in a week. One stone represented one-ninth of his body: a body, moreover, with little flesh to spare. He achieved the loss on time through starvation, running and sweating, and still had enough strength to hold half a ton of horse on the wing.

Noel Murless had engaged a jockey who would put himself through wringers to win races. Noel Murless would settle for the odd bumping and boring charge that would surely lie ahead, if he could reserve for his stable that will, that skill, that unwavering passion.

# Crepello, Carrozza and Petite Etoile

Crepello came into Noel Murless's yard as a yearling towards the end of 1955, and right from the beginning looked a horse with a sparkling future.

Inheriting Sir Gordon Richards' job at Warren Place, Noel Murless's great training establishment in Newmarket, Lester had a tremendous 1955 season, beating a century of winners for the first time and finishing third behind Doug Smith and Scobie Breasley on the jockeys' list.

The Never Say Die suspension was firmly behind him. The Never Say Die triumph in the Derby was what people remembered of 1954: the flashing presence rather than the disputed absence.

While there were no Classic Piggott wins in 1955, there were others of interest, the biggest single prize being the Eclipse Stakes at Sandown, where Lester brought home Darius, which had finished third in Never Say Die's Derby.

On Nucleus, owned by Miss Dorothy Paget and trained by Helen Johnson Houghton at Blewbury in Berkshire (though the horses ran under the name of her friend, Charles Jerdein, as it was in the old-fashioned days before the Jockey Club granted training licences to women) Lester won four races. The third of these wins was at Royal Ascot in the King Edward VII Stakes, a sweet victory, as it was in that race a year earlier that the Rashleigh/Garter/Never Say Die collision occurred. The fourth Nucleus winner of the season was the prestigious Jockey Club Stakes at Newmarket late in September.

Besides these, the year's highlights were Little Cloud's winning of the Northumberland Plate for Sir Victor Sassoon, and the same owner's Elopement taking the Hardwicke Stakes at Royal Ascot, both horses trained by Noel Murless: and also Lester's first winner for the Queen, Annie Oakley at York in October.

Lester survived 1955 without a suspension or even a caution: perhaps everyone had learned something from the year before.

With the advent of the 1956 season, the training of both Crepello and Carrozza began in earnest. Crepello had been bred by Sir Victor Sassoon as a stayer to go two miles, being by Donatello II, who had won the Ascot Gold Cup. The colt was not, on his breeding, regarded as a top prospect for the Derby even though he had been prudently entered at birth for the big race.

A good-looking chestnut with a short neck on a big body, Crepello appeared as strong to the eye as he proved under the saddle. Always easy to ride, he would go without trouble wherever Lester wanted, and from very early on produced mouth-opening speeds on the gallops at home.

Training him was, in most respects, easy, but in one respect difficult: there was always the suspicion that one of the tendons in his forelegs would give way, which would mean effectively the end of his racing career. Accordingly throughout his life, Crepello wore strong supportive bandages on his forelegs, the sort called Newmarket Boots, which were made of doeskin and sewn on tightly, semi-permanent. They had to be turned round on the legs every day to dislodge any piece of grit which might have slipped inside.

Noel Murless decided to run Crepello in June, which was fairly early for a juvenile of that breeding, and consequently sent him to Royal Ascot for the 5-furlong Windsor Castle Stakes. He told Lester to go carefully and not to push him too hard, and Lester, following instructions, was just beaten by the good Fulfer, trained by Geoffrey Brooke.

Lester's words: 'Noel told me to be easy with him. I could have won otherwise. But I didn't punish him at all. It wouldn't have done him good for the future.'

Noel was very pleased with the way Crepello ran, but instead of making haste to capitalise, he let down the colt for a while and brought him back to full training in September for the

Middle Park Stakes at Newmarket. In that race, Crepello met some of the proven best of the season's two-year-olds, and was beaten into fourth place behind Pipe of Peace. The result was considered disappointing, even though the opposition had been stiff, the race fast and the distances at the end very short between the first four horses.

Noel Murless gave Crepello another rest and then ran him over seven furlongs in the Dewhurst Stakes, also at Newmarket, on 1 November. Crepello ran well and won by three-quarters of a length from the Queen's Doutelle, but still appeared not tremendously impressive.

'He was always a bit lazy,' Lester says. 'When he got to the front, he never did more than he had to.'

Noel Murless, nonetheless satisfied, put Crepello away for the winter after what had been a basically undemanding two-year-old programme, and concentrated on keeping the suspect legs strong for the heights ahead.

It's no easy matter to train a horse into tip-top form for the Two Thousand Guineas, run at Newmarket at the beginning of May, without a preliminary race first. Noel Murless, however, planned to do exactly that with Crepello, and feeling no doubt that it was now-or-never with the legs, galloped him hard and often on the Heath. The companions in these gallops were two good Murless four-year-olds and also the three-year-old Arctic Explorer, which Lester later that year took to victory in both the King Edward VII Stakes (again) and the Eclipse. The gallops were almost races in themselves, and by 1 May, the day of the Two Thousand Guineas, Noel Murless was confident that the colt was ready.

The Two Thousand Guineas turned out to be no easy race. For a start Crepello had the worst draw of all, number fifteen, on the outside. At Newmarket, the horses running the straight Rowley Mile come by preference down what is technically the outer rail of the track, that is to say, along the rail nearest to the stands. Crepello, drawn furthest away from the stands rail, was at a great disadvantage. Next, the opposition contained Pipe of Peace (the favourite) which had beaten Crepello on the same course the previous year, and also a good French horse, Tyrone, of which much was expected. Third, there were two delays to the start of the race, one horse bolting on the canter down, and three jockeys later being unseated by colliding with the starting tapes as the horses came under orders. Two of these horses were remounted, but Chevastrid decamped into the next parish and was eventually counted out.

When the race finally started, Lester solved the bad draw by coming over towards the stands rail, even though it meant tucking in near the rear of the field. There he stayed until he was nearing the Bushes, those few hawthorns on the far side of the track two or three furlongs from the winning post, where the horses meet rising ground.

At that point, Lester pulled Crepello out a little and shook him up; and he says, 'I just went through them so easily, it was hard to believe'. Crepello reached the front but 'went a bit lazy again', leaving Lester the task of holding off Pipe of Peace and the faster finishing Quorum (who in the end took second place), both horses having been at Crepello's heels for longer than was comfortable. The three battlers flashed across the line with no daylight between them, the official distances being half a length and a short head. The French horse Tyrone finished fourth, a good way back.

Crepello was immediately made favourite for the Derby, his reputation based not just on having won the Two Thousand Guineas, but on the persistence with which he'd fought off the challenge of Pipe of Peace over the last stages, and on the visible power and presence of his muscular body. Crepello, in fact, was *exciting*.

There has hardly been another horse of which more was confidently expected at Epsom, despite a pessimistic 'knocking' campaign by a section of the Press. 'Finding one to beat Crepello' became the slightly mournful quest of would-be punters not liking the 6–4 available: and they would have been even less hopeful if they'd heard Lester's own opinion.

'Crepello worked very well before the Derby, as well as any horse I've ever seen. His gallops were terrific. He was one of the very best of horses.'

Crepello went like a king to Epsom and with majesty took his crown. Lester let him go along easily in seventh or eighth place and as in the Guineas made no early move. Coming round

Tattenham Corner, he was tucked indistinguishably behind a cluster including Brioche, Eudaemon and Chevastrid (back from the next parish). Not until two furlongs out, as in the Guineas, did Lester move, and then, as before, the incredible acceleration set the stands roaring.

Crepello sliced through the Derby field and won by a length and a half in 2 minutes $35\frac{2}{5}$th seconds, only $1\frac{3}{5}$th seconds outside Mahmoud's long-standing 1936 record. A few carping critics nevertheless said it hadn't been a 'good' Derby because Crepello had beaten 'nothing'. But he had. The horse which finished second was the then little known Ballymoss, whose starry future victories included the Irish Derby, the St Leger, the King George VI and Queen Elizabeth Stakes and the Prix de l'Arc de Triomphe. Pipe of Peace again came third.

Sir Victor Sassoon had already won the Derby with Pinza, but he had bred Crepello, which made the second winner sweet. Plans were immediately laid for the St Leger, with the King George and Queen Elizabeth Stakes along the way.

Crepello worked faultlessly again at home and went to Ascot for the King George as odds-on ante-post favourite. Then, while he stood waiting in the Ascot stables, the heavens opened and rain bucketed down on the racecourse. By the time of the first race, the going was 'heavy'.

Noel Murless struggled with a dilemma. The ante-post market meant that if he withdrew the horse, those who had already backed him would lose their money. If he ran the horse, the tug of the sticky turf might be too much for the suspect tendons. The legs had so far stood up to everything asked of them, but always on good ground.

For the sake of Crepello, for the sake perhaps of the St Leger and the Triple Crown, Noel Murless withdrew him an hour before the big race. The decision was greeted with howls of rage by the disappointed crowd and with resignation by Lester. The horse went home sound to Newmarket and was given a short rest before preparing for the St Leger.

It was then, after a gallop at home, that the worst happened. Crepello went irretrievably lame, the tendon stretching ominously, ready to tear if stressed. The days of speed and glory were depressingly over.

Crepello ran in only five races in his life. Lester puts him in the top five horses he ever rode, and thinks he would have been unbeaten after the Derby. At stud, perhaps because of his own long-distance breeding, Crepello was not immediately notable. His colt foals were in general moderate, the fillies better. The fillies went on to make good brood-mares, and themselves produced many winners.

Noel Murless's stable in 1957 was solidly packed with outstanding equine talent, but all of his lesser horses ran into winning form also, as if inspired by the great. The mystery of being 'in form' can never be scientifically explained, but when the heavens smile it's best not to waste time.

Lester's sixth winner of the season was Carrozza for the Queen in the Princess Elizabeth Stakes at Epsom in April, an early announcement if ever there was one of the filly's intentions. Despite her small size – a shade under 15 hands – she proved game and determined throughout her career.

By Dante, Carrozza was owned by the National Stud and leased by Her Majesty, an arrangement common for many years. Latterly, the National Stud (theoretically owned by the taxpayers) has kept only stallions and brood-mares, with no horses of tip-top racing age. The Queen for years sent the National Stud horses to Noel Murless to train, while those she herself owned were with Sir Cecil Boyd Rochfort.

During 1956, Carrozza as a two-year-old had won early on for Noel Murless at Hurst Park, ridden by Lester, but in general there was more public interest in the Queen's very own filly of the same age, Mulberry Harbour. After her early two-year-old win, besides, Carrozza was off the racecourse for weeks, having tangled with her rug in her box at home, injuring herself severely.

In 1957, after her first three-year-old win, she ran with promise but without distinction to finish fourth in the One Thousand Guineas (ridden by Bill Rickaby) and it was Mulberry Harbour who went to the Oaks with more expected. Mulberry Harbour carried the Queen's first colours: Harry Carr wore the black velvet cap with the gold fringe, while Lester's cap was white with a gold tassel. Neither was favourite, that honour going to the Aga Khan's French-trained filly Rose Royale II at 11–10. Mulberry Harbour, next best, set off at 11–4.

In the race itself, however, Mulberry Harbour faded unusually under pressure, having rounded Tattenham Corner in a good second position. Carrozza, going well, came down the hill against the rails with two or three others in front. One of those, Taittinger, well fancied, tired a little and came away from the rails, leaving a gap. Lester took Carrozza through it like a dart before the crowd could draw breath and they were suddenly out in front, sprinting for home.

The favourite Rose Royale II took up the battle, but couldn't pass. An Irish horse, Silken Glider, ridden by Jimmy Eddery (father of Pat, Paul, Michael and David) next got into top gear and began overhauling Carrozza. The crowd held its breath. Lester kept little Carrozza going with every resource of his artistry, with Silken Glider gaining inexorably. So close were they as they passed the post that neither jockey was certain who had won, though in three strides more there would have been no problem as Silken Glider shot ahead before pulling up.

The judge called for a photograph, and after a nail-biting pause Carrozza was named the winner by a short head. The Queen, to delighted applause, led in her first Classic winner and people began searching for new adjectives to apply to Lester.

Lester and Noel Murless together won forty-five races in 1957, headed of course by the Two Thousand Guineas, the Derby and the Oaks. Seven of those races were won for the Queen, twenty for Sir Victor Sassoon. Of the 122 winners Lester rode that year, over half started favourite. Carrozza at 100–8 was the longest price of all.

It was also the year of Lester's first Ascot Gold Cup, won on Zarathustra, trained not by Noel Murless but by Cecil Boyd Rochfort. Cecil Boyd Rochfort had two runners in the race, the other being Atlas, for the Queen. He gave his stable jockey, Harry Carr, the choice of mounts and, as every jockey has done too often for comfort, Harry Carr chose the wrong one. Zarathustra's long-distance record in earlier years had been excellent, but as a six-year-old he had not so far won. Against that, Atlas had won last time out. The wrong choice was easy to make. Lester rode Zarathustra that time only, taking the lead more than a furlong out and comfortably staying ahead to win by one and a half lengths. Zarathustra retired on his considerable laurels, and never raced thereafter.

The very next year, 1958, Lester won the Ascot Gold Cup again, this time on Gladness, trained in Ireland by Vincent O'Brien. It was Lester's first ever ride for Vincent, and certainly neither of them foresaw the close partnership they would one day reach.

Gladness took the lead two furlongs out, and won the Gold Cup by a length, unpressed. Vincent next ran her in the Goodwood Cup, Lester leading most of the way to win easily, and after that sent her to the Ebor at York, where she obliged at a canter. That Gold Cup, that Ebor Handicap, were Lester's top wins of the 1958 season.

Gladness was a great galloper, Lester says, though one wouldn't have expected it. She was a big rough-looking mare, bred like a jumper, who ran first at the end of her three-year-old season and blossomed marvellously only at four. At five, she won only one small race in Ireland, but went on later to be a great brood-mare, all of her progeny proving winners.

During 1958, Noel Murless's stable reached none of the great heights of the year before, but contained instead a clutch of two-year-old fillies of great promise for the future, among them Prince Aly Khan's grey twinkler, Petite Etoile. Lester won two two-year-old races on Petite Etoile, none of them top events, and also lost twice against better horses. Consequently, he approached 1959 without overwhelming faith in the little grey star.

First time out in 1959 she won the Free Handicap at Newmarket. Lester rode one for the Queen in that race, and could judge Petite Etoile's performance only from afar, but saw nothing to enthuse him.

Noel Murless had entered his three best fillies in the One Thousand Guineas, and gave Lester as stable jockey his pick of them: Petite Etoile, Rose of Medina and Collyria. Lester had won races on all three and was undecided, but he eventually chose Sir Victor Sassoon's Collyria, who was galloping splendidly for him at home.

All jockeys choose the wrong horse now and again, and as Harry Carr had done before him, Lester got it wrong. Doug Smith, engaged for Petite Etoile, won the One Thousand Guineas – rather to the astonishment of her owner, Prince Aly Khan, who had expected his other runner, the French-trained Paraguana, to take the honours. Collyria ran badly, and throughout her career afterwards proved unpredictable, sometimes brilliant, sometimes dull.

Coming up to the Oaks five weeks later, Lester was given the identical choice: Collyria, Rose of Medina, Petite Etoile.

This time, although the One Thousand Guineas success was still considered surprising and although there were doubts that Petite Etoile would stay a mile and a half, Lester took thought of the speed she could produce and concluded that he shouldn't turn her down. 'I thought if she got the trip she would be able to beat them all. So I rode her, and she won very easily that day. She was a pretty good filly.'

The 'pretty good filly' was followed home at a distance of three lengths by the favourite Cantelo (trained by Bill Elsey), who won the St Leger later that year, and then by stable-mates Rose of Medina and Collyria: Noel Murless's trio had finished first, third and fourth.

Lester rode Petite Etoile steadfastly from then on, and with her during the rest of the season collected three other substantial prizes, the Sussex Stakes, the Yorkshire Oaks and finally the Champion Stakes at Newmarket in October.

(Interestingly, in an autumn race not involving Petite Etoile, Lester again had to choose between Rose of Medina and Collyria. He chose Rose of Medina, and Collyria won. Life's full of ironies.)

There were only three runners in the dramatic Champion Stakes. Lester, at the point where he had to start his winning dash, made a move to go through a space between the Irish-trained Barclay on the outside and a French colt, Javelot, nearer the rails. Both horses were ahead of him, and when Barclay's jockey saw Lester coming, he pulled over to shut him off. Lester had the choice of steering round to the outside, or squirting through the small gap between Javelot and the rails. Being Lester, he chose the gap. Petite Etoile shot through like a grey javelin and took the race by half a length, leaving the French jockey Freddie Palmer furiously shaken to his roots and Noel Murless and Prince Aly Khan gasping with shock on the stands.

There was a lot of general shouting but no enquiry. Petite Etoile had neither bumped nor hampered Javelot, and Freddie Palmer was erroneously credited with having let her through out of the goodness of his heart. Noel Murless had wanted 'a nice quiet race' and got instead a last-second victory snatched with breath-stopping audacity. The quiet Mr Piggott shrugged and turned his deaf ears to the fuss. He had taken his chance, got through his gap, won his race: end of story.

Petite Etoile snoozed the winter away and came back in 1960 to take her limelight as a four-year-old. The brilliant 'little star', who was not actually small like her name but on the contrary notably sturdy, ran first in 1960 at Kempton in May, bringing home odds of 7–1 on.

In June, on the day after St Paddy's Derby, Petite Etoile with her long white nose strode away at Epsom with the Coronation Cup: and it was the last time Prince Aly Khan rejoiced in a winner, as he was killed a fortnight later in a car smash. For a while the news shattered the spirits of the stable, although nothing could stop the flow of winners. Noel Murless decided to run Petite Etoile, who had been inherited by the new Aga Khan (Prince Aly's son) in the King George and Queen Elizabeth Stakes at Ascot in July.

The race was not among Lester's happiest experiences. Everyone unrealistically expected the mare to be invincible, but she had recently been coughing, and in a large field on soft ground she couldn't make her way early enough to the front. Lester attracted a good deal of criticism from people who couldn't ride a donkey and as usual took it stoically. He had tried to win. Petite Etoile had tried to win. They hadn't managed it, for once. They had a lot of ground to make up in the straight, and they lost by half a length to Aggressor.

Petite Etoile retired for a lengthy rest while her trainer pondered long-term tactics and possibilities for the following year.

In April 1961, Petite Etoile, now five years old, had to struggle hard at Sandown to beat moderate opponents, but again took the Coronation Cup at Epsom in June, with more elan, and a fortnight later won at Royal Ascot, each time starting an odds-on favourite.

Next time out, she ran at an evening meeting at Kempton Park, in the Aly Khan International Memorial Cup, with perhaps too much at stake. The race in memory of her former owner proved sadly to be the one she couldn't win, and she was unexpectedly beaten two full lengths by a horse belonging to Sir Winston Churchill, High Hat. This time no one could criticise Lester's riding. The great-hearted mare had been given every chance and hadn't been able to produce her flying last-minute speed.

She had won nearly all of her races by one length or less, with Lester often thought to have left her winning run too late. She was a racer, however, who came always with late acceleration, and was not at her best if left too long in front. In Lester she had the perfect jockey, cool enough to wait, confident enough to set her flying just in time.

She ran again in 1961 after the Aly Khan Memorial, and won, still at odds-on, at Doncaster in September. Later the same month, she ran in the Queen Elizabeth II Stakes at Ascot, but in spite of Lester's best efforts she was without her old withering speed at the end, and lost by half a length. The reign – and the career – of one of racing's greatest mares was over: the sparkling little star went out.

Behind the headlines and the ballyhoo, the late nineteen-fifties were the worst years of Lester's constant battle against weight. Between the years of twenty and twenty-four he suffered unforgiving hunger pains day after day, denying his body the normal consolidation of young manhood, facing the stark choice between career and physical deprivation.

It's easy to underestimate what many jockeys endure for the sake of their jobs. Most people wanting to lose weight go on a comparatively gentle reducing diet and expect to revert to more normal food fairly soon. They do not unremittingly starve and sweat and still turn in top athletic performances, knowing that it will last for as long ahead as their talents and their bodies can stand it.

In his late teens and early twenties Lester used to let himself off the worst hunger pangs after the end of the Flat season, with the result that each winter his weight crept up ten or more pounds in four months. Each spring, he was then faced with the same task as in 1954, at the end of the Never Say Die suspension, the quick and agonising reduction of an already sparse body.

Finally he decided the partial let-up of winter wasn't worth the increasing difficulty he found each spring, and from about 1959 onwards he maintained his full spartan regime year round. His method was simple: eat what you like, but very little of anything. Take small portions and leave half. Drink half a cup of sugared coffee, black. Half a cup of tea. A few sips of Coca-Cola. Half a glass of champagne. He used to drink half a gin-and-tonic, but less as time went on.

Shellfish, lamb cutlets, chicken, smoked salmon, all in tiny amounts, he likes. Disliked are potatoes, cake and curry. Ice-cream is adored, but the trouble with that, he says disgustedly, is that four ounces of ice-cream produce in him a pound of body weight, which he holds neither logical nor fair.

Around four large cigars a day take the place of further food, as also does sunshine, when he can get it. One needs to eat less in the sun.

At about thirty years of age, Lester's weight finally stabilised on this regime at roughly 8 st 5 lb, enabling him to ride at a little under that if essential. Back in 1957, however, he was still at the grindingly horrific stage of shaping his body to suit his will, and apart from eating too little, was also reducing his body fluids violently.

Many jockeys sweat away their mornings in saunas. Lester hit on a less time-wasting solution and turned his own car into a sweat box, driving to meetings in mid-summer with the windows closed and the heater full on. In addition, he wore several layers of absorbent T-shirts under a rubber sweat suit, and on top of that, an ordinary shirt, jacket and trousers. On arrival in the changing room, he peeled the whole lot off and hoped to make the weight on the scales.

Those sweltering journeys, his wife said later, were not the best way for her to arrive at Royal Ascot looking cool, fresh and uncreased.

# Susan, Maureen and Tracy

Susan Armstrong met Lester Piggott when he was fifteen and she was eleven. They each went to the Doncaster Sales with their parents in 1951 and stayed in the same hotel, the Mount Pleasant, on the road between Doncaster and Bawtry.

Susan's mother and father knew Keith and Iris Piggott well: the four of them had been close friends in earlier years, but in successive house-moves had drifted apart.

Susan's mother, born Maureen Greenwood, was living in Letcombe Regis with *her* mother when the newly-married Keith and Iris built their first home opposite her own. The three of them played tennis together often, a trio later turned into a foursome when Sam Armstrong, who trained horses at Middleham in Yorkshire, began visiting Maureen Greenwood in the mid nineteen-thirties.

Maureen's mother remarried (to Bob Thorburn, a racehorse owner), Maureen later in her turn marrying Sam Armstrong and going off with him to the north, moving eventually to Newmarket when he transferred his stable there in 1945. Because of the distances from Berkshire, and because private travelling was discouraged during the Second World War, Maureen saw little of the Piggotts for many years.

The two families had, however, known each other well enough and for long enough for the common ground to lie there between Susan and Lester, waiting.

Neither remembers anything particular about their first meeting: they just know where and when it occurred. Neither, unsurprisingly, felt irresistibly drawn to the other. Lester went on racing, Susan went back to school, and that was that.

Someone gave Susan a Horselover's Calendar with a picture of Lester sitting on a bucket looking up at a horse that was looking down at him. 'By this time he was pretty well known,' she says. The calendar must even so have been important to her, because she remembers it.

She left school at fifteen and went to a finishing school in Switzerland for nine months. At sixteen she was home in Newmarket, working full-time for her father in almost every possible capacity: assistant trainer, teacher of apprentices and secretary. She rode out at exercise every morning. She shepherded the apprentices at race meetings, and she saddled her father's runners at the races. She did office work in the evenings. All this was before she was old enough to learn to drive.

She says herself that she had almost no social life and no close personal friends, an exception being the four daughters of jockey Edgar Britt, who rode regularly for her father: but they still lived in the north, and she saw them seldom. She led a hardworking life, partly from force of circumstances but clearly also because she enjoyed it. She didn't want to go out to parties: she disliked parties then and does so still.

She was therefore in many important ways already a perfect match for Lester Piggott. Like him, she came from a busy racing family who took hard work for granted. She liked a quiet private life. She was intelligent, and doing a job most people might have considered her too young for, with competence of a high order. The reputation her father enjoyed for training apprentices was largely Susan's work. She it was who day by day taught Wally Swinburn, Paul Tulk and 'Kipper' Lynch, and gave further help to Josh Gifford, who had come from Cliff Beechener's stable, having won his first race at eleven.

Susan knew a great deal about horses and rode excellently herself; and beyond all that she was (and is) extremely pretty.

Lester, one day early in 1957, went round to the Armstrong house to collect a pair of shoes which Wally Swinburn had brought back for him from India, where the two of them had been riding during the winter. By then Lester knew Susan pretty well by sight because she was so often at the races. He said something to her about taking her out, sometime. She said she would go, but heard no more.

Their first significant meeting came a little later in the same spring when the Britt girls came down from the north to go with Susan to the eighteenth birthday dance of Anne Carr, daughter of Harry Carr, then the Queen's jockey.

Joe Mercer was there, who later married Anne Carr, and Jimmy Lindley, and a whole bunch of the young generation, including Lester. They all spent an euphoric evening and Lester again said something to the seventeen-year-old Susan about taking her out, but again did nothing about it.

Although they talked to each other often on race days after that, it was more than a year later before the decisive move was made. Lester invited Susan to go to the musical 'My Fair Lady' and then to dinner, the occasion to take place on the first evening of the Derby meeting in June.

Susan accepted. Lester picked her up from where she was staying near the Epsom course with her parents, drove her to London and delivered her back to them afterwards. The event had been a success.

'After that,' Susan says, 'the friendship developed. We saw each other all the time at the races, and he was often in Newmarket because of riding for Noel Murless.'

They went to the pictures, went out to dinner. 'It just became an understood thing between us that we would get married. It wasn't a sudden thing. It was just understood.'

They took their time. Lester had had other girl friends: Susan much enjoyed what she was doing. Marriage, as for many a couple, meant for him responsibility and for her the prospect of abandoning a job where she was outstanding and, instead, running a house and cooking, which for all her abilities she knew nothing about and didn't relish.

They decided eventually that February 1960 would be a suitable time. Susan would be twenty, Lester twenty-four. There would be time for a honeymoon before Lester prepared for the new Flat season in March.

As neither of them much enjoyed parties, they decided against a big wedding in Newmarket when 'all the world' would come, and also against Lester's home town, Lambourn, settling instead on neutral ground in London. Accordingly, with a minimum of ballyhoo and with eighty relatives and friends (and a press photographer) in attendance, Lester and Susan married on 22 February 1960 at St Mark's church, North Audley Street.

Susan wore a flowered silk dress with a hat made of petals, Lester wore a navy blue pin-striped suit: they looked apprehensively happy. The reception was held at Brown's Hotel, where Susan's parents had held theirs also, and the new couple went away to the south of France for two weeks afterwards.

Returning, they moved into the house they had bought in The Avenue, Newmarket, and named it Florizel, after a horse trained by Keith Piggott that Susan had ridden a year or two earlier in the Newmarket Town Plate. In that event, she had been beaten by Julie Murless (Noel Murless's daughter, later wife of Henry Cecil) but had been fond enough of the horse to choose its name for her first married home.

Domesticity sat oddly on the young Piggotts. Susan learned to cook chicken, which they ate most of the time. Lester mowed the lawn. Susan says that at least her ignorance in the kitchen had one excellent result: Lester never had *quite* so much trouble with his weight after he'd married her.

Susan came from a family where everything was geared to the needs of her father. Sam's training operation was the most important element: Maureen organised the whole of life around it. Susan and her brother Robert, four years younger, were accustomed to giving their father's needs absolute priority without question. Lester came from a family which put *his* needs first, which organised life around his comings and goings, which fed him at times which suited him and provided a comprehensive support system with undemanding devotion.

When they left these backgrounds and came together, the young pair simply continued in their accustomed life roles. Susan smoothed the way for Lester instead of for her father; Lester moved from his mother's solicitude to his wife's.

It was a dove-tailing pattern and a foundation which weathered the strains and storms inevitable in every marriage, which carried them through in fundamental accord to a silver wedding day and beyond, and which shows no sign of cracking.

This is not to say there is never nowadays a cross word. With a life lived at the pace and stress of the Piggotts', it would be unnatural if there weren't sometimes a frustrated edge to the voices. The constantly-ringing telephone, interrupting every conversation, is picked up often with gritted teeth.

They each, however, come from long-lasting families, and one of the strengths of such families is that they pass on the *expectation* of stability to the next generation.

Neither Lester nor Susan ever rebelled against their parents. Susan sought advice often from her mother and deeply admired her father. Lester in later years built a bungalow for Keith and Iris a few steps from his own house. With family affiliations so strong on each side, the habit of affection between Lester and Susan became the solid rock of the Piggott marriage, trustable by tradition under their feet.

In the June after the wedding, Lester won the Derby for the third time and later in the year Susan became pregnant. Their first daughter, named Maureen after Susan's mother, was born in May 1961, during the week of Chester races.

Lester was in Chester, of course. He returned to his newly extended family in a happy state of semi-intoxication, having celebrated the arrival not just with his fellow jockeys but also with most of the visiting Australian cricket team, notably Keith Miller, a favourite friend.

Soon after the birth, Susan went back to riding her father's racehorses out at morning exercise, a part of her life she had missed, and later that year, and again in 1963, she won the Newmarket Town Plate.

In 1965, Susan gave birth to their second daughter, Tracy, completing the family; and a few years later, her old habit of managerial hard work resurfacing after a long period of domesticity, she began to operate as a bloodstock agent. Slowly, cautiously at first, but over the years with increasing skill and confidence, she turned her deep knowledge of horses into a tangible asset, developing a sizeable and respected business.

Both Lester and Susan believed always in keeping their children with them and in showing them the world, and consequently from a very young age the two girls travelled several times to the Bahamas, South America and the Caribbean, and towards the end of their schooldays to Singapore, Malaysia, Hong Kong and throughout Europe. At every destination, Lester made excursions to nearby courses to ride winners, mildly continuing the tradition that work comes first with pleasure as its consequence.

The whole family became expert travellers, not least because they all positively enjoy it. There is probably no one on earth faster through an airport than Lester, who seems to carry the floor plans of dozens of them in his head.

On one occasion, his speed got him into trouble. He and Susan (without the girls) were travelling from Hong Kong to Singapore where he was due to ride in one of the island's most important races, the Lion City Cup. He had won the race the year before, and many were hoping that on Blue Star he would do it again.

The Piggotts had to change planes en route at Bangkok, and there, intead of flying straight on, they were delayed for a whole night. Flying on the next morning, they touched down at Singapore at about the time Lester should have been changing into his colours out at the racecourse.

'Get the bags,' Lester said succinctly to Susan, sprinting first off the aeroplane and finding an escalator leading upwards through an apparent side door. Susan went through the health check desk and through immigration with wide-eyed stunned officials saying, 'Did you see that man? He didn't go through the health desk, he didn't go through immigration, he didn't go through customs!'

'Dear me,' Susan said. 'How extraordinary,' and didn't say she knew him.

Lester ran right through the airport buildings and caught a taxi. Susan composedly collected the suitcases as instructed, was met as arranged by friends, booked in at the hotel and finally arrived on the racecourse.

The Lion City Cup was over. Lester had won. The appreciative crowd was counting its winnings.

Retribution appeared later in the afternoon in the shape of three forbidding young immigration officials who threatened deportation, but fortunately by the next morning a few words had been quietly dropped in high places, mainly to the effect that Lester had had an obligation to fulfil and it wasn't his fault he'd been delayed; and the champion overland traveller got off with a caution.

Ask Maureen and Tracy if their father was strict with them as children, and they laugh, the idea is so alien. Lester undemandingly loves his daughters, is proud of them, anxious for them sometimes, hoping they'll be happy. They have grown up with the pleasant sort of beauty that any father would delight in, with sweet natures speaking volumes for their source of upbringing.

To be the child of a household name has destroyed many, but Lester and Susan's down-to-earth manner and simple tastes cooled the greenhouse of success like air conditioning. In their house, there was Lester the living Dad, not Lester the living legend.

For Maureen it was never a problem to have a famous father: she accepted it from birth as part of life. For Tracy perhaps it wasn't quite as simple, and for a while during her teens she preferred, when among strangers, for them not to find out who she was. Both of the girls naturally learned to ride, but were never forced. Maureen in her teens took to eventing, and Tracy rides exercise on racehorses. Neither has shown any desire to be a professional jockey. Both are supportive, proud and protective of their father.

After fifteen years, Lester and Susan left their first house and built a new one on the opposite side of Newmarket, where there was room also to build stables. Influenced by a house they had seen in Hollywood, and another in Australia, they designed a one-storey U-shaped house round a swimming pool, and with them from one home to the other they took both their telephone number and the name Florizel.

From the road, shielded by bushes along a curving drive, the low house is easy to overlook. Inside, it is spacious without trying to be grand, comfortable without opulence, built purposefully for a busy life, with 'his' and 'hers' offices.

Lester's workplace at home in summer consists mainly of a garden chair in an airy sunroom beside a telephone with office clothes consisting of swimming shorts and a cigar.

A man's house, family, habits of life are always a reflection of his essence. There is no pretension in Lester's.

# St Paddy

The colt developing as a two-year-old in 1959 in Noel Murless's stable sent a ripple of anticipation through an establishment that was already enjoying a brilliant year. There was not only Petite Etoile's unbroken run of six wins including the One Thousand Guineas and the Oaks, but also the multiple winners Primera and the Queen's Pindari, who took the Ebor and the Voltigeur in a magnificent double at York on the same afternoon. Noel Murless's prize-winnings soared ahead of Cecil Boyd Rochfort's, and Lester finished the 1959 season with 142 winners, a great improvement on 1958's 83 from much the same number of rides.

Underlying all was the promise of St Paddy.

St Paddy was by Aureole, a great sire of many winners who nevertheless frequently passed on his volatile and unreliable temperament. No one therefore was much surprised when St Paddy proved to be highly strung and easily frightened: the problem was basically to release his speed while staying in control.

Lester rode him often at exercise on the Heath. 'He bolted a few times. A bird would fly up, and he'd be off and go two or three furlongs before I could stop him.'

Trusting to no birds flying up from the track itself, Noel Murless sent his hard-pulling two-year-old to York in August for his first public outing on the day Petite Etoile won the Yorkshire Oaks, and such was St Paddy's reputation for speed at home that he was backed down to favourite.

The worst happened. St Paddy came out of the paddock gate onto the course and straightaway bolted. He went three furlongs flat out before Lester could pull him up, throwing away all chance of winning the race. Lester took him to the start and set off, but there was no use pressing the colt hard, so he tucked him in behind to teach him how to settle, and they finished in the ruck, about ninth of eighteen.

After that débâcle, jockey and trainer decided to try a crossed noseband next time out—a sort of bridle which gives much stronger control of a horse's head. Noel Murless sent St Paddy to Ascot for the 1-mile Royal Lodge Stakes in late September, and Lester took him down early to the start, trotting sedately. Let off, St Paddy immediately ate up the ground with his fearsome speed, and won by five lengths. Derby-prospect watchers sat up and took notice, and Noel Murless sighed with relief.

During the winter, the trainer mapped out his plan of campaign, deciding that St Paddy should take his chance in the Two Thousand Guineas but that, unlike Crepello, he could not be trained to the minute to win. St Paddy was a stuffily-breathing horse who needed a very great deal of work, and more preparation than the scant six weeks between the beginning of the Flat season and the first two classics allowed.

Considering that he really needed a longer distance and hadn't been trained very hard, St Paddy ran well in the 1-mile Two Thousand Guineas to finish sixth. Noel Murless, not expecting a win, knew contentedly that the colt would improve on this Newmarket performance, and two weeks later ran him in the Dante Stakes at York, which St Paddy obligingly won easily.

Before both of those races, Lester had ridden the good-looking dark bay down to the start in a crossed noseband which he had taken off at the post: the crossed noseband was thought too severe for racing in because, once the tapes had gone up, the horse had to be free to stretch his head forward and develop his rocket speed unhindered.

Approaching the Derby, Lester's chief fear was that when the horses turned to canter back past the stands at the end of the parade, St Paddy would blast off at a hundred miles an hour, and to avoid that he used a dropped noseband with hooks at the side. 'You can hold anything in that.'

St Paddy went in subdued fashion to the start, and the restraints were there removed. Perhaps because of his easily frightened nature and his comparative unreadiness in the Two Thousand Guineas, he started at 7–1, by no means favourite. The opposition included two Irish colts, Kythnos and Alcaeus, and the French runner, Angers, the best backed.

The race itself proved to be without complication for Lester. He took St Paddy into the front bunch at the start and simply stayed there, always going easily in third or fourth place. With coolness and great timing, he urged St Paddy to the front two furlongs out and let the colt stride away freely, keeping him ahead without problem, riding him with hands and heels only.

The two Irish colts came second and third, the faster finishing Alcaeus passing the more fancied Kythnos a short distance from the post. The French hope, Angers, cast gloom over the Epsom Downs by breaking a hind leg before reaching Tattenham Corner and having to be destroyed, a sad end to a great horse.

It was a fast Derby, only a shade outside Crepello's time: the fourth victory for Sir Victor Sassoon, the second for Noel Murless, the third of course for Lester. After these giddy heights, St Paddy went back to Newmarket for a well-earned rest, his next race not to be until Goodwood at the end of July. Again, as for the Guineas, he could not be trained back to his absolute peak in time for Goodwood, and was beaten there in the 1-mile 3-furlong Gordon Stakes by Kipling.

Lester's opinion of St Paddy as a whole is that the colt was a speed machine but unintelligent. Of riding him, he says, 'He was a great horse when he was running away in a race, when he was pulling against his bit. If he wasn't pulling, he wouldn't race. If you had to let him off the bit, he'd get frightened and it was the end, he wouldn't win. It was better to hold the reins tight, to keep him pulling, even if you knew he wasn't going to go any faster. It gave him a bit of courage.'

Lester's victories on St Paddy looked inevitable from the stands and his losses sometimes inexplicable: the key to both lay in the quirks of the nervous equine mind, and the complete understanding of them in the thoughtful mind of his jockey.

After Goodwood, St Paddy went to York fully prepared for the Great Voltigeur, and won easily. Ahead then lay the St Leger, the one classic neither Lester nor Sir Victor had won so far.

The field opposing St Paddy at Doncaster lacked much glitter and, in the event, on perfect going, the colt ran the easiest race of his life. He won by three lengths, unstretched, pulling so hard against his bit that the Press dubbed it 'runaway St Leger', and 'just too simple'. Lester kept his council, and everyone in the Murless camp was naturally ecstatic, particularly the owner, who had bred the horse himself.

Sir Victor Sassoon was not in good health and came to the St Leger in a wheel-chair, frail but smiling broadly: with other winners such as Sunny Way, Tudor Love and Off Key, he finished the season overwhelmingly as the leading owner. Noel Murless similarly topped the trainers' list, and the great Aureole commandingly led the sires. St Paddy the schizophrenic warily ate his hay and continued to be frightened by birds.

Lester, his St Paddy season augmented by the four-year-old successes of Petite Etoile and by a stream of further Murless winners, was also supported by a whole host of other trainers hungry for his talents. Disappointing few of them he rode with constant inspiration and mastery, his very presence on a horse abruptly shortening its odds; and despite not being able to ride half the horses running because of his weight, he won 170 races from 640 rides and became champion jockey for the first time.

Marriage, the Derby, the championship, all in one year. The Gods were smiling. What could possibly go wrong?

In the next season, 1961, Pinturischio went wrong.

Pinturischio was the equivalent of Crepello and St Paddy, a colt with everything it took to win the Derby. Owned like the others by Sir Victor Sassoon, and coming to hand early, he won a mile race at Newmarket in April 1961, starting at a justified 5–2 on.

Secrets are impossible on Newmarket Heath. The work-watchers with their powerful binoculars, the bookmakers' runners, the inquisitive Press, all had seen for themselves the developing power of the potential world beater, and large bets were already being struck on his winning the Derby in June.

Sired by Sir Victor Sassoon's Derby winner Pinza, Pinturischio started favourite in the Two Thousand Guineas, and although he didn't win, he did enough in finishing a good fourth to keep expectations high. Owner, trainer and jockey looked forward to another Derby success. The public confidently piled on the ante-post bets.

Others were less pleased at the prospects. Three weeks before the Derby, someone broke into the Murless stable and gave Pinturischio a massive dose of a diarrhoea-producing drug. The colt, in a sorry state, nevertheless recovered in time for Noel Murless to resume his Derby preparation, and it was thought that the nobbling attempt had failed. Everyone underestimated the villains' determination. Despite increased security, the stables were again penetrated, another and stronger dose of physic being administered to Pinturischio.

This time, the colt was desperately ill. Not only had he no chance of running in the Derby, he never properly recovered at all, and was unable ever to race again. This wicked destruction of a great animal cast a cloud over the whole racing year for those concerned.

Lester himself watched the Derby on television in his sitting-room and saw Psidium, on whom he had once won, and could, if he had chosen, have ridden in the big race, beat a poor field at the outside price of 66–1.

It was considered at the time likely that someone in the stable had helped Pinturischio's nobblers; had shown them a way in and pointed them to the right horse. Not until four or five years later was this theory proved correct, when the villains were finally detected. The inside man proved to Lester's and everyone's disgust to be one of the best lads in the stable. He had cared for one great horse and at the same time ruined another. He had taken owners' compliments and thanks and cynically robbed Sir Victor Sassoon behind his back not only of another possible Derby but of the colt's future at stud.

St Paddy, having wintered well and developed, proved one of the stable's top 1961 earners, going from strength to strength. For openers he went to Sandown to run against only two opponents, one of which was his own pacemaker, Sunny Way. As St Paddy was thought to be quietening down with age, Lester rode him to the start without the dropped noseband. A mistake. St Paddy gave signs of his old trick of taking charge and, to stop him, Lester guided him towards one of the steeplechase fences. St Paddy immediately began to measure his stride to jump, and

Lester had to pull him out again. They did reach the start in fair control, however, and in the race St Paddy cantered nonchalantly home to win, untaxed.

Next time out (restrained down to the start), he went to Royal Ascot and dealt equally disdainfully with three contestants in the Hardwicke Stakes (one of them again Sunny Way), leaving Vincent O'Brien's Die Hard, on which Lester later that year won the Ebor, struggling helplessly in his wake.

St Paddy next went to the Eclipse Stakes at Sandown in July where he led from start to finish, Lester smoothly holding off the supporting cast of six. Press reports noted that all three wins were 'easy', because St Paddy was never off the bit.

Considered unbeatable, St Paddy set off in the King George VI and Queen Elizabeth Stakes in soft going on a windy day at Ascot later the same month, and there met his Waterloo in the shape of the French horse Right Royal V, who won by three clear lengths.

'He murdered me,' Lester says succinctly. St Paddy, in desperation let off the bit, still couldn't quicken. A four-year-old, he was giving a stone in weight to his three-year-old conqueror.

On this downbeat note, one of the era's great racing partnerships came to an end: in August the news came that Sir Victor Sassoon, at seventy-nine, had died of a heart attack at home in the Bahamas.

Reeling from this second great blow, the Murless stable again rallied and went on with business.

Aurelius, who had missed the Derby because of the hard ground and had won the King Edward VII Stakes instead (that race again!), went forth and doggedly clung on to a one and a half length lead in the St Leger, bringing home at least one Classic as consolation.

St Paddy, now carrying the colours of Lady Sassoon, came out again in September, and (strongly held) won the Jockey Club Stakes at Newmarket, conclusively beating High Hat who had earlier defeated Lester and Petite Etoile in the Aly Khan Memorial. St Paddy finally ran in Newmarket's Champion Stakes in October, but again he was outrun by a French horse, this time the practically unknown Bobar II. St Paddy couldn't quicken at the end and lost by three-quarters of a length.

A line was drawn under a brilliant career, and St Paddy went to stud. Because of his own insecurities, his progeny were seldom bold and the runaway star was not an outstanding sire. Connaught, second in the 1968 Derby, was the best of his 'get'.

Lester rode St Paddy in all of his races: two also-rans, three seconds and nine firsts.

# Injuries: Part 1

Racehorses are not safe, and no one who rides them over a long period escapes injury of some sort. It's considered inevitable that jump jockeys should get hurt occasionally, but the level of risk accepted by Flat race jockeys is curiously underestimated. There they are, perched over the shoulders of half a ton of athletic muscle travelling at up to forty miles an hour, with nothing but their sense of balance between them and the crunching crash. Flat race jockeys look at the risk clearly: much of the public doesn't see it at all.

For Lester, the first serious involuntary dismount at top speed occurred on 31 March 1951, when he was fifteen.

On the day of the Lincolnshire Handicap in which he was due to ride Seconds Out, owned by Jack Solomons the boxing promoter, Lester rode in the afternoon's first event, the Castle Plate. His mount, a filly, Pandite, started favourite and ran reasonably well, with Lester in third place fifty yards from the winning post going flat out for the finish. Without warning, Pandite went down, hurling Lester to the ground. Pandite lay helplessly on her side, sorely injured with a broken leg. Lester lay beside her, cradled in the arms of two ambulancemen who went to his aid; and on them all, as so often in Britain, it poured with rain.

Pandite was put out of her misery on the spot. Lester, clutching a badly broken collar-bone, was carried by the ambulancemen off the course, and driven from there to Lincoln County Hospital for X-rays, bone setting and strapping. Iris, of course, went with him and later that day drove her sore and shaken son home to Lambourn, whose only consolation was that he hadn't missed winning the Lincoln. Seconds Out lost on points, finishing well down the field.

By the next morning, Lester was comfortable, smiling, planning to keep fit by walking, and determining on the earliest possible come-back. He made that in two weeks and two days, riding in five races at Birmingham on his first day's reappearance, and winning the last on Grey Magic, beating the odds-on favourite.

At fifteen, a lifelong pattern was in this way set: the real agonising pain dealt with as quickly as possible, the recovery speedy, the courage intact. The list of Lester's subsequent injuries, long chiefly because of his long career, would have horrified and deterred many a strong man: Lester simply thinks it amazing that anyone should consider tumbling off horses any sort of reason for not getting back on immediately.

For all self-employed jockeys, the inducement to return to the saddle is ostensibly two-fold. First, it's boring sitting around doing nothing. Second, sitting around doing nothing is expensive. Self-employed people cannot claim unemployment benefits, and no work means no income. All the same, to say that the indecent scramble back to the saddle of almost every jockey, not just Lester, is fired by finance is to misunderstand the underlying psychology. The need to earn is often given as the public reason for the fastest possible return, because the need to earn is easily understood. The deeper need for speed, for competition, for exercising one's skill, for winning—all that lies in a shadowy compulsive area of self-fulfilment that can be destroyed by too much dissection.

When the compulsion fades, when it's gone, the jockey stops riding in races. Money in itself is not motivation enough. Lester himself says jockeyship is 'just a job', a statement his actions belied. For Lester, the post-injury urge to return to race-riding was instinctive and not to be analysed. Enough to say that in him it had been from the beginning consistently and overwhelmingly strong.

Lester's 1951 season ended even worse than it began, with another and much more prolonged sojourn in hospital.

In August, in the last race at Lingfield, the favourite, Persian

Wood, fell without warning coming round the last bend into the straight, bringing down Lester on No Light who was tracking him closely. Eph Smith, riding Persian Wood, broke his collar-bone and some ribs, and Persian Wood, with a broken leg, had to be put down.

Lester's severe injuries were caused not so much by the fall itself as by hitting at high speed one of the concrete posts supporting the rails. Those concrete uprights were over and over again the source of terrible damage to jockeys and horses, and it took thirty years from Lester's accident for them to be replaced on most courses by plastic posts which would snap in a collision, not mangle the bodies of man or beast.

Lester broke his leg, his hip and his collar-bone, multiple injuries which put him in East Grinstead Hospital for three weeks and plaster for three months. Once the bone-setting operations were over he was cosseted like mad by the East Grinstead nurses and given no-frills devotion in Lambourn by his parents, but, legs being notoriously slow to mend, it was not until well after the Flat season ended in November that he was able to get back on a horse.

After these dramatic goings on, it was thirteen years before anything more serious than cuts and bruises came Lester's way, but on 27 September 1964, in Paris, the run of good luck drastically ended.

By then he was adult (twenty-eight), married, a father, and set fair to become champion jockey for the second time. The championship was very important to him at that point as, since winning it for the first time in 1960, he had seen it appropriated for the following three years by Scobie Breasley. On the day he rode in Paris, Lester's score stood at 135, with another Australian jockey, Ron Hutchinson, at his heels on 123, and Scobie third at 118. Lester was hungry to regain the crown, and he couldn't know that it would be his own for the next eight years.

He rode Persian Garden for Noel Murless in the Prix Henry Delamarre at Longchamp, and at about half way, when lying about fifth, his mount crumpled and fell. Lester says he thinks he was squeezed for room and that his horse caught the heels of another. In any case, he was pitched straight off, and the two horses immediately behind fell on top of him.

Lester, unconscious for half an hour, was carried off on a stretcher to go to hospital, lying white and silent under a fringed car rug. One of the other fallen jockeys, Marcel Depalmas, went with him. The third, Roger Poincelet, walked away unhurt and later the same day won the Prix de Sablonville on The Marshall.

The Stewards, holding a subsequent enquiry, blamed Yves Saint-Martin, riding Acer, for the squeeze and handed out a month's suspension, saying at the same time that they didn't think he had caused the disaster intentionally. Either one is guilty, or one is not!

Lester and his French champion-elect counterpart were thus both in one incident prevented from riding in the 1964 Arc de Triomphe, run the following Sunday, but in the event neither Saint-Martin's mount, Jour et Nuit, nor Lester's, Royal Avenue, added to their intended jockeys' disappointments.

Lester, still unconscious, and Depalmas, concussed and delirious, were taken to the Clinique Jouvenet at St Cloud, always the care centre for racing mishaps. One enterprising journalist described Depalmas as on his feet and giving a lucid account of the triple fall after a 'check-up' at the hospital, but in fact the lightweight Frenchman was talking disjointed nonsense in a southern French accent in a two-bed ward shared with the non-speaking and badly battered Lester.

Julie Murless, Noel's daughter, telephoned to Susan back home in Newmarket, and in tears told her that Lester might have fractured his skull. Susan, four and a half months pregnant with their second child, was taken by a close friend, Charles St George, in a private plane to Paris the following day, and went to the clinic knowing only that Lester was alive. She found him in the hallway outside the ward, not only alive but sleepily conscious and sitting in a wheel-chair. That was the good news. The bad, which she and Lester successfully hid from the Press, was that Lester's face was cut and severely bruised, and all the left shoulder, arm and side of his body the same, and that he had double vision and an intense persisting headache.

'A spokesman' at the hospital helpfully and publicly announced that there was 'no fracture'. Both Lester and Susan say there was a hairline fracture at the base of the skull, and in view of the severity and persistence of that fall's effect on his brain, they are certainly right.

The English newspapers were predicting Lester to be 'Out for six weeks' or 'Out for the rest of the season'. The season would end on 31 October, less than five weeks ahead. Lester, his mind on his fragile lead in the championship, had other ideas.

Susan moved into the clinic to be near to tend her husband, and the delirious Depalmas was moved to another ward, but because he didn't really know where he was, he kept wandering back in again, as in a farce; at least he kept the Piggotts' sense of humour alive through the anxious days.

With his customary resilience, Lester was back on his feet by Friday and on the Saturday, six days after the crash and the day before the Arc, he and Susan flew back to Heathrow. They were worried about dodging the airport photographers, as Lester, with his groggily shaky legs and severely cut and bruised face, didn't want the world in general to see him. He was saved, as it happened, by the Beatles, who were flying in from America on the same day. All the photographers pointed their waiting lenses the Beatles' way, and Lester brought his frail state of health home unnoticed.

He rested for almost a week, the double vision and the headaches persisting, and then rode a hack on Newmarket Heath, intending to race the next day. On his return from the exercise, however, he announced he was 'not satisfied with his condition', which literally meant 'can't see, head thumping, sore and stiff and too weak to win'. He would be thoroughly fit to ride on the following Wednesday, he said firmly: and Ron Hutchinson meanwhile closed the championship gap to five.

Wednesday came and went, but by the following Friday the fitness was more or less a fact, and in the Houghton Stakes at Newmarket Lester rode with paramount strength to get Alan Adare home by a head.

Poor Ron Hutchinson got to within two of Lester's total during the last week of the season, but in the end Lester won by four, at 140 to Ron's 136. Scobie Breasley finished third with 123.

Very probably under the strict rules later introduced to prevent jockeys from riding with insufficiently mended injuries,

Lester would have been forced to sit around for longer than the nineteen days it took him to get back to winning. The modern rules might possibly have given Ron Hutchinson the championship. But there it is; Lester successfully suppressed the seriousness and extent of the damage, and he could make his own choices, and he did by will-power take his title.

The double vision lasted a month. The headaches went on for fifteen years, recurring at periods of stress, and often during flights, and unpredictably at other times. Although a faintly anxious severity had for long been his accustomed public face, it is possible that for fifteen years the headaches accounted for the extra strain apparent in so many photographs. It has been noticeable in latter years that the Piggott smile is a more common occurrence, and that Lester is much more relaxed. It's possible it is the *headaches* which relaxed: they plough no more furrows in his forehead.

# Suspensions: Part 2

Between the restoration of his licence in 1954 and the spring of 1962, Lester had been before the Stewards at scattered intervals for a bunch of various and repeated misdemeanors, such as 'anticipating the start', 'excessive use of the whip', 'starting in the wrong place', 'not keeping a straight course' and 'not riding out for third place'. The last infringement is common to all jockeys, who hate to be hard on a horse if it can't win. The betting public on the other hand rises to understandable peaks of fury when their place bets go visibly down the drain. The rules insist a horse must be ridden right out, regardless of whether or not a hard finish will exhaust or sicken the horse for the future. Maybe the rules are right, maybe they are not: the argument goes constantly on.

Lester was also cautioned for a broken stirrup leather (should look after his equipment properly), for being two minutes late in weighing out (allowed to race), and for forgetting to weigh in when finishing fourth (fined 10 sovs.).

Only in 1959, however, was he actually suspended, and again, strangely enough, because of an incident involving his cousin, Bill Rickaby. No one nowadays can check with Bill Rickaby about his impressions of this or any other race, as very sadly he was involved some years ago in a car crash in Hong Kong, which left his memory impaired.

At an evening meeting at Nottingham in June, Lester, riding Astrador, swerved left suddenly against Bill Rickaby's Roi de Perse, but then straightened and went on to finish second, by a neck. Roi de Perse, hampered, couldn't recover to come in better than fifth in a close-packed field. There were barely two lengths between the first and fifth.

Astrador (trained by Noel Murless) was disqualified and placed last, and Lester was suspended for the rest of the two-day meeting for rough riding. No one seems to have taken into account the fact that on its previous running, Astrador had similarly swerved left with no warning. Horses, as Lester says, are unpredictable, and do not run on rails.

The suspension followed less than a week after he had brilliantly won the Oaks on Petite Etoile.

The events of 1962 were grimmer and altogether different, and again left Lester white-faced and bitter.

He had ridden many times over the years for a trainer called Bob Ward who had a stable at Hednesford in Staffordshire. Bob Ward was in general suspected by the Stewards of not running his horses fairly; of sending them out for 'easy' races to do no good and be reduced in the handicap, and then running them to win carrying a lighter weight and all the stable's money.

Bob Ward was by no means alone in this practice which went on, to some extent, in most stables in the land, and had done from time immemorial. In Bob Ward's case, however, the Stewards considered it blatant, and they were out to catch him. Nemesis was waiting around like a whole new thunderstorm looking for an excuse to happen, and it was Lester's bad luck that time that he got struck by its lightning.

Bob Ward decided to run two of his horses, Ione and Polly Macaw, in a selling race for three-year-olds at the Lincoln evening meeting on 30 May. It was the first race on the card, and the distance was five furlongs. Ward engaged Peter Robinson to ride Polly Macaw, and asked Lester to ride Ione.

Lester had won on Ione a year earlier on her first appearance on a racecourse. She had started favourite at 5–4 on (certainly because Lester was on board) and just lasted out to beat a poor field by half a length. Between then and the fateful Lincoln meeting, she had run nine more times unsuccessfully, once coming second with Lester but otherwise finishing nowhere with a variety of other jockeys.

Selling races, more common in those days than now, were designed for bad horses, to give them a chance of a win. Running a good horse in a seller meant that the owner or trainer could be fairly sure of winning, and could make a large profit from gambling. Lester knew that Bob Ward had a habit of running better-class horses in selling races, but he didn't mind riding them, precisely because of their good prospects of winning.

After becoming champion jockey in 1960, Lester lost the 1961 title at the very last minute to Scobie Breasley, so in the spring of 1962 he set out deliberately to win all the races he could, in order to take it back. He rode anything that was offered to him, and he agreed without question to ride Ione. He says, 'I never used to think of reasons why I shouldn't accept any particular ride, if it looked as though it might win. What jockey would?'

On the day of the race, Ione,with her string of non-successes behind her, was quoted in the morning papers as favourite at 6–4 on. This was certainly only because Lester was riding, as odds automatically shortened for him always. Still, betting forecasts are anyway just that: forecasts. Often wrong.

Polly Macaw, Bob Ward's other runner, was forecast at 3–1. She had won a modest three-year-old handicap at Ayr earlier in the season (at 11–8 on), and as a two-year-old had won four times, three times in addition being placed. She was, in fact, a better horse than Ione.

Between the publication of the morning papers and the moment of the start of the race in the evening, Bob Ward and others heaped their money on the better horse, and the prices changed round. The starting price of Polly Macaw was returned at evens; that of Ione at 11–8.

Lester knew none of this. In the parade ring just before the race, Bob Ward mentioned that he thought Polly Macaw would win. Lester felt no premonition, saw no reason to be wary. He went out to ride Ione as in any other race. He rode to win, to add to his score, which was the only reason he was on the horse at all.

In the event, of course, he lost. Polly Macaw ran away with the race and won by two lengths, pulling up. Ione, second, came in three lengths ahead of the rest, having gone sluggishly throughout the five furlongs, which was in itself an odd distance and too short, as most selling plates for three-year-olds are longer. In the auction afterwards, Polly Macaw was sold to a Mr R. Stevenson for 220 guineas, and the punters collected their winnings.

At that point the thunderstorm burst. Bob Ward, Lester and Peter Robinson were invited to explain the result before the Stewards in London.

It looked bad, Lester admits. The total change-round in the betting appeared damning. So did the fact that Polly Macaw had been pulling up at the end: if Peter Robinson had gone flat out over the line instead of sitting up and looking back, it would have been much better. He would have shown that winning wasn't easy. As it was, the Stewards interpreted his relaxation as proof that he knew Ione wouldn't challenge and pass him.

Lester, too, by the end, was standing up in his stirrups, pulling up. He never in all his racing life drove a horse hard when it could do no good. 'If I'd murdered her,' he says, 'I still couldn't have beaten Polly Macaw.'

The Stewards said Lester appeared not to be trying to win. They also suggested that Bob Ward had given him non-win instructions, and that Lester had followed them. Lester protested his innocence in vain. The Stewards, who over and over again had vigorously reproved and punished him for trying *too hard* to win, wouldn't believe, on this occasion, that he had tried at all.

They suspended his licence for two months which meant he would miss both the Derby and Royal Ascot. As for Bob Ward, who was probably the prime target, the Stewards withdrew his training licence altogether, with no limit for a return. No action was taken against Peter Robinson, because he had ridden the winner.

Bob Ward was away from racing for eight years before he got his licence back. And then, to Lester's consternation, the same thing happened again. Bob Ward asked him to ride a horse which therefore started as a short-priced favourite: Lester took the mount and got beaten by another well-backed runner from the same stable. There was no enquiry that time, but Lester decided it might be prudent not to ride again for Bob Ward.

When Polly Macaw eventually retired after a long successful career and went to stud, she proved a great brood-mare, one of her progeny, Right Tack, winning both the 1969 English and Irish Two Thousand Guineas.

Back in 1962, shocked and angry, Lester took Susan to the south of France to while away his suspension in a holiday, and came back to race again on 30 July at Windsor.

After the Never Say Die suspension, the crowd had cheered Lester to the echo when he won his first race back. In 1962, when he reappeared after what many considered an even more unjust exile, the crowd applauded and cheered him all the way from the weighing-room to the parade ring *on his way out to race*: a spontaneous, extraordinary, unique outpouring of affection and trust.

The Bob Ward case was naturally not the last time L. Piggott came before the Stewards. Two or three times most years afterwards there were fines or cautions for minor infringements of the rules, but this is not unusual in jockeys riding upwards of six hundred races a year.

As for actual suspensions, in the twenty-three years during which Lester rode after 1962, he was 'off' six times in England each for a few days only, and always for 'jostling', 'rough riding', 'bumping', 'taking someone's ground', trying too hard to win. As Lester says, 'All good jockeys get suspensions. It's the law of averages.' He has no complaints.

Suspensions nowadays are altogether more common than they were. Also they are longer: most are now for a week, not a day. Modern racing is quite severely regulated, and Lester doesn't think it a bad thing. It makes everyone careful, he says, and this is good. Even if one is careful, one runs into trouble. It is impossible to do everything right all the time.

Some of Lester's brushes with authority happened when he thought the instructions he was given were unreasonable. He was cautioned, for instance, both for 'not leaving the paddock when instructed' and another time for 'leaving the paddock without permission'. Lester always did what he considered best for the horse he was riding at that moment. Officialdom came second in importance in his estimation, and officialdom didn't like it. Athletes and sportsmen of all sorts kick against being over-coerced, and jockeys are no exception. On one occasion I myself heard and saw an official publicly give Lester a totally unnecessary order very rudely, and I sympathised entirely with Lester's deaf-eared non-compliance. Lester knew that obeying would be bad for his horse. The official reported him. Lester got a caution.

Probably the most significant clash between Lester's professional judgment and the authoritarianism that equally wanted its own way occurred at Bath in 1968.

Lester considered, as he cantered down to the starting gate, that his mount was going lame behind, that it couldn't move properly and could easily break down. At the post, he asked permission to withdraw without coming under starter's orders, and was refused. Lester protested. A vet was called; he watched the horse being led at a trot up and down and pronounced it sound. Lester was instructed to line up and start. Lester said that if he were forced to line up and start, he would do so, but he would not urge his horse to race.

He was sharply instructed to line up. He did so. The race began and Lester took no part, steadying his horse to a walk immediately, and later trotting back.

All sorts of fury were heaped upon his head but Lester unwaveringly stuck to his guns: to race could have been disastrous to the horse, he said, and that was that. The Stewards at Bath referred the matter to the Stewards of the Jockey Club, who held their own enquiry. They concluded there should be no suspension, but they 'severely cautioned' Lester and fined him £100 for making no attempt to take part in the race. The horse, incidentally, was found to be not only lame but incapable of galloping properly even when sound. It was only its second appearance on a racecourse, and it never ran again.

One has some sympathy for the officials: they were not accustomed to dealing with anyone so tough in mind. But on the other hand, if any official in any walk in life wants respect, he has to earn it. There were always individual officials and stewards whose commonsense Lester respected, and from them he would accept judgments without question. He has never been against authority itself, only against its imperfections and misuse.

Lester's last lengthy suspension, years later, was pure French farce.

By 1979, the increasingly frequent suspensions handed out to all busy jockeys were no longer instantly put into effect but were always for a period starting nine days ahead. 'Seven days' suspension to be in operation from such and such a date.' This was for the sake of trainers whose plans used to be much hampered by the abrupt disappearances of their jockeys.

Lester was given a five-days suspension late in August 1979 for not keeping straight on Thatching in the William Hill Sprint Championship at York, and during the nine days before this suspension came into effect he went over to ride at the seaside holiday town of Deauville in France. It so happened that on the morning of the Grand Prix de Deauville, there was a meeting on the course of Stewards from all over the world, including some from England. French pride in this gathering ran strong.

During the prestigious race, Lester on African Hope and Alain Lequeux alongside on Jeune Loup almost simultaneously picked up their whips to make a challenge on the one horse ahead of them, First Prayer. Alain Lequeux with his whip in his left hand gave his horse a smack and in doing so accidentally struck Lester's whip with his own. Lester, raising his whip in his right hand, hadn't yet tightened his grip on the handle: hit at that time, his whip flew straight out of his grasp and dropped to the ground.

It looked as if Jeune Loup was beaten and that African Hope might win, so it occurred to Lester he might borrow the necessary encouragement from his neighbour. Accordingly, he reached over and put his hand enquiringly on Lequeux's whip, more or less asking for the loan, and Lequeux, after a second or two, let him take it. There was no 'snatch', as widely reported in the Press.

As it happened, Lester could make no impression on the leader and Jeune Loup finished strongly after all. Lester, second, gave Alain Lequeux, third, his whip back after the winning post, and both jockeys returned to the weighing-room grinning. It wasn't Alain Lequeux who complained at all, but the trainer of Jeune Loup. He alone was angry, and he made a fuss.

The laughter hung lightheartedly over the holiday meeting for the whole afternoon, but didn't seep into the Stewards' room. Tut tut and dear dear, this was no joking matter. This had happened in front of the Stewards from all over. French pride demanded serious retribution. The placings of the second and third horses were swapped round, and Lester was sentenced to twenty days suspension, which meant missing the whole of the St Leger meeting.

The English Stewards told Lester they wouldn't have suspended him themselves and the French jockeys urged him to appeal against so harsh a sentence, but with little faith in appeals he skipped off to the sun with Susan and had a rest.

The whip in question was auctioned four years later at a Charity Race Day at Ascot, making £8,400 for the Invalid Children's Aid Society. Someone, at least, had a sense of humour!

Earlier in the same year, Lester had to pay a colossal fine in Hong Kong for pushing away with his hand the head of a horse crowding him. Foul riding, they called it. Commonsense, Lester thought.

Funny life, a jockey's.

# Sir Ivor

Many and varied were the changes and upheavals of the years between Lester's third and fourth Derby winners, St Paddy in 1960 and Sir Ivor in 1968, most momentous of all being the champion's parting from Noel Murless.

That partnership had looked to be solid forever. The two protagonists had acted together in great accord, trusting each other, appreciative and companionable, oblivious to a great extent of the difference in age. As far as Noel was concerned, Lester had a place for life. Lester, growing from eighteen, when the Murless job had been an offer beyond dreams, arrived ten years later at a point where he felt confined and, despite all his triumphs, unfulfilled.

Noel looked at the yardful of horses at Warren Place. Lester looked at the world.

Noel's roots were in the gentlemanly tradition where success was its own reward, but Lester frankly wanted to make money. Noel's owners, charming and friendly, were nevertheless not financially the best to ride for. Jockeys' fees weren't stunningly large, nor were their percentages of winning prize money generous. After tax, in spite of Press reports to the contrary, even the champion was making no fortune.

'The papers didn't bother to do their sums,' Lester said of that time. 'I read that I was a millionaire. But six hundred rides a year at £10 a ride, that was £6,000, and winning percentages at 7½% came to £7,500, if I won £100,000 in prizes. Take tax off. How could I possibly be a millionaire? It was rubbish.'

He was missing also the financial advice he had occasionally received from banker Sir Victor Sassoon during his annual summer trips to England, and was unable to find anyone else to help him with money management. 'You have to learn to do it yourself,' he says: and he began to put his mind to it seriously.

No athlete or sportsman, amateur or professional, can be sure how long his career will last. It's considered normal nowadays to make what one can while the peaks of youth allow, and in the nineteen sixties, particularly after his crash in Paris, Lester began to see consolidation as his number one target. Winning itself was fine, but he had Susan, Maureen and Tracy and his own future to provide for, and at thirty he couldn't have imagined that his supremacy would march on for another twenty years.

He wanted freedom. He didn't actually want to leave Noel Murless, but he wanted liberty to choose other horses in preference if he thought they had more chance of winning any particular big race than the home-grown offerings. Noel wanted a jockey totally loyal to his stable. He expected Lester as a matter of course to ride whatever horses the stable ran, and only to ride for other trainers when not required at home. A retainer binds a jockey to do just that, and Noel had retained Lester's services for eleven years.

In 1966, Lester, by his own choice, took no retainer from Noel. The old arrangement still appeared on the surface to be working, but there was no binding contract between them, only habit.

As often happens in racing stables after several consecutive tremendous years, Noel's yard went through a comparatively quiet period after 1961. Winners came in plenty, of course, but there were no St Paddys or Crepellos, no dizzy heights. In 1965, Lester had handsomely hung on to his title with 160 wins, of which twenty-eight had been Murless trained; but his own summits of the season had been the Ascot Gold Cup on Fighting Charlie, trained by Farnham (Freddy) Maxwell, and the King George VI and Queen Elizabeth Stakes, also at Ascot, on Paddy Prendergast's runner, Meadow Court.

In 1966 Noel Murless decided to run Varinia in the Oaks, requesting Lester to ride. Varinia had won her previous race but not with Lester who had excused himself to go to Ayr instead, to ride and win on Aegean Blue for Fulke Johnson Houghton in the Usher-Vaux Gold Tankard. Lester said that in the Oaks he would prefer to ride Valoris, owned by Charles Clore and trained by Vincent O'Brien. Vincent had asked him, and Lester intended to accept.

There were no raised voices. There was silence between them; hurt, on Noel Murless's part, determined on Lester's. The trainer told the Press that the partnership was at an immediate end, and the jockey regretted it but stuck to his decision.

Valoris was the third of three O'Brien runners at Epsom, all with Lester aboard, all backed down to favourite. The first two, Right Noble in the Derby and Donato in the Coronation Cup, ran very listlessly, each being beaten not by a hard-driven half-length into second place, but finishing sixth or seventh by a distance. Lester went out to the Oaks uncomfortably aware that he might have thrown away his friendship with Noel Murless for the sake of a stable going through the general doldrums.

For most of the race it may have seemed that way to the Epsom crowd. Varinia, the spurned filly, set off well, made a good but sensible pace and led for one mile and two furlongs. Only with two furlongs to go did Lester seriously move on Valoris, but from then on there was no doubt. The O'Brien filly went into the lead a furlong out and with Lester riding collectedly sped easily past the post first, with Berkeley Springs running on into second place.

Varinia finished third. Lester had made his point, but no one was sure at what cost.

During the weeks ahead, it became clear it had been at very little cost at all. Lester continued to win races almost daily, fuelled by the whole bunch of trainers he normally rode for when not wanted by Noel Murless. He rode three winners at Royal Ascot, and with a flourish brought home Pieces of Eight in the Eclipse for Vincent O'Brien, earning prize money not so very far behind the Oaks.

Three days before the Eclipse, Lester rode again for Noel Murless. Neither had wanted the open split, and in quiet and in private they patched it up. Lester reserved his right to choose his mounts in big races and Noel offered him the stable hope, Aunt Edith, in the King George VI and Queen Elizabeth Stakes.

Aunt Edith was one Lester was definitely not going to turn down. The sedate name did no justice to the zipalong four-year-old filly which Lester had ridden to easy victory in the Yorkshire Cup just before the Valoris/Varinia affair. Since then, she had flopped at Royal Ascot (with Scobie Breasley), but Lester harked back to her three-year-old days when she and he had skipped lightheartedly away with a big race at Goodwood and then the much bigger Prix Vermeille at Longchamp, prize money £30,485.

Lester rode Aunt Edith in the King George in the simple and well-tried pattern: take her to the front fairly early and just stay there. Stay there he did, although Aunt Edith this time was sorely pressed by the favourite, Sodium, which in the last stages of the race was gaining with every stride. Lester, riding all out, saved the day by an exhausted half-length, and later in the afternoon won twice more, making a Murless treble.

After that triumph, all seemed to go on as before in Warren Place, but to the trainer's repeated offer of a retainer and a binding contract for the following year, the jockey said no. Lester very much wanted to continue with the stable, but on his own terms. Noel not surprisingly felt that he had to have a jockey he could be sure of for big events. With nothing resolved they continued their normal winning progress, and in October, all hatchets buried, Lester won on Varinia at Ascot.

During the latter half of the season two especially significant things happened. First, in the Champion Stakes (October, Newmarket), Lester chose to ride Vincent O'Brien's Eclipse winner, Pieces of Eight, in preference to Hill Rise on which he had won the Queen Elizabeth II Stakes by a neck last time out for Noel Murless. Again, Lester chose right.

Second, Lester rode two winners on the Murless-trained two-year-old Royal Palace which was showing definite promise. Lester, however, didn't think the colt was anything really special because on the second occasion, in the Royal Lodge Stakes, the horse refused to start properly and was left by six lengths, and later wanted to run out instead of straightening after the bend: Lester was put off, and that time he was wrong.

Royal Palace, the following year, won the Two Thousand Guineas and the Derby, without Lester on board. During the early part of the winter, Noel again asked Lester to commit himself to Warren Place. Lester still preferred freedom of choice. Noel finally decided he needed the certainty of a contracted jockey more than life with an unpredictable wizard, and he invited George Moore to come from Australia to take the post.

George Moore accepted, and the long scintillating Murless–Piggott era finally came to an end. 'I left a year too soon,' Lester said later. 'But I never regretted leaving.'

During that last season, Lester won 191 races, more than in any other year, thirty-five of them, despite the hiatus in the middle, for Noel Murless.

Many predicted that Lester had made a fool of himself, as it was considered that no jockey, however good, could successfully freelance. The last who had tried it, Steve Donoghue, had promptly and permanently lost his well-established champion status to Gordon Richards. Lester, it was said, had consigned himself to oblivion.

Lester took no notice of the pessimists who presumably hadn't done any sums either. Of Lester's 191 winners, 156 had been for trainers *other* than Noel Murless, and the champion had every hope those trainers would still employ him.

Naturally, they did. When the best jockey is to be had for the asking, one asks. Lester had always ridden for his father-in-law, Fred (Sam) Armstrong, when he could and in 1967 he could most of the time. There were other regulars like Fulke Johnson Houghton and Freddy Maxwell, and many occasionals such as Dick Hern, Ryan Price, Sam Hall and Pat Rohan.

With mixed feelings and a stoical exterior, Lester back down the field watched Royal Palace win the Two Thousand Guineas, and the next day rode Noel Murless's second runner, Royal Saint, in the One Thousand Guineas, coming ninth in a close-packed finish behind the stable's first string winner, Fleet.

Ah, said the know-alls with malicious grins, serve him right. He could have won two classics, they said.

Lester doggedly went on winning a good many smaller races, giving more than value for money, and by sheer force of appearing constantly in the frame began to silence the critics. The Derby, all the same, was a wry experience. George Moore won on Royal Palace: Lester rode Ribocco for Fulke Johnson Houghton and finished second by two and a half lengths. Every chance, not quite enough speed. The critics still smirked.

Ribocco, by Ribot, had been an outstanding two-year-old but in his first three-year-old outings had run below his promise. In the Derby itself, his old form had swept back encouragingly, and he and Lester were sent to the Irish Sweeps Derby at the Curragh three weeks later.

There Ribocco beat a Murless horse, Sucaryl, into second place, and the critics were more or less silenced. A few grins broke out again when Noel's Busted won the King George VI and Queen Elizabeth Stakes with Lester on Ribocco third, but when Ribocco and Lester scorched ground to defeat Noel's excellent Hopeful Venture within the last furlong of the St Leger, there was nothing more to be said. Lester had made the 'impossible' transition, had won at least one of the classics, and had emerged still as champion. He had cemented important ties with Ribocco's owner, American Charles Engelhard, and had survived with a minimum of official troubles—to wit, two mild cautions for being late into the parade ring and one for 'jostling' in a race.

Besides all that, he had won both the Gimcrack and the Middle Park Stakes, top races for two-year-olds, on his father-in-law's best horse, Petingo.

Petingo, owned by Captain Marcus Lemos, a good friend of Lester's, represented Sam Armstrong's strongest-ever hope of winning both the Two Thousand Guineas and the Derby, and everyone assumed that Lester would be out there putting his genius to familial use. They reckoned without Vincent O'Brien, fate . . . and Sir Ivor.

Lester had no contract of any sort with Vincent O'Brien, just an understanding that when the Irish trainer ran a good horse outside Ireland, Lester would be asked to ride. It was an agreement that suited them both well, and it had been in operation since Gladness's win in the Ascot Gold Cup back in 1958.

Accordingly, when Vincent asked Lester to go to France to ride Sir Ivor in the Grand Criterium at Longchamp in October, Lester accepted; however, as it was only a week before the race, it meant getting himself off another horse, Timmy My Boy, that he had been engaged for.

Lester had never seen Sir Ivor and knew nothing about him, but Vincent's opinion that he was 'a hell of a horse' was enough. A glance at the form books showed reasonable wins in two races in Ireland after a modest first outing, all ridden by the O'Brien retained jockey, Liam Ward.

So Lester went to France and met Sir Ivor, and they won the Grand Criterium easily from opposition that proved to be of the very highest class. Bella Paola, second, went on the following year to win all the French fillies' classics, and Timmy My Boy, third, finished second the next year in the French Derby.

Lester returned thoughtfully to England and wrestled with his problem. Petingo was family, Petingo had won easily every time out, and Petingo wouldn't stay the Derby distance of a mile and a half. Sir Ivor was very good indeed and Sir Ivor would very possibly stay. Petingo might beat Sir Ivor in the Two Thousand Guineas, but Sir Ivor could win the Derby, and other races after.

When he decided on Sir Ivor, Lester's popularity in the family suffered a temporary dent. Lester, all the same, had been consistent. Having gone through all the trauma of extricating himself from the constraints of obligation at Warren Place, he was not going to surrender his hard-won freedom of choice to fetters of blood. He told Sam Armstrong early in the winter, as soon as he had decided, so as to give his father-in-law time to find another jockey with whom to plan Petingo's spring campaign.

Vincent sent Sir Ivor to Pisa for the worst of the winter, thinking Italy might be warmer for the American-bred colt. Whether or not it made any difference, Sir Ivor came back into training and won the Two Thousand Guineas Trial at Ascot early in April 1968.

No one was deeply impressed. Over a distance of seven furlongs, too short for him, Sir Ivor had had to struggle hard to get home by half a length, Lester slipping the field a furlong out by just enough to keep his nose ahead at the post. He had started at 15–8 on and hadn't looked worth the confidence.

Eyebrows were raised even higher when, a week later, Petingo came out for his first race and with Joe Mercer won easily by four lengths at Newmarket. Speculation arose that L. Piggott had got himself off two classic champions in a row, and Lester himself, in the quiet of the night, could only sweat and hope.

Sir Ivor had been taken back to Ireland to train for the Two Thousand Guineas, but Vincent O'Brien was dissatisfied with his colt's progress, chiefly because of his tendency to pull himself up before the end of a gallop. Vincent decided to send Sir Ivor over to Newmarket ten days before the Guineas so that Lester could gallop him on the Heath and test his fitness.

With Sir Ivor came two other of Vincent's good horses, to make the work-out both strong and private, and the gallop was held unobtrusively at the southernmost end of the schooling grounds, heading away from the town, seven to eight furlongs alongside the Devil's Dike, ending down by the golf course beside the road to Cambridge.

Jockey Brian Taylor, who had come to ride one of the pacemakers, was wearing exercise boots and couldn't get his feet into the stirrups of the racing saddle Vincent had supplied. Lester told him prosaically to take off his boots and ride in bare feet. Lester's solutions to many problems are breathtakingly direct.

So with a bare-footed Brian Taylor in the racing saddle of one, the two pacemakers set off in front with Sir Ivor behind, Lester mindful of Vincent's instruction to follow the other two until about two furlongs from the end, and thus make Sir Ivor work hard.

Two furlongs from the end, Lester urged Sir Ivor to accelerate, and he felt for the first time the stunning ability of that splendid colt to switch on extra speed as if with booster rockets. Sir Ivor passed the other two as if they'd been standing still and by the end of the gallop had opened up a lead of a hundred yards. It was, Lester says, the best training gallop he rode in his whole life.

Much relieved, Vincent and Lester rested more peacefully, both of them in Lester's house, as Vincent wasn't returning to Ireland before the Two Thousand Guineas.

Vincent and Sam Armstrong were very good friends, having in the past been partners in a bloodstock agency. After the Sir Ivor gallop it so happened that Susan, driving Vincent home, noticed that Petingo was about to be given his own work-out on a different training ground on the other side of the road. With interest she stopped the car, and she and Vincent watched Joe Mercer give Petingo as smooth and satisfactory a gallop as any trainer could wish. There was clearly going to be no easy task ahead for Sir Ivor.

Lester by now had come to understand the horse's preferences. Sir Ivor, he says, was a lovely horse to ride, very easy and intelligent, willing to do whatever his rider asked. Racing excited him, and he would signal his approval with a kick and a buck in the paddock. He carried his head low and liked to be ridden on a long rein. Diametrically opposite to St Paddy, he dropped his bit immediately a race started and went along on his own. He knew that when Lester stopped riding him hard, the race was over, and he would pull himself up in a few strides. He stopped indeed so fast that other horses behind sometimes ran into the back of him. With most Flat horses, it's the exact reverse: they don't understand about winning posts, and stopping them afterwards can be a problem.

Lester pondered the likes, dislikes and intelligence of Sir Ivor and worked out how to ride him to best effect: an effect that left racing crowds gasping and believing every time that Sir Ivor would get beaten because Lester had left his winning run too late.

The Two Thousand Guineas in 1968 was a hot race packed with good horses. So Blessed went off fast in front and led for six of the eight furlongs and, significantly from Lester's point of view, sped straight down the centre of the course, not swerving over to the stands' rails, as happens in most races. The other runners followed So Blessed, so that the stands' rails were left clear.

At the Bushes, two to three furlongs out, Lester and Sir Ivor were almost last. Petingo took up the running from So Blessed, and the contest looked over.

Lester shook up Sir Ivor and steered him into the untenanted lane alongside the rails; and Sir Ivor flew as he had in the gallop, leaving the others standing. He reached the front a very short distance from the winning post, streaking darkly past the hard-driven Petingo by one and a half lengths. He hadn't won, Lester thought privately, by as much as he had expected. The point, however, had been made. He had truly chosen his winner.

Raymond Guest, Sir Ivor's owner, was the American ambassador to Ireland. He greeted his magnificent winner in the unsaddling enclosure with breathless excitement, and immediately with Vincent began making plans for the Derby.

Lester's plans were already made: to ride Sir Ivor as before, to hold him up until the last minute, tucked in behind other runners, and to get him to switch on the after-burners not too soon and not too late. Lester was certain Sir Ivor would win, and uncharacteristically said so publicly several times. Asked before the Guineas what could defeat him, he had said 'a fall'. Approaching the Derby, even that possibility was discounted.

No one knew for certain that Sir Ivor would actually get the mile and a half because he had never worked or galloped more than a mile and a quarter, and besides, on his breeding his best distance should have been a mile, as in the Guineas.

At Epsom, Lester carried out his plan to perfection, taking up a handy position at sixth or seventh with Sir Ivor well tucked in and relaxed. Straightening up after Tattenham Corner, Connaught took the lead by two or three clear lengths, with Lester tracking Remand, which he thought a great danger. About a furlong and a half from the post, he could see Remand would have no chance of catching Connaught, now five lengths ahead, so he pulled out Sir Ivor to give him a free run, and told him to go.

Nothing happened. For fifty precious yards, Sir Ivor seemed not to understand what was wanted. Lester thinks he'd got the horse so well settled that the change-gear message took a while to get through. When it did, though, the flying machine overhauled Connaught effortlessly in the last hundred yards and beat him by an easy one and a half lengths.

The American ambassador to Ireland wasn't there to cheer. He was watching the race on a television set on a long lead on a lawn in Ireland while he awaited the arrival of the President of Eire to the opening of the John F. Kennedy Memorial Park in County Wexford. That day had been chosen because it had been John F. Kennedy's birthday. Too bad for Raymond Guest! The President of Eire's car drove in through the gates a few seconds after Sir Ivor had passed the post, a marked piece of tact and diplomacy between two friendly powers.

The next time Sir Ivor ran, which was in the Irish Sweeps Derby, Lester didn't ride him, as Liam Ward was retained for all Vincent O'Brien's horses in Ireland. Lester rode Ribero, which he thought was a waste of time, but he agreed from regard for his owner Charles Engelhard, whom he liked and for whom he had won on Ribocco and many others. Ribero had had to be taken out of the Epsom Derby because of a foot injury, but Lester had ridden him at Royal Ascot later and finished eight lengths behind Connaught, who had been second to Sir Ivor at Epsom. On the face of it, Ribero had absolutely no chance against Sir Ivor at The Curragh.

Lester all the same was as usual out to do his best. He took the Johnson Houghton-trained colt early into third place and halfway up the straight was in front and going for home. He glanced back to see Sir Ivor coming and about a furlong from home he urged every fraction of speed from Ribero to counter the inevitable as best he could.

The inevitable didn't happen. Sir Ivor approached Ribero's quarters and stayed there, the two horses racing flat out to the winning post. Ribero won by two lengths, which was, Lester says, one of the mysteries of all time.

Poor Liam Ward came in for a great deal of criticism, which Lester thinks was bad luck. A mile and a half was Sir Ivor's limit, and Liam Ward, Lester says, was probably doing what he thought was safest, taking the horse to the outside as they came into the straight to give him a clear run. But Sir Ivor, Lester knew, didn't like to see too much daylight too soon. 'Those horses,' he says, 'that have that terrific speed at the end, you don't want to let them see anything until it's time to let them go, otherwise they won't produce it. Even the best horses can get beaten if there's a certain way they want riding, and you don't ride them that way.'

Riding any horse the way Lester did, it should be said, presupposes the jockey also had Lester's nerve and acute sense of timing besides being able to read a horse's mind.

Next time out one week later, Lester and Sir Ivor were beaten in the one and a quarter mile Eclipse. Lester thinks it was probably a mistake to run there, even though it was the horse's best distance, as the ground was very hard. The colt wasn't a hundred per cent happy and wasn't moving very well. In addition, he was taking on Royal Palace and Taj Dewan, both four-year-olds.

Royal Palace (Derby winner the previous year) won by a short head from Taj Dewan, with Lester, unable to catch them, three quarters of a length third.

The Eclipse jarred Sir Ivor badly and it was touch and go whether he ever raced again. It took Vincent from July to October to get him right, barely in time for the Arc de Triomphe. Two weeks before the Arc, he ran in the Prix du Prince d'Orange, finishing an encouraging second and looking fit and ready for the bigger prize. In the mile-and-a-half Arc itself, Lester says Sir Ivor ran very well, but he couldn't make any impression at the end and came second by four lengths to Vaguely Noble who was, after all, bred to be a true mile-and-a-half horse.

Back to himself in every way, Sir Ivor went next to Newmarket and won the Champion Stakes at a canter, incidentally beating Taj Dewan out of sight.

After that, Vincent sent him to America to run in the Washington International at Laurel racecourse, which is situated halfway between Baltimore, Maryland, and Washington D.C. The weather was terrible, the going like a bog. No one knew how Sir Ivor was going to run a mile and a half in such conditions as he barely made it in good.

Lester rode him exactly as he had in the Two Thousand Guineas and the Derby, tucking him in tight in about fifth place and biding his time. It wasn't until the last hundred yards that he asked him to go, and then Sir Ivor gave it all, sweeping past the leaders and winning by three quarters of a length in the last few strides. Fifty yards past the post, he had stopped. He and Lester were covered with mud and the colt was exhausted. 'I've never seen a horse so tired after a race,' Lester says. 'He'd given everything. He was the best horse I'd ever ridden.'

The American racing press were crushingly critical of tactics they didn't understand. American jockeys don't ride waiting races. Lester was accused of having almost thrown away the prize, and no one paid attention when he tried to explain that that was the only way the horse could win. Not until the following year when he went back and won in the same way on another horse, Karabas, did they begin to understand and respect him.

Sir Ivor's great career was at an end, but his marvellous power is on record for posterity. A film was made that year, at first intended merely to publicise racing, but later focussing on and following the fortunes of the winner of the Guineas and the Derby. Lovingly photographed and called simply 'The Year of Sir Ivor', it was shown to public acclaim by the BBC.

The year of Sir Ivor was also, for Lester, the year of Petingo. Once his friend Marcus Lemos and his father-in-law Sam Armstrong had forgiven him for choosing to beat them in the Two Thousand Guineas, they put him back pretty rapidly on the stable's best. Ten days before Sir Ivor's Derby, Lester rode Petingo in the Prix Lupin at Longchamp, regrettably without results. Next time out, however, in the St James's Palace Stakes at Royal Ascot, he led for the whole mile to win comfortably, and six weeks later produced a repeat performance in the richly-endowed Sussex Stakes at Goodwood. In his final race for the year, he finished second, hard ridden, and was retired to go to stud.

In the 1968 summing-up statistics, Petingo finished eighth on the table of leading winners. Sir Ivor came first, Royal Palace second, Ribero third. Lester again kept his championship, followed by Sandy Barclay, who had replaced George Moore as Noel Murless's stable jockey. Noel Murless was leading trainer, with Vincent O'Brien (British stake money only) runner-up, Fulke Johnson Houghton third and Sam Armstrong sixth. Raymond Guest headed the owners, H. J. Joel (owner of Royal Palace) came second, Charles Engelhard third, Marcus Lemos tenth.

Lester had won the Two Thousand Guineas, the Derby and the St Leger (on Ribero), the Irish Derby, the Cesarewitch, the Dewhurst, the Champion Stakes and the Washington International.

It hadn't been a bad year, all in all, for a freelance.

# Nijinsky

In the year between Sir Ivor and Nijinsky there were no Classic wins for Lester, but 1969 had its compensations, one of which was the bay mare Park Top.

Lester had begun riding for Bernard van Cutsem, who had moved his horses into Lord Derby's Stanley House stables and was training for his friends, among them the Duke of Devonshire and Lord Derby himself. Bernard van Cutsem was one of the old and now rare breed of trainers, those who were independently rich and who trained for the satisfaction of the occupation rather than from a need to make a living.

Bernard van Cutsem had his eye on young Willie Carson who had recently finished his apprenticeship with Sam Armstrong and was riding first jockey for Lord Derby. Van Cutsem intended Willie to be his full stable jockey when he was more experienced, but meanwhile he gave some rides to Willie and engaged Lester for the rest. Lester thus rode for the stable for only two or three summers, one of which was Park Top's five-year-old season.

Owned by the Duke of Devonshire, she hadn't run at two, and Lester hadn't ridden her either at three or four when she had won several times. His first acquaintance with her was in a small race in France in May 1969, which she won very easily.

Lester was impressed. She looked like an old gelding, she was modestly bred and she had cost about £500 as a yearling, but she never fussed, she was a beautiful ride and she understood exactly what was required. Very much like Sir Ivor, she needed to be ridden from far back so as to come with a great burst of speed at the end. Like him, she would pull herself up when she'd reached the front.

Lester rode her in the Coronation Cup at Epsom and won with a rush in the last few yards by three-quarters of a length, making it all look easy. It was Park Top's biggest win to date, and it was decided she should run next in the Eclipse. Lester had prior obligations for the Eclipse, in the shape of his Derby mount Ribofilio, owned by Charles Engelhard and trained by Fulke Johnson Houghton, so Geoff Lewis was engaged for Park Top.

A week before the Eclipse, Ribofilio started coughing and had to be withdrawn, leaving Lester without a ride. Ruefully he agreed to partner the five-year-old Wolver Hollow which he had ridden once before but not to much effect. The horse had had a middling-successful career which was drawing to a close.

Sir Cecil Boyd Rochfort had trained Wolver Hollow originally, and the horse's owner, Mrs C. O. Iselin, American and very old, was leaving him to the trainer in her will. Henry Cecil, Cecil Boyd Rochfort's stepson, had taken over the licence by 1969, and although Wolver Hollow had been entered in the Eclipse he was also entered in a handicap on the same day, a race in which he had far more chance. It was Cecil Boyd Rochfort himself who chose the Eclipse against his stepson's preference for the handicap: and so Lester got his mount.

The only chance he had, he thought, was to ride Wolver Hollow to stay the distance, which meant from the rear of the field, conserving energy. Accordingly he set off right at the back, behind even Park Top, who had also of course to be ridden from behind. The pair of them came round into the Sandown straight last and second last, and the horses in front all swung slightly wide, pulling out to challenge each other. Geoff Lewis went up fast on their inside, with Lester following: and Geoff, realising he was reaching the front too soon, eased back a shade and in doing so came off the rails.

'I nipped through on the inside of him,' Lester says. 'Caught him unawares.' Lester sympathised with Geoff's dilemma and thought he'd had bad luck. But Lester on Wolver Hollow was through and away, snatching the seemingly impossible victory by an easy looking two and a half lengths. Park Top, her effort spent too early, just couldn't quicken at the end.

Mrs Iselin, happy, died soon after. Cecil Boyd Rochfort retired Wolver Hollow and sent him to stud, where he proved to be worth a fortune.

Bernard van Cutsem put Lester back on Park Top for the King George VI and Queen Elizabeth Stakes, run two weeks after the Eclipse. Lester set out of course to win at the last possible second, but slightly to his horror found himself in the same position as Geoff Lewis in the Eclipse. The field of twelve swung wide coming round the last bend, the gaps opened up, and Park Top went up the straight with a free run on the rails.

Lester says, 'I was up behind the leaders, running away. I was there too early but I had to go through with it, it was no good stopping. I was in front a whole furlong out. She did pull up a bit over the last hundred yards, but she was so much the best horse that she still won.'

Next time out she won a nice race at Longchamp and then went to the same track for the Prix de l'Arc de Triomphe. Lester rode to the winning formula, but on this occasion without success. Coming into the straight well back, he judged he had things set up right for beating them all. Then out of the pack sprinted Levmoss, slipping them unexpectedly and setting up a three- to four-length lead. Park Top had that much further to make up, and just failed to reach the front by half a length.

'Levmoss!' Lester exclaims disgustedly. 'A 50–1 shot. He won the Ascot Gold Cup which is for long distance stayers, and then he goes and wins the Arc.'

Lester all the same had his compensations that day. He might have been second in the big one, but he won four of the other Longchamp races, cheered so hard by the French crowd one could have heard them on the far side of Paris.

Park Top ran once more that year, in the Champion Stakes at Newmarket, but when Lester asked her to fly, she couldn't produce. 'Nothing happened,' Lester says: and she finished second to an unfamiliar three-year-old from France.

The following year at six she won early in France but after coming second in the Coronation Cup at Epsom had some trouble with her fetlocks. She ran twice more towards the end of the season, but by then she had had enough.

It was in 1969 that Karabas turned into a really good racehorse, Lester winning five useful events on him for Lord Iveagh and Bernard van Cutsem on his way to the critic-silencing display in the Washington International. One of the American writers, praising that win, capitulated totally to say, 'In our opinion, Lester, because of his great strength, skill, intelligence and courage, is the world's greatest jockey.' All a good deal different from before the race, when another writer had published his opinion that with Lester Piggott on his back, Karabas was running under a 10-lb penalty.

A disappointment of the year was Ribofilio, of which much had been expected in the way of classics. Owned by Charles Engelhard and trained by Fulke Johnson Houghton, he was sadly tailed off pulling up in the Two Thousand Guineas, fifth in the Epsom Derby and second in the Irish Sweeps Derby, each time starting favourite. Apart from his very first outing, when he won a three-horse Guineas trial with Joe Mercer, his only visit to the winner's enclosure was at Goodwood where he won a two-horse race with Lester at 7–1 on.

In 1969, Lester rode again a few times for Noel Murless (Sandy Barclay having hurt his shoulder) their joint winner, Paddle Boat, being greeted by huge cheers from an approving crowd. Noel and Lester had never actually quarrelled and retained affection and respect for each other always.

On the down side, the first day of Royal Ascot brought Lester a suspension that was described by the Press, owners and public alike as 'staggering', 'too severe', 'unjustified' and 'pointless'. This was the time that Geoff Lewis was 'severely cautioned for giving false evidence', to the effect that Lester had not materially interfered with his (Geoff's) winner. In the very last flat-out fifty yards of the St James's Palace Stakes, Lester's horse had closed on and touched the rump of Geoff's, and the Stewards lodged an objection.

Lester's supposed and contended 'crime' was to swerve unexpectedly on Habitat and perhaps prevent Geoff on Right Tack (out of Polly Macaw!) from winning by as far as he might otherwise have done. 'What Habitat did,' Lester said, 'was to try to bite Right Tack. He lunged at him in a split second. Horses aren't angels, and I had no possibility of pulling him off. It didn't affect the outcome of the race.'

Habitat's attempt at biting Right Tack got Lester suspended for seven days, Polly Macaw and her offspring thus completing a double (*see* page 96), and Geoff Lewis was furious at being officially called a liar.

Lester's suspension was announced on the Wednesday morning as starting on Friday, the last day of the Royal meeting. Lester went straight out and won Wednesday's Royal Hunt Cup on Kamundu to thunderous applause, the crowd loudly expressing its disgust. Habitat, presumably without biting anybody, won four races for Lester during the season, ending on the four-in-a-day triumph at Longchamp.

In the dying fall of the year, halfway through October, the shape of things to come in 1970 was unwrapped at Newmarket. Nijinsky, already an unbeaten star in Ireland, four times a two-year-old winner with Liam Ward, came over for the Dewhurst Stakes.

Lester rode. Starting at 3–1 on, Nijinsky took the lead inside the final furlong, quickened from there and won smoothly by three lengths: and a whole brave new world could clearly be seen on the horizon.

Nijinsky was bred in Canada by the famed E. P. Taylor, owner of Nijinsky's sire, Northern Dancer. The well-grown bay was sold as a yearling to Charlie Engelhard for $84,000. The new owner, a commodity tycoon dealing in platinum, decided he should be trained in Ireland by Vincent O'Brien; in England, of course, his horses were mostly trained by Fulke Johnson Houghton at Blewbury. Lester's companionship with Charlie Engelhard, already strong, was about to be deeply strengthened.

The American had come into racing fairly late in life, Lester riding his first ever winner, and also, it turned out later, his last. 'He was,' says Lester, 'a marvellous owner, one of the very best, a wonderful man. He started with only three or four horses and then bought several yearlings by Ribot and had great success.'

Nijinsky was a great big horse, which was surprising as the

fabled Northern Dancer is small. Nijinsky was the first to bear witness to the extraordinarily prolific prize-winning blood lines carried by his Canadian sire. Even at twenty-two, Northern Dancer is still siring top-class winners; a sturdy, punchy, glossy character cantering nonchalantly to greet visitors in his white railed paddock on the Taylors' more southerly stud farm in Maryland.

Unlike many big horses, Nijinsky was handy to ride and could move himself collectedly round a small track or a downhill turn like Tattenham Corner. He would fuss and sweat before races, being highly strung, but was fairly sensible and would do what his jockey asked. Lester thought him not very clever but very well trained: if he'd been with anyone but Vincent he might not have excelled.

First time out in 1970 he won in Ireland, ridden by Liam Ward, and next came over for the Two Thousand Guineas. There, in majestic style, he fulfilled all the prophesies, making it look easy. With his great size and his smooth ground-gobbling action he seemed a breed apart, and Lester, Vincent, Charlie Engelhard and a delighted E. P. Taylor began to look forward with confidence to the Derby.

Two days after the Two Thousand Guineas, Lester completed the classic double by winning his first One Thousand Guineas on Humble Duty, owned by Jean, Lady Ashcombe and trained by Peter Walwyn. Lester was deputising for Duncan Keith, away ill from too much weight and water reduction, and not for the first or last time coaxed a chance ride to an easy-seeming major win.

Four days before the Derby, Lester himself came near to fainting from dehydration, having wasted down to 8 st 4 lb, his limit. After a tremendously strenuous week's travelling, riding in France and Ireland as well as in England in a heat wave, he forgot to drink his customary half-glass of water between races, a precaution of his when doing very light.

Riding Gem Stone hard for two furlongs, he began to ease up in the last hundred yards of the fourth race at Newmarket, knowing anyway he couldn't win as he was eight lengths behind the leader. The Stewards called him in, as so often, for an explanation. Lester, drooping with fatigue, told them he'd stopped riding because he felt tired and unwell, which they thought a reasonable answer. They despatched him to the doctor who said Lester could go on riding but, after one more unsuccessful circuit, he gave it up and went home to rest. Such was the resilience of his iron body that next day he flew to Paris and lost by a nose at Longchamp on Karabas. By Sunday evening he was home, feeling fit, but saying he might just take it easy until Wednesday.

As for Sir Ivor two years earlier, Derby day dawned sweet, fair and sunny, and again everything went well. In a small field of eleven, Nijinsky lay about sixth until two furlongs out. Then Lester took him without pressure into the lead and sped inexorably further and further away, with the good French horse Gyr puffing in his wake. The official distances between the first six horses were two and a half lengths, three lengths, half a length, two and a half lengths, ten lengths: a procession.

Lester thought that except for Gyr, the opposition wasn't as good as most years, but as Nijinsky's time, untroubled, came within two seconds of Mahmoud's record, one must reckon the colt would have beaten anything that offered.

Nijinsky went back to Ireland and with Liam Ward in the saddle won the Irish Sweeps Derby. Lester rode Meadowville which had come fifth behind Nijinsky at Epsom. This time, however, there was to be no dramatic upset. Meadowville finished second by three lengths, undisgraced.

Lester's next outing on Nijinsky was the King George VI and Queen Elizabeth Stakes at Ascot. This was the colt's most tremendous performance of all, as he won the six-horse 1½-mile star event literally at a canter. The previous year's Derby winner, Blakeney, hard ridden, came in two lengths back, with Lester's old friend Karabas fourth.

With the Two Thousand Guineas and the Derby in the bag, Charlie Engelhard decided to go for the St Leger, hoping Nijinsky would be the first to win the Triple Crown of classics since Bahram in 1935. Before the Doncaster race, however, Nijinsky contracted American ringworm, which had recently been infecting horses in Britain. It takes the form of small lumps under the skin which can spread all over a horse's body. In Nijinsky, who had it badly, it also broke out in spots and made him very irritable.

He wouldn't have a saddle on for a while and after he'd recovered it was a rush to get him ready in time for the St Leger.

The extra distance of the fifth classic – 1 mile 6½ furlongs – was also a problem, and Vincent and Lester decided he should wait with Nijinsky as long as possible and ask him for speed only at the end.

With perhaps all this in his mind, Lester fell off at the start of the race before the St Leger, his horse Leander decamping into the middle distance and leaving him stranded. Immediately, as from nowhere, policemen were suddenly running towards him to find out if he was all right. Bewildered, he said yes. He hadn't known until then that an escaped lunatic had been making death threats against himself and Nijinsky. Doncaster executives, who didn't want his corpse on their turf, were taking it seriously. Impressed, Lester returned horseless to change into Nijinsky's colours. His saddle, still on Leander, still loose, couldn't be retrieved in time, so he rode with one he borrowed.

After all these alarms, the race itself went much as planned. Lester waited and waited with Nijinsky and asked him for speed right at the end. It looked an easy win to the crowd, but Lester knew the colt couldn't have gone any further or any faster and had finished extremely tired. Meadowville, as in the Irish Derby, came in second, only a length behind.

Nijinsky went exhausted back to Ireland where it was found that he had lost forty pounds in weight from the race and the journey, and he was a horse who rarely lost weight at all.

Charlie Engelhard, all the same, had his splendid Triple Crown, and Nijinsky, with a run of eleven unbroken wins, looked invincible.

He went to France for the Arc de Triomphe a month later, and because of the French President and his large entourage crowding into the parade ring at Longchamp, he became very fussed, sweating copiously. In Susan's words, 'The world's Press and TV were allowed into the paddock and they *devoured* Nijinsky. A Japanese TV man even put a microphone to the horse's mouth. It was a disgrace, and has never been allowed to happen since. It ruined the horse's nerves and he was white with sweat by the time they reached the course.'

In the race itself, he showed none of his easy early speed and

Lester didn't push him because he thought he would pick up later. Turning into the straight a good way back, Lester had to decide whether to go between other horses or switch to the outside. He chose the outside and took Nijinsky to the front with a hundred yards to go to the post.

Nijinsky was tired, but Lester thought he would hang on long enough. Then Nijinsky started to drift to the left off a straight line, which he had never done before, and Sassafras, one of the horses he had already passed, caught him in the last stride and won by a head.

It was, Lester says, a big disappointment, a tragedy, and he spent ages afterwards agonising about whether he should have gone through the field, not round the outside, and whether he should have left it even later, inside the last fifty yards, to hit the front. But Nijinsky was stone cold and drifting left, and Yves Saint-Martin, riding the French Derby winner, simply seized his chance.

Thirteen days later Nijinsky, seeming none the worse, ran in the Champion Stakes at Newmarket. The public made him an odds-on favourite as usual, but to Lester this great colt had no life left. When he tried to take the lead a furlong out, there was no quickening response. He lost to Lorenzaccio, and had trouble even in finishing second. Nijinsky the spectacular dancer had had enough, and had given his last performance.

Lester still believes that but for the draining ordeal of the St Leger, he might have won both the Arc and the Champion Stakes. What is certain is that Nijinsky's progeny will go on winning for generations, as he has proved a mighty sire.

It was at Newmarket in April 1971 that Lester rode Charlie Engelhard's last winner, Mansingh. The great sportsman, multi-millionaire head of a minerals empire, died suddenly in Florida aged only fifty-four.

# The Row Over Roberto

'Derby Storm over Piggott' roared the headlines in early June 1972. 'Piggott sparks big race row'. Critics wrote letters signed 'Disgusted' to the newspapers and journalists jumped in severely with vitriolic condemnations.

Bill Williamson, who had originally been engaged to ride Roberto, had been told two days before the race that he would be replaced by Lester. The darling of British racing was instantly re-cast as an unsportsmanlike villain, and as usual offered no explanation or defence. Sympathy for Bill Williamson was universal. Lester was booed at the races, which he didn't clearly hear. He had done nothing wrong. He felt none of the shame everyone was busy heaping upon him.

Lester was often accused of stealing other jockeys' mounts but, in reality, this is impossible. It isn't the jockey who decides. A jockey can say he is available and willing: the decision as to whether or not to put him up rests perhaps with the trainer but ultimately with the owner of the horse. Many, if not most, champion jockeys cast their attention in the direction of horses they would like to ride, if they could. They know that where the stable has a secure top jockey retained, it's pointless going any further, but where the position is less clear, it isn't considered unreasonable to indicate interest.

Sir Gordon Richards, for instance, did it all the time. His announcements of availability were greeted with unconfined joy, and Gordon rode on hundreds of backs where others had sat before. Everyone knew but no one openly complained, and if the jocked-off jockeys resented it, they suffered their hurt feelings in silence. There isn't a jockey present or past who hasn't been jocked off now and again. It's a fact of life. It's bitter when it happens, but it's the owner's prerogative.

To take an unheated view of the uproar which surrounded Lester's engagement to ride Roberto in the 1972 Derby, one has first to understand Roberto's owner and then to look straightly at the facts.

The owner – and breeder – was John W. Galbreath, a trim good-looking American, at that time seventy-three, the owner of the Pittsburg Pirates baseball team and a long-time racing enthusiast who had already owned two winners of the Kentucky Derby. He is a nice man, a great sportsman, powerful in opinion and decision.

'Anyone who doesn't consider the Epsom Derby one of the greatest sports events in the world must be out of his mind,' he was reported as saying.

He had named Roberto after Roberto Clemente, one of the greatest of baseball hitters, and now in 1972 it was time to go for the greatest of all home runs.

The standing of the Epsom Derby had prompted those other great Americans, Raymond Guest and Charles Engelhard, to send their horses over the ocean to Vincent O'Brien, and John Galbreath dearly wanted Roberto up on the record boards with Sir Ivor and Nijinsky. He would have done anything in his power to achieve it.

The facts were that Lester could have been on Roberto from the beginning, like the others, as Vincent, after three wins in Ireland with his new retained jockey Johnny Roe, sent the two-year-old Roberto to the Grand Criterium at Longchamp in the autumn for Lester's assessment.

Lester thinks Roberto could have won the French race, but he was beaten into fourth place for three good reasons, all understandable only in retrospect. First, Vincent told Lester the horse liked to be ridden from behind: Lester rode that way but found too late that it was getting him beaten. Second, Roberto was developing a strong preference for left-handed tracks, and Longchamp is right-handed. Third, at that time the French had a ruling that all foreign horses had to be put through the starting stalls before they raced. Roberto was accordingly put through the stalls either on the morning of the race or the day before. (Lester can't remember which; he wasn't on him.) An excitable horse and always on his toes, Roberto was put through the stalls twice. The first time was all right, but the second time he reared and went over backwards, taking skin off his rump as his back went under the gates. It didn't help him much, Lester says, when it came to the actual race.

Lester all the same would have agreed at once to ride Roberto in the Two Thousand Guineas and the Derby had it not been for Crowned Prince, a fine colt trained by Bernard van Cutsem. Crowned Prince also was American-bred and owned and, with Lester at the helm, had in the 1971 season won both the Champagne Stakes and the Dewhurst Stakes, two of the very top juvenile contests. Lester, along with many others, considered Crowned Prince the better Classic prospect and, by the beginning of the 1972 season, he had committed himself to partnering him. The Australian Bill Williamson, who hadn't so far ridden Roberto in a race, was engaged in place of Lester for the Guineas and the Derby.

First time out, two weeks before the Two Thousand Guineas, disaster struck Crowned Prince. Starting favourite in the Craven Stakes at Newmarket, he produced no response when asked by Lester, and was afterwards found to have developed the breathing troubles known as a soft palate. He had to be taken out of training and never ran again.

However much they might both regret it, it was too late for Vincent to put Lester back on Roberto. Bill Williamson was not replaced.

Lester eventually took a ride for Bill Marshall in the Two Thousand Guineas but finished, as he'd expected, in the ruck. Roberto was beaten half a length by Willie Carson on Hard Top, Bernard van Cutsem's stable-mate of Crowned Prince.

Twelve days before the Derby, Bill Williamson fell heavily in a race at Kempton, chipping a bone in his shoulder and cutting his face. He was unable to ride the following week, and it was debatable whether or not he would be fit again in time for Epsom. If he weren't, Lester would be back on Roberto.

Lester had been casting about philosophically for a mount in the Derby. He couldn't ride Roberto, and the other two he fancied, Lyphard and Yaroslav, were similarly taken by other jockeys. Lester talked to Vincent about Manitoulin, the O'Brien second string, and Vincent invited him to go to Ireland to ride a gallop on him. Lester went. Manitoulin, a decent previous winner, belonged to John Galbreath's wife: he worked well in the gallop but finished behind Roberto at less than the Derby distance. Lester liked the feel of him well enough, and reflecting also that if Bill Williamson did get fit he at least wouldn't be watching from the stands, he took the ride.

Bill Williamson naturally did everything he could to get fit, and that was how things stood the weekend before the Derby when the owner John Galbreath came over from America to see his colt perform. He had been slightly out of touch and didn't know the extent of forty-nine-year-old Bill Williamson's injuries. Despite the jockey's protestation that he had mended and was fit, John Galbreath was alarmed. He wanted so very much to win that Derby, not just for the kudos but also for the stud value afterwards. He knew about athletes – his baseball team had recently won the World Series, equivalent of the World Cup in soccer – and he considered that no jockey could be totally fit after a twelve-day absence from the saddle recovering from a fall.

Fairly, he asked Bill Williamson to ride a trial gallop on Epsom Downs, but Bill Williamson didn't turn up, saying he had overslept. John Galbreath also arranged for him to go for an assessment to the London clinic of Bill Tucker, the sports injury specialist to whom many jockeys took their cracks and sprains. Bill Tucker said after an examination that in his opinion Bill Williamson was fit, but the owner was unconvinced. He wouldn't have fielded a ball-player in a big game on those terms. He thought it over and told Bill Williamson and Vincent at a meeting in London's Claridges Hotel that he wanted to take Lester off his wife's horse Manitoulin and put him on Roberto; and he promised the sorely disappointed Australian an equal percentage with Lester of the Derby prize, if Lester should win. On Monday evening, after this meeting, Vincent told the Press of the change of plans.

Lester knew nothing of this. Far from having with machiavellian cunning got Bill Williamson jocked off, he had been out of the country altogether for two days, riding in France and winning the French Derby. When he returned home on Monday evening, Susan told him Vincent had telephoned to say he would be on Roberto, not Manitoulin, and Lester with some contentment ate his dinner, unaware of the howls of accusation about to break over his head. On Manitoulin he'd had little chance, on Roberto he had more, but he wasn't himself convinced that he would win, not as on Sir Ivor and Nijinsky. To Lester, it was all on a lower key.

The papers broke the news with scandalised fanfares on Tuesday morning and Bill Williamson, to prove his point, rode in a selling race at Salisbury that afternoon, finishing seventh of eight. This result was an inconclusive pointer to his state of fitness, but he was clearly back in the saddle; and on Wednesday Lester went to Epsom for his date with history, his name unjustly blackened as never before.

All Bill Williamson said to Lester was, 'I don't mind, I'm getting the money anyway,' but some of the Press inflamed anti-Piggott feeling by inventing bitter tirades that Bill Williamson never uttered. Although of course he had wanted to ride in the Derby, he had not been over-enthusiastic about Roberto before the Two Thousand Guineas, and not much more after losing that race injudiciously by half a length. He knew also, naturally, that he wouldn't have been on Roberto at all except for Crowned Prince. He was not, in short, an established stable jockey being jocked off by an intruder, and he accepted the revised situation with more resignation than most people gave him credit for.

As a result of the Press's views, however, one can say that no one except Bill Williamson, the Galbreaths, Vincent and Lester himself really wanted Lester to win that Derby. Certainly the bookmakers didn't, as however much the public might disapprove, they still piled their money on the maestro, and Roberto had been backed down to 3–1 favourite by the 'off'.

Roberto, Lester remembers, was a rough, tough-looking horse, not very big, who never felt as if he was doing all he could. He rode him out at Epsom the day before the Derby to refresh their acquaintanceship, and Lester and Vincent agreed that this time

Roberto should be up with the leaders from the beginning so as not to leave too much to make up in the closing stages. Roberto ran most of the race in fourth or fifth place behind Pentland Firth and Meadow Mint, and made headway coming to the last two furlongs. Neither Lyphard nor Yaroslav figured as they had been expected to, and it was Pentland Firth and ultimately Rheingold with which Lester had to contend.

Rheingold, ridden by Ernie Johnson, was racing on the outside of Roberto and hanging badly to the left, squeezing Lester towards Pentland Firth. A bump or two occurred before Rheingold and Roberto shed Pentland Firth in their wake. Rheingold then continued to hang heavily towards Roberto while remaining about a neck in the lead. As if locked together, though not in fact touching, they sprinted the last furlong side by side, Lester by superhuman strength seeming just at the end to lift the whole weight of Roberto, to drive and inspire and force him to one last-second effort. The straining pair flashed across the line in such close proximity that neither jockey knew which had won.

Lester dismounted and unsaddled Roberto out on the course, in the placed horses' unsaddling area, and carried his saddle from there to the weighing room. 'There's no point in riding into the winner's circle at Epsom unless you're certain you've won,' he said.

He walked through muted crowds who were silent partly from uncertainty about the result and very definitely from disapproval of the last-minute jockey switch. Lester had produced one of the most remarkable riding feats of his whole brilliant career, but at that moment no one applauded. Lester himself, walking in unmoved by the atmosphere, was thinking mainly that even if Rheingold had stayed on and won, he might still lose the race if there were an enquiry. The photograph, however, showed that Roberto had indeed come first – by a nostril, by a scant four inches – and the Stewards immediately announced their enquiry.

The subject was Rheingold's failure to keep a straight line, and his hampering and bumping of Roberto. For twenty-two long minutes, the Stewards kept everyone agonising before announcing that the placings would remain unchanged. No action was to be taken against Rheingold which was confirmed as second. Roberto had safely won his Derby, and John Galbreath was the happiest man on the Turf.

There were critics who said Lester had been too hard on Roberto and had thrashed him unmercifully to get his win. 'Well,' Lester says, 'of course I was hard on him. I had to be, at the end. I felt he could go faster, if only he would. I suppose it looked worse just because I didn't have room to use my whip. Rheingold was too close.'

Vets examined Roberto afterwards, and there were no whip marks on him. Whatever persuasion Lester had used over those last gruelling fifty yards, it hadn't been a beating.

By the following morning, the Press were conceding that the owner had been right, that no one but Lester could have won that race on Roberto, that the change of jockey had been devastatingly demonstrated to be wise, that Lester was supreme.

The cheers on Derby day itself however were all for 'Weary Willie' Williamson who displayed some I-told-you-so fitness by winning two races later in the afternoon, with Lester both times on the favourite in the pack behind him. No one in their hearts believed by then that Bill Williamson would have won on Roberto, but he did have his compensations in the shape of underdog-sympathy and Galbreath cash.

How valuable is loyalty? How much should one expect?

Loyalty comes low down on the list of priorities in professional team games: the fittest and best get to play. Loyalty may be admirable or it may be sentimental mush or a refusal to face facts. Loyalty may be courageous and it may be costly and it may be stupid.

John Galbreath was realistic, not disloyal. He had no long-term ties with Bill Williamson, only the brief encounter of one lost race. In his own mind, his loyalty was primarily to the horse which he had bred on his own stud farm and had known much longer. In effect, he paid Bill Williamson not to ride, and never then or afterwards regretted an action seen unsympathetically by many as disgraceful.

Other trainers and owners after him wanted and demanded Lester in place of their former jockeys, often with equally furious consequences. The rows thundered on with great storms of indignation but, as Lester says, 'If someone asks you to ride a good horse, you don't say "No, no, let so-and-so ride it." You say, "Yes, all right."'

Lester's friendships with many powerful owners, besides, ran deep. They liked him and trusted him, and it was to *him* they wished to show loyalty, if they could. They understood he couldn't be on their horses everywhere, but if they could have him, they would.

Modern racing is big business, like it or not. The stud fees beckon. If you are an owner with many thousands invested in bloodstock, the winning of big Flat races means more than the pride of leading in your darlings and beaming at prize-givings. Losing gracefully brings nothing but sighs. It may be sad or it may be good for a vigorous industry. The fact is that if you own expensive Flat racers and seriously want to win big races, you seek to engage the best jockey available.

Lester, free-lancing, available, needed only to be asked.

# The Roberto, Rheingold and Hard to Beat Circus

Among his fellow jockeys Lester was liked and very much respected. His constant courage, commonsense, calm temperament and astringent wit were appreciated and relied upon, and although he was never a jolly extrovert in the mould, say, of Willie Carson, his quiet camaraderie with his colleagues in the changing-room was a daily fact.

Most trainers and almost all owners deferred to him, leaning forward to hear better what he said. His down-to-earth clear-sighted opinions were seldom ignored, his understanding of horses being second to none. Many owners, indeed, were and are slightly in awe of him, perhaps because of his often detached manner and his unconscious aura of power.

Lester himself was unaware for a very long time of the effect his presence has on people, and probably even now scarcely understands it. His sort of power is hard to perceive from the inside. As far as he's concerned, he is merely doing a job.

It was in the year of Roberto's Derby that he deliberately walked away from his champion's crown. He stopped chasing around the country day in and day out in the search for numbers. He rode a great deal abroad, even more than usual, and he remained cool when Willie Carson led the jockeys' list by a substantial margin halfway through the season. In the eight preceding years, if someone had headed him, he had flown and driven inexhaustibly to catch up and prevail. In 1972, it was as if he had grown past needing the number one slot, and without a pang let it go.

'When you're Champion,' he says, 'and you're ten winners in front in June, you think that when you're thirty in front you can take a day off. It's not much fun. I decided that whenever possible I wouldn't ride on Mondays or Tuesdays, to have some time to myself.'

In other ways, the 1972 season was a switchback affair, up with satisfying highs and down with good decisions gone wrong. There were some splendid successes such as Boucher winning the St Leger for Vincent O'Brien and owner Ogden Phipps, and Noble Decree taking the richly-endowed Observer Gold Cup for Bernard van Cutsem and Nelson Bunker Hunt. Both of these horses, like Roberto, were American bred and American owned. Lester always did particularly well with American imports, drawing out their toughness and speed as if in response to his own.

It was Roberto, however, who dominated Lester's year; Roberto, Rheingold and a French horse, Hard to Beat. These three met often that season and the next, their mixed results appearing incomprehensible and their jockeys playing musical chairs.

Lester to begin with went four times to France to ride Hard to Beat who, in spite of his name, was French bred and was trained by a Frenchman, Richard Carver, at Chantilly near Paris. He was a great horse but had three powerful idiosyncracies: he would race well only on right-handed tracks, he hated to travel and he suffered from claustrophobia.

He and Lester won their preliminary race easily enough and started hot favourites in the French equivalent of the Two Thousand Guineas. Hard to Beat always had to be put into the starting stalls last, because he so hated being locked into the small space that, once inside, he would continually plunge forwards and hit the front gates, which in their turn would knock him backwards.

In the French Guineas, the gates opened while he was on the rebound, rocking backwards, which lost him what proved to be a crucial length over the turning Longchamp mile. Hard to Beat didn't run well and everybody was unhappy.

Next time out, he won easily in the Prix Lupin and the Stewards wanted to know how he had improved so much.

The fourth of the French races was the Prix du Jockey Club (the French Derby) in early June. This was the one and only ideal race for Hard to Beat, held as it was at right-handed Chantilly, near where he was trained – no travel to get there in claustrophobic horse-boxes. He and Lester won the race easily; and Lester believes that if Hard to Beat could have run at Chantilly all his life, he would never have been beaten.

Winning the French Derby on Hard to Beat was what Lester was doing on the Sunday John Galbreath arrived in London to enquire into Bill Williamson's fitness for Roberto.

After his remarkable Epsom Derby the victorious Roberto ran abysmally in the Irish Sweeps Derby on 1 July (ridden by luckless Johnny Roe), finishing twelfth and nearly last, with stable mate Manitoulin sixth. Roberto wouldn't go at all and Vincent sought frustratedly for reasons.

At Saint-Cloud, the day after the Irish Derby, Yves Saint Martin on Rheingold showed his heels to Lester on Hard to Beat. Trainer Barry Hills had discovered that Rheingold ran better in France, for reasons known only to the colt, and now had his post-Derby sights set on the Arc de Triomphe.

Lester reckoned it a mistake for Hard to Beat to have been sent to Saint-Cloud (a left-hand track) in preference to the Grand Prix de Paris at Longchamp (right-handed) where he would have won easily. The Grand Prix de Paris prize money was also larger, and the field wouldn't have included the big danger, Rheingold, but the new Japanese owner, who had bought Hard to Beat after his victory in the French Derby, insisted on the Grand Prix de Saint-Cloud because it was another of the French classics.

When it came to the Benson and Hedges Gold Cup at York in August, Lester had been invited by Barry Hills to ride Rheingold, and had accepted, Yves Saint-Martin being claimed elsewhere. Roberto also had been entered in the Benson and Hedges Gold Cup, but after the Irish Derby flop Vincent didn't want to run him, especially as the event was dominated by the unbeaten Brigadier Gerard.

John Galbreath, however, insisted a few days before the race that Roberto should take his chance. Lester couldn't ride him as he was already engaged for Rheingold, so the mount was offered to Bill Williamson, who turned it down. Very well, John

Galbreath said, I'll send a jockey from America; and he sent a champion, the Panamanian Braulio Baeza.

The York race was a sensation. Baeza on Roberto jumped out of the gate at a tremendous pace and kept right on going, breaking the course record. The scintillating Brigadier Gerard for the first and last time met his match and finished a tired second by three lengths. Rheingold ran like a dead horse and trailed in fourth of the five runners, 13 or so lengths behind Roberto.

Everyone retired in slight embarrassment (except Baeza and John Galbreath) and considered the implications.

Lester couldn't understand Rheingold's failure, as he had ridden him seven furlongs at half-speed on Newbury racecourse the Saturday before and had found him in terrific form. Barry Hills took Rheingold home to Lambourn and didn't run him again that year, as the horse – and the dreams of the Arc – had gone all to pieces. (Barry Hills, incidentally, had bought and expanded the Lambourn yard where Lester had been brought up.) Roberto went back to Ireland to be prepared for the Prix Niel at Longchamp a month later. Braulio Baeza was to return to ride.

Lester was engaged in the race for Hard to Beat who was returning from the lay-off that had followed his defeat at Saint-Cloud. Baeza jumped off again smartly on Roberto, and Lester, pulling out all stops, beat him rousingly by a length. Baeza came in for criticism and Lester for glory, but, he says, 'It was just one of those things.'

The two colts met for the last time that season in the Arc de Triomphe, Baeza again on Roberto, Lester on Hard to Beat. Roberto set off so fast that the whole field ran most of the race off the bit, pushing. Neither he nor Hard to Beat did much good in the end, finishing seventh and eighth behind San San, ridden by Freddie Head. Rheingold moped in Lambourn under his trainer's worried eye.

Next year, the three colts, now four years old, resumed the circus. Lester, back on Roberto, won the Coronation Cup at Epsom in perhaps the horse's easiest race ever. With only five runners, none of the others of his class, Roberto made a good deal of the running and finished five lengths ahead at a canter.

Epsom, Lester points out, is a left-hand track, as is York, and Roberto too was a different horse when going the way he liked.

On the day before the Coronation Cup, Lester had come second in the Derby on Cavo Doro, beaten half a length by Morston.

Rheingold, restored to tremendous health, won four straight races for Yves Saint-Martin in the first few months of the season, and Barry Hills with confidence sent him to Ascot in July for the King George VI and Queen Elizabeth Stakes. Yves Saint-Martin was to ride.

Hard to Beat came over from France for the race, Jimmy Lindley engaged for the saddle.

Roberto also lined up, ridden by Lester.

It had all the makings of a hot contest, and so it proved, but none of them won. They were all beaten by the brilliant three-year-old filly Dahlia, ridden by Bill Pyers, owned by Nelson Bunker Hunt and trained by Maurice Zilber in France. The nearest to her skittish heels was Rheingold, six lengths second. Hard to Beat, too far from his home stable, came ninth, while Roberto, who had reached the front five furlongs out, weakened sadly to finish almost last. Ascot is right-handed, like Longchamp, and again it made all the difference.

It was Roberto's last race. He had been withdrawn from the Eclipse earlier because of monsoon-type rains on the morning of the race, and although he was expected to repeat his Benson and Hedges win at York, Vincent again withdrew him at the last moment because of soft going. John Galbreath took him home to his U.S. stud farm, where he proved to be among the top flight of sires.

For Rheingold, the King George was by no means the end of the road. With Lester riding (as a run-up to the Arc de Triomphe, in which Yves Saint-Martin was already booked for Allez France), he ran a month later at York in the Benson and Hedges Gold Cup, but couldn't quicken at the end and finished third. As in the year before, he seemed to fall apart after that, and it looked miserably doubtful whether he could be got right for his again planned target of the Arc de Triomphe in October.

Barry Hills rested him well before re-starting strong work, and then asked Lester to ride him at Lambourn and give his opinion.

Lester said Rheingold was the same as at York: lifeless. Barry Hills in despair again set to work on his colt and Lester shortly went off to the south of France for a few days' rest in the sun.

'Barry rang up about September 25th, ten days before the Arc,' Lester says. 'He said come and ride him again, so I went back in the middle of the night and rode him work in the morning, and he was a different horse.' With that, Rheingold returned to France, where he had never been beaten, and took his place in the Arc de Triomphe.

After all the ups and downs and tribulations, the event itself went smoothly. Rheingold was drawn well, and Lester set off promptly to ride from near the front, quickening into the lead with impressive ease two furlongs out and cruising home by two and a half lengths from Yves Saint-Martin on the French star filly Allez France. The big Rheingold, Lester said, was ideal for that sort of race.

It was Lester's fifteenth ride in the race and his first win, his first triumphant Triomphe. There was relief as well as joy in his broad smile when Rheingold was led in by his owner, Henry Zeisel. The long dream of Barry Hills had at last come true. Hard to Beat, soldiering on, ran into third place, ridden this time by Gerard Thiboeuf.

It was the final time out for both colts: the circus was over and time moved on.

# Empery

The years between the Derbys of Roberto (1972) and Empery (1976) reverberated in Lester terms with names like Apalachee, Cellini, Abergwaun and Thatch, all trained by Vincent O'Brien, with Steel Heart for Dermot Weld, Giacometti for Ryan Price, Sagaro for François Boutin and Juliette Marny for Jeremy Tree. Above all, there was Dahlia who had made mincemeat of Roberto, Rheingold and Hard to Beat in the King George VI and Queen Elizabeth at Ascot.

Abergwaun, owned by Lester's long-time friend Charles St George, won rompingly at Royal Ascot in 1973 three days after owner John Mulcahy had taken the St James's Palace Stakes with Thatch; and Thatch later won the Sussex Stakes at Goodwood in fine style.

Less happy in a way were the careers of Apalachee and Cellini, though each won more in prize money. This pair seemed, as two-year-olds, to be the natural successors to Vincent's string of great Derby winners, both having at the end of 1973 shown brilliant promise. Lester won the Dewhurst Stakes on Cellini, followed by the Observer Gold Cup on Apalachee, and it seemed merely to be a toss-up which took the more classics come 1974.

Then, first time out as a three-year-old, Apalachee set off at the Curragh at 6-1 on and Lester had a struggle to win by a neck. He went all the same to the Two Thousand Guineas at Newmarket; started favourite and finished third; and, to everyone's dismay, he showed no more development and had to be withdrawn before the Derby, never racing again.

Cellini scraped home in two preliminary races and started favourite in the Irish Two Thousand Guineas, also finishing third. He had one more outing, unsuccessful, at Royal Ascot, and that was that. Brilliant two-year-olds do occasionally fizzle out for no discernible reason, and even the O'Brien touch couldn't conjure miracles from spent rockets.

Steel Heart, owned by Ravi Tikkoo, had a great two-year-old season in 1974, culminating in a defeat by Grundy in the Dewhurst, no disgrace: but he too made less mark at three.

Unbeaten as a two-year-old, Giacometti came second in the 1974 Two Thousand Guineas, third in the Derby (both with Tony Murray up) and second in the St Leger (with Lester), a great horse knocking continually on the classic door. Owner Charles St George finally led in his winner after the Champion Stakes in October, Giacometti and Lester scoring in fine style, unchallenged.

Juliette Marny, sired by 1969 Derby winner Blakeney, bred and owned by James Morrison, and partnered by Lester, won Lingfield's Oaks Trial Stakes by a head in May 1975, followed by the Oaks itself in June. A bright bay filly who carried her head high, she wasn't Lester's original choice for the Oaks. He had the pick of her or her better regarded stablemate Brilliantine, Jeremy Tree having the faith to leave the choice entirely to his jockey. The racecard on the day actually had L. Piggott down to ride both horses, with asterisks explaining that he would ride either one. It wasn't until noon on the baking hot day of the Oaks, three and a quarter hours before the 'off', and on the telephone to Jeremy, that Lester made his choice. James Morrison, on his way to the course, didn't find out until Susan Piggott told him. Lester had decided on that morning that the going was likely to be too firm for Brilliantine but would suit Juliette Marny, and he was right. Juliette Marny, running in blinkers for the first time to concentrate her mind, won breezily by a margin of four lengths. Brilliantine, hating the ground, came in eleventh.

It was never his riding alone that made Lester unique as a jockey but his thought-out judgments and understanding of what horses liked. He chose wrong sometimes, inevitably, but only a fraction of the number of times that he chose right.

Before the Irish Guinness Oaks, he had a choice of the three best fillies: Juliette Marny, the French filly Nobiliary, and Vincent O'Brien's Tuscarora. He chose Juliette Marny again, and in a desperate finish sent her shooting to the front in the last two or three strides to overhaul Tuscorora by a neck, with Nobiliary an undisgraced third. One could hardly be *more* right.

In 1975, a year crowned for him by the award of the OBE, Lester took his sixth Ascot Gold Cup, and altogether won eight of the Royal meeting's twenty-four races. Vincent O'Brien trained six winners, four with Lester and the other two with lightweight Sardinian Gianfranco Dettori, an unusual choice of jockey made at Lester's suggestion.

Dahlia it was, however, who became the overall star of those years, although Lester didn't ride her regularly until half way through her four-year-old season. He partnered her only once before that, in her very first outing when she won a good 5-furlong race at Deauville for her French trainer Maurice Zilber and American owner Nelson Bunker Hunt. She ran three more times without winning at two, but at three had much success, chiefly in the hands of stable jockey Bill Pyers, but sometimes in Yves Saint-Martin's. The only filly consistently to beat her was the flashing Allez France, owned by Daniel Wildenstein, trained by Albert Klimscha and also ridden by Yves Saint-Martin.

Lester often rode Nelson Bunker Hunt's English-trained horses, especially those with Bernard van Cutsem, and it was at the owner's behest that Lester took the ride when Dahlia came over for the King George VI and Queen Elizabeth Stakes at Ascot in July 1974. Trainer Maurice Zilber, always keen on Lester, was totally in favour. As in the year before, when she had skipped away from Rheingold, Dahlia made her way through the field, hit the front a good way from home and stayed on to win with ease by two and a half lengths.

Next time out, she won the Benson and Hedges Gold Cup by the same margin at York, and then crossed the Atlantic to run at Belmont Park in New York. Ron Turcotte, a Canadian jockey, rode and won on her there, but two weeks later Lester was back in the saddle for the Canadian International Championship at Toronto.

Lester, arriving from England a few scant hours in advance,

rode one of those races guaranteed to be bad for a watching owner's heart, appearing to be hopelessly shut in too near to home and then streaking through a late opening to win at high speed. Dahlia's time at Toronto was a record for the Woodbine course.

A year earlier, Dahlia had unaccountably come nowhere in the Arc de Triomphe (behind Lester on Rheingold) but had then gone to Laurel and with Bill Pyers won the Washington International. After the Toronto win, she again ran at Laurel, Lester flying over for the second time in a fortnight, but this time she met her match.

Lester's two journeys were a clear statement that he was no longer fighting to be champion. By late October, he and Pat Eddery were both within reach of the honour, the younger jockey very slightly in front. Lester went off to Canada and Washington in search of big prizes, Pat turning down a ride at Laurel to concentrate on numbers at home. In the next few years after he stopped chasing the crown, Lester's places on the jockeys' list were: in 1972, fourth; in 1973, second; in 1974, second; and in 1975, third. If one counted in his overseas wins, nothing much had changed.

Dahlia and Lester again won the Benson and Hedges Gold Cup in 1975, her last success in Europe. In all, she amassed well over a million and a half dollars in prize money for Nelson Bunker Hunt, and had won in every country she visited – France, England, Canada and her original homeland, the United States.

She ran best when she'd been travelling, Lester says, as, unlike many horses, she seemed to enjoy it. She was tough and game and keen to race, pulling quite hard. She liked and was much better in a fast-run race, and she was never ready to produce anything much until the weather was warm, from mid-June onwards. After her European career, her owner sent her for a year to be trained in California where she continued to win many big races; and Lester sums her up simply as 'tremendous'.

Empery, like Dahlia, was sired by Vaguely Noble, owned by Nelson Bunker Hunt and trained in France by Maurice Zilber.

Maurice Zilber was by birth Egyptian and had been twelve times leading trainer in his native country before leaving there with nothing during the Nasser upheavals. Arriving penniless in

France, he immediately set about gathering together a new stable, and such was his skill, his forcefulness and his persuasive tongue that he was back high on the racing map in exceedingly short time.

A trainer of the very highest class, he is somewhat volatile in temperament and sometimes on non-speaking terms with his owners because of differences of opinion as to how the horses should be run. Among them on occasion was Nelson Bunker Hunt. Nevertheless, the two strong-minded men, both of a sturdy presence, scored a long string of successes together, glued in spite of irritations.

Nelson Bunker Hunt at that time had countless horses in training and on stud farms in Europe and America and was at the height of the era of his success. Empery was not, in fact, reckoned to be his best colt in 1976: he had another charismatic three-year-old in Youth.

Empery ran three times as a two-year-old, winning one small race and making not much show in the Grand Criterium. First time out in his three-year-old season Lester rode him in the Prix d'Essai des Poulains, the French equivalent of the Two Thousand Guineas, but although he ran well he finished fourth. Next time out, much the same result. On the third try, with Bill Pyers, he finished third in the Prix Lupin, the race being won by his stable-mate Youth. Youth, ridden as usual by Freddie Head, then went on to win the Prix du Jockey Club (French Derby) on the Sunday after Empery ran at Epsom.

Although useful and in Lester's words 'a nice horse', Empery had up to that time made no particular mark, and it was only because Lester had accepted the ride on him that he was in the news much at all. As in Joe Lawson's days, it was the trainer alone whose faith was unshaken.

Lester himself thought it likely he would be beaten by Wollow, which had fought indomitably to seize the Two Thousand Guineas for Henry Cecil, with Gianfranco Dettori in the saddle. Wollow, sired by Lester's old friend and winner, Wolver Hollow, was proving the prolific winner he was to be all his racing life. Lester said aloud that it would take a gunshot to stop Wollow winning the Derby. Maurice Zilber got to hear of Lester's published opinions and telephoned to tell him strongly in his

French-Egyptian accent that Empery had much improved during the past week and was in peak form to win: and Lester again set off at Epsom with the trainer's confidence overriding his doubts.

Lester did most particularly want to win, as if he did he would set an all-time record of seven victories in the big race. He already shared the record with Steve Donoghue and Jem Robinson, but being ahead on his own meant much more. Empery was, of course, unknown to British racegoers as all his runs had so far been in France, and because of this he started at a generous 10-1, with Wollow, the only one better backed, a hot favourite at 11-10.

Lester rode the Derby to his well-tried pattern, Empery being easy to ride with no wayward quirks of temperament. He set off well, stayed in fourth or fifth place until the last two furlongs, then quickened in a flying straight line well away from the rails to win in the end with apparent ease by three lengths from Relkino, with Oats third.

The supposedly unbeatable Wollow finished an undistinguished fifth, to post-mortem mutterings of 'ground too soft'; and subsequently Wollow and his Italian jockey retrieved their dignity by winning the Eclipse (on a disqualification), the Sussex Stakes and the Benson and Hedges Gold Cup.

Empery still isn't considered by some to have been a truly great horse, but on his day he beat the greater Wollow out of sight. Nelson Bunker Hunt wasn't there to lead in his risen star, his daughter Betsy deputising. The owner himself listened to the race on the telephone back home in Dallas where his wife had arranged a silver wedding party, oblivious to the clash of dates.

Empery had one more run, in the Irish Sweeps Derby three weeks after Epsom. This time he started favourite but couldn't quicken when challenged and was beaten two and a half lengths by another American-bred, French-trained horse, Malacate. Empery, his Derby reputation more or less intact, went back over the ocean to stud.

In 1976, Lester rode a great deal for Sir Noel Murless, the old partnership reasserting itself for one last flourish as the great trainer was to retire at the end of the season. Together, they won twenty-three more races, notably the Royal Hunt Cup at

Royal Ascot with Jumping Hill, and the Richmond Stakes and the Laurent-Perrier Champagne Stakes with a warmly promising two-year-old J.O. Tobin.

Lester's last ever-win for Noel was Tinsley Green at Lingfield on 2 November, a small prize but a big milestone, charged with nostalgic mutual memories of great moments shared.

In numbers of wins, 1976 wasn't notable for Lester: he scored only 87 from a small (for him) pool of 402 races in Great Britain. In prestige they were colossal, as apart from the Derby he won the Yorkshire Cup on Bruni, the Coronation Cup on Quiet Fling and the Ascot Gold Cup, as in the previous year, on Sagaro. Also the Nassau Stakes with Roussalka and the Cesarewitch with John Cherry.

The decade of the seventies saw a great expansion of commercial sponsorship of races. New races arose, old races were adopted, the pattern of prize money changed. Historic old races, those left without sponsors, lost some of their standing, while others advanced in importance. The Cheveley Park Stakes and the Dewhurst Stakes, both for top two-year-olds, were adopted and endowed by bookmaker William Hill, and in 1976 Lester won them both.

As the familiar Murless name faded away, a new name began to appear, heralding a whole new age. Lester won the Cheveley Park on Durtal, trained by Barry Hills, and the Dewhurst on Vincent's new white hope, The Minstrel.

Both horses were owned by the newcomer: Robert Sangster.

# The Minstrel and Alleged

The ink on the Press huzzas for Lester's seventh victory in the Derby was hardly dry when he set out on the path to the eighth. Among Vincent O'Brien's large 1976 intake of two-year-old colts, the best looked like being not only The Minstrel but also Be My Guest, Valinsky, Artaius and Alleged.

Be My Guest, like The Minstrel, was sired by Northern Dancer, and Valinsky was by Nijinsky, himself also by Northern Dancer. Artaius's sire was Round Table, Alleged's was Hoist the Flag: all five colts had thus crossed the Atlantic.

During 1976, Lester won on all of the first three, all in Ireland. Alleged came to hand very late indeed and won his only two-year-old race on 1 November, ridden by Thomas Murphy. Artaius, too, ridden by the same jockey, ran once and late and was beaten by Orchestra. They, it was clear, were unlikely to be ready for the Derby.

Opening the 1977 campaign, Vincent first of all sent his unbeaten three-time winner The Minstrel to Ascot for what the betting public expected to be an odds-on doddle; and to all appearances, things went well. The horse won. From Lester's viewpoint, though, that race did The Minstrel no good. The ground was soft which drained a lot of the colt's stamina. He had to struggle a bit to win, and near the end he was drifting slightly to the left, often a sign of fatigue.

When The Minstrel came over for the Two Thousand Guineas, Lester didn't think he looked in top condition, but hoped it was because of the cold wet spring which hadn't been helpful to horses in general. The Minstrel ran fairly well but could produce no finishing speed, and in a hard race was beaten into third place by two lengths.

Vincent took him home to Ireland and decided to try for the Irish Two Thousand Guineas three weeks later. Lester says this was again a very hard race, which The Minstrel was unlucky to lose. Nebbiolo, who finished third, ran into the back of him a furlong and a half out, unbalancing him, and Pampapaul, a moderately good performer trained in Ireland by Noel Murless's brother Stuart, came with a strong run on the outside and beat him by a short head. As preparation for the Derby, the three hard races in a row, two of them lost, were all fairly discouraging.

Be My Guest made a much more positive show first time out, coming over for the Epsom Spring Meeting and winning the Ladbroke Blue Riband Trial Stakes by a clear three lengths, untroubled. Next time out, though, he like Artaius lost by two lengths to Orchestra, a useful horse but not Derby class.

Valinsky came out at The Curragh in May and in a trial race was soundly beaten by Alleged; definitely not what had been expected. Vincent by now was scratching his head and wondering which, if any, he could send to Epsom for the big race. It was unthinkable for him not to be represented at all, but if all his colts looked like flopping, maybe it would be better for everyone's reputation if he kept them at home. The owners disagreed. Sir Charles Clore wanted Valinsky to run and Mrs A. Manning felt the same about Be My Guest, sink or swim. Vincent decided at that point to let only those two take their chances. However, after discussing with Lester the whys and wherefores of the Irish Two Thousand Guineas, it was decided The Minstrel should also take his place at Epsom and he, Lester, would ride. Vincent, with enormous respect for Lester's judgment, revised his plans and shipped all three, misgivings or not.

The Minstrel was a bright chestnut with a white face and four white socks, markings often considered undesirable until the 'handsome is as handsome does' rule takes over. He was jointly owned by Robert Sangster, Vincent and two or three others, but ran always in the increasingly familiar Sangster colours of blue, green and white. The Sangster silks and The Minstrel's hide made a shiningly vivid combination; impossible to miss.

The Minstrel was in addition excitable by nature, and Vincent was afraid the noise of the Epsom crowds would upset him. As a solution, he stuffed cotton-wool into the colt's ears in the saddling boxes, with Lester removing the O'Brien-style tranquilliser once he'd arrived unfussed at the start.

Many hearts sank when the ultra-visible pair set off slowly from the Derby gate. The Minstrel was never a quick starter, Lester says, but much else that day was in his favour. The ground was hard, which the little horse liked, and the track was left-handed, the way he went best. Blushing Groom, a very good unbeaten French horse, winner of the French Two Thousand Guineas, started hot favourite, but Lester, who had been beaten by him in the Grand Criterium the previous autumn, didn't think he would stay the longer distance at Epsom, which The Minstrel might.

Starting willy-nilly at the rear of the large field, Lester reckons he had fifteen horses ahead to beat when they had gone a third of the way. By the downhill approach to Tattenham Corner, he had passed a few but still lay about tenth.

Hot Grove, ridden by Willie Carson, came past Lester on the outside and began to make a run. Lester, thinking Hot Grove a danger because of having won the Chester Vase on him only four weeks earlier, decided it would be best to stay close, and went after him. Both horses, on the curve, shot up to be level with the leaders, passing ten horses inside a furlong. There was a bit of interference on the inside, Lester says, but on the outside he and Willie had a clear run.

When the field straightened after Tattenham Corner, Hot Grove went into the lead, with Lester on his outside still following. All the way up the straight, The Minstrel chased Hot Grove, and for most of the way that's how it looked to Lester that they would finish. He could make no impression until inside the last furlong, when slowly the gap began to close. At one hundred yards from the post, The Minstrel was second by three-quarters of a length and the jockey was hopeful: at fifty yards, by half a length, and the jockey was sure; and in the last twenty-five yards they broke Willie Carson's heart.

Lester says The Minstrel won (by a neck) because he outran Hot Grove over the distance. To Lester, it was always the horse that won, not himself. He says, 'He won', not 'I won'.

The Minstrel, he says, was a good tough horse who, at the time of the Derby, was developing fast and just coming to his full strength. Pampapaul, who had beaten him in Ireland only two weeks earlier, could finish no nearer than fifteen lengths back. Valinsky finished tenth with Be My Guest on his heels, eleventh. Blushing Groom came third by five lengths, not making the distance, as Lester had thought.

The Minstrel's golden time of harvest lasted seven and a half dramatic weeks. After the Epsom fireworks, the next outing was the Irish Sweeps Derby in the second half of June where Lester and The Minstrel lined up at The Curragh in a field of fifteen. The race went sweetly enough until near the end, when The Minstrel, leading by a clear margin, swerved suddenly across the path of Lucky Sovereign who was chasing him home. Naturally enough, Lucky Sovereign's jockey, Frankie Durr, lodged an objection, saying he had been hampered, his horse having had to shorten his stride. The Stewards debated for a tense half-hour before announcing, to Vincent's vast relief, that the result would stand. The Minstrel, it was reckoned, had been far enough in front for his crossing of Lucky Sovereign's path to have had no effect on the outcome.

The Minstrel, one of those many horses with a left-hand preference, had swerved left on the right-hand Curragh, an echo perhaps of his drift leftwards first time out at Ascot.

It was to Ascot all the same that he went next, to the King George VI and Queen Elizabeth Diamond Stakes a month after the Irish Derby. On the very hot and humid day, The Minstrel's coat was shining with sweat, and as usual he was slow out of the stalls. As in the Derby, the Sangster colours bobbed along in the rear for about half a mile before making a move forward, but this time Lester came round the bend into the straight no nearer than sixth. He continued to make smooth progress and passed the long-time leader Orange Bay a furlong from the post. It looked all over bar the cheering.

Orange Bay, however, ridden by Pat Eddery, behaved as if insulted and refused to give in. He was on the rails, to his advantage, with Lester on the outside; and he fought back all the way. It was the hardest of battles of balance, and endurance, two horses and two jockeys united in art, strength and inbred indomitable will to win.

It could have gone either way. It went to Lester and The Minstrel by a short head; perhaps by an inch or two further than Roberto had won the Derby. Lester this time, however, was confident and rode into the winner's enclosure to ecstatic acclaim.

The Queen, in her Silver Jubilee year, presented the de Beers diamond prizes, and later in the afternoon Lester thanked her by riding her a winner on her own horse, Valuation. Pictures of the Queen with Lester always show them both smiling: no doubt they usually meet in moments of victory, but their shared understanding and devotion to racing comes over clearly as a positive warmth.

The five owners of The Minstrel debated and argued for quite a while over the colt's future programme, but in the end he ran no more races. E.P. (Eddie) Taylor, who had bred him in Canada, bought a half-share back for four and a half million dollars, and The Minstrel departed in a hurry to his Maryland farm in September. The haste was owing to an equine genital disease which had temporarily closed (among others) the National Stud: no one wanted The Minstrel to be stranded if the Americans, like the Australians, put a ban on the import of stallions from Britain.

The Minstrel ran nine races in all. Lester rode him every time except the first: lost two, won six.

The whole of Jubilee year was for Lester a right royal procession, his quicksilver last-second finishes bringing off hats and coups from Goodwood to York.

Vincent's other best colts all had their days, including the beaten Derby pair, Valinsky and Be My Guest. In August, Sir Charles Clore saw Valinsky do him proud in the Geoffrey Freer Stakes at Newbury, and at Goodwood two weeks later Mrs Manning lived through one of Lester's heart-stoppers when Be My Guest brought her the Waterford Crystal Mile by a hard-ridden head. Be My Guest turned out later to be a prolific sire of first class winners, ironically topping The Minstrel.

The late-developers, Artaius and Alleged, grew in prowess every month, Artaius coming to a glorious peak at Sandown in July, when he made all the running and broke the course record in winning the Joe Coral Eclipse Stakes for Mrs George Getty II. Still on a high, he equally dominated the Sussex Stakes at Goodwood, Lester dictating the whole pace and shape of the race from start to finish.

If Artaius was great, Alleged was greater – in the end. Although he won his first three races of the season, they were all pitched low to match his current abilities, and no one thought a great deal of him. Not until the middle of August, when it was as if he had metamorphosed into a different horse: and he never did well, it transpired, until late in the year.

Vincent decided he was ready for the Great Voltigeur at York, the faithful public instantly making him second favourite with nothing much to go on. Best backed was Hot Grove, who had given The Minstrel so much trouble in the Derby. The new Alleged made mincemeat of Hot Grove and everything else. Lester took him straight into the lead at the beginning and he coolly stayed there, accelerating when asked three furlongs out and winning literally at a canter by seven lengths. Hot Grove finished fourth, and Orchestra, who had beaten Be My Guest, finished fifth. A good many eyes opened very wide indeed, and Alleged's forthcoming appearance in the St Leger was all of a sudden taken to be a formality.

Everyone reckoned without the Jubilee. The year was the Queen's own and her greatest in terms of classics. Her great battling filly Dunfermline had won the Epsom Oaks, but having shown no speed in the Yorkshire Oaks later, went to Doncaster as a query spent force.

Willie Carson demonstrated that she was no such thing. Alleged took the lead easily entering the straight and looked a winner until two furlongs from home, when Lester found himself working to keep his position. Dunfermline passed him a furlong and a half out and won decisively by one and a half lengths. The cheers erupted for the Queen, and a thoughtful Vincent took Alleged back to Ireland and wondered about the Arc de Triomphe. The owner in whose colours the colt had run, Californian Bob Fluor, sold most of his one-fifth share in disappointment to Robert Sangster who already owned two-fifths.

Alleged, Lester says, was one of the very easiest of horses to ride. He would always do as he was asked, always give whatever he was capable of at any particular moment. Lester liked to ride him in front because that way he could set the pace himself. Many jockeys don't like to lead and many trainers and owners don't like to see their horses in front early on, but with the right mount, it's the way to stage-manage the whole play.

Because of Lester, the 1977 Arc de Triomphe was to begin with a comparatively slow-run race. After two furlongs, he took the lead which no one else wanted, then dictated the pace he felt right and shook up Alleged coming into the straight, surprising and slipping the field and sprinting to victory.

To the crowd it looked all too easy. So does conducting a symphony to anyone but a musician.

Alleged, the home camp felt, would go from strength to strength as a four-year-old, and in some ways they were right. He was faster at four, a late developer coming to his peak.

First time out in 1978, he won a modest race at the Curragh in May against four opponents, starting at 7–1 on. This was planned as a step on the way in his preparation for Epsom's Coronation Cup, but the firm ground at the Curragh almost put an end to the horse's career, Alleged jarring himself to such an extent that Vincent was unable to do much with him until the approach of autumn. Then, as in the previous year, he seemed to change entirely, his vigour flooding in on a healthy tide.

The Arc de Triomphe again was his target, one of the few major races left. Sharpening him to fitness a scant two weeks before, Vincent sent him to Longchamp for the Prix du Prince d'Orange, generally accepted as a suitable preliminary. Alleged and Lester not only won easily against good opponents but broke the course record.

Sighing with relief, Vincent took his revitalised horse home and returned him to France for the Arc itself on 1 October. On the day, Lester was afraid the ground would be too soft for Alleged because the colt liked good ground to be at his best, but he had the highest regard for his speed. 'He could have won a six-furlong sprint when he was a four-year-old, he was that good.'

For the second year running, the Arc was a slow-run race, playing right into Lester's hands. He didn't need to lead because another horse was prepared to, and he sat poised in second or third place until two furlongs out. When he set Alleged going, it was quickly all over. He swept to the front and could have gone further away. The winning margin was officially two lengths, and the effort involved was 'comfortable'.

It was Alleged's last race. In spite of discussions about the Champion Stakes and the Washington International, it was felt that he had already done enough, and he was syndicated for stud. Thanks to Vincent's care in choosing suitably moderate races within his early powers, Alleged was beaten only once. He was, Lester considers, the easiest to ride of all the great horses he partnered.

Back in Jubilee year, with the double 'Arc' still unthought of, Lester won the Ascot Gold Cup for the third time on Sagaro. It has become fashionable to decry Flat horses that can stay over distances of two and a half miles. Encouraged by generous sponsorship, the rage is all for nippy two-year-olds, for three-year-olds who can barely make the Derby distance, for fast turnovers and quick results. Stayers can be treated with condescension.

Sagaro changed all that, at least for one day, producing at six years such juvenile speed as to leave a distinguished field of younger horses looking foolish. Trained by François Boutin in France, Sagaro made his third Ascot raid look easiest of all, although it was the first time ever since the race was inaugurated in 1807 that it had been won three times by one horse.

'The pace was pretty well flat out all the way,' Lester says, 'and Sagaro could have gone round again. Most of the others could hardly walk at the finish.'

Between the heights of 1977 there were, as usual, depths. Into the 'most gloomy' category came the loss of his driving licence for six months, the result of two speeding offences, far apart in time of occurrence, coming into court within three days of each other. He got off the first time but the second lot of magistrates thought enough was enough. He'd been clocked at 91 mph and the police had had a job to catch him.

Into the 'most dangerous' category came Durtal, the filly who could have lost him his life.

# Injuries: Part 2

The size, noise and nearness of the Epsom crowd in Silver Jubilee mood on Oaks day, 1977, stirred the excitable filly Durtal to a state near hysteria. (A pity she had no cotton-wool in her ears.) Trained by Barry Hills, owned by Robert Sangster, and having won the Cheveley Park Stakes most promisingly as a two-year-old, Durtal started her three-year-old season well with a win in the Fred Darling Stakes at Newbury in April and a third in the French One Thousand Guineas on 1 May.

At Epsom, after the parade past the stands, Durtal set off back towards the start of the Oaks at a canter which quite soon quickened to a runaway gallop, impervious to all stop signals from her jockey. At a point up on the far side of the parade ring at Epsom, one has to steady to a walk and bear left to go along a lengthy railed stretch of Downs to reach the starting point of the Oaks and the Derby; it's a stretch which isn't wide as it's used for access only, not in races, and it can't be seen from the stands.

Durtal showed no signs at all of understanding the situation and pulling herself up. Lester, faced with a head-on crash against the far end of the parade ring area, hauled her head towards the path to the start. Durtal turned, crashed against the rails, and didn't stop. All that happened was that her saddle slipped backwards, leaving Lester without any possible control over her panic. Her pace increased. Lester tried desperately to remain on her back, lurching first to the left and then to the right. The saddle slipped completely down Durtal's right side, taking Lester with it. His foot slid through the stirrup and the stirrup leather twisted.

It happened at such speed that he could do nothing to avoid it.

The bolting Durtal dragged him at a full flat-out gallop along the ground for almost a hundred yards, her sharp hooves slashing the air all around him. Lester, trapped in the most dangerous of all riding configurations, had time to think that he would quite likely be killed.

His deliverance was as accidental as his predicament. Durtal, frenzied, crashed again against the rails and, by incredible luck, the stirrup iron around Lester's ankle hit a post and broke. Lester fell free to the ground and Durtal fell over the rails, staking herself in the leg and then bleeding.

Lester wasn't bleeding. He went back to the weighing-room, had a cup of tea, rode again a couple of races later and won the last race, cool as cool.

It was afterwards that the shock really hit him: when he turned white at the thought of what he'd survived, and spoke about it with fear tightening his vocal chords, sharpening the pitch of his voice. Now, years later, he refers to the brush with death calmly as 'something that happened', but I talked with him soon after, while the experience was fresh, when his mind was still filled with remembered horror, and at that time he thought it the worst that could ever happen.

He's changed his mind, since.

The worst, in Lester's history, faced a good deal of stiff competition, even before 1977.

After the 1964 crash in Paris, there were some relatively accident-free years, but in 1966, on the evening before he was due to ride Charles Engelhard's Right Noble in the Derby, he began to suffer excruciating pains in his side. A doctor, called in, said Lester had a kidney stone on the move, which he would pass or not pass; one would have to wait and see.

Lester spent the night in recurring bouts of great pain as the stone moved down through the abdomen, and the next morning, in the same state, went to Epsom. This was the very year when he was making the stand to leave Noel Murless. This was the very week of the Oaks he had gambled his future on winning on Valoris. There was no way, that week, that he was going to be ill in bed.

He won the first race of the day, but in the Derby itself, Right Noble, not the best of Vincent's stars, could finish no nearer than seventh behind Charlottown. The jockey seemed to feel nothing during the races, and sometime afterwards – before the Oaks – got rid of the kidney stone in the normal course of events.

Several people thought him more taciturn than usual, that Derby day.

In 1970, when Lester was cantering back after a race, a horse stumbled and threw him over its head.

It was the last race at Newbury on a Wednesday in June, and Lester, picking himself up, thought nothing much had happened. By the time he'd changed, however, he couldn't put his foot to the ground without pain and could hardly walk. He went immediately to see the orthopaedic surgeon Bill Tucker in London, who gave Lester two sticks to support him, telling him to come back for investigation and treatment the next day.

It transpired that Lester had broken the long bones in his foot, but in such a way that although he could hardly walk, he could – and did – ride horses.

Bill Tucker, that invaluable patcher-up of countless injured jockeys, worked habitually on the principle that if someone *believed* they could ride, then they could, broken bones or not. Fitness, in his eyes, was as much a state of mind as of body, which was one of the reasons he passed Bill Williamson as fit to ride Roberto, and why, in my own case, he once made a removable plaster for a broken forearm, to take off for racing and to fasten back for support after.

Bill Tucker strapped Lester's foot tightly in supportive adhesive bandage, not in plaster, and told him to keep it cold.

Lester, in a larger-sized shoe and unable to walk without help, went over to Ireland to ride Meadowville in the Irish Derby. That was on Saturday, three days after his fall. David Robinson, owner of Meadowville, was horrified. Lester, he said, couldn't possibly ride with a broken foot. Certainly he could, Lester said.

Riding was quite different from walking. His foot didn't hurt him, on a horse.

David Robinson and trainer Michael Jarvis helplessly and in bewilderment agreed to let him ride. Lester sat in the changing-room at The Curragh with his foot in a bucket of ice until race time, then he put on one of his grandfather Ernie's racing boots – which were larger than his own – and, holding onto someone for support, hobbled and hopped out to the parade ring.

It was as he'd said. He was all right on a horse. Meadowville didn't win only because he was beaten by three lengths into second place by Liam Ward on the all-conquering Nijinsky, not through any inability in his jockey.

Lester was due to ride two more horses for David Robinson the following afternoon in Paris. Unable, in face of proof to the contrary, to say Lester was incapable of performing, the owner compromised by removing his jockey from one horse only, that running in a long-distance race. Lester, accordingly, accompanied everywhere by ice-packs and followed by Susan and friends carrying his saddles and other gear, limped at high speed by air to Orly and Longchamp. The race he was still to ride was the Grand Prix de Paris; the horse, Roll of Honour. Helped like a cripple out to the parade ring, Lester confounded all doubters by winning by a neck.

From France, Lester and Susan went to Spain for him to ride in more races: and Spain was so hot that the ice-packs melted between hotel and racecourse.

The foot took a while to get better, Lester says, but of course it did in the end. He walked out with scarcely a wince in July to win the King George VI and Queen Elizabeth Stakes on Nijinsky.

Several of Lester's injuries were less public, although giving him equal trouble. In the year of The Minstrel, for instance, a few weeks before the frightening escapade on Durtal, he badly hurt his thumb at Lingfield, in the Derby Trial. His horse reared in the stalls, tangling Lester's hand in the barred metal walls and wrenching the thumb backwards so forcefully that a main tendon was stretched beyond being able to function. Lester couldn't afterwards bring his thumb across to touch any finger: it flapped uselessly, without strength.

Very sore and swollen, the hand was seen at Newmarket by an orthopaedic surgeon who came privately from Cambridge. He didn't know much about racing, he said. Would Lester please explain when he next wanted to ride.

Immediately, Lester said. Tomorrow. The Derby would occur in two weeks.

The orthopaedic surgeon was of the opinion that the thumb needed three weeks' complete rest, and even then, he warned doubtfully, the tendon might never recover. He put on some strapping encouragingly, and went away.

Lester continued to ride uninterruptedly and two weeks later won the Derby on The Minstrel. A week later, the orthopaedic surgeon called again at Newmarket to see how the thumb was doing.

'By the way,' he said, 'I saw you won that race you were so worried about. What was it called?'

Lester's thumb never did return to its former shape, though the tendon in the end recovered. His grandfather's hands, he says, were much worse. Ernie Piggott broke his fingers often.

In January 1976, on one of his many winter excursions, Lester fell in the straight in a race in Kuala Lumpur, Malaysia. He was riding a horse called Uncle Ivor (trained in Singapore by his close friend Ivan Allan) which clipped the heels of the horse in front and came down when everyone was going at flat-out speed to the finish.

Lester, tumbled along under the flying hooves, was taken to hospital for checks. From there, he telephoned to Susan who was in Singapore, saying he might have cracked a rib but was otherwise all right. In the morning, apparently recovered, he went back to the racecourse and rode in the first race.

Finding it too painful to continue, however, he flew to Singapore to join Susan who says he looked 'shaken' when he arrived. The next day, Lester consulted a doctor as he was due to fly to New Zealand to ride in the Air New Zealand Cup, and thought his ribs might need strapping. The doctor, after examining him, said dryly that Lester really shouldn't fly anywhere, let alone to New Zealand to race; he had indeed broken not one but two ribs, one of which had punctured his lung. Better, the doctor said, to rest in Singapore for two weeks. *Essential*, he said, if Lester intended to go on living.

Geoff Lewis, who happened to be in Hong Kong, went to New Zealand in Lester's place, while Lester for once listened to good advice and peacefully mended.

In September 1980, back in England, he fell on his shoulder in September at York. It looked nothing much. It happened just as he passed the winning post, finishing half way back, not engaged with the leaders. His stirrup leather broke just at the instant when he'd stopped riding hard and hadn't begun to pull up. Sooner, or later, he could have managed. At that moment, though, he was unbalanced and fell off.

He picked himself up slightly embarrassed and seemingly unharmed, but he had damaged the socket of his shoulder and pinched a nerve which for the rest of the season troubled him with shooting pains down his arm.

Bill Tucker had retired and gone to live in Bermuda and was not around to consult. In addition, strict rules had recently been introduced to prevent jockeys riding when unfit. Medical cards had to be carried and be produced every race day for the racecourse doctor to check. All but minor injuries incurred mandatory lay-offs. Riding with broken feet was out. Lester kept his shoulder troubles private and before the end of the season had won 156 races in England alone.

The shooting pains continued until November when Lester, happening to be in California with Susan and Maureen, consulted a recommended doctor there. The doctor injected him several times, and the pains subsided.

The affair of Lester's ear at Epsom's Spring Meeting in 1981 was public in the extreme.

There had been no cameras at the point where Durtal had dragged him in 1977, but four years later they were steadily focussed on the starting stalls when Lester lined up there on a Thursday afternoon on Winsor Boy for a 5-furlong sprint.

The horses were all in the stalls, excited and keen, the starter on the point of letting them go. Lester was gathering his reins but hadn't yet a firm hold. Winsor Boy, totally without warning, went back, bang, against the closed doors behind him, then dived down to the ground in front. Never before or since, Lester says, has he known a horse to go underneath the gates. Winsor Boy went down and underneath in a flash, taking Lester with him.

In the horse's passage under the still closed gates, Lester's right ear was all but torn off: only a small flap of skin held it on.

Winsor Boy scrambled to his feet, leaving his jockey on the ground, and galloped for two furlongs up the course. Then he swerved left, crashed through the rails and dropped dead of a heart attack, falling unfortunately on a spectator in a wheelchair, who survived.

Lester was told this afterwards. At the time, he lay bleeding on the turf while most people fussed over his ear and he himself – and the racecourse doctor – worried that his back was broken.

'There was so much blood from my ear, but I hardly felt it. My back was worst. Terrible . . . Terrible.'

The bottom of the gate had scraped all down the knobs of his backbone and battered his muscles, leaving him in agony and unable to move. In the ambulance on the way to Epsom hospital, he felt more pain than from any other injury ever.

When he arrived at the hospital, his back was immediately X-rayed, and he felt reassured, though not much better, when he was told there were no fractures.

Susan had not been at the racecourse. She heard of the accident by telephone when Dr Michael Allen, who had been appointed chief racecourse medical officer when the medical cards were introduced, reached her in London. He was kind, Susan says. He told her that Lester had been transferred to Roehampton Hospital and that they were trying to locate a particular plastic surgeon who worked there, Patrick Whitfield, who was good with almost-severed ears.

By eight in the evening the ear was sewn back in place. Susan slept across two chairs that night by Lester's bedside and the Press began to camp in droves in the corridors downstairs.

Journalists used every ruse they could think of to reach Lester, but he was well guarded by doctors and nurses who repeatedly asked the Press to leave, to no avail. There's no one as persistent as a journalist whose editor has told him not to come back without a story, particularly when all the editors in London have issued the same orders.

Lester and Susan, wanting to go home quietly, uninterviewed, plotted with one of their friends to create a diversion. The friend arrived in her car at the hospital's front door, loudly announcing she had come to collect Lester. The gentlemen of the Press focussed their cameras and got out their notebooks, and Lester, shuffling, his head heavily bandaged, was smuggled by the nurses out of a back door to be whisked off unseen in a car driven by Susan.

After Bill Tucker retired, Lester had begun being treated by an osteopath, Johnny Johnson, and it was to him that he turned now for repairs. But for Johnny Johnson's frequent assistance, Lester and Susan say, Lester's career might not have lasted so long. He worked that time on the sore backbone and deeply-bruised muscles intensively day after day in London until Lester could again move normally with returning strength.

By the following Tuesday, home in Newmarket, Lester thought it time to get back on a horse: but in case he wasn't as much recovered as he believed, it was decided he should sit only on a pony. A pony was duly borrowed from a small girl (with her entire permission) and to everyone's satisfaction Lester rode it round in an indoor school with no ill effects.

Susan had been to Lillywhites sports shop in London to find something for Lester to wear over his bandaged ear, returning with a red, white and blue woollen headband, originally designed for skiers. Resplendent in this, and equipped with a larger size in helmets, he reappeared on a racecourse six days after the accident, getting his medical card signed to endorse his fitness and riding two horses at Ascot, an also-ran and a second.

On the seventh day, on Fairy Footsteps, he won the One Thousand Guineas.

In August 1984, Lester went to Yarmouth to ride a not-too-brilliant gelding, Royal Octave, in a two-year-old selling race. He was trained by Ben Hanbury who had formerly rented Lester's newly-built yard in Newmarket and for whom Lester often rode when asked.

Royal Octave led for a good deal of the way but he produced no finishing speed and was beaten into third place, earning his owner the princely sum of £88.60. Lester pulled him up in the normal way, turned and began to trot back, the reins loose in his hands and lying on the horse's neck. Something abruptly scared him at that point and he shied violently, whipping round in a 180-degree turn, flinging Lester out sideways.

Lester's foot, as before with Durtal, went through the stirrup iron, and Royal Octave, already alarmed, set off at a renewed gallop with Lester hanging helplessly by his caught ankle. For a good fifty yards, he dragged him along the hard ground, his hind feet thudding into him repeatedly while he tried frantically to free his foot. Again ... again ... he thought he would be killed.

He saved himself. He survived not by getting his foot back through the stirrup, but by pulling his foot out of his boot. He fell free, badly battered, while the gelding hurtled onwards until his panic died. There was no chance that time that, after a cup of tea, Lester would be riding in the next race as one of the horse's kicks had damaged his hip, knocking a chunk off the top of his femur. Jockeys' bones, as one can see, are close to the surface under the skin.

Lester went home for a good deal of treatment from Johnny Johnson and also from two devoted physiotherapists in Newmarket, Fiona Morton and her partner Barbara. Lester particularly wants to thank those two and their assistants for all their help, acknowledging that he owed to them his comparatively fast return to the saddle.

It was on 8 August that Royal Octave dragged him. On 1 September, he returned with a winner ... a 6–4 favourite two-year-old, Oh So Sharp.

Within five weeks, but not until after he'd won the St Leger on Commanche Run, Kanz, trained by Guy Harwood, clipped the heels of a runner in front and fell with him two furlongs from the start of the Sun Chariot Stakes at Newmarket. Lester rolled over in several somersaults owing to the fast speed, and was helped to his feet by a doctor following the field with an ambulance. The doctor put in a report that Lester had appeared dazed after his fall, and Dr Allen had no choice but to act on this and require Lester not to race again for two days.

Two days might not normally matter, but this fall occurred on a Saturday afternoon, and the Prix de l'Arc de Triomphe was on the next day, Sunday.

When Dr Allen insisted Lester miss the Arc, Lester thoroughly lost his temper. He asked Dr Allen to examine his (Lester's) eyes, which he did: there was no sign of concussion. Dr Allen all the same said he couldn't overthrow the judgment of his colleague. Lester, who had raced with double vision, with a broken foot, a punctured lung and a kidney stone, who had struggled back countless times with half-healed hurts, was totally furious at being stood down when he felt all right.

Susan, alerted at home by telephone, drove along to the racecourse and went to the first-aid room, and there found her husband covered in mud, blazing with anger, arguing strongly and looking anything, she says, but dazed.

There was nothing to be done. No possibility of appeal. Lester and Susan went home, she to telephone pleadingly to a neurologist who said that even if Lester was completely all right – and who wouldn't be dazed for a second or two after somersaulting from a horse at thirty-five miles an hour – even *if*, he too couldn't overthrow the opinion of a colleague.

Lester had been going to ride Rainbow Quest for Jeremy Tree in the Arc but his disappointment could have been worse. Until a day earlier, his intended mount had been the great Teenoso on whom he won the 1983 Derby, but an old injury of Teenoso's had flared up, causing him to be withdrawn at the last minute. The offer of Rainbow Quest had been a bonus and a consolation. In the event, ridden instead by Tony Murray, the colt finished well back; and if Lester had been on his back, it might well have been said that Lester shouldn't have been allowed to ride after his fall. (Ironically, Rainbow Quest won the Arc – on an objection – in 1985, ridden this time by Pat Eddery.)

The odd thing, Lester says now with a smile, was that in all the fuss at Newmarket over whether or not he was dazed, no one noticed the thing that was actually wrong. The thumb he had injured before was in the wars again, and his whole hand was numb. 'I stood there arguing with Dr Allen,' Lester says, 'and I couldn't feel my hand at all. But if he had let me ride ... I could have ridden like that.' And after all else, one has to believe it.

He worked on his numb hand all evening, until the feeling gradually came back, and concedes now that two days' rest didn't do him much harm.

In spite of his fury on that occasion, he does think the modern medical rules are fairly sensible. It is mostly for head injuries that compulsory rest periods are imposed: two days for dizziness and a week for a simple knock-out are normal. A whole lot of punch-drunk jockeys, so the thinking goes, would do the industry no good.

Dr Michael Allen is in fact a thoroughly pleasant and humane man walking a difficult tightrope, with fiercely indignant jockeys on the one hand and the interests of owners, trainers, punters and the Injured Jockeys Fund on the other.

Lester, who hid his worst injuries better than most, has no disabilities or lasting effects today.

# Trainers

'Good trainers are good to ride for. Bad trainers make good horses bad. The best trainers make the easy things look easy,' Lester said.

'Don't you mean,' I asked mildly, 'that the best trainers make the *difficult* things look easy?'

No, Lester didn't. Bad trainers, he said, make the easy things look difficult. 'Some trainers make their horses stupid. They rush them and don't give them a chance to learn good manners, because they can't afford to pay people to teach them. A good trainer's horses are always better rides.'

He must have ridden for more trainers than any other jockey, and he sees the differences between them as mostly in the trainers' own personalities, not in the fitness of their charges. Most trainers can turn out a reasonably fit horse: if they couldn't, they'd be out of business. Success lies in unmeasurable things like commonsense, imagination, patience and flair.

Of the trainers Lester rode for most significantly, the first (except for his father) were Frank and Ken Cundell. Frank and his cousin Ken were, as young men, joint assistants to their uncle, Leonard Cundell, who trained in the racing village (then Berkshire, now Oxfordshire) of Aston Tirrold. Returning from the Second World War, Frank took over Leonard's yard while Ken set up on his own, ten miles away at Compton in Berkshire.

I myself (Dick Francis) rode jumpers for both cousins for many years, especially for Frank after Ken had turned more and more to the Flat. Frank, who trained Zina for the 1950 Cambridgeshire, later concentrated on jumpers, and I rode for him until I retired in 1957. He was a great friend, whose death in 1983 the whole racing world mourned.

For four years from 1949, I rented from Ken a house which looked out into his yard. I rode his horses at morning exercise, raced them in the afternoons and acted for him in any capacity I could. One can say that I knew him well, and we have remained friends ever since. Retired now, he is kind and generous, with forthright views unhesitatingly expressed.

When Lester was still a smallish bundle of raw fourteen-year-old talent, Ken was heard regularly saying, 'That boy is going to be the greatest jockey who ever lived, mark my words,' and, thirty-six years later, beaming with pleasure, he finishes the sentence, 'and I was right.'

Back in 1950, he saw the talent clearly and, knowing Keith Piggott well, had no trouble in engaging his son.

It was Ken, training Zucchero, who gave Lester at fifteen his first ride in the Derby. Zucchero represented Ken's first and best chance of winning the most prestigious race in the world, and for him to have chosen a semi-child as a jockey was a remarkable proof of his faith.

The waywardly brilliant colt came into Ken's yard because his owner, Charles Stuart, grown sick of the two-year-old's infuriating habit of refusing to start, offered him to his bookmaker, George Rolls, to clear a debt of £800. George Rolls relayed this to Ken, who happened to be there in the Rolls office when the offer was made by telephone. 'You take Zucchero,' Ken said at once, 'and I'll make him start'; and so the bargain was struck.

Ken was usually successful in the matter of starting (*see* page 29) but Zucchero was too moody for his own good. 'He used to sulk,' Ken says. 'I could feel him sulking just before the Derby. They had to walk in towards the tapes twice before the starter let them go, and Zucchero didn't like it.'

One evening later in the year, when Ken was in the colt's box, Zucchero tried to bite him. Ken, infuriated, took hold of his head-collar and punched Zucchero hard in the ribs. 'I punched him several times as hard as I could. I fought him ... and he behaved better to me after. A difficult horse, but he was never so much trouble after that.'

Of Lester's suspension on Never Say Die, Ken says, 'It was extremely unfair. A most wicked decision. I was there. I was particularly watching Rashleigh because he was owned by Charles Stuart who had originally owned Zucchero, and I clearly saw Gordon pull across to close the gaps. He took the next horse (Garter) with him onto Lester while Lester was making his move forward, and it wasn't Lester's fault that the horses bumped.'

When Lester was reinstated, Ken put him up again straightaway, and was moved when Iris Piggott came across to him at the races and thanked him for his faith. There had been no question of anything else, in Ken's mind.

'Not only did horses go well for him,' Ken says, 'but he would come back afterwards and give you a sensible opinion. His judgment and understanding were most useful, extraordinary in a boy so young. He rode all those good horses for me, Tancred, Cool Shamrock, Longstone, March Past.... The first time he rode March Past, he amused me by telling me he thought the horse might win a seller. He didn't know March Past wasn't fit and was just out for a run.'

March Past's wins included the Solario Stakes at Sandown, the Greenham at Newbury and the Wokingham at Royal Ascot, and eventually he became great at stud, siring, among others, Queen's Hussar, the sire of Brigadier Gerard.

Ken was a trainer who liked to bet, relying on his winnings for income. It was a common practice in very many stables for horses to run unfit (a practice fined into virtual extinction nowadays) so that they could come bursting out highly-tuned later to win at long odds.

Lester says, 'Ken Cundell hated to talk to the Press. He'd never tell them anything. He thought they would spoil the market for him, which they did. He used to ask me to ride and say, "Don't tell the Press," so there would be a blank against the jockey's name in the papers. You can't do that now, of course.

'He was a good trainer, very clever. Zucchero was a great horse. He would have won the King George VI and Queen

Elizabeth Stakes easily but for his stubbornness at the start, and any horse that can win that race has to be great.'

Noel Murless in his young days rode as a jump jockey, chiefly as an amateur but for one year as a professional. Too big and too heavy to continue, he turned to training in Hambleton near Thirsk, in Yorkshire. From there, he moved to Beckhampton in Wiltshire, taking over the stables of the legendary Fred Darling during the latter's failing health, and from there to Newmarket, improving in skill all the way.

When Sir Gordon Richards retired, in 1954, Noel started negotiations for the services of another senior jockey, which pleased his owners well enough except for the Aga Khan. 'The old Aga,' Noel says, 'wanted a good young jockey, either Lester or Manny Mercer. He wouldn't have an older one. Gordon (who was setting up as a trainer at Ogbourne in Wiltshire) wanted Lester also, but I'm glad to say he decided to come to me, fortunately. He was only eighteen at the time, but he was already an accomplished jockey.'

Noel and Lester were always on very friendly and relaxed terms although, Noel says, 'He was always respectful. He still is, couldn't be more so. He's very modest, as you know.'

I asked Noel what he thought of Lester's suspensions, those that occurred after Never Say Die.

He replied, 'For many years, Lester had a rough deal from the Stewards. They were always after him for stupid little things. In those days they were more autocratic than they are now.

'I remember him riding Primera here at Newmarket in the Princess of Wales Stakes. It was a very close thing, and as they were approaching the winning post, Lester hit him just once. Anyway, some time after the race, my travelling head-lad came to me and said the Stewards had ordered Primera to be taken out of the horse-box into which he'd been loaded for the journey home, because they wanted to examine him. I was blazing because, coming down the ramp, he could have hurt himself. It's always a risk. They had an enquiry with Lord Derby in the chair, and he went on about the whip mark on the horse, but I pointed out that at that time of the year (mid-summer), young horses' coats mark so easily you can mark them with your finger when they're hot and steaming like that. That's the sort of thing Lester had to put up with a lot in his early days.

'I don't think it had any effect on his riding, but it affected him mentally for a time, and I think it's very much one of the reasons why he won't converse with people.'

A steady diet of injustice, one might say, inhibits the tongue.

I asked Noel about Lester's riding, and any races he particularly remembered. He replied, 'Like Gordon, Lester is an absolute genius, but very different. If you put Gordon on a highly-strung horse, it was like putting an electric battery on top, they'd get really worked up. But Lester's very relaxed himself, therefore his mounts relaxed too.

'One race which stands out in my mind is Carrozza's Oaks. She came round Tattenham Corner tucked in behind. Then the opportunity presented itself and Lester grabbed it with both hands by picking the filly up and shooting her through all the opposition. He came through on the inside and rode a fantastic race on her. He always knew just when to make his effort and he knew exactly where the winning post was.

'I don't recall him losing any race, certainly not one of any importance, which he should have won. A lot of people blamed him for losing the King George VI and Queen Elizabeth Stakes on Petite Etoile, but I certainly didn't. She didn't get a mile and a half very well. As the race was run, if he had stuck to the inside, trailing Aggressor, he might perhaps have won, but in my way of thinking he did exactly the right thing in bringing his mount to the outside.

'She was never the same mare after she'd had the cough the next year. We were forced to keep her on and run her at five because Prince Aly Khan had died and the family wanted to encourage the young Aga to be keen on racing. She was very difficult to train at five. She was a right monkey at the best of times, but of course Lester knew her to absolute perfection.

'He was pretty good on any course, but he was marvellous round Epsom because he had the pattern absolutely fixed in his mind. He knew exactly where he'd got to be at any moment, and he was there. If the horse was good enough, well, he'd come on and win. He did that everywhere, but it was more apparent at Epsom.'

I asked Noel if he remembered anything amusing which happened between Lester and the owners.

He laughed, and said, 'I remember when Lester was riding a horse for old Colonel Giles Loder at Brighton one day, in Lester's first year with us. Old Loder was a steward there and he was having this conversation with Lester and neither could hear what the other was saying. I said, "Come on, Lester, get up," and he said, "What was Colonel Loder saying to me?" I replied, "Oh, never mind about that, just get up." Anyway, the horse won the race and the old man was of course delighted, and said to me, "Lester did just what I told him to, exactly!"

'Another time, Lester rode a horse for Prince Aly in France and he had a bit of trouble with one of those French jocks. They got to using their whips on each other, instead of on their horses. Lester gave him a couple of right cracks and there was a bit of a row about it at Chantilly. The next week at Ascot, he was riding one for the Queen which I was running. As the Queen was walking away after our pre-race chat in the parade ring, she turned to wish Lester a good ride in the race. Lester asked me, "What did the Queen say to me?" I said, "She said, you aren't to bugger the French jockeys about." So with a perfectly straight face he just said, "All right, I won't touch 'em this week." He has a great sense of humour, in a quiet way.'

Inevitably, finally, I asked Noel how he'd felt when Lester left, and how it had happened.

Noel said, 'Lester came up to the house one night at the end of 1965 and said he'd like to go freelance. I said I felt he owed it to everyone to carry on with the stable, and of course he did, mostly, until the 1966 Oaks. But, looking back, I think my attitude was wrong. He was quite entitled to go freelance, and I'm sure now he did the right thing. Strangely enough, we both had our best years immediately afterwards.

'I felt that with the horses I had there, I had to have a stable jockey, so that's why we got George Moore over from Australia. But racing was never the same to me, quite, after Lester and I split up. It was very easy before. We knew each other so well. It was a great shame really, but there we are, it happened. I think if Lester had stayed with us through 1967, we could have won all five Classics.'

The tone of Noel's voice when he speaks of Lester is affectionate and humorous, tinged a little with regret but more with pride. They were easy together and a great team. 'It was a fantastic thing for me as a trainer,' he says, 'to have first Gordon Richards and then Lester Piggott.'

Of the many other very good British trainers Lester rode for often during the Murless years and beyond, he would class among the most rewarding from his own point of view people like Helen Johnson Houghton, Jeremy Tree, Freddy Maxwell, Barry Hills, and Pat Rohan, people he could rely on for steady bread and butter and frequent jam.

One must mention particularly Susan's father, Fred (Sam) Armstrong, an exceedingly nice man as well as a highly efficient trainer. At one point, both he and Noel Murless trained in Middleham in Yorkshire, travelling regularly together to race meetings as close friends.

From Lester's angle, Sam's one drawback was his habit of not making up his mind until the last minute about where or whether he would be running his horses, leaving Lester unable to make riding plans with other trainers, a habit he shared incidentally with his great friend Vincent O'Brien.

When Sam retired in favour of his son Robert, the Armstrong-Piggott success story continued unabated.

There were the great French trainers, notably the volatile Maurice Zilber, who swaps his jockeys around as the whim takes him and who precipitated another row for Lester by announcing to the Press that Lester would ride his horse Mississipian in the English Derby, without first informing a) Lester, b) his stable jockey Bill Pyers, or c) the owner, Nelson Bunker Hunt. Bill Pyers not unreasonably kicked up a terrible fuss, the headlines thundered indignantly away and the owner finally decided not to run the horse at all. Great stuff!

Among other foreign trainers, Lester's longest and most fruitful association and friendship has probably been with Ivan Allan of Singapore. Lester rates him as a trainer in the class of Noel Murless, Vincent O'Brien and Henry Cecil, and says he has an eye for bloodstock as good as any in the world. He bought Commanche Run, for instance, for £9,000.

Born a mixture of English, Scottish, Indian and Malaysian, Ivan Allan is a shrewd, quiet, thoughtful perfectionist who brings off great coups for his gambling Eastern owners. 'In England,' Lester says, 'winning big races is what matters. Out where Ivan trains, it's winning big bets; and I don't know which is more difficult.' It was for Allan that Lester won the Lion City Cup by dodging the immigration desk at Singapore.

Lester won sporadically over many years for Paddy Prendergast, the flamboyant and excitable Irishman who, if anything displeased him in a race, would go screaming off to the Press saying, 'Lester will *never* ride for me again,' only to ring up to re-engage Lester three or four weeks later as if nothing had happened.

Towards the end, Lester returned to Warren Place to ride for Noel Murless's son-in-law, Henry Cecil (*see* next chapter) and also teamed up frequently with the young Italian Luca Cumani (*see* the chapter on Commanche Run).

The years from 1966 to 1980 were Vincent O'Brien's.

Vincent rode in amateur races as a young man, but Lester has never seen him on a horse. Lester would think it essential for a trainer to ride out with his string, if it weren't that Vincent doesn't do it.

Quiet and retiring, Vincent lives comfortably at Ballydoyle, County Tipperary, a hundred miles south-west of Dublin. Early in his training career, he had only jumpers, scoring marvellous and seemingly never-ending successes, with four Cheltenham Gold Cups, three Champion Hurdles, and three Grand Nationals. It wasn't until 1957 that he began to turn seriously to the Flat.

Lester's approval of his methods is unbounded.

'Vincent is the best,' he says. 'He does everything right in a commonsense way, and he has great insight into his horses. He thinks of what will please them. He makes life interesting for them so that they'll enjoy what they're doing. Like Noel used to, he thinks about his horses all the time and nothing else matters. He doesn't like to make up his mind very long before a race whether to run or not. The ground has to be just right. He pays great attention to detail. He *makes* good horses: some of his best winners wouldn't have been great if they'd been trained by anyone else.'

Way back in 1958, when Vincent asked twenty-two-year-old Lester to partner Gladness in the Ascot Gold Cup, he had never met him or seen him race, as he hadn't been Flat racing in England much by then.

Having picked his jockey on reputation alone, Vincent then had Lester come to a hotel in Ascot on the morning of the race, and for an hour in a private room showed him films of all Gladness's former outings. He told Lester about her character and her likes and dislikes, and how she might best be ridden. Lester watched and listened, went along to the course and won the Gold Cup. It was the opening day of the great partnership, which took further steps forward later in the year when Lester and Gladness won the Goodwood Cup and also the Ebor at York.

Lester says, 'Often afterwards Vincent showed me films if I was going to ride a horse for him that I hadn't seen. Once I'd ridden a horse, he never said any more. He knew I'd know what to do. He shows films to other jockeys, too. Attention to detail, all the time.'

Vincent's views on Lester are equally unequivocal and admiring. 'There's no question he's an absolute genius,' Vincent says. 'I don't believe there's ever been a jockey who thinks more about what he's ridden and what he's going to ride. I very much appreciated his views on my horses. Sometimes he wouldn't give an opinion immediately, and it might be the next week, when I met him, that he'd say something that really cleared my mind on any doubts I had regarding a horse. He'd give me an explanation of why it had run the way it had. He was rarely wrong in his assessment.

'And he was so smart; he discovered how to ride the Ribot horses. So many of that stock were mean devils and ungenerous, and they wouldn't go any pace early on in races, and Lester would sit with them and let the field go ahead until he felt them beginning to pick up, and then he'd get them to go, and I saw him win races you couldn't believe he could possibly win from where he was.

'For me, there was nobody else who could really ride the Ribots – Ribocco, Ribofilio, Ribero, all those.'

Of the Roberto affair, Vincent says, 'After Bill Williamson had the fall, I was immediately afraid he wouldn't be fit to ride in the Derby, and up until the Monday before the Derby Bill Tucker in London wasn't at all happy with Bill Williamson's progress. John Galbreath set up the appointment to see Bill Williamson at Claridge's Hotel at five o'clock but Bill arrived early, and when I got there at five John Galbreath had already told him he didn't want him to ride. John Galbreath had said that, as an athlete, there was no way he was going to be fit, and so it was settled. I rang up the Press Association from Claridge's and told them Lester would be riding Roberto.'

Of the Derby itself, Vincent says, 'Unless Roberto might by some miracle have done more for another jockey, no one but Lester could have won. Lester said to me that night, late on, at the celebration party, "He wasn't doing much for me, you know."' But, Vincent laughs, 'Perhaps he'd have done less for anyone else.'

Of Sir Ivor and Nijinsky, Vincent says, 'They were two great horses, and it would be hard for me to say which was the better. There was a real doubt about their getting a mile and a half because they were both American bred, and the Americans breed their horses for a mile and a quarter, the distance of their top classic races. Sir Ivor and Nijinsky were both best at a mile and a quarter.'

I mentioned that Lester still thinks Sir Ivor the best horse he ever rode, and Vincent said, 'I can imagine him saying that because there were no problems with Sir Ivor. He must have been a grand horse to ride, he was as tough as could be, he didn't care, the crowd didn't bother him a bit, the other horses being on their toes didn't trouble him. During a race he didn't pull, he'd settle and go anywhere you wanted, and where you asked him, he'd go, just like that. Whereas Nijinsky got tensed up and sweated. Once he was out of the stalls, Lester said, he was fine. He'd drop his bit and be perfectly all right, but the waiting about beforehand always upset him. Of course, having a horse like that under you doesn't help, it's bound to get you tensed up. I'm sure Lester liked Sir Ivor better.'

He went on, 'Lester revolutionised race-riding, you know. Before Lester, if there was no pace, if no one wanted to take up the running, no jockey would go on, and the horses would crawl. But Lester finished all that because if nothing went, *he* went, and you never see slow-run races any more. The others picked it up from him, but he was the one who started it. It's a good thing, because the public were very critical of a slow early pace.

'Lester was a truly, truly great jockey and it was incredible that at fifty he was riding better than ever. His brain had matured, his thinking was so good. I think at the end, he was the best he'd ever been.'

Vincent and his wife Jacqueline were afraid, after I'd talked with them for a while, that they'd said so many nice things about Lester he might seem an insipid goody-goody, so they cast around for a few derogatory remarks, without any noticeable success. Their voices throughout were as affectionate as Sir Noel Murless's had been, the good memories crowding in.

The worst they could find to say was that when Lester went over to Ireland to work Vincent's horses on the gallops, he would be trying to find out which of the Ballydoyle horses were best and which were fit, which Vincent wouldn't always want him to know in case Lester used the knowledge to get off his horses and onto those of other trainers. A duel of wits would ensue, with Lester usually and craftily finding out what he wanted to know.

'I would tell him,' Vincent says with a laugh, 'to set off up the gallops with the others, but he would manage to get left, so he could come along from more than six lengths behind and find out how his horse compared. He'd do diabolical things and then say, "Sorry about that." '

'Vincent would come into the house in a terrible temper sometimes, saying he'd never get Lester to ride work again,' Jacqueline says, 'and then five minutes later, they'd be bosom friends as usual.

'Lester's sweet,' Jacqueline says. 'Something very dear about him. And so *funny*. Also he's considerate and thoughtful about people in ways you wouldn't expect. For instance, we were staying in Florida with him once and I had our youngest child there, who was only three. We were staying also with the Galbreaths, actually. Lester was concerned whenever our son was getting cold in the water or sunburnt, and would look after him – things you wouldn't expect him to worry about or be interested in. When my own hip was bad, he was always asking how I was, very kindly, and he's always so fond of his two girls.'

From Vincent's point of view, Lester's overall knowledge of racing has been invaluable.

Vincent says, 'He knows other horses from running against them. He's very intelligent. I'm a bit away from things here and I can ring up Lester and ask him what he thinks of any race coming up, and he can tell me. His judgment is superb. He knows how the other jockeys react and what they're likely to do. It's as if he's been playing poker every night with the same half-dozen fellows; he's got them all sized up.'

Neither Lester nor Vincent lost any regard for each other, but towards 1980 things began to change. There was no one dramatic circumstance which caused the ending of the great partnership, only several small factors of relatively minor importance which together led toward an amicable conclusion.

For a start, Lester grew tired of the continual journeys to Ireland, beginning after all the years to find them irksome. Then, Vincent says, with himself growing slightly deaf and the telephone lines from Ireland quite often crackling, he was finding it harder to understand what Lester was saying. Communication grew more difficult; even frustrating. They occasionally misunderstood each other completely.

Vincent also had, at the insistence of some of his owners, got Lester some time earlier to sign an agreement to ride the Ballydoyle horses when required and, again as in years past, Lester had begun to chafe.

'He signed the agreement,' Vincent says, 'but I always knew that if a better horse came on the scene, Lester would be on the phone. He would come up with all sorts of unbelievable reasons why he shouldn't ride one of mine when he'd got a better prospect. He always made us laugh. But then one of my owners insisted on running a particular horse in one of the classics, and also insisted that Lester should ride it, and since it had no chance, none at all, he was a bit fed up.

'Lester and I agreed that it was no good him going on being tied down. He had to be free. He was best that way. He had to be a freelance, it suited his nature. He was in a bracket on his own. He had been riding occasionally for Henry Cecil (and in 1979 won the Ascot Gold Cup for him on Le Moss) and as Henry lived just along the road from him in Newmarket, he didn't have to cross the Irish Sea to ride work.

'I, of course, wanted a jockey who could ride every horse I ran, so we talked it over and an amicable parting of the ways came about. Indeed, Lester concurred with my decision to approach Pat Eddery to take his place.'

Funnily enough, while I was in Vincent's house in 1985, Pat Eddery happened to telephone about future plans. There was a horse of Vincent's he couldn't ride because he was still nursing an injury, and he suggested Lester should this time take *his* place. Between the jockeys, there was accord.

Lester's parting from Vincent brought the usual misleading and hurtful headlines: 'Piggott sacked'. 'Piggott snubbed'. 'Piggott out, Eddery in'. Presumably no one asked Vincent for the truth; and he's not easy to reach, to be fair. He's as reserved and private as Lester, and equally unwilling to bare his soul to the Press.

Looking back and looking forward, Vincent says now with conclusive sincerity, 'I have the greatest admiration for Lester, as a man and as a jockey, and as a friend.'

# Teenoso

By the autumn of 1980, the complex pattern of Lester's life had melted and reformed yet again.

Early in September most people were still happily drawing the wrong conclusions about his parting with Vincent only to be thrown into doubt and reverse by the announcement that he would ride first jockey the following year for Henry Cecil. Henry Cecil's former main jockey, Joe Mercer, who lived near Newbury, had negotiated to ride for the nearer stable of Peter Walwyn once Peter Walwyn's former jockey, Pat Eddery, had gone to Vincent. Lester proposed to Henry Cecil that he, Lester, should take Joe Mercer's place, and Henry immediately, and with awakening interest, agreed. The three jockeys thus moved round in a ring in a manner convenient to each, with none of them a loser.

At about the same time, it became clear that Lester, without particularly trying, was again in contention to be champion jockey, his total creeping nearer that of Willie Carson who was leading. Lester, thinking it might be a satisfaction to regain the crown he'd abdicated, tried hard from then on, but not to the point of sacrificing absolutely everything to the chase. He left the field to Willie in the last week of the season in November and went to ride again in the Washington International.

His mount, three-year-old Argument, trained in France by Maurice Zilber, had been placed but hadn't won all season in good class races. Lester, booked only a few days before the International for a horse he'd never ridden, nevertheless came up with a game plan for Laurel that brought the American crowd to its feet. Tucked in tight on the rails for most of the way, Lester brought Argument wide on the last bend and with a flick passed with seeming effortlessness the three horses who had been battling each other for the lead: and it was after this resounding triumph that he finally sought treatment for his injured shoulder and painful arm (*see* page 158).

Willie won the championship conclusively with a flurry of late winners from John Dunlop whose horses had all come roaring back into form after a bout with a virus, but the year overall had been good for Lester. No classics, but many big successes like the Coronation Cup, the Yorkshire Oaks, the Great Voltigeur, the Cheveley Park and the Middle Park Stakes and the Tote Cesarewitch.

In addition, there had been Moorestyle, trained by Susan's brother Robert Armstrong, owned by Moores International Furnishings, which had started by winning the Tote Free Handicap at Newmarket in April and in splendidly untroubled fashion won four more top sprints in England and two in France – the Prix de l'Abbaye on Arc day and another Group I race later in October – totting up prize money of roughly £160,000. Moorestyle had been picked out and bought by Susan, acting for the owners, and it was this success which above all consolidated her high rating as a bloodstock agent.

It had been a great year altogether for the brother-in-law partnership: they won nineteen races together in England alone, with Robert finishing sixth on the trainers' list.

There were frissons of the future, if only one could have felt them. In July, Lester won on Winsor Boy who left the starting stalls normally and showed no signs of diving out underneath, and in September, engaged as quite often by Newmarket trainer Michael Stoute, he rode and won a small race on a first-time-out two-year-old colt – Shergar.

By the following season, Shergar was being ridden by nineteen-year-old Walter Swinburn who had risen from the apprenticeship ranks with tremendous panache to be Michael Stoute's stable jockey. Shergar and Walter Swinburn shot away with the Derby to win by a staggering ten lengths: and almost immediately after-

Lester with his father Keith. *Photo Source/Fox*

Zucchero refuses to start in the 1952 Derby, with Ken Cundell pointing the way! *Daily Mail*

The last hurdle at Sandown, Autumn 1953. Dick Francis ahead, Lester jumping. Number 4 won.

The last bend at Sandown. *Gerry Cranham*

**The Queen leading in Carozza after the 1957 Oaks.** *Sport & General*

**Lester after riding work at Singapore racecourse.** *Mary Francis*

**Lester on Nijinsky in the starting stalls for the 1970 St. Leger.** *Gerry Cranham*

**Sir Ivor exercising at Epsom on the day before the 1968 Derby.**
*Press Association*

The autograph queue at Nottingham, 29 October 1985. Lester's last day of racing in the United Kingdom.
*Sporting Pictures (UK)*

The Queen greets Lester after his win on The Minstrel in the 1977 King George VI and Queen Elizabeth stakes.
*Bernard Parkin*

The author and Lester working hard on this book, Penang 1980.
*Mary Francis*

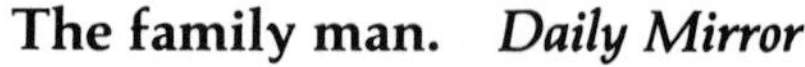
The family man. *Daily Mirror*

**The Queen Mother with Lester; John Oaksey on the left, Lester's wife Susan on the right.** *Doug McKenzie*

**Lester and Susan drinking from a coconut on the beach at Penang.** *Mary Francis*

1950: fourteen year old Lester going down to the start at Newbury with anxiety in his face and all the skill in the world in those hands.

The man he became, calm and secure. *Gerry Cranham*

wards, as if 1954 were happening all over again, the acclaimed teenage conqueror was handed a suspension for careless riding. The offence occurred, almost unbelievably, in *exactly the same race*, the King Edward VII Stakes at Royal Ascot.

Walter Swinburn, riding Centurius, bumped Bustomi. Centurius finished second to Bustomi subsequently and was disqualified. Walter Swinburn got six days off for the bump, which was better than Lester's six months but the designated six days included the upcoming Irish Sweep's Derby.

Lester, who had ridden Shergar in both his two-year-old races, was the natural choice to take Walter Swinburn's place at The Curragh, which he did, winning at a saunter without getting out of breath.

For Lester, 1981 began, proceeded and ended well, all except for the small matter of having his ear nearly torn off in April.

His appetite whetted by his nearness to the jockeys' championship the year before, he set out deliberately in 1981 to get his title back. Just to prove he could. Just to state that, forty-five or not, he still had it in him.

He returned to the gruelling treadmill of travelling, travelling, travelling. He rode everything that offered and quite a few that he asked for. It is true that he was helped to his goal by Willie Carson unfortunately falling out of the contest from injury in August, but he looked almost impishly happy throughout, and from riding an astonishing 703 races in England alone, he made it to the top again, for the tenth time, with 179 wins. In 113 other races he came second, and in 87, third. His winning percentage was 25.46, meaning that more than a quarter of his mounts came in first.

He was helped on the way to these highly impressive results by the sheer size of Henry Cecil's stable and by the full maturing of the trainer's talents. Lester rates him on a par with Vincent and says he is tremendously good at picking the right races for his horses. Together they won 75 races in England as well as others in Ireland and France in what was by far the most prolific partnership of Lester's career.

As Henry Cecil had moved into his father-in-law's stable when Sir Noel Murless retired in 1976, Lester was in a sense returning home, back to the bricks and mortar of Warren Place. Back also to many of the same owners as in the Murless days, notably H. J. (Jim) Joel, who owned Fairy Footsteps.

Ridden by Pat Eddery, the filly had won her final race as a two-year-old. Lester partnered her for the first time when she was three, in an April race at Newmarket. She won so obligingly that she was instantly made favourite for the One Thousand Guineas, and it was because he thought so much of her that Lester scrambled through his recovery from the ear and back-bone damage.

The fillies' classic was a desperately hard race with six of the fourteen runners almost line-abreast at the finish. Lester, believing Fairy Footsteps could outstay them all, had led from the beginning, but he found in the last stages that he couldn't get her away cleanly from the bunch of challengers, and it was only because of his sheer driving force and refusal to lose that he kept her in front. The very short distances between the first six horses were a neck, a neck, half a length, a short head, half a length. Fairy Footsteps had given her best performance and didn't train on for the Oaks. Lester won the Oaks nevertheless on Blue Wind, trained in Ireland by Dermot Weld.

There was the usual sort of fuss because the able Irish trainer chose to put the prime Epsom specialist on the filly that represented his first and best real chance of an English classic, instead of staying with his regular jockey, young Walter Swinburn's father, Wally.

Lester had often won for Dermot Weld in the past, and the fuss over Blue Wind, as one astute newspaperman pointed out, only occurred afterwards, and only because Lester won. The engagement in itself had raised no comment ten days earlier, and in fact Wally Swinburn had agreed to the switch, acknowledging that for such a chance one had to have the best. He himself had lost by a short head on Blue Wind the previous time out, and may have felt he didn't want to repeat that in the Epsom Oaks.

Blue Wind in the event won comfortably, but it hadn't looked as if it would be that way on paper beforehand: Lester slipped the field with a fierce burst of acceleration two furlongs out, and after that no one could catch him. Wally Swinburn was back on Blue Wind when she won the Irish Oaks six weeks later, a decent consolation.

Ardross, bought as a five-year-old by Lester's friend, Charles St George, provided a whole row of successes for the Cecil stable, including Lester's tenth Ascot Gold Cup; also the Yorkshire Cup, the Goodwood Cup, the Geoffrey Freer Stakes at Newbury and the Prix Royal Oak at Longchamp in September.

As a six-year-old, this incredible horse gave an almost complete repeat performance, preluding it this time by a sturdy half-length win in the Jockey Club Stakes at Newmarket in April 1982. Then came in turn the Yorkshire Cup, the Henry II Stakes at Sandown, the Ascot Gold Cup and the Geoffrey Freer Stakes. Also the Doncaster Cup; and, finally, by only a head he lost the Arc de Triomphe. As a two-year concord between great horse, consistent trainer and super jockey, Ardross's record can seldom have been excelled.

In 1982, Lester also gave his own personal encore, riding even more winners than in 1981 and hanging on undisputedly to his position at the top of the heap, with at 188 his second-highest total ever.

There were no classics and indeed, for the first time in twenty years, he didn't ride in the Derby. His intended mount, Simply Great, winner of the Mecca Dante for Henry Cecil and Daniel Wildenstein, hurt his heel on the Friday before the Derby and left the field to the co-favourite and eventual winner, Vincent O'Brien's Golden Fleece. Lester spent the Derby commentating on the runners with Brough Scott for ITV.

Apart from riding more winners (again) than anyone else at Royal Ascot - six - he scored in a dozen or more big races, including the Yorkshire Oaks on Awaasif, owned by Sheikh Mohammed, trained by John Dunlop. The year ended on a great note of promise as two of the Cecil two-year-old colts, Diesis and Dunbeath, won William Hill's two highly-endowed races for juveniles, the Dewhurst and Futurity Stakes respectively.

One can never really tell, though, in racing. Neither Diesis nor Dunbeath made it into the winner's enclosure again, Diesis and Lester being beaten into eighth place in the 1983 Two Thousand Guineas and coming second to Steve Cauthen on The Noble Player at Kempton in May. Dunbeath, similarly, never regained his two-year-old speed.

As the very wet spring of 1983 progressed, it became clear that

Henry Cecil wouldn't be putting forward a contender for the Derby, and other trainers with chances cast their eyes towards Lester. Chief among them was Lester's personal friend Geoffrey Wragg, who had recently taken over the licence from his father, Harry, and was training Teenoso.

Lester had been Geoffrey Wragg's first choice for Teenoso's first wins but Lester, then, had been needed by Henry Cecil. Teenoso had therefore won twice when ridden by Steve Cauthen, but Steve was retained by owner Robert Sangster and trainer Barry Hills, and would be partnering their horse, The Noble Player, in the Derby.

Lester had ridden winners for the Wraggs often (as he had for almost every top trainer by that time) and was definitely interested in Teenoso. He might never have been on the colt's back himself, but he had ridden *against* him four times, twice winning from him as a two-year-old, twice being beaten by him at three. It doesn't take as much as that for Lester to sum up any horse: he knew the bay long-legged Teenoso pretty well.

On the other hand, he had also been asked to ride Tolomeo who had finished second in the Two Thousand Guineas for trainer Luca Cumani. To find out about Tolomeo's suitability for Epsom, Luca Cumani and Lester set up a gallop on the racecourse at Newmarket two weeks before the big race. The gallop was to begin where the 5-furlong races started from, but to go the wrong way round the course so that Tolomeo would experience a downhill left-hand turn similar to that which he would meet at Epsom. After the turn, the gallop would end at a distance of a mile and a quarter from the start. Three other horses took part, to give Tolomeo a lead. Lester was supposed to go on and beat them at the finish, but when he asked for the effort, Tolomeo produced nothing and was in effect tailed off.

In retrospect, Lester realised it was probably because Tolomeo, usually a hard worker, was being asked to gallop going away from his home stable. 'He wasn't stupid, you know!' It was lucky for him, Lester says, that Tolomeo worked badly, because otherwise he would have chosen him over Teenoso.

Teenoso, sired by Empery's stable-mate Youth, was one of those racehorses who positively act well on soft ground, and the ground in Derby week was still sodden. He liked to take a good hold of his bit and pull, but he would do nothing quickly: it wasn't any use expecting a fierce burst of acceleration. In the Derby, Lester accordingly let him pull his way towards the lead fairly early on, hitting the front a good three furlongs from the winning post, from where he ran on strongly to beat Carlingford Castle by three lengths.

As so often with Lester, it all looked tantalisingly easy but he had again chosen the right horse (Tolomeo finished ninth) and he had read his mount's capabilities and preferences correctly before they set out. Tolomeo was actually a very good horse. Later in the year, ridden by Pat Eddery, he won the Budweiser Million at Arlington Park, Chicago.

Teenoso ran twice more in 1983; in the Irish Sweeps Derby and the Great Voltigeur later at York. The ground for the Irish Derby was firm, and Teenoso towards the end of the race (in which he finished third) hung badly to the right. It was put down to the hard ground, but after he had come third again at York he was found to have a hairline fracture in one of his joints.

He raced no more that season, but recovered to run the following year, heaping upon himself all sorts of further glory. After a close third, with Lester, in a preliminary in April, he won at Chester for Pat Eddery (Lester injured) and then, with Lester back in the saddle, won the Grand Prix de Saint-Cloud on 1 July. The ground at the Paris track was firm, but Teenoso's joints survived. It was the jockey who suffered damage: he rode with blood running down his face, the result of Teenoso tossing his head at the end of the parade past the stands, and opening cuts above and below Lester's right eye.

He ran last of all in the King George VI and Queen Elizabeth Diamond Stakes at Ascot four weeks later where, on firm ground, Lester repeated the tactics that had won them the sodden Derby. He let Teenoso pull his way to the front almost at once, then steadied him for a while behind another horse, then let him take the lead again when he wanted to, a good half-mile from home. He had to ride Teenoso hard during the last stages but they sped on together to win by two and a half lengths from Sadler's Wells: and Tolomeo, incidentally, finished third.

Teenoso was retired by his owner, Eric Moller, to the Highclere Stud in Hampshire following his inability to run in the Arc (*see* p. 162), his first progeny due to be seen racing in 1987.

Back in 1983, his ninth Derby sitting comfortably in the record books, Lester struck trouble at Glorious Goodwood, on Vacarme. Trained by Henry Cecil, owned by Daniel Wildenstein, the two-year-old chestnut Vacarme had won first time out at Ascot, but at Goodwood, Lester, having dropped him in behind other horses to steady him, found it difficult to get through.

Lester saw enough room along the rails and made his move that way, at which point the bunch of horses racing on Lester's left drifted in towards the rails, narrowing the space. Vacarme and Pacific King bumped, then Vacarme went on through to lead easily and win at a canter.

Behind him, Pacific King having dropped back, the other horses continued to drift to the right to the extent that Godstone, now on the rails, was severely squeezed and could finish only third instead of second.

There were objections all round. The rider of the third, Godstone, objected to the second, and their placings were switched. Vacarme, for earlier colliding with Pacific King, was disqualified altogether and placed last, and Lester got a suspension of five days for careless riding. As he says, it was the three horses drifting towards the rails that caused both lots of trouble, but it was he, characteristically taking his chance, who got the chop.

The owner and his son were furious with Lester about the disqualification, saying that Lester could have won just as easily on the wide outside, which is where he should have been. Lester said nothing but reflected that two-year-olds given a clear view on the outside sometimes get frightened and stop racing.

Vacarme and Lester were back in the winner's enclosure after the Mill Reef Stakes at Newbury in September, Lester having again held up the colt until entering the last furlong. (And it is perhaps worth noting that, although ridden subsequently by other jockeys, Vacarme never won a big race for anyone else.)

With the shape of the Arc de Triomphe on the horizon (the Trusthouse Forte Prix de l'Arc de Triomphe), Lester was asked about six weeks in advance by John Dunlop to partner Sheikh Mohammed's Awaasif. The filly hadn't won since Lester had ridden her to victory in the Yorkshire Oaks the previous August, but with Willie Carson she had finished third immediately behind Lester on Ardross in the 1982 Arc de Triomphe, demonstrating she could act at Longchamp on a good day. There was a slight question mark over her fitness in early autumn 1983, but Lester engaged himself to ride her if she should prove sound and ready in a final gallop on the Thursday before the race.

On the Sunday (one week) before the Arc, before the Awaasif gallop could take place, trainer Patrick Biancone telephoned to Lester from France and offered him the ride on the filly All Along, owned by Daniel Wildenstein. Lester had never ridden All Along, but of course he regularly rode the horses Daniel Wildenstein had in training in England with Henry Cecil. (Vacarme was one.)

Lester told Patrick Biancone about the gallop on Awaasif and said he could ride All Along only if Awaasif wasn't fit. Between Biancone's grasp of English and Lester's indistinct speech, the message was misunderstood. The French trainer told the French Press that Lester would definitely be riding All Along and it was printed in the papers the next morning.

When Lester heard of it, he pointed out that Patrick Biancone had got it wrong. If Awaasif were fit, he was committed to ride her. Daniel Wildenstein, a Parisian art dealer, threw one of his well-known tantrums. 'Lester Piggott will never ride for me again,' he told the Press.

Patrick Biancone next told the papers (or else they printed it without asking him) that the American jockey currently riding in France, Cash Asmussen, who had also ridden often for Daniel Wildenstein, would partner All Along in the Arc. When Cash Asmussen heard the news, he said no, he wouldn't, he was riding Welsh Term.

'Cash Asmussen will never ride for me again,' Daniel Wildenstein said.

Neither Lester nor Cash Asmussen had, in any case, been first choice for the ride; Freddie Head had been asked first, but he was riding Lovely Dancer. Nor were Lester and Cash Asmussen the first jockeys to displease Daniel Wildenstein. Yves Saint-Martin and Pat Eddery had both in earlier years been discarded. ('Eddery will never ride for me again.')

'There wasn't much between the two fillies on paper,' Lester says. 'All Along had beaten me on Awaasif once as a three-year-old, but Awaasif had run well in the Yorkshire Oaks. I could have ridden either of them, but I stuck with Awaasif. You can't get it right *every* time.'

Ruefully he finished thirteenth on Awaasif while All Along scored her first win of the season in unbeatable style with young Walter Swinburn.

With only his pride dented, Lester went to Milan a fortnight later and on Awaasif won the Gran Premio del Jockey Club, one of Italy's best races. She was a good tough filly, Lester says, but the Arc just wasn't her day.

All Along's career took wings. She crossed the Atlantic and won both Internationals – the Rothman's at Woodbine, Toronto, and the Washington DC, at Laurel, Maryland – as well as the Turf Classic at Aqueduct, New York; and in the following year proved equally brilliant. Walter Swinburn partnered her throughout until one day he lost, and was replaced.

Choosing horses, Lester says philosophically, is like the three-card trick. Try as you may, you can miss the queen.

# Choosing the Horses, Riding the Courses

'Obviously a freelance can only ride two or three or perhaps four of the horses in a big race, because the others have retained jockeys on them.' (Lester talking) 'If there was a good horse who hadn't got a retained jockey on it, they'd ask me. It was a great advantage.'

Perhaps three to four hundred horses are entered each year in each of the classics, more particularly in those for colts. The bigger the number entered, the larger the prize, as these races are sweepstakes. The entries have to be made three to four months in advance of the races, which means that anyone who has a good two-year-old cannot afford not to enter it, in case it should have developed miraculously through the winter and be a world-beater at three. Everyone has learned from Brigadier Gerard who might have won the Derby if only he'd been entered: but on his breeding, he hadn't looked a possible.

Even though the entries for all five classics have to be made before the opening of the Flat season (the rules change from time to time), the actual *runners* aren't known for sure until sometimes a week or a few days before the events. Running and riding plans may tentatively be made a long time in advance, but often, for all big races, not only the classics, there are last-minute decisions on all sides. The results of all the preliminary races and trials have to be taken into account, as do last-minute health problems, and deluges or droughts.

It would often be at a point close to a big race that Lester would be asked by two or three trainers for his services. Sometimes the free horse would be so good it would be accepted by Lester immediately. More often, a choice between two would have to be made, a process which began with his own knowledge and observation, not in reading the form book. He had almost always ridden the possibles himself or had ridden against them: he knew their likely capabilities at first hand.

Taken into consideration was whether the distance of the race suited the horse, what the ground would be like, hard or soft, and whether the horse was likely to feel well in himself. It might not be sensible to choose a horse who'd had a very hard race recently, even if he had won; he might be half-dead next time out.

If the choice came near the beginning of the year, Lester wouldn't be looking just at the one big race, but at what might happen later. He would favour a horse likely to go on to win big races after.

In choosing between two in the Derby, say, he might be faced with a seasoned campaigner on the one hand and on the other a horse who'd only run twice. The experienced horse would know better what to do, but the beginner might go further and faster on the day. Assessing them could be tricky.

If the choices appeared altogether level, Lester would pick the better trainer. It wouldn't matter so much who the trainer was for an ordinary race, but the better trainers seem to have a higher average in big races. There was also the owner to be considered, as, if there were no other deciding factors, Lester tended to choose any particular horse because of liking the owner.

On the financial side, there might be an owner who would offer more than the 7½% share of the winning prize money, or more than the usual riding fee, or both. The offer would be decisive only if everything else were more or less equal: first and foremost, Lester's aim was to win.

'You have to listen to what everyone says and take it all in, or you'd never do anything right, but you mustn't be swayed by people trying to persuade you. You can make some awful mistakes by being sentimental and not looking at things as they really are. That's so easy. No, you've got to be pretty tough about it, really.'

Juggling all the variables, he would arrive in a day or two at his decision, often unsure even after the die was cast. He never acted on intuition, which he found unreliable. Evidence and reason led him on, and most times they were right.

Even when he had said 'Yes' to one trainer, he'd sometimes keep the second dangling with 'I'll ride yours if So-and-so doesn't run.' And the second trainer might engage another jockey with the proviso that 'Lester rides instead of you if So-and so doesn't run.' The owner of the second horse would be praying for So-and-so to go lame. There are only so many Derbys in anyone's life.

Practically none of this agonising went into riding plans for smaller races. If an offered horse had a reasonable chance, Lester accepted it. If a much better offer came along, he would probably get off the first and onto the other: this was no heinous crime but a common practice among almost all jockeys when not needed by their home stable. All the great jockeys of the past built their winning totals on this method, including Sir Gordon Richards and the legendary Fred Archer, who averaged one winner in three rides throughout his career.

Being a jockey is like any other business, and getting oneself onto winners is the point of the trade. Many a trainer had the jitters until L. Piggott's name was actually up there safely on the number boards.

Lester did occasionally get himself *off* what turned out to be the winner. Horses can make fools of the brightest.

Lester knows horses like other people know people. He recognises their faces, learns their heads. They all look different to him. Once he's met them and got to know them, he's familiar with them and can identify them anywhere instantly.

Horses know him in return. 'They can't say hello,' he says, 'but you know they know you because of the way they look at you.'

'Sir Ivor always knew Lester,' Vincent O'Brien assured me. 'Whenever he heard his voice, he'd look round. He'd always look at him if he was near. All horses know Lester if he's ridden them.'

Every stable-lad who looks after a racehorse for a long time knows it infallibly and is known, but in the much shorter contact of horse and jockey it's less usual, even in a champion, and Lester's quick affinity with horses is at the root of his success. He takes it for granted. Part of life. There's no mush. He talks of horses as individuals, but in a very down to earth fashion.

'A lot of them are stupid. A lot are intelligent. They vary in the same way that people do. There's no point in getting irritated with the stupid ones. They can't help it. Some horses like to do something wrong all the time. Even when they've run very often, they'll jump all over the place, pull too hard, try not to go into the stalls ... they make life hard for themselves, but they keep on with it. Some people are like that, too.

'Not every horse can run fast, the same way that people can't. It's unreasonable to expect it. Intelligence has nothing to do with speed. Some very slow horses are intelligent, some good ones aren't. If a horse has an ache or a pain he can't go fast, but as he can't tell you, it's probably never found out.

'At least sixty percent of horses don't really want to do their best. Winning doesn't mean all that much to them. You have to try to humour them to get them to do what they can. I've ridden some very good horses who were so good it didn't matter that they wouldn't do their best, they could win anyway. Like Roberto. He was a terrific horse going left-handed, but he was half-hearted in his Derby; he should have won by a couple of lengths.

'There's a vast difference between a really good horse and a bad horse. People don't realise. It's not a matter of twenty lengths difference, it's a furlong. If you get a horse who's very fast, very intelligent and wants to race, it's a revelation. On one of those you can beat the world.'

Top flat race jockeys ride five, six, sometimes seven hundred races a year. The turnover of flat race horses is so rapid – they race at two, at three, less often at four, rarely at five – that more than half of the time the jockey will be going out to the parade-ring to ride a horse he hasn't ridden before.

'Some of them are boats,' Lester says. 'Big slow boats.'

The type of horse and race Lester rode most was to some extent governed by his weight. He could do 8st 4lbs if he had to, but was more comfortable at 8st 7lbs. This cut out half the horses in most handicap races, limiting his options to the top weights and explaining why he seldom won the big handicaps like the Lincoln and Cambridgeshire.

When engaged to ride a horse he hadn't ridden before and hadn't ridden against, Lester would read the form book carefully. 'If the horse had won once, no matter how long ago, I'd look to see what happened that day, when things went right. The going, the pace, where he was during the greater part of the race and when he made a move. Because the horse liked it, that time. So you try to make everything the same for him again, and it often works.

'I've seen useless horses win races. Horses you wouldn't believe, win races. One day the horse is going to feel all right, and if he runs enough times, every week perhaps, he'll win. There's a race for nearly every horse. A horse won a good race at Sandown not long ago who'd run *thirty times* without winning. Some owners just keep on running them, hoping. If the horse has ever shown any sort of promise, there's always a chance.'

Trainers like Richard Hannon are good for horses like that: he thinks nothing of running the same horse four times in three weeks. That's at the far end of the scale from Sir Noel Murless who with a horse that had its limitations would patiently wait, running it lightly or not at all until everything was right. Then if the horse won that one race, that would be enough, the programme would have been a success, the horse would retire. Not many trainers now have owners as patient as Noel had trained his to be. Quite often his owners didn't even know their horses were running until they looked in the morning papers, as he would forget to tell them. Noel's favourite sort of owner (and one suspects Lester's henceforth also) was one who brought him good horses, paid the bills regularly and expected little conversation.

Lester says he *will* let his owners know when their horses are running.

Only fair, he thinks.

Lester's style of riding has been to a great extent dictated by his height, and as he has said when comments have been made about the famous behind sticking up in the air, 'Well, I've got to put it somewhere.'

The shortness of his stirrup leathers, now universally copied, was not much to do with serious theories of race-riding but mostly the result of the introduction of starting stalls.

The English variety of stalls are narrow, and inside have a small ledge along each side which a jockey can step onto if he needs to. With longer stirrup leathers, too much of the leg lies below the ledge: Lester got tired of bumping his knees on it as his mounts plunged out of the stalls, and shortened his leathers to bring them up higher. His knees escaped battery and a new style was born.

He rode with longer leathers out at exercise and for trial gallops, but found the very short leathers beneficial to the horse for racing: the jockey's weight is poised above the horse's shoulder, where it causes least interference to the horse's action.

When Lester was first a jockey there were only about eight big races each year; now there are at least twenty-five.

He says he always got tense before the Derby, especially if he had any sort of chance, and reckoned that it probably helped because when he's tense he thinks faster, but it became impossible to live in twenty-five states of tension each year, and he tended to be less and less affected by big occasions. His great asset, anyway, had always been his capacity to keep cool in any form of stress and to go out to the most demanding examination with his brain functioning clearly. Stage-fright wasn't a problem. Anxiety to succeed . . . always, yes.

The anxiety, as every jockey knows, wasn't for his own sake alone, but for the owner's, the trainer's, the lad's and that of everyone else whose thought and work had gone into producing a horse ready to run for its everlasting reputation.

The training path to the Derby is fairly well marked. A colt that has shown speed and willingness as a two-year-old gets himself entered for the big race, and entered also for the Two Thousand Guineas.

The first two classics occur early in the season – too early, Lester thinks – leaving a scant five weeks for preparatory three-year-old races. There is only time really for one outing, and only four races in the calendar at present are of sufficient class to be considered true trials. If a colt does well, or at least isn't disgraced, in one of these, he'll take his place in the Two Thousand Guineas at the beginning of May at Newmarket.

Newmarket, where Lester has lived since his marriage in 1960, is a Suffolk country town set on a bleak, almost treeless heath scoured by winds off the North Sea. An unforgiving place for thoroughbreds, cold in the spring, hard and testing. If the weather's bad, the thousands of horses trained there face extra difficulties in developing.

(Blame King Charles II. All his fault. He loved the town and held court there, making hapless foreign ambassadors travel uncomfortably northwards by coach to present their credentials; probably, who knows, on the racecourse itself. In the 1660s, he made Newmarket the headquarters of the new sport of horse racing, and so it has remained ever since.)

The Two Thousand Guineas is run on the Rowley Mile (after King Charles II's nickname, 'Old Rowley') which is straight, wide, undulating, bare and searching. Only a very fit horse can win. The distance, one mile, is only two-thirds of the Derby, but the Two Thousand Guineas winner is almost automatically made favourite for Epsom.

The programme for fillies is a replica of the colts'. A preliminary test, then the 1-mile One Thousand Guineas at Newmarket, then at Epsom the 1½-mile Oaks. Lester thinks fillies are harder to train, and in spite of his understandings with Petite Etoile, Carrozza, Park Top, Dahlia and the others, he preferred to ride colts.

He also preferred riding on the other course at Newmarket, the July Course, used chiefly in mid-summer. 'It's warmer,' is the succinct reason. Like everyone with only a paper-thin insulating layer of subcutaneous fat, Lester feels the cold.

When he was young and struggling painfully against his own weight, he used to get extremely tired by the end of a hard race. He would ride all out to win, and maybe lose, and think exhaustedly that he'd got to go straight out and do it again ... and again. By the end of a busy afternoon, if he'd been concerned in several close finishes, he hardly had the strength to walk to his car.

This went on throughout his twenties, and it wasn't until he reached thirty that he reckons he arrived at his full physical stamina. At roughly the same time, his body weight stabilised at 8st 6lbs, a balanced compromise at last between what was normal and what he wanted. At one time he had touched 10st 2lbs, but from thirty onwards he never put on more than a pound or two during periods of comparative inactivity, and says he could have ridden twenty hard races in a row and then sprinted to his car.

He weighed himself every day at home but didn't go to the extreme of carting scales along with him abroad. He can tell his weight, he says smiling, by the waistband of his trousers.

After the rigours of the Guineas meeting, but before the Derby, there is Chester week.

Chester is a circular track almost completely on the turn, with a very short 1-furlong straight. The form book gets all upset at Chester because of the turns. Some horses like it there but don't do well afterwards; others can't act there at all.

'You often get three-year-olds going to Chester,' Lester says, 'who have never galloped round a turn in their life. Two-year-old races elsewhere are mostly straight, and if they're trained at Newmarket, the training gallops are all straight, too. When they get to Chester, half of them don't know what to do.'

Horses can either gallop round turns or they can't, he says. A horse can't be taught how to turn; either it comes naturally, or he's awkward. Sometimes a horse can turn easily one way but not the other – like Never Say Die. Smaller horses can turn more easily, very big ones seldom can. But if a big horse *can*, like Rheingold, he'll do well.

At Chester, although one wouldn't think so, it's possible to come from a long way back and get up to win. It's possible, Lester says, because horses tend to run races at a faster pace there because it's a small track, and if you know this and you're riding a horse that can turn, you can increase the speed even more at the right point and win.

It's best to be drawn with a low number in every race there, which puts one on the inside of the left-handed track. There are seldom more than fourteen runners in most races because of the lack of room, but more are allowed in the Chester Cup. Chester is a meeting Lester always enjoyed.

From Chester to Epsom. 'Whoever thought of putting that racecourse where it is must have been an idiot,' Lester says. 'If it wasn't for the Derby, no one would run a good horse there. A lot of it is downhill. Horses aren't supposed to gallop downhill. It's not so bad if the going is good or soft, but if it's hard, Epsom can break a horse down.' That said, he adds, 'There's nothing wrong with Tattenham Corner. It looks sharp, but it isn't. Horses turn well there; they hardly notice it.

'The ideal way to win the Derby is first of all to be drawn in the middle, or middle to outside. The horses on the inside have to go faster after the start to keep their position, and those on the outside have a job to close in. The large size of the field most years is in itself the first problem. The middle horses have the better chance to be where they need to be, which is towards the right-hand side of the track for a couple of furlongs, so gaining the advantage of the early right-hand bend. The runners then gradually come back to the left, and it is at this point that it's necessary to be in a good position. On a horse with a bit of speed one can reach and keep a good place here, in the first ten.

'The order then usually doesn't change much until Tattenham Corner. On the run down towards the corner there may be one or two bad horses dropping back from in front, which one has to miss, and round the turn there will be one or two more dropping back. Coming into the straight, the winner will be in the first six.

'From there, it depends on what the horse likes and what he can do. If he can run flat out for the last three furlongs, that's the place to start accelerating from. If he can only go for a furlong and a half, it's useless to start too soon. If he doesn't like to be in front very long, one has to wait until the final two hundred yards. If the horse can't quicken all that much, he has to be brought to the front early on.'

The Derby was one of the few races Lester preferred not to win along the rails. Even with a horse like Sir Ivor, who had to be covered up until the last minute, he preferred to win away from the rails, not only to avoid being shut in but because the ground slopes in towards the rails quite sharply and can upset a horse's balance crucially at the worst moment.

'The Derby nearly always goes to an experienced horse

(though Morston had run – and won – only once before his big day), because it is a rough, tough race. There are a lot of runners, there's fierce competition and no one gives an inch. If a horse has run only twice beforehand, he may react nervously, and only a horse that can get in there and have a go will win.'

Oddly enough, excitable horses do well at Epsom. Empery, The Minstrel, Nijinsky, all sweated there before they turned their temperaments to explosive speed.

After Epsom, Royal Ascot. A good track, Lester says; the straight perhaps a shade too short. He had the shape, distance and desirable speeds of all the races there so clearly in his mind that he was top (or joint-top) rider at the Royal meeting eighteen times. On each occasion since 1979 he was presented with a handsome lidded crystal vase. Nine of them stand in glittering rows on his bookshelves, and one on the coffee table contains books of matches for lighting cigars.

Ascot, Lester says, has the best jockeys' changing-rooms in the country. Ascot also, at the July meeting, holds the country's best race.

This, he reckons, is the King George VI and Queen Elizabeth Diamond Stakes, which is roughly England's equivalent to the Prix de l'Arc de Triomphe. By the time the 'Diamond' Stakes is run, the horses have sorted themselves out and one knows the really good ones. Then, too, top three-year-olds run against top four-year-olds and upwards, which makes it very fast and a great test of the best horse overall. It may not have the absolute prestige of the Derby, but these days it offers more in prize-money.

Lester won it seven times.

Of the other big tracks, he thinks Newbury the fairest and best: a really superb racecourse. It can accommodate large fields, and the ground is always good.

Kempton is great to ride on, though not as popular with the public as it should be. The evening meetings there (Lester didn't like evening racing much) offer races that are probably easier to win than anywhere else, chiefly because a lot of trainers don't like evening meetings either.

Sandown, where the Eclipse is run in July, has a stiff uphill finish. One can easily get into trouble with that, Lester says, and also one has to remember and allow for the fact that the winning line seems to be at an angle, and the horses nearest the stands will be favoured if there's a close finish on the more-used round course. The straight 5-furlong track up the middle of the course is stiff too, but the result is easier to judge with the naked eye.

In late July there is Glorious Goodwood, with everyone in a holiday mood and many jockeys and their families staying the week in seaside hotels.

Lester says the dilemma of whether or not to water the Goodwood course in the summer heat sometimes results in the field on the round course crossing right over away from the watered and then rained-on part of the track and racing on drier ground against the stands' rails, which makes the distance covered longer and cuts up the ground used for the straight races. Watering is always a problem on the hilltop of the Sussex South Downs.

In between the big race meetings, there are of course dozens at other scattered tracks, many of which Lester went to often, and where he liked to ride, places like Lingfield, Haydock and Nottingham. Salisbury, with its springy downland turf, was built by one of his ancestors, a Cannon of Stockbridge.

In August, there's York, one of Lester's favourites. There too in later years, there was an award for the top jockey of the August meeting, which Lester won several times.

You can't fault the place, he says. It is one of the great tracks. The Benson and Hedges Gold Cup has been a pinnacle race of the season, but since Benson and Hedges have withdrawn their support, the race will have a different sponsor and title in future.

And so to September and the St Leger meeting at Doncaster. On the straight course there, Lester says, a good draw is essential, the higher numbers on the stands' rails having the better chance, but in the St Leger, on the round course, it doesn't matter.

Most of the racecourses nowadays have saunas to help with jockeys' weight problems: the one installed at Doncaster didn't work for several years because the electric wiring in the weighing-room couldn't deliver enough current. Satirical letters of protest flew in a barrage from the Jockeys' Association to the hapless Clerk of the Course who could make no decision as it's a council-run track, and the sauna stood there, mute and cold for some years. It is all right now, though.

All through the year, the pattern changes. Horses come and go, some emerging, some fading, some returning. It's impossible for a horse to stay at the very top of his form for the whole seven and a half months.

'Quite often you think a horse is going to be a big challenge,' Lester says. 'Then when you get to the races, you have a look at him and you can see he's not going to trouble you.

'I think jockeys see this more than the people who look after the horses at home, because those people don't see the change as much as someone seeing the horse maybe once a week, or every two weeks. You see a horse at his peak, and you know what that looks like, you know how he should be. Then at other times you can see he's lost weight or he's too fat, and you know he won't win. Towards the end of the season especially, you see horses that have lost their condition. It's very hard to describe it to someone who doesn't really know what you're talking about, because to most ordinary people every horse looks the same.'

Few people have been less ordinary in that matter than Lester Keith Piggott.

# Travels

Lester saw the whole world as his racetrack, and with the ability to match the vision he donned his silks in a total of thirty-three countries outside Great Britain.

The results in winners of this truly astonishing globe-trotting are as follows:

| | | | |
|---|---|---|---|
| Argentina | 3 | Japan | 0 |
| Australia | 19 | Jersey | 2 |
| Austria | 0 | Kenya | 1 |
| Bahrein | 2 | Malaysia | 30 |
| Belgium | 4 | New Zealand | 7 |
| Brazil | 1 | Norway | 7 |
| Canada | 1 | Puerto Rico | 0 |
| Denmark | 3 | Rhodesia | 3 |
| France | 352 | Singapore | 45 |
| Germany | 27 | South Africa | 19 |
| Greece | 11 | Spain | 5 |
| Holland | 0 | Sweden | 7 |
| Hong Kong | 29 | Switzerland | 0 |
| India | 8 | Trinidad | 1 |
| Ireland | 176 | U.S.A. | 12 |
| Italy | 36 | Venezuela | 0 |
| Jamaica | 11 | | |

The minimum total of overseas races won is 821. For principal races won in each country, *see* the Appendix on page 321. The real significance of this long tribute to stamina and versatility is that for every six winners scored in Britain, Lester rode another overseas.

His easy embrace of other countries stemmed perhaps from the example of his grandfather, Ernie, who lived and raced for many years in France. Lester has always felt particularly at home there, and except for England preferred riding there to anywhere else.

After the First World War, a good many English racing jockeys and trainers settled in France, their names – Carver, Head, Cunnington, Bartholomew, Palmer – persisting to this day. Many of these families still speak English fluently, and Lester has had no language problems in France. He reads French himself better than he speaks it, but sign language makes up for what he can't say. Many racing terms, anyway, are the same in both languages, and enquiries (those unavoidable hurdles) are conducted for the English in English.

Lester says that when he first went to ride in France there were some very excitable jockeys who were the roughest riders in the world. It was to deal with the wilder excesses of this tribe that the French Jockey Club, during the 1970s, brought in severe new interpretations of the rules. There was to be no more selfish criss-crossing during races: everyone was to race in a dead straight line; and if keeping straight meant losing the race, too bad.

For some time, the suspension rate rose to the point where trainers found it difficult to find a good jockey in possession of his licence. 'Eight days, eight days, all the time,' is how Lester describes it. In the end, and as a result, the French Jockey Club made racing literally straight.

Of the modern French jockeys, Lester thinks Yves Saint-Martin far and away the best. If he had freelanced, Lester says, he could have ridden any horse anywhere in the world: 'Everyone would have been happy to put him up.' The two jockeys rode against each other for many years, both in England and France, and respected and liked each other throughout.

Lester much appreciated the conditions in French changing-rooms: far more comfortable than in Britain. The valets there are employed by the racecourses, not by a pool of jockeys, and he never, as on bank holidays and other multiple race-days in

England, found his breeches and sets of colours hung on a nail with all dressing, changing and packing of weight cloths to be done in a hurry by himself. One valet to two or three jockeys is normal in France, with someone else to see to the weighing out. With six or more races to be changed for in an afternoon, jockeys value such help.

On account of trainers in general vying for the best for the best, Lester's tally world-wide of classic-equivalents is phenomenal. In France alone he won seven; and it might be helpful to explain what the French classics are called on their home Turf.

The One Thousand Guineas equivalent is the Poule d'Essai des Pouliches (fillies): the Two Thousand Guineas is the Poule d'Essai des Poulains (colts). Both are held at Longchamp.

The Derby equivalent is the Prix du Jockey Club: the Oaks is the Prix de Diane. Both are run at Chantilly.

The St Leger equivalent is the Prix Royal Oak, held at Longchamp.

The shape of the French racing year is as familiar to Lester as the British, culminating of course in the Prix de l'Arc de Triomphe in October, which he won three times (Rheingold once, Alleged twice).

Alleged, who was never beaten in France, gave Lester his most intense satisfactions in that country, but he remembers also with pleasure the wonderfully prolific Moorestyle, who won the prestigious Prix de la Forêt twice, the Prix Maurice de Gheest at Deauville and carried off the big 5-furlong event (Prix de l'Abbaye) on Arc day, besides finishing second in the Poule d'Essai des Poulains.

The real impetus to Lester's wider travels was the spread of the concept of international jockey team races. These were originally started by Australia in the nineteen fifties, where three of the states invited teams from the rest of the world to ride against teams of Australians. Harry Carr was one of the first of the British jockeys to go, and soon the contests were popular.

Lester much enjoyed team racing, which took him to places he might not have seen. He learned a great deal about people he would never have met and saw the similarities everywhere in the widespread and ancient pastime of racing horses. His increasing familiarity with the globe prompted him finally to say, 'When you've been so often to so many places, it's all much like going to Brighton.'

Lester first went abroad in a team in December 1957, travelling to Australia as the English representative in an international team of one jockey from each of England, Italy, Germany, Hungary, South Africa, India and France. He won down under to great acclaim, being extravagantly described as 'the Glamour Boy of Racing', 'the Prince of the Pigskin'.

Curiously his saddles were seized and fumigated by customs officials when he arrived in case the leather was carrying foot and mouth disease! Lester later came across a man in Australia who made perfect lightweight racing saddles. He bought twenty of them and used them for years, but could get no more when the last had worn out as the maker had meanwhile won the state lottery and stopped work.

On his way home from that first visit to Australia, Lester rode and won his first race in India, at Calcutta, but in between he made a brief detour to Malaysia. 'I like it here,' he was reported as saying after riding at Penang. 'I hope to come back.'

Come back he did, eventually, and in the end almost every year afterwards.

Like other British jockeys, he developed a great fondness for racing in Hong Kong and Singapore ('Nice places'), and would always fly from Singapore to the Malaysian tracks – Penang, Kuala Lumpur, Ipoh – with alacrity. One weekend at Kuala Lumpur he won eight races, four each day.

He often rode work for Ivan Allan in the mornings round Singapore's great Bukit Timah racecourse; the course where they test every horse's urine in the morning before it runs in the afternoon, and where nicotine turned up once in a sample because a stable-lad who smoked had got tired of waiting for his charge to perform!

Lester won six Singapore classics, five of them for Ivan Allan. In between such triumphs, he sunbathed round the pool of the Goodwood Park Hotel, entertained friends, had suits made for him practically overnight. Staying with him there for a week once, I could see why he liked it.

As a member of a team, he went several times to South Africa, riding in Durban, Pietermaritzburg, Cape Town and Johannesburg. The tours there used to last for a good two weeks, and once in Cape Town his horse broke a blood vessel in the very first race, falling and injuring Lester's knee. To his great disgust, he had to spend the whole of the rest of the visit hobbling around on crutches, watching his colleagues have all the fun.

Teams from other countries have given good value also in England, huge crowds for instance flocking to places like Sandown Park to see America's great Willie Shoemaker matched with Lester, to see Angel Cordero and Lafitt Pincay take on Pat Eddery and Willie Carson.

In races like these, the jockeys usually draw for the available mounts, which means that they're almost always on horses they've never seen before. There's a good mixture of luck, therefore, in the results, although the theory is that it's here that the jockeyship counts. Serious gamblers, not surprisingly, keep their money in their pockets.

The problem with team racing, of course, is that none of the races themselves are of huge stature with prize money to match. Owners are considered gallant for lending their horses, though what they have to fear from the top ranks of any country's jockeys has always seemed to me to be nothing. The success of any series of invitation races depends very largely on the mounts on offer being reasonably good.

Although Lester went once or twice to the United States as part of a team, it was as an individual he made most mark. He would have ridden more there were it not that the weights are lower than in Britain. The top weight in very many races is 8st 4lb, Lester's absolute lower limit; and in consequence there are now very few American-born jockeys, most coming from the shorter and lighter peoples of places like Panama and Puerto Rico.

It was often in turf races (as opposed to dirt) that Lester triumphed, including his three Washington DC Internationals at Laurel on Sir Ivor (1968), Karabas (1969) and Argument (1980).

Of racing there in general he says, 'Nobody bothers much about being on the inside in America. The horses always swing wide coming into the straight and it's easy to get a run through wherever you like. Usually the best horse wins, as they go so fast right from the beginning. Often the first three-quarters of a race are faster than the finish. Lots of races are framed to attract the best horses, because those are the ones who bring in the customers. A very good horse won't be handicapped out of running: there's never more than 20lb. between top and bottom weight. Entries in most races have to be made only two days before, except for big races like the Kentucky Derby.'

It's all faster, more fluid than in England, congenial to someone who could choose his Oaks mount four hours before racetime on the basis of the baking morning sunshine on the course.

At one of Lester's last meetings in America, the Breeders' Cup day at Aqueduct, New York, in November 1985, I went down to the jockeys' changing area to find him. He wasn't there, and he should have been, as in the U.S. jockeys are not allowed to wander around freely between races, as in England. The official in charge there was most annoyed that he was missing.

Lester, as it happened, was at that moment being fêted, honoured and thanked for the pleasure he'd given everyone for so long by the President of the racecourse and the assembled executives and Stewards. I was still waiting when he returned from this back-slapping interlude and when he explained where he'd been, the aggrieved official gave him a right ticking off all the same!

Sublime to ridiculous, I thought: and a summary of the way Lester had been treated a great deal too often.

Apart from an official or two, there is worldwide regret that the long fellow won't be back to take away breaths in a tight finish. Apart perhaps also from jockeys worldwide, who won't have to beat him any more and can sleep more easily in their beds.

Lester has been the most international of all jockeys, a forerunner in demolishing barriers, unequivocally welcomed, trusted, and everywhere cheered. There hasn't been much of the backbiting abroad that he's had to put up with at home: as the Bible says, a prophet is not without honour, save in his own country.

Lester's standing overseas is high. He was an exceptional voyager; an ambassador, in his own way, for what's best in sport.

# Commanche Run and After

Lester made a slowish start in 1984, accelerating from zero to full operating speed only in the second half of April and not winning any big races until late in May: but then, in a space of two weeks, he won four. The first two were a double on Khaled Abdulla's Adonijah, first in the Brigadier Gerard Stakes at Sandown and next in Derby week, in the Pacemaker Diomed Stakes, the opening event of the Epsom meeting. Two days later on the same course Sheikh Mohammed's Prince of Peace obliged in the Northern Dancer handicap, both of the Arab-owned horses being trained by Henry Cecil.

The fourth big race, momentously for Lester, was the Oaks.

He'd had no success in the year's Classics until then, neither of his Guineas mounts producing much and his Derby hope, Alphabatim, coming in fifth. In the run up to the Oaks, John Dunlop asked Lester to partner Circus Plume whom he had taken to victory, first time out, in the Sir Charles Clore Stakes at Newbury three weeks earlier. With no Henry Cecil runner to cloud the issue, Lester accepted.

On paper, it looked an open race with no foregone conclusions, and so it proved in the event. Optimistic Lass, ridden by Walter Swinburn, started favourite at 7–2, with Circus Plume, owned by Sir Robin McAlpine, second favourite at 4–1. Poquito Queen, with Steve Cauthen, came next.

These three fillies all moved forward three furlongs out, as did a fourth, the 66–1 outsider Media Luna, ridden by Paul Cook. Circus Plume took the lead about 2 furlongs from the winning post and looked certain to stay there. Then Media Luna, the unexpected, sharpened her pace and put her nose decisively in front, and it took all Lester's force and resolution to regain his advantage. He won with not many yards to spare, by a neck.

There was more to that win for Lester than just another Classic. It was his twenty-seventh, the all-important figure which drew him level with a record that had stood for a hundred and fifty-seven years. Frank Buckle, between 1792 and 1827, won the Two Thousand Guineas five times, the One Thousand Guineas six times, the Derby five times, the Oaks nine times and the St Leger twice. A jockey of incredibly durable talent, he went on riding until he was sixty-five, and until Lester came along it looked as if his record would be safe for ever. There are far more runners now than the small fields of four, five and six that Buckle had to beat, also more trainers, more jockeys, more money poured into bloodstock. In a different world, equalling the ancient record was a triumph indeed. The Epsom crowd, which knew the score, made the welkin ring.

Not that, for Lester, twenty-seven were enough. A dead-heat wasn't the same as a clear lead. With time running out as he came into the homestretch of his career, he began thinking of twenty-eight.

With the St Leger runners still a misty line of possibles, however, he filled in time with a continuing flurry of big prizes such as the Queen Anne Stakes at Royal Ascot, the Lancashire Oaks and the Princess of Wales Stakes at Newmarket. Next came the blazing highlight of Teenoso's King George VI and Queen Elizabeth Diamond Stakes and, after that, three days later, he won the Gordon Stakes at Goodwood on Commanche Run.

Commanche Run, owned by Lester's Singapore friend Ivan Allan and trained by Luca Cumani, had earlier in the season been ridden to victory by Darrel McHargue, the American jockey newly working as Cumani's stable jockey, but when Lester rode the colt at Goodwood, Darrel McHargue was sitting out a suspension.

Lester had won for Luca Cumani several times over the eight years the young Italian had been training in Newmarket, and he had won much oftener for trainer Ivan Allan, principally in Malaysia and Singapore. His tally of Singapore classics for Ivan

Allan stood at five: the Queen Elizabeth II Cup in 1972, the Lion City Cup twice, in 1976 and 1977, the Tunku Gold Cup, 1979, and the Singapore Derby, also 1979.

The professional association and personal friendship between Ivan Allan and Lester was of long standing and great depth. Lester had often ridden the horses the Singapore trainer owned in England. It wasn't unreasonable, in the face of all these facts, that Ivan Allan should want Lester to ride Commanche Run in the St Leger.

Luca Cumani, notwithstanding Lester's 5-length win on the horse at Goodwood, wanted his stable jockey Darrel McHargue to be back on Commanche Run for the Doncaster classic. There was a severe and public clash of loyalties, with Lester as usual being allotted the blame. Ivan Allan's loyalty was to Lester, Luca Cumani's to Darrel McHargue; but the owner who pays the training fees has the right to decide.

Three days before the St Leger, with the fuss over riding plans raging away, Commanche Run fell on the road while out at morning exercise and cut and grazed his knees. Luca Cumani had to work night and day to get him to the post, skilfully keeping infection and swelling at bay with icepacks, and he delivered Commanche Run fit and well – but untypically sweating – to the test.

The opposition he faced was formidable, including Alphabatim, Lester's Derby mount, and Baynoun, on which Lester had won early in the season. As usual, he knew almost a third of the field of eleven at first hand, and had raced against several of the others. He thought the question marks over his chances were, first, the grazed knees and, second, whether the distance of 1¾ miles would be too far for his mount.

In the race, riding with inspiration, he rubbed out the question marks in no uncertain fashion. He designed the first of the sort of races later so familiar to Commanche Run watchers, taking the lead after entering the straight and challenging all else to pass. Baynoun ahead of Alphabatim struggled to do just that all the way up the long straight, Steve Cauthen riding at full stretch, but with strength and willpower Lester got Commanche Run home by a neck.

Alphabatim, Crazy and Shernazar (Shergar's half-brother)

followed in a bunch, less than two lengths covering the first five horses. It had been a hard, remarkable race, and with no disrespect to Darrel McHargue everyone at Doncaster could see clearly that Lester and only Lester could have kept Commanche Run's nose in front.

He was cheered over and over as he was led in, as he dismounted, as he unsaddled. He was smiling non-stop. He had beaten history and Frank Buckle. He'd amassed the magic twenty-eight. It was, for everyone there, a tremendous day.

Lester's own words, discussing the event with me in retrospect, were simply, 'He ran a very game race and he was able to win.'

Never one for histrionics, Mr Piggott.

Luca Cumani, greatly pleased, made no complaint about Lester riding Commanche Run ever after. He is, Lester says, a very good trainer with a great sense of humour. They first met in Italy, when Lester won the Italian Derby on Luca's father's horse, Cerreto. Luca, six feet tall, was at that time riding a lot of winners himself; a first rate amateur jockey, Lester says.

In Lester's final season, 1985, Commanche Run developed splendidly in scope and power. First time out, at Sandown Park, he won very easily by 12 lengths. After that he went to Royal Ascot for the Princess of Wales Stakes, but he didn't seem to be himself that day. He got worked up before the race and didn't run well, finishing third to Bob Back and Pebbles, beaten 1½ lengths and a short head. When a horse doesn't feel well, it's often impossible to know the reason.

Next time out, Commanche Run went down to the start for the Coral Eclipse Stakes at Sandown, but Lester dismounted when he reached the stalls, feeling that his mount was lame. Lester thought the problem might be in the horse's stifle (a joint high on the groin) and the starter didn't demur. The horse was trotted round, and it was clear all wasn't well.

Lester, and the starter also, looked at the horse's feet, but could see no trouble there. There was nothing to be done, however, but to withdraw without coming under starter's orders, disappointing though it was for Ivan Allan who had come from Singapore for the event.

Commanche Run went home to Newmarket where it was found that one of the nails securing his racing plates had penetrated a foot: and it took a long while to heal as the horse didn't have very good feet in the first place. He had to miss the King George VI and Queen Elizabeth Diamond Stakes because it was still bothering him, and he couldn't run again until the Benson and Hedges Gold Cup at the York meeting in the middle of August.

'He wasn't a hundred percent that day,' Lester says. 'I was trying to save the horse a bit, knowing that he wasn't really wound up. I didn't want to go too fast on him. The other jockeys let me set my own pace, though, which suited me, and when I quickened up in the straight he just had enough at the end to last. But if someone had taken me along faster all the way, he'd never have got the trip.'

The win looked easy. 'It wasn't, really,' Lester says.

From York to Ireland for the Phoenix Champion Stakes. Commanche Run was feeling all right that day and won easily without problems. Lester was most impressed with him, as the going was soft. As a three-year-old, the bay colt won twice on very hard ground which it was supposed he liked best. 'To be able to gallop as well as he did in the soft ground, he had to be an exceptional horse. So few good horses can act on both.'

There was a good deal of excitement after that race as the three respective racecourses had jointly offered a £1,000,000 bonus to any horse winning all three of the Benson and Hedges, the Phoenix Park and the Newmarket Dubai Champion Stakes. With two down and one to go, Commanche Run really looked as if the treble were possible. The million possibility had been covered by insurers whose cheque in good faith was on show at the three race meetings. After Ireland, they were definitely anxious!

Alas for the Midas hopes. By the time the Dubai Champion Stakes came around at Newmarket in October, Commanche Run, who liked warm weather, had gone over the top, and never troubled the first and second, the One Thousand Guineas winner Pebbles, and the Derby winner Slip Anchor.

It was Commanche Run's last race: there was to be no great Indian Summer. He stands now at stud at John Magnier's Coolmore Stud in Co. Tipperary.

At the end of 1984, Lester and Henry Cecil had regretfully come to the end of their partnership. They had both wanted and intended it to last until Lester's retirement, but the dissolution was brought about a year early because of Daniel Wildenstein's continuing refusal to have Lester ride his horses. (The owner who pays the bills has the right to decide.)

When Daniel Wildenstein had said, 'Eddery shall never ride for me again,' his then trainer Peter Walwyn had replied that in that case he wouldn't be able to train the Wildenstein horses, and asked for them to leave. Henry Cecil didn't feel he could do that to an owner who had entrusted to him more than twenty good horses. He was, however, finding it very irksome always having to seek out and engage other jockeys whenever the Wildenstein horses ran. 'A nightmare,' he said.

He had intended anyway to ask Steve Cauthen to take Lester's place after he retired and, for the sake of Daniel Wildenstein, brought this plan forward a year. Lester went back to freelancing, and Steve Cauthen moved from Barry Hills to Henry Cecil, from Lambourn to Newmarket.

Daniel Wildenstein rewarded Henry Cecil for his loyalty by announcing, in Derby week 1985, that he was taking all his horses away anyway, as he thought he'd like to have them trained in France.

An odd business, loyalty.

Lester announced in the spring of 1985 that that would be his last season, and Edward Gillespie, manager of Cheltenham racecourse, came up with the brilliant idea of arranging a match race between the two retiring jockey superstars, Lester and jump racing's long-time champion, John Francome.

The race was to be on the Flat, and to be called the Walton Hall Duel of the Champions. The place, Warwick racecourse; the date, Saturday 18 May, the time 7.45 pm – during the normal evening jump-racing programme.

Warwick racecourse had never seen anything like it. The capacious car parks filled and overspilled and shut their gates. When I arrived just after the first race, the nearest kerbside spot I could find in the crowded surrounding streets was over half a mile from the action.

The stands were packed, people seeming to be hanging out of the balconies from the press of those behind. More people, on the ground, lined the paddock rails three deep. And all this on a dreadful day of dark clouds, heavy showers, rough wind and diving temperatures. November weather; no fine light warm May evening.

John Francome, six weeks after hanging up the seven-league boots in which he had jumped his way into folklore, John Francome with his curls, his huge grin, his unmistakable voice and his megawatt personality was already there, spreading light.

Lester was to come by helicopter from Coventry airport, having flown there after riding in Ireland that afternoon. The buzz went round that he had been delayed and hadn't arrived, and instinctively everyone looked at the sky, a tempest-tossed jumble of clouds black enough to deter the most resolute pilot. Loudspeakers announced the race would be put back half an hour, to give him more time.

It poured. Everyone huddled in inadequate shelters, shivering, pulling padded jackets close. The evening's regular races damply proceeded, and eventually the drenching shower passed.

A scant hour before the postponed match time, the brave helicopter swept in below the clouds and landed in the centre of the course, and there Lester was, to everyone's great relief, walking composedly across the track, light, neat, a comet with a tail of running children.

Spirits rose. More rain fell. By 8.15 pm, the light was so bad they would have drawn stumps at Lords ten times over.

Lester rode The Liquidator, John, Shangoseer.

Lester's mount at 10st 2lb had been set to carry 10lb less than John's. They had been handicapped by computer.

The rain stopped again, just in time. The wet crowd emerged from under the overhangs of roofs, and the jockeys, Lester in silk, John in wool, paraded their mounts past the enthusiastic stands. The bookmakers had made The Liquidator favourite; no disrespect to John. The race started in front of the paddock, so that everyone could see. The distance ahead, 1¾ miles, 180 yards. John Francome set off fast, knowing it was probably his only chance, but Lester within the first quarter mile caught and passed him.

All round the track they went in the same order, with never much more than a length between them. Round the final bend,

John, driving Shangoseer hard, closed the gap to half a length, his horse's nose at Lester's saddle. The crowd roared. John used his whip. Lester sat dead still. It looked for a moment as if John might prevail, but The Liquidator kept right on going. His winning margin, three-quarters of a length, had been unchanged all along the straight.

To many, Lester's win as usual looked easy, but it hadn't been. He told me afterwards that he'd had to lead almost from the beginning because The Liquidator, once headed, tended to lose interest and stop. 'I knew if John caught up with me again it would be all over. I had to sit there and just keep my horse going. I couldn't ride him any harder, he wouldn't have liked it. If I'd used my whip, he would have stopped. He couldn't go any faster. It was a close thing, really.'

The 10-lb advantage in weight had very likely proved the decisive factor, and it was the computer, one might say, who took the prize.

With wet hair, wet clothes and smiles to shame the sun, the great satisfied crowd drifted home. Rain or not, it had been, like Agincourt, a battle not to be missed.

Two weeks before the Warwick race, Lester had ridden in his last Two Thousand Guineas. He had been going to ride Luca Cumani's Bairn, on whom he had decisively won the preliminary Greenham Stakes at Newbury, but at the last minute these plans were changed.

Bairn was owned by Sheikh Mohammed. His elder brother, Sheikh Maktoum al Maktoum, also had a runner in the race; Shadeed, trained by Michael Stoute. Eleven days before the Two Thousand Guineas, Shadeed's usual jockey, Walter Swinburn, was involved in an incident in the Blue Riband Stakes at Epsom, in which it was judged that in finishing second he had interfered with the horse which finished fourth.

To the consternation of the stable, Walter Swinburn wasn't just disqualified from second place but was given a three-week suspension. Against this harsh sentence (uncomfortably reminiscent again of the slap-down-the-young-star syndrome), trainer and jockey appealed. (They appealed also against a different suspension later in the year and got the sentence then *increased*.)

The Blue Riband appeal was turned down, and Shadeed was without a jockey. Lester was engaged to ride Bairn, but there's a tradition amongst Arabs that the older brother has preference. The younger must give the elder whatever he wants. Maktoum al Maktoum exercised this right and chose to have Lester on his horse, the younger brother yielding him up as a matter of course. Luca Cumani, resigned, engaged Willie Carson for Bairn. Lester took the switch philosophically as he didn't mind which of the horses he rode. He had seen Shadeed win the Craven Stakes and thought him brilliant.

The Two Thousand Guineas is always a hard race, and Shadeed, Lester says, was never going as well as he had in the Craven. Lester feared he would be beaten, and beaten moreover by Bairn, who had been slowly away from the gate but was uncomfortably close with Willie Carson scenting victory. In another of those rocketting finishes, entirely in tune with his horse, Lester won on Shadeed by a head.

'It was lucky for me,' he says, grinning.

Lucky too for Michael Stoute and the elder Maktoum. Lester won't have it that he would have won on Bairn anyway if he hadn't been switched to Shadeed, but he's fairly alone in that opinion.

Winning the Two Thousand Guineas put his classic record up another notch to twenty-nine, and that's where it will stand now for perhaps another 157 years, or indeed for ever.

The final tally of English classic wins is:

*Two Thousand Guineas*
Crepello, 1957
Sir Ivor, 1968
Nijinsky, 1970
Shadeed, 1985

*One Thousand Guineas*
Humble Duty, 1970
Fairy Footsteps, 1981

*Derby*
Never Say Die, 1954
Crepello, 1957
St Paddy, 1960
Sir Ivor, 1968
Nijinsky, 1970
Roberto, 1972
Empery, 1976
The Minstrel, 1977
Teenoso, 1983

| *Oaks* | *St Leger* |
|---|---|
| Carrozza, 1957 | St Paddy, 1960 |
| Petite Etoile, 1959 | Aurelius, 1961 |
| Valoris, 1966 | Ribocco, 1967 |
| Juliette Marny, 1975 | Ribero, 1968 |
| Blue Wind, 1981 | Nijinsky, 1970 |
| Circus Plume, 1984 | Athens Wood, 1971 |
| | Boucher, 1972 |
| | Commanche Run, 1984 |

Lester won one more classic in his last season, the French Oaks on Lypharita. Throughout the whole of the summer, he rode as much in France as in England, actually winning more races there than at home.

Everywhere he went, there were the 'last' races to be ridden. The last Derby, the last time at The Curragh, the final chance at the Arc. Everywhere too there were presentations and speeches, and not only in England but in Ireland, Sweden, Italy and France.

There were cheers and champagne and damp eyes: photographs of Lester and Vincent with their arms round each other's shoulders; a procession of thanksgiving for joys present and past. No one wanted him to finish, and everyone knew that he must.

Nottingham racecourse invited him to go there on 29 October for his last day's racing in England, and put on a special programme to do him honour. A hundred or more telegrams arrived for him there on the day, one notably from the Queen Mother wishing him good fortune and saying how much he would be missed.

Lester came by helicopter with Maureen and Tracy: Susan had to be on business at a bloodstock sale.

The huge crowd, positively willing him to ride a winner, had to wait only until the second race. Then Full Choke, which just about described the state of half the onlookers' throats, triumphantly took him past the post, and for the last time in England the hats came off and the cheers rang out. He rode three more races, second, eighth and again second; and quite suddenly it was all over. Nothing in English racing would be the same, ever again.

Nottingham racecourse designed a special racecard for the

event, with a portrait of Lester on the front. People beseiged him all afternoon for autographs, waiting patiently in hundreds for the famous scrawl. One of the cards that he and a number of his fellow jockeys signed was for ex-jump-jockey turned expert commentator, Richard Pitman. A month later, Richard generously gave his racecard to be auctioned to raise money for Children in Need. Those few sheets of paper were sold for £1100, an eloquent tribute to Lester's stature in history.

Nottingham wasn't entirely the end of the road. The foreign travels continued, with races ridden and won in America later in the autumn, and spring in the Far East still beckoning with promise. It seemed as if Lester wanted no sudden cut-off, as if he would go on riding sporadically with no ending in mind, until one day, looking back, he could see that *that* race, *there*, had been the last. As if he didn't want to know it was finally over until after it was.

By December 1985, his spacious stables in Hamilton Road, Newmarket - Eve Lodge - were alive and bustling with yearlings, the dying fall of one career revitalising like the phoenix into a new incarnation. Lester the jockey was going, Lester the trainer arriving: he looked forward to the new life with zest.

It would take two years, he said, to wind up to full pitch. In his first season, all the yearlings would be running as two-year-olds, in the next season at three, and thereafter the crops would rotate smoothly. He has room for a hundred horses in the substantial main stable blocks which are built on the barn system under huge sheltering roofs. Accommodation for another forty is available next door, when needed.

Successions of tenants disclosed the need for slight modifications to the original design, and during the summer of 1985 building work progressed to prepare the yard as a modern, efficient, thoroughly high-standard establishment ready to take on the world.

Great jockeys don't automatically make great trainers, but Lester has two prime advantages: first, that as the son of a trainer he's known the job from birth, and second, that he's married to someone who knows what's needed at least as well as he does. Susan, assistant trainer at sixteen: Susan, bloodstock agent. She knows the necessary organisation like the alphabet.

Lester continues to ride work in the mornings, assessing his charges' readiness from the saddle. The insights he gave to other trainers about their horses he applies now to his own.

He expects jockeys who ride for him to report fully, as he used to himself. He never could understand trainers who wouldn't listen to details of how their horses had run. 'Didn't want to hear the worst, I suppose!'

I have read speculations that Lester won't succeed as a trainer because he can't 'blarney' the owners.

Quite right. Lester believes his owners deserve better than blarney.

They'll get the truth.

# The Man Inside The Myth

The public's perception of Lester Piggott as a jockey was always unerringly accurate. They saw the dash, the balance, the courage, the judgment and the searing finishes. They understood the compulsion to win and the troubles it led to. They expected honesty, a run for their money, a hard man in the saddle. They laid out their cash on those qualities from the time he was twelve.

He gave them fair return. Except at the very beginning when, as he says, 'If you wanted rides, you did as you were told', he was impervious to instructions or inducements not to win. It was axiomatic among trainers that if you wanted a race lost by the jockey, you didn't engage L. Piggott. If you wanted it won – totally different matter.

The public are not fools. They approved of Lester. They ignored damaging criticism. They saw their man clearly, and extended to him a durable affection of such power that the vocal expression of it at race meetings towards the end of his last season brought him very close to tears.

The public's perception of Lester's off-track personality has always been dependent on the Press, and the Press's perception has too often been wrong. This isn't necessarily the journalists' fault. They have been trying for decades to extract from an introvert all sorts of personal revelations which he is unwilling and probably unable to give.

Reading through press cuttings in bulk for this book, I have been struck by the amount of awe expressed by the sportswriters, by the admiration, the informed praise and the generous celebration of genius.

But also there's an undercurrent from some of them sometimes of semi-stifled malice, of pique that Lester wouldn't dance to their tune, of sly pleasure taken in his discomfitures. They were getting back at him, one supposes, for his refusal to talk to them when they wanted him to. Lester at the races was working, had his mind on what he was doing, and didn't care for interruptions.

The effort involved in Lester's listening to questions out in the noisy open air has always been underestimated. Often he didn't answer pressmen's questions because he didn't know what they were asking. If they spoke to the side or back of his head, he didn't know they were there. The pause between asking Lester something and receiving a reply is often taken up by his sorting out unfamiliar lip movements into words. Some cynics think he can always hear if he wants to, but he can't: he couldn't, for instance, hear the Queen wish him a good race in the paddock at Ascot.

To Lester, what was written about him as a jockey was simply part of the job. He took it for granted that newspapers would print what they liked. He neither thanked them for their compliments nor complained of their criticism. He shrugged when they got facts wrong, and he didn't put them right. Few sportsmen have had to stand up to such ruthless and relentless dissection, but Lester takes it in his stride.

Sensationalism, he knows, sells papers. An ill-natured headline rivets attention as pats on the back do not. 'You can't blame the Press,' he says. 'They have to think up a story on days when nothing's happened. They have to fill up that space every day. It must be hard.' All the same, he says, many of the pressmen have invented a lot of things he never said or did. 'Some of them should be writing "True Confessions".' For instance, one of them wrote a story about a robbery at Lester's home in which £3000 was stolen from under the floorboards. This story, often repeated since, was pure fiction. No robbery of any kind took place.

Among the journalists he approved of were Peter O'Sullevan, John Oaksey and Peter Scott, and for those he would make an effort. Also at one time, he collaborated with Brough Scott in a 'Lester Piggott' column in London's *Evening Standard*.

During his many appearances in London before the Stewards, what he mostly thought of was how to escape from the Jockey Club premises without being intercepted by the Press. On the day of the 1962 Bob Ward suspension, he found himself hemmed in on the pavement by determined scribblers, at which point Peter O'Sullevan drove up (timing it to the second), opened his car door and invited Lester within.

Lester left the rest of the Fourth Estate swallowing impotent fury while Peter O'Sullevan, driving away with the prize, offered a hundred pounds from the *Daily Express* for an exclusive interview. Lester took the money, Peter got his story, and each, from the perspective of years, looks back to the incident with amusement.

Only once did Lester actually sue anybody for libel, and that was a French magazine which accused him of having links with the Mafia. He won his case and was paid damages, along with Charles Engelhard and Charles St George who had also been mentioned.

'The Press could say what they liked about my riding,' he says, 'but that was different.'

The French Press are regulated far less strictly than the British, French newspapers make up scurrilous stories as a matter of course, and only provably outrageous damaging lies get taken to court.

In England, because Lester has so seldom refuted anything written, the misconceptions abound, and constant repetition of the same mistakes has turned them into widely held beliefs. Most of the population of Great Britain, for instance, believes that Lester seldom smiles. The legend of 'old stone-face' has been reinforced by every scowling photograph any editor could dig up.

The fact actually is that Lester *often* smiles and often laughs, and there are hundreds of smiling photographs on record. He smiles, however, from pleasure, and never to placate. He has felt no need, ever, to placate the Press, which is perhaps why they don't often print him smiling.

He pointed one day, while we were taping for this book, to a Press photograph of himself being led in on one of his Derby winners.

'I was smiling there,' he said, positively.

I looked at the grave pictured face. 'That isn't exactly a beam, Lester,' I said.

'Well ... I was smiling before that, and I was smiling after that. There, I was smiling *inside*.'

There's a general misconception, partly because of the straight-faced photographs, that for Lester being a jockey was a grim humorless business. All wrong. He passionately loved it. 'I couldn't have done it if I hadn't. You've got to have fun if you want to win.'

Fun is a constant word in his vocabulary. 'It wasn't much fun' has always been a reason for his not repeating any experience. It wasn't much fun, in the end, making endlessly repeated journeys to Ireland, his chief reason for leaving Vincent O'Brien. 'It's very important to want to go where you're going,' Lester says. 'If you don't, it's time to find a reason for not going.'

Fun, for Lester, means enjoyment, not giggles. His desire and capacity for enjoyment has seldom been mentioned, undoubtedly because so much of it goes on inside his head, unexpressed. He thought it would have been ridiculous, after he'd won races, to jig about and laugh a lot. 'Everyone would have thought I was an idiot.' Perhaps more importantly, he would have seemed an idiot to himself.

There's an uneasy misconception that Lester doesn't care for anyone except himself, which is perhaps of all the misconceptions the most hurtful. His quiet kindnesses to all sorts of people get little publicity, but the recipients do sometimes talk.

Martin Blackshaw, for instance, the jump jockey, was once hurt and in hospital in France after a fall. Lester found the number and telephoned, asking if he were all right, asking if he needed any money or any other help. Martin Blackshaw was surprised and grateful enough to tell the Press.

A fan of Lester's, an elderly lady called Florrie Ramsey, once sent him a box of chocolates when he himself was injured long ago. Lester called in to see her when he was racing at York, near her home, and continued to do so sporadically for many years.

Every fan letter gets answered, a considerable time-consumer. Many of the fans have been writing for years and are to Lester old friends. His handwriting is small, neat, legible, and slopes forward. He never minds signing autographs at race meetings, his only complaint being about children. 'They come up to you and push their books under your nose, and I wouldn't mind that except that they will stand on your toes.' (His toes, in paper-thin racing boots, were unprotected and highly vulnerable!) 'I like children, and I like to see them at the races. It's good for racing that they come.'

Lester has paid bills for people in trouble and often visited injured colleagues in hospital, and every time, if a journalist has got to hear of it, such an act has been greeted with vast surprise, whereas the truth is that Lester isn't and never has been the chunk of flint he's repeatedly been reported to be.

Certainly, mindful of his mother's teaching, he's not a soft touch, but where he likes, and where he loves, he is constantly generous. He built a comfortable one-storey house for Keith and Iris about two hundred yards from his own in Newmarket, and when he's at home sees them at least once daily, taking good care of them in their eighties.

He and Susan provide their elder daughter Maureen with horses for eventing, and he overtly delights in her company. To Tracy, their younger, he gives with an open hand and can't suppress a smile when he looks at her. One of the things that most exasperates his daughters is hearing their father called mean.

I understand when people complain that Lester is inconsistent in his behaviour towards them, because he is; but it should be borne in mind that a) if he doesn't answer, he hasn't heard the question; b) if the answer is a grunt, he is concentrating on something else and doesn't want to be distracted; and c) he never talks for the sake of talking. Silence is natural to him, not a sign of boredom.

He occasionally gets depressed. ('Everyone gets depressed, don't they?') His depressions have nothing to do with actual events, nothing to do with reverses, disappointments or injury. Low periods come for no identifiable reason, but usually when he has too little to do. They may last for two or three days, during which he may be quieter than ever.

At scattered times he may relax, be great company, expansive, full of jokes. There's no point in wondering if it's the silent or the talkative fellow that's the true Lester. They both are. His outer mood may swing from one to the other, but it doesn't follow that his inner feelings change at all. He doesn't see why anyone should be disconcerted, and it doesn't bother him if they are.

When he's grown tired of anything he's doing, he still tends to walk away from it, just as he did from the children his mother asked to tea. When he's interested, his energy and stamina are endless. When he wants something, he is tenacious in pursuit.

He is not self-analytical. He turns his perceptions outward, and is acutely, unselfconsciously observant. He still sees what goes on around him with the sharp uncluttered objective freshness of childhood, and he doesn't interpret or bend what he sees to match some preconceived theory.

He is obliging and easy-going most of the time (which some pressmen will find amazing), and the things which irritate him are what irritate most people, like having to wait about.

Central to his character is his pleasure in speed. He often says that if he hadn't been a jockey he would have been a racing driver, and for years he drove as if British roads were race-tracks. Two six-month suspensions for speeding and one for three months were the result. A miracle in those days, his friends said, for him to hold his driving and riding licences simultaneously.

Lester's views of other people are remarkably tolerant. '*Too* tolerant,' Susan says, emphatically.

In all the years we worked on this book, Lester never said anything nasty about anybody. His most stringent criticism took the form of 'He's mad, you know', and once only he (justifiably) described someone in four anatomical letters. The only alterations he asked me to make to what I'd written, apart from errors of fact, were deletions to two separate paragraphs in which I described how people had done him positive harm when he had in no way harmed *them*.

Of the first, he said, 'It's a bit strong. Couldn't you cut that a bit?'

'But Lester,' I protested, 'it's true.'

'Yes, I know,' he said, 'but he's still around. That won't do him any good. He's got a living to make, you know.'

On the second occasion, the man in question was dead. 'Yes,' Lester said, 'but his son isn't. I don't want to hurt him.'

I watered down the paragraphs.

Vincent O'Brien says, 'Lester could afford to say nasty things about people, and probably with good reason. Such a good trait, that he doesn't.'

Even-tempered and normally in a good humour, Lester never lets his brief furies against reverses and injustices linger on as grudges and resentments. 'I never stay angry long. I soon forget it. You can't do anything about what's happened. Being angry does no good.' He likes peace in his mind, in fact, so that he can think of something constructive, like how to win tomorrow.

It's all part of his preference for damped-down emotion that he likes cats and dislikes dogs. Cats come and go in his house, tolerated, gently ignored. He says the first of them was acquired long ago to please the children, but they are like him, walking quietly and independently about their business, self-sufficiently arranging their own lives. Dogs, which demand much, are alien.

Lester's views on the human race are simple. 'I don't care whether they're black, white or yellow, everybody's the same. I've travelled so much, and colour doesn't matter. I don't dislike people. They don't bother me. I get along with people pretty well. It's stupid not to.

'I got on well with nearly all the other jockeys, especially Gordon, but most of all with Scobie Breasley. I like him. We rode together every day for probably twenty years. I was closer to him than to anyone else. He was a good jockey, very tough. I think he was the best of all the Australian jockeys I've seen, including George Moore, who I think was next best.'

Pressed to say who he *didn't* like, Lester came up with not a name but a category. 'I don't like people who can't stop talking. I go the other way when I see them coming.'

His closest friends have tended to be older than himself, among them several of the owners he rode for, people of power and substance, enjoying racing as a pastime but basically of serious mind. Some of these friendships, like that with Charles St George, have lasted thirty years. Others, like that with Charles Engelhard, the great gusty tycoon addicted to Coca-Cola, ended only in death.

Early among these friendships came that with Sir Victor Sassoon. Although usually in a wheel-chair as a result of injuring his back in a flying accident, Sir Victor would come to Britain each summer from his home in the Bahamas and often walk into the winner's enclosure with the help of sticks. He was a knowledgeable breeder who owned four Derby winners, Hard Ridden, Pinza, Crepello and St Paddy.

In the year of Lester and Susan's marriage, he invited them to stay with him in Nassau, and he was, they affirm, the kindest and most generous of men. His death in 1961 was to them, as to the Murless family and racing in general, a dreadful blow.

When he had owned horses in China (before the revolution) and Hong Kong and India, Sir Victor had raced them under the pseudonym of 'Mr Eves'. He called both his stud farm and his house in Nassau 'Eves'. When Lester and Susan built their yard in Newmarket, they called it 'Eve Lodge' as a tribute to his memory.

Lady Sassoon is Maureen's godmother: Maureen's full name is Maureen Iris Eve. When Lester was hurt in Paris, Lady Sassoon was there to drive Susan to the hospital and generally look after her. The affections have run strong and deep.

Mrs Hue Williams, then Mrs Vera Lilley, owner of Lester's 1961 St Leger winner, Aurelius, is another good friend, as was Prince Aly Khan.

Newmarket is a town where people spin separately in their own little orbits, not mixing a great deal socially. Everyone knows everyone, everyone meets at the races, and that's where it rests. Among Lester's closest contemporary local friends are probably Henry and Julie (Murless) Cecil and Trish and Geoffrey Wragg, the trainer of Teenoso. Julie Cecil, who was a child when Lester first went to ride for her father, says she always knew when he was trying to get out of riding one of the stable's horses. 'He used to sit on the window seat in the sitting-room of Warren Place and start swinging his legs.'

Geoffrey Wragg, Lester says, was at one time more interested in putting radio sets together than in training horses. Trish Wragg clips news stories about Lester and makes up his cuttings books. Trish and Susan are close friends.

Lester himself doesn't spend much time thinking about people.

He thinks most about horses but also a fair amount about world affairs. He reads the local newspapers when he's in Australia, Singapore, America ... wherever they're printed in English. He's thoughtful and well-informed. In England, he reads the *Sporting Life* and *The Daily Telegraph*.

I have known Lester on and off for a very long time. I am fifteen years and five days older than he is, so that from age and also from geography - Newmarket is a hundred miles from where I live in Oxfordshire - we have never been contemporary neighbourly companions. Our lives, on the other hand, have touched at many and varied points, and we have grown to know each other well.

It was when we rode against each other as jump jockeys that I first became aware that the brash aggressive character of the newspapers didn't square with the polite unassuming reality in the changing-room. He wasn't surly, he wasn't uncooperative; he was thoroughly sensible in outlook and manner. He would race against anyone without quarter, but that was fine, so did we all.

For several years when Lester and I rode regularly for the same trainers, Frank and Ken Cundell (he on their Flat horses, I on their jumpers), we rode out together occasionally at morning exercise, and I gave him legs-up onto Zucchero in parade rings while Ken Cundell was waiting at the starting gates.

I wrote a bit about Lester during the sixteen years I worked for the *Sunday Express*, but not a great deal as my column was chiefly about jumping.

When my wife Mary and I owned (and she managed) an air charter business ferrying owners, trainers and jockeys to race meetings, Lester was one of our most frequent passengers. Others included Jimmy Lindley, Joe Mercer and Pat Eddery, but it was Lester, eventually, who with Susan became directors of the company, and remained so until we sold the business in late 1975.

The charter flights were always made by professional commercial pilots, but my wife once flew Lester herself - just the two of them - on a private flight from Oxford airport to Shoreham in Sussex. When our insurance advisors got to hear of it, they flung up their hands in horror. 'Don't do it!' they cried, 'Lester Piggott is the second hottest property to the Queen'.

The second hottest property thought it a great joke.

It was early in 1973, while he was a director of the air business, and while I was still writing for the *Sunday Express* but had already published eleven novels, that Lester first asked me to write this book. A contract was drawn up to last for ten years, which seemed ages at the time, but we were well into the second ten-year contract before he retired.

During that time, we worked a good deal together, taping conversations in various places, in his home and mine, and in London, America and Penang.

In Penang because, in 1980, Mary and I with Lester and Susan and Maureen and Tracy spent three weeks' holiday together in Penang and Singapore. Also in Penang were Susan's brother Robert Armstrong and his wife Mary Ann; and the whole lot of us passed a warm and agreeable time going on beach picnics by speedboat, fishing, swimming, dining and lazing about eating (gorgeous) ice cream. The tapes Lester and I made there under the palm trees are loud with birdsong.

He wanted in this book to have someone say for him what he has been unable to say for himself; to write the truth, even if some who read it prefer still to cling to the misconceptions. He wanted someone to write it who understood his way of life, who'd suffered some of the same disappointments, who'd felt the same urge to pursue winners at whatever physical cost, who'd had the same sort of moments of total fulfilment.

I don't pretend to know Lester absolutely: he's a complex human being and there are impenetrable parts of the forest. I write of him as I know him at first hand. I write of the level-headed man who has emerged from the transcripts of dozens of hours of recordings. I listen to the truths in his recorded voice. I've written what he has said, and what I've seen.

Back in 1950, as a fourteen-year-old child competing on adult terms, aware of his skill but still groping for social sureness, his rounded face mirrored his anxieties. To see Lester as he is now, look at the dust jacket of this book: a mature, secure, calm man of good sense, with humour and humanity in his eyes.

That's the true Lester; the product of the journey.

He told me in January 1984 that he thought he would ride for only two more seasons. He had been saying 'two or three more' for about ten years, but this sounded more positive.

I asked why he should stop when he was riding as well as ever.

After a while he said, 'I think I win now chiefly from experience. From knowing where to be, and what to do. I may think I'm as strong as I was ten years ago . . . I may feel that I am . . . but I'm probably not. I'll have to stop sometime. I think I'll stop when I'm fifty.'

He didn't sound sad, but I felt it.

How long, I asked him, would he have gone on being a jockey if it hadn't been for growing older, if he could have stopped time and stayed young.

A wry smile. No hesitation.

'A thousand years,' he said.

# Appendices

# Lester Piggott – British Wins

Whilst we have striven to present these statistics as accurately as possible, one or two errors are bound to have been overlooked during the production of such a mammoth list, and for these we apologise.

| Date | Race Course | Horse | Race | Value £ | Dist Fur | Owner | Trainer | S/P |
|---|---|---|---|---|---|---|---|---|
| 1948 | | | | | | | | |
| 18 Aug | Haydock | The Chase | Wigan Lane S Hcp 8F Sellig Hcp | 294 | 8 | Mrs B J R Lavington | K Piggott | 10/1 |
| 1948: 1 win; 2 2nds; 24 rides | | | | | | | | |
| 1949 | | | | | | | | |
| 20 Aug | Newbury | Forest Glade | | 207 | 7 | Mrs B J R Lavington | K Piggott | 6/1 |
| 1 Sept | Bath | Secret Code | | 188 | 12 | Mrs B J R Lavington | K Piggott | 7/2F |
| 26 Sept | Birmingham | Gold Sandal | | 207 | 8 | Mrs T Lilley | F Templeman | 5/2F |
| 21 Oct | Newbury | Variety Girl | Didcot Nursery Hcp | 552 | 7 | E Thornton-Smith | F Templeman | 100/6 |
| 28 Oct | Thirsk | Flurry | | 267 | 5 | E Strong | F Hartigan | 100/8 |
| 9 Nov | Liverpool | Little Bonnet | | 414 | 6 | J Olding | H Persse | 15/2 |
| 1949: 6 wins; 8 2nds; 10 3rds; 120 rides | | | | | | | | |
| 1950 | | | | | | | | |
| 10 Apl | Kempton | Extra-Dry | | 347 | 12 | W Harvey | K Piggott | 6/1 |
| 1 May | Bath | Cool Shamrock | | 276 | 8 | J Hallinan | K Cundell | 100/8 |
| 12 May | Kempton | Tancred | Queen Elizabeth | 855 | 5 | S L Sheldrick | K Cundell | 5/1 |
| 31 May | Chepstow | Green Tipperary | | 188 | 10 | Mrs B J R Lavington | K Piggott | 6/1 |
| 5 June | Lewes | Humanity | | 207 | 5 | E Thornton-Smith | F Templeman | 2/1F |
| 21 June | Newbury | Humanity | Empire Hcp | 690 | 5 | E Thornton-Smith | F Templeman | 100/7 |
| 23 June | Sandown | Lanarth* | | 305 | 13½ | R T Fox-Carlyon | W Pratt | 9/4F |
| 3 July | Nottingham | Brickworth Belle | | 207 | 5 | T Venn | H Whiteman | 10/1 |
| 5 July | Salisbury | Alizarene | | 207 | 8 | R O Girling | K Cundell | 9/2 |
| 14 July | Sandown | Wild Chancellor | | 345 | 8 | W Van De Stadt | K Cundell | 8/1 |
| 22 July | Hurst Park | Alizarene | | 276 | 8 | R O Girling | K Cundell | 10/3 |
| 25 July | Goodwood | Vidi Vici | Craven Stks | 650 | 10 | P G Thompson | T R Rimell | 6/1 |
| 29July | Worcester | Star of Clubs | | 410 | 6 | J G Dimond | K Cundell | 5/1 |
| 1 Aug | Birmingham | Fair Betty | | 277 | 10 | W J Rimell | T R Rimell | 10/1 |
| 2 Aug | Bath | Tai-Yat | | 438 | 17 | S G Banks | G Todd | 10/3 |
| 7 Aug | Chepstow | Trigennie | | 207 | 10 | G A Lister | K Cundell | 20/1 |

* Dead Heat

| Date | Race Course | Horse | Race | Value £ | Dist Fur | Owner | Trainer | S/P |
|---|---|---|---|---|---|---|---|---|
| 8 Aug | Chepstow | Gold Sandal | | 207 | 8 | E Thornton-Smith | F Templeman | 7/1 |
| 10 Aug | Brighton | Star of Clubs | | 287 | 6 | J G Dimond | K Cundell | 11/2 |
| 11 Aug | Lewes | Moorish Spangle | | 138 | 12 | Mrs W R Tarrant | G Bennett | 10/1F |
| 14 Aug | Folkestone | Blue Sapphire | | 313 | 12 | Maharajah of Baroda | G Duller | 3/1 |
| 14 Aug | Folkestone | No Light | | 207 | 10 | Lord Abergavenny | W Payne | 5/1 |
| 17 Aug | Windsor | Trigennie | | 220 | 12 | G A Lister | K Cundell | 5/4 |
| 23 Aug | Salisbury | Barman | | 292 | 5 | W A Jackson | J G Waugh | 3/1 |
| 24 Aug | Salisbury | New Pioneer | | 207 | 12 | J Ismay | M Blackmore | 8/1 |
| 25 Aug | Lingfield | Lancashire Lassie | Hever Stks | 527 | 7 | G R Beard | R Smyth | 6/1 |
| 26 Aug | Lingfield | Blue Sapphire | | 227 | 12 | Maharajah of Baroda | G Duller | EvF |
| 30 Aug | Brighton | Humanity | | 310 | 6 | E Thornton-Smith | F Templeman | 11/2 |
| 31 Aug | Brighton | Sun Flame | | 717 | 12 | Lt Col D T Wallis | K Cundell | 5/1 |
| 1 Sept | Folkestone | Don's Fancy | | 138 | 15 | C Braham | W Payne | 2/1F |
| 1 Sept | Folkestone | Queen's Prize | | 138 | 12 | Mrs E J Lewis | J C Waugh | 5/1 |
| 2 Sept | Folkestone | White Ant | | 207 | 6 | O/trainer | G N Bennett | 4/5F |
| 11 Sept | Wolver'ton | Curly Cut | | 207 | 8 | P B Raymond | M Collins | 10/3 |
| 14 Sept | Bath | Finalis | | 188 | 12 | O/trainer | F Templeman | 7/1 |
| 16 Sept | Kempton | Sun Flame | | 365 | 12 | Lt Col D T Wallis | K Cundell | 6/4F |
| 20 Sept | Brighton | Zina | Brighton Autumn Cup | 992 | 12 | Lady I Guinness | F Cundell | 11/2 |
| 21 Sept | Ascot | Tancred | Buckingham Palace Stks | 1,090 | 5 | S L Sheldrick | K Cundell | 5/1F |
| 22 Sept | Ascot | Moorish Spangle | Wild Boar Stks | 653 | 12 | Mrs W R Tarrant | G Bennett | 4/1 |
| 23 Sept | Ascot | Abraham's Star | Swinley Forest Hcp | 483 | 7 | P G Thompson | T R Rimell | 6/1 |
| 26 Sept | Newmarket | Horatia | Abington Mile Nursery Stks | 700 | 8 | F C Bailey | K Cundell | 10/1 |
| 28 Sept | Newmarket | Holm Bush | Jockey Club Stks | 5,372 | 10 | Sir D Bailey | A Budgett | 5/1 |
| 30 Sept | Newbury | Finalis | | 485 | 12 | O/trainer | F Templeman | 100/8 |
| 30 Sept | Newbury | Extra-Dry | | 483 | 16 | W Harvey | K Piggott | 100/6 |
| 4 Oct | Lingfield | Eldoret | | 207 | 16 | T G Johnson | W Payne | 9/2 |
| 7 Oct | Ascot | Damrémont | | 483 | 7 | P G Thompson | T R Rimell | 5/1 |
| 11 Oct | Newmarket | Golden Quip | | 362 | 7 | Maj D J Vaughan | F Cundell | 7/1F |
| 13 Oct | Warwick | Taor | | 196 | 16 | R O Girling | K Cundell | 11/2 |
| 13 Oct | Warwick | Fancy Inn | | 138 | 5 | Lady Baron | W Payne | 7/4F |
| 13 Oct | Warwick | No Light | | 198 | 8 | Lord Abergavenny | W Payne | 4/1 |
| 16 Oct | Wolver'ton | Moorish Spangle | | 276 | 12 | Mrs W R Tarrant | G Bennett | 2/1F |
| 18 Oct | Hurst Park | Pre-War | | 414 | 14 | Mrs M H McAlpine | V Smyth | 11/8F |
| 21 Oct | Newbury | Zina | | 420 | 10 | Lady I Guinness | F Cundell | EvF |
| 21 Oct | Newbury | Horatia | | 552 | 8 | P C Bailey | K Cundell | 9/2 |

1950: 52 wins; 45 2nds; 39 3rds; 404 rides

| 1951 | | | | | | | | |
|---|---|---|---|---|---|---|---|---|
| 27 Mar | Kempton | Breath of Spring | | 356 | 5 | M Wilson | J Powell | 25/1 |
| 27 Mar | Kempton | Tancred | | 418 | 5 | S L Sheldrick | K Cundell | 15/2 |
| 29 Mar | Lincoln | Nuts and Wine | | 196 | 5 | Maj G M Harbord | J Powell | 5/4F |
| 30 Mar | Lincoln | Roydon | | 198 | 12 | Mrs E G Williams | J Powell | 8/1 |
| 17 Apl | Birmingham | Grey Magic | | 207 | 5 | Mrs P Reynolds | W Payne | 6/1 |
| 23 Apl | Wolver'ton | Poolfix | | 207 | 5 | O/trainer | F Hartigan | 5/2 |
| 24 Apl | Epsom | Barnacle | Great Metropolitan | 1,204 | 18 | A Aman | A Budgett | 10/1 |
| 26 Apl | Epsom | Zucchero | Blue Riband Trial Stks | 2,439 | 8 | G Rolls | K Cundell | 7/1 |
| 28 Apl | Worcester | Game Boy | | 207 | 10 | O/trainer | R Sturdy | 4/1 |
| 30 Apl | Worcester | Palm Grove | | 383 | 5 | O/trainer | F Hartigan | 20/1 |
| 15 May | Birmingham | Dashwood | | 277 | 6 | H Wragg | C Pratt | 15/2 |
| 16 May | Salisbury | Wild Boy | | 312 | 5 | Lady Baron | W Payne | 6/1 |
| 16 May | Salisbury | Sun Flame | | 310 | 12 | Lt Col D T Wallis | K Cundell | 100/8 |

| Date | Race Course | Horse | Race | Value £ | Dist Fur | Owner | Trainer | S/P |
|---|---|---|---|---|---|---|---|---|
| 16 May | Salisbury | Fancy Inn | | 207 | 6 | T Organ | W Payne | 9/2 |
| 21 May | Warwick | Manhattan | | 198 | 7 | Mrs S Jacobson | K Cundell | 8/11F |
| 26 May | Hurst Park | No Light | | 276 | 10 | Lord Abergavenny | W Payne | 2/1F |
| 28 May | Wolver'ton | Prince Marika | | 276 | 5 | M V Everett | T Farmer | 9/4F |
| 29 May | Epsom | Barnacle | Rosebery Memorial Hcp | 690 | 18 | Mrs J Bailward | A Budgett | 7/1 |
| 29 May | Epsom | Deerslayer | | 420 | 7 | Sir W Waldron | T Farmer | 8/1 |
| 1 June | Epsom | Grani | | 345 | 10 | G C Vandervell | J C Waugh | 10/1 |
| 4 June | Warwick | The Woodstock Gate | | 196 | 5 | Mrs G M Harbord | J Powell | 13/8F |
| 7 June | Brighton | Wild Chancellor | | 276 | 8 | W Van de Stadt | K Cundell | 10/3 |
| 9 June | Lingfield | Grey Magic | | 207 | 6 | Mrs P Reynolds | W Payne | 9/4 |
| 11June | Leicester | Moulan | | 287 | 6 | Mrs J Drabble | K Piggott | 10/11F |
| 18 June | Birmingham | High Number | | 207 | 5 | Maj G Glover | F Cundell | 7/1 |
| 19 June | Birmingham | Chiaroscuro | Midland Breeders Foals Stks | 1,356 | 10 | H R Hobson | F Cundell | 100/8 |
| 21 June | Newbury | Vidi Vici | Newbury Summer Cup | 1,149 | 12 | P G Thompson | T R Rimell | 10/3 |
| 23 June | Worcester | Greenstone | | 207 | 5 | R H Holbech | T Yates | 11/4F |
| 30 June | Alex Palace | Yogi | | 207 | 5 | Mrs S Sanger | T Carey | 5/1 |
| 2 July | Folkestone | Bobby Brooks | | 188 | 6 | Mrs E G Williams | J Powell | 5/1 |
| 3 July | Folkestone | Don's Fancy | | 207 | 15 | C Braham | W Payne | 8/1 |
| 4 July | Brighton | Damrémont | Brighton Mile Champion Cup | 690 | 8 | P G Thompson | T R Rimell | 5/2F |
| 6 July | Windsor | Sun Flame | | 276 | 12 | Lt Col D T Wallis | K Cundell | 5/1 |
| 7 July | Windsor | Zucchero | | 276 | 12 | G Rolls | K Cundell | 11/10F |
| 10 July | Salisbury | Pyrgos | | 388 | 12 | B Samuel | W Payne | 6/1 |
| 13 July | Sandown | Zucchero | Commonwealth Stks | 1,196 | 13 | G Rolls | K Cundell | 11/10F |
| 14July | Sandown | Mystery IX | Eclipse | 9,445 | 10 | Mrs V Esmond | P Carter(F) | 100/8 |
| 17 July | Newmarket | Damrémont | Thurston | 526 | 10 | P G Thompson | T R Rimell | 11/4 |
| 18 July | Bath | Kibitzer | | 207 | 6 | J A de Rothschild | D Watson | 10/1 |
| 18 July | Bath | Chiaroscuro | | 291 | 10 | H R Hobson | F Cundell | 3/1 |
| 19 July | Bath | Wayland | | 276 | 10 | G C Vandervell | J C Waugh | 6/1 |
| 20 July | Ascot | Setare Andakhian | Balmoral | 684 | 12 | J B Townley | P Beasley | 9/4F |
| 27 July | Hurst Park | No Light | | 345 | 10 | Lord Abergavenny | W Payne | 4/1F |
| 3 Aug | Goodwood | Grani | Chesterfield Cup | 1,502 | 10 | G C Vandervell | J C Waugh | 8/1 |
| 7 Aug | Chepstow | Cloonane | | 207 | 10 | Mrs H S Martin | T Yates | 12/5F |
| 7 Aug | Chepstow | Moulan | | 138 | 6 | Mrs J Drabble | K Piggott | 11/8 |
| 14 Aug | Nottingham | Belle of Colombo | | 277 | 15 | V Oliver | P Nelson | 10/1 |
| 16 Aug | Bath | Solperion | | 312 | 5 | A Summers | F Cundell | 2/1F |
| 17 Aug | Newbury | Whinsaire | | 310 | 12 | O/trainer | J R Neill | 5/2F |
| 18 Aug | Newbury | Port Desire | | 207 | 6 | Lt Col T R Badger | F Templeman | 100/7 |
| 22 Aug | York | Grani | | 198 | 9 | G C Vandervell | J C Waugh | 10/1 |

1951: 51 wins; 36 2nds; 40 3rds; 432 rides

1952

| Date | Race Course | Horse | Race | Value £ | Dist Fur | Owner | Trainer | S/P |
|---|---|---|---|---|---|---|---|---|
| 25 Mar | Lincoln | Amberley | | 345 | 16 | J U Baillie | J C Waugh | 7/1 |
| 5 Apl | Liverpool | Pol Roger* | | 220 | 10 | W Churchill | W Nightingall | 9/4F |
| 7 Apl | Newmarket | What Happened | | 370 | 6 | Mrs J V Rank | W Nightingall | 13/2 |
| 18 Apl | Newbury | Uricon | | 420 | 5 | Miss P Aspinall | F Cundell | 25/1 |
| 21 Apl | Wolver'ton | Colourist | | 287 | 8 | P G Thompson | T R Rimell | 7/2F |
| 29 Apl | Newmarket | Queen's Bench | First Spring Stks (2-y-o) | 715 | 5 | P Hatvany | F Day | 100/8 |
| 30 Apl | Newmarket | Indubitably | | 414 | 6 | Mrs J V Rank | W Nightingall | 9/2 |

* Dead Heat (F) = France

| Date | Race Course | Horse | Race | Value £ | Dist Fur | Owner | Trainer | S/P |
|---|---|---|---|---|---|---|---|---|
| 1 May | Newmarket | Court Guide | Newmarket Stks (2-y-o) | 633 | 5 | Mrs J C Humphreys | J A Waugh | 33/1 |
| 8 May | Sandown | Reminiscence | | 413 | 5 | Mrs J V Rank | W Nightingall | 6/5F |
| 10 May | Kempton | Honey | | 408 | 11 | Brig J M J Evans | K Cundell | 5/2F |
| 12 May | Birmingham | Stranger | | 345 | 6 | Lady Baron | W Payne | 7/1 |
| 14 May | Bath | Triangle | | 419 | 10 | Mrs J V Rank | N Cannon | 11/10F |
| 15 May | Bath | Demonstrate | | 311 | 10 | Mrs J V Rank | N Cannon | 2/1 |
| 19 May | Wolver'ton | Percussion | | 276 | 5 | J E Ferguson | J C Waugh | 7/1 |
| 21 May | Salisbury | Gay Time | | 410 | 10 | Mrs J V Rank | N Cannon | 4/7F |
| 22 May | Salisbury | Honey | | 333 | 12 | Brig J M J Evans | K Cundell | 6/4F |
| 23 May | Hurst Park | Indubitably | | 207 | 6 | Mrs J V Rank | W Nightingall | 3/1 |
| 30 May | Epsom | Enrapt | Ebbisham Stks | 1,754 | 8 | Mrs J V Rank | N Cannon | 5/1 |
| 5 June | Windsor | Taranto | | 276 | 12 | O/trainer | H Blagrave | 100/7 |
| 6 June | Sandown | Running Water | | 477 | 8 | Mrs J V Rank | H Persse | 5/4F |
| 7 June | Sandown | Part du Lyon | | 405 | 10 | D W Molins | W Nightingall | 6/1 |
| 10 June | Lewes | Ardena | | 188 | 5 | A Summers | F Cundell | 3/1 |
| 10 June | Lewes | Stranger | | 286 | 8 | Lady Baron | W Payne | 6/4F |
| 20 June | Royal Ascot | Malka's Boy | Wokingham | 1,582 | 6 | H E Elvin | W Nightingall | 100/6 |
| 26June | Newbury | Manas | | 473 | 13 | O/trainer | H Blagrave | 3/1 |
| 1 July | Wolver'ton | Chiaroscuro | Southern Hcp | 528 | 12 | H R Hobson | F Cundell | 6/1 |
| 3 July | Newmarket | Zucchero | Princess of Wales Stks | 2,945 | 12 | G Rolls | W Payne | 20/1 |
| 8 July | Salisbury | Canardeau | | 464 | 6 | O/trainer | H Blagrave | 3/1F |
| 12 July | Sandown | Windsor Star | Star Stks | 689 | 5 | Lady Baron | M Beary | 3/1 |
| 16 July | Newmarket | Indubitably | | 303 | 6 | Mrs J V Rank | W Nightingall | 6/5F |
| 18 July | Ascot | Grey Magic | Balmoral | 638 | 12 | Mrs P Reynolds | W Payne | 10/1 |
| 23 July | Kempton | Heroism | | 437 | 8 | A Summers | F Cundell | 100/8 |
| 23 July | Kempton | March Past | | 430 | 5 | Mrs G Trimmer-Thompson | K Cundell | 4/1 |
| 25 July | Hurst Park | Priory Way | | 490 | 7 | Mrs J V Rank | W Nightingall | 2/1F |
| 29 July | Goodwood | Longstone | Craven | 623 | 10 | Mrs C Evans | K Cundell | 11/4F |
| 30 July | Goodwood | Jaymah | Charlton Hcp | 681 | 8 | G L Hobbs | K Cundell | 7/1 |
| 2 Aug | Worcester | Trigennie | | 207 | 11 | G A Lister | K Cundell | 10/11F |
| 4 Aug | Chepstow | Miss Ping | | 138 | 5 | G Armstrong | F Cundell | 8/1 |
| 5 Aug | Chepstow | Taranto | | 331 | 12 | O/trainer | H Blagrave | 1/9F |
| 5 Aug | Chepstow | Jonquil | | 138 | 5 | A E Stigwood | F Cundell | 10/11F |
| 7 Aug | Brighton | Belvoir Street | | 287 | 6 | G O Johnson | F Cundell | 4/6F |
| 11 Aug | Folkestone | Wyedale | | 237 | 10 | C C Wootton | H Whiteman | 10/11F |
| 13 Aug | Salisbury | Ben Tinto | | 207 | 14 | O/trainer | H Blagrave | 7/4F |
| 13 Aug | Salisbury | Sun Glory | | 422 | 6 | O/trainer | H Blagrave | 9/4F |
| 13 Aug | Salisbury | Longstone | | 207 | 10 | Mrs C Evans | K Cundell | 11/10F |
| 14 Aug | Salisbury | Nullabor | | 388 | 5 | G Armstrong | F Cundell | 12/5F |
| 14 Aug | Salisbury | Pyrgos | | 276 | 5 | B Samuel | W Payne | 5/1 |
| 18 Aug | Warwick | Belvoir Street | | 294 | 5 | Mrs K Leary | F Cundell | 4/1 |
| 19 Aug | York | Zucchero | Rose of York | 1,700 | 8 | G Rolls | W Payne | 13/2 |
| 20 Aug | Bath | Dutchman | | 138 | 6 | H Sumner | F Cundell | 10/1 |
| 20 Aug | Bath | Sam's Folly | | 207 | 8 | Miss A M Masters | I Anthony | 10/1 |
| 20 Aug | Bath | Eastern Ocean | | 138 | 10 | H Sumner | F Cundell | 9/4 |
| 21 Aug | Lingfield | Intriganse II | | 207 | 6 | Mrs J V Rank | R Warden | 8/1 |
| 25 Aug | Worcester | Carmo | | 290 | 5 | Mrs E Stevens | F Cundell | EvF |
| 2 Sept | Lewes | Liproar | | 276 | 12 | L A Abelson | V Smyth | 5/2F |
| 3 Sept | Bath | Coral Reef | | 207 | 10 | O/trainer | H Blagrave | 4/7F |
| 4 Sept | Bath | March Past | | 207 | 6 | Mrs G Trimmer-Thompson | K Cundell | 11/8F |
| 4 Sept | Bath | Bell Buoy | | 138 | 10 | J W Case | J Dines | 5/2 |
| 5 Sept | Folkestone | Non-Stop | | 138 | 15 | W Churchill | W Nightingall | 13/8F |
| 5 Sept | Folkestone | Silvergreen | | 237 | 6 | Mrs E G Williams | J Powell | 6/4F |
| 5 Sept | Folkestone | Daytime | | 245 | 10 | W F Bates | W Nightingall | 5/1 |
| 8 Sept | Warwick | Blazing | | 138 | 5 | G H Fairhurst | D Candy | 10/1 |

| Date | Race Course | Horse | Race | Value £ | Dist Fur | Owner | Trainer | S/P |
|---|---|---|---|---|---|---|---|---|
| 13 Sept | Doncaster | March Past | Doncaster Produce Stks | 1,818 | 6 | Mrs G Trimmer-Thompson | K Cundell | 8/1 |
| 13 Sept | Doncaster | Barnacle | Rufford Abbey Hcp | 778 | 18 | Mrs J Bailward | A Budgett | 9/1 |
| 19 Sept | Kempton | Wild Boy | Avington Stks | 589 | 6 | Lady Baron | M Beary | 5/1F |
| 24 Sept | Salisbury | Globetrotter | | 269 | 8 | A K Macomber | C Pratt | 6/1 |
| 27 Sept | Ascot | Prince D'or | Kensington Palace Stks | 716 | 6 | G H Fairhurst | D Candy | 10/1 |
| 27 Sept | Ascot | Ben Tinto | Red Deer Hcp | 1,243 | 12 | O/trainer | H Blagrave | 8/1 |
| 29 Sept | Birmingham | Minstrel Girl | | 207 | 5 | O/trainer | H Blagrave | 8/1 |
| 1 Oct | Newmarket | Peter Barty | Boscawen Stks | 517 | 6 | Mrs H E Elvin | W Nightingall | 6/4 |
| 3 Oct | Newmarket | Apple Chutney | | 425 | 6 | J F Duff | R Day | 10/1 |
| 18 Oct | Sandown | March Past | Solario | 1,544 | 7 | Mrs G Trimmer-Thompson | K Cundell | 9/2 |
| 20 Oct | Wolver'ton | Cheyne | | 276 | 16 | O/trainer | S Wootton | 9/4F |
| 24 Oct | Newbury | Chivalry | | 400 | 7 | P Hatvany | W Wightman | 6/1 |
| 28 Oct | Newmarket | Morning Trial | Rutland | 526 | 12 | H S Lynch | J Bisgood | 8/1 |
| 1 Nov | Sandown | SS Commando | | 345 | 5 | O/trainer | Capt S Carlos-Clarke | 100/9 |
| 3 Nov | Birmingham | Imprudent | | 207 | 13 | J G de Pret-Roose | Capt S Carlos-Clarke | 8/13F |
| 11 Nov | Leicester | Happy Flight | | 276 | 10 | H E Pretyman | W Payne | 5/1 |
| 15 Nov | Lingfield | Oscar | | 276 | 12 | J Rogerson | R Perryman | 6/1 |
| 1952: 79 wins; 47 2nds; 70 3rds; 620 rides | | | | | | | | |
| 1953 | | | | | | | | |
| 26 March | Liverpool | Terrorist | | 193 | 6 | W J Rimell | T R Rimell | 4/1F |
| 1 Apl | Nottingham | Sun Suit | | 277 | 5 | Mrs L Hawkins | Capt S Carlos-Clarke | 100/7 |
| 7 Apl | Birmingham | Imprudent | | 285 | 13 | J G de Pret-Roose | Capt S Carlos-Clarke | 5/2F |
| 9 Apl | Leicester | Rocky Lane | | 207 | 12 | Mrs L Hawkins | Capt S Carlos-Clarke | 10/3F |
| 13 Apl | Windsor | Windsor Star | | 276 | 8 | Lady Baron | W Payne | 100/7 |
| 17 Apl | Hurst Park | Tangle | | 276 | 10 | Lady Baron | W Payne | 100/8 |
| 23 Apl | Epsom | SS Commando | | 330 | 5 | O/trainer | Capt S Carlos-Clarke | 13/2 |
| 2 May | Newbury | Vello D'oro | | 476 | 5 | J L C Pearce | V Smyth | 7/2 |
| 4 May | Warwick | SS Commando | | 291 | 5 | O/trainer | Capt S Carlos-Clarke | 1/7F |
| 6 May | Sandown | Tangle | | 456 | 10 | Lady Baron | W Payne | 5/1 |
| 8 May | Kempton | Approval | | 343 | 16 | L A Abelson | V Smyth | 6/1 |
| 12 May | Newmarket | Vello D'oro | | 305 | 5 | J L C Pearce | V Smyth | 10/3 |
| 25 May | Hurst Park | Ever-Ready | | 483 | 5 | Sir M McAlpine | V Smyth | 20/1 |
| 27 May | Windsor | Vital Spark | | 207 | 5 | Sir M McAlpine | V Smyth | 2/1F |
| 1 June | Leicester | Carola Pride | | 207 | 8 | A W Macnamara | K Piggott | 4/1 |
| 5 June | Epsom | Zucchero | Coronation Cup | 3,732 | 12 | G Rolls | W Payne | 100/7 |
| 16 June | Royal Ascot | Absolve | Gold Vase | 2,709 | 16 | Sir M McAlpine | V Smyth | 20/1 |
| 23 June | Folkestone | Stone Ginger | | 138 | 10 | Mrs M Smorfitt | H Brown | 10/3 |
| 26 June | Windsor | Cote d'Or | | 294 | 5 | H E Pretyman | W Payne | 5/1 |
| 27 June | Windsor | Zucchero | | 204 | 12 | G Rolls | W Payne | 1/5F |
| 29 June | Wolver'ton | Don Rickardo | | 276 | 5 | B Mavroleon | W Payne | 9/4 |
| 8 July | Salisbury | Carola Pride | | 207 | 7 | A W Macnamara | K Piggott | 6/1 |
| 10 July | Sandown | Blarney Stone | Sandown July Stayers Stks | 543 | 16 | M H MacAlpine | V Smyth | 13/8F |
| 15 July | Bath | Westerlands Champagne | | 274 | 10 | Mrs F Nagle | H Brown | 4/6F |

| Date | Race Course | Horse | Race | Value £ | Dist Fur | Owner | Trainer | S/P |
|---|---|---|---|---|---|---|---|---|
| 16 July | Bath | Forbear | | 313 | 5 | Dr M V Murray | T Fitzgeorge-Parker | 9/2 |
| 21 July | Leicester | Della's Choice | | 277 | 6 | C Braham | K Cundell | 2/1F |
| 15 Aug | Newbury | Longstone | | 276 | 10 | Mrs C Evans | K Cundell | 4/1 |
| 18 Aug | York | Zucchero | Rose of York | 1,670 | 8 | G Rolls | W Payne | 15/8 |
| 31 Aug | Lewes | Belle Esprit | | 138 | 12 | J A Scrimgeour | T Yates | 2/1F |
| 4 Sept | Folkestone | Nordest | | 242 | 16 | H V Cozens | J Bisgood | 10/1 |
| 11 Sept | Doncaster | Globetrotter* | | 312 | 6 | Mrs C Pratt | C Pratt | 6/1F |
| 12 Sept | Alex Palace | Della's Choice | | 276 | 5 | C Braham | K Cundell | 2/1F |
| 16 Sept | Brighton | Globetrotter | | 376 | 8 | Mrs C Pratt | C Pratt | 11/2 |
| 19 Sept | Chepstow | Manas | Welsh Cesarewitch | 549 | 16 | O/trainer | H Blagrave | 10/3F |
| 29 Sept | Newmarket | Forbear | | 449 | 5 | Dr M V Murray | T Fitzgeorge-Parker | 11/4 |
| 3 Oct | Warwick | Double Comfort | | 196 | 5 | E Bee | T Yates | 10/1 |
| 3 Oct | Warwick | Aer Lingus | Autumn Breeders Stks | 781 | 8 | Mrs C A Blyth | J Fawcus | 11/8F |
| 16 Oct | Newmarket | Sunnybrae | | 474 | 8 | J A de Rothschild | D Watson | 6/1F |
| 21 Oct | Hurst Park | Loll | | 392 | 5 | D Nossez | M Pope | 7/2 |
| 31 Oct | Sandown | Prince Haven | | 336 | 5 | W L Hall | T Yates | 100/6 |
| 13 Nov | Lingfield | Longstone | | 254 | 10 | Mrs C Evans | K Cundell | 13/8F |

1953: 41 wins; 32 2nds; 45 3rds; 441 rides

| Date | Race Course | Horse | Race | Value £ | Dist Fur | Owner | Trainer | S/P |
|---|---|---|---|---|---|---|---|---|
| 1954 | | | | | | | | |
| 25 Mar | Liverpool | Richmond Street | | 193 | 6 | Mrs H Nadler | T R Rimell | 2/1F |
| 29 Mar | Nottingham | Itajuru | | 277 | 8 | A Portman | G Kennedy | 100/9 |
| 31 Mar | Leicester | Prince Haven | | 207 | 6 | W L Hall | T Yates | 100/8 |
| 31 Mar | Leicester | Spinster's Luck | | 276 | 5 | Mrs H B Brassey | Capt S Carlos-Clarke | 11/4F |
| 3 Apl | Windsor | Flying Argosy | | 276 | 8 | S L Sheldrick | K Cundell | 100/6 |
| 9 Apl | Newbury | Babylonian | | 420 | 13 | G H Dowty | T R Rimell | 3/1F |
| 23 Apl | Sandown | Longstone | Twickenham | 572 | 10 | Mrs C Evans | K Cundell | 10/3 |
| 1 May | Newbury | Ciao | | 473 | 5 | Mrs J Stanley | H Wragg | 6/4F |
| 4 May | Chester | Dicer | | 376 | 10 | J M Nadler | T R Rimell | 3/1F |
| 5 May | Chester | Wise Folly | Great Cheshire Hcp | 790 | 10 | R S Clark | J Lawson | 10/1 |
| 8 May | Chepstow | Flagship | | 188 | 5 | Sir B Mountain | P Nelson | 10/1 |
| 8 May | Chepstow | Proud Scot | | 307 | 12 | Major T Adam | P Nelson | 6/1 |
| 10 May | Birmingham | Dazzler | | 277 | 8 | Mrs W H Dunnett | P Nelson | 100/8 |
| 12 May | Bath | March Past | | 207 | 8 | Mrs G Trimmer-Thompson | K Cundell | 7/2 |
| 13 May | Bath | Long Hope | | 188 | 5 | O/trainer | Capt S Carlos-Clarke | 15/8F |
| 13 May | Bath | Copernic | | 320 | 10 | Mrs F W Wignall | C Jerdein | 10/3 |
| 20 May | Salisbury | Spinster's Luck | | 305 | 5 | Mrs H B Brassey | Capt S Carlos-Clarke | 20/5 |
| 20 May | Salisbury | Hectic | | 402 | 10 | H Samuel | W Payne | 11/4F |
| 24 May | Lewes | Salmon Prince | | 207 | 10 | Mrs E N Cohen | T Yates | 2/5F |
| 27 May | Kempton | Pierobello | Mentmore Hcp | 751 | 8 | H J Jones | J Lawson | 13/8F |
| 29 May | Kempton | Copernic | Halliford | 548 | 11 | Mrs F W Wignall | C Jerdein | 3/1 |
| 31 May | Leicester | The Deacon | | 207 | 10 | Miss D Paget | C Jerdein | 8/15F |
| 2 June | Epsom | Never Say Die | The Derby | 16,959 | 12 | R S Clark | J Lawson | 33/1 |
| 2 June | Epsom | Damrémont | Epsom Stks | 629 | 10 | T H Degg | T R Rimell | 9/2F |
| 4 June | Epsom | Big Berry | Ebbisham | 2,444 | 8 | Maj Gen J Combe | J Lawson | 8/11F |
| 4 June | Epsom | Proud Scot | Nonsuch | 5,496 | 12 | Maj T Adam | P Nelson | 3/1 |
| 5 June | Warwick | Condensed | | 138 | 5 | Miss V Pratt | T Yates | 6/1 |
| 5 June | Warwick | Easter Bride | | 138 | 5 | W J Rimell | T R Rimell | 11/8F |
| 7 June | Chepstow | Mulgrave | | 138 | 6 | Mrs H French | A French | 2/1F |
| 9 June | Windsor | Ciao | | 207 | 6 | Mrs J Stanley | H Wragg | 11/2 |

* Dead Heat

| Date | Race Course | Horse | Race | Value £ | Dist Fur | Owner | Trainer | S/P |
|---|---|---|---|---|---|---|---|---|
| 9 June | Windsor | Alarm Call | | 207 | 12 | Mrs Z E Lambert | G Bowsher | 10/1 |
| 12 June | Worcester | Blue Sandal | | 287 | 6 | H Cox | T Yates | 20/1 |
| 12 June | Worcester | Copernic | | 207 | 10 | Mrs F Wignall | C Jerdein | 10/11F |
| 29 Sept | Newmarket | Cardington King | Isleham Stks | 535 | 7 | C W Rawlins | R Jarvis | 5/1F |
| 1 Oct | Newmarket | Sunny Brae | | 495 | 9 | J A de Rothschild | D Watson | 4/1F |
| 2 Oct | Newbury | Pierobello | | 361 | 8 | H J Jones | J Lawson | EvF |
| 6 Oct | York | Evening Trial | | 362 | 8 | Sir V Sassoon | N Murless | 12/1 |
| 8 Oct | Ascot | Wordsworth | Sandwich | 749 | 6 | Duke of Norfolk | W Smyth | 100/7 |
| 12 Oct | Newmarket | Princely Gift | | 471 | 6 | Sir V Sassoon | N Murless | 2/1F |
| 16 Oct | Sandown | Rashleigh | Wheatsheaf | 816 | 10 | C Stewart | N Murless | 5/4F |
| 22 Oct | Newbury | Pierobello | | 379 | 7 | H J Jones | J Lawson | 9/4 |
| 27 Oct | Newmarket | Raging Storm | | 425 | 7 | W E Haynes | R Day | 11/2 |

1954: 42 wins; 38 2nds; 30 3rds; 262 rides

| Date | Race Course | Horse | Race | Value £ | Dist Fur | Owner | Trainer | S/P |
|---|---|---|---|---|---|---|---|---|
| 1955 | | | | | | | | |
| 21 Mar | Lincoln | Flame Royal | | 138 | 12 | L H Dowling Snr | M Moroney | 7/1 |
| 23 Mar | Lincoln | Crawthorne Wood | | 138 | 6 | Maj J D Summers | A Budgett | 10/1 |
| 28 Mar | Leicester | Biberwis | | 277 | 7 | L M Parnes | K Piggott | 9/1 |
| 29 Mar | Leicester | Mardis | | 277 | 5 | F G Robinson | A Budgett | 13/8F |
| 16 Apl | Hurst Park | King Bruce | | 306 | 7 | W C Tarry | P Hastings-Bass | 100/7 |
| 18 Apl | Wolver'ton | Time to Reason | | 234 | 8 | R S Clark | A Budgett | 4/6F |
| 19 Apl | Wolver'ton | Nucleus | | 207 | 7 | Miss D Paget | C Jerdein | 4/6F |
| 20 Apl | Epsom | Harbour Bar | | 420 | 8 | Maj J H Paine | C Jerdein | 6/1 |
| 26 Apl | Newmarket | Raging Storm | Hasting | 589 | 10 | W E Haynes | R Day | 11/2 |
| 30 Apl | Newbury | Little Cloud | | 420 | 13 | Sir V Sassoon | N Murless | 7/1 |
| 2 May | Alex Park | Fisher's Tale | | 188 | 5 | J H Hawes | J Lawson | 4/5F |
| 10 May | Newmarket | Five Aces | Wilburton Hcp | 716 | 7 | C Steuart | N Murless | 7/1 |
| 11 May | Bath | Master Silver | | 173 | 5 | H Hall | N Henesy | 11/4 |
| 12 May | Newmarket | Montauk | Bedford Stks | 630 | 5 | Miss M R Cox | J Lawson | 12/1 |
| 19 May | Salisbury | Molten Lava | | 420 | 5 | Sir V Sassoon | N Murless | 4/1 |
| 19 May | Salisbury | Rose Knight | | 299 | 8 | Mrs M D Herniman | N Henesy | 9/2 |
| 19 May | Salisbury | Persian Fox | | 336 | 14 | T E Morel | M Feakes | 4/1F |
| 20 May | Hurst Park | Copernic | | 390 | 15 | Mrs F W Wignall | C Jerdein | 7/1 |
| 23 May | Leicester | Crowland Bridge | | 332 | 8 | A Parkinson | J A Waugh | 11/4 |
| 23 May | Leicester | Indian Ruler | | 207 | 12 | Major R M Coles | T Yates | 100/7 |
| 28 May | Hurst Park | Nucleus | Tudor Rose Hcp | 840 | 10 | Miss D Paget | C Jerdein | 9/4F |
| 28 May | Hurst Park | Longstone | | 306 | 10 | Mrs C Evans | K Cundell | 3/1 |
| 30 May | Doncaster | Judicial | | 345 | 5 | Sir V Sassoon | N Murless | 4/11F |
| 30 May | Doncaster | Poke Bonnet | | 365 | 5 | Sir P Loraine | N Murless | 5/4F |
| 31 May | Chepstow | Florus | | 395 | 12 | D Prenn | J Goldsmith | 11/2 |
| 31 May | Chepstow | Paper Chase | | 138 | 8 | Mrs D M Evans-Bevan | R J Colling | 6/4F |
| 1 June | Windsor | Happy Worker | | 287 | 8 | E Bee | T Yates | 10/1 |
| 3 June | Kempton | Noble Charger | Windsor Castle Stks | 509 | 6 | Miss Z Daniels | J Beary | 3/1 |
| 6 June | Nottingham | Sensation | | 207 | 5 | G A Gilbert | W Dutton | 11/10F |
| 7 June | Lewes | Woodworm | | 207 | 5 | Mrs A E Johnson | W Payne | 10/1 |
| 8 June | Brighton | Bois le Roi | Pavilion Hcp | 592 | 12 | Lt Col R Taylor | N Murless | 9/2 |
| 10 June | Thirsk | Scollata | | 207 | 8 | Sir V Sassoon | N Murless | 6/5F |
| 20 June | Folkestone | Woodworm | | 138 | 5 | Mrs A E Johnson | W Payne | 15/8F |
| 21 June | Birmingham | Evening Trial | | 277 | 10 | Mrs L E Hatton | D Butchers | 6/5F |
| 24 June | Lingfield | Poise | | 422 | 10 | Miss D Paget | C Jerdein | 8/1 |
| 25 June | Newcastle | Little Cloud | Northumberland Pl | 2,065 | 16 | Sir V Sassoon | N Murless | 13/2 |
| 27 June | Brighton | The Moat | | 409 | 5 | G G Johnson | K Cundell | 4/1F |
| 27 June | Brighton | AA | | 373 | 6 | Sir V Sassoon | N Murless | 2/1 |
| 28 June | Newmarket | Princely Gift | | 302 | 6 | Sir V Sassoon | N Murless | 11/4F |

| Date | Race Course | Horse | Race | Value £ | Dist Fur | Owner | Trainer | S/P |
|---|---|---|---|---|---|---|---|---|
| 29 June | Newmarket | Knightly Valiant | Stud Produce Stks | 849 | 5 | Prince Aly Khan | N Murless | 5/4F |
| 1 July | Newmarket | Seph | | 340 | 5 | Mrs R Macdonald-Buchanan | N Murless | 5/1F |
| 1 July | Newmarket | Rose Fair | Princess Stks | 1,328 | 6 | Lady Ralli | J A Waugh | 4/1 |
| 1 July | Warwick | Manor Lane | | 392 | 5 | H Andrews | F Cundell | 9/2 |
| 2 July | Alex Palace | Lady Supreme | | 207 | 5 | T Lilley | N Murless | 4/5F |
| 5 July | Nottingham | Crowland Bridge | | 207 | 8 | A Parkinson | J A Waugh | 1/9F |
| 6 July | Salisbury | Redway | | 207 | 7 | J D Kyle | W Payne | 9/4 |
| 6 July | Salisbury | King Conkers | | 207 | 14 | T G Johnson | W Payne | 2/1F |
| 7 July | Salisbury | Abervale | | 364 | 5 | | N Murless | 9/4F |
| 9 July | Sandown | Darius | Eclipse | 9,296 | 10 | Sir P Loraine | H Wragg | 11/10F |
| 12 July | Royal Ascot | Nucleus | King Edward VII Stks | 5,186 | 12 | Miss D Paget | C Jerdein | 4/1 |
| 12 July | Royal Ascot | Elopement | Hardwicke | 3,995 | 12 | Sir V Sassoon | N Murless | 6/5F |
| 18 July | Leicester | Game Chip | | 138 | 5 | A J Tompsett | M Feakes | 5/1 |
| 21 July | Bath | Rose Knight | | 207 | 12 | Mrs M D Herniman | N Henesy | 5/6F |
| 21 July | Bath | Silver Robert | | 303 | 5 | Mrs T Yates | T Yates | 15/8F |
| 22 July | Doncaster | Don Basilio | | 317 | 6 | B Mavroleon | M Feakes | 7/4F |
| 25 July | Alex Palace | The Beadle | | 188 | 8 | N S C Collin | N Murless | 5/2 |
| 27 July | Goodwood | Alibi II | Warren Stks | 585 | 11 | D Morris | C Pratt | 10/3 |
| 29 July | Goodwood | Princely Gift | Chichester Stks | 593 | 6 | Sir V Sassoon | N Murless | 11/8F |
| 2 Aug | Brighton | Mithoo | | 386 | 10 | D Nossel | K Piggott | 10/3 |
| 2 Aug | Brighton | Greenheart | August Stks | 811 | 12 | Sir V Sassoon | N Murless | 2/9F |
| 2 Aug | Brighton | Band Practice | | 342 | 5 | Sir V Sassoon | N Murless | 5/2F |
| 3 Aug | Brighton | Peruke | | 369 | 5 | Mrs R Macdonald-Buchanan | N Murless | 9/4 |
| 4 Aug | Brighton | Amber Glass | Brighton Sprint Hcp | 865 | 6 | Capt A S Wills | P Nelson | 9/4F |
| 4 Aug | Brighton | Sun Sparkle | | 344 | 5 | T Lilley | N Murless | 4/1 |
| 6 Aug | Newmarket | Raging Storm | | 522 | 10 | W E Haynes | R Day | 7/2F |
| 9 Aug | Nottingham | Game Chip | | 207 | 5 | A J Tompsett | M Feakes | 5/1F |
| 10 Aug | Haydock | Sensation | | 207 | 5 | G A Gilbert | W Dutton | 10/11F |
| 11 Aug | Salisbury | Racketeer | | 296 | 5 | Sir V Sassoon | N Murless | 4/9F |
| 12 Aug | Newbury | Pappagena | | 420 | 8 | Mrs C Evans | C Jerdein | 2/1F |
| 12 Aug | Newbury | Princely Gift | Hungerford Stks | 533 | 7 | Sir V Sassoon | N Murless | 2/1 |
| 13 Aug | Newbury | Silver Robert | | 276 | 5 | Mrs T Yates | T Yates | 6/4F |
| 17 Aug | Sandown | Hook Money | | 287 | 5 | R S Clark | A Budgett | 11/8F |
| 18 Aug | Sandown | Alibi II | Poulsen | 521 | 13 | D Morris | C Pratt | 4/1 |
| 18 Aug | Sandown | Preamble | | 330 | 13 | Lt Col G Loder | N Murless | EvF |
| 19 Aug | Lingfield | Polkemmet | | 396 | 10 | J U Baillie | H Price | 8/13F |
| 19 Aug | Lingfield | Woodworm | | 274 | 5 | Mrs A E Johnson | W Payne | 4/1 |
| 22 Aug | Worcester | Redress | | 207 | 6 | J U Baillie | J A Waugh | 4/6F |
| 24 Aug | York | Seph | Wykeham Hcp | 1,395 | 6 | Mrs R Macdonald-Buchanan | N Murless | 10/1 |
| 25 Aug | Brighton | Funny Business | | 298 | 5 | Sir V Sassoon | N Murless | 1/7F |
| 25 Aug | Brighton | Canardeau | | 273 | 7 | G Varnavas | H Price | 9/2 |
| 27 Aug | Windsor | Silver Robert | | 276 | 5 | Mrs T Yates | T Yates | 4/5F |
| 29 Aug | Lewes | Sun Sparkle | | 207 | 5 | T Lilley | N Murless | 2/7F |
| 29 Aug | Lewes | Grass Cubes | | 237 | 12 | Sir V Sassoon | R Swash | 4/1F |
| 1 Sept | Bath | Rain Cloud† | | 248 | 10 | Prince Aly Khan | N Murless | |
| 8 Sept | Doncaster | Princely Gift | Portland Hcp | 2,575 | 5 | Sir V Sassoon | N Murless | 5/2F |
| 15 Sept | Yarmouth | Sensation | | 207 | 6 | G A Gilbert | W Dutton | 1/2F |
| 19 Sept | Leicester | Saphos | | 285 | 10 | J Collier | P Nelson | 4/7F |
| 23 Sept | Ascot | Final Court | Waterford | 854 | 6 | Mrs E Longton | P Nelson | 9/4F |
| 26 Sept | Birmingham | Private Lives | | 277 | 6 | E D Midwood | P Nelson | 5/2F |
| 29 Sept | Newmarket | Annie Oakley | | 236 | 8 | The Queen | N Murless | 7/2 |
| 29 Sept | Newmarket | Nucleus | Jockey Club Stks | 4,765 | 14 | Miss D Paget | C Jerdein | EvF |
| 5 Oct | York | Prairie Emblem | | 436 | 6 | F E White | W Dutton | 2/1 |
| 5 Oct | York | Annie Oakley | | 385 | 8 | The Queen | N Murless | 11/10F |

† Walkover

| ate | Race Course | Horse | Race | Value £ | Dist Fur | Owner | Trainer | S/P |
|---|---|---|---|---|---|---|---|---|
| Oct | York | Alibi II | Aske Stks | 691 | 16 | D Morris | C Pratt | 11/10F |
| Oct | York | Camus-an-Eilean | | 367 | 6 | Capt A S Wills | P Nelson | EvF |
| Oct | Warwick | Fluvius | | 207 | 8 | F E White | J Lawson | EvF |
| Oct | Sandown | Poke Bonnet | Heather Stks Hcp | 540 | 5 | Sir P Lorraine | N Murless | 100/9 |
| Oct | Wolver'ton | Saphos | | 335 | 11 | J Collier | P Nelson | 11/8F |
| Oct | Wolver'ton | Prairie Emblem | | 207 | 5 | F E White | W Dutton | 6/4F |
| Oct | Newmarket | Ragd | | 364 | 12 | Mrs J Forrestal | P Prendergast(I) | 2/1 |
| Oct | Kempton | Saphos | | 500 | 11 | J Collier | P Nelson | 9/2 |
| Nov | Birmingham | Kandy Sauce | | 207 | 6 | Sir V Sassoon | N Murless | 8/1 |
| Nov | Birmingham | Chunkara | | 277 | 7 | J Hylton | A Smyth | 25/1 |

55: 103 wins; 84 2nds; 77 3rds; 530 rides

56

| ate | Race Course | Horse | Race | Value £ | Dist Fur | Owner | Trainer | S/P |
|---|---|---|---|---|---|---|---|---|
| Mar | Hurst Park | High Lustre | Primrose Cup | 840 | 7 | C W Bell | W Nightingall | 2/1F |
| Apl | Wolver'ton | Pa Bear | | 276 | 7 | T Holland-Martin | C Jerdein | 9/4F |
| Apl | Wolver'ton | Nysos | | 207 | 7 | Mrs W H Dunnett | P Nelson | 2/7F |
| Apl | Hurst Park | High Force | | 306 | 5 | Brig J M S Evans | K Cundell | EvF |
| Apl | Hurst Park | Nucleus | | 448 | 14 | Miss D Paget | C Jerdein | 5/4F |
| Apl | Worcester | Courtney | | 207 | 6 | Miss D Paget | H Nicholson | 9/4F |
| Apl | Sandown | The Box* | | 199 | 5 | J U Baillie | K Cundell | 20/1 |
| Apl | Birmingham | Pillow Fight | | 277 | 8 | O/trainer | S Mercer | 5/2 |
| Apl | Birmingham | Prairie Emblem | | 207 | 6 | F E White | W Dutton | 4/9F |
| May | Newmarket | Polish Lancer | | 320 | 6 | Sir B Mountain | P Nelson | 7/2 |
| May | Newmarket | Golden Leader | | 333 | 8 | A Rose | W Dutton | 4/9F |
| May | Newmarket | Affiliation Order | Denton Stks | 558 | 10 | N Harmsworth | C Jerdein | 13/8 |
| May | Nottingham | Gamesmanship | | 277 | 10 | J R Munson | P Nelson | 4/1 |
| May | Nottingham | Right Boy | | 207 | 5 | G R Gilbert | W Dutton | 5/1 |
| May | Kempton | Vigo | Queen Elizabeth Stks | 664 | 5 | T H Farr | W Dutton | 2/1F |
| May | Kempton | The Box | | 314 | 5 | J U Baillie | J A Waugh | 7/4F |
| May | Kempton | Gay Priscilla | | 321 | 5 | M Ostrer | K Piggott | 25/1 |
| May | Kempton | Nucleus | | 626 | 12 | Miss D Paget | C Jerdein | 5/1F |
| May | Wolver'ton | Woodworm | | 207 | 5 | Mrs T G Johnson | W Payne | 5/4F |
| May | Newmarket | Broke Bey‡ | | 388 | 5 | Mrs J R Mullion | R Day | 8/15F |
| May | Hurst Park | Carrozza | | 390 | 5 | The Queen | N Murless | 100/7 |
| May | Hurst Park | High Lustre | Tudor Rose Hcp | 840 | 10 | C W Bell | W Nightingall | 7/1 |
| May | Hurst Park | Nucleus | Winston Churchill Stks | 2,595 | 16 | Miss D Paget | C Jerdein | 2/1 |
| May | Hurst Park | Saykash | | 306 | 10 | C F Hughesdon | P Nelson | 2/1F |
| May | Birmingham | Right Boy | | 207 | 5 | G A Gilbert | W Dutton | 1/6F |
| May | Birmingham | Tottenham | | 207 | 8 | A Gilbourne | G Spann | 10/1 |
| May | Manchester | Racin' Plaid | | 276 | 5 | Mrs E Goldson | W Dutton | 15/8F |
| May | York | Pasture | | 410 | 8 | Sir V Sassoon | N Murless | 11/10F |
| May | York | Ante Lip | | 292 | 5 | Sir V Sassoon | N Murless | 10/1 |
| June | Epsom | Mansbridge | Woodcote | 2,053 | 6 | Col B Hornung | N Murless | 100/9 |
| June | Epsom | High Lustre | Durdans | 514 | 10 | C W Bell | W Nightingall | 4/1 |
| June | Epsom | Knight Valiant | Royal | 625 | 7 | Prince Aly Khan | N Murless | 11/8F |
| June | Yarmouth | Right Boy | | 207 | 6 | G A Gilbert | W Dutton | 1/4F |
| June | Yarmouth | My Pal | | 207 | 5 | G A Gilbert | W Dutton | 5/1F |
| June | Kempton | Saphos | Derby Memorial | 1,059 | 16 | J Collier | P Nelson | 100/9 |
| June | Kempton | Tarsus | Rivermead | 687 | 6 | T Lilley | N Murless | 100/8 |
| June | Kempton | Rich Bloom | | 493 | 11 | C W Bell | W Nightingall | 11/4 |
| June | Leicester | Mainswitch | | 207 | 6 | Capt A S Willis | P Nelson | 5/4F |
| June | Leicester | Honey Harvest | | 206 | 10 | O/trainer | R C Sturdy | 5/1 |
| June | Lingfield | Alcorab | | 394 | 12 | N W Purvis | E Parker | 11/2 |
| June | Lingfield | Pa Bear | | 276 | 10 | T Holland-Martin | C Jerdein | 4/1 |
| June | Doncaster | Ogwen | | 207 | 5 | Sir V Sassoon | N Murless | 5/2 |
| June | Doncaster | Hunter's Horn | | 436 | 8 | Sir V Sassoon | N Murless | 11/4F |

Dead Heat ‡On objection

| Date | Race Course | Horse | Race | Value £ | Dist Fur | Owner | Trainer | S/P |
|---|---|---|---|---|---|---|---|---|
| 16 June | Doncaster | Welsh Weaver | | 262 | 6 | Mrs F Williams | W Dutton | 11/10F |
| 18 June | Lewes | Broken Ranks | | 173 | 8 | Mrs I Bullen | F Cundell | 15/8 |
| 20 June | Royal Ascot | Pharsalia | Queen Mary Stks | 3,788 | 5 | Major L B Holliday | H Cottrill | 100/7 |
| 21 June | Royal Ascot | Court Command | King Edward VII | 4,480 | 12 | Mrs V Lilley | N Murless | 100/7 |
| 23 June | Ascot Heath | Grounded | Fenwolf | 861 | 6 | H Warner | N Murless | 15/2F |
| 26 June | Birmingham | Otava | | 207 | 6 | Lady H Svejdar | P Prendergast (I) | 4/7F |
| 27 June | Newbury | Preamble | | 276 | 13 | F F Tuthill | N Murless | 5/2F |
| 29 June | Newcastle | Deck Tennis | Fawdon | 501 | 6 | The Queen | N Murless | 8/13F |
| 29 June | Newcastle | Vigo | Gosforth Park Cup | 765 | 5 | T H Farr | W Dutton | 11/8F |
| 29 June | Newcastle | Hunter's Horn | | 416 | 8 | Sir V Sassoon | N Murless | 4/9F |
| 2 July | Brighton | Preza | | 356 | 5 | The Queen | P Nelson | 5/2 |
| 2 July | Brighton | Teneretta | | 371 | 12 | The Queen | N Murless | 2/7F |
| 3 July | Wolver'ton | Bowerchalke | | 207 | 5 | S J Gillings | M Beary | 4/1 |
| 3 July | Wolver'ton | Lacloche | | 230 | 8 | Miss D Paget | C Jerdein | 4/7F |
| 4 July | Newmarket | Accumulator | | 242 | 8 | D W Molins | W Nightingall | 9/4F |
| 4 July | Newmarket | Epsom Lady | | 464 | 6 | Mrs M Benson | S Ingham | 9/4F |
| 5 July | Newmarket | Right Boy | Exeter | 627 | 6 | G A Gilbert | W Dutton | 13/8F |
| 6 July | Newmarket | Gladiolus | | 487 | 5 | A Plesch | H Leader | 100/8 |
| 6 July | Stockton | Hunter's Horn | | 308 | 9 | Sir V Sassoon | N Murless | 8/100F |
| 9 July | Alex Palace | Guinea | | 207 | 5 | Mrs D M Fitzpatrick | N Murless | 2/1F |
| 10 July | Nottingham | Hunter's Horn | | 207 | 8 | Sir V Sassoon | N Murless | 4/9F |
| 10 July | Salisbury | Mongol Warrior | | 207 | 10 | B Mavroleon | M Feakes | Ev/F |
| 10 July | Salisbury | Saphos | | 338 | 12 | J Collier | P Nelson | 7/4F |
| 11 July | Salisbury | Cuba | | 207 | 7 | Lord Sefton | P Hastings-Bass | 6/5F |
| 11 July | Salisbury | Sylphide | | 344 | 5 | T Lilley | N Murless | 100/6 |
| 12 July | Salisbury | Sun Flight | | 429 | 5 | Mrs C G Lancaster | S Tree | 2/1 |
| 13 July | Sandown | Rich Bloom | Commonwealth | 1,226 | 13½ | C W Bell | W Nightingall | 4/1 |
| 16 July | Birmingham | Preamble | | 323 | 16 | F F Tuthill | N Murless | 1/2F |
| 16 July | Lewes | Melody Fair | | 315 | 8 | J Crow | R Sturdy | 7/2F |
| 16 July | Lewes | Bowerchalke | | 276 | 5 | S J Gillings | M Beary | 11/2 |
| 17 July | Newmarket | Ogwen | | 551 | 5 | Sir V Sassoon | N Murless | 10/11F |
| 19 July | Bath | Pneumatic | | 207 | 5 | Contessa Di Sant Elia | W Wightman | 13/8F |
| 21 July | Doncaster | Near Star | | 391 | 8 | R S Grierson | A Barclay | 7/1 |
| 21 July | Doncaster | Space Ship | | 276 | 11 | Sir V Sassoon | N Murless | 11/10F |
| 21 July | Doncaster | Adventuress | | 207 | 5 | Sir V Sassoon | N Murless | 7/4F |
| 23 July | Leicester | Joyeux II | | 207 | 12 | Mrs F W Wignall | C Jerdein | 2/1 |
| 26 July | Kempton | Queen's Bench | Blackbird S | 670 | 6 | Sir P Hattvany | F Cundell | 5/1F |
| 27 July | Hurst Park | Space Ship | | 306 | 14 | Sir V Sassoon | N Murless | 8/11F |
| 30 July | Birmingham | Prince Tarquin | | 207 | 6 | F Humphreys | W Dutton | 4/5F |
| 30 July | Birmingham | Jomarbet | | 366 | 5 | M Cowley | R Ward | 11/10F |
| 7 Aug | Brighton | Sculptor | Brighton Hcp | 874 | 8 | Lord Sefton | P Hastings-Bass | 13/8F |
| 7 Aug | Brighton | King's Love | | 300 | 12 | Mrs F Bullock | F Cundell | 5/1 |
| 7 Aug | Brighton | Starlit Moonlight | | 324 | 5 | Prince Aly Khan | N Murless | 6/5F |
| 8 Aug | Brighton | Riseborough | | 275 | 8 | Sir V Sassoon | N Murless | 5/2 |
| 9 Aug | Brighton | Abercorn | | 299 | 9 | Col B Hornung | N Murless | 1/5F |
| 10 Aug | Redcar | Jomarbet | | 485 | 5 | M Cowley | R Ward | 5/4F |
| 11 Aug | Redcar | Closed Doors | | 345 | 5 | Mrs J Y Watson | W Gray | 8/13F |
| 13 Aug | Nottingham | Space Ship | | 207 | 13 | Sir V Sassoon | N Murless | 1/25F |
| 14 Aug | Nottingham | Guinea | | 207 | 5 | Mrs D M Fitzpatrick | N Murless | 9/4 |
| 15 Aug | Salisbury | Kriss Kringle | | 207 | 6 | L Lipton | J Cligott | 9/2 |
| 15 Aug | Salisbury | Canardeau | | 336 | 7 | G Varnavas | H Price | 3/1 |
| 16 Aug | Salisbury | Melody Fair | | 207 | 10 | J Crow | R Sturdy | 6/4 |
| 17 Aug | Newbury | Blue Owen | | 386 | 6 | M Ostrer | K Piggott | 10/1 |
| 18 Aug | Newbury | Court Command | Oxfordshire Stks | 1,073 | 13 | T Lilley | N Murless | 5/2F |
| 20 Aug | Warwick | Couag | | 138 | 7 | Capt A S Wills | P Nelson | 7/4F |
| 23 Aug | York | Meldon | Convivial | 1,470 | 5 | Mrs J C B Cookson | P Beasley | 7/2 |
| 25 Aug | Worcester | Mr McTaffy | | 207 | 11 | T Holland-Martin | C Jerdein | 6/4F |
| 25 Aug | Worcester | Mardis | | 276 | 6 | F Parker | P Doherty | 11/8F |

(I) = Ireland

| Date | Race Course | Horse | Race | Value £ | Dist Fur | Owner | Trainer | S/P |
|---|---|---|---|---|---|---|---|---|
| 29 Aug | Brighton | Amber Glass | | 392 | 6 | Capt A S Wills | P Nelson | 7/4 |
| 29 Aug | Brighton | Space Ship | | 317 | 10 | Sir V Sassoon | N Murless | 6/100F |
| 30 Aug | Brighton | Abercorn | | 327 | 8 | Col B Hornung | N Murless | 11/10F |
| 31 Aug | Windsor | Sun Flight | | 276 | 5 | Mrs G G Lancaster | J Tree | 9/2 |
| 4 Sept | Lewes | Emporium | | 188 | 10 | A Hambury | C Hook | 3/1 |
| 4 Sept | Lewes | The Cobra | | 173 | 5 | P Bartholomew | F N Winter | 100/9 |
| 8 Sept | Salisbury | Nixon | | 366 | 10 | J R Mullion | P Nelson | 11/4 |
| 15 Sept | Sandown | Kandy Sauce | Atalanta Stks | 505 | 10 | Sir V Sassoon | N Murless | 5/4F |
| 19 Sept | Brighton | Meerschaum | | 315 | 10 | Sir V Sassoon | N Murless | 4/1 |
| 24 Sept | Windsor | Nixon | | 276 | 10 | J R Mullion | P Nelson | 1/3F |
| 25 Sept | Leicester | Keybag | | 277 | 5 | Capt A S Wills | P Nelson | 5/4F |
| 25 Sept | Leicester | Mainswitch | | 138 | 5 | Capt A S Wills | P Nelson | 11/2 |
| 29 Sept | Ascot | Miracle World | Kensington Palace Stks | 640 | 6 | C W Bell | W Nightingall | 7/1 |
| 2 Oct | Newmarket | Kandy Sauce | Old Rowley Stks | 779 | 8 | Sir V Sassoon | N Murless | 4/5F |
| 4 Oct | Newmarket | Maelstrom | | 232 | 8 | C W Bell | W Nightingall | 11/10F |
| 9 Oct | Nottingham | Golden Gittell | Cowley Park | 666 | 8 | M Kingsley | N Scobie | 13/8F |
| 11 Oct | York | Near Star | | 407 | 9 | R S Grierson | A Barclay | 9/2 |
| 13 Oct | Ascot | Tudor Jinks | | 483 | 8 | A J Tompsett | M Feakes | 9/2 |
| 15 Oct | Warwick | Robert's First | | 294 | 16 | M Sack | W Marshall | 8/1 |
| 17 Oct | Newmarket | Redress | | 259 | 6 | J U Baillie | A Kerr | 9/1 |
| 27 Oct | Doncaster | Coote Hill | | 196 | 18 | G A Gilbert | W Dutton | 7/1 |
| 27 Oct | Doncaster | My Pal | | 207 | 5 | G A Gilbert | W Dutton | 5/2F |
| 30 Oct | Nottingham | Pelican Peat | | 376 | 6 | N Hall | E Cousins | 100/8 |
| 30 Oct | Nottingham | Kandy Sauce | Limekiln Stks | 979 | 10 | Sir V Sassoon | N Murless | 7/4F |
| 1 Nov | Nottingham | Dewhurst | | 1,943 | 7 | Sir V Sassoon | N Murless | 1/2F |
| 3 Nov | Kempton | Keybag | Willow Stks | 511 | 5 | Capt A S Wills | P Nelson | 6/1 |
| 7 Nov | Birmingham | The Box | | 477 | 8 | J U Baillie | J A Waugh | 11/8F |
| 17 Nov | Manchester | Golden Gittell | Lancashire Nursery Hcp | 765 | 6 | M Kingsley | N Scobie | 9/2 |

1956: 129 wins; 79 2nds; 75 3rds; 642 rides

| Date | Race Course | Horse | Race | Value £ | Dist Fur | Owner | Trainer | S/P |
|---|---|---|---|---|---|---|---|---|
| 1957 | | | | | | | | |
| 8 Apl | Alex Palace | Barton Street | | 207 | 8 | J U Baillie | A Kerr | 9/4F |
| 11 Apl | Newmarket | Shearwater | Craven | 734 | 8 | Lt Col G Loder | N Murless | 10/1 |
| 13 Apl | Newbury | Sijui | Fred Darling | 1,207 | 7 | Sir V Sassoon | N Murless | 20/1 |
| 16 Apl | Wolver'ton | Dented Pride | | 207 | 5 | Mrs A J O'Donohoe | P Nelson | 9/2 |
| 16 Apl | Wolver'ton | Davidal | | 207 | 7 | J Collier | P Nelson | 4/5F |
| 25 Apl | Epsom | Carrozza | Princess Elizabeth Stks | 6,461 | 8 | The Queen | N Murless | 10/1 |
| 27 Apl | Sandown | Sun Charger | Royal | 1,727 | 10 | Col B Hornung | N Murless | 7/1 |
| 27 Apl | Sandown | King's Barn | Marcus Beresford Stks | 592 | 8 | Col B Hornung | N Murless | 4/1 |
| 30 Apl | Newmarket | Arctic Explorer | Hastings | 546 | 10 | Lt Col G Loder | N Murless | 13/8 |
| 1 May | Newmarket | Crepello | 2000 Guineas | 13,598 | 8 | Sir V Sassoon | N Murless | 7/2 |
| 4 May | Nottingham | Master of Boyden | | 207 | 5 | Mrs T C Claydon | H Leader | 8/13F |
| 15 May | Newmarket | Arctic Explorer | | 371 | 12 | Lt Col G Loder | N Murless | 6/5F |
| 15 May | Newmarket | Sun Charger | | 1,786 | 10 | Col B Hornung | N Murless | 11/4 |
| 18 May | Haydock | Baby Brother | | 490 | 5 | A Rose | W Dutton | 8/11F |
| 21 May | York | Jomarbet | | 398 | 6 | M Cowley | R Ward | 15/2 |
| 24 May | Manchester | Ouragain | | 207 | 5 | W G Brabin | W Dutton | 11/10F |
| 24 May | Manchester | Prairie Emblem | | 345 | 6 | F E White | W Dutton | 11/8F |
| 24 May | Manchester | My Gem | | 207 | 10 | Mrs G Miller Mundy | P Walwyn | 5/4F |
| 29 May | Lincoln | Caroli | | 138 | 6 | F E White | W Dutton | 13/8F |
| 30 May | Lincoln | Kellys Castle | | 138 | 5 | A Reese | W Dutton | 8/1 |
| 30 May | Lincoln | Pelican Peat | | 276 | 7 | O/trainer | N Hall | 4/1 |
| 5 June | Epsom | Crepello | The Derby | 18,659 | 12 | Sir V Sassoon | N Murless | 6/4F |
| 7 June | Epsom | Carrozza | The Oaks | 16,101 | 12 | The Queen | N Murless | 100/8 |

| Date | Race Course | Horse | Race | Value £ | Dist Fur | Owner | Trainer | S/P |
|---|---|---|---|---|---|---|---|---|
| 10 June | Birmingham | Dented Pride | | 207 | 5 | Mrs A J O'Donohoe | P Nelson | 2/5F |
| 11 June | Birmingham | Vigo | Festival Stks | 1,174 | 6 | T H Farr | W Dutton | EvF |
| 11 June | Birmingham | Cameo | | 276 | 5 | A G Samuel | P Walwyn | 11/8F |
| 12 June | Kempton | Mustapha | Princess Stks | 984 | | Miss H Jacobson | E Parker | 7/1 |
| 13 June | Manchester | North British | | 292 | 5 | E A Brown | R Ward | 4/6F |
| 13 June | Manchester | Right Boy | Beaufort Hcp | 692 | 5 | G A Gilbert | W Dutton | 11/4F |
| 14 June | Manchester | Mansbridge | Red Rose | 1,325 | 6 | Col B Hornung | N Murless | 5/1 |
| 15 June | Alex Palace | Addax | | 207 | 8 | Lord Howard de Warden | J A Waugh | 5/4F |
| 17 June | Leicester | Dented Pride | | 207 | 5 | Mrs A J O'Donohoe | P Nelson | 2/7F |
| 17 June | Royal Ascot | Abelia | Queen Mary Stks | 3,558 | 5 | Col B Hornung | N Murless | 11/2 |
| 20 June | Royal Ascot | Zarathustra | Ascot Gold Cup | 11,587 | 20 | T J S Gray | Sir C Boyd Rochfort | 6/1 |
| 20 June | Royal Ascot | Arctic Explorer | King Edward VII | 5,101 | 12 | Lt Col G Loder | N Murless | 6/1 |
| 21 June | Royal Ascot | Right Boy | King's Stand | 1,484 | 5 | G A Gilbert | W Dutton | 4/1 |
| 22 June | Ascot Heath | Flake White | Fenwolf | 725 | 6 | The Queen | N Murless | 9/4F |
| 25 June | Birmingham | Pelican Peat | | 276 | 7 | O/trainer | N Hall | 8/13F |
| 26 June | Newbury | Baby Flinders | Berkshire Foal Stks | 1,535 | 5 | Sir V Sassoon | N Murless | 15/8F |
| 26 June | Newbury | Street Singer | Empire Hcp | 840 | 6 | Maj J H Paine | P Walwyn | 4/1F |
| 27 June | Newbury | Starboard | | 276 | 6 | Sir B Mountain | P Nelson | 13/8F |
| 27 June | Newbury | Rue de Romance | Newbury Summer Cup | 1,026 | 12 | W G Turriff | G Todd | 4/1F |
| 27 June | Newbury | L'Amir II | | 442 | 13 | Sir B Mountain | P Nelson | 9/4 |
| 28 June | Newcastle | Satan's Slide | | 503 | 6 | Sir V Sassoon | N Murless | EvF |
| 28 June | Newcastle | Cornplaster | | 503 | 6 | J Hanson | D Gunn | 7/4F |
| 28 June | Newcastle | Impala | | 384 | 8 | The Queen | N Murless | 8/11F |
| 29 June | Newcastle | Pinched | Seaton Delaval | 2,360 | 5 | Sir V Sassoon | N Murless | 10/11F |
| 1 July | Brighton | Billy Muggins | | 425 | 6 | D Morris | C Pratt | 5/1 |
| 2 July | Brighton | Harbour Bar | | 373 | 10 | A G Samuel | P Walwyn | EvF |
| 3 July | Newmarket | Abelia | July Stks | 2,085 | 5 | Col B Hornung | N Murless | 1/2F |
| 4 July | Newmarket | Tudor Grand | | 320 | 7 | P Winstone | W Nightingall | 9/2 |
| 4 July | Newmarket | Baby Flinders | Plantation | 599 | 5 | Sir V Sassoon | N Murless | 2/7F |
| 4 July | Newmarket | Sylphide | | 428 | 7 | T Lilley | N Murless | 8/13F |
| 6 July | Newmarket | Sweet Angel | | 800 | 13 | Sir V Sassoon | N Murless | 11/2F |
| 6 July | Newmarket | Vigo | | 1,194 | 6 | T H Farr | W Dutton | 7/2 |
| 6 July | Newmarket | Hedonist | | 348 | 12 | F Sykes | P Nelson | 5/2 |
| 8 July | Alex Palace | Birthday Present | | 489 | 13 | Mrs D E Purvis | E Parker | 7/4F |
| 8 July | Nottingham | Skelbo Star | | 277 | 8 | Mrs R Grosvenor | P Walwyn | 3/1 |
| 12 July | Manchester | Dark Heron | Dockers Derby | 1,072 | 12 | G W Brown | W Dutton | 6/1 |
| 13 July | Sandown | Frogmorton | | 409 | 8 | Mrs G T S Houghton | P Walwyn | 9/1 |
| 13 July | Sandown | Arctic Explorer | Eclipse | 7,673 | 10 | Lt Col G Loder | N Murless | 10/3 |
| 15 July | Birmingham | Her Ladyship | | 276 | 10 | O/trainer | R Sturdy | 9/2 |
| 15 July | Birmingham | Pierian Springs | | 276 | 8 | Mrs V G Cardy | F Walwyn | 5/2F |
| 17 July | Newmarket | Sylphide | Falmouth | 1,357 | 8 | T Lilley | N Murless | 11/2 |
| 17 July | Newmarket | Light Harvest | | 304 | 6 | Lt Col D Forster | J A Waugh | 13/8 |
| 19 July | Doncaster | Skish | | 207 | 18 | J Westoll | G Barling | 11/4F |
| 19 July | Doncaster | Cornplaster | Red House | 930 | 5 | J Hanson | D Gunn | 10/11F |
| 22 July | Leicester | Rose Bag | | 207 | 5 | Capt A S Wills | P Nelson | 10/11F |
| 22 July | Leicester | Skelbo | Star | 262 | 8 | Mrs R Grosvenor | P Walwyn | 1/2F |
| 22 July | Leicester | Game Star | | 207 | 8 | Mrs T Baron | J C Waugh | 13/2 |
| 23 July | Folkestone | Harbour Bar | | 138 | 12 | A G Samuel | P Walwyn | 10/11F |
| 24 July | Windsor | Golden Gittell | | 276 | 6 | M Kingsley | K Piggott | 5/1 |
| 29 July | Alex Palace | Oedipus | | 336 | 13 | Miss M L Pinder | P Walwyn | 6/1 |
| 30 July | Goodwood | Abelia | Molecomb | 2,974 | 5 | Col B Hornung | N Murless | 1/5F |
| 2 Aug | Goodwood | Rue De Romance | Trundle | 1,362 | 11 | W G Turriff | G Todd | 11/10F |
| 3 Aug | Epsom | Street Singer | Diomed Hcp | 727 | 7 | Major J H Paine | P Walwyn | 5/4F |
| 3 Aug | Epsom | Arabesque | | 356 | 12 | Sir V Sassoon | R Swash | 11/4F |
| 6 Aug | Brighton | Boccaccio | | 407 | 6 | Sir V Sassoon | N Murless | 4/5F |
| 8 Aug | Brighton | Candytuft | | 470 | 5 | The Queen | N Murless | 6/1 |

| Date | Race Course | Horse | Race | Value £ | Dist Fur | Owner | Trainer | S/P |
|---|---|---|---|---|---|---|---|---|
| 9 Aug | Newmarket | Stoneborer | | 476 | 8 | Sir V Sassoon | N Murless | 7/4F |
| 10 Aug | Redcar | Vigo | Redcar Hcp | 1,185 | 6 | T H Farr | W Dutton | 8/11F |
| 10 Aug | Redcar | Sunsque | | 345 | 6 | Mrs R D Peacock | R Peacock | 10/11F |
| 12 Aug | Folkestone | Spinosa | | 207 | 10 | Lord Sefton | P Hastings-Bass | 2/1 |
| 14 Aug | Haydock | So-Long-Boy | | 392 | 8 | H E Jones | R Ward | 7/1 |
| 14 Aug | Haydock | Arcandy | Cavalier Hcp | 1,170 | 6 | Mrs M V Linde | G Beeby | 6/4F |
| 15 Aug | Sandown | Court Command | | 510 | 13 | Mrs V Lilley | N Murless | 4/5F |
| 16 Aug | Newbury | Meissa | St Hugh's Stks | 696 | 5 | T Roberts | A Budgett | 3/1 |
| 17 Aug | Stockton | Roman Nose | | 297 | 6 | Sir V Sassoon | N Murless | 10/11F |
| 19 Aug | Warwick | Billy Muggins | Little Breeders Stks | 577 | 5 | D Morris | C Pratt | 6/4F |
| 23 Aug | Newmarket | Risborough | | 290 | 8 | Sir V Sassoon | N Murless | 9/4 |
| 27 Aug | Folkestone | Stunning | | 173 | 6 | Mrs M Hutchison | C Jerdein | 4/6F |
| 28 Aug | Brighton | Angel Baby | | 463 | 6 | Mrs V Lilley | N Murless | 7/2 |
| 29 Aug | Brighton | Madam Recorder | | 439 | 5 | C Steuart | N Murless | 4/6F |
| 29 Aug | Brighton | Prince Moon | August Hcp | 943 | 12 | Sir V Sassoon | N Murless | 9/1 |
| 3 Sept | Birmingham | Candytuft | | 276 | 6 | The Queen | N Murless | EvF |
| 4 Sept | Bath | Nile King | | 541 | 5 | H S Persse | C Jerdein | 2/1F |
| 6 Sept | Manchester | Stoneborer | | 534 | 8 | Sir V Sassoon | N Murless | 6/1 |
| 7 Sept | Kempton | Queen's Bench | | 577 | 5 | P Hatvany | F Cundell | 10/3F |
| 7 Sept | Kempton | Satan's Slide | | 677 | 8 | Sir V Sassoon | N Murless | 7/1 |
| 9 Sept | Warwick | Hortensio | | 207 | 7 | O/trainer | T Yates | 3/1 |
| 10 Sept | Doncaster | Golden Gittell | Fitzwilliam Stks | 656 | 6 | M Kingsley | K Piggott | EvF |
| 18 Sept | Yarmouth | Strung-Up | | 1,974 | 5 | Sir V Sassoon | N Murless | 9/4 |
| 20 Sept | Kempton | Barton Street | Hayden S Stks | 591 | 12 | J U Baillie | A Kerr | 6/4F |
| 21 Sept | Kempton | Pin-Wheel | Imperial Produce Stks | 6,931 | 6 | Sir V Sassoon | N Murless | 6/1 |
| 23 Sept | Windsor | Mother Goose | | 276 | 5 | E Littler | W Nightingall | 8/1 |
| 24 Sept | Windsor | Nile King | | 138 | 6 | H S Persse | C Jerdein | 5/2F |
| 24 Sept | Windsor | Holiday Time | | 276 | 5 | Sir W Churchill | W Nightingall | 5/2F |
| 24 Sept | Windsor | Amber Glass | | 233 | 8 | H S Lester | G Todd | 7/4 |
| 26 Sept | Ascot | Barleycroft | Clarence House | 678 | 6 | Col B Hornung | N Murless | 8/1 |
| 27 Sept | Ascot | Pinched | Royal Lodge | 3,840 | 8 | Sir V Sassoon | N Murless | EvF |
| 28 Sept | Ascot | Brilliant Stone | Blue Seal | 1,565 | 6 | Lt Col R Taylor | N Murless | 7/4F |
| 5 Oct | Newbury | Boccaccio | Autumn Foal Stks | 1,997 | 6 | Sir V Sassoon | N Murless | 11/10F |
| 12 Oct | Ascot | Abelia | Cornwallis | 1,578 | 5 | Col B Hornung | N Murless | 5/4F |
| 14 Oct | Warwick | Militaire II | | 285 | 10 | H R Hobson | C Jerdein | 11/4 |
| 15 Oct | Newmarket | Cheetah | | 345 | 10 | O/trainer | N Murless | 9/4F |
| 15 Oct | Newmarket | Cameo | | 309 | 5 | A G Samuel | P Walwyn | 7/2 |
| 17 Oct | Newmarket | Meissa | | 358 | 5 | T Roberts | A Budgett | 10/1 |
| 26 Oct | Doncaster | Rockaline | | 452 | 12 | S S Niarchos | H Leader | 5/2F |
| 30 Oct | Newmarket | Snow Cat | | 327 | 7 | The Queen | N Murless | 10/1 |
| 30 Oct | Newmarket | Melody Fair | | 275 | 8 | J Crow | R Sturdy | 5/2 |
| 9 Nov | Windsor | Mother Goose | | 345 | 6 | E Littler | W Nightingall | 3/1 |
| 9 Nov | Windsor | Truecode | | 438 | 10 | Mrs C Evans | K Cundell | 9/4F |

1957: 122 wins; 92 2nds; 83 3rds; 577 rides

1958

| Date | Race Course | Horse | Race | Value £ | Dist Fur | Owner | Trainer | S/P |
|---|---|---|---|---|---|---|---|---|
| 31 Mar | Nottingham | Scargill | | 296 | 7 | B W Grainger | W Dutton | 8/1 |
| 7 Apl | Kempton | Mother Goose | 1000 Guineas Trial Stks | 1,294 | 7 | E Littler | W Nightingall | 4/7F |
| 15 Apl | Newmarket | Loyal Lady | | 426 | 5 | O/trainer | T Carey | 100/7 |
| 16 Apl | Newmarket | Primera | | 285 | 12 | C H Dracoulis | N Murless | 7/4 |
| 17 Apl | Newmarket | Basaltic | | 254 | 5 | D Deyong | H Leader | 11/8F |
| 24 Apl | Epsom | Morin | Epsom Hcp | 754 | 5 | S Wootton | J Sirett | 7/2 |
| 26 Apl | Sandown | Arctic Explorer | Coronation Stks | 984 | 10 | Lt Col G Loder | N Murless | 11/4 |
| 26 Apl | Sandown | Snow Cat | Royal Stks | 1,744 | 10 | The Queen | N Murless | 11/2 |
| 5 May | Nottingham | Scargill | | 296 | 8 | B W Grainger | W Dutton | 4/9F |

| Date | Race Course | Horse | Race | Value £ | Dist Fur | Owner | Trainer | S/P |
|---|---|---|---|---|---|---|---|---|
| 6 May | Chester | Prince Moon | Great Cheshire Hcp | 976 | 10 | Sir V Sassoon | N Murless | EvF |
| 7 May | Chester | Sandiacre | Chester Cup | 2,556 | 18 | M Cowley | W Dutton | 15/2 |
| 7 May | Chester | Lawrence | | 488 | 5 | J Ismay | D Rogers (I) | 5/2F |
| 8 May | Chester | Primera | Eaton Hcp | 757 | 12 | G H Dracoulis | N Murless | 11/8F |
| 12 May | Birmingham | Rose's Reject | | 276 | 6 | G A Gilbert | W Dutton | 6/5F |
| 14 May | Newmarket | Cameo | | 303 | 5 | A G Samuel | P Walwyn | 3/1F |
| 23 May | Sandown | Loyal Lady | | 414 | 5 | T R Carey | T Carey | 3/1 |
| 24 May | Sandown | Abelia | Alington | 1,184 | 5 | Col B Hornung | N Murless | 3/1 |
| 27 May | Hurst Park | Noeboi | | 276 | 5 | M Ostrer | K Piggott | 7/4F |
| 3 June | Epsom | Master Sands | Ashtead Stks | 650 | 7 | H K Henly | F Walwyn | 10/1 |
| 4 June | Epsom | Pinched | St James's Stks | 2,431 | 8 | Sir V Sassoon | N Murless | 4/6F |
| 10 June | Nottingham | Two Tails | | 284 | 5 | A Rose | W Dutton | 6/1 |
| 11 June | Brighton | The Tuscar | | 1,005 | 12 | J Lewis | T Carey | 5/1 |
| 12 June | Brighton | Illinois | Brighthelmstone | 1,052 | 10 | C F Hughesdon | P Nelson | 100/6 |
| 13 June | Lincoln | Last Order | | 207 | 5 | F E White | W Dutton | 4/1 |
| 13 June | Lincoln | Melody Fair | | 276 | 10 | J Crow | R Sturdy | 9/2F |
| 19 June | Royal Ascot | Right Boy | Cork & Orrery | 1,668 | 6 | G A Gilbert | W Dutton | 5/6F |
| 19 June | Royal Ascot | Gladness | Ascot Gold Cup | 10,950 | 20 | J McShain | M V O'Brien(I) | 3/1F |
| 20 June | Royal Ascot | Carnoustie | Windsor Castle | 2,071 | 5 | Lt Col G Loder | N Murless | 25/1 |
| 21 June | Ascot Heath | Primera | Churchill | 1,369 | 12 | G H Dracoulis | N Murless | 10/11F |
| 25 June | Newbury | Flash Past | | 366 | 8 | Mrs G Trimmer-Thompson | K Cundell | 13/2 |
| 27 June | Doncaster | Ten Time | | 193 | 6 | Mrs B Marshall | B Marshall | 8/11F |
| 27 June | Doncaster | Briar Close | | 207 | 5 | Lady Boyle | W Dutton | 11/2 |
| 28 June | Newcastle | Scargill | | 362 | 9 | B W Grainger | W Dutton | 9/2 |
| 2 July | Liverpool | Arctic's Ration | | 390 | 13 | J Bullock | S Hall | 15/8F |
| 2 July | Liverpool | Burtonwood | | 300 | 5 | A Monk | W Dutton | 4/9F |
| 3 July | Liverpool | Houndstooth | | 207 | 5 | Mrs E Goldson | W Dutton | 10/11F |
| 3 July | Liverpool | Miss McTaffy | | 336 | 13 | T Holland-Martin | P Walwyn | 4/9F |
| 4 July | Warwick | Signal Boy | | 294 | 5 | A Bott | R Ward | 13/8F |
| 5 July | Newmarket | Right Boy | July Cup | 1,177 | 6 | G A Gilbert | W Dutton | 4/5F |
| 8 July | Nottingham | Rhythmic | Dukeries Hcp | 690 | 6 | Maj A C Straker | W Dutton | 3/1 |
| 9 July | Salisbury | Obvious Answer | | 435 | 5 | H D H Wills | P Walwyn | 7/2 |
| 10 July | Doncaster | Euphorbia | | 207 | 5 | Lord Feversham | W Dutton | 2/7F |
| 12 July | Sandown | Petite Etoile | Star Stks | 630 | 5 | Prince Aly Khan | N Murless | 7/2 |
| 15 July | Newmarket | Dame Melba | | 339 | 6 | T Lilley | N Murless | 8/1 |
| 19 July | Ascot | Parrotia | Princess Margaret | 993 | 5 | Lt Col G Loder | N Murless | 8/15F |
| 21 July | Leicester | Hindu Slipper | | 207 | 5 | F Slater | F Walwyn | 4/1 |
| 28 July | Birmingham | Clear Evidence | | 188 | 5 | J A Sutton | F Walwyn | 5/2 |
| 29 July | Goodwood | Firestreak | New Ham Flat Stks | 2,561 | 6 | J Lewis | T Carey | 2/1F |
| 30 July | Goodwood | Right Boy | King George Stks | 1,038 | 5 | G A Gilbert | W Dutton | 8/13F |
| 31 July | Goodwood | Carnoustie | Rous Memorial Stks | 1,207 | 6 | Lt Col G Loder | N Murless | 6/1 |
| 31 July | Goodwood | Gladness | Goodwood Cup | 3,413 | 16 | J McShain | M V O'Brien(I) | 1/2F |
| 2 Aug | Epsom | Rose Pale | | 336 | 5 | Prince Aly Khan | N Murless | 4/1 |
| 4 Aug | Epsom | Prince Moon | | 525 | 12 | Sir V Sassoon | N Murless | 1/5F |
| 5 Aug | Brighton | Halfway House | | 529 | 5 | Mrs E D Benson | H Price | 7/1 |
| 6 Aug | Brighton | Salute | | 514 | 8 | J A Luke | H Price | 7/2 |
| 7 Aug | Brighton | Soliptic | | 551 | 12 | Col B Hornung | N Murless | EvF |
| 7 Aug | Brighton | Persian Water | | 502 | 8 | The Queen | N Murless | 2/9F |
| 8 Aug | Redcar | Spice | | 485 | 5 | G A Gilbert | W Dutton | 11/10F |
| 8 Aug | Redcar | Jomarbet | | 308 | 6 | M Cowley | W Dutton | 4/1F |
| 11 Aug | Nottingham | Games | | 296 | 5 | A G Samuel | P Walwyn | 5/4F |
| 13 Aug | Sandown | High Fidelity | | 287 | 8 | E J Parker | E Parker | 2/1F |
| 13 Aug | Sandown | Petite Etoile | | 523 | 5 | Prince Aly Khan | N Murless | 1/6F |
| 14 Aug | Sandown | Miss McTaffy | | 301 | 13 | T Holland-Martin | P Walwyn | 2/11F |
| 15 Aug | Newbury | Short Sentence | St Hugh's | 1,221 | 5 | The Queen | N Murless | 9/4F |

(I) = Ireland

| Date | Race Course | Horse | Race | Value £ | Dist Fur | Owner | Trainer | S/P |
|---|---|---|---|---|---|---|---|---|
| 18 Aug | Warwick | Clear Evidence | | 294 | 5 | J A Sutton | F Walwyn | 2/7F |
| 19 Aug | York | Right Boy | Nunthorpe | 1,600 | 5 | G A Gilbert | W Dutton | 8/100F |
| 20 Aug | York | Gladness | Ebor | 10,214 | 14 | J McShain | M V O'Brien(I) | 5/1F |
| 25 Aug | Worcester | My Pal | | 361 | 8 | G A Gilbert | W Dutton | 4/1 |
| 25 Aug | Worcester | Honey Parrot | | 207 | 12 | T Holland-Martin | P Walwyn | 5/1 |
| 29 Aug | Windsor | Rare Quality | | 345 | 6 | H D H Wills | P Walwyn | 11/2 |
| 29 Aug | Windsor | Frederique II | | 345 | 8 | O/trainer | W Nightingall | 10/3 |
| 1 Sept | Birmingham | Valiant Effort | | 276 | 5 | H D H Wills | P Walwyn | 13/2 |
| 2 Sept | Birmingham | Right Boy | | 494 | 6 | G A Gilbert | W Dutton | 2/5F |
| 13 Sept | Sandown | Pindari | Solario | 1,952 | 7 | The Queen | N Murless | 20/1 |
| 15 Sept | Wolver'ton | Painters Green | | 188 | 7 | Sir E Hanmer | W Dutton | 3/1 |
| 18 Sept | Brighton | High Fidelity | | 519 | 8 | O/trainer | E Parker | 4/1F |
| 23 Sept | Windsor | Pine Tree | | 276 | 6 | Sir V Sassoon | N Murless | 2/1F |
| 29 Sept | Birmingham | Plead | | 188 | 6 | A G Samuel | P Walwyn | 13/8 |
| 2 Oct | Haydock | Tropicana | | 207 | 8 | G A Oldham | H Wragg | 4/1 |
| 4 Oct | Newbury | Donna | | 840 | 5 | Lord Rosebery | J Sirett | 8/1 |
| 6 Oct | Nottingham | My Pal | | 356 | 8 | G A Gilbert | W Dutton | 5/1 |
| 9 Oct | Liverpool | Plead | | 294 | 6 | A G Samuel | P Walwyn | EvF |
| 7 Nov | Liverpool | Who You | | 207 | 6 | J McLean Jnr | J Fawcus | 7/1 |

1958: 83 wins; 81 2nds; 64 3rds; 537 rides

| Date | Race Course | Horse | Race | Value £ | Dist Fur | Owner | Trainer | S/P |
|---|---|---|---|---|---|---|---|---|
| 1959 | | | | | | | | |
| 28 Mar | Kempton | Gentiana | Princess Royal | 683 | 5 | Mrs G Davis | T Carey | 11/2 |
| 28 Mar | Kempton | Frasco | | 538 | 11 | Miss M L Pinder | P Walwyn | 5/1 |
| 10 Apl | Hurst Park | Miss McTaffy | | 390 | 15 | T Holland-Martin | P Walwyn | 5/1 |
| 13 Apl | Alex Palace | Top Lady | | 276 | 5 | O/trainer | T Carey | 5/1 |
| 14 Apl | Newmarket | Pindari | Craven | 758 | 8 | The Queen | N Murless | 6/1 |
| 16 Apl | Newmarket | Pinicola | | 342 | 7 | C Steuart | N Murless | 100/8 |
| 19 Apl | Thirsk | Carnoustie | Classic Trial | 1,164 | 8 | Lt Col G Loder | N Murless | 7/4F |
| 21 Apl | Epsom | Miss McTaffy | Great Metropolitan | 1,515 | 18 | T Holland-Martin | P Walwyn | 10/1 |
| 22 Apl | Epsom | Frasco | | 456 | 12 | Miss M L Pinder | P Walwyn | 7/4F |
| 23 Apl | Epsom | Magic Moment | | 509 | 7 | Mrs J Benskin | A Budgett | 7/4F |
| 23 Apl | Epsom | Rose of Medina | Princess Elizabeth | 5,806 | 8 | J R Hindley | N Murless | 5/12 |
| 4 May | Nottingham | Jacintha | | 207 | 6 | M Russell | T Corbett | 5/2 |
| 4 May | Nottingham | Clarendon Pete | | 296 | 8 | K O Boardman | P Rohan | 13/2 |
| 5 May | Chester | Boccaccio | Great Cheshire Hcp | 1,024 | 10 | Sir V Sassoon | N Murless | 4/1F |
| 5 May | Chester | Golden Light | Prince of Wales Stks | 1,074 | 5 | Mrs F Williams | P Walwyn | 7/1 |
| 7 May | Chester | Primera | Ormonde | 2,346 | 13 | C H Dracoulis | N Murless | 11/8F |
| 8 May | Kempton | Blackbeard | | 553 | 11 | Sir V Sassoon | N Murless | 100/7 |
| 11 May | Wolver'ton | Scargill | | 268 | 8 | B D Grainger | P Rohan | 11/4F |
| 12 May | Wolver'ton | Dark Heron | | 276 | 16 | E W Brown | P Rohan | 9/4 |
| 13 May | Newmarket | Collyria | Haverhill | 631 | 9 | Sir V Sassoon | N Murless | 11/10F |
| 18 May | Hurst Park | Dance Time | | 598 | 5 | Prince Aly Khan | N Murless | 6/1 |
| 19 May | Hurst Park | Dona Ana | | 699 | 10 | Col B Hornung | N Murless | 100/6 |
| 21 May | Manchester | White House | | 207 | 12 | The Queen | N Murless | 8/13F |
| 22 May | Manchester | My Pal | Isonomy Hcp | 1,030 | 8 | G A Gilbert | P Rohan | 6/1 |
| 23 May | Manchester | Open Sky | | 578 | 11 | T Lilley | N Murless | 7/2 |
| 25 May | Alex Palace | Game Lady | | 207 | 5 | Mrs G Miller | P Walwyn | 7/2 |
| 26 May | York | Bleep | | 559 | 9 | Sir V Sassoon | N Murless | 10/3 |
| 26 May | York | Tin Whistle | Knavesmire | 604 | 5 | B W Grainger | P Rohan | 3/1F |
| 28 May | York | Kelso Queen | | 503 | 5 | W Beswick | R Ward | 15/2 |
| 30 May | Newbury | Dame Melba | Sandeford Priory | 1,133 | 10 | T Lilley | N Murless | 2/1F |
| 4 June | Epsom | Nagamm | Coronation Cup | 3,265 | 12 | Mrs A Plesch | H Wragg | 5/4 |
| 5 June | Epsom | Petite Etoile | The Oaks | 21,135 | 12 | Prince Aly Khan | N Murless | 11/2 |
| 6 June | Kempton | Beau Court | River Mead Stks | 779 | 6 | T Lilley | N Murless | 100/8 |

(I) = Ireland

| Date | Race Course | Horse | Race | Value £ | Dist Fur | Owner | Trainer | S/P |
|---|---|---|---|---|---|---|---|---|
| 10 June | Brighton | Sheesmine | | 475 | 8 | M Ostrer | K Piggott | 1/3F |
| 12 June | Birmingham | Plead | | 257 | 8 | A G Samuel | P Walwyn | 8/13F |
| 12 June | Birmingham | College Queen | | 307 | 13 | B Samuel | P Walwyn | 6/4 |
| 13 June | Birmingham | Time and Chance | | 276 | 6 | H L L Morriss | P Walwyn | 4/1 |
| 13 June | Birmingham | The Golden Age | | 345 | 6 | Capt H Price | B Marshall | 3/1 |
| 18 June | Royal Ascot | Right Boy | Cork and Orrery | 1,740 | 6 | G A Gilbert | P Rohan | 11/4 |
| 18 June | Royal Ascot | Pindari | King Edward VII | 5,237 | 12 | The Queen | N Murless | 13/8F |
| 22 June | Birmingham | Motorist | | 276 | 10 | C Nicholson | P Walwyn | 2/1F |
| 23 June | Birmingham | Clarendon Pete | | 276 | 7 | K O Boardman | P Rohan | 11/10F |
| 24 June | Newbury | The Welshman | Foxhill Hcp | 1,120 | 10 | Mrs F Williams | P Walwyn | 7/1 |
| 26 June | Doncaster | Miss Phoebe | | 193 | 6 | E A Brown | R Ward | 9/4 |
| 26 June | Doncaster | Inga | | 207 | 5 | Mrs N Murless | N Murless | 30/100F |
| 26 June | Doncaster | Gaymoss | | 540 | 12 | R A Smith | S Hall | EvF |
| 26 June | Doncaster | Dover | | 438 | 8 | Lt Col H L V Beddington | P Rohan | 9/4 |
| 27 June | Newcastle | Tin Whistle | Seaton Delaval | 1,805 | 5 | B Grainger | P Rohan | 4/9F |
| 29 June | Wolver'ton | Clarendon Boy | | 276 | 11 | K O Boardman | P Rohan | 4/6F |
| 1 July | Liverpool | Poynton Lass | | 246 | 5 | A Bernie | R Ward | 4/9F |
| 3 July | Newmarket | Primera | Princess of Wales | 2,588 | 12 | C H Dracoulis | N Murless | 4/5F |
| 4 July | Newmarket | Right Boy | July Cup | 1,930 | 6 | G. Gilbert | P Rohan | 11/10F |
| 6 July | Nottingham | Brandy Sauce | | 326 | 5 | R G Johnson | P Rohan | 1/2F |
| 6 July | Lewes | Motorist | | 207 | 10 | G Nicholson | P Walwyn | 2/5F |
| 6 July | Nottingham | Clarendon Pete | | 444 | 8 | K O Boardman | P Rohan | 7/4F |
| 7 July | Nottingham | Brother Stephen | | 207 | 5 | Mrs E M R Dutton | P Rohan | 5/4F |
| 7 July | Nottingham | Chanticleer | | 266 | 5 | A Bernie | R Ward | EvF |
| 9 July | Salisbury | Firestreak | | 425 | 6 | J Lewis | P Nelson | 7/100F |
| 10 July | Sandown | High Fidelity | | 475 | 7 | O/trainer | E Parker | 3/1 |
| 11 July | Sandown | Motorist | | 475 | 10 | G Nicholson | P Walwyn | 5/6F |
| 13 July | Alex Palace | Legal Star | | 207 | 5 | Mrs R Grosvenor | P Walwyn | 5/4F |
| 15 July | Doncaster | Poynton Lass | | 391 | 5 | A Bernie | R Ward | 4/9F |
| 15 July | Doncaster | Inga | Red House | 863 | 5 | Mrs N Murless | N Murless | 4/11F |
| 15 July | Doncaster | Plead | | 207 | 8 | A G Samuel | P Walwyn | 11/4 |
| 16 July | Doncaster | Lucky Stream | | 291 | 11 | J R Hindley | N Murless | 1/2F |
| 17 July | Ascot | Sandiacre | Brown Jack | 1,124 | 22 | M Cowley | P Rohan | 7/2F |
| 20 July | Nottingham | Dover | | 207 | 8 | Lt Col H L V Beddington | P Rohan | 3/1 |
| 22 July | Kempton | Nero's Love | | 530 | 7 | G P Graham | K Cundell | 3/1 |
| 24 July | Hurst Park | Grasp | | 765 | 8 | C Nicholson | P Walwyn | 1/3F |
| 25 July | Hurst Park | Lucky Stream | Virginia | 549 | 10 | J R Hindley | N Murless | 15/8F |
| 28 July | Goodwood | Primera | Bentinck | 1,102 | 14 | S Joel | N Murless | 4/6F |
| 28 July | Goodwood | Court Prince | Charlton | 1,124 | 8 | T Lilley | N Murless | 8/1 |
| 29 July | Goodwood | Petite Etoile | Sussex | 2,730 | 8 | Prince Aly Khan | N Murless | 1/10F |
| 29 July | Goodwood | Right Boy | King George Stks | 1,119 | 5 | G A Gilbert | P Rohan | 8/13F |
| 30 July | Goodwood | Enticement | Lavant | 587 | 5 | Lord Norrie | P Walwyn | 13/8 |
| 1 Aug | Thirsk | Poynton Lass | | 292 | 5 | A Bernie | R Ward | 8/11F |
| 1 Aug | Thirsk | Daybrook Lad | | 345 | 16 | A H Rostance | D Gunn | 11/10F |
| 3 Aug | Chepstow | Pacifico | | 515 | 6 | G C Vandervell | J A Waugh | 3/1 |
| 3 Aug | Chepstow | Grasp | | 369 | 6 | C Nicholson | P Walwyn | 1/7F |
| 3 Aug | Chepstow | Scampette | | 207 | 8 | Mrs H H Renshaw | A Budgett | 2/5F |
| 4 Aug | Ripon | Sherwood | | 291 | 6 | A H Rostance | D Gunn | 9/2 |
| 5 Aug | Brighton | Illinois | Brighton Cup | 1,969 | 12 | F Sykes | P Payne-Gallwey | 7/1 |
| 5 Aug | Brighton | Astrador | | 558 | 6 | Mrs V Lilley | N Murless | 2/1F |
| 6 Aug | Brighton | Mead | | 574 | 5 | Miss F M Prior | W Wightman | 5/1 |
| 6 Aug | Brighton | Pure Pitch | | 519 | 8 | Sir V Sassoon | N Murless | EvF |
| 7 Aug | Newmarket | Saucy Queen | | 472 | 8 | Sir V Sassoon | N Murless | 10/1 |
| 10 Aug | Nottingham | Clarendon Pete | | 296 | 8 | K O Boardman | P Rohan | EvF |
| 12 Aug | Sandown | Ticklish | | 307 | 16 | C W Engelhard | P Walwyn | 15/8 |
| 13 Aug | Sandown | Dambuster | | 303 | 8 | O/trainer | E Parker | 5/1 |

| Date | Race Course | Horse | Race | Value £ | Dist Fur | Owner | Trainer | S/P |
|---|---|---|---|---|---|---|---|---|
| 14 Aug | Newbury | Sleipner | | 361 | 12 | Sir V Sassoon | N Murless | 5/1 |
| 14 Aug | Newbury | Nero's Love | | 840 | 8 | G P Graham | F Cundell | 11/2 |
| 15 Aug | Newbury | Carpaccio | | 420 | 6 | T Holland-Martin | P Walwyn | 7/1 |
| 15 Aug | Newbury | Astrador | Washington Singer | 1,102 | 6 | Mrs V Lilley | N Murless | 4/1 |
| 17 Aug | Warwick | Plead | | 207 | 8 | A G Samuel | P Walwyn | 3/1 |
| 17 Aug | Warwick | Jacintha | | 207 | 7 | M Russell | T Corbett | 13/8F |
| 18 Aug | York | Petite Etoile | Yorkshire Oaks | 1,176 | 5 | Prince Aly Khan | N Murless | 2/15F |
| 18 Aug | York | Right Boy | Nunthorpe | 2,207 | 5 | H D Wills | P Rohan | 4/9F |
| 19 Aug | York | Primera | Ebor | 10,093 | 14 | S Joel | N Murless | 6/1 |
| 19 Aug | York | Pindari | Great Voltigeur | 10,508 | 12 | The Queen | N Murless | 11/10F |
| 22 Aug | Newmarket | Red Pins | | 352 | 12 | Sir V Sassoon | N Murless | 7/4F |
| 25 Aug | Folkestone | Legal Star | | 206 | 5 | Mrs R Grosvenor | P Walwyn | 10/11F |
| 26 Aug | Brighton | Short Sentence | Preston Park Hcp | 910 | 7 | The Queen | N Murless | 2/1F |
| 26 Aug | Brighton | Red Pins | | 497 | 12 | Sir V Sassoon | N Murless | 11/10F |
| 26 Aug | Brighton | Mandolina | | 542 | 6 | T Lilley | N Murless | 1/4F |
| 27 Aug | Brighton | Illinois | August Hcp | 932 | 12 | F Sykes | P Payne-Gallwey | 7/4F |
| 28 Aug | Windsor | Saucy Queen | | 345 | 12 | Sir V Sassoon | N Murless | 4/1F |
| 29 Aug | Windsor | Astrador | Star & Garter Pl | 690 | 6 | Mrs V Lilley | N Murless | 8/13F |
| 1 Sept | Birmingham | Keryl | | 276 | 6 | Lord Fairhaven | R Jarvis | 10/3 |
| 5 Sept | Hurst Park | Saint Anne | | 390 | 6 | A G Samuel | P Walwyn | 3/1 |
| 7 Sept | Windsor | Open Sky | | 345 | 10 | T Lilley | N Murless | 2/1 |
| 11 Sept | Doncaster | Jacintha | Corporation S Hcp | 1,153 | 6 | M Russell | T Corbett | 7/2F |
| 14 Sept | Wolver'ton | Overtown | | 207 | 11 | A G Samuel | P Walwyn | 9/4 |
| 17 Sept | Ayr | Court Prince | Tote Investors | 2,253 | 10 | T Lilley | N Murless | 15/8F |
| 18 Sept | Kempton | Red Pins | | 556 | 12 | Sir V Sassoon | N Murless | 10/3F |
| 18 Sept | Kempton | Astrador | | 524 | 6 | Mrs V Lilley | N Murless | 6/4F |
| 18 Sept | Kempton | Alice Delysia | | 511 | 11 | A Butt | P Walwyn | 9/4 |
| 21 Sept | Edinburgh | Illinois | Edinburgh Gold Cup | 828 | 12 | M F Sykes | P Payne-Gallwey | 10/11F |
| 24 Sept | Ascot | Whipsnade | Marlborough House Stks | 1,068 | 8 | J A Sutton | N Murless | 4/1 |
| 25 Sept | Ascot | Rose of Medina | Princess Royal | 2,398 | 12 | J R Hindley | N Murless | 8/13F |
| 25 Sept | Ascot | St Paddy | Royal Lodge | 3,082 | 8 | Sir V Sassoon | N Murless | 11/4F |
| 26 Sept | Ascot | High Ditch | Blue Seal | 2,355 | 6 | Lt Col G Loder | N Murless | 9/1 |
| 28 Sept | Birmingham | Koga | | 276 | 5 | Mrs C W Gordon | A Budgett | 4/9F |
| 30 Sept | Newmarket | Pacifico | | 921 | 6 | G C Vandervell | J A Waugh | 100/7 |
| 1 Oct | Newmarket | Court Prince | Jockey Club Stks | 4,431 | 14 | T Lilley | N Murless | 10/3 |
| 2 Oct | Newbury | Boccaccio | Falkland Hcp | 699 | 10 | Sir V Sassoon | N Murless | 3/1F |
| 2 Oct | Newbury | Banyan | | 371 | 8 | Mrs A Plesch | H Wragg | 7/1 |
| 5 Oct | Nottingham | High Fidelity | | 351 | 8 | O/trainer | E Parker | 4/5F |
| 7 Oct | York | Laminate | Malton | 646 | 5 | Sir V Sassoon | N Murless | EvF |
| 9 Oct | Ascot | All Honesty | Sandwich | 1,211 | 6 | H D H Wills | P Walwyn | 5/4F |
| 9 Oct | Ascot | Sleipner | | 523 | 16 | C Carlow | N Murless | 11/4F |
| 10 Oct | Warwick | Schatzi | | 207 | 10 | S L Green | W Payne | 8/1 |
| 10 Oct | Warwick | Barbary Pirate | | 207 | 8 | Miss B Cavendish-Bentinck | R Sturdy | 5/4F |
| 16 Oct | Newmarket | Saucy Queen | Southfield Hcp | 600 | 14 | Sir V Sassoon | N Murless | 10/3 |
| 17 Oct | Newmarket | Petite Etoile | Champion | 10,406 | 10 | Prince Aly Khan | N Murless | 2/11F |
| 17 Oct | Newmarket | Keryl† | Histon Stks | 687 | 7 | Lord Fairhaven | R Jarvis | |
| 20 Oct | Wolver'ton | Honey Lamb | | 207 | 11 | A Kennedy | P Walwyn | 9/4 |
| 22 Oct | Newbury | Ides of March | | 420 | 6 | M P Davis | R Jarvis | 10/3F |
| 24 Oct | Doncaster | Silver King | | 207 | 6 | J Phang | S Hall | 2/1F |
| 24 Oct | Doncaster | Red Pins | Irwin Hcp | 1,226 | 12 | Sir V Sassoon | N Murless | 11/10F |
| 3 Nov | Birmingham | Pin Table | | 276 | 6 | Sir V Sassoon | N Murless | 9/2 |
| 6 Nov | Windsor | Grey Ghost | | 276 | 5 | G H Chandler | T Carey | 6/1 |
| 13 Nov | Manchester | Sovereign Path | | 556 | 6 | O/trainer | R Mason | 15/2 |

1959: 142 wins; 96 2nds; 85 3rds; 559 rides

† Walkover

| Date | Race Course | Horse | Race | Value £ | Dist Fur | Owner | Trainer | S/P |
|---|---|---|---|---|---|---|---|---|
| 1960 | | | | | | | | |
| 27 Mar | Lincoln | Barbary Pirate | | 207 | 10 | Miss B Cavendish-Bentinck | R Sturdy | 10/3 |
| 29 Mar | Nottingham | Afghanistan | | 690 | 10 | Mrs J F C Bryce | F Armstrong | 100/9 |
| 6 Apl | Newmarket | Afghanistan | | 292 | 12 | Mrs J F C Bryce | F Armstrong | 6/4F |
| 9 Apl | Newbury | New Move | | 386 | 5 | C Nicholson | P Walwyn | 3/1F |
| 11 Apl | Wolver'ton | Io | | 207 | 8 | H L L Morriss | P Walwyn | 2/1F |
| 16 Apl | Kempton | Palatina | | 605 | 5 | R Scully | F Armstrong | 10/11F |
| 16 Apl | Kempton | Falls of Shin | Rosebery | 1,693 | 10 | O/trainer | E Parker | 10/1 |
| 16 Apl | Kempton | Soldanella | | 594 | 11 | M Russell | T Corbett | 20/1 |
| 19 Apl | Epsom | Nelocette* | | 194 | 5 | P B Raymond | K Piggott | 5/2F |
| 20 Apl | Epsom | Firestreak | City and Suburban | 2,627 | 10 | J Lewis | P Nelson | 11/4F |
| 20 Apl | Epsom | New Move | | 623 | 5 | C Nicholson | P Walwyn | 8/13F |
| 21 Apl | Epsom | Plump | Princess Elizabeth | 6,410 | 8 | Sir V Sassoon | N Murless | 6/4F |
| 22 Apl | Sandown | Dairialan | Sandown Cup | 973 | 10 | C Gardiner | F Armstrong | 2/1 |
| 23 Apl | Nottingham | Mirage | | 345 | 12 | Lord Howard de Walden | J A Waugh | 5/4F |
| 25 Apl | Nottingham | Silver Sand | | 306 | 8 | E D Cooke | F Armstrong | 9/2F |
| 30 Apl | Warwick | Golden Bowler | | 294 | 5 | Mrs A Donaldson | K Cundell | E/F |
| 30 Apl | Warwick | Mirage | | 462 | 12 | Lord Howard de Walden | J A Waugh | 4/5F |
| 30 Apl | Warwick | Barbary Pirate | | 207 | 10 | Miss B Cavendish-Bentinck | R Sturdy | 1/5F |
| 3 May | Chester | Tin Whistle | Prince of Wales Stks | 1,041 | 5 | B W Grainger | P Rohan | 5/1F |
| 4 May | Chester | Io | Grosvenor Stks | 825 | 10 | H L L Morriss | P Walwyn | 5/4F |
| 7 May | Kempton | Petite Etoile | Victor Wild Stks | 574 | 12 | Prince Aly Khan | N Murless | 1/7F |
| 7 May | Kempton | Laughing Cheese | | 480 | 5 | G Davis | T Carey | 7/2 |
| 9 May | Birmingham | Indian Princess | | 414 | 5 | Maj C H Reynard | P Rohan | 9/4 |
| 11 May | Bath | Grasp | | 432 | 10 | C Nicholson | P Walwyn | 6/4F |
| 13 May | Hurst Park | Legal Note | | 465 | 5 | R B Moller | P Walwyn | 5/1 |
| 16 May | Wolver'ton | Daynor | | 251 | 8 | Mrs J Stuart Goitar | P Rohan | 4/7F |
| 17 May | York | New Move* | Zetland | 632 | 5 | C Nicholson | P Walwyn | 4/6F |
| 17 May | York | Canticle | | 427 | 9 | G L Lloyd | P Walwyn | 10/1 |
| 18 May | York | St Paddy | Dante | 1,875 | 10½ | Sir V Sassoon | N Murless | 8/11F |
| 18 May | York | Radio Pye | | 631 | 6 | Mrs L McVey | S Hall | 9/4F |
| 19 May | York | Ambergris | | 686 | 5 | Sir P Loraine | H Wragg | 4/11F |
| 20 May | Pontefract | Nereid | | 207 | 5 | E G Harrison | R Curran | 3/1F |
| 20 May | Pontefract | Monkey Minor | | 390 | 8 | Mrs E M Crossfield | F Armstrong | 4/6F |
| 21 May | Lingfield | Ides of March | Tote Investors | 1,916 | 10 | M P Davis | R Jarvis | 5/1F |
| 23 May | Alex Palace | Velocette | | 267 | 5 | P B Raymond | K Piggott | 5/2 |
| 23 May | Alex Palace | Legal Star | | 207 | 5 | T Holland-Martin | P Walwyn | 11/2 |
| 23 May | Nottingham | T-M | | 267 | 8 | Lord Howard de Walden | L Hall | 5/4F |
| 23 May | Nottingham | Noah | | 207 | 5 | Lt Col H L V Beddington | P Rohan | 5/2 |
| 25 May | Windsor | Bambola | | 345 | 5 | R F Scully | F Armstrong | 10/1 |
| 25 May | Lincoln | Daynor | | 207 | 8 | B Jenks | P Rohan | 4/1 |
| 26 May | Lincoln | Coconut Palmetto | | 237 | 5 | Mrs J F C Bryce | F Armstrong | 1/2F |
| 26 May | Lincoln | Silver Sand | | 257 | 12 | E D Cooke | F Armstrong | 8/11 |
| 27 May | Newbury | Sovereign Path | Lockinge | 1,203 | 8 | O/trainer | R Mason | 7/4F |
| 27 May | Newbury | Sunny Way | | 420 | 12 | Sir V Sassoon | N Murless | 4/1 |
| 28 May | Newbury | Favorita* | | 465 | 5 | Mrs V Lilley | N Murless | 5/4F |
| 30 May | Lewes | Legal Star | | 271 | 5 | T Holland-Martin | P Walwyn | 11/4F |
| 31 May | Epsom | Velocette | | 589 | 5 | P B Raymond | K Piggott | 5/4F |
| 31 May | Epsom | Firestreak | Craven | 1,068 | 8 | J Lewis | P Nelson | 4/9F |
| 1 June | Epsom | Dairialatan | Egmont Hcp | 998 | 10 | Sir C Gardiner | F Armstrong | 3/1F |
| 1 June | Epsom | St Paddy | The Derby | 53,052 | 12 | Sir V Sassoon | N Murless | 7/1 |
| 2 June | Epsom | Petite Etoile | Coronation Cup | 2,966 | 12 | Prince Aly Khan | N Murless | 1/3F |

* Dead Heat

| Date | Race Course | Horse | Race | Value £ | Dist Fur | Owner | Trainer | S/P |
|---|---|---|---|---|---|---|---|---|
| 2 June | Epsom | Indigeneus | Tadworth Hcp | 987 | 5 | T D Grimes | R Thrale | 9/4F |
| 2 June | Epsom | Prince Moon | Abbot's Hill Hcp | 960 | 8 | O/trainer | T Carey | 100/7 |
| 3 June | Epsom | Munificent | Mickleham | 1,131 | 6 | O/trainer | T Corbett | 11/4F |
| 4 June | Kempton | Sind | | 598 | 8 | Sir P Loraine | H Wragg | 9/4F |
| 8 June | Brighton | Illinois | Pavilion Hcp | 962 | 12 | F Sykes | P Payne-Gallwey | 11/4 |
| 9 June | Brighton | Musical March | | 352 | 7 | R O Girling | K Cundell | 8/1 |
| 9 June | Brighton | Favorita | | 421 | 5 | Mrs V Lilley | N Murless | 8/15F |
| 11 June | Sandown | Dairialatan | Loraine Hcp | 932 | 10 | Sir C Gardiner | F Armstrong | 5/4F |
| 11 June | Sandown | Dolgelley | | 345 | 5 | Col B Hornung | N Murless | 7/2 |
| 11 June | Sandown | Lady Advocate | | 992 | 5 | Mrs W C Pegley | W Nightingall | 7/4 |
| 16 June | Royal Ascot | Tin Whistle | Cork and Orery | 1,629 | 6 | B W Grainger | P Rohan | 8/1F |
| 16 June | Royal Ascot | New Move | Cheshire Stks | 1,697 | 5 | C Nicholson | P Walwyn | 7/1 |
| 16 June | Royal Ascot | Sunny Way | King George Stks | 1,770 | 12 | Sir V Sassoon | N Murless | 7/1 |
| 17 June | Royal Ascot | Firestreak | Rous Memorial Stks | 1,553 | 8 | John Lewis | P Nelson | 8/11F |
| 20 June | Folkestone | Raymoss | | 207 | 10 | D Devong | H Leader | 1/3F |
| 20 June | Birmingham | Pass | | 257 | 6 | A Portman | G Kennedy | 100/8 |
| 20 June | Birmingham | Raoul | | 276 | 13 | H Garrood | L Hall | 11/4F |
| 21 June | Birmingham | Saint Anne | Midland Breeders | 1,406 | 10 | G A Gilbert | P Walwyn | 1/25F |
| 23 June | Newbury | Crowded Room | | 420 | 6 | C W Engelhard | P Walwyn | 6/1 |
| 24 June | Windsor | Luminarch | | 345 | 8 | B Walsh | R Read | 13/2 |
| 24 June | Windsor | Canticle | | 345 | 12 | C L Lord | P Walwyn | 7/4 |
| 25 June | Windsor | Speed Bird | | 345 | 5 | O/trainer | F Armstrong | 100/8 |
| 25 June | Windsor | Laughing Cheese | | 690 | 6 | G Davis | T Carey | 4/1 |
| 27 June | Brighton | Grasp | Brighton M Stks | 1,416 | 8 | C Nicholson | P Walwyn | 10/1 |
| 27 June | Brighton | Golden Cheers | | 524 | 12 | C Payne-Crofts | H Price | 4/1 |
| 27 June | Brighton | Prince Nick | | 611 | 7 | Mrs F Chandler | T Carey | 3/1 |
| 27 June | Wolver'ton | Walker | | 207 | 12 | Lt Col H L V Beddington | P Rohan | 5/4F |
| 29 June | Liverpool | Dairialatan | Waterloo Pl | 1,012 | 10 | Sir C Gardiner | F Armstrong | 5/4F |
| 30 June | Newmarket | Favorita | July Stks | 1,549 | 5 | Mrs V Lilley | N Murless | 10/3 |
| 1 July | Newmarket | Gallant Deal | | 397 | 8 | I Allen | F Armstrong | 4/5F |
| 1 July | Newmarket | Primera | Princess of Wales | 2,775 | 12 | S Joel | N Murless | 9/4F |
| 1 July | Newmarket | Past Experience | | 297 | 6 | H D H Wills | P Walwyn | 2/1 |
| 1 July | Warwick | Furcero | | 294 | 5 | M Cowley | K Piggott | 4/5F |
| 1 July | Warwick | Cheetah Peter | | 207 | 12 | Mrs A Johnson | H Hannon | 5/1 |
| 1 July | Warwick | Pride of Kilmallock | | 207 | 5 | O/trainer | D Whelan | 9/4 |
| 2 July | Newmarket | Tin Whistle† | July Cup | 2,130 | 6 | B G Grainger | P Rohan | |
| 4 July | Nottingham | Monkey Minor | | 390 | 8 | Mrs E M Crosfield | F Armstrong | 10/11F |
| 4 July | Nottingham | Coconut Palm | | 207 | 6 | Mrs J F C Bryce | F Armstrong | 1/6F |
| 5 July | Nottingham | Port O' Christo† | | 458 | 5 | O/trainer | R Ward | |
| 5 July | Nottingham | Punchinello | | 207 | 8 | J S Gerber | W O'Gorman | 10/11F |
| 8 July | Sandown | Exar | | 487 | 16 | Dr C Vittadini | N Murless | 4/7F |
| 11 July | Kempton | Faust | Crazy Gang Stks | 1,787 | 12 | S Joel | N Murless | EvF |
| 12 July | Nottingham | Green Opal | Falmouth Stks | 1,354 | 8 | Lt Col G Loder | N Murless | 9/4 |
| 12 July | Nottingham | King's Son | | 587 | 5 | Mrs V Lilley | N Murless | 6/1 |
| 14 July | Nottingham | Cawston Tower | | 347 | 5 | C Haddon | R Read | 7/4F |
| 15 July | Ascot | Sunny Way | | 568 | 12 | Sir V Sassoon | N Murless | 9/4 |
| 19 July | Folkestone | Coconut Palmetto | | 207 | 6 | Mrs J F C Bryce | F Armstrong | 5/1 |
| 18 July | Leicester | Monkey Minor | | 267 | 8 | Mrs E M Crosfield | F Armstrong | 1/3F |
| 20 July | Kempton | Brass Nail | | 519 | 5 | Sir G Bailey | K Cundell | 5/4F |
| 22 July | Hurst Park | Crowded Room | | 765 | 6 | C W Engelhard | P Walwyn | 8/13F |
| 25 July | Alex Park | Unanimity | | 287 | 8 | Mrs C H Pratt | C Pratt | 7/4 |
| 25 July | Birmingham | Steve Grey | | 276 | 6 | F E White | P Rohan | 7/4F |
| 28 July | Goodwood | Exar | Goodwood Cup | 3,137 | 21 | Dr C Vittadini | N Murless | 4/9F |
| 30 July | Epsom | Alcazar | | 363 | 8 | Sir P Loraine | N Murless | 8/11F |
| 1 Aug | Folkestone | Cheongsam | | 207 | 10 | J R Mullion | G Richards | EvF |

† Walkover

| Date | Race Course | Horse | Race | Value £ | Dist Fur | Owner | Trainer | S/P |
|---|---|---|---|---|---|---|---|---|
| 2 Aug | Brighton | Eddy | | 488 | 5 | A Johnstone | N Murless | 7/4F |
| 6 Aug | Newmarket | Tudor Love | | 291 | 8 | Sir V Sassoon | N Murless | 10/11F |
| 8 Aug | Nottingham | Favorita | Nottinghamshire Breeders Stks | 1,128 | 5 | Mrs V Lilley | N Murless | 8/15F |
| 9 Aug | Nottingham | Adonius | | 207 | 5 | Mrs V Lilley | N Murless | 5/1 |
| 9 Aug | Alex Palace | French Beam | | 282 | 8 | M Ostrer | K Piggott | 11/8F |
| 10 Aug | Sandown | Imperial Gray | | 332 | 8 | M Sobell | G Richards | 4/1F |
| 11 Aug | Sandown | Pandofell | | 314 | 13 | H W Daw | F Maxwell | 10/11F |
| 11 Aug | Sandown | Princely Folly | | 454 | 5 | Lt Col G Loder | N Murless | 6/1 |
| 11 Aug | Sandown | Exar | | 484 | 13 | Dr C Vittadini | N Murless | 7/100F |
| 12 Aug | Newbury | Sweet Lola | | 420 | 6 | Mrs V Lilley | N Murless | 8/1 |
| 12 Aug | Newbury | Nero's Love | Russley Hcp | 840 | 8 | Mrs G P Graham | K Cundell | 5/2 |
| 12 Aug | Newbury | Eblouissante | St Hugh's Stks | 1,332 | 5 | L H H Moody | A Budgett | 10/11F |
| 15 Aug | Warwick | New Move | | 559 | 5 | C Nicholson | P Walwyn | 9/4F |
| 15 Aug | Warwick | Master Lou | | 207 | 8 | L Gilmore | H Hannon | 2/1F |
| 16 Aug | York | Ambergris | | 1,276 | 5 | Sir P Loraine | H Wragg | 10/3 |
| 17 Aug | York | St Paddy | Great Voltigeur | 5,951 | 12 | Sir V Sassoon | N Murless | 4/11F |
| 20 Aug | Lingfield | Thames Trader | Queen Elizabeth Cup | 765 | 7 | H S Persse | S Ingham | 8/13F |
| 19 Aug | Newmarket | Keld | | 323 | 5 | Mrs N Murless | N Murless | 11/8F |
| 19 Aug | Newmarket | Sunflake | | 313 | 8 | Maharani of Baroda | F Armstrong | 7/2 |
| 22 Aug | Worcester | Chevertons | | 207 | 5 | T J Isbill | H Hannon | 8/1 |
| 22 Aug | Worcester | Punchinello | | 276 | 8 | J S Gerber | W O'Gorman | EvF |
| 22 Aug | Worcester | Cadenza II | | 207 | 6 | R B Moller | P Walwyn | 4/11F |
| 24 Aug | Brighton | Princess Lioi | | 550 | 6 | Lady U Vernon | N Murless | 8/11F |
| 26 Aug | Sandown | Nero's Love | Bear Hcp | 742 | 8 | Mrs B Graham | K Cundell | 7/2 |
| 27 Aug | Sandown | Apostle | Lyons Maid Stks | 2,930 | 10 | Mrs D Montagu | S Ingham | 4/6F |
| 29 Aug | Birmingham | Adonius | | 276 | 6 | Mrs V Lilley | N Murless | EvF |
| 30 Aug | Alex Palace | Andromache | | 276 | 5 | Mrs E Dawson Miller | M Bolton | 7/4F |
| 2 Sept | Hurst Park | Brass Nail | | 366 | 6 | Sir G Bailey | K Cundell | 7/4F |
| 3 Sept | Manchester | Sariegail | | 207 | 10 | O/trainer | J Weston-Evans | 11/4F |
| 3 Sept | Manchester | Dommie | | 292 | 5 | J E Clout | T Dent | 4/9F |
| 3 Sept | Manchester | Favorita | Autumn Breeders Stks | 1,757 | 5 | Mrs V Lilley | N Murless | 4/6F |
| 7 Sept | Doncaster | Palatina | Glasgow Paddocks Hcp | 1,136 | 5 | R F Scully | F Armstrong | 11/10F |
| 7 Sept | Doncaster | Blast | | 1,183 | 8 | R N Richmond-Watson | A Budgett | 9/2F |
| 8 Sept | Doncaster | Exar | Doncaster Cup | 3,390 | 18 | Dr C Vittadini | N Murless | 6/100F |
| 9 Sept | Doncaster | Michael's Trigger | | 1,232 | 6 | I Allan | F Armstrong | 9/2F |
| 10 Sept | Doncaster | St Paddy | St Leger | 30,378 | 14 | Sir V Sassoon | N Murless | 4/6F |
| 13 Sept | Yarmouth | V Flight | | 207 | 6 | Lt Col N E Friege | H Wragg | 11/10F |
| 14 Sept | Brighton | Macquario | | 427 | 10 | Lord Feversham | N Murless | 9/1 |
| 14 Sept | Brighton | Indigenous | | 501 | 5 | T D Grimes | R Thrale | 11/8F |
| 15 Sept | Brighton | Sue Set | | 519 | 6 | C G Crook | A Smyth | 5/1 |
| 16 Sept | Kempton | Colour Blind | | 592 | 5 | J U Baillie | T Corbett | 2/1 |
| 19 Sept | Leicester | Fire Raiser | | 267 | 10 | O/trainer | F Maxwell | 11/4 |
| 19 Sept | Leicester | Cherambsca | | 207 | 8 | Mrs P B Raymond | K Piggott | 10/3 |
| 20 Sept | Leicester | Royal Heiress | | 207 | 5 | I Allan | F Armstrong | 6/4F |
| 20 Sept | Leicester | Sariegail | | 207 | 10 | O/trainer | J Weston-Evans | 2/1 |
| 20 Sept | Leicester | Pandofell | | 332 | 11 | H W Daw | F Maxwell | 8/100F |
| 23 Sept | Ascot at Newbury | Green Opal | Princess Royal Stks | 2,368 | 12 | Lt Col G Loder | N Murless | 3/1 |
| 30 Sept | Newbury | Anise | | 512 | 6 | A G Samuel | P Walwyn | 4/1 |
| 4 Oct | Nottingham | Palatable | | 207 | 5 | Miss M L Pinder | P Walwyn | 2/5F |
| 7 Oct | Ascot at Kempton | Psidium | Duke of Edinburgh | 2,500 | 6 | Mrs A Plesch | H Wragg | 9/4 |
| 8 Oct | Ascot at Kempton | Favorita | Cornwallis | 2,181 | 5 | Mrs V Lilley | N Murless | 11/10F |

| Date | Race Course | Horse | Race | Value £ | Dist Fur | Owner | Trainer | S/P |
|---|---|---|---|---|---|---|---|---|
| 8 Oct | Ascot at Kempton | Ides of March | Buckhounds | 511 | 12 | M P Davis | R Jarvis | 4/7F |
| 10 Oct | Warwick | Resora | | 207 | 12 | F J Honour | F Cundell | 7/2 |
| 12 Oct | Newmarket | Blue Palm | | 602 | 13 | J S Gerber | W O'Gorman | 6/5F |
| 15 Oct | Wolver'ton | Ides of March | Wm Butler Trophy | 1,455 | 11 | M P Davis | R Jarvis | 5/4F |
| 15 Oct | Wolver'ton | Atlantic Ocean | | 276 | 16 | W J Rimell | T F Rimell | 4/5F |
| 15 Oct | Wolver'ton | Kalkoura | | 270 | 8 | Mrs J A Cecil-Wright | W Wightman | 5/4 |
| 17 Oct | Wolver'ton | Como Fair | | 345 | 5 | G W Brown | P Rohan | 11/10F |
| 22 Oct | Newbury | Mime | | 350 | 12 | G C Judd | H Price | 4/11F |
| 3 Nov | Liverpool | Chrysler III | | 626 | 14 | Sir A Jarvis | P Walwyn | 100/6 |
| 4 Nov | Liverpool | Atlantic Ocean | | 420 | 14 | W J Rimell | T F Rimell | 6/1 |
| 11 Nov | Manchester | Dommie | | 292 | 6 | J E Clout | J Dent | 9/4F |
| 11 Nov | Manchester | White Beam | | 207 | 10 | S W Nicholson | E Gifford | 100/8 |
| 12 Nov | Manchester | Beau Rossa | | 207 | 10 | B Kerr | S Hall | 11/8F |

1960: 170 wins; 107 2nds; 75 3rds; 640 rides

| Date | Race Course | Horse | Race | Value £ | Dist Fur | Owner | Trainer | S/P |
|---|---|---|---|---|---|---|---|---|
| 1961 | | | | | | | | |
| 21 Mar | Lincoln | Resora | | 207 | 10 | F J Honour | F Cundell | 13/8F |
| 22 Mar | Lincoln | Lucky Harry | | 392 | 5 | J O'Loughlin | M Connelly(I) | 5/4 |
| 22 Mar | Lincoln | Fight On | | 291 | 6 | J Muldoon | M Connelly(I) | 2/5F |
| 23 Mar | Liverpool | Fulminate | | 207 | 14 | G A Tachmindi | F Armstrong | 4/1 |
| 24 Mar | Liverpool | Ione | | 298 | 5 | B W Grainger | R Ward | 4/5F |
| 27 Mar | Nottingham | Bonny Creeper | | 207 | 5 | B W Grainger | R Ward | 11/4 |
| 3 Apl | Kempton | Aidos | | 575 | 8 | Duchess of Norfolk | G Smyth | 7/2F |
| 4 Apl | Birmingham | Frimley | | 257 | 6 | C F Smith | R Ward | 5/4F |
| 5 Apl | Hurst Park | Westlands | | 502 | 10 | Miss J L Mitchell | D Whelan | 4/1 |
| 6 Apl | Hurst Park | Whimsical | | 585 | 8 | C W Engelhard | F Johnson Houghton | 7/1 |
| 7 Apl | Windsor | Palatina | | 345 | 6 | R F Scully | F Armstrong | 9/4F |
| 10 Apl | Leicester | Tico | | 267 | 5 | Capt T E Langton | R Ward | EvF |
| 10 Apl | Leicester | Chevertons | | 207 | 7 | T J Isbill | H Hannon | 3/1 |
| 11 Apl | Newmarket | Aurelius | Craven Stks | 724 | 8 | Mrs V Lilley | N Murless | 8/1 |
| 11 Apl | Newmarket | River Chanter | | 503 | 5 | R J Sigtia | G Todd | 7/4 |
| 13 Apl | Newmarket | Pinturischio | | 559 | 8 | Sir V Sassoon | N Murless | 2/5F |
| 14 Apl | Newbury | Sovrango | | 420 | 10 | G A Oldham | H Wragg | 3/1F |
| 15 Apl | Newbury | Sudden Thought | | 397 | 5 | Lord Norrie | F Johnson Houghton | 5/2F |
| 15 Apl | Newbury | Souieda | | 363 | 5 | S L Green | W Payne | 11/8F |
| 17 Apl | Wolver'ton | Miss Primrose | | 336 | 5 | B W Grainger | R Ward | 8/100F |
| 19 Apl | Epsom | Scots Fusilier | | 734 | 5 | O/trainer | T A Corbett | 7/2 |
| 21 Apl | Sandown | Admiral's Lark | Sandown Cup | 837 | 10 | Mrs J C Armitage | D Whelan | 11/2 |
| 22 Apl | Sandown | Petite Etoile | Coronation Stks | 986 | 10 | Aga Khan | N Murless | 4/9F |
| 22 Apl | Sandown | Pre-emptive | | 655 | 8 | H H Renshaw | A Budgett | 100/8 |
| 27 Apl | Newmarket | Dunker | | 572 | 5 | J U Baillie | T Corbett | 4/7F |
| 2 May | Chester | Bonny Creeper | | 523 | 5 | B W Grainger | R Ward | 2/1 |
| 4 May | Chester | Beau Ideal | | 969 | 10 | Mrs G G Scobie | D Gunn | 9/4F |
| 6 May | Kempton | Moitie | | 500 | 5 | G R Smith | M Pope | 11/10F |
| 6 May | Kempton | Scottish Prince | | 550 | 5 | O/trainer | D Whelan | 15/2 |
| 8 May | Alex Palace | Phaeidippides | | 300 | 8 | B Shine | M Pope | 4/6F |
| 9 May | Leicester | Principal | | 207 | 5 | E B Benjamin | F Armstrong | 11/8F |
| 9 May | Leicester | Afghanistan | | 345 | 11 | Mrs J R C Bryce | F Armstrong | E/F |
| 9 May | Leicester | Timimi | | 207 | 8 | S L Green | W Payne | 13/1 |
| 13 May | Haydock | Little Buskins | John Davies Hcp | 1,699 | 12 | T Gray | Sir C Boyd Rochfort | 11/4 |
| 13 May | Haydock | Tender Colt | | 525 | 7 | G A Gilbert | A Vasey | 7/4F |
| 15 May | Wolver'ton | Moat Plat | | 207 | 8 | W N Wilfred | J Fawcus | 9/4F |
| 16 May | York | Aiming High | Glasgow Stks | 951 | 9 | The Queen | N Murless | 3/1F |

(I) = Ireland

| Date | Race Course | Horse | Race | Value £ | Dist Fur | Owner | Trainer | S/P |
|---|---|---|---|---|---|---|---|---|
| 16 May | York | Tin Whistle | Micklegate Hcp | 808 | 5 | B W Grainger | P Rohan | 15/8F |
| 17 May | York | Bonny Creeper | Scarbrough | 814 | 5 | B W Grainger | R Ward | 9/1 |
| 17 May | York | Ambergris | Musidora Stks | 1,186 | 10 | Sir P Loraine | H Wragg | 4/9F |
| 17 May | York | Pandofell | Yorkshire Cup | 1,760 | 16 | H Warwick | F Maxwell | 11/4F |
| 18 May | York | Miss Primrose | Dringhouses S | 948 | 5 | B W Grainger | R Ward | 4/1 |
| 20 May | Sandown | Favorita | Alington Stks | 1,061 | 5 | Mrs V Lilley | N Murless | 13/8F |
| 20 May | Sandown | St Paddy | Coombe Stks | 1,011 | 13 | Sir V Sassoon | N Murless | 1/6F |
| 22 May | Hurst Park | Magic Court | | 580 | 13 | Mrs V Lilley | N Murless | 6/1 |
| 23 May | Redcar | Killiney Hill | | 207 | 11 | T S Lucas | F Armstrong | 11/4 |
| 24 May | Liverpool | Blue Over | | 345 | 6 | Mrs W Whittaker | F Armstrong | 8/11F |
| 24 May | Liverpool | Wrangle | June Rose Hcp | 704 | 8 | J A Shelfim | S Hall | 8/13F |
| 24 May | Liverpool | Scabiosa | | 207 | 5 | M Batthyany | F Armstrong | 15/8F |
| 24 May | Liverpool | Nautical Lad | | 276 | 14 | A H Moralee | J Ormston | 4/7F |
| 25 May | Manchester | Layer | | 292 | 5 | J Kendrick | R Ward | 9/4 |
| 25 May | Manchester | Riguada | | 514 | 10 | Maharani of Baroda | F Armstrong | 15/8F |
| 29 May | Lewes | William F | | 277 | 8 | O/trainer | E J Parker | EvF |
| 29 May | Wolver'ton | Dime | | 265 | 16 | E J Luckin | I Benstead | 6/1 |
| 29 May | Wolver'ton | Royal Stripe | | 345 | 8 | T G Johnson | W Payne | 6/4F |
| 30 May | Epsom | Apostle | Craven | 1,561 | 10 | Mrs S Montagu | S Ingham | 8/11F |
| 1 June | Epsom | Petite Etoile | Coronation Cup | 3,894 | 12 | Aga Khan | N Murless | 2/5F |
| 2 June | Epsom | Crazy Grey | Mickleham S | 1,202 | 6 | Mrs T H Carey | T Carey | 100/7 |
| 3 June | Kempton | Pyrmont | | 547 | 10 | S Wootton | S Ingham | 5/12F |
| 7 June | Brighton | Illinois | Pavilion Hcp | 978 | 12 | F Sykes | P Payne-Gallwey | 7/4 |
| 7 June | Brighton | Perdix | | 460 | 6 | The Queen | N Murless | 7/1 |
| 9 June | Sandown | Sunny Way | HWFA Williams Hcp | 1,089 | 16 | Sir V Sassoon | N Murless | 6/4F |
| 12 June | Lewes | Timimi | | 235 | 8 | S L Green | W Payne | EvF |
| 14 June | Royal Ascot | Favorita | Jersey | 1,910 | 7 | Mrs V Lilley | N Murless | 5/4F |
| 14 June | Royal Ascot | Aiming High | Coronation | 3,562 | 8 | The Queen | N Murless | 100/8 |
| 15 June | Royal Ascot | Abermaid | New Stks | 2,420 | 5 | Sir P Loraine | H Wragg | 3/1F |
| 15 June | Royal Ascot | Pandofell | Gold Cup | 11,205 | 20 | H Warwick Daw | F Maxwell | 100/8 |
| 15 June | Royal Ascot | Aurelius | King Edward VII Stks | 3,499 | 12 | Mrs V Lilley | N Murless | 11/4 |
| 16 June | Royal Ascot | Petite Etoile | Rous Memorial | 1,527 | 8 | Aga Khan | N Murless | 2/15F |
| 16 June | Royal Ascot | St Paddy | Hardwicke | 2,504 | 12 | Sir V Sassoon | N Murless | 4/9F |
| 19 June | Folkestone | Cash 'n Carry | | 314 | 5 | Mrs H J Heinz | F Walwyn | 6/4F |
| 19 June | Folkestone | Mrs Flurry | | 207 | 10 | T K Cooper | F Walwyn | 2/1 |
| 20 June | Birmingham | Our Sam | | 257 | 6 | B W Grainger | P Rohan | EvF |
| 20 June | Birmingham | Vintner | | 276 | 10 | T H Farr | P Rohan | 11/10F |
| 24 June | Newcastle | Carnival Dancer | | 355 | 7 | J F D Ward | H Blackshaw | 13/2 |
| 23 June | Doncaster | Our Sam | | 287 | 6 | B W Grainger | P Rohan | 2/11F |
| 23 June | Doncaster | Blue Over | | 323 | 6 | Mrs W Whittaker | F Armstrong | 5/2 |
| 26 June | Brighton | Wise Love | | 568 | 7 | B Davis | T Carey | 6/4F |
| 27 June | Wolver'ton | Frigor | | 215 | 8 | J F de Rothschild | P Walwyn | 8/13F |
| 28 June | Alex Palace | Westham | | 287 | 5 | J H A Greenland | D Whelan | 11/10F |
| 30 June | Newmarket | Apostle | Princess of Wales | 2,511 | 12 | Mrs P Montagu | S Ingham | 4/6F |
| 3 July | Nottingham | Scollop | | 277 | 8 | T H Farr | P Rohan | 10/11F |
| 4 July | Nottingham | Private Eye | | 207 | 5 | T H Farr | P Rohan | 1/4F |
| 5 July | Yarmouth | Buxus | | 345 | 10 | Mrs A Plesch | H Wragg | 5/1 |
| 5 July | Yarmouth | Hestia | | 314 | 8 | Maj G Bradstock | H Wragg | 15/8F |
| 6 July | Yarmouth | Feathers | | 277 | 8 | Mrs B A Waller | F Cundell | 4/5F |
| 6 July | Yarmouth | Principal | | 411 | 6 | E B Benjamin | F Armstrong | 9/4F |
| 6 July | Yarmouth | Bay of Persia | | 325 | 10 | R F Scully | F Armstrong | 8/1 |
| 7 July | Sandown | Sunny Way | | 491 | 16 | J Barker | W Wharton | 8/15F |
| 8 July | Sandown | Off Key | | 587 | 13 | Sir V Sassoon | N Murless | 2/1F |
| 8 July | Sandown | St Paddy | Eclipse | 17,055 | 10 | Sir V Sassoon | N Murless | 2/13F |
| 8 July | Sandown | A and N | | 504 | 10 | B Sunley | S Ingham | 4/1 |
| 10 July | Birmingham | Aseret | | 257 | 5 | G A Gilbert | B Foster | EvF |

| Date | Race Course | Horse | Race | Value £ | Dist Fur | Owner | Trainer | S/P |
|---|---|---|---|---|---|---|---|---|
| 11 July | Newmarket | Illinois | | 418 | 12 | F Sykes | P Payne-Gallwey | 5/2 |
| 12 July | Newmarket | Caerphilly | | 484 | 5 | Mrs N Murless | N Murless | 6/4F |
| 12 July | Newmarket | Raconteuse | | 421 | 8 | E C Bland | F Johnson Houghton | 7/1 |
| 13 July | Newmarket | Young Lochinvar | | 474 | 6 | Sir V Sassoon | N Murless | 100/8 |
| 13 July | Doncaster | Chestergate | | 207 | 6 | K O Boardman | W O'Brien | 5/4F |
| 13 July | Doncaster | Souieda | | 207 | 5 | S L Green | W Payne | 11/8F |
| 14 July | Ascot | Golden Sands | Red Oaks | 1,110 | 8 | P Oppenheimer | O Elliott | 8/1 |
| 15 July | Ascot | Parquetta | Princess Margaret | 1,496 | 5 | Mrs J A Dewar | H Wragg | 10/3 |
| 17 July | Leicester | Principal | | 207 | 6 | E B Benjamin | F Armstrong | 3/1 |
| 17 July | Leicester | Cave of Dracan | | 267 | 8 | Capt J E Langton | R Ward | 4/9F |
| 18 July | Leicester | Afghanistan | | 224 | 11 | J F C Bryce | F Armstrong | EvF |
| 18 July | Alex Palace | Cash 'n Carry | | 207 | 5 | Mrs H J Heinz | F Walwyn | 9/4F |
| 19 July | Kempton | Mrs Flurry | | 528 | 12 | T K Cooper | F Walwyn | 6/1 |
| 20 July | Kempton | Pinicola | | 474 | 8 | S Steuart | N Murless | 5/4 |
| 24 July | Birmingham | Two Fiddlers | | 276 | 5 | F G Rissbrook | S Everitt | 11/4F |
| 27 July | Goodwood | Caerphilly | Lavant | 646 | 5 | Mrs N Murless | N Murless | 3/1F |
| 27 July | Goodwood | Tipstaff | Arundel Castle Private Sweepstake | | 6 | Lord Porchester | T Corbett | 5/2 |
| 29 July | Warwick | Aseret | | 294 | 5 | G A Gilbert | B Foster | EvF |
| 29 July | Warwick | Overdue | | 207 | 6 | C Nicholson | F Johnson Houghton | 5/2F |
| 29 July | Warwick | Cinzano | | 207 | 8 | A G Samuel | F Johnson Houghton | 5/2F |
| 31 July | Folkestone | Grey Ghost | | 238 | 6 | C H Chandler | T Carey | 6/5F |
| 1 Aug | Alex Palace | Bright Biddy | | 287 | 5 | F E Hardy | R Read | 10/3 |
| 1 Aug | Alex Palace | Admiral's Candy | | 207 | 5 | Mrs J C Armitage | D Whelan | 8/1F |
| 1 Aug | Redcar | Off Key | Vaux Gold Tankard | 10,460 | 14 | Sir V Sassoon | N Murless | 100/7 |
| 7 Aug | Epsom | Overdue | | 590 | 6 | C Nicholson | F Johnson Houghton | 2/1 |
| 9 Aug | Brighton | Wimbledon | | 512 | 5 | The Queen | N Murless | 11/10F |
| 12 Aug | Newmarket | Secret Session | | 412 | 8 | Mrs V Lilley | N Murless | 1/10F |
| 12 Aug | Newmarket | Melodious Charm | | 521 | 5 | J R Hindley | N Murless | 5/2F |
| 12 Aug | Newmarket | Silver Kumar | | 405 | 5 | Mrs R Read | R Read | 5/4 |
| 14 Aug | Nottingham | Caerphilly | Nottinghamshire Breeders Yearlings | 885 | 5 | Mrs N Murless | N Murless | 10/11F |
| 14 Aug | Nottingham | Timimi | | 276 | 8 | S L Green | W Payne | 9/4 |
| 14 Aug | Nottingham | Pannier | | 276 | 10 | Mrs R Macdonald-Buchanan | J A Waugh | 5/6F |
| 16 Aug | Salisbury | Lyonado | | 425 | 5 | E J M Jones | K Piggott | 10/3 |
| 16 Aug | Salisbury | Tipstaff | | 493 | 7 | Lord Porchester | T Corbett | 7/4F |
| 19 Aug | Newbury | Mere Worth | Washington Singer | 1,472 | 6 | Mrs E B Holmes | N Murless | 9/1 |
| 21 Aug | Worcester | T. M. | | 317 | 8 | C T Whiting | R Ward | 7/4F |
| 21 Aug | Worcester | Silver Stream | | 207 | 6 | Mrs J A Dewar | H Wragg | 2/1F |
| 23 Aug | York | Die Hard | Ebor | 10,039 | 14 | Maj L Gardner | M V O'Brien(I) | 11/2F |
| 24 Aug | Lingfield | Grey Ghost | | 390 | 6 | C H Chandler | T Carey | 11/4 |
| 26 Aug | Newcastle | Nymphea | | 291 | 12 | Mrs A Plesch | H Wragg | 2/11 |
| 30 Aug | Ripon | Sparrows Nest | | 415 | 5 | R G Cable | R Ward | 11/8F |
| 1 Sept | Manchester | Gendarme | | 326 | 6 | O/trainer | S W Everitt | 4/1 |
| 1 Sept | Manchester | Secret Session | | 468 | 8 | Mrs V Lilley | N Murless | 1/2F |
| 2 Sept | Manchester | Battle Station | | 207 | 5 | R F Scully | F Armstrong | 2/9F |
| 5 Sept | Windsor | Prince Nick | | 370 | 6 | Mrs F Chandler | T Carey | 5/2F |
| 7 Sept | Doncaster | Pandofell | Doncaster Cup | 3,174 | 18 | H Warwick Daw | F Maxwell | 9/4F |
| 8 Sept | Doncaster | Aznip | September Stks | 1,680 | 7 | Lt Col G Loder | N Murless | 11/10F |
| 9 Sept | Doncaster | Petite Etoile | Scarborough | 1,196 | 8 | Aga Khan | N Murless | 4/7F |

(I) = Ireland

| Date | Race Course | Horse | Race | Value £ | Dist Fur | Owner | Trainer | S/P |
|---|---|---|---|---|---|---|---|---|
| 9 Sept | Doncaster | Aurelius | St Leger | 29,817 | 14 | Mrs V Lilley | N Murless | 9/2 |
| 11 Sept | Wolver'ton | Fairy Wood | | 207 | 7 | G Drinkwater | H Hannon | 9/4F |
| 11 Sept | Wolver'ton | Nymphea | | 207 | 11 | Mrs A Plesch | H Wragg | 4/5F |
| 13 Sept | Brighton | Barbary Pirate | | 402 | 10 | Miss B Cavendish-Bentinck | R Sturdy | 2/1F |
| 14 Sept | Brighton | Mysticism | | 514 | 6 | R F Watson | N Bertie | 7/4F |
| 16 Sept | Kempton | Will Reward | | 524 | 7 | G Baylis | S Ingham | 11/10F |
| 18 Sept | Leicester | Pannier | | 345 | 10 | Lady Z Wernher | Sir C Boyd Rochfort | 2/1 |
| 19 Sept | Windsor | Palmete | | 276 | 8 | Lord Howard de Walden | J A Waugh | 4/1 |
| 30 Sept | Newmarket | St Paddy | Jockey Club Stks | 2,282 | 14 | Sir V Sassoon | N Murless | 4/6F |
| 2 Oct | Nottingham | Tenebre | | 207 | 7 | R A L Cohen | R Day | 100/6 |
| 2 Oct | Nottingham | Columbus | | 351 | 10 | O/trainer | F Armstrong | 6/1F |
| 2 Oct | Nottingham | Abundance | | 276 | 8 | Lord Howard de Walden | J A Waugh | 13/8F |
| 2 Oct | Nottingham | Nymphea | | 276 | 10 | Mrs A Plesch | H Wragg | EvF |
| 3 Oct | Nottingham | Impelo | | 276 | 8 | M F Cutler | H Price | 6/1 |
| 4 Oct | York | Flower Drum | | 615 | 12 | Lord Elveden | H Wragg | 15/8F |
| 6 Oct | Ascot | Pellegrino | Sandwich | 1,322 | 6 | Col B Hornung | N Murless | 7/2F |
| 14 Oct | Newmarket | Silver Kumar | Queensberry Hcp | 1,014 | 5 | Mrs R Read | R Read | 6/1 |
| 21 Oct | Doncaster | Golden Voice | | 207 | 8 | Col B Hornung | N Murless | 4/1 |
| 30 Oct | Birmingham | Panthera | | 276 | 6 | Mrs V Lilley | N Murless | 3/1 |
| 30 Oct | Birmingham | Luciole | | 276 | 13 | Lord Carnarvon | N Bertie | 9/4 |
| 4 Nov | Liverpool | George's Girl | | 207 | 6 | B Coleman | M Connolly(I) | 4/5F |
| 9 Nov | Newbury | Prince Tudor | William Clark Hcp | 840 | 6 | O/trainer | J Weston-Evans | 8/1 |
| 9 Nov | Newbury | Sublime | | 420 | 13 | Lady Rowlandson | R Jarvis | 8/11F |

1961: 164 wins; 108 2nds; 73 3rds; 703 rides

| Date | Race Course | Horse | Race | Value £ | Dist Fur | Owner | Trainer | S/P |
|---|---|---|---|---|---|---|---|---|
| 1962 | | | | | | | | |
| 26 Mar | Lincoln | Vilbar | | 294 | 6 | M Ostrer | K Piggott | 9/1 |
| 26 Mar | Lincoln | Lyonado | | 375 | 5 | E M Jones | K Piggott | 10/1 |
| 26 Mar | Lincoln | Ronic | | 375 | 7 | J U Baillie | J A Waugh | 9/2 |
| 28 Mar | Lincoln | Smokey Gem | | 207 | 7 | J Kendrick | R Ward | 11/4F |
| 30 Mar | Liverpool | Rigvada | Liverpool Spring Cup | 765 | 10 | Maharani of Baroda | F Armstrong | 9/2 |
| 2 Apl | Nottingham | Melozza | | 318 | 8 | M Batthyany | F Armstrong | 2/1F |
| 2 Apl | Nottingham | Gendarme | | 207 | 7 | O/trainer | S W Everitt | 8/1 |
| 2 Apl | Nottingham | Bronze Brae | | 276 | 8 | O/trainer | R Day | 5/2F |
| 4 Apl | Hurst Park | White Park Bay | | 390 | 14 | E D Midwood | P Payne-Gallwey | 7/4F |
| 6 Apl | Windsor | Queen's Hussar | | 276 | 5 | Lord Carnarvon | T Corbett | 4/7F |
| 18 Apl | Pontefract | Melozza* | | 142 | 8 | Mrs E Glynn | E Gifford | 7/4F |
| 18 Apl | Pontefract | Golden Cognac | | 207 | 5 | J Barker | W Wharton | 3/1 |
| 24 Apl | Epsom | Grand Applause | | 567 | 7 | E Rudd | H Cottrill | 11/4F |
| 25 Apl | Epsom | Queen's Hussar | Cuddington | 763 | 5 | Lord Carnarvon | T Corbett | 11/10F |
| 28 Apl | Sandown | Ferneley | Royal Stks | 1,825 | 10 | Lt Col G Loder | N Murless | 4/1 |
| 3 May | Newmarket | Peroxide | | 665 | 9 | R F Scully | F Armstrong | 13/2 |
| 4 May | Hurst Park | Flashing Light | | 390 | 5 | M Berol | T Corbett | 5/2F |
| 4 May | Hurst Park | Samothraki | | 1,336 | 10 | J M Mason | F Maxwell | 9/4F |
| 7 May | Alex Palace | Sweet Molly | | 207 | 8 | S Bates | D Whelan | 4/1 |
| 8 May | Chester | Ann Boleyn | Lily Agnes Stks | 1,180 | 5 | Lord Carnarvon | T Corbett | 2/5F |
| 9 May | Chester | Mona Louise | Stewards' Stks | 1,038 | 7 | O/trainer | R E Mason | 4/1 |
| 12 May | Kempton | Golden Inca | | 639 | 5 | O/trainer | J Weston-Evans | 10/1 |
| 12 May | Kempton | Vijay | | 555 | 5 | I J Chouls | K Piggott | 7/2 |

* Dead Heat (I) = Ireland

| Date | Race Course | Horse | Race | Value £ | Dist Fur | Owner | Trainer | S/P |
|---|---|---|---|---|---|---|---|---|
| 15 May | York | Romantic | Zetland | 836 | 5 | Lt Col G Loder | N Murless | 5/2 |
| 17 May | York | See See | Dringhouses S | 1,024 | 8 | C I Whiting | R Ward | 9/4F |
| 17 May | Sandown | Goa | | 547 | 7 | R V Stone | D Thom | 9/4F |
| 19 May | Sandown | Aurelius | Coombe Stks | 1,025 | 13 | Mrs V Lilley | N Murless | 6/4F |
| 21 May | Birmingham | Pornic | | 276 | 5 | W S Dugdale | T Corbett | 11/10F |
| 22 May | Birmingham | Sharuk | | 276 | 5 | Sir C Dowty | F Armstrong | 7/4F |
| 25 May | Lingfield | Romancero | | 390 | 10 | F C Thrush | T Carey | 5/1 |
| 28 May | Leicester | Faerie Ring | | 201 | 5 | Mrs J F C Bryce | F Armstrong | 2/5F |
| 28 May | Leicester | Livin' Doll | | 267 | 10 | J Foulds | D Thom | 9/4F |
| 29 May | Leicester | Pannier | | 345 | 10 | Mrs R Macdonald-Buchanan | J A Waugh | 11/10F |
| 1 June | Newbury | Icarus | | 420 | 12 | The Queen | N Murless | 8/1 |
| 1 June | Newmarket | Peroxide | | 670 | 8 | R F Scully | F Armstrong | EvF |
| 1 June | Newmarket | Panjandrum | | 311 | 14 | Lord Howard de Warden | J A Waugh | 4/1 |
| 1 Aug | Goodwood | Romantic | Richmond | 3,215 | 6 | Lt Col G Loder | N Murless | 8/11F |
| 2 Aug | Goodwood | Princess Cecilia | Lavant | 612 | 5 | Lt Col G Loder | N Murless | 9/4 |
| 3 Aug | Goodwood | Picador | Foxhall | 689 | 6 | Lord Carnarvon | T Corbett | 9/4F |
| 4 Aug | Epsom | Park Hill Boy | Tattenham Hcp | 705 | 6 | E S Dixon | E Davey | 13/2 |
| 4 Aug | Epsom | Zaragoza | | 568 | 10 | Maj H P Holt | R Greenhill | 10/1 |
| 4 Aug | Epsom | True North | Box Hill | 935 | 7 | E B Benjamin | F Armstrong | 2/1 |
| 4 Aug | Epsom | Principal | Diomed Hcp | 961 | 8 | H A Greenland | D Whelan | 7/4F |
| 6 Aug | Newcastle | Koshka | | 355 | 5 | Aga Khan | N Murless | 4/9F |
| 6 Aug | Newcastle | Ribot Light | | 415 | 8 | Lady Sassoon | N Murless | 1/10F |
| 8 Aug | Brighton | Tour de France | | 543 | 10 | Mrs J Goldsmith | H Goldsmith | 4/1 |
| 14 Aug | Alex Palace | Ravello | | 277 | 8 | Mrs A Saville | R Kennett | 2/1F |
| 14 Aug | Alex Palace | Blue Over | | 257 | 8 | Mrs W Whittaker | F Armstrong | 4/11F |
| 18 Aug | Newbury | Grand Applause | | 345 | 7 | E Rudd | H Cottrill | 6/1 |
| 20 Aug | Lewes | Barbary Pirate | | 275 | 8 | G J Horton | R Sturdy | 11/2 |
| 24 Aug | Lingfield | Picador | | 390 | 6 | Lord Carnarvon | T Corbett | 4/11F |
| 24 Aug | Lingfield | Senta | | 306 | 16 | Miss P Wolf | D Marks | 13/8F |
| 25 Aug | Lingfield | Tudor Tale | | 470 | 12 | P Winstone | H Cottrill | 10/11F |
| 25 Aug | Lingfield | Dangerfield | Frant Pl | 765 | 7 | S Joel | H Cottrill | 10/1 |
| 27 Aug | Warwick | Mellors | | 376 | 6 | Mrs J F C Bryce | F Armstrong | 4/7F |
| 27 Aug | Warwick | Snap Decision | | 207 | 8 | C B Duguid | R Read | 11/2 |
| 29 Aug | Beverley | Principal | George Habbershaw Hcp | 603 | 10 | E B Benjamin | F Armstrong | EvF |
| 29 Aug | Beverley | Golden Inca | | 278 | 7 | O/trainer | J Weston-Evans | 2/1 |
| 30 Aug | Beverley | Sharuk | | 207 | 7 | Sir G Dowty | F Armstrong | EvF |
| 30 Aug | Beverley | Paulis Plume | | 207 | 5 | W Dickie | E Davey | 3/1F |
| 31 Aug | Hurst Park | Thames Trader | Nonsuch Pl | 790 | 13 | S Wootton | S Ingham | 11/2 |
| 3 Sept | Pontefract | St Maur | | 207 | 6 | A Dormer | C Elliott | 4/9F |
| 3 Sept | Pontefract | Fauvist | | 207 | 5 | Dr M L Slotover | F Armstrong | 8/11F |
| 3 Sept | Pontefract | Chanora | | 276 | 12 | Mrs E M Crosfield | F Armstrong | 13/8F |
| 4 Sept | Birmingham | Mbarara | | 276 | 7 | M W Wickham-Boynton | N Murless | 6/4F |
| 4 Sept | Birmingham | Saint Levantine | | 276 | 13 | Miss M L Pinder | F Johnson Houghton | EvF |
| 7 Sept | Sandown | Aurelius | Atalanta Stks | 822 | 10 | Mrs V Lilley | N Murless | 1/4F |
| 7 Sept | Sandown | Douvarme | | 345 | 8 | Maj H R Broughton | J A Waugh | 6/1 |
| 7 Sept | Sandown | Senta | | 587 | 16 | Miss P K Wolf | D Marks | 5/2F |
| 11 Sept | Doncaster | Tudor Tale | Great Yorkshire Hcp | 2,198 | 14 | P Winstone | H Cottrill | 8/1 |
| 11 Sept | Doncaster | Albatros | Clumber Stks | 1,243 | 11 | Lt Col G Loder | N Murless | 11/10F |
| 17 Sept | Edinburgh | Valedictory | | 205 | 5 | J E Clout | T Dent | 6/4F |
| 17 Sept | Edinburgh | Blue Over | | 434 | 8 | Mrs W Whittaker | F Armstrong | 10/11F |
| 17 Sept | Edinburgh | Afghanistan | | 517 | 12 | Mrs J F C Bryce | F Armstrong | 3/1 |
| 17 Sept | Edinburgh | Craigs of Kyle | | 207 | 7 | Maj W D Montgomerie | A Barclay | 13/2 |

| Date | Race Course | Horse | Race | Value £ | Dist Fur | Owner | Trainer | S/P |
|---|---|---|---|---|---|---|---|---|
| 21 Sept | Kempton | Charmer | | 659 | 7 | Lt Col G Loder | N Murless | 10/1 |
| 3 Oct | Newmarket | Thames Trader | Victory Hcp | 1,010 | 12 | S Wootton | S Ingham | 6/4F |
| 6 Oct | Newmarket | Follow Suit | Dewhurst | 4,500 | 7 | Lt Col G Loder | N Murless | 10/1 |
| 9 Oct | Nottingham | Grey Mop | | 276 | 8 | T West | S Hall | 7/2 |
| 11 Oct | York | Angel's Head | | 516 | 8 | Lady Sassoon | N Murless | 10/1 |
| 11 Oct | York | El Gallo | | 510 | 6 | C A B St George | N Murless | 11/8F |
| 15 Oct | Wolver'ton | Grey Jet | | 276 | 5 | K O Boardman | W O'Brien | 9/2 |
| 15 Oct | Wolver'ton | Church Stretton | | 345 | 8 | K O Boardman | W O'Brien | 11/4 |
| 15 Oct | Wolver'ton | Hot Dish | | 276 | 5 | Lord Ranfurly | H Cottrill | 3/1F |
| 17 Oct | Newmarket | Bonnie Girl | | 367 | 5 | Mrs S Bonny | H Blackshaw | 9/4F |
| 18 Oct | Newmarket | Young Lochinvar | | 433 | 8 | Lady Sassoon | N Murless | 4/9F |
| 18 Oct | Newmarket | Granville Greta | Queensberry Hcp | 655 | 5 | E S Dixon | E Davey | 10/1 |
| 20 Oct | Warwick | Fauvist | | 291 | 5 | Dr M Slotover | F Armstrong | 9/4F |
| 20 Oct | Warwick | St Gulliver | | 375 | 12 | Sir G Dowty | F Armstong | 4/9F |
| 22 Oct | Birmingham | Mustavon | | 690 | 8 | Mrs L McVey | S Hall | 4/1F |
| 27 Oct | Stockton | Bonnie Girl | | 293 | 5 | Mrs S Bonny | H Blackshaw | 4/9F |
| 27 Oct | Stockton | Raccolto | | 207 | 10 | L G Lazarus | S Hall | 4/5F |
| 1 Nov | Liverpool | Fauvist | | 207 | 5 | Dr M L Slotover | F Armstrong | 10/3F |
| 1 Nov | Liverpool | Invasion | | 207 | 13 | R J Sigtia | S Hall | 3/1 |
| 9 Nov | Manchester | Sublime | Delamere Hcp | 735 | 16 | Lady Rowlandson | R Jarvis | 7/1 |
| 10 Nov | Manchester | Raccolto | | 345 | 10 | L G Lazarus | S Hall | 6/4F |

1962: 96 wins; 77 2nds; 50 3rds; 458 rides

| Date | Race Course | Horse | Race | Value £ | Dist Fur | Owner | Trainer | S/P |
|---|---|---|---|---|---|---|---|---|
| 1963 | | | | | | | | |
| 29 Mar | Liverpool | Forgotten Dreams | | 383 | 13 | Mrs P Meehan | A Thomas | 11/4F |
| 2 Apl | Nottingham | Crumpet | | 402 | 7 | A C D Ingleby-MacKenzie | A Freeman | 4/1 |
| 5 Apl | Windsor | Vijay | | 401 | 6 | I J Chouls | K Piggott | 15/2 |
| 13 Apl | Kempton | Turbo Jet | 2000 Guineas Trial | 2,067 | 7 | J McShain | M V O'Brien(I) | 7/4F |
| 15 Apl | Newcastle | Shantam | | 375 | 5 | J Wilcox | H Blackshaw | 11/10F |
| 22 Apl | Alex Palace | Fair Occasion | | 403 | 8 | Mr E Thornton-Smith | F Armstrong | 100/8 |
| 25 Apl | Epsom | Paramour | | 510 | 7 | Mrs J F C Bryce | F Armstrong | 5/2 |
| 25 Apl | Epsom | Amorella | Princess Elizabeth Stks | 4,436 | 8 | Lady Sassoon | N Murless | 11/2 |
| 27 Apl | Sandown | Light Thrust | Guildford Hcp | 1,102 | 13 | Col F T Halse | W Nightingall | 3/1F |
| 29 Apl | Wolver'ton | Aerosol | | 276 | 5 | Mrs R Macdonald-Buchanan | J A Waugh | 5/1 |
| 30 Apl | Newmarket | Siesta Time | | 578 | 5 | W Clarke | D Thom | 9/1 |
| 3 May | Ascot | Siesta Time | | 611 | 5 | W Clarke | D Thom | 11/8F |
| 6 May | Alex Palace | Placate | | 207 | 5 | Mrs B Myers | D Whelan | 5/2F |
| 6 May | Alex Palace | Mig | | 419 | 8 | E Weigan | D Thom | 11/2 |
| 7 May | Chester | Christmas Island | Chester Vase | 2,253 | 12 | Lord Ennisdale | P Prendergast(I) | 100/8 |
| 7 May | Chester | The Creditor | Stewards' Stks | 1,024 | 7 | Lady Sassoon | N Murless | 2/1F |
| 13 May | Birmingham | Siesta Time | | 414 | 5 | W Clarke | D Thom | 8/11F |
| 13 May | Birmingham | Technue | | 257 | 5 | O/trainer | S Everitt | 9/4 |
| 13 May | Birmingham | Selly Oak | | 402 | 6 | H Andrews | F Cundell | 6/4F |
| 14 May | York | Basan | Zetland | 828 | 5 | O/trainer | D Griffiths | 6/1 |
| 20 May | Leicester | Silas | | 403 | 8 | T H Farr | F Armstrong | 11/8F |
| 21 May | Alex Palace | Marguerite | | 276 | 5 | C A B St George | H Wallington | 10/11F |
| 22 May | Sandown | Crepes D'Enfer | | 512 | 10 | Lady Sassoon | N Murless | 2/1 |
| 22 May | Sandown | Shovel | | 445 | 5 | O/trainer | J Sutcliffe | 4/1 |
| 25 May | Worcester | Storm Trooper | | 345 | 16 | Lord Crawshaw | F Armstrong | 6/4F |
| 25 May | Worcester | White Rajah | | 449 | 6 | C W Engelhard | F Johnson Houghton | 2/1F |
| 25 May | Worcester | Thank You | | 207 | 5 | Mrs G T Johnson Houghton | F Johnson Houghton | 4/5F |
| 28 May | Epsom | Fauvist | | 597 | 5 | Dr M L Slotover | F Armstrong | 11/2 |

(I) = Ireland

| Date | Race Course | Horse | Race | Value £ | Dist Fur | Owner | Trainer | S/P |
|---|---|---|---|---|---|---|---|---|
| 1 June | Doncaster | El Gallo | | 383 | 6 | C A B St George | N Murless | 11/10F |
| 5 June | Kempton | Lovely Money | Falcon S | 1,072 | 8 | E Thornton-Smith | F Armstrong | 9/2 |
| 8 June | Manchester | Lynda's Own | | 422 | 5 | B Grainger | E Cousins | 8/15F |
| 8 June | Manchester | Petty Gift | | 443 | 11 | W Hill | W Elsey | 13/2 |
| 8 June | Manchester | Espresso | Manchester Cup | 4,159 | 12 | G Oldham | H Wragg | 3/1F |
| 8 June | Manchester | Red Chorus | Lancashire Oaks | 2,223 | 11 | J R Hindley | N Murless | 9/4 |
| 10 June | Nottingham | Rochidious | | 257 | 10 | A T Izzard | D Thom | EvF |
| 10 June | Nottingham | Bally Royal | | 401 | 13 | Mrs V Hue-Williams | N Murless | 7/1 |
| 10 June | Nottingham | Fideve | | 403 | 6 | Lady Sassoon | N Murless | 11/2 |
| 12 June | Lincoln | Pow Wow | | 294 | 5 | D Bernie | R Barons | 9/2 |
| 13 June | Lincoln | Legal Tangle | | 294 | 7 | N Hetherton | H Blackshaw | 11/8F |
| 13 June | Lincoln | Paramour | | 372 | 7 | Mrs J F C Bryce | F Armstrong | 4/7F |
| 14 June | Sandown | Bannockburn | | 595 | 10 | Mrs R Macdonald-Buchanan | J A Waugh | 7/2 |
| 19 June | Royal Ascot | The Creditor | Jersey Stks | 1,816 | 7 | Lady Sassoon | N Murless | 11/2F |
| 19 June | Royal Ascot | Spaniards Close | Royal Hunt Cup | 3,960 | 8 | Mrs B Davis | F Winter | 25/1 |
| 19 June | Royal Ascot | Raccolto | Bessborough | 1,731 | 12 | L G Lazarus | S Hall | 11/4 |
| 20 June | Royal Ascot | El Gallo | Cork and Orrery | 1,642 | 6 | C A B St George | N Murless | 20/1 |
| 20 June | Royal Ascot | Twilight Alley | Gold Cup | 10,397 | 20 | Lady Sassoon | N Murless | 10/3 |
| 21 June | Royal Ascot | Majority Rule | King's Stks | 2,083 | 5 | J Muldoon | W O'Gorman | 100/8 |
| 21 June | Warwick | French Vintage | | 346 | 6 | L Doubleday | F Winter | 4/11F |
| 21 June | Warwick | Be Hopeful | | 347 | 8 | G P Williams | P Walwyn | 5/6F |
| 24 June | Birmingham | Fideve | Warwickshire Breeders Stks | 1,866 | 6 | Lady Sassoon | N Murless | 6/5F |
| 25 June | Birmingham | Tom Tit | | 402 | 16 | Mrs F W Ward | F Cundell | 11/4 |
| 26 June | Newbury | Morning Calm | | 511 | 10 | Aga Khan | N Murless | 7/2 |
| 27 June | Newcastle | Tudor Grey | Gosforth Park Cup | 1,135 | 5 | E B Benjamin | F Armstrong | 4/1 |
| 28 June | Windsor | Tech Girl | | 287 | 6 | O/trainer | S W Everitt | 5/2 |
| 28 June | Windsor | Lyonado | | 378 | 6 | E J Jones | K Piggott | 5/1F |
| 29 June | Newcastle | Der Ring | | 401 | 7 | Lady Sassoon | N Murless | 4/5F |
| 1 July | Brighton | Souieda | | 382 | 7 | S L Green | W Payne | 10/1 |
| 3 July | Liverpool | Techland | | 294 | 5 | O/trainer | S W Everitt | 6/4 |
| 3 July | Liverpool | Lanarkshire | | 421 | 5 | Miss P J B S Finlay | W Elsey | 2/7F |
| 6 July | Nottingham | Costmary | | 403 | 5 | T H Farr | F Armstrong | 4/5F |
| 6 July | Nottingham | Colour Blind | | 403 | 13 | J U Baillie | T Corbett | 8/13F |
| 11 July | Yarmouth | Feathers | | 277 | 8 | Mrs B A Waller | F Cundell | EvF |
| 11 July | Doncaster | Monkey Palm | | 403 | 6 | Mrs E M Crosfield | F Armstrong | 1/5F |
| 11 July | Doncaster | Crept In | | 520 | 7 | Mrs J R Hindley | N Murless | 3/1 |
| 12 July | Manchester | Folding Money | | 485 | 6 | G Ainscough | M Connolly(I) | 1/2F |
| 13 July | Sandown | Bannockburn | | 432 | 10 | Mrs R Macdonald-Buchanan | J A Waugh | 4/1 |
| 17 July | Kempton | Teetotal | | 502 | 8 | Mrs M Lawson | W Payne | 11/4F |
| 19 July | Pontefract | Pursued | | 345 | 10 | J Banks | A Cooper | 11/10F |
| 19 July | Pontefract | Royal Tree | | 346 | 8 | O/trainer | M J Moroney | 5/4F |
| 19 July | Pontefract | Milburn | | 347 | 6 | R C Cockburn | E Davey | 10/3 |
| 19 July | Pontefract | Holly Lame | | 347 | 6 | C T Whiting | E Davey | 3/1 |
| 19 July | Pontefract | Cresside | | 346 | 5 | Mrs R Digby | J Clayton | 3/1 |
| 20 July | Ascot | Romancero | Black Nest Hcp | 1,028 | 8 | F C Thrush | T Carey | 10/1 |
| 20 July | Ascot | Faberge II | Virginia Water | 1,117 | 5 | N H Wachman | F Maxwell | 13/8F |
| 20 July | Ascot | Arctic Vale | Sunninghill Park | 933 | 16 | Mrs E Goring | P Prendergast(I) | 9/2 |
| 20 July | Wolver'ton | Tudor Times | | 346 | 7 | Dr M L Slotover | F Armstrong | 7/4F |
| 22 July | Leicester | Bannockburn | | 402 | 12 | Mrs R Macdonald-Buchanan | J A Waugh | 1/4F |
| 23 July | Leicester | Tudorama | | 402 | 5 | M I Leaver | F Armstrong | 11/10 |
| 23 July | Leicester | Therma | | 272 | 6 | O/trainer | S W Everitt | 1/8F |
| 23 July | Leicester | Acclaim | | 414 | 8 | H Dare | F Cundell | 4/1 |
| 23 July | Leicester | Colour Blind | | 403 | 12 | J U Baillie | T Corbett | 4/6F |
| 24 July | Sandown | Serendipity | | 500 | 5 | Mrs J F C Bryce | F Armstrong | 4/11F |
| 24 July | Sandown | Casablanca | | 702 | 7 | Col B Hornung | N Murless | 5/1 |

(I) = Ireland

| Date | Race Course | Horse | Race | Value £ | Dist Fur | Owner | Trainer | S/P |
|---|---|---|---|---|---|---|---|---|
| 24 July | Sandown | Loidien | | 488 | 10 | M W Wickham-Boynton | N Murless | 11/8F |
| 25 July | Sandown | Bally Royal | | 640 | 13 | Mrs V Hue-Williams | N Murless | 4/5F |
| 26 July | Newbury | Dieu Soleil | | 504 | 6 | Mrs V Hue-Williams | N Murless | 6/1 |
| 27 July | Newbury | Sweet Moss | Donnington Castle Stks | 1,625 | 7 | Lady Sassoon | N Murless | 11/10 |
| 27 July | Newbury | Zingaline | | 640 | 5 | F R Hue-Williams | N Murless | EvF |
| 29 July | Birmingham | Tudor Times | | 402 | 6 | Dr M L Slotover | F Armstrong | 1/2F |
| 29 July | Birmingham | Taste of Honey | | 414 | 10 | Mrs A M Palmer | F Maxwell | 7/4F |
| 31 July | Goodwood | Corinth | | 607 | 6 | A J Macdonald-Buchanan | J A Waugh | 2/1 |
| 31 July | Goodwood | St Gulliver | Chesterfield Cup | 2,131 | 10 | Sir G Dowty | F Armstrong | 4/1F |
| 2 Aug | Goodwood | Tudorama | Findon S | 1,182 | 5 | M I Leaver | F Armstrong | 6/5F |
| 3 Aug | Newmarket | Creation | | 381 | 8 | Mrs V Hue-Williams | N Murless | 8/11F |
| 3 Aug | Newmarket | Bally Royal | | 898 | 14 | Mrs V Hue-Williams | N Murless | 10/3 |
| 5 Aug | Ripon | Matatina | Great St Wilfred Hcp | 3,925 | 6 | Mrs R C Wilson | F Armstrong | 5/6F |
| 6 Aug | Brighton | Zingaline | Channel Stks | 800 | 6 | F R Hue-Williams | N Murless | EvF |
| 6 Aug | Brighton | Romancero | | 401 | 10 | F C Thrush | T Carey | EvF |
| 10 Aug | Redcar | E J | Bedale Stks | 965 | 7 | D Murray | P Rohan | 2/1F |
| 10 Aug | Redcar | Connamara Kid | | 379 | 9 | K O Boardman | W O'Brien | 11/2 |
| 12 Aug | Nottingham | Monkey Palm | | 690 | 6 | Mrs E M Crosfield | F Armstrong | 11/2 |
| 13 Aug | Nottingham | Luxury Sport | | 257 | 10 | Mrs F H Higgins | J Mulhall | 7/2 |
| 13 Aug | Nottingham | Umgeni Poort | | 403 | 6 | C Nicholson | F Armstrong | 1/6F |
| 14 Aug | Haydock | Richard's Spur | | 402 | 10 | D O'Dell | W Lyde | 5/2 |
| 15 Aug | Haydock | Pickapepper | | 401 | 8 | Mrs J F C Bryce | F Armstrong | 9/4F |
| 16 Aug | Stockton | Tudorama | | 403 | 5 | M I Leaver | F Armstrong | EvF |
| 17 Aug | Newbury | Peter le Grand | Washington Singer Stks | 1,438 | 6 | F Hue-Williams | N Murless | 2/1F |
| 17 Aug | Newbury | Aria Royal | Kenneth Robertson Hcp | 3,120 | 12 | A Turner | E Weymes | 100/9 |
| 17 Aug | Newbury | Farida Jenks | Shrivenham Hcp | 840 | 5 | Miss H Monteith | I Walker | 15/2F |
| 19 Aug | Lewes | Magic Mist | | 247 | 5 | J I Taubman | W Combes | 7/4 |
| 19 Aug | Lewes | Be Hopeful | | 347 | 8 | G P W Williams | P Walwyn | 6/4F |
| 19 Aug | Lewes | Glamorous | | 346 | 12 | Lord Carnarvon | T Corbett | 6/4F |
| 19 Aug | Lewes | March Hare | | 346 | 10 | J Sheffield | P Walwyn | EvF |
| 20 Aug | York | Matatina | Nunthorpe | 3,945 | 5 | Mrs R C Wilson | F Armstrong | 7/2 |
| 22 Aug | York | Talahesse | Gimcrack | 7,260 | 6 | H Loebstein | T Corbett | 11/8F |
| 23 Aug | Lingfield | L'Etranger | | 401 | 6 | J Cohen | D Hanley | 5/2 |
| 24 Aug | Newmarket | The Creditor | | 1,247 | 8 | Lady Sassoon | N Murless | 11/10F |
| 24 Aug | Newmarket | Monkey Palm | | 634 | 6 | Mrs E M Crosfield | F Armstrong | 7/4F |
| 26 Aug | Warwick | Rainy Day | | 392 | 7 | O/trainer | E Davey | 9/2 |
| 29 Aug | Brighton | St Gulliver | August Hcp | 1,836 | 12 | Sir G Dowty | F Armstrong | 4/5F |
| 29 Aug | Brighton | Der Ring | | 418 | 7 | Lady Sassoon | N Murless | 11/2 |
| 31 Aug | Sandown | El Gallo | Daily Mirror Hcp | 1,763 | 5 | C A B St George | N Murless | 100/8 |
| 2 Sept | Lewes | Tondo | | 347 | 8 | E C Bland | F Armstrong | 4/5F |
| 2 Sept | Lewes | Fair Decision | | 346 | 8 | E Thornton-Smith | F Armstrong | 9/2 |
| 3 Sept | Birmingham | Rochidious | | 257 | 10 | A T Izzard | D Thom | 11/8F |
| 4 Sept | Ripon | Bluebottle | | 351 | 5 | J R Mullion | F Armstrong | 4/6F |
| 7 Sept | Epsom | Palm | Heathcote Nursery Hcp | 2,054 | 7 | A Plesch | J Rogers(I) | 8/1 |
| 7 Sept | Epsom | Crepes D'Enfer | Redhill Stks | 916 | 10 | Lady Sassoon | N Murless | 10/11F |
| 9 Sept | Warwick | Quo Banco | | 347 | 7 | J R Mullion | F Armstrong | 5/4F |
| 9 Sept | Warwick | Golden Ruffle | | 678 | 5 | J Muldoon | W O'Gorman | 11/8F |
| 9 Sept | Warwick | Mellors | | 346 | 12 | Mrs J F C Bryce | F Armstrong | 3/1 |
| 11 Sept | Doncaster | Passenger | Town Moor Hcp | 1,182 | 7 | W R Kinsey | P Moore | 10/3 |
| 11 Sept | Doncaster | Umgeni Poort | Prince of Wales Nursery Handicap | 1,048 | 8 | G Nicholson | F Armstrong | 9/4F |

(I) = Ireland

| Date | Race Course | Horse | Race | Value £ | Dist Fur | Owner | Trainer | S/P |
|---|---|---|---|---|---|---|---|---|
| 16 Sept | Lewes | Rose Barker | | 347 | 8 | S J Gillings | W Payne | 5/2 |
| 18 Sept | Ayr | Snow Vista | | 402 | 8 | O/trainer | E Weymes | 6/4F |
| 18 Sept | Ayr | Wrangle | Royal Caledonian Hunt Hcp | 1,095 | 8 | J A Shellim | S Hall | 2/1F |
| 19 Sept | Brighton | Arbutus | | 393 | 8 | The Queen | N Murless | EvF |
| 19 Sept | Brighton | Soueida | | 404 | 8 | S L Green | W Payne | 2/1F |
| 20 Sept | Kempton | Crepes D'Enfer | Tangiers Stks | 943 | 11 | Lady Sassoon | N Murless | 4/6F |
| 21 Sept | Kempton | Royal Unity | | 548 | 8 | B Myers | J Sutcliffe | 4/1F |
| 21 Sept | Kempton | Derring-Do | Imperial Stks | 6,702 | 6 | Mrs H H Renshaw | A Budgett | 2/1F |
| 23 Sept | Leicester | Cloudbreak | | 402 | 5 | Mrs D Wigan | N Murless | 2/5F |
| 23 Sept | Leicester | Lucky Harry | | 346 | 10 | N Mundy | B Foster | 15/8 |
| 23 Sept | Leicester | Marchakin | | 414 | 12 | Mrs G Trimmer-Thompson | K Cundell | 5/4F |
| 23 Sept | Leicester | Margit | | 402 | 8 | W J Kelly | G Smyth | 3/1F |
| 25 Sept | Pontefract | Hail Duke | | 346 | 10 | W N Wilfred | L Hall | 5/6F |
| 25 Sept | Pontefract | Monkey Palm | | 347 | 6 | Mrs E M Crosfield | F Armstrong | 2/5F |
| 25 Sept | Pontefract | Snow Vista | | 346 | 8 | O/trainer | E Weymes | 2/1F |
| 26 Sept | Pontefract | St Gulliver | | 690 | 12 | Sir G Dowty | F Armstrong | 11/8F |
| 27 Sept | Ascot (at Newbury) | Vhairi | Princess Royal Stks | 1,194 | 12 | H Leggat | P Beasley | 11/4F |
| 27 Sept | Ascot (at Newbury) | Casabianca | Royal Lodge | 3,851 | 8 | Col B Hornung | N Murless | 4/1 |
| 28 Sept | Ascot (at Newbury) | Impact | Clarence House | 568 | 6 | Mrs V Hue-Williams | N Murless | 6/11 |
| 28 Sept | Ascot (at Newbury) | The Creditor | Queen Elizabeth II | 5,186 | 8 | Lady Sassoon | N Murless | 5/4F |
| 30 Sept | Birmingham | Eighty Draws | | 257 | 7 | Mrs D Wickins | H Price | 11/8F |
| 4 Oct | Haydock | Lanconello | | 434 | 12 | Marchese Incisa Della Rocchetta | J Clayton | 5/1 |
| 4 Oct | Haydock | Death Ray | Copeland Hcp | 953 | 8 | R A Budgett | A Budgett | 3/1F |
| 4 Oct | Haydock | Umgeni Poort | | 402 | 8 | C Nicholson | F Armstrong | 13/8F |
| 7 Oct | Nottingham | Precarious | | 414 | 8 | Capt G H Drummond | R Greenhill | 11/4 |
| 7 Oct | Nottingham | Sublime | | 552 | 16 | Lady Rowlandson | R Jarvis | 10/11F |
| 8 Oct | Nottingham | Passenger | | 552 | 8 | W R Kinsey | P Moore | 9/4F |
| 15 Oct | Wolver'ton | Golden Ruffle | | 346 | 5 | J Muldoon | W O'Gorman | 5/4F |
| 15 Oct | Wolver'ton | African Drum | | 345 | 8 | K O Boardman | W O'Brien | 9/4F |
| 16 Oct | Kempton | Sabra | | 651 | 6 | B Myers | D Whelan | 4/9F |
| 16 Oct | Kempton | Royal Avenue | Mentmore Stks | 992 | 11 | C A B St George | N Murless | 4/5F |
| 18 Oct | Newmarket | Royal Desire | Houghton Stks | 1,787 | 7 | Mrs M E Whitney-Tippett | N Murless | 11/10F |
| 19 Oct | Newmarket | Legal Court | Rous Mem | 702 | 6 | Miss O Bridges | R Day | 6/5 |
| 19 Oct | Newmarket | Nos Royalistes | AFA Security Bell Hcp | 2,680 | 16 | Lady Sassoon | J Rogers(I) | 11/4F |
| 21 Oct | Birmingham | Pure Bog | | 257 | 7 | Mrs R Watson | P Rohan | 5/4F |
| 21 Oct | Birmingham | Whitley Court | | 402 | 13 | B W Grainger | P Rohan | 4/1 |
| 23 Oct | Sandown | Flow-Kaj | | 411 | 13 | J M Wolf | E Reavey | 13/8F |
| 26 Oct | Doncaster | Nos Royalistes | Cantelo Stks | 1,328 | 14 | Lady Sassoon | J Rogers(I) | 8/13F |
| 7 Nov | Manchester | Royal Avenue | | 401 | 10 | C A B St George | N Murless | 9/2 |
| 8 Nov | Manchester | Sublime | | 631 | 16 | Lady Rowlandson | R Jarvis | 11/4 |
| 9 Nov | Manchester | Near the Line | | 403 | 10 | Mrs H L L Morriss | H Wragg | 1/2F |
| 9 Nov | Manchester | Fury Royal | | 401 | 10 | A Turner | E Weymes | 7/2 |

1963: 175 wins; 109 2nds; 71 3rds; 657 rides

| Date | Race Course | Horse | Race | Value £ | Dist Fur | Owner | Trainer | S/P |
|---|---|---|---|---|---|---|---|---|
| 1964 | | | | | | | | |
| 28 Mar | Kempton | Water Baby | | 577 | 5 | Lord Porchester | T Corbett | 11/10F |
| 28 Mar | Kempton | Close Call | | 572 | 5 | M Bonsor | T Corbett | 10/3 |
| 30 Mar | Birmingham | Persinglass | | 549 | 10 | C Clore | P Nelson | 11/2 |

(I) = Ireland

| Date | Race Course | Horse | Race | Value £ | Dist Fur | Owner | Trainer | S/P |
|---|---|---|---|---|---|---|---|---|
| 4 Apl | Windsor | Siliconn | | 276 | 5 | C Pollock | T Corbett | 13/8F |
| 10 Apl | Lingfield | Polyfoto | | 544 | 5 | Mrs C Reavey | E Reavey | 7/1 |
| 10 Apl | Lingfield | Spare Filly | | 547 | 10 | Mrs R Read | R Read | 100/9 |
| 11 Apl | Lingfield | Siesta Time | Leigh Hcp | 1,211 | 7 | W Clarke | D Thom | 10/3 |
| 15 Apl | Newmarket | Ruby's Princess | | 478 | 5 | E A Holt | W O'Gorman | 7/2 |
| 15 Apl | Newmarket | Polyfoto | | 309 | 5 | Mrs C J Reavey | E Reavey | 5/4F |
| 18 Apl | Newbury | Grecian Jet | | 429 | 5 | Mrs F Wilkinson | T Corbett | 11/10F |
| 18 Apl | Newbury | Royal Avenue | John Porter | 1,966 | 12 | C A B St George | N Murless | 100/8 |
| 18 Apl | Newbury | Rajen | | 504 | 8 | Mrs I J Chouls | K Piggott | 4/1 |
| 23 Apl | Epsom | Be Hopeful | Great Surrey Hcp | 1,000 | 6 | G P Williams | P Walwyn | 100/7 |
| 29 Apl | Newmarket | Rajen | | 472 | 12 | Mrs I J Chouls | K Piggott | 5/2F |
| 6 May | Chester | Persian Garden | Grosvenor Stks | 1,179 | 10 | Lt Col G Loder | N Murless | 20/1 |
| 7 May | Chester | Arctic Vale | Ormonde | 1,976 | 13 | Mrs E Goring | P Prendergast (I) | 6/5F |
| 7 May | Chester | Sweet Moss | Grosvenor | 2,420 | 10 | Lady Sassoon | N Murless | 5/4F |
| 9 May | Haydock | Crepes Braves | | 398 | 10 | Lady Sassoon | N Murless | 4/9F |
| 14 May | Salisbury | Merry Madcap | | 553 | 5 | Mrs H O H Freyling-huysen | F Maxwell | 100/8 |
| 16 May | Kempton | Confinement | | 515 | 5 | R Davies | W Holden | 4/5F |
| 20 May | Lincoln | Gram of Gold | | 345 | 10 | Mrs B Pearce | W O'Gorman | 9/2 |
| 21 May | Lincoln | Hasty Cast | | 207 | 5 | Mrs J S Crosfield | F Armstrong | 2/5F |
| 22 May | Lingfield | Gay Enchantment | | 390 | 5 | F Woolff | W Payne | 11/2 |
| 22 May | Liverpool | Birdbrook | | 294 | 8 | Mrs J F C Bryce | F Armstrong | 4/5F |
| 22 May | Liverpool | St Gulliver | Summer Cup | 1,109 | 10 | Sir G Dowty | F Armstrong | 11/4F |
| 25 May | Worcester | Tudor Summer | | 438 | 6 | L Thompson | W O'Gorman | 6/1 |
| 25 May | Worcester | Souieda | | 345 | 8 | S L Green | W Payne | 1/4F |
| 25 May | Worcester | Silent Trust | | 207 | 5 | I Allan | F Armstrong | 1/5F |
| 26 May | York | Sweet Moss | Dante | 2,790 | 10 | Lady Sassoon | N Murless | 3/1F |
| 26 May | York | Majority Rule | | 791 | 5 | J Muldoon | W O'Gorman | 9/2 |
| 27 May | York | Royal Unity | Hambleton Hcp | 822 | 8 | B Myers | J Sutcliffe | 11/10F |
| 30 May | Newbury | Tintinabula | Hermitage Pl S | 980 | 5 | C A B St George | H Wallington | 5/1 |
| 30 May | Newbury | The Creditor | Lockinge | 2,316 | 8 | Lady Sassoon | N Murless | 10/11F |
| 30 May | Leicester | Asado | | 207 | 5 | Lord Howard de Walden | J A Waugh | 1/3F |
| 2 June | Epsom | Goldendale | Ladbroke Gold Cup | 2,824 | 8 | Mrs B Hornung | N Murless | 4/1 |
| 5 June | Epsom | Very Nice | | 692 | 6 | L A Abelson | N Smyth | 10/1 |
| 6 June | Kempton | Diplopia | | 590 | 5 | O/trainer | N Smyth | 7/1 |
| 9 June | Alex Palace | Priadasee | | 414 | 5 | Maharani of Baroda | F Armstrong | 100/6 |
| 10 June | Brighton | Operatic Society | Pavilion Hcp | 1,374 | 12 | R Pears-Walker | C Benstead | 5/2 |
| 10 June | Brighton | Mwanza | | 446 | 8 | J R Hindley | N Murless | 10/3 |
| 12 June | Sandown | Queen's Hussar | | 787 | 8 | Lord Carnarvon | T Corbett | 1/2F |
| 12 June | Sandown | Golden Ruffle | | 559 | 5 | J Muldoon | W O'Gorman | 5/2F |
| 12 June | Bath | Young Rowette | | 345 | 5 | C W Hanks | R Read | 13/8F |
| 15 June | Leicester | Hasty Cast | | 345 | 6 | Mrs J S Crosfield | F Armstrong | 1/2 |
| 15 June | Leicester | King's Petition | | 345 | 8 | F Thrush | C E Pratt | 9/4 |
| 16 June | Royal Ascot | Roan Rocket | St James's Palace Stks | 9,049 | 8 | T F C Frost | G Todd | 5/4F |
| 17 June | Royal Ascot | Young Christopher | Jersey | 1,829 | 7 | J McShine | F Maxwell | 5/4F |
| 20 June | Worcester | Harvest Child | | 425 | 10 | Brig M Gordon-Watson | F Maxwell | EvF |
| 22 June | Birmingham | Silent Trust | | 690 | 6 | I Allan | F Armstrong | 4/6F |
| 24 June | Newbury | Democratic Fair | Test S Pl | 980 | 8 | W Crayden | K Gethin | 5/4F |
| 24 June | Newbury | Peter Piper | Netheravon Hcp | 840 | 13 | Mrs V R Phillips | R Mason | 4/1 |
| 24 June | Newbury | Siliconn | Berkshire Stks | 1,099 | 5 | C Pollock | T Corbett | 7/2 |
| 24 June | Newbury | Versailles | | 536 | 10 | Mrs V Hue-Williams | N Murless | 7/1 |
| 25 June | Newbury | Crepes D'Enfer | Summer Cup | 1,591 | 12 | Lady Sassoon | N Murless | 7/2F |
| 25 June | Newbury | Merry Madcap | | 597 | 5 | Mrs H O H Freling-huysen | F Maxwell | 15/8F |

(I) = Ireland

| ate | Race Course | Horse | Race | Value £ | Dist Fur | Owner | Trainer | S/P |
|---|---|---|---|---|---|---|---|---|
| June | Wolver'ton | Fire Worship | | 345 | 5 | Col A W Newman | F Armstrong | 7/4 |
| June | Wolver'ton | Right Game | | 345 | 5 | Mrs B Bray | F Armstrong | 5/2 |
| June | Brighton | Crepes Braves | | 421 | 10 | Lady Sassoon | N Murless | 1/2F |
| July | Sandown | Light Thrust | | 629 | 13 | Col F T Halse | W Nightingall | 3/1 |
| July | Sandown | Joyful | | 414 | 5 | Lt Col G Loder | N Murless | 4/7F |
| July | Nottingham | Mwanza | | 414 | 8 | J R Hindley | N Murless | 1/2F |
| July | Windsor | Tondo | | 414 | 12 | E Cooper Bland | F Armstrong | 15/8F |
| July | Windsor | Talahasse | | 332 | 8 | H Loebstein | T Corbett | 1/8F |
| July | Lingfield | Coolroy | | 457 | 10 | A Kennedy | W Nightingall | 3/1 |
| July | Lingfield | Amfissa | Equestrian Stks | 1,518 | 10 | M W Wickham-Boynton | N Murless | 4/6F |
| July | Lingfield | Touroy | John Bishop Wine Co | 898 | 10 | A Kennedy | W Nightingall | 3/1F |
| July | Lingfield | Dieu Soleil | Town and Country Cup | 2,400 | 12 | Mrs V Hue-Williams | N Murless | 9/4F |
| July | Birmingham | Prince of Norway | | 414 | 13 | C Clore | P Nelson | 2/1F |
| July | Birmingham | First Prize | | 681 | 6 | Mrs M Bonsor | T Corbett | 4/11F |
| July | Kempton | Silent Trust | | 470 | 7 | I Allen | F Armstrong | 2/1F |
| July | Doncaster | Merry Madcap | | 500 | 5 | Mrs H O H Freling-huysen | F Maxwell | 5/4F |
| July | Doncaster | Palm | | 482 | 7 | A Plesch | N Murless | 5/2 |
| July | Yarmouth | Leonardo | | 345 | 6 | C A B St George | N Murless | 10/11F |
| July | Yarmouth | Good Shooting | | 277 | 7 | J Simmons | R Read | 2/1F |
| July | Yarmouth | Ballycotton | | 345 | 7 | O/trainer | W O'Gorman | 6/4F |
| July | Ascot | Holborn | Granville | 865 | 5 | C W Engelhard | F Johnson Houghton | 5/1 |
| July | Leicester | Absalom | | 345 | 5 | Lt Col J Hornung | J A Waugh | 5/6F |
| July | Leicester | Hasty Cast | Worksop Manor | 828 | 6 | Mrs J S Crosfield | F Armstrong | 3/10F |
| July | Leicester | Pickapepper | | 345 | 8 | Mrs J F C Bryce | F Armstrong | 8/13F |
| July | Leicester | Arbutus | | 346 | 10 | The Queen | N Murless | 8/11F |
| July | Sandown | Tinto | Lane Pl S | 965 | 5 | O/trainer | W O'Gorman | 10/3 |
| July | Sandown | Palm | | 469 | 7 | A Plesch | N Murless | 4/6F |
| July | Newbury | Merry Madcap | | 964 | 6 | Mrs H O H Freling-huysen | F Maxwell | 2/1F |
| July | Newbury | Persian Garden | Morland Breweries Hcp | 1,535 | 13 | Lt Col G Loder | N Murless | 5/1 |
| July | Birmingham | Billy Betts | | 344 | 5 | A E Havill | A Smyth | 10/11F |
| July | Birmingham | Soueida | | 474 | 8 | S L Green | W Payne | 4/11F |
| July | Goodwood | Roan Rocket | Sussex Stks | 15,010 | 8 | T F C Frost | G Todd | 4/6F |
| July | Goodwood | Matatina | King George Stks | 1,421 | 5 | Mrs R C Wilson Jnr | F Armstrong | EvF |
| July | Goodwood | Sweet Moss | Gordon Stks | 4,962 | 11 | Lady Sassoon | N Murless | 11/2 |
| Aug | Epsom | Evemaled | | 580 | 6 | O/trainer | R Read | 11/10F |
| Aug | Epsom | Dieu Soleil | Earle Dorling Mem Hcp | 835 | 12 | Mrs V Hue-Williams | N Murless | 11/10F |
| Aug | Epsom | Leonardo | Box Hill Stks | 872 | 7 | C A B St George | N Murless | 5/6F |
| Aug | Epsom | Palm | Diomed Hcp | 824 | 8 | A Plesch | N Murless | 9/4F |
| Aug | Epsom | Palmroy | | 467 | 5 | A Kennedy | W Nightingall | 1/2F |
| Aug | Epsom | Hasty Cast | Paddock Hcp | 875 | 6 | Mrs J S Crosfield | F Armstrong | 1/2F |
| Aug | Brighton | Royal Desire | Brighton Hcp | 1,838 | 8 | Mrs M E Whitney Tippett | N Murless | 6/1 |
| Aug | Brighton | Astrellita | | 761 | 6 | Mrs L McVey | N Murless | 6/5F |
| Aug | Redcar | Tuning Fork | | 690 | 12 | R B Moller | H Wragg | 8/15F |
| Aug | Redcar | Alley Cat | | 414 | 6 | J R Hindley | N Murless | 4/5F |
| Aug | Redcar | Fireworship | | 414 | 5 | Col A W Newman | F Armstrong | 4/7F |
| Aug | Redcar | Passenger | William Hill Gold Cup | 6,540 | 8 | W R Kinsey | P Moore | 8/1 |
| 1 Aug | Nottingham | Atonement | | 414 | 5 | J A Sutton | N Murless | 2/5F |
| 2 Aug | Haydock | Money for Nothing | | 414 | 5 | T Holland-Martin | F Johnson Houghton | 10/11F |

| Date | Race Course | Horse | Race | Value £ | Dist Fur | Owner | Trainer | S/P |
|---|---|---|---|---|---|---|---|---|
| 12 Aug | Haydock | Tante Louise | | 414 | 10 | C Loyd | F Johnson Houghton | 7/4 |
| 13 Aug | Haydock | Rowdy Boy | | 414 | 6 | A H Rostance | E Weymes | EvF |
| 13 Aug | Haydock | Souieda | | 414 | 10 | S L Green | W Payne | 4/11F |
| 14 Aug | Newbury | Light Thrust | | 414 | 13 | Col F T Halse | W Nightingall | 9/4F |
| 14 Aug | Newbury | High Sun | | 690 | 5 | W F Bates | S Ingham | 4/5F |
| 17 Aug | Lewes | No Dope | | 345 | 5 | P L Stafford | F Winter | 5/6F |
| 20 Aug | York | Patti | Galtres Stks | 1,426 | 12 | Lady Granard | P Prendergast (I) | 8/15F |
| 22 Aug | Newbury | Leonardo | Dynastron | 1,245 | 7 | C A B St George | N Murless | 6/1 |
| 24 Aug | Warwick | Gold Span | | 345 | 7 | O/trainer | J P Bartholomew | 10/11F |
| 24 Aug | Warwick | Abscond | | 345 | 6 | C W Engelhard | F Johnson Houghton | 10/11F |
| 26 Aug | Brighton | Mozetta | | 404 | 10 | Sir W Pigott-Brown | F Cundell | 4/1 |
| 27 Aug | Brighton | Der Ring | | 797 | 7 | Lady Sassoon | N Murless | 13/8F |
| 27 Aug | Brighton | Casabianca | | 406 | 8 | Lt Col J Hornung | N Murless | 11/10F |
| 28 Aug | Sandown | London Melody | | 746 | 8 | B Delfont | W Nightingall | 6/1 |
| 29 Aug | Sandown | Passenger | James Upton Stks | 1,878 | 8 | W R Kinsey | P Moore | 9/4 |
| 4 Sept | Epsom | Dion | Epsom Cup | 1,485 | 18 | P Bull | W Elsey | 7/2 |
| 4 Sept | Epsom | Astrellita | | 795 | 6 | Mrs L McVey | N Murless | 8/13F |
| 5 Sept | Epsom | Leonardo | Stanley | 1,893 | 7 | C A B St George | N Murless | 1/3F |
| 7 Sept | Folkestone | Aegean Blue | | 374 | 5 | Lt Cmdr P S Emmet | F Johnson Houghton | 7/4F |
| 10 Sept | Doncaster | Linacre | | 888 | 10 | F More O'Ferrall | P Prendergast(I) | 8/13F |
| 11 Sept | Newbury | Moonlighter | | 414 | 13 | P Mellon | I Balding | 4/5F |
| 11 Sept | Newbury | Crepes D'Enfer | | 425 | 10 | Lady Sassoon | N Murless | 7/1F |
| 12 Sept | Newbury | Holborn | | 690 | 5 | C W Engelhard | F Johnson Houghton | 7/2F |
| 16 Sept | Brighton | Arthur Duffy | | 467 | 5 | C A B St George | N Murless | 8/13F |
| 16 Sept | Brighton | Impact | | 391 | 10 | Mrs V Hue-Williams | N Murless | 7/4F |
| 17 Sept | Brighton | Persian Garden | Autumn Cup | 1,831 | 12 | Lt Col G Loder | N Murless | 6/4F |
| 17 Sept | Brighton | Der Ring | | 420 | 8 | Lady Sassoon | N Murless | 5/2F |
| 22 Sept | Leicester | Franc | | 345 | 10 | C Loyd | F Johnson Houghton | 10/1 |
| 22 Sept | Leicester | Fast Company | | 327 | 12 | G Trapani | C Mitchell | 8/11F |
| 24 Sept | Ascot | Vercussia | | 552 | 6 | F R Hue-Williams | N Murless | 11/4 |
| 26 Sept | Ascot | Perspective | | 439 | 6 | R B Moller | H Wragg | 5/6F |
| 26 Sept | Ascot | Linacre | Queen Elizabeth Stks | 5,449 | 8 | F More O'Ferrall | P Prendergast (I) | 11/10F |
| 16 Oct | Newmarket | Alan Adare | Houghton Stks | 939 | 7 | Lt Col G Loder | N Murless | 11/8F |
| 17 Oct | Newmarket | Monaco Princess | | 404 | 10 | Lady Sassoon | N Murless | 5/2 |
| 22 Oct | Newbury | Impact | | 398 | 12 | Mrs V Hue-Williams | N Murless | 85/40 |
| 29 Oct | Liverpool | Aria Royal | | 414 | 13 | A Turner | E Weymes | 4/1F |
| 30 Oct | Lingfield | Flying Muzzle | | 414 | 6 | R Zether | D Hanley | 9/4F |

1964: 140 wins; 106 2nds; 70 3rds; 626 rides

| Date | Race Course | Horse | Race | Value £ | Dist Fur | Owner | Trainer | S/P |
|---|---|---|---|---|---|---|---|---|
| 1965 | | | | | | | | |
| 24 Mar | Doncaster | Panariver | | 420 | 7 | Mrs J E Gilbert | B Foster | 11/4F |
| 27 Mar | Liverpool | Fighting Charlie | | 383 | 15 | Lady M Bury | F Maxwell | 4/9F |
| 3 Apl | Catterick | Gay Palm | | 273 | 5 | S W Everitt | P Rohan | 4/11F |
| 3 Apl | Catterick | Fletch | | 368 | 11 | M Clayton | P Rohan | 6/4F |
| 8 Apl | Newbury | Money for Nothing | | 455 | 5 | T Holland-Martin | F Johnson Houghton | 7/2F |
| 10 Apl | Newbury | Yankee Clipper | | 414 | 8 | C W Engelhard | J Tree | 5/1 |
| 20 Apl | Birmingham | Friary Court | | 276 | 5 | C W Engelhard | J Tree | 8/11F |
| 22 Apl | Epsom | Miba | Princess Elizabeth | 4,004 | 8 | P Oppenheimer | H Cottrill | 11/4 |

(I) = Ireland

| Date | Race Course | Horse | Race | Value £ | Dist Fur | Owner | Trainer | S/P |
|---|---|---|---|---|---|---|---|---|
| 26 Apl | Windsor | She's Sweet | | 207 | 5 | T Holland-Martin | F Johnson Houghton | 6/1 |
| 29 Apl | Newmarket | Flying Muzzle | Bretby Hcp | 789 | 6 | R E Zelker | D Hanley | 4/1 |
| 1 May | Ascot | Anselmo | Paradise | 1,833 | 16 | B Fury | K Piggott | 10/11F |
| 1 May | Ascot | Friary Court | | 452 | 5 | C W Engelhard | F Johnson Houghton | 5/2 |
| 3 May | Lanark | Fighting Charlie | | 414 | 15 | Lady M Bury | F Maxwell | 1/3F |
| 5 May | Chester | Minipal | | 417 | 5 | Lord Leverhulme | F Johnson Houghton | 5/2 |
| 6 May | Chester | Aegean Blue | | 775 | 12 | Lt Cmdr P S Emmet | F Johnson Houghton | 7/2 |
| 10 May | Windsor | Lover's Pool | | 345 | 12 | L A Abelson | P Smyth | 9/4F |
| 12 May | Alex Palace | Martinet* | | 304 | 13 | G A Gilbert | K Piggott | 2/1F |
| 14 May | Sandown | Madcap* | | 292 | 5 | Mrs H O H Freling-huysen | F Maxwell | 8/1 |
| 17 May | Brighton | Riot Act | Spring Hcp | 1,824 | 10 | Mrs J F C Bryce | F Armstrong | 2/1F |
| 17 May | Brighton | Hetty | | 432 | 6 | D D Delgado | F Armstrong | 7/4F |
| 19 May | York | Tin King | | 762 | 5 | C W Engelhard | F Johnson Houghton | 7/1 |
| 21 May | Lingfield | Bally Russe | | 524 | 10 | F R Hue-Williams | N Murless | 100/8 |
| 25 May | Alex Palace | Welsh Harvest | | 276 | 5 | Sir E McAlpine | F Armstrong | 4/5F |
| 25 May | Alex Palace | Warsite | | 276 | 5 | J Allen | F Armstrong | 1/3F |
| 28 May | Wolver'ton | Grigio | | 252 | 5 | A Bernie | R Barnes | 5/1 |
| 28 May | Newbury | Tin King | | 414 | 5 | C W Engelhard | F Johnson Houghton | 8/11F |
| 29 May | Leicester | The Traveller | | 345 | 7 | W L Shrive | J Hartigan | 5/2 |
| 29 May | Leicester | Diplopia | | 414 | 12 | Sir C C Cumming | P Smyth | 9/4 |
| 29 May | Leicester | Bally Conneely | | 320 | 10 | Mrs V Stux Rybar | F Maxwell | 2/1F |
| 4 June | Epsom | Kew | Acorn | 880 | 5 | Mrs J R Mullion | F Armstrong | 10/3F |
| 5 June | Kempton | Arctic Kanda | | 821 | 16 | A J Allen | W Nightingall | 5/2 |
| 5 June | Kempton | Brave Knight | | 447 | 11 | Lady Marks | W Nightingall | 10/11F |
| 7 June | Sandown | Golden Ruffle | | 782 | 5 | L Thompson | W O'Gorman | 4/7F |
| 8 June | Sandown | Merry Madcap | | 834 | 5 | Mrs H O H Freling-huysen | F Maxwell | 11/10F |
| 10 June | Haydock | Tipacoup | | 414 | 7 | Mrs A Phipps | P Rohan | 3/1F |
| 10 June | Haydock | Mad Oliver | | 392 | 6 | B P Jenks | P Rohan | 1/6F |
| 10 June | Haydock | Naval Sound | | 373 | 5 | B P Jenks | P Rohan | 1/3F |
| 15 June | Royal Ascot | Young Emperor | Coventry | 5,967 | 6 | Mrs P Poe | P Prendergast (I) | 9/4F |
| 16 June | Royal Ascot | Casabianca | Royal Hunt Cup | 5,332 | 8 | Lt Col J Hornung | N Murless | 100/9 |
| 16 June | Royal Ascot | Bracey Bridge | Ribblesdale | 9,147 | 12 | M W Wickham-Boynton | N Murless | 5/1 |
| 17 June | Royal Ascot | Tin King | New Stks | 5,400 | 5 | C W Engelhard | F Johnson Houghton | 4/7F |
| 17 June | Royal Ascot | Fighting Charlie | Gold Cup | 10,801 | 20 | Lady M Bury | F Maxwell | 6/1 |
| 17 June | Royal Ascot | Swift Harmony | Chesham | 2,200 | 6 | P G Finlinson | E Reavey | 6/1 |
| 17 June | Royal Ascot | Brave Knight | King George | 1,558 | 12 | Lady Marks | W Nightingall | 6/1 |
| 18 June | Royal Ascot | Sweet Moss | Rous Memorial | 1,137 | 8 | Lady Sassoon | N Murless | 4/1 |
| 19 June | Ascot | Gallic | Erroll | 1.405 | 5 | C Loyd | F Johnson Houghton | 4/1F |
| 21 June | Birmingham | London Way | Letherby and Christopher Hcp | 1,276 | 10 | D Robinson | B Hobbs | 9/2 |
| 21 June | Birmingham | Selly Oak | | 414 | 5 | H Andrews | F Cundell | 11/8F |
| 21 June | Folkestone | Sunshine Story | | 247 | 10 | T Holland-Martin | F Johnson Houghton | 10/11F |
| 22 June | Alex Palace | Call to Arms | | 414 | 8 | C W Engelhard | F Johnson Houghton | 5/1 |
| 22 June | Alex Palace | Catamaran | | 414 | 3 | Sir G Dowty | F Armstrong | 7/1 |

* Dead Heat (I) = Ireland

| Date | Race Course | Horse | Race | Value £ | Dist Fur | Owner | Trainer | S/P |
|---|---|---|---|---|---|---|---|---|
| 25 June | Windsor | Aultroy | | 345 | 8 | A J A Kennedy | W Nightingall | 6/1 |
| 28 June | Brighton | Giuro | | 404 | 6 | T Holland-Martin | F Johnson Houghton | 11/8 |
| 28 June | Brighton | Jan | | 423 | 12 | W Barnett | D Candy | 7/2 |
| 28 June | Brighton | Ballyconneelly | | 470 | 10 | Mrs V Stux-Rybar | F Galba | 4/7F |
| 28 June | Brighton | Nereus | | 390 | 7 | Mrs G Trimmer-Thompson | K Cundell | 7/2 |
| 29 June | Brighton | Patron Saint | | 431 | 10 | Mrs J F C Bryce | F Armstrong | 4/1 |
| 30 June | Alex Palace | Tromba | | 414 | 8 | Sir R Sykes | F Armstrong | 1/10F |
| 30 June | Salisbury | Wimpole Street | Bibury Cup | 419 | 12 | Dr D A Fermont | D Thom | 9/2 |
| 30 June | Alex Palace | Polynia | | 414 | 8 | A R Davison | T Gosling | EvF |
| 1 July | Salisbury | Coup | | 401 | 8 | C Loyd | F Johnson Houghton | 5/2 |
| 2 July | Sandown | Hallucination | | 414 | 13 | Maj H S Cayzer | W Wightman | 3/1F |
| 3 July | Nottingham | Freda's Legacy | | 251 | 8 | W E Neesham | J Hartigan | 10/11F |
| 3 July | Nottingham | Welsh Harvest | | 414 | 6 | Sir E McAlpine | F Armstrong | 4/5F |
| 5 July | Nottingham | Dizzy Dolly | | 254 | 6 | Dr P A Knight | F Cundell | 4/7F |
| 5 July | Nottingham | Mernian | | 414 | 8 | Mrs I Bellamy | F Cundell | 4/5F |
| 5 July | Folkestone | Bronze Anchor | | 345 | 6 | G W Harris | W Nightingall | 7/2 |
| 7 July | Newmarket | Ballyconneelly | | 402 | 10 | Mrs V Stux-Ryber | F Maxwell | 6/4F |
| 8 July | Newmarket | Track Spare | | 457 | 5 | O/trainer | R Mason | 4/6 |
| 8 July | Warwick | Thirty Bob | | 345 | 5 | W N Wilfred | S Ingham | 6/1 |
| 9 July | Chester | Wordona | | 389 | 6 | C Chambers | R Mason | 5/4 |
| 9 July | Chester | Darfur | | 419 | 10 | The Queen | N Murless | 13/8F |
| 9 July | Lingfield | Haymaking | | 509 | 6 | C Nicholson | F Johnson Houghton | 10/11F |
| 10 July | Chester | Zahedan | Gold Star Stks | 813 | 5 | Aga Khan | N Murless | 11/2 |
| 10 July | Chester | Clarity | Red Rose Stks | 827 | 12 | Lord Dulverton | N Murless | EvF |
| 12 July | Windsor | Patron Saint | | 345 | 12 | Mrs F J C Bryce | F Armstrong | 4/5F |
| 14 July | Kempton | Hotroy | | 811 | 10 | A J A Kennedy | W Nightingall | 4/1 |
| 15 July | Kempton | Aultroy | Worthington Stks | 1,989 | 11 | A J A Kennedy | W Nightingall | 10/3 |
| 15 July | Kempton | Touchdown | Allan Taylor Stks | 842 | 6 | D Prenn | J Winter | 7/1 |
| 17 July | Ascot | Soft Angels | Princess Margaret Stks | 2,230 | 6 | Lady Sassoon | N Murless | 10/3 |
| 17 July | Ascot | Meadow Court | King George VI and Queen Elizabeth | 31,206 | 12 | G M Bell | P Prendergast (I) | 6/5F |
| 17 July | Wolver'ton | Street Bookmaker | | 252 | 8 | W N Wilfred | R Thrale | 6/5F |
| 17 July | Wolver'ton | Extortion | | 345 | 11 | Mrs S Sokolow | K Piggott | 9/4 |
| 19 July | Leicester | Lumley Road | | 345 | 6 | J R Measures | F Armstrong | 15/8F |
| 19 July | Leicester | Sherwood Melody | | 414 | 6 | C T Whiting | E Davey | 13/8F |
| 19 July | Leicester | Croft What's Wanted | | 345 | 5 | J R Measures | F Armstrong | 4/7F |
| 19 July | Leicester | Patron Saint | | 414 | 12 | J F C Bryce | F Armstrong | 5/4F |
| 21 July | Sandown | Zaheedan | National Stks | 8,057 | 5 | Aga Khan | N Murless | 11/8F |
| 22 July | Sandown | Street Bookmaker | | 420 | 8 | W N Wilfred | R Thrale | 5/4 |
| 26 July | Nottingham | Cost Mary | | 414 | 13 | T H Farr | F Armstrong | 10/11F |
| 28 July | Goodwood | Pugnacity | King George Stks | 4,430 | 5 | L B Holliday | W Wharton | 9/4 |
| 29 July | Goodwood | Irish Guard | Lavant Stks | 790 | 5 | Col W Stirling | P Prendergast (I) | 9/4F |
| 30 July | Goodwood | Aunt Edith | Nassau | 2,948 | 10 | Lt Col J Hornung | N Murless | 7/4F |
| 31 July | Epsom | Stock Beck | | 797 | 12 | J R Hindley | N Murless | 5/2F |
| 2 Aug | Newcastle | Purple Hills | | 383 | 12 | John McDonald | E Weymes | 7/1 |
| 3 Aug | Brighton | Cornflower | | 459 | 5 | Mrs D Wigan | N Murless | 5/2 |
| 3 Aug | Brighton | Miss Rosa | Channel Stks | 1,807 | 6 | Mrs S Beatty | N Murless | 5/2 |
| 4 Aug | Pontefract | Saints and Sinners | | 345 | 6 | J R Mullion | F Armstrong | 7/4F |
| 4 Aug | Pontefract | My Sweet Afton | | 257 | 6 | Mrs J R Mullion | F Armstrong | 2/5F |
| 4 Aug | Pontefract | Tromba | | 345 | 8 | Sir R Sykes | F Armstrong | 9/4F |
| 10 Aug | Alex Palace | Princesse D'Albe | | 414 | 8 | W Harvey | W Nightingall | 5/6F |

(I) = Ireland

| Date | Race Course | Horse | Race | Value £ | Dist Fur | Owner | Trainer | S/P |
|---|---|---|---|---|---|---|---|---|
| 10 Aug | Alex Palace | Just Lucky II | | 414 | 5 | C H Palmer | F Armstrong | EvF |
| 11 Aug | Haydock | Every Blessing | | 414 | 5 | M W Wickham-Boynton | N Murless | 2/1 |
| 11 Aug | Haydock | Freda's Legacy | | 291 | 8 | Lady Lilford | D Charlesworth | 8/11F |
| 12 Aug | Haydock | Stock Beck | Colonel Ashton Hcp | 824 | 12 | J R Hindley | N Murless | 8/11F |
| 12 Aug | Haydock | El Commandante | | 414 | 6 | C A B St George | N Murless | 11/4F |
| 13 Aug | Newbury | Roan Rocket | Hungerford Stks | 1,883 | 7 | T F C Frost | G Todd | 1/2F |
| 16 Aug | Windsor | Aultroy | | 345 | 10 | A J A Kennedy | W Nightingall | 2/1F |
| 16 Aug | Windsor | Costmary | | 345 | 12 | T H Farr | F Armstrong | 3/1 |
| 18 Aug | York | Ragazzo | Great Voltigeur | 4,524 | 12 | E R More O'Ferrall | P Prendergast (I) | 13/8F |
| 19 Aug | York | Young Emperor | Gimcrack | 6,809 | 6 | Mrs P Poe | P Prendergast (I) | 5/6F |
| 21 Aug | Newmarket | Hetty | | 409 | 5 | D D Delgado | F Armstrong | 5/1 |
| 25 Aug | Brighton | Riot Act | Preston Park Hcp | 1,363 | 8 | Mrs J F C Bryce | F Armstrong | 7/4F |
| 27 Aug | Brighton | Democratic Fair | | 424 | 8 | W Crayden | K Gethin | 4/1 |
| 27 Aug | Brighton | Just Lucky II | | 420 | 6 | C H Palmer | F Armstrong | 6/5F |
| 28 Aug | Leicester | Held Firm | | 346 | 8 | D Morris | H Wallington | 7/2 |
| 28 Aug | Leicester | Seymour | | 345 | 6 | Miss P Major | H E Smyth | EvF |
| 28 Aug | Leicester | Chiltern Miss | | 414 | 8 | H H Renshaw | A Budgett | 2/1F |
| 28 Aug | Leicester | Costmary | | 329 | 12 | T H Farr | F Armstrong | 8/100F |
| 30 Aug | Epsom | Ermalad | | 559 | 8 | Mrs A Laurence | R Read | 5/2F |
| 1 Sept | York | Marcus Brutus | | 486 | 6 | C A B St George | S Hall | 2/1 |
| 2 Sept | Chester | Minera | | 392 | 6 | Duke of Westminster | N Murless | 4/1F |
| 2 Sept | Chester | Free Boy | | 782 | 12 | E Sjoo | W O'Gorman | 9/4F |
| 2 Sept | Chester | Balbi | | 538 | 13 | Lady Sassoon | N Murless | 5/4 |
| 4 Sept | Sandown | King of Thule | Billy Butlin S Pl | 1,980 | 5 | O/trainer | W O'Gorman | 7/1 |
| 7 Sept | Doncaster | Celtic Song | Champagne Stks | 5,168 | 7 | M Rayne | P Prendergast (I) | 2/1 |
| 10 Sept | Doncaster | Bracey Bridge | Park Hill Stks | 3,929 | 14 | M W Wickham-Boynton | N Murless | 7/2 |
| 10 Sept | Doncaster | Jet Aura | Feversham | 846 | 8 | C Clore | P Prendergast (I) | 8/11F |
| 14 Sept | Goodwood | Double-U-Jay | | 858 | 6 | G Harwood | J Winter | 13/8 |
| 14 Sept | Goodwood | Lindosa | Chisledown | 1,101 | 8 | J R Hindley | N Murless | 4/9F |
| 15 Sept | Ayr | Hetty | | 414 | 5 | D D Delgado | F Armstrong | 7/4F |
| 17 Sept | Haydock | Regal Bell | Buggins Farm Hcp | 866 | 8 | J R Mullion | F Armstrong | 11/4 |
| 17 Sept | Haydock | Miss Lane | | 414 | 7 | Lady Sassoon | N Murless | 6/4F |
| 17 Sept | Haydock | Patron Saint | | 414 | 12 | Mrs J F C Bryce | F Armstrong | 6/4F |
| 18 Sept | Ayr | Princess Imgard | | 366 | 6 | O/trainer | E Davey | 4/1F |
| 18 Sept | Ayr | Every Blessing | Firth of Clyde | 827 | 6 | M W Wickham-Boynton | N Murless | 8/11F |
| 20 Sept | Edinburgh | Costmary | Edinburgh Gold Cup | 419 | 12 | T H Farr | F Armstrong | 11/10F |
| 23 Sept | Ascot | Bracey Bridge | Princess Royal Stks | 1,948 | 12 | M W Wickham-Boynton | N Murless | 6/4F |
| 25 Sept | Ascot | Soft Angels | Royal Lodge Stks | 5,687 | 8 | Lady Sassoon | N Murless | 5/2F |
| 27 Sept | Wolver'ton | Splurge | | 252 | 7 | A Plesch | F Armstrong | 10/3 |
| 28 Sept | Alex Palace | Parole Board | | 414 | 5 | C G Glover | M Pope | EvF |
| 2 Oct | Newmarket | Lindosa | | 524 | 8 | J R Hindley | N Murless | 3/10F |
| 4 Oct | Nottingham | Lumley Road | | 414 | 8 | J R Measures | F Armstrong | 100/9 |
| 5 Sept | Nottingham | September | | 207 | 5 | A R R Tenty | R Sturdy | 7/2F |
| 6 Oct | York | Costmary | | 514 | 12 | T H Farr | F Armstrong | 6/1F |
| 6 Oct | York | Shipyard† | | 580 | 8 | E Cooper Bland | F Armstrong | 9/4F |
| 7 Oct | York | Pomato | | 547 | 8 | A Plesch | N Murless | 6/1 |
| 7 Oct | York | Marcus Brutus | | 575 | 6 | C A B St George | S Hall | 9/4F |
| 9 Oct | Ascot | Tin King | Cornwallis | 1,884 | 5 | C W Engelhard | F Johnson Houghton | 8/11F |
| 13 Oct | Kempton | Lumley Road | | 551 | 7 | J R Measures | F Armstrong | 5/2F |

† Walkover (I) = Ireland

| Date | Race Course | Horse | Race | Value £ | Dist Fur | Owner | Trainer | S/P |
|---|---|---|---|---|---|---|---|---|
| 13 Oct | Kempton | Tamerslip | | 775 | 12 | R H New | F Maxwell | 11/2 |
| 13 Oct | Kempton | Siliconn | | 429 | 8 | C Pollock | T Corbett | 9/4F |
| 14 Oct | Newmarket | Bolting | | 418 | 5 | Mrs D Wigan | N Murless | 5/2 |
| 14 Oct | Newmarket | Temeraire | | 471 | 6 | R C Wilson | F Armstrong | 9/2 |
| 15 Oct | Newmarket | Edelo | | 388 | 10 | Lady Sassoon | N Murless | 4/11F |
| 22 Oct | Newbury | Lumley Road | | 690 | 8 | Mrs J R Mullion | F Armstrong | 13/8F |
| 27 Oct | Ascot | Court Milliner | | 431 | 8 | Mrs J R Mullion | F Armstrong | 15/8F |
| 29 Oct | Lingfield | Swiftest | | 414 | 7 | C Nicholson | F Armstrong | 4/7F |
| 29 Oct | Lingfield | Gettysburg | | 414 | 6 | J R Mullion | F Armstrong | 10/1 |
| 29 Oct | Lingfield | Pardoric | | 414 | 12 | Mrs L R Wald | D Hastings | 100/7 |

1965: 160 wins; 110 2nds; 81 3rds; 655 rides

| Date | Race Course | Horse | Race | Value £ | Dist Fur | Owner | Trainer | S/P |
|---|---|---|---|---|---|---|---|---|
| 1966 | | | | | | | | |
| 22 Mar | Doncaster | Costmary | | 414 | 10 | T H Farr | F Armstrong | 13/8F |
| 22 Mar | Doncaster | Rackham | | 414 | 12 | Miss A E Abbott | R Hobson | 9/2 |
| 24 Mar | Liverpool | Lumley Road | | 463 | 8 | J R Measures | F Armstrong | 8/13F |
| 25 Mar | Liverpool | Patron Saint | Liverpool Spring Cup | 845 | 10 | Mrs J F C Bryce | F Armstrong | 6/4F |
| 26 Mar | Liverpool | Fair Play II | | 463 | 13 | Major D Wigan | H Price | 4/6F |
| 28 Mar | Nottingham | Obrigada | | 328 | 5 | N W Purvis | T Waugh | 4/6F |
| 1 Apl | Ascot | Althrey Don | Thames Stks | 806 | 6 | J A Done | P Rohan | 11/2 |
| 1 Apl | Ascot | Maldavan | | 494 | 8 | Mrs G M Sandiford | J Goldsmith | 5/2F |
| 18 Apl | Edinburgh | Costmary | Edinburgh Spring Cup | 828 | 12 | T H Farr | F Armstrong | 1/2F |
| 21 Apl | Epsom | Every Blessing | Princess Elizabeth Stks | 2,724 | 8 | M W Wickham-Boynton | N Murless | 5/1 |
| 27 Apl | Newmarket | Capital Charge | | 492 | 7 | Mrs J A de Rothschild | J Clayton | 2/1F |
| 28 Apl | Newmarket | Touchdown | Bretby Hcp | 884 | 6 | D Prenn | J Winter | 3/1F |
| 29 Apl | Ascot | Right Noble | White Rose Stks | 2,370 | 12 | C W Engelhard | M V O'Brien(I) | 11/4 |
| 29 Apl | Ascot | Smooth | | 436 | 5 | Mrs D A Rasbotham | R Houghton | 6/4F |
| 30 Apl | Ascot | Enrico | Victoria Cup | 3,274 | 7 | D Robinson | J Thompson | 11/2 |
| 2 May | Windsor | Lumley Road | | 345 | 8 | J R Measures | F Armstrong | 8/15F |
| 3 May | Chester | Klonogue | | 426 | 5 | R J McAlpine | P Rohan | 13/8F |
| 4 May | Chester | Aegean Blue | Chester Cup | 5,348 | 18 | Lt Cmdr P S Emmett | R Houghton | 22/1 |
| 4 May | Chester | Watergate | Grosvenor Stks | 897 | 10 | Duke of Westminster | N Murless | 5/6F |
| 5 May | Chester | Lady Jester | | 393 | 5 | B P Jenks | P Rohan | 2/7F |
| 5 May | Chester | Biomydrin | Ormonde Stks | 1,425 | 13 | Lady Sassoon | N Murless | 11/2 |
| 6 May | Haydock | Fighting Charlie | | 378 | 16 | Lady M Bury | F Maxwell | 1/8F |
| 7 May | Haydock | Hob-Hob | | 414 | 8 | G B Turnbull | W Hall | 10/3 |
| 11 May | Alex Palace | Bay Pardan | | 343 | 8 | R Chinn | J Sutcliffe | 5/1 |
| 11 May | Alex Palace | Costmary | | 403 | 5 | T H Farr | F Armstrong | 11/8F |
| 12 May | York | Aunt Edith | Yorkshire Cup | 3,043 | 14 | Lt Col J Hornung | N Murless | 4/5F |
| 13 May | Pontefract | Sky Lustre | | 207 | 5 | S Terry | R Jarvis | EvF |
| 13 May | Pontefract | Tzigelina | | 345 | 6 | O/trainer | A W Goodwill | 3/1F |
| 14 May | Ayr | Aegean Blue | Usher-Vaux Gold Tankard | 4,430 | 15 | Lt Cmdr P S Emmett | R Houghton | 6/4F |
| 17 May | Alex Palace | Vijay | | 414 | 8 | R F P Boss | E Goodard | 3/1 |
| 20 May | Newbury | Zend Avesta | Ross Group Stks | 855 | 13 | G Kindersley | W Payne | 6/1 |
| 20 May | Newbury | Tin King | Butlin Hcp | 958 | 6 | C W Engelhard | R Houghton | 9/1 |
| 23 May | Windsor | Smooth | | 207 | 5 | Mrs D A Rasbotham | R Houghton | 8/13F |
| 25 May | Epsom | Caterina | Stewards Hcp | 873 | 5 | R F Scully | F Armstrong | 13/8F |
| 26 May | Epsom | On Your Mark | Great Surrey Stks | 788 | 5 | C H Palmer | F Armstrong | 9/4 |
| 27 May | Epsom | Valoris | The Oaks | 35,711 | 12 | C Clore | M V O'Brien (I) | 11/10F |
| 27 May | Epsom | Cambridge | Nonsuch Hcp | 839 | 12 | D Robinson | J Thompson | 11/4F |
| 28 May | Kempton | Haymaking | | 552 | 8 | C Nicholson | R Houghton | 8/11F |
| 30 May | Redcar | Fully-Charged | | 361 | 5 | T E Boothby | A Hobson | 10/3 |
| 31 May | Sandown | Chrona | | 427 | 8 | H D H Wills | R Houghton | 9/4F |

(I) = Ireland

| Date | Race Course | Horse | Race | Value £ | Dist Fur | Owner | Trainer | S/P |
|---|---|---|---|---|---|---|---|---|
| 1 June | Kempton | Golden Horus | Sceptre Stks | 867 | 6 | Mrs D M Solomon | W O'Gorman | 11/8F |
| 4 June | Lingfield | Blue Carnation | (Wills) Hickstead Prize Stks | 1,486 | 16 | P B Raymond | K Piggott | 7/4F |
| 7 June | Alex Palace | Old Frame | | 414 | 8 | C Nicholson | R Houghton | 4/5F |
| 8 June | Beverley | Lady Jester | Hilary Needler Trophy | 1,811 | 5 | B P Jenks | P Rohan | 2/1F |
| 9 June | Beverley | Solar Call | Robert B Massey Group | 933 | 5 | G N Sutherland | P Rohan | 11/10F |
| 9 June | Brighton | Abscond | | 409 | 10 | C W Engelhard | R Houghton | 4/6F |
| 10 June | Sandown | Bluebeard's Slipper | | 414 | 8 | Lord Leverhulme | R Houghton | 6/4F |
| 11 June | Sandown | Hiding Place | Raynes Pl | 821 | 8 | Lord Porchester | J Clayton | 5/4F |
| 16 June | Royal Ascot | Falcon | New Stks | 5,204 | 5 | C W Engelhard | R Houghton | 11/8F |
| 16 June | Royal Ascot | Marcus Brutus | King George V | 1,596 | 12 | C A B St George | S Hall | 11/2 |
| 17 June | Royal Ascot | On Your Mark | Windsor Castle | 1,861 | 5 | C H Palmer | F Armstrong | 9/4F |
| 18 June | Ascot | Lomond | Churchill Stks | 1,507 | 12 | W Ruane | R Jarvis | 6/1 |
| 22 June | Yarmouth | Venture Boy | | 267 | 8 | S Bates | J Sutcliffe | 5/4F |
| 24 June | Doncaster | Swiftest | Chesterfield Hcp | 831 | 8 | C Nicholson | F Armstrong | 6/4F |
| 24 June | Doncaster | Italiano | | 414 | 10 | D Robinson | J Thompson | 2/5F |
| 25 June | Doncaster | Streakie | | 423 | 6 | D Robinson | J Thompson | 13/8F |
| 29 June | Thirsk | Marble Court | | 414 | 6 | G S Yell | P Rohan | 1/4F |
| 30 June | Carlisle | Friar's Mary | | 277 | 6 | A Bernie | R Barnes | 20/1 |
| 30 June | Carlisle | Costmary | Cumberland Plate | 1,110 | 12 | T H Farr | F Armstrong | 2/1F |
| 1 July | Haydock | Fully-Charged | | 291 | 7 | T E Boothby | R Hobson | 5/1 |
| 2 July | Haydock | Fable Amusant | | 380 | 8 | Mrs L Carver | E Cousins | 2/5F |
| 4 July | Edinburgh | Quoff | | 341 | 8 | A C Leggat | T Robson | 7/1 |
| 4 July | Edinburgh | Retz-Canoy | | 344 | 5 | J H Wyllie | E Carr | 4/5F |
| 7 July | Doncaster | Florescence | | 414 | 5 | J R Mullion | F Armstrong | 2/9F |
| 8 July | Sandown | Costmary | | 782 | 13 | T H Farr | F Armstrong | E/F |
| 8 July | Sandown | Italiano | | 414 | 10 | D Robinson | J Thompson | 11/8F |
| 9 July | Sandown | Pieces of Eight | Eclipse | 27,326 | 10 | Comtessa de la Valdene | M V O'Brien (I) | 15/2 |
| 9 July | Sandown | Smokey Dish | | 414 | 7 | D Robinson | J Thompson | 3/1F |
| 13 July | Newmarket | Pink Gem | | 495 | 6 | H J Joel | N Murless | 9/2F |
| 13 July | Newmarket | Showoff | Bunbury Cup | 2,108 | 7 | D Prenn | J Winter | 9/1 |
| 13 July | Newmarket | Golden Horus | July Stks | 1,471 | 6 | Mrs D M Solomon | W O'Gorman | 2/1 |
| 14 July | Newmarket | Bindibu | | 453 | 7 | Mrs J F C Bryce | F Armstrong | 100/8 |
| 14 July | Newmarket | Chrona | | 781 | 8 | H D H Wills | R Houghton | 9/1 |
| 15 July | Ascot | Tordo | Hyperion | 2,897 | 6 | C W Engelhard | M V O'Brien (I) | 8/13F |
| 15 July | Ascot | Tatarin | Cranbourn Chase | 845 | 12 | F R Hue-Williams | N Murless | 5/6F |
| 16 July | Ascot | Aunt Edith | King George VI & Queen Eliz | 29,167 | 12 | Lt Col J Hornung | N Murless | 7/2 |
| 16 July | Ascot | Fleet | Princess Margaret | 1,996 | 6 | R C Boucher | N Murless | 4/6F |
| 16 July | Ascot | Bally Russe | Sunninghill Park | 751 | 16 | F R Hue-Williams | N Murless | EvF |
| 18 July | Leicester | Mossy | | 414 | 12 | C Loyd | R Houghton | 15/8 |
| 19 July | Leicester | Bloody Mary | | 345 | 5 | Mrs J F C Bryce | F Armstrong | 13/8 |
| 19 July | Leicester | Hi-Yu | | 296 | 6 | R L Heaton | J Hartigan | 11/8F |
| 19 July | Leicester | Old Frame | | 414 | 10 | C Nicholson | R Houghton | 13/8 |
| 19 July | Leicester | Parthian Shot | | 345 | 10 | Mrs J F C Bryce | F Armstrong | 11/8F |
| 19 July | Leicester | Chestergate | | 345 | 12 | K O Beardman | R Hollinshead | 2/15 |
| 20 July | Sandown | Falcon | National Stks | 6,951 | 5 | C W Engelhard | R Houghton | 8/13F |
| 22 July | Newbury | Ribocco | | 470 | 6 | C W Engelhard | R Houghton | 5/4F |
| 22 July | Newbury | Smooth | St Catherine's Stks | 813 | 6 | Mrs D A Rasbotham | R Houghton | 11/12 |
| 23 July | Newbury | Speed of Sound | Dennington Castle | 890 | 7 | F R Hue-Williams | N Murless | 13/2 |
| 23 July | Newbury | Abbeyfield | | 476 | 5 | Mrs S Beatty | N Murless | 8/13F |
| 25 July | Alex Palace | Red Favourite | | 414 | 5 | Mrs J R Mullion | F Armstrong | 13/8F |
| 25 July | Alex Palace | Aglojo | | 414 | 5 | A W Peisa | F Armstrong | 1/3F |
| 26 July | Goodwood | Smooth | Molecomb Stks | 1,846 | 5 | Mrs D A Rasbotham | R Houghton | 9/2 |

(I) = Ireland

| Date | Race Course | Horse | Race | Value £ | Dist Fur | Owner | Trainer | S/P |
|---|---|---|---|---|---|---|---|---|
| 26 July | Goodwood | Starry Halo | New Ham | 859 | 6 | D Robinson | J Thompson | 7/2 |
| 29 July | Goodwood | Haymaking | Nassau Stks | 2,006 | 10 | C Nicholson | R Houghton | 13/2 |
| 29 July | Goodwood | Winkie | Findon | 845 | 5 | D Robinson | J Thompson | 10/11F |
| 3 Aug | Pontefract | Castellano | | 345 | 6 | Lady Ashcombe | P Walwyn | 10/3 |
| 3 Aug | Pontefract | Hard Water | | 345 | 5 | J R Brown | P Rohan | 7/2 |
| 3 Aug | Pontefract | On Probation | | 345 | 8 | R F Scully | F Armstrong | 4/11F |
| 3 Aug | Pontefract | The Ark | | 345 | 12 | W J Jones | D Rayson | 11/8 |
| 5 Aug | Newmarket | Florescence | | 417 | 5 | J R Mullion | F Armstrong | 4/6F |
| 6 Aug | Newmarket | Herbaceous | | 354 | 8 | Mrs N Murless | N Murless | 5/1 |
| 8 Aug | Leicester | Midsummer Dream | | 345 | 5 | Mrs D Robinson | J Thompson | 1/5F |
| 8 Aug | Leicester | Loose Cover | | 414 | 8 | Mrs J F C Bryce | F Armstrong | 4/9F |
| 8 Aug | Leicester | Valentino | | 345 | 12 | H T Smith | P Moore | 10/11F |
| 9 Aug | Leicester | Bloody Mary | | 345 | 5 | Mrs J F C Bryce | F Armstrong | 4/5F |
| 10 Aug | Haydock | Aglojo | | 560 | 7 | A W Peisa | F Armstrong | E/F |
| 11 Aug | Haydock | Edolo | | 400 | 10 | Lady Sassoon | N Murless | 11/7F |
| 11 Aug | Haydock | Crocus | Colonel Ashton | 895 | 12 | Lady M Bury | F Maxwell | 7/2 |
| 12 Aug | Newbury | Petite Marmite | | 690 | 8 | Mrs V Cripps | E Lambton | 7/2 |
| 13 Aug | Newbury | Ribocco | | 3,853 | 6 | C W Engelhard | R Houghton | 8/11F |
| 15 Aug | Nottingham | Sharp Work | | 414 | 5 | Capt N Peto | J Dennistoun | 13/8F |
| 16 Aug | York | Royal Palace | Acomb Stks | 1,408 | 6 | H J Joel | N Murless | 7/2 |
| 16 Aug | York | Parthian Glance | Yorkshire Oaks | 4,490 | 12 | W H D Riley-Smith | G Todd | 3/1 |
| 16 Aug | York | Caterina | Nunthorpe | 3,754 | 5 | R F Scully | F Armstrong | 13/2 |
| 16 Aug | York | Mintmaster | Lonsdale Hcp | 1,354 | 16 | E Collington | A Cooper | 2/1F |
| 16 Aug | York | Florescence | Prince of Wales | 1,254 | 5 | J R Mullion | F Armstrong | 4/6F |
| 17 Aug | York | Fancy Smith | Rous S | 1,208 | 5 | R A Cattle | P Rohan | 2/1F |
| 19 Aug | Lingfield | Full Stretch | | 414 | 6 | J A Sutton | N Murless | 1/2F |
| 19 Aug | Lingfield | Astral Green | | 456 | 10 | Lady Sassoon | N Murless | 2/1F |
| 20 Aug | Newmarket | Last Case | | 772 | 8 | Mrs R Grosvenor | P Nelson | 2/1 |
| 20 Aug | Newmarket | Sharp Work | | 424 | 6 | Capt N Peto | J Dennistoun | 9/4 |
| 24 Aug | Brighton | Royal Saint | | 475 | 7 | Mrs V Hue-Williams | N Murless | 11/10F |
| 24 Aug | Brighton | Loose Cover | Preston Park Hcp | 1,341 | 8 | Mrs J F C Bryce | F Armstrong | 5/6F |
| 24 Aug | Brighton | Old Bailey | | 411 | 6 | E Ostrer | I Walker | 5/4F |
| 24 Aug | Brighton | Svenno | | 404 | 10 | Mrs M Gordon-Watson | E Parker | 4/11 |
| 25 Aug | Beverley | Above Water | | 381 | 5 | V C Watts | J Watts | 6/4F |
| 25 Aug | Beverley | Petite Marmite | | 791 | 8 | Mrs V Cripps | E Lambton | 4/6F |
| 26 Aug | Goodwood | Tubalcain | Bentinck | 1,167 | 19 | H Fellowes | E Goddard | 11/4F |
| 27 Aug | Goodwood | Greek Streak | | 382 | 8 | C F Hughesdon | P Nelson | 11/8 |
| 27 Aug | Goodwood | King Log | | 769 | 11 | Mrs W H D Riley-Smith | G Todd | 8/11F |
| 29 Aug | Epsom | London Boy | | 424 | 6 | D Robinson | J Thompson | 8/15F |
| 29 Aug | Epsom | Green Halo | Fifinella | 1,421 | 10 | E Loder | N Murless | 1/3F |
| 30 Aug | Epsom | My Mary | | 427 | 7 | G P Williams | P Walwyn | 9/4F |
| 30 Aug | Epsom | Astral Green | | 393 | 10 | Lady Sassoon | N Murless | 1/2F |
| 31 Aug | York | Marble Court | | 521 | 6 | G S Yell | P Rohan | 4/11F |
| 31 Aug | York | James | | 498 | 6 | C A B St George | S Hall | 11/10F |
| 2 Sept | Sandown | Revelation | | 414 | 5 | O/trainer | W O'Gorman | 7/2 |
| 2 Sept | Sandown | Speed of Sound | Solario | 1,802 | 7 | F R Hue-Williams | N Murless | 4/7F |
| 5 Sept | Warwick | Biobet | | 465 | 5 | Mrs J F C Bryce | F Armstrong | 7/2 |
| 5 Sept | Warwick | Field Mouse | | 345 | 5 | Mrs J F C Bryce | F Armstrong | 5/2F |
| 5 Sept | Warwick | Castellano | | 345 | 7 | Jean Lady Ashcombe | P Walwyn | 3/1F |
| 5 Sept | Warwick | Tueuerama | | 363 | 10 | Maj H Cayzer | F W Wightman | 11/8F |
| 5 Sept | Warwick | On Probation | | 345 | 8 | R F Scully | F Armstrong | 10/11F |
| 7 Sept | Doncaster | Barnie's Image | Fitzwilliam S | 1,258 | 6 | R A Smith | S Hall | 13/8F |
| 7 Sept | Doncaster | Uncle Tittlefeet | Corporation | 1,038 | 8 | Mrs W A Richardson | W A Stephenson | 8/13F |
| 9 Sept | Doncaster | Parthian Glance | Park Hill Stks | 3,901 | 14 | Mrs W H D Riley-Smith | G Todd | 4/5F |
| 12 Sept | Goodwood | Red Favourite | | 482 | 5 | Mrs J R Mullion | F Armstrong | 2/1F |
| 12 Sept | Goodwood | Full Stretch | | 462 | 6 | J A Sutton | N Murless | 8/15F |

| Date | Race Course | Horse | Race | Value £ | Dist Fur | Owner | Trainer | S/P |
|---|---|---|---|---|---|---|---|---|
| 12 Sept | Goodwood | Medaea | | 389 | 11 | Mrs W H D Riley-Smith | G Todd | 5/4 |
| 13 Sept | Goodwood | Suez Canal | | 459 | 8 | T L R Holland | T Corbett | 5/2F |
| 13 Sept | Goodwood | Bates | | 462 | 8 | G H Richards | A Budgett | 5/1 |
| 14 Sept | Brighton | Doushiska | | 444 | 12 | Lord Carnarvon | P Nelson | 6/5F |
| 14 Sept | Brighton | Bolting | | 624 | 6 | Mrs D Wigan | N Murless | 11/10F |
| 15 Sept | Ayr | Plotina | | 454 | 7 | Maj S Vernon | N Murless | 4/5F |
| 15 Sept | Ayr | St Chad | Ladykirk | 806 | 5 | Mrs N Murless | N Murless | 1/3F |
| 16 Sept | Kempton | Be Hopeful | Tangiers | 809 | 8 | G P Williams | P Walwyn | 7/12 |
| 16 Sept | Kempton | Valentino | | 596 | 12 | H T Smith | P Moore | 9/4F |
| 17 Sept | Kempton | Drevno | | 493 | 11 | Mrs F Maxwell | F Maxwell | 11/8F |
| 19 Sept | Leicester | Field Mouse | | 345 | 5 | Mrs J F C Bryce | F Armstrong | 9/100F |
| 19 Sept | Leicester | Old Bailey | | 345 | 6 | E Ostrer | I Walker | EvF |
| 20 Sept | Leicester | Bonne Surprise | | 345 | 6 | R F Scully | F Armstrong | 15/8F |
| 20 Sept | Leicester | Donoric | | 342 | 7 | Mrs L R Waud | D Hastings | 11/4F |
| 22 Sept | Ascot | Royal Saint | Chertsey | 922 | 6 | Mrs V Hue-Williams | N Murless | 10/11F |
| 23 Sept | Ascot | Royal Palace | Royal Lodge Stks | 5,500 | 8 | H J Joel | N Murless | 6/4F |
| 23 Sept | Ascot | Aglojo | | 434 | 7 | A W Peisa | F Armstrong | 7/4F |
| 24 Sept | Ascot | Fab | Blue Seal | 1,996 | 6 | Mrs S Beatty | N Murless | 4/11F |
| 24 Sept | Ascot | Hill Rise | Queen Elizabeth II | 5,203 | 8 | G A Pope Jnr | N Murless | 7/2 |
| 27 Sept | Alex Palace | Karesuando | | 414 | 13 | H B Ely | F Armstrong | 9/4 |
| 27 Sept | Alex Palace | Hiue | | 247 | 5 | J R Mullion | F Armstrong | 11/4F |
| 28 Sept | Newmarket | Fleet | Cheveley Park Stks | 9,467 | 6 | R C Boucher | N Murless | 5/2F |
| 29 Sept | Newmarket | Ambericos | Severals | 802 | 8 | Mrs A Ford | M V O'Brien(I) | 5/6F |
| 29 Sept | Newmarket | Langley Park | | 425 | 9 | M Sobell | G Richards | 11/4F |
| 30 Sept | Windsor | Polmak | | 340 | 12 | H B Ely | F Armstrong | 8/13F |
| 3 Oct | Newbury | Whirled | | 540 | 6 | Mrs H O H Frelinghuysen | F Maxwell | 5/2F |
| 3 Oct | Newbury | Teesdale | | 426 | 10 | Mrs S Beatty | N Murless | 7/2 |
| 5 Oct | York | Plotina | | 594 | 8 | Maj S Vernon | N Murless | 13/8F |
| 5 Oct | York | Scottish Mary | | 752 | 6 | Mrs J W Hanes | Sir C Boyd Rochfort | 3/1 |
| 6 Oct | Ascot | Varinia | | 792 | 12 | M W Wickham-Boynton | N Murless | 11/10F |
| 7 Oct | Ascot | Petite Marmite | | 758 | 8 | Mrs V Cripps | E Lambton | 4/7F |
| 10 Oct | Nottingham | Nelion | | 414 | 8 | M W Wickham-Boynton | N Murless | 5/2F |
| 13 Oct | Newmarket | Minho | Tattersall N/H | 1,030 | 7 | Lord Grimthorpe | P Rohan | 10/1 |
| 15 Oct | Newmarket | Pieces of Eight | Champion Stks | 26,972 | 10 | Comtessa de la Valdene | M V O'Brien(I) | 5/4F |
| 15 Oct | Newmarket | Love for Sale | Houghton | 1,693 | 7 | Lady Sassoon | N Murless | 11/4 |
| 17 Oct | Windsor | Polmak | | 340 | 12 | H B Ely | F Armstrong | 11/10F |
| 22 Oct | Doncaster | Ribocco | Observer Gold Cup | 20,155 | 8 | C W Engelhard | R Houghton | 4/9F |
| 24 Oct | Nottingham | Penny Regina | | 394 | 6 | I J Chouls | R Houghton | 8/1 |
| 24 Oct | Nottingham | Capacity | | 414 | 13 | Mrs J A de Rothschild | J Clayton | 11/10F |
| 26 Oct | Ascot | Plotina | | 415 | 8 | Maj S Vernon | N Murless | 2/5F |
| 26 Oct | Ascot | Aglojo | | 503 | 7 | A W Pejsa | F Armstrong | 4/1 |
| 28 Oct | Lingfield | Que Guapo | | 414 | 7 | J Straus | S Ingham | EvF |
| 29 Oct | Lingfield | Whaddon Green | | 414 | 6 | P J King | D Hanley | 6/11 |

1966: 191 wins; 89 2nds; 101 3rds; 682 rides

| Date | Race Course | Horse | Race | Value £ | Dist Fur | Owner | Trainer | S/P |
|---|---|---|---|---|---|---|---|---|
| 1967 | | | | | | | | |
| 25 Mar | Doncaster | On Your Mark | | 373 | 8 | C H Palmer | F Armstrong | 1/5F |
| 27 Mar | Kempton | Starry Halo | Coventry | 1,221 | 8 | D Robinson | J Thompson | 8/13F |
| 28 Mar | Nottingham | Caruso | | 372 | 8 | J Thornton Jnr | Denys Smith | 2/1F |
| 5 Apl | Doncaster | Golden Horus | | 414 | 8 | N B Hunt | W O'Gorman | 1/3F |
| 6 Apl | Liverpool | Miss Peseta | | 276 | 5 | B P Jenks | P Rohan | 4/6F |
| 6 Apl | Liverpool | Major Rose | | 414 | 14 | R Heaton | H Price | 5/2F |

(I) = Ireland

| Date | Race Course | Horse | Race | Value £ | Dist Fur | Owner | Trainer | S/P |
|---|---|---|---|---|---|---|---|---|
| 21 Apl | Newbury | Royal Saint | Fred Darling | 2,316 | 7 | Mrs V Hue-Williams | N Murless | 8/11F |
| 21 Apl | Newbury | Londoner | | 593 | 11 | D Robinson | J Thompson | 7/1 |
| 25 Apl | Epsom | Starry Halo | Blue Riband Stks | 3,222 | 8 | D Robinson | J Thompson | 8/13F |
| 29 Apl | Sandown | Sun Rock | Royal | 1,263 | 10 | Mrs V Hue-Williams | N Murless | 9/4F |
| 2 May | Newmarket | Sea Treasure | | 441 | 8 | Mrs J R Mullion | F Armstrong | 4/1F |
| 4 May | Newmarket | Jenny | | 478 | 5 | Mrs V Hue-Williams | N Murless | 100/8 |
| 11 May | Chester | David Jack | Ormonde | 1,156 | 13 | J Fisher | E Lambton | 8/13F |
| 17 May | York | Carlburg | | 680 | 16 | D Robinson | J Thompson | 7/1 |
| 17 May | York | Lunar Princess | | 643 | 6 | Mrs A S Smith | D Rayson | 10/3 |
| 20 May | Lingfield | Waterloo Place | Cosmopolitan Cup | 852 | 10 | Mrs J Rogerson | H Thomson Jones | 6/1 |
| 27 May | Kempton | Sing Again | | 636 | 5 | Capt M D Lemos | F Armstrong | 4/9F |
| 29 May | Leicester | Bamboozle | | 617 | 12 | E Cooper Bland | F Armstrong | 1/2F |
| 29 May | Leicester | Chico | | 272 | 5 | Lady M Fitzalan-Howard | J Dunlop | 4/11F |
| 29 May | Leicester | Boot Camp | | 378 | 7 | R F Scully | F Armstrong | 4/11F |
| 30 May | Sandown | Falcon | | 793 | 5 | C W Engelhard | R Houghton | 6/1 |
| 2 June | Newbury | Supreme Lady | | 488 | 5 | B J Roberts | F Maxwell | 7/4F |
| 3 June | Newmarket | Petingo | | 420 | 5 | Capt M D Lemos | F Armstrong | 6/1 |
| 8 June | Epsom | Sing Again | Great Surrey | 782 | 5 | Capt M D Lemos | F Armstrong | 11/8F |
| 8 June | Epsom | Turn Coat | Royal Hcp | 816 | 6 | Mrs J R Mullion | F Armstrong | 10/1 |
| 12 June | Folkestone | Soverena | | 345 | 5 | L D S Clarke | F Armstrong | 11/4F |
| 21 June | Royal Ascot | Polmak | Bessborough | 1,392 | 12 | H B Ely | F Armstrong | 9/2F |
| 26 June | Leicester | Equal Chance | | 345 | 5 | R C Wilson Jnr | F Armstrong | 11/10F |
| 26 June | Leicester | Game All | | 353 | 10 | Mrs J F C Bryce | F Armstrong | 4/9F |
| 28 June | Salisbury | Razia | | 407 | 5 | I J Chouls | R Houghton | 4/11 |
| 28 June | Salisbury | Lord Sing | | 414 | 10 | Lord Leverhulme | R Houghton | 8/11F |
| 30 June | Doncaster | Fully-Charged | | 207 | 7 | T E Boothby | R Hobson | 4/1F |
| 30 June | Doncaster | Pandear | | 414 | 10 | J Muldoon | F Carr | 10/11F |
| 30 June | Lingfield | Persian Raider | | 453 | 12 | F R Hue-Williams | K Cundell | 5/2 |
| 3 July | Wolver'ton | Soverena | | 334 | 5 | L D S Clarke | F Armstrong | 4/9F |
| 4 July | Kempton | Chasmarella | | 419 | 11 | A R Davison | T Gosling | 8/1 |
| 5 July | Kempton | Drevno | | 600 | 16 | O/trainer | F Maxwell | 9/2 |
| 6 July | Kempton | Last Shot | | 435 | 6 | D Prenn | J Winter | 4/1 |
| 6 July | Yarmouth | Melmark | | 207 | 5 | M Walters | F Armstrong | 7/2 |
| 8 July | Yarmouth | Molly Morgan | | 414 | 6 | Lord Crawshaw | F Armstrong | 7/4F |
| 8 July | Yarmouth | London Boy | | 378 | 6 | D Robinson | J Thompson | 6/1 |
| 10 July | Folkestone | Crossbow | | 324 | 10 | C W Engelhard | R Houghton | 11/4F |
| 11 July | Windsor | Splice the Mainbrace | | 345 | 12 | Mrs T Hartman | M Pope | 4/1 |
| 12 July | Doncaster | Field Mouse | | 414 | 5 | Mrs J F C Bryce | F Armstrong | 8/11F |
| 12 July | Doncaster | King of Rhodes | | 485 | 7 | O/trainer | W O'Gorman | 4/7F |
| 13 July | Doncaster | Soverena | | 366 | 5 | L D S Clarke | F Armstrong | 4/11F |
| 13 July | Doncaster | Ohio | | 414 | 12 | E Sjoo | W O'Gorman | 5/4F |
| 17 July | Nottingham | Gusty Girl | | 320 | 6 | Mrs A Phipps | P Rohan | 5/2F |
| 17 July | Windsor | Arras | | 345 | 10 | Lady Macdonald-Buchanan | J A Waugh | 10/1 |
| 19 July | Sandown | Whirled | St James's Fillies | 779 | 8 | Mrs H O H Freyling-huysen | F Maxwell | 4/5F |
| 24 July | Leicester | London Boy | | 364 | 6 | D Robinson | J Thompson | 13/8F |
| 24 July | Leicester | Green Son | | 345 | 5 | D Robinson | F Winter | 9/2 |
| 25 July | Leicester | Coonbeam | | 345 | 5 | Mrs C Smith-Bingham | P Walwyn | 8/13F |
| 26 July | Goodwood | Miss McLairon | Selsey | 800 | 6 | E Holland-Martin | R Houghton | 7/1 |
| 31 July | Newcastle | Sky Rocket | Seaton Delaval | 1,617 | 5 | Mrs J F C Bryce | F Armstrong | 5/1 |
| 31 July | Newcastle | Arms Park | | 403 | 6 | C A B St George | S Hall | 4/5F |
| 2 Aug | Yarmouth | Patron Saint | | 690 | 10 | Mrs J F C Bryce | F Armstrong | 5/2F |
| 7 Aug | Nottingham | Vittangi B | | 414 | 7 | H B Ely | F Armstrong | 6/4F |
| 8 Aug | Redcar | French Comedy | | 251 | 10 | E W Fattorini | F Hartigan | 10/11F |
| 14 Aug | Nottingham | Sky Rocket | | 414 | 5 | Mrs J F C Bryce | F Armstrong | EvF |

| ate | Race Course | Horse | Race | Value £ | Dist Fur | Owner | Trainer | S/P |
|---|---|---|---|---|---|---|---|---|
| Aug | Nottingham | Dicker | | 381 | 10 | Mrs J F C Bryce | F Armstrong | 5/6F |
| Aug | Nottingham | Uncrowned | | 414 | 5 | C Loyd | R Houghton | 2/1F |
| Aug | Goodwood | Arctic Jelly | | 505 | 6 | Dr M L Slotover | F Armstrong | 2/5F |
| Aug | Yarmouth | Gold Piece | | 232 | 5 | Capt M D Lemos | F Armstrong | 7/2 |
| Aug | Yarmouth | Patriotic Alibi | | 414 | 6 | J B Watriss | F Armstrong | 15/2 |
| Aug | Pontefract | Flibbertigibbet | | 414 | 10 | Mrs J F C Bryce | F Armstrong | 3/1F |
| Aug | Pontefract | Drevno | | 319 | 12 | Mrs F Maxwell | F Maxwell | 2/5F |
| Aug | York | Miss Tarara | Convivial | 1,359 | 6 | Sir F Cassell | R Houghton | 100/8 |
| Aug | York | Bamboozle | Galtres | 986 | 12 | E Cooper Bland | F Armstrong | 7/4F |
| Aug | York | Petingo | Gimcrack | 5,078 | 6 | Capt M D Lemos | F Armstrong | 7/4F |
| Aug | Windsor | Flibbertigibbet | | 339 | 12 | Mrs J F C Bryce | F Armstrong | 8/13F |
| Aug | Windsor | Dicker | | 366 | 10 | Mrs J F C Bryce | F Armstrong | 1/5F |
| Aug | Epsom | Field Mouse | | 796 | 5 | Mrs J F C Bryce | F Armstrong | 2/1 |
| Aug | Epsom | St Paul's Girl | Fifinella | 1,163 | 10 | S Joel | H Cottrill | 4/1F |
| Aug | Epsom | Belinda Jane | | 445 | 7 | K Dodson | S Ingham | 11/2 |
| Aug | Epsom | Duperion | | 392 | 10 | Mrs M S Gilbert | H Wallington | 2/7F |
| Sept | Sandown | Remand | Solario | 1,710 | 7 | J J Astor | W Hern | 8/15F |
| Sept | Warwick | Killam | | 345 | 8 | C A B St George | F Armstrong | 5/2 |
| Sept | Warwick | Easter Island | | 273 | 12 | J Ward | D Leslie | 7/4F |
| Sept | York | Bull Run | | 461 | 16 | J J Astor | W Hern | 13/1 |
| Sept | Wolver'ton | Dicker | | 326 | 12 | Mrs J F C Bryce | F Armstrong | 2/13F |
| Sept | Goodwood | Miss Tarara | | 413 | 6 | Sir F Cassell | R Houghton | 4/7F |
| Sept | Goodwood | Haymaking | | 753 | 10 | C Nicholson | R Houghton | 13/8 |
| Sept | Doncaster | Ribocco | St Leger | 42,695 | 14 | C W Engelhard | R Houghton | 7/2F |
| Sept | Doncaster | Fair Samela | Town Moor Hcp | 1,413 | 7 | Mrs O S Johnston | E Weymes | 11/2F |
| Sept | Pontefract | Thereby | | 345 | 6 | T H Farr | F Armstrong | 4/7F |
| Sept | Pontefract | Valairon | | 277 | 8 | W H Lockwood | M W Easterby | 5/2F |
| Sept | Pontefract | Palariba | | 339 | 8 | R F Scully | F Armstrong | 11/8F |
| Sept | Pontefract | Dicker | | 347 | 10 | Mrs J F C Bryce | F Armstrong | 4/6F |
| Sept | Haydock | Crocus | Haydock Park Stayers Hcp | 853 | 16 | Lady M Bury | F Maxwell | 5/4F |
| Sept | Haydock | Naval Sound | | 282 | 5 | B P Jenks | P Rohan | EvF |
| Sept | Haydock | Easter Island | Tote Investors Trophy | 1,128 | 12 | J Ward | D Leslie | 4/1 |
| Sept | Haydock | Marcotte | | 389 | 8 | J Muldoon | F Carr | 6/4F |
| Sept | Beverley | Pennant | Ronald Fell Hcp | 1,259 | 10 | The Late R Fell | S Hall | 6/4F |
| Sept | Beverley | Field Mouse | | 395 | 5 | Mrs J F C Bryce | F Armstrong | 5/2F |
| Sept | Beverley | Naval Sound | | 364 | 5 | B P Jenks | P Rohan | 5/4F |
| Sept | Ascot | Bamboozle | Princess Royal Stks | 1,724 | 12 | E Cooper Bland | F Armstrong | 7/2F |
| Sept | Ascot | Denosa | Blue Seal | 1,920 | 6 | C Clore | M V O'Brien(I) | 15/8F |
| Sept | Ascot | Remand | Royal Lodge | 3,742 | 8 | J J Astor | W Hern | 13/8F |
| Oct | Nottingham | Aberdeen | | 690 | 8 | S Joel | H Cottrill | 7/1 |
| Oct | Nottingham | Hit the Beach | | 414 | 8 | Mrs H O H Frelinghuysen | F Maxwell | 10/3 |
| Oct | Newmarket | Fly Past | | 428 | 7 | C W Engelhard | R Houghton | 8/1 |
| Oct | Newmarket | Lalibella | Cheveley Park | 7,742 | 6 | J P Philipps | M V O'Brien(I) | 5/1 |
| Oct | Newmarket | Petingo | Middle Park | 7,908 | 6 | Capt M D Lemos | F Armstrong | 1/4F |
| Oct | Teesside | Irish Friendship | | 207 | 7 | J C Raisbeck | F Armstrong | 3/1F |
| Oct | Windsor | Paddy Boy | | 345 | 10 | D Robinson | P Davey | 6/1 |
| Oct | Ascot | Crossbow | | 429 | 10 | C W Engelhard | R Houghton | 6/1 |
| Oct | Ascot | Whirled | Marlborough House | 814 | 8 | Mrs H O H Frelinghuysen | F Maxwell | 13/8F |
| Oct | Ascot | Bamboozle | Mornington | 834 | 12 | E Cooper Bland | F Armstrong | 2/1 |
| Oct | Newmarket | Forlorn River | Challenge | 2,326 | 6 | Mrs W A Richardson | W A Stephenson | 6/4F |
| Oct | Newmarket | Italiano | | 432 | 12 | D Robinson | P Davey | 5/1 |
| Oct | Nottingham | Viroy | | 436 | 10 | N Capon | H Price | 5/2F |
| Oct | Beverley | Sir Blast | | 345 | 7 | R Boyles | A Vasey | 7/2F |
| Oct | Beverley | Apelles | | 345 | 7 | O/trainer | F Maxwell | 5/2F |
| Oct | Newbury | Path | | 550 | 6 | C Loyd | R Houghton | 2/1F |

=Ireland

| Date | Race Course | Horse | Race | Value £ | Dist Fur | Owner | Trainer | S/P |
|---|---|---|---|---|---|---|---|---|
| 3 Nov | Haydock | Shaka | | 306 | 8 | N B Stephenson | H Jones | 10/1 |
| 4 Nov | Haydock | Ribero | | 386 | 6 | C W Englehard | R Houghton | 2/5F |

1967 117 wins; 100 2nds; 64 3rds; 557 rides

1968

| Date | Race Course | Horse | Race | Value £ | Dist Fur | Owner | Trainer | S/P |
|---|---|---|---|---|---|---|---|---|
| 26 March | Doncaster | My Swanee | | 363 | 12 | Mrs L Napier | W Marshall | 7/4 |
| 28 March | Liverpool | Galesian | | 276 | 5 | M Gallacher | E Grassick(I) | 4/1 |
| 5 Apl | Ascot | Sir Ivor | Two Thousand Guineas Trial | 1,290 | 7 | R R Guest | M V O'Brien(I) | 8/15F |
| 13 Apl | Doncaster | London Boy | | 239 | 6 | D Robinson | P Davey | 94F |
| 13 Apl | Doncaster | River Peace | | 411 | 5 | D Robinson | P Davey | 8/11F |
| 15 Apl | Nottingham | Rollicker | | 408 | 13 | Mrs J Bricken | B Hobbs | 5/2 |
| 15 Apl | Nottingham | Sunrust | | 363 | 5 | P E Booth | D Thom | 8/13F |
| 16 Apl | Newmarket | Kiss Me | | 398 | 5 | D Robinson | M Jarvis | 4/7F |
| 23 Apl | Epsom | Pick Me Up | Great Metropolitan | 1,730 | 18 | B P Jenks | T F Rimell | 6/1F |
| 24 Apl | Epsom | Hibernian | Cherkley | 2,556 | 12 | J Cox Brady | M V O'Brien(I) | 9/4F |
| 24 Apl | Epsom | My Swanee | City and Suburban | 2,059 | 10 | Mrs L Napier | W Marshall | 11/2 |
| 24 Apl | Epsom | River Peace | | 395 | 5 | Mrs D Robinson | P Davey | 1/3F |
| 26 Apl | Beverley | Golden Scythe | | 377 | 16 | D Prenn | J Winter | 7/4 |
| 27 Apl | Sandown | Chimney | | 487 | 5 | P Oppenheimer | H Cottrill | 7/1 |
| 27 Apl | Sandown | Bread and Wine | | 462 | 5 | A C Saer | P Canty | 7/4F |
| 30 Apl | Newmarket | Game All | | 584 | 10 | Mrs J F C Bryce | F Armstrong | 6/1 |
| 1 May | Newmarket | Sir Ivor | Two Thousand Guineas | 22,586 | 8 | R R Guest | M V O'Brien(I) | 11/8F |
| 2 May | Newmarket | London Boy | Bretton Hcp | 806 | 6 | D Robinson | P Davey | 6/5F |
| 3 May | Ascot | Silverware | | 564 | 5 | C Nicholson | R Houghton | 7/2 |
| 3 May | Ascot | Marmaduke | Crocker Bulteel Stks | 2,012 | 7 | Mrs G Trimmer-Thompson | K Cundell | 11/2 |
| 3 May | Ascot | Flying Legs | | 491 | 12 | D Robinson | M Jarvis | 10/1F |
| 7 May | Alex Palace | Sunrust | | 516 | 5 | P E Booth | D Thom | 4/5F |
| 7 May | Chester | River Peace | Lily Agnes | 835 | 5 | D Robinson | P Davey | 1/3F |
| 8 May | Chester | Master Rose | | 4,895 | 18 | R L Heaton | H Price | 11/4F |
| 10 May | Leicester | Laxmi | | 345 | 5 | Prince Sayajirao Gaekwar of Baroda | F Armstrong | 2/1F |
| 13 May | Wolver'ton | Silk II | | 390 | 9 | Mrs J A de Rothschild | J Clayton | 10/3 |
| 14 May | York | Silverware | Tattersall's Yorkshire Stks | 912 | 5 | C Nicholson | R Houghton | 8/15F |
| 18 May | Newmarket | Grey Portal | | 497 | 5 | D Prenn | J Winter | 11/4 |
| 18 May | Newmarket | Saintly Den | | 444 | 6 | Lord Leverhulme | R Houghton | 100/9 |
| 21 May | Alex Palace | Rose Petition | | 300 | 5 | Mrs G D Mottram | R Read | 10/11F |
| 22 May | Goodwood | Star Story | | 400 | 5 | Mrs D A Rasbotham | R Houghton | 4/7F |
| 22 May | Goodwood | Lucky Match | | 450 | 11 | C Clore | H Price | 1/2F |
| 27 May | Windsor | Little Gaston | | 207 | 5 | Mrs R Lamb | G Beeby | 11/10F |
| 28 May | Epsom | Silverware | Woodcote | 1,662 | 6 | C Nicholson | R Houghton | 4/7F |
| 29 May | Epsom | Sir Ivor | The Derby | 58,525 | 12 | R R Guest | M V O'Brien(I) | 4/5F |
| 29 May | Epsom | Berber | St James's | 3,273 | 8 | M Sobell | Sir G Richards | 6/1 |
| 1 June | Newmarket | Quicksilver | | 490 | 5 | H B Ely | F Armstrong | 9/2 |
| 1 June | Newmarket | Thereby | | 572 | 8 | T H Farr | F Armstrong | 11/2 |
| 1 June | Newmarket | Backgammon | | 397 | 6 | D Cottage | K Cundell | 2/1F |
| 3 June | Redcar | Naval Sound | | 335 | 5 | Mrs D M Solomon | F Carr | E/F |
| 3 June | Redcar | Helen Nichols | | 415 | 5 | Mrs C A B St George | S Hall | 4/11F |
| 4 June | Sandown | Sidon | Westbury | 1,654 | 10 | Mrs D B Brewster | Sir G Richards | 4/6F |
| 6 June | Brighton | Soverena | | 464 | 5 | L D S Clarke | F Armstrong | 5/11F |
| 8 June | Windsor | Affric | | 400 | 5 | D H Wills | R Houghton | 11/4F |
| 8 June | Windsor | Emperor Menelik | | 460 | 10 | R F Watson | Sir G Richards | 9/4F |
| 10 June | Folkestone | Exiled | | 451 | 6 | W H White | P Supple | 2/1F |
| 10 June | Folkestone | Marsica | | 428 | 10 | J R S Coggan | R Houghton | 9/4 |

(I) = Ireland

| Date | Race Course | Horse | Race | Value £ | Dist Fur | Owner | Trainer | S/P |
|---|---|---|---|---|---|---|---|---|
| 10 June | Nottingham | Brightness | | 381 | 13 | T W Smith | E Goddard | 11/10F |
| 10 June | Nottingham | Tilius | | 690 | 10 | O/trainer | J Walker | 7/2 |
| 11 June | Wolver'ton | Firechief | | 249 | 5 | R Lingham | P Supple | 11/10F |
| 11 June | Alex Palace | Sebastapol | | 377 | 8 | Lady Wyford | Sir G Richards | 6/1 |
| 11 June | Wolver'ton | Royal Artillery | | 337 | 11 | H J Joel | T Waugh | 8/13F |
| 12 June | Kempton | Camilous | | 876 | 8 | C W Engelhard | R Houghton | 4/1F |
| 12 June | Kempton | Belted | Wm Hill Diamond Hcp | 2,000 | 16 | J Ismay | K Cundell | 3/1F |
| 14 June | Bath | Star Story | | 345 | 5 | Mrs D A Rasbotham | R Houghton | 6/4 |
| 17 June | Leicester | Court Photo | | 381 | 8 | Sir J Dean | P Supple | 9/4F |
| 18 June | Royal Ascot | Petingo | St James's Palace | 4,311 | 8 | Capt M D Lemos | F Armstrong | 10/11F |
| 20 June | Royal Ascot | Mountain Call | Cork and Orrery | 1,299 | 6 | I E Kornberg | B van Cutsem | 8/15F |
| 20 June | Royal Ascot | Ribofilio | Chesham | 2,020 | 6 | C W Engelhard | R Houghton | 7/2 |
| 1 July | Brighton | Calshot | | 459 | 6 | A Plesch | F Armstrong | 8/13F |
| 3 July | Folkestone | Milengo | | 267 | 10 | Capt M D Lemos | F Armstrong | 5/2F |
| 3 July | Folkestone | Chateau D'If | | 412 | 6 | Sir R Macdonald-Buchanan | D Sirett | 4/1 |
| 3 July | Folkestone | High Marshal | | 370 | 15 | D Prenn | J Winter | 6/4F |
| 6 July | Sandown | Flying Legs | | 750 | 5 | D Robinson | M Jarvis | 3/1 |
| 6 July | Sandown | Privy Seal | Sandown Anniversary Hcp | 1,500 | 8 | Maj G Glover | T Waugh | 9/4F |
| 11 July | Newmarket | Laxmi | | 464 | 5 | Prince Sayajirao Gaekwar of Baroda | F Armstrong | 4/1 |
| 11 July | Doncaster | Sica Dan | | 376 | 5 | W A S Russell | W O'Gorman | 9/100F |
| 13 July | York | Stung | Milkmaid | 1,662 | 5 | Lord Leverhulme | R Houghton | 4/7F |
| 15 July | Windsor | Heyboy | | 345 | 6 | Mrs A J Saville | J E Sutcliffe | 11/8F |
| 15 July | Brighton | Tyronera | | 345 | 477 | C Clore | Miss M Nightingall | 5/1 |
| 22 July | Folkestone | Redon | | 373 | 12 | C A B St George | R Armstrong | 6/4F |
| 22 July | Windsor | Rose Petition | | 246 | 10 | Mrs G D Mottram | A Read | 11/8F |
| 25 July | Sandown | Woodlands Boy | | 414 | 10 | Mrs S Barnes | T Gosling | 5/11 |
| 26 July | Ascot | Mount Melody | Granville | 550 | 5 | C W Engelhard | R Houghton | 8/11F |
| 26 July | Chester | Admiral's Quill | | 477 | 10 | Mrs D Bowlby | P Walwyn | 5/6F |
| 27 July | Ascot | Star Story | Princess Margaret | 1,920 | 6 | Mrs D A Rasbotham | R Houghton | 4/11 |
| 29 July | Alex Palace | Seato | | 399 | 5 | O/trainer | W O'Gorman | 5/1 |
| 30 July | Goodwood | Flying Legs | Molecombe Stks | 1,700 | 5 | D Robinson | M Jarvis | 4/1 |
| 31 July | Goodwood | Petingo | Sussex Stks | 12,113 | 8 | Capt M D Lemos | F Armstrong | 6/4F |
| 2 Aug | Goodwood | Grasper | Findon M | 830 | 5 | P Nicholson | R Houghton | 8/13F |
| 5 Aug | Windsor | Welsh Whistler | | 345 | 5 | C A Blackwell | J Winter | 8/13F |
| 7 Aug | Yarmouth | Soroca | | 419 | 6 | Capt M D Lemos | F Armstrong | EvF |
| 7 Aug | Yarmouth | Hector Heathcote | | 414 | 7 | S C Booth | D Thom | 7/2 |
| 8 Aug | Yarmouth | Chateau D'If | | 483 | 7 | Sir R Macdonald-Buchanan | J Sirett | 4/5F |
| 9 Aug | Newmarket | Exalt | | 470 | 7 | C W Engelhard | R Houghton | 3/1 |
| 12 Aug | Windsor | Laxmi | | 345 | 5 | Prince Sayajirao Gaekwar of Baroda | F Armstrong | 10/11F |
| 13 Aug | Windsor | Chasmarella | | 320 | 11 | A R Davison | T Gosling | 8/13F |
| 13 Aug | Nottingham | Backgammon | Nottingham Stewards Hcp | 2,522 | 6 | D Cottage | K Cundell | 8/1 |
| 16 Aug | Newbury | Keep Going | St Hugh's | 873 | 5 | Miss S J Hayward | T Leader | 11/2 |
| 20 Aug | York | Petros | Rose of York | 2,632 | 8 | F W Burman | B van Cutsem | 11/2 |
| 20 Aug | York | Dieudonne | Acomb Stks | 1,158 | 6 | Sir F Cassell | R Houghton | 3/1F |
| 24 Aug | Lingfield | Grey Goose | Nizefella M | 1,073 | 6 | Lord Porchester | J Clayton | 7/11 |
| 26 Aug | Alex Palace | Haute Couture | | 415 | 13 | G Rosen | J Walker | 4/11F |
| 27 Aug | Folkestone | Golden Helmet | | 480 | 6 | C W Engelhard | R Houghton | 7/2 |
| 27 Aug | Yarmouth | Balidar | | 414 | 6 | D Prenn | J Winter | 4/5F |
| 28 Aug | Brighton | Word from Lundy | | 571 | 7 | E Holland-Martin | R Houghton | 11/2 |

(I) = Ireland

| Date | Race Course | Horse | Race | Value £ | Dist Fur | Owner | Trainer | S/P |
|---|---|---|---|---|---|---|---|---|
| 29 Aug | Brighton | Pirate Pete | | 360 | 5 | L J Nutt | R Sturdy | 11/2 |
| 29 Aug | Brighton | Exiled | | 486 | 6 | W H White | P Supple | 100/8 |
| 30 Aug | Goodwood | Big Sir | | 346 | 14 | D W Molins | K Cundell | 2/1F |
| 30 Aug | Goodwood | Dino | | 367 | 8 | C W Engelhard | J Tree | 2/1 |
| 2 Sept | Epsom | Benroy | | 782 | 8 | A J A Kennedy | Miss M Nightingall | 6/4F |
| 2 Sept | Epsom | Welshman | | 796 | 5 | S Bridge | F Cundell | 3/1F |
| 2 Sept | Epsom | Mahal | Fifinella | 1,115 | 10 | Mrs D Bowlby | P Walwyn | 11/2 |
| 3 Sept | Chepstow | Dark Court | | 331 | 10 | Mrs M Sobell | Sir G Richards | 5/4F |
| 4 Sept | York | Sica Dan | Talahasse | 1,327 | 5 | A J Russell | W O'Gorman | 4/6F |
| 4 Sept | York | Parley | | 451 | 16 | Mrs J A de Rothschild | J Clayton | 2/1F |
| 5 Sept | Haydock | Equal Change | | 388 | 5 | R C Wilson Jnr | F Armstrong | 11/1 |
| 7 Sept | Sandown | Keep Going | Billy Butlins | 1,636 | 5 | Mrs S S Hayward | T Leader | 8/11F |
| 9 Sept | Windsor | Chasmarisha | | 327 | 11 | R Davison | T Gosling | 8/13F |
| 10 Sept | Doncaster | Paul-Mary | | 985 | 9 | O/trainer | W O'Gorman | 7/2 |
| 10 Sept | Doncaster | Ribofilio | Champagne | 5,273 | 7 | C W Engelhard | R Houghton | 7/2 |
| 11 Sept | Doncaster | Ribero | St Leger | 33,437 | 14 | C W Engelhard | R Houghton | 10/3 |
| 12 Sept | Doncaster | Oraculus | Fitzwilliam | 940 | 8 | P B Raymond | K Cundell | 13/8F |
| 13 Sept | Newbury | Myrtus | | 468 | 13 | N Cohen | H Price | 11/10F |
| 13 Sept | Newbury | Grey Portal | Fairhurst Nursery Hcp | 908 | 7 | D Prenn | J Winter | 6/1 |
| 14 Sept | Newbury | George Stubbs | | 474 | 5 | R Green | R Jarvis | 3/1F |
| 19 Sept | Yarmouth | Court Photo | | 483 | 8 | Sir J Dean | P Supple | 4/1 |
| 19 Sept | Yarmouth | High Marshal | | 383 | 14 | D Prenn | J Winter | 7/2 |
| 19 Sept | Yarmouth | Ben Novus | | 367 | 10 | J N Peatt | W Hide | 6/4F |
| 20 Sept | Kempton | Madlin | | 445 | 6 | T C Vigors | J Tree | 13/8 |
| 20 Sept | Kempton | Mountain Call | | 645 | 5 | I E Kornberg | B van Cutsem | 1/5F |
| 21 Sept | Kempton | First Pick | | 429 | 11 | D Morris | H Wallington | 2/1F |
| 25 Sept | Lingfield | Chasmarella | | 424 | 12 | A R Davison | T Gosling | 4/6F |
| 28 Sept | Ascot | Peace | Blue Seal | 1,844 | 6 | J H Whitney | J Tree | 9/2 |
| 3 Oct | Newmarket | Keep Going | | 492 | 5 | Mrs S S Hayward | T Leader | 6/1 |
| 5 Oct | Newmarket | Major Rose | Cesarewitch | 5,447 | 20 | R L Heaton | H Price | 9/1F |
| 9 Oct | Lingfield | Synella | | 506 | 5 | J R S Coggan | R Houghton | 11/4F |
| 9 Oct | Lingfield | Harbour Flower | | 414 | 6 | R F Scully | F Armstrong | 11/2F |
| 10 Oct | York | Royal Wink | | 440 | 8 | C W Engelhard | R Houghton | 4/1 |
| 10 Oct | York | Erne | | 628 | 8 | J H Whitney | J Tree | 9/2 |
| 17 Oct | Newmarket | Ribbocare | Jockey Club Cup | 2,330 | 16 | C W Engelhard | J Tree | 6/1 |
| 18 Oct | Newmarket | Mountain Call | Challenge | 2,372 | 6 | I E Kornberg | B van Cutsem | 2/1F |
| 18 Oct | Newmarket | Ribofilio | Dewhurst | 8,570 | 7 | C W Engelhard | R Houghton | 8/11F |
| 19 Oct | Newmarket | Sir Ivor | Champion | 14,673 | 10 | R R Guest | M V O'Brien(I) | 8/11F |
| 19 Oct | Newmarket | Laxmi | | 507 | 5 | Prince Sayajirao Gaekwar of Baroda | F Armstrong | 11/4F |
| 21 Oct | Leicester | Chip | | 414 | 5 | C Loyd | R Houghton | 13/2 |
| 23 Oct | Sandown | Varma | | 474 | 5 | C Clore | T Masson | 11/4 |
| 25 Oct | Newbury | Erne | | 604 | 8 | J H Whitney | J Tree | 5/1 |
| 8 Nov | Haydock | Notonia | | 404 | 12 | A Plesch | F Armstrong | 13/8F |

1968: 139 wins; 98 2nds; 75 3rds; 580 rides

| Date | Race Course | Horse | Race | Value £ | Dist Fur | Owner | Trainer | S/P |
|---|---|---|---|---|---|---|---|---|
| 1969 | | | | | | | | |
| 24 Mar | Doncaster | New Charter | Batthyany | 929 | 5 | G P Goulandris | F Armstrong | 13/2 |
| 25 Mar | Doncaster | My Swanee | | 414 | 10 | A G M Stevens | W Marshall | 11/2F |
| 5 Apl | Kempton | Fordie | | 534 | 11 | Lord Cadogan | C Bewicke | 3/1F |
| 8 Apl | Newcastle | Petrus | Tweed Stks | 1,215 | 9 | F W Burmann | B van Cutsem | 4/11F |
| 15 Apl | Newmarket | Medina Boy | | 430 | 5 | J Strauss | S Ingham | 7/4F |
| 18 Apl | Newbury | Jukebox | | 621 | 5 | D Morris | H Wallington Jnr | 7/4F |
| 18 Apl | Newbury | Rossendale | | 702 | 8 | J H Thursby | J Clayton | 3/1F |

(I) = Ireland

| Date | Race Course | Horse | Race | Value £ | Dist Fur | Owner | Trainer | S/P |
|---|---|---|---|---|---|---|---|---|
| 19 Apl | Newbury | Emerilo | Newbury Spring Cup | 1,756 | 7 | J W Hickman | D Hanley | 3/1F |
| 23 Apl | Epsom | Karabas | City and Suburban | 2,489 | 10 | Lord Iveagh | B van Cutsem | 9/1 |
| 27 Apl | Newmarket | Karabas | Turn of the Lands | 1,234 | 10 | Lord Iveagh | B van Cutsem | 9/4F |
| 1 May | Newmarket | Constans | | 1,293 | 6 | Miss M Sheriffe | J Tree | 9/2 |
| 1 May | Newmarket | Chagrin Falls | | 690 | 5 | C Lassen | J Winter | 11/4 |
| 2 May | Ascot | Soroco | Crocker Bulteel | 2,068 | 7 | Capt M D Lemos | R Armstrong | 100/9 |
| 2 May | Ascot | Light Fire | White Rose | 2,068 | 10 | Mrs Grosvenor | P Nelson | 10/3 |
| 16 May | Lingfield | The Elk | Derby Trial | 2,617 | 12 | Miss M Sheriffe | J Tree | 10/1 |
| 20 May | Alex Palace | Bar of Gold | | 276 | 8 | Mrs E Bednash | W Marshall | 6/4F |
| 23 May | Haydock | Habitat | | 552 | 8 | C W Engelhard | R Houghton | 8/11F |
| 29 May | Brighton | Buff's Own | | 633 | 12 | Mrs J A de Rothschild | J Clayton | EvF |
| 31May | Newmarket | Camina Boy | | 482 | 5 | Capt M D Lemos | F Armstrong | 9/4F |
| 3 June | Windsor | Almacest | | 518 | 5 | E B London | F Armstrong | 11/4F |
| 5 June | Epsom | Park Top | Coronation Cup | 11,457 | 12 | Duke of Devonshire | B van Cutsem | 11/4 |
| 6 June | Epsom | Quarry Knowe | | 797 | 5 | Lord Weir | H Price | 15/8 |
| 7 June | Epsom | Marsascala | Mickleham | 834 | 6 | Capt T E Langton | P Rohan | 11/10F |
| 9 June | Wolver'ton | Buff's Own | | 483 | 11 | Mrs J A de Rothschild | J Clayton | 4/9F |
| 10 June | Alex Palace | Jolly Rocker Girl | | 510 | 5 | S Sherman | S Ingham | 11/8F |
| 11 June | Kempton | Balidar | Matador Hcp | 1,352 | 6 | D Prenn | J Winter | 5/4F |
| 11 June | Yarmouth | My Solo | | 518 | 5 | F W Burmann | B van Cutsem | 1/6F |
| 11 June | Yarmouth | Solarel | | 552 | 14 | Lord Derby | B van Cutsem | 11/2 |
| 11 June | Yarmouth | Ditamba | | 452 | 10 | C A Blackwell | J Winter | 4/1 |
| 13 June | Sandown | Ballysampson | | 694 | 8 | W Ellis | J Winter | 8/1 |
| 14 June | Newmarket | Barton Mills | | 690 | 6 | D Montagu | B van Cutsem | 4/6F |
| 14 June | Newmarket | Parcel | | 607 | 14 | K Mason | B van Cutsem | 11/10F |
| 14 June | Newmarket | Ra | | 816 | 7 | J B Wattriss | F Armstrong | 3/1F |
| 17 June | Royal Ascot | Lexicon | Ascot Stakes | 3,144 | 20 | G P Eliot | H Price | 10/1 |
| 18 June | Royal Ascot | Kamundu | Royal Hunt Cup | 4,353 | 8 | J Banks | F Carr | 7/1 |
| 27 June | Kempton | Grisaille | | 818 | 7 | Mrs J A de Rothschild | J Clayton | 7/2 |
| 30 June | Brighton | Paddle Boat | | 546 | 12 | Mrs J R Hindley | N Murless | 8/11F |
| 1 July | Brighton | Sixfiveseven | | 613 | 7 | C A Blackwell | J Winter | 5/2 |
| 1 July | Brighton | Tintagel II | | 677 | 12 | Mrs R C Sturdy | R C Sturdy | EvF |
| 3 July | Yarmouth | Emma Canute | | 450 | 7 | Lady D Vyner | G Barling | 2/5F |
| 3 July | Pontefract | Suecol | | 552 | 6 | J McShane | F Maxwell | Ev |
| 5 July | Sandown | Tudor Boy | | 813 | 5 | H Loebstein | T Corbett | 4/6 |
| 5 July | Sandown | My Swanee | Sandown Anniv Hcp | 1,534 | 8 | A G M Stevens | W Marshall | 3/1 |
| 5 July | Sandown | Wolver Hollow | Eclipse | 25,029 | 10 | Mrs C O Iselin | H Cecil | 8/1 |
| 7 July | Nottingham | Wincrock | | 483 | 5 | H L Rawcliffe | F Maxwell | 11/4 |
| 8 July | Newmarket | Coevers | | 504 | 16 | E B Benjamin | G Barling | 7/2 |
| 10 July | Newmarket | Malika | | 772 | 14 | O/trainer | M W Easterby | 5/2 |
| 10 July | Newmarket | Vital Match | Falmouth | 2,203 | 8 | O/trainer | H Blagrave | 3/10 |
| 10 July | Doncaster | Darunda | | 690 | 12 | Maj E T Baring | F Maxwell | 4/9 |
| 11 July | Newbury | Pyrenean | | 600 | 6 | A R C Hobbs | F Maxwell | 11/2 |
| 12 July | Wolver'ton | Pannaletta | | 479 | 5 | E H L Rawcliffe | F Maxwell | 8/13 |
| 12 July | Wolver'ton | Threshoon | Wolverhampton Stks | 859 | 16 | W G Wilcox | W A Stephenson | 8/11 |
| 12 July | York | My Swanee | Magnet Cup | 3,775 | 10½ | A G M Stevens | W Marshall | 5/2 |
| 12 July | York | Raffingora | Rievaulx Hcp | 701 | 5 | A G M Stevens | W Marshall | 10/3 |
| 12 July | York | Indomitable | | 665 | 12 | Mr W H D Riley-Smith | H Price | 2/9F |
| 15 July | Kempton | Bosairun† | | 795 | 7 | J Gavaghan | W Marshall | |
| 16 July | Kempton | Quarry Knowe | | 578 | 6 | Lord Weir | H Price | 4/5F |
| 18 July | Pontefract | John's Key | | 352 | 12 | R E Harrison | E Magner | 2/1F |
| 21 July | Windsor | Elatria | | 518 | 5 | C P Goulandris | F Armstrong | 6/4 |
| 21 July | Windsor | Detonator (USA) | | 518 | 6 | Maj H Cayzer | W Wightman | 13/8F |
| 21 July | Leicester | Overlord | | 474 | 5 | Col W Stirling | J Dunlop | 15/8 |
| 21 July | Leicester | Sayes | | 518 | 6 | E B London | F Armstrong | 11/7F |
| 22 July | Alex Palace | Macadamia | | 485 | 5 | A Plesch | F Armstrong | 4/9F |

† Walkover (USA) = America

| Date | Race Course | Horse | Race | Value £ | Dist Fur | Owner | Trainer | S/P |
|---|---|---|---|---|---|---|---|---|
| 22 July | Alex Palace | Kirisama | | 555 | 13 | Miss M Price | F Armstrong | 5/1 |
| 22 July | Alex Palace | Cabouchon | | 269 | 13 | F J Hart | W Marshall | 4/9F |
| 23 July | Sandown | Vital Match | | 761 | 8 | O/trainer | H Blagrave | 4/9F |
| 26 July | Ascot | Park Top | King George VI and Queen Elizabeth | 31,122 | 12 | Duke of Devonshire | B van Cutsem | 9/4F |
| 28 July | Newcastle | Another Guitarist* | | 217 | 6 | F F Watts | Mrs R Lomax | 3/1 |
| 1 Aug | Goodwood | Medina Boy | Rous Memorial | 1,078 | 6 | J Straus | S Ingham | 1/2F |
| 4 Aug | Wolver'ton | Many a Mickle | | 207 | 5 | H G Thompson | J Hardy | EvF |
| 4 Aug | Wolver'ton | Kimi | | 489 | 8 | R More O'Ferrall | J Dunlop | 4/5F |
| 8 Aug | Newmarket | Camina Bay | | 587 | 6 | Capt M D Lemos | F Armstrong | EvF |
| 8 Aug | Newmarket | Emerilo | | 566 | 8 | J W Hickman | D Hanley | 4/5F |
| 9 Aug | Redcar | Premiette | | 537 | 7 | Mrs M Marginson | M W Easterby | 13/2 |
| 9 Aug | Redcar | Dumana | | 468 | 6 | A Bosley | W Marshall | 5/1 |
| 9 Aug | Nottingham | Quentanner | | 446 | 5 | J Britton | W A Stephenson | 13/8F |
| 9 Aug | Windsor | Lutine | | 518 | 10 | G Biggs | F Maxwell | 9/4 |
| 13 Aug | Haydock | Christmas Gold | | 715 | 7 | Mrs L Brotherton | L Shedden | 9/4 |
| 14 Aug | Alex Palace | All Royal | | 523 | 8 | I J Chouls | R Houghton | 11/4 |
| 14 Aug | Haydock | Pyremean | | 505 | 6 | A R C Hobbs | F Maxwell | 1/2 |
| 14 Aug | Haydock | Arctic Judge | | 467 | 10 | Mrs J A McDougald | I Balding | 11/4 |
| 16 Aug | Newbury | Raffingora | Shrivenham | 804 | 5 | A G M Stevens | W Marshall | 5/2 |
| 16 Aug | Newbury | Medina Boy | Washington Singer | 1,149 | 6 | J Straus | S Ingham | 4/5 |
| 16 Aug | Newbury | Gold Lane | | 649 | 7 | L A H Ames | G Hunter | 8/1 |
| 18 Aug | Windsor | Greenhills | | 519 | 10 | C Payne-Crofts | H Price | 9/2 |
| 19 Aug | York | My Swanee | Rose of York | 2,692 | 8 | A G M Stevens | W Marshall | 8/1 |
| 19 Aug | York | Blue Yonder | Eglinton | 1,348 | 12 | J H Whitney | J Tree | 9/4 |
| 19 Aug | York | Raffingora | Harewood | 1,473 | 5 | A G M Stevens | W Marshall | 15/8F |
| 21 Aug | York | Tower Walk | Nunthorpes | 3,552 | 5 | V W Hardy | G Barling | 7/1 |
| 22 Aug | Haydock | Catriona | | 498 | 5 | Col J Berry | I Balding | 10/11F |
| 22 Aug | Haydock | Wishoon | | 552 | 10 | D Robinson | M Jarvis | 7/4F |
| 22 Aug | Haydock | Smokey Rockett | Buggins Farm | 1,188 | 7 | D Robinson | M Jarvis | 10/11F |
| 22 Aug | Haydock | Polsky | | 512 | 6 | D Robinson | P Davey | 3/1 |
| 22 Aug | Windsor | Elatria | | 518 | 5 | C P Goulandris | F Armstrong | 7/2 |
| 23 Aug | Newmarket | Mount Melody | | 598 | 6 | C W Engelhard | R Houghton | 2/1F |
| 25 Aug | Pontefract | Efficacy | | 318 | 10 | O/trainer | W A Stephenson | 11/10 |
| 25 Aug | Pontefract | Soroco | Darley Brewery | 1,858 | 10 | Capt M D Lemos | F Armstrong | 10/3 |
| 26 Aug | Folkestone | Dumana | | 446 | 6 | A Bosley | W Marshall | 6/1 |
| 26 Aug | Folkestone | Olympic | | 283 | 10 | Mrs D C Marshal | W Marshall | 9/4F |
| 26 Aug | Folkestone | Queen Flavia | | 498 | 15 | Mrs D Riley-Smith | H Price | 5/2 |
| 29 Aug | Windsor | Swinging Again | | 518 | 5 | R C Wilson Jnr | F Armstrong | 5/2F |
| 29 Aug | Windsor | Gaberdine | | 463 | 11 | Mrs J A de Rothschild | J Clayton | 11/10 |
| 30 Aug | Goodwood | Habitat | Wills Mile | 7,507 | 8 | C W Engelhard | R Houghton | 9/2 |
| 30 Aug | Goodwood | Ribofilio | | 1,714 | 14 | C W Engelhard | R Houghton | 1/7 |
| 1 Sept | Newcastle | Rake Wood | Embassy | 914 | 9 | O/trainer | W A Stephenson | 3/1 |
| 1 Sept | Newcastle | Askalan | Parkins Memorial | 862 | 6 | J B Wharton | W A Stephenson | 4/11F |
| 1 Sept | Newcastle | Parradell | Virginia Stks | 840 | 10 | F G B Fleetwood-Hesketh | G Barling | 4/9F |
| 2 Sept | Epsom | Blue Yonder | Chessington | 649 | 10 | J H Whitney | J Tree | 4/9F |
| 2 Sept | Epsom | Karabas | | 574 | 10 | Lord Iveagh | B van Cutsem | 1/2F |
| 3 Sept | York | Calamus | | 745 | 16 | Lord Vestey | F Maxwell | 4/1 |
| 4 Sept | York | Cleona | Tadcaster | 835 | 6 | E B C Driffield | E Weymes | 11/4 |
| 4 Sept | York | Christmas Gold | | 766 | 7 | Mrs L Brotherton | L Shedden | 6/4 |
| 4 Sept | York | Gaberdine | Rufford | 951 | 12 | Mrs J A de Rothschild | J Clayton | 7/4F |
| 4 Sept | York | Emma Canute | | 706 | 6 | Lady D Vyner | G Barling | 10/11 |

* Dead Heat

| Date | Race Course | Horse | Race | Value £ | Dist Fur | Owner | Trainer | S/P |
|---|---|---|---|---|---|---|---|---|
| 5 Sept | Chester | Runzara | | 520 | 5 | D Prenn | J Winter | 8/13F |
| 5 Sept | Chester | Side Hill | | 554 | 7 | Duke of Devonshire | B van Cutsem | 1/2F |
| 5 Sept | Chester | Word From Lundy | | 574 | 12 | E Holland-Martin | R Houghton | 7/2 |
| 8 Sept | Windsor | Varma | | 518 | 10 | C Clore | M Masson | 3/10F |
| 9 Sept | Doncaster | Wardie | Glasgow Paddocks | 907 | 5 | K Dodson | E Davey | 6/4F |
| 9 Sept | Doncaster | Smokey Rockett | Rous N/H | 1,457 | 7 | D Robinson | M Jarvis | 9/4 |
| 9 Sept | Doncaster | Agenor | Clumber | 1,024 | 12 | Count C Seilern | J Clayton | 100/9 |
| 10 Sept | Doncaster | Tribal Chief | Norfolk | 4,167 | 5 | J L Swift | B Swift | 4/11 |
| 10 Sept | Doncaster | Green Shoon | Autumn | 1,019 | 10 | D Robinson | P Davey | 11/4 |
| 10 Sept | Doncaster | Mountain Call | Portland | 3,631 | 5 | I E Kornberg | B van Cutsem | 11/4 |
| 11 Sept | Doncaster | Karabas | Scarbrough | 1,274 | 10 | Lord Iveagh | B van Cutsem | 4/1 |
| 12 Sept | Doncaster | Karoo | Feversham | 1,184 | 7 | F W Burmann | B van Cutsem | 2/1F |
| 12 Sept | Doncaster | Purple Haze | Cleveland | 1,335 | 9 | D Robinson | P Davey | 2/1F |
| 13 Sept | Newbury | Hartley Court | | 701 | 5 | R K Richards | D Hanley | 20/1 |
| 13 Sept | Newbury | Principal Boy | Peter Hastings | 4,373 | 10 | Lady Hothfield | J Clayton | 4/1 |
| 13 Sept | Newbury | My Solo | Highclere | 851 | 5 | F W Burmann | B van Cutsem | 13/8F |
| 16 Sept | Yarmouth | Rea | | 207 | 7 | J D Ashenheim | F Armstrong | 9/2 |
| 16 Sept | Yarmouth | Sweet Perfume | | 562 | 6 | D Robinson | M Jarvis | 11/8F |
| 18 Sept | Ayr | Wilfrid | Shaw Memorial | 853 | 8 | Mrs E P Mathews | S Hall | 5/1 |
| 18 Sept | Ayr | Quarry Knowle | Ladykirk | 1,682 | 5 | Lord Weir | H Price | 11/8F |
| 20 Sept | Kempton | Yellow God | Imperial | 8,011 | 6 | D Robinson | P Davey | 4/5F |
| 20 Sept | Kempton | Jukebox | | 484 | 6 | D Morris | H Wallington Jnr | 4/5F |
| 20 Sept | Kempton | Regal Path | | 510 | 11 | N Cohen | H Price | 11/8F |
| 24 Sept | Haydock | Quadrant | | 552 | 5 | A Wetherall | F Maxwell | 11/8 |
| 24 Sept | Haydock | Slingsby | | 544 | 8 | J R Mullion | F Armstrong | 9/4 |
| 26 Sept | Ascot | Sayes | | 690 | 7 | E B London | F Armstrong | 5/1 |
| 26 Sept | Ascot | Winton Hotel | | 676 | 16 | S Winton | P Ashworth | 4/1 |
| 26 Sept | Ascot | Miss Dorothy | | 207 | 5 | Mrs J H Pugh | R Houghton | 7/4 |
| 29 Sept | Hamilton | Lucky Shoes | | 701 | 5 | P Davey | L Brown | 9/2 |
| 29 Sept | Hamilton | Pride of India | | 454 | 10 | B Widener | H Cecil | 4/5F |
| 29 Sept | Hamilton | Rain in the Face | Royal Caledonian Hunt Hcp | 518 | 8 | J H Whitney | H Cecil | 3/1F |
| 29 Sept | Hamilton | Silver Shoe | | 503 | 8 | Mrs L Brotherton | L Shedden | 10/3 |
| 2 Oct | Newmarket | Coming of Age | | 690 | 6 | A Willingston | D Smith | 5/1 |
| 2 Oct | Newmarket | Mercian | Severals | 859 | 8 | J Westoll | G Barling | 3/1 |
| 6 Oct | Wolver'ton | Barrettown Joy | | 483 | 5 | G Weston | H Cecil | 9/4F |
| 7 Oct | Lingfield | Argot | | 552 | 7 | Mrs I L Tooth | R Houghton | 8/13F |
| 7 Oct | Lingfield | Varma | | 552 | 10 | C Clore | M Masson | 9/2F |
| 7 Oct | Lingfield | Sweet Song | | 556 | 6 | Mrs D Robinson | M Jarvis | 5/1 |
| 9 Oct | York | Slingsby | | 667 | 8 | J R Mullion | F Armstrong | 2/1 |
| 10 Oct | Ascot | Karabas | | 656 | 10 | Lord Iveagh | B van Cutsem | 1/3F |
| 11 Oct | Ascot | Ribston | Sandwich | 1,198 | 7 | C W Engelhard | J Tree | 7/2 |
| 16 Oct | Newmarket | Smokey Rockett | Somerville Tatts | 925 | 7 | D Robinson | M Jarvis | 7/2 |
| 17 Oct | Newmarket | Nijinsky (Can) | Dewhurst | 10,576 | 7 | C W Engelhard | M V O'Brien(I) | 1/3F |
| 18 Oct | Newmarket | Mysolo | Suffolk N/H | 1,027 | 5 | F W Burmann | B van Cutsem | 1/4F |
| 20 Oct | Leicester | Lucky Shoes | | 414 | 6 | D Robinson | P Davey | 3/1F |
| 24 Oct | Newbury | Pizzicato | | 743 | 12 | L B Holliday | W Hern | 10/1 |
| 25 Oct | Doncaster | Tintagel II | Manchester Stks | 4,217 | 12 | O/trainer | R Sturdy | 15/2 |
| 31 Oct | Newmarket | Honorius | | 706 | 8 | Mrs J F C Bryce | F Armstrong | 11/10F |
| 1 Nov | Haydock | Xan II | | 207 | 12 | Count C Seilern | J Clayton | 15/8F |

1969: 163 wins; 95 2nds; 87 3rds; 600 rides

1970

| Date | Race Course | Horse | Race | Value £ | Dist Fur | Owner | Trainer | S/P |
|---|---|---|---|---|---|---|---|---|
| 23 Mar | Doncaster | Major Blue | Batthyany Hcp | 898 | 5 | D Robinson | P Davey | 4/1 |
| 23 Mar | Doncaster | Lord Gayle(USA) | | 690 | 7 | R N Webster | F Armstrong | 2/1 |
| 24 Mar | Doncaster | Tin Guard | | 406 | 5 | D Robinson | P Davey | 8/11F |

(I) = Ireland (Can) = Canada

| Date | Race Course | Horse | Race | Value £ | Dist Fur | Owner | Trainer | S/P |
|---|---|---|---|---|---|---|---|---|
| 24 Mar | Doncaster | Green Shoon | | 690 | 10 | D Robinson | P Davey | 85/40F |
| 28 Mar | Kempton | Yellow God | Two Thousand Guineas Trial | 1,578 | 7 | D Robinson | P Davey | 6/4F |
| 28 Mar | Kempton | Slingsby | | 512 | 8 | J R Mullion | F Armstrong | 5/2F |
| 30 Mar | Kempton | Miss Skyscraper | One Thousand Guineas Trial | 1,508 | 7 | O J Simms | R Jarvis | 2/1 |
| 31 Mar | Newcastle | Windstorm | | 447 | 5 | Miss R Hurst | M W Easterby | 7/4F |
| 2 Apl | Liverpool | Lucky Shoes | | 466 | 8 | D Robinson | P Davey | 15/8F |
| 2 Apl | Liverpool | Pelham | | 483 | 14 | J Banks | F Carr | 11/8F |
| 4 Apl | Liverpool | Northern Wizard | | 504 | 8 | Mrs R I Nielson | W C Marshall | 6/1 |
| 4 Apl | Liverpool | Palm Beach | | 523 | 13 | C Haynes | T F Rimell | 9/2 |
| 11 Apl | Ascot | Major Blue | | 734 | 5 | D Robinson | P Davey | 3/1F |
| 15 Apl | Newmarket | Meadowville | Wood Ditton | 930 | 8 | D Robinson | M Jarvis | 9/4F |
| 18 Apl | Newbury | Leander | | 682 | 8 | C W Engelhard | J Tree | 9/2 |
| 21 Apl | Epsom | Decies | Blue Riband Trial | 3,645 | 8 | N B Hunt | B van Cutsem | 2/1 |
| 22 Apl | Epsom | Flight Dancer | | 660 | 5 | Mrs M A Moore | R Houghton | 8/1 |
| 22 Apl | Epsom | Tin Guard | | 585 | 5 | D Robinson | P Davey | 4/11F |
| 22 Apl | Epsom | Gay Baby | | 619 | 5 | D Robinson | M Jarvis | 2/1F |
| 23 Apl | Epsom | Raffingora | | 740 | 5 | A G M Stevens | W Marshall | 4/1 |
| 24 Apl | Sandown | Pleaseme | | 552 | 5 | Mrs M Adams | P Ashworth | 13/8F |
| 24 Apl | Sandown | Leander | | 738 | 8 | C W Engelhard | M Tate | 2/1F |
| 25 Apl | Sandown | Nice Music | | 675 | 5 | D Robinson | P Davey | 5/1 |
| 25 Apl | Ascot (at Newmarket) | Only a Wish | White Rose | 2,048 | 10 | Miss M Sheriffe | J Tree | 10/1 |
| 28 Apl | Newmarket | Karoo | | 960 | 8 | F Burmann | B van Cutsem | 2/1F |
| 29 Apl | Newmarket | Fireside Chat | | 690 | 5 | C W Engelhard | R Houghton | 6/5F |
| 29 Apl | Newmarket | Nijinsky (Can) | Two Thousand Guineas | 28,295 | 8 | C W Engelhard | M V O'Brien(I) | 4/7F |
| 30 Apl | Newmarket | Balidar | Bretby Hcp | 1,245 | 6 | D Prenn | J Winter | 2/1F |
| 30 Apl | Newmarket | Humble Duty | One Thousand Guineas | 21,015 | 8 | Jean Lady Ashcombe | P Walwyn | 3/1F |
| 1 May | Ascot (at Newmarket) | Flight Dancer | | 581 | 5 | Mrs M A Moore | R Houghton | 4/5F |
| 5 May | Chester | Green Shoon | | 631 | 10 | D Robinson | P Davey | 4/6F |
| 8 May | Kempton | Mysolo | Queen Elizabeth | 837 | 15 | F W Burmann | B van Cutsem | 10/11F |
| 8 May | Kempton | Northern Wizard | | 536 | 8 | Mrs R I Nelson | W Marshall | 7/2 |
| 8 May | Leicester | Festino | | 520 | 7 | H Loebstein | T Corbett | 11/2 |
| 8 May | Newcastle | Martial Bliss | | 587 | 5 | A Cooper | H B T Jones | 7/2 |
| 12 May | York | My Swallow | Zetland Stks | 752 | 5 | D Robinson | P Davey | 8/13F |
| 12 May | York | Raffingora | Micklegate | 740 | 5 | A G M Stevens | W Marshall | EvF |
| 13 May | Salisbury | The Wynk | | 345 | 8 | C B Stewardson | W Marshall | 3/1F |
| 15 May | Lingfield | Leander | | 552 | 10 | C W Engelhard | J Tree | 6/4F |
| 20 May | Goodwood | Green God | | 633 | 5 | D Robinson | M Jarvis | 11/10F |
| 21 May | Goodwood | Lucky Cheat | | 428 | 5 | D Prenn | J Winter | 5/1 |
| 22 May | Haydock | Flight Dancer | | 428 | 5 | Mrs M A Moore | R Houghton | 3/10F |
| 22 May | Haydock | Tom Gate (USA) | | 552 | 8 | C W Engelhard | R Houghton | 8/15F |
| 23 May | Doncaster | King's Catch | | 437 | 5 | D Robinson | P Davey | 2/5F |
| 23 May | Doncaster | Hunter Jet | | 725 | 8 | J A Sutton | F Maxwell | 11/10 |
| 26 May | Sandown | Raffingora | Temple | 1,487 | 5 | A G M Stevens | W Marshall | 4/1 |
| 27 May | Brighton | Manxman | | 371 | 6 | Lord Leverhulme | R Houghton | 3/1F |
| 27 May | Brighton | Huzoor | | 635 | 12 | P B Raymond | K Cundell | 4/1 |
| 3 June | Epsom | My Swallow | Woodcote | 2,427 | 6 | D Robinson | P Davey | 8/13F |
| 3 June | Epsom | Nijinsky (Can) | The Derby | 62,311 | 12 | C W Engelhard | M V O'Brien(I) | 11/8F |
| 4 June | Epsom | Pleaseme | Carew | 8,904 | 6 | Mrs N Adams | P Ashworth | 8/11F |
| 4 June | Epsom | Great Gale | Carshalton | 8,624 | 10 | Lord Carnarvon | P Nelson | 7/2 |
| 5 June | Epsom | Raffingora | Cherkley Sprint | 3,970 | 5 | A G M Stevens | W Marshall | 9/4F |
| 6 June | Epsom | Brabant | Abbot's Hill | 1,532 | 8 | Count C Seilern | J Clayton | 10/11F |

(I) = Ireland (USA) = America (Can) = Canada

| Date | Race Course | Horse | Race | Value £ | Dist Fur | Owner | Trainer | S/P |
|---|---|---|---|---|---|---|---|---|
| 9 June | Hamilton | Nice Music | | 796 | 5 | D Robinson | P Davey | 2/7F |
| 9 June | Hamilton | Bora Bora | | 880 | 8 | R Ohrstrom | H B T Jones | 1/3F |
| 9 June | Hamilton | Quayside | | 825 | 10 | T Robson | D Smith | 6/4 |
| 9 June | Hamilton | Sovereign Gleam | | 888 | 6 | D Robinson | M Jarvis | 5/4F |
| 10 June | Kempton | Double First | | 556 | 11 | C W Engelhard | J Tree | 4/11F |
| 10 June | Kempton | Pleaseme | | 624 | 5 | Mrs M Adam | P Ashworth | 6/4 |
| 12 June | Sandown | Tandeo | | 820 | 14 | Col J D Clague | C Benstead | 15/8 |
| 12 June | Sandown | Honorius | | 595 | 10 | Count C Seilern | J Clayton | 1/2F |
| 13 June | Sandown | Silver Fish | | 771 | 5 | D Robinson | M Jarvis | 2/5F |
| 13 June | Sandown | Granados | Arthur Lorraine Hcp | 1,173 | 10 | E B Benjamin | G Barling | 5/2 |
| 18 June | Royal Ascot | Karabas | Hardwicke | 9,601 | 12 | Lord Iveagh | B van Cutsem | 11/8F |
| 20 June | Warwick | Longfield Boy | | 320 | 6 | C Drinkwater | R Hannon | 8/13F |
| 20 June | Warwick | Night Traffic | | 599 | 5 | Mrs M A Moore | R Houghton | 1/2F |
| 20 June | Royal Ascot | Welsh Saint | Cork and Orrery | 2,684 | 6 | J P Philipps | M V O'Brien(I) | 15/8 |
| 20 June | Royal Ascot | Swing Easy | New | 4,274 | 5 | J H Whitney | J Tree | 5/2 |
| 22 June | Windsor | Rambling Rose | | 518 | 5 | Mrs J F C Bryce | F Armstrong | 8/11F |
| 22 June | Nottingham | Stay on Five | | 279 | 6 | Mrs E Bednash | W Marshall | 8/13F |
| 22 June | Nottingham | The Fair | | 445 | 13 | O/trainer | W A Stephenson | 5/4F |
| 24 June | Newbury | Tandeo | | 607 | 13 | Col J D Clague | C Benstead | 8/13F |
| 3 July | Haydock | Raffingora | | 835 | 5 | A G M Stevens | W Marshall | 5/4F |
| 4 July | Sandown | Hunting Song | | 831 | 7 | Lord Carnarvon | P Nelson | 7/2 |
| 4 July | Sandown | Seventh Hussar | | 1,557 | 8 | Mrs H Poyser | H Price | EvF |
| 4 July | Sandown | Tandeo† | | 2,168 | 14 | Col J D Clague | C Benstead | |
| 6 July | Nottingham | Caius | | 448 | 8 | J B Winter | D Smith | 4/6 |
| 6 July | Nottingham | Segrev | | 483 | 16 | C Rudkin | M H Easterby | 7/4F |
| 8 July | Newmarket | Swing Easy | July Stks | 2,728 | 6 | S H Whitney | J Tree | 10/11F |
| 8 July | Doncaster | Barbary Chief | | 690 | 6 | Mrs R Tikkoo | F Armstrong | 4/9F |
| 8 July | Doncaster | Tirconail | | 630 | 18 | R N Webster | F Armstrong | 4/9F |
| 8 July | Doncaster | Sweet Date | | 648 | 5 | D Robinson | R Smart | 3/1 |
| 8 July | Doncaster | Romany Music | | 652 | 7 | D Robinson | P Davey | 7/4F |
| 9 July | Doncaster | Soroco | | 832 | 10 | Capt M D Lemos | F Armstrong | 5/2 |
| 9 July | Doncaster | Sovereign Gleam | | 625 | 7 | D Robinson | M Jarvis | 4/7F |
| 9 July | Doncaster | Silver Dream | | 673 | 7 | D Robinson | H Smart | 2/5F |
| 11 July | York | Trasi Girl | Milk Maid | 1,690 | 5 | D Head | B W Hills | 4/7F |
| 13 July | Windsor | Rambling Rose | | 518 | 5 | Mrs J F C Bryce | F Armstrong | 1/3F |
| 16 July | Nottingham | Constans | | 884 | 5 | Miss M Sheriffe | J Tree | 5/1 |
| 16 July | Nottingham | Barton Mills | | 1,511 | 7 | D Montagu | B van Cutsem | 7/4F |
| 16 July | Nottingham | Honorius | Mark Lane Hcp | 920 | 10 | Count C Seilern | J Clayton | 11/8 |
| 16 July | Nottingham | Flagon | | 690 | 13 | Mrs A J Scratchley | J Dunlop | 4/6F |
| 17 July | Chester | Tintangel II | | 611 | 12 | O/trainer | R Sturdy | 5/4F |
| 21 July | Leicester | Cheval | | 456 | 12 | Mrs Burdett-Coutts | J Dunlop | 3/10F |
| 25 July | Ascot | Night of Darkness | | 862 | 8 | Mrs R Nelson | B Swift | 3/1F |
| 25 July | Ascot | Nijinsky (Can) | King George VI and Queen Elizabeth | 31,993 | 12 | C W Engelhard | M V O'Brien (I) | 40/85F |
| 25 July | Ascot | Hickleton | Brown Jack Stks | 1,362 | 22 | R Dawson | B W Hills | 1/4F |
| 27 July | Newcastle | It's the Finish | | 387 | 6 | E W Shepherd | R Sturdy | 13/2 |
| 28 July | Goodwood | Juke Box | Spillers Stewards Cup | 6,603 | 6 | D Morris | H Wallington | 100/6 |
| 29 July | Goodwood | Raffingora | King George | 1,882 | 5 | A G M Stevens | W Marshall | 4/1 |
| 29 July | Goodwood | Swing Easy | Richmond | 7,135 | 6 | J H Whitney | J Tree | 4/5F |
| 1 Aug | Goodwood | Saratoga Skiddy | | 865 | 6 | A G M Stevens | W Marshall | 3/1F |
| 1 Aug | Goodwood | Super Honey | Pilgrim | 1,064 | 5 | Mrs M Slade | H Price | 5/2 |
| 1 Aug | Windsor | Zamberex | | 269 | 8 | L Page | V Cross | 4/1 |
| 1 Aug | Windsor | Rambling Moss | | 476 | 5 | Mrs J F C Bryce | F Armstrong | 4/5F |
| 3 Aug | Windsor | Little Goose | | 518 | 5 | Lord Porchester | J Clayton | 3/1 |

† Walkover (I) = Ireland (Can) = Canada

| Date | Race Course | Horse | Race | Value £ | Dist Fur | Owner | Trainer | S/P |
|---|---|---|---|---|---|---|---|---|
| 4 Aug | Brighton | Fair Astrolle | | 625 | 6 | W McEnery | S Ingham | 10/3 |
| 4 Aug | Brighton | Wasmiyah | | 632 | 7 | Mrs B Marshall | B Swift | 5/2F |
| 4 Aug | Brighton | Gone Gay | | 471 | 10 | O/trainer | H Blagrave | 4/5F |
| 4 Aug | Brighton | Welshman | | 612 | 5 | H Dare | F Cundell | 4/11F |
| 5 Aug | Brighton | Uncle Sol | | 565 | 6 | C W Engelhard | J Tree | 4/9F |
| 5 Aug | Brighton | Macaw | | 536 | 8 | Mrs E P Courdeau | P Dawson | 11/2 |
| 7 Aug | Newmarket | Torna Sunda | | 849 | 6 | D Ridley | A M Kerr | 6/4F |
| 8 Aug | Redcar | Lord Gayle(USA) | Wm Hill Gold Cup | 6,130 | 8 | R Webster | F Armstrong | 7/4F |
| 10 Aug | Windsor | Sharp Eyes | | 471 | 8 | D Robinson | P Davey | 5/4F |
| 17 Aug | Windsor | Royal Wash | | 518 | 6 | D Robinson | B Smart | 5/2F |
| 17 Aug | Windsor | Klemperer | | 518 | 10 | J Whitney | J Tree | 15/8 |
| 18 Aug | York | Constans | Harewood Hcp | 1,350 | 5 | Miss M Sheriffe | J Tree | 9/4F |
| 19 Aug | York | Tintagel II | Johnnie Walker Ebor | 8,613 | 14 | Mrs R C Sturdy | R Sturdy | 6/1F |
| 19 Aug | York | Meadowville | Great Voltigeur | 3,976 | 12 | D Robinson | M Jarvis | 8/13F |
| 20 Aug | York | Pretty Puffin(USA) | Galtres | 1,836 | 12 | R F Scully | F Armstrong | 6/5F |
| 24 Aug | Pontefract | Karoo | Darley Brewery Hcp | 1,942 | 10 | F W Burmann | B van Cutsem | 5/2F |
| 25 Aug | Folkestone | Persian Don | | 575 | 15 | D Fitzgerald | J Tree | 15/8 |
| 25 Aug | Folkestone | Soroco | | 761 | 10 | Maj J L Mitchell | F Armstrong | 11/4F |
| 29 Aug | Goodwood | Hazy Idea | March | 1,534 | 14 | L B Holliday | W Hearn | 9/4 |
| 29 Aug | Goodwood | Saratoga Skiddy | | 595 | 6 | A G M Stevens | W Marshall | 5/1 |
| 29 Aug | Windsor | Red House | | 623 | 7 | Mrs D Price | H Price | 2/1F |
| 31 Aug | Newcastle | Magna Carta | W D & H O Wills | 3,383 | 16 | The Queen | I Balding | 11/10F |
| 31 Aug | Newcastle | Caius | | 974 | 8 | J B Winter | D Smith | 3/10F |
| 1 Sept | Epsom | Plaintive Melody | | 651 | 7 | D Robinson | P Davey | 8/11F |
| 2 Sept | York | Saratoga Skiddy | | 664 | 5 | A G M Stevens | W Marshall | |
| 3 Sept | Brighton | La Corsaire | | 502 | 5 | Mrs J F L Denny | R Houghton | 2/9F |
| 3 Sept | Brighton | Tintagel II† | Sydney Thomson Mem Hcp | 1,056 | 12 | Mrs R G Sturdy | R G Sturdy | |
| 4 Sept | Sandown | Night and Day | | 670 | 10 | Lady Hothfield | J Clayton | 10/11F |
| 5 Sept | Sandown | Noirmont Point | Myra Miller S | 1,611 | 5 | K Dodson | S Ingham | 11/10 |
| 5 Sept | Sandown | Close Combat | | 1,635 | 16 | D Howard | B W Hills | 5/4 |
| 5 Sept | Sandown | Maraschino | Daniel Prenn Stks | 2,204 | 10 | J Whitney | J Tree | 3/1F |
| 7 Sept | Windsor | Russian Reward | | 284 | 5 | P Gallagher | W Marshall | 11/4 |
| 10 Sept | Doncaster | Sea Friend | Feversham M | 1,252 | 7 | Mrs J R Mullion | P Prendergast(I) | 7/4F |
| 10 Sept | Doncaster | Sparkler | Bradgate Park Hcp | 1,480 | 6 | J R Mullion | F Armstrong | 5/4F |
| 11 Sept | Doncaster | Calpurnius | Scarborough | 1,270 | 10 | C W Engelhard | J W Watts | 8/15F |
| 12 Sept | Doncaster | Nijinsky(Can) | St Leger | 37,082 | 14 | C W Engelhard | M V O'Brien(I) | 2/7F |
| 12 Sept | Doncaster | Zingari(USA) | Town Moor Hcp | 1,385 | 7 | C W Engelhard | R Houghton | 10/3 |
| 17 Sept | Ayr | Gaberdine | | 690 | 13 | Mrs J A de Rothschild | J Clayton | 5/2 |
| 18 Sept | Ayr | Romardia | | 613 | 7 | H D Hill | A Vasey | 9/2 |
| 24 Sept | Ascot | Golden Orange | Buckingham Palace | 1,293 | 8 | Lady Clifden | K Cundell | 3/1 |
| 24 Sept | Ascot | Park Top | Cumberland Lodge | 2,999 | 12 | Duke of Devonshire | B van Cutsem | 4/5F |
| 2 Oct | Haydock | Valley Farm | | 528 | 6 | O/trainer | W Carr | 7/2 |
| 2 Oct | Haydock | Major Rose | | 964 | 16 | K Wheldon | H Price | 10/1 |
| 3 Oct | Newmarket | Popkins | Sun Chariot | 4,355 | 10 | R B Moller | H Wragg | 4/7F |
| 8 Oct | York | Coursier | | 803 | 8 | Mrs S Nichols | F Armstrong | 11/2 |
| 8 Oct | York | Buff's Own | | 957 | 12 | Mrs J A de Rothschild | J Clayton | 10/3F |
| 8 Oct | York | Effulgence | | 696 | 8 | R Howse | W Marshall | 4/1 |
| 9 Oct | Ascot | Lord Gayle | | 630 | 10 | Mrs C Dickson | F Armstrong | 5/4F |
| 9 Oct | Ascot | Sovereign Gleam | Tankerville Hcp | 1,134 | 7 | D Robinson | M Jarvis | 7/4F |
| 10 Oct | Ascot | Staincross | | 964 | 6 | M Clayton | P Rohan | 5/2 |
| 12 Oct | Warwick | Hypatia | | 380 | 8 | P Bull | S Ingham | 10/3F |
| 16 Oct | Newmarket | Chiseldon | | 615 | 16 | G Lister | K Cundell | 85/40F |

† Walkover (I) = Ireland (USA) = America (Can) = Canada

| Date | Race Course | Horse | Race | Value £ | Dist Fur | Owner | Trainer | S/P |
|---|---|---|---|---|---|---|---|---|
| 29 Oct | Newmarket | Sparkler | Potter Trophy | 1,380 | 7 | J R Mullion | F Armstrong | 13/2 |
| 30 Oct | Newmarket | Tula Rocket | | 414 | 7 | D Montagu | B van Cutsem | 7/4F |
| 31 Oct | Haydock | Coral Diver | | 456 | 16 | B P Jenks | T F Rimell | 4/5F |

1970: 162 wins; 110 2nds; 68 3rds; 586 rides

| Date | Race Course | Horse | Race | Value £ | Dist Fur | Owner | Trainer | S/P |
|---|---|---|---|---|---|---|---|---|
| 1971 | | | | | | | | |
| 26 Mar | Doncaster | Winden | | 690 | 10 | A G M Stevens | W Marshall | 11/2F |
| 26 Mar | Doncaster | Prince of Daroun | | 604 | 12 | A Kilpatrick | C Bewicke | 6/1 |
| 26 Mar | Doncaster | Quayside | | 590 | 10 | T Robson | D Smith | 4/9F |
| 30 Mar | Wolver'ton | Sea Tale | | 380 | 12 | D Robinson | M Jarvis | 9/4 |
| 2 Apl | Liverpool | Phaestus | | 407 | 13 | Mrs J Dillon | T F Rimell | 4/1 |
| 6 Apl | Leicester | High Meadow | | 276 | 5 | Mrs R Hodges | F Carr | 5/2F |
| 10 Apl | Teesside | High Meadow | | 310 | 5 | Mrs R Hodges | F Carr | 1/2F |
| 10 Apl | Teesside | Grisaille | | 421 | 7 | S Everitt | W Marshall | 10/11F |
| 14 Apl | Newmarket | Honorius | | 569 | 12 | Count C Seilern | J Clayton | 7/2 |
| 15 Apl | Newmarket | Super Honey | Nell Gwyn | 2,315 | 7 | Mrs M Slade | H Price | 2/1 |
| 16 Apl | Newbury | Mansingh (USA) | | 513 | 5 | C W Engelhard | R Houghton | 13/8F |
| 16 Apl | Newbury | Master Gwynne | | 690 | 11 | J Whitney | J Tree | 4/6F |
| 20 Apl | Epsom | Gaberdine | | 771 | 10 | Mrs J A de Rothschild | J Clayton | 13/8 |
| 21 Apl | Epsom | Tandy | City Suburban | 2,424 | 16 | B Shine | B Swift | 11/4 |
| 22 Apl | Epsom | Super Honey | Princess Elizabeth | 3,725 | 8 | Mrs M Slade | H Price | 11/8 |
| 22 Apl | Epsom | Constans | | 752 | 5 | Miss M Sheriffe | J Tree | 4/1 |
| 23 Apl | Sandown | Song of the Sea(USA) | | 688 | 8 | Mrs C W Engelhard | R Houghton | 11/8 |
| 23 Apl | Sandown | Boulette | | 745 | 10 | R B Moller | H Wragg | 10/1 |
| 24 Apl | Sandown | Melody Rock | | 677 | 14 | R Woods | H Price | 7/2 |
| 27 Apl | Brighton | Barbary Chief | | 572 | 10 | Mrs R Tikkoo | F Armstrong | 9/4F |
| 27 Apl | Brighton | Sacramento Song | | 813 | 12 | C A B St George | H Price | 7/2F |
| 28 Apl | Ascot | Mansingh(USA) | | 632 | 5 | Mrs C W Engelhard | R Houghton | 10/11F |
| 1 May | Newmarket | Communication | Palace House | 2,723 | 5 | G van der Ploeg | W Marshall | 10/1 |
| 4 May | Chester | Smoke Rocket | | 660 | 7 | P Rackham | D Weeden | 15/2 |
| 5 May | Chester | Adorable Cyril | | 656 | 10 | Mrs S C Reakes | F Carr | 15/8F |
| 6 May | Chester | Quayside | Ormonde | 2,281 | 13 | T Robson | Denys Smith | 6/4F |
| 7 May | Kempton | Brambleberry (USA) | | 512 | 5 | Mrs C W Engelhard | R Houghton | 8/13F |
| 7 May | Kempton | King Penguin (USA) | | 621 | 5 | Mrs C W Engelhard | R Houghton | 9/4 |
| 8 May | Kempton | Sacramento Song | | 827 | 12 | C A B St George | H Price | 8/11F |
| 8 May | Kempton | Harland | | 505 | 8 | Lord Weir | H Price | 2/11F |
| 11 May | York | Deep River | Tattersalls Yorkshire Stks | 960 | 5 | D Robinson | P Davey | 2/5F |
| 11 May | York | Plaintive Melody | | 774 | 7 | D Robinson | P Davey | 11/2 |
| 12 May | York | Joshua | Spring Cup | 2,516 | 7 | G R Rickman | A Kerr | 5/1 |
| 12 May | York | Most Secret | | 829 | 5 | Mrs K M Carmichael | M W Easterby | 10/3 |
| 13 May | York | The Brianstan | Duke of York Stks | 2,520 | 6 | N Powell | J Sutcliffe | EvF |
| 14 May | Lingfield | Maina | Oaks Trial | 2,315 | 12 | H J Joel | N Murless | 3/1 |
| 18 May | Brighton | Coursier | | 817 | 12 | Mrs S Nichols | F Armstrong | 11/10 |
| 19 May | Goodwood | Levanter | | 1,274 | 12 | H L Vickery | H Price | 10/11F |
| 20 May | Goodwood | Mountain Storm | | 432 | 5 | A D Shead | P Smyth | 5/1 |
| 21 May | Newbury | Bright Fire | | 904 | 7 | Mrs R Grosvenor | P Nelson | 3/1F |
| 21 May | Newbury | Musicale | | 498 | 5 | Lt Col J Charles-Pole | B W Hills | 5/4F |
| 22 May | Newbury | Grisaille | | 911 | 8 | S Everitt | W Marshall | 9/2F |
| 26 May | Brighton | Takawin | | 540 | 5 | E R Hill | P Supple | 2/1F |
| 28 May | Haydock | The Klonarides Kid | | 343 | 5 | Mrs A Banks | F Carr | 2/1F |
| 28 May | Haydock | Phantom Major (USA) | | 726 | 8 | Mrs C W Engelhard | R Houghton | 8/15F |

(USA) = America

| Date | Race Course | Horse | Race | Value £ | Dist Fur | Owner | Trainer | S/P |
|---|---|---|---|---|---|---|---|---|
| 28 May | Haydock | King Penguin (USA) | | 380 | 5 | Mrs C W Engelhard | R Houghton | 4/7F |
| 2 June | Epsom | Red Laser | | 905 | 5 | W D Tremaine | F Armstrong | 8/11F |
| 2 June | Epsom | Sparkler | Diamed | 4,797 | 8 | J R Mullion | F Armstrong | EvF |
| 3 June | Epsom | Sasha | | 880 | 10 | Count C Seilern | J Clayton | 7/2 |
| 4 June | Epsom | Ndabibi | | 762 | 8 | Lady Delamere | B van Cutsem | 8/13F |
| 4 June | Epsom | The Klonarides Kid | Tattenham CL | 1,192 | 6 | Miss M Sheriffe | F Carr | 6/4F |
| 4 June | Epsom | Constans | Cherkley Sprint | 3,849 | 5 | Miss M Sheriffe | J Tree | 2/1 |
| 4 June | Epsom | Green God | Headley Hcp | 1,196 | 6 | D Robinson | M Jarvis | 10/1 |
| 5 June | Epsom | Grisaille | Abbot's Hill | 4,496 | 8 | S Everitt | W Marshall | 4/1 |
| 11 June | Sandown | Grisaille | | 623 | 7 | S Everitt | W Marshall | 4/1 |
| 11 June | Sandown | Green God | | 835 | 5 | D Robinson | M Jarvis | 11/10F |
| 12 June | York | Roy Bridge | | 778 | 6 | Maj Gen Sir R Feilden | J Oxley | 5/4F |
| 12 June | York | Algarve | | 731 | 10 | Lord Margadale | J Tree | 15/8 |
| 14 June | Leicester | Royal Ride | | 578 | 5 | D Robinson | J Powney | 11/4 |
| 14 June | Leicester | Silly Billy | | 518 | 6 | late J H Farr | F Armstrong | 11/10F |
| 14 June | Brighton | Barton Mills | | 801 | 8 | D Montagu | B van Cutsem | 1/3F |
| 17 June | Royal Ascot | Meadow Mint (USA) | Chesham | 2,958 | 6 | R N Webster | F Armstrong | 6/5 |
| 18 June | Royal Ascot | Hickleton | Queen Alexandra | 2,154 | 22 | W Ward | B W Hills | 5/2 |
| 18 June | Royal Ascot | Swing Easy (USA) | King's Stand | 4,571 | 5 | J H Whitney | J Tree | 7/1 |
| 19 June | Warwick | Cider With Rosie | | 556 | 12 | A V Mullings | S Ingham | 5/2F |
| 21 June | Nottingham | Hard Slipper | | 524 | 13 | J B Harvey | R Sturdy | 11/2 |
| 21 June | Nottingham | Sharpen Up | | 518 | 5 | O/trainer | B van Cutsem | 3/8 |
| 21 June | Windsor | Pollster | | 518 | 5 | Lady Wilson | J Tree | 15/8F |
| 21 June | Windsor | Royal Captive | | 521 | 6 | L H Rumhold | R Smyth | 3/1F |
| 23 June | Newbury | Proof Positive | | 1,202 | 5 | J H Whitney | J Tree | 6/1 |
| 23 June | Newbury | Gaberdine | | 625 | 13 | Mrs J A de Rothschild | J Clayton | 8/11F |
| 23 June | Newbury | Sea Coral | | 632 | 10 | D Prenn | J Winter | 2/1F |
| 25 June | Doncaster | Diamond Joe | | 690 | 6 | D Robinson | M Jarvis | 4/1 |
| 25 June | Doncaster | Fireside Chat (USA) | | 688 | 6 | Mrs C W Engelhard | R Houghton | 5/2 |
| 25 June | Kempton | Grisaille | | 487 | 8 | S Everitt | W Marshall | 12/1 |
| 25 June | Kempton | Tickled Pink | | 566 | 12 | D Robinson | R Jarvis | 13/8F |
| 24 June | Newbury | Buff's Own | Newbury Summer Cup | 1,980 | 12 | Mrs J A de Rothschild | J Clayton | 11/10F |
| 30 June | Salisbury | Winning Double | | 518 | 10 | Lady E Longman | J Tree | 11/2 |
| 1 July | Yarmouth | Apelles | | 207 | 8 | Mrs B May | J Edwards | 11/2 |
| 1 July | Yarmouth | Silly Billy | | 515 | 7 | late J H Farr | F Armstrong | 4/7F |
| 1 July | Yarmouth | Misty Light | | 506 | 10 | R F Scully | F Armstrong | 4/6F |
| 2 July | Beverley | Comedy Star (USA) | Welbred | 2,504 | 8 | Mrs C W Engelhard | R Houghton | 11/4 |
| 2 July | Haydock | Maina | Lancashire Oaks | 2,418 | 12 | H J Joel | N Murless | 1/2F |
| 3 July | Sandown | Tilario | | 887 | 7 | H Loebstein | T Corbett | 2/1 |
| 9 July | Newbury | Grisbi | | 625 | 8 | Mrs J A de Rothschild | J Clayton | 4/7F |
| 9 July | Newbury | Green God | | 594 | 6 | D Robinson | M Jarvis | 11/8 |
| 10 July | York | Bar Silvero | | 707 | 12 | J Barsby | W Wharton | 7/4F |
| 10 July | York | Mansingh (USA) | | 676 | 5 | Mrs C W Engelhard | R Houghton | 4/9F |
| 12 July | Windsor | Shoolerville | | 518 | 6 | Mrs J F C Bryce | F Armstrong | 4/5F |
| 12 July | Windsor | Exclaim | | 578 | 10 | Lady Beaverbrook | A Breasley | 4/1F |
| 15 July | Nottingham | Pisces | | 553 | 5 | A G M Stevens | L G Kennard | 1/5F |
| 15 July | Nottingham | Laujo | | 523 | 7 | Mary Lady Delamere | D Stephenson | 6/1 |
| 16 July | Lingfield | Blue River Wonder | | 552 | 6 | O/trainer | P Smyth | 4/5F |
| 16 July | Chester | Mrs Moss | | 511 | 5 | Sir W Pigott-Brown | R Houghton | 5/2F |
| 17 July | Doncaster | Ndabibi | Vernon Sangster Gold Cup | 4,308 | 8 | Mary Lady Delamere | B van Cutsem | 13/8F |

(USA) = America

| Date | Race Course | Horse | Race | Value £ | Dist Fur | Owner | Trainer | S/P |
|---|---|---|---|---|---|---|---|---|
| 17 July | Doncaster | Swing Easy | Daniel Prenn | 1,576 | 5 | J H Whitney | J Tree | 8/13F |
| 21 July | Sandown | Buffo | | 690 | 7 | Lord Howard de Walden | H Cecil | 11/8F |
| 21 July | Sandown | Great Charter | | 601 | 5 | Mrs E T Colley | R Jarvis | 4/5F |
| 22 July | Sandown | Comedy Star (USA) | | 516 | 7 | S Everitt | R Houghton | 11/8F |
| 22 July | Sandown | Lochwinnoch Lisa | | 690 | 10 | Mrs J Maddocks | J Winter | 13/8 |
| 24 July | Ascot | Secret Kiss (USA) | Princess Margaret | 1,976 | 6 | Mrs M Fogarty | N Fogarty(I) | 2/1F |
| 26 July | Windsor | Star Trek | | 482 | 8 | A Berry | P Nelson | 5/1 |
| 28 July | Goodwood | Constans | King George Stks | 2,424 | 5 | Miss M Sheriffe | J Tree | 9/4 |
| 29 July | Goodwood | Some Hand | Foxhall Maiden | 1,084 | 6 | Mrs M Haggas | J Hindley | 7/1 |
| 29 July | Goodwood | Mansingh (USA) | Wills Embassy | 3,628 | 5 | Mrs C W Engelhard | R Houghton | 2/1F |
| 29 July | Goodwood | Green God | Singleton | 1,291 | 5 | D Robinson | R Jarvis | 11/4 |
| 30 July | Goodwood | Valmara(USA) | | 926 | 5 | G Oldham | H Wragg | 5/4F |
| 30 July | Goodwood | Sea Music | Rous Memorial | 1,362 | 6 | Lady M Bury | H Cecil | 4/1 |
| 31 July | Windsor | Intelligentsia | | 681 | 6 | R R Guest | F Armstrong | 9/4F |
| 31 July | Goodwood | Maximilian | Pilgrim | 1,089 | 5 | Lady Iveagh | P Prendergast (I) | EvF |
| 31 July | Goodwood | Baby Princess | | 620 | 8 | J Ashenheim | R Houghton | 5/1 |
| 4 Aug | Brighton | Pollster | | 505 | 5 | Lady Wilton | J Tree | 9/4 |
| 4 Aug | Brighton | Baochica | | 499 | 8 | J N Gifford-Mead | R Sturdy | 6/5F |
| 5 Aug | Brighton | Finesse | | 546 | 12 | G F Mathieson | S Ingham | 4/1 |
| 9 Aug | Windsor | Minio(F) | | 518 | 10 | Marchesa Incisa Della Rochetta | J Clayton | 11/10F |
| 9 Aug | Newcastle | Rambling Rose | Northumberland Sprint Trophy | 2,575 | 5 | Mrs J F C Bryce | F Armstrong | 4/7F |
| 10 Aug | Nottingham | Native Majesty | | 518 | 5 | F McMahon | B van Cutsem | 4/5F |
| 17 Aug | York | Billy Bremner | Acomb | 1,647 | 6 | Mrs A Banks | F Carr | 7/1 |
| 18 Aug | York | Athens Wood | Great Voltigeur | 1,405 | 12 | Mrs J Rogerson | H B T Jones | 13/8 |
| 19 Aug | York | Mansingh (USA) | Prince of Wales | 1,708 | 5 | Mrs C W Engelhard | R Houghton | 1/4F |
| 19 Aug | York | Swing Easy | Nunthorpe | 3,613 | 5 | J H Whitney | J Tree | 2/1 |
| 20 Aug | Lingfield | Exclaim | | 803 | 10 | Lady Beaverbrook | A Breasley | 11/8F |
| 23 Aug | Windsor | Bold and Free | | 518 | 5 | D Robinson | P Davey | 5/1 |
| 23 Aug | Windsor | Black Sky | | 436 | 11 | G Newman | C Benstead | 11/8F |
| 23 Aug | Windsor | Minio(F) | | 518 | 10 | Marchesa Incisa Della Rochetta | J Clayton | 4/9F |
| 26 Aug | Brighton | Marechal Drake | | 785 | 12 | D Prenn | J Winter | 11/4 |
| 26 Aug | Brighton | Uncle Sol | | 476 | 10 | Mrs C W Engelhard | J Tree | 2/5F |
| 28 Aug | Goodwood | Klavier | | 672 | 12 | J I Morrison | J Tree | EvF |
| 28 Aug | Goodwood | Royal Captive | | 621 | 6 | W R Rumbold | R Smyth | 15/8 |
| 30 Aug | Ripon | High Top | Champion 2-y-o Trophy | 1,431 | 6 | Sir J Thorn | B van Cutsem | 4/7F |
| 31 Aug | Epsom | Mujon | | 615 | 6 | Mrs M Johnson | K Cundell | 5/2 |
| 1 Sept | York | Amplifier (USA) | | 672 | 6 | J H Whitney | J Tree | 4/6F |
| 2 Sept | York | Red Signal(F) | | 857 | 6 | H J Joel | N Murless | 4/6F |
| 2 Sept | York | Billy Bremner | | 650 | 6 | Mrs A Banks | F Carr | 5/2 |
| 4 Sept | Sandown | Sol D'Argent | Sportsman Club Hcp | 1,625 | 16 | Mrs C Harris | T Gosling | 10/1 |
| 4 Sept | Sandown | Calpurnius | William Hill Stks | 2,294 | 8 | Mrs C W Engelhard | J W Watts | 10/11F |
| 6 Sept | Windsor | Knockroe | | 454 | 11 | Maj V McCalmont | P Nelson | EvF |
| 6 Sept | Windsor | Harland | | 515 | 10 | Lord Weir | H Price | No SP |
| 8 Sept | Doncaster | Crowned Prince (USA) | Champagne | 5,413 | 7 | F McMahon | B van Cutsem | 11/10F |
| 9 Sept | Doncaster | Example | Park Hill | 4,442 | 14 | The Queen | I Balding | 11/2 |
| 11 Sept | Doncaster | Athens Wood | St Leger | 35,742 | 14 | Mrs J Rogerson | H B T Jones | 5/2 |
| 13 Sept | Wolver'ton | Kinsman | | 483 | 5 | Lady Mountain | P Nelson | 11/10F |
| 13 Sept | Wolver'ton | Corrieghall | | 468 | 12 | C Cleary | T F Rimell | 8/15F |
| 13 Sept | Wolver'ton | Gold Strike | | 480 | 9 | E Sjoo | W O'Gorman | 8/1 |
| 14 Sept | Goodwood | Spirit in the Sky | | 669 | 6 | M Howard | B W Hills | 5/6F |

(I) = Ireland (F) = France (USA) = America

| Date | Race Course | Horse | Race | Value £ | Dist Fur | Owner | Trainer | S/P |
|---|---|---|---|---|---|---|---|---|
| 17 Sept | Ayr | Irish Love | | 690 | 6 | D Robinson | M Jarvis | 1/8F |
| 18 Sept | Kempton | Red Mask | Ladbroke Cambridgeshire Trial | 1,208 | 8 | W Maskell | A Kerr | 11/10F |
| 23 Sept | Ascot | Knockroe | Cumberland Lodge | 3,774 | 12 | Maj V McCalmont | P Nelson | 1/2F |
| 25 Sept | Ascot | Calve | Blue Seal | 2,136 | 6 | Beatrice Lady Granard | P Prendergast (I) | 4/5F |
| 25 Sept | Ascot | Abergwaun | Diadem | 3,688 | 6 | C A B St George | M V O'Brien(I) | 15/2 |
| 25 Sept | Ascot | Sol D'Argent | Red Deer | 1,317 | 12 | Mrs G Harris | T Gosling | 4/1 |
| 27 Sept | Nottingham | Chadleigh | | 503 | 16 | J E Bigg | W Wharton | 7/11F |
| 30 Sept | Newmarket | Old and Wise | | 860 | 8 | D Robinson | P Davey | 6/4 |
| 6 Oct | York | Relkaum | | 749 | 5 | R B Moller | H Wragg | 1/2F |
| 7 Oct | York | Sacramento Song | | 715 | 12 | C A B St George | H Price | 9/2 |
| 9 Oct | Ascot | Capriole | Kensington Palace | 1,064 | 6 | Mrs A Collins | P Beasley | 6/4 |
| 14 Oct | Newmarket | Clean Bowled | | 690 | 6 | R E Sangster | E Cousins | 11/1 |
| 15 Oct | Newmarket | Crowned Prince | Dewhurst | 10,408 | 7 | P McMahon | B van Cutsem | 4/9F |
| 21 Oct | Newbury | Disguise | | 5,512 | 7 | Lord Porchester | B W Hills | 3/1 |
| 30 Oct | Haydock | Meicle (USA) | | 639 | 5 | R N Webster | R Armstrong | EvF |
| 30 Oct | Haydock | Green God | Vernons Spring Cup | 6,603 | 6 | D Robinson | M Jarvis | 7/4 |
| 30 Oct | Haydock | Hickleton | | 619 | 16 | W Ward | B W Hills | 8/13F |

1971: 162 wins; 120 2nds; 93 3rds; 631 rides

| Date | Race Course | Horse | Race | Value £ | Dist Fur | Owner | Trainer | S/P |
|---|---|---|---|---|---|---|---|---|
| 1972 | | | | | | | | |
| 27 Mar | Leicester | Charladouce | | 597 | 12 | C A B St George | H Cecil | EvF |
| 28 Mar | Leicester | Suecol | | 576 | 12 | J McShane | R Hollinshead | 5/1 |
| 28 Mar | Leicester | The Go-Between | | 276 | 5 | Mrs D Heimann | J Hindley | 4/1 |
| 1 Apl | Kempton | Lord David | Rosebery | 2,949 | 9 | G Marks | S Ingham | 10/1 |
| 1 Apl | Kempton | Widower Brown | | 515 | 12 | Mrs C McSweeney | J Hindley | 5/4F |
| 4 Apl | Warwick | Air Pocket | | 207 | 5 | Maj P Ness | J Hindley | EvF |
| 4 Apl | Warwick | Brother Scot | | 440 | 8 | Mrs A Banks | F Carr | 9/2 |
| 6 Apl | Liverpool | The Go-Between | | 276 | 5 | Mrs D Heimann | J Hindley | 8/11F |
| 11 Apl | Newmarket | Irvine | | 965 | 14 | C A B St George | H Cecil | 6/4F |
| 12 Apl | Newmarket | Lord David | Rubbing House | 2,301 | 9 | G Marks | S Ingham | 4/7F |
| 12 Apl | Newmarket | Double Tot | | 690 | 7 | Mrs C W Engelhard | J Tree | 14/1 |
| 20 Apl | Epsom | The Go-Between | | 807 | 5 | Mrs D Heimann | R Akehurst | 5/6F |
| 20 Apl | Epsom | Club Talk | | 791 | 8 | T Haynes | A Pitt | 4/1 |
| 24 Apl | Warwick | Bretton Woods | | 207 | 10 | E Tudo | J Hindley | 10/11F |
| 27 Apl | Newmarket | Claudius | May M Plate | 1,035 | 5 | Capt J Macdonald-Buchanan | J Oxley | 10/3 |
| 28 Apl | Newmarket | Newway | | 690 | 5 | C Nicholson | R Houghton | 9/2 |
| 28 Apl | Newmarket | Sandal | Turn of the Lands Hcp | 1,293 | 10 | Maj A Stoute | M Stoute | 7/2 |
| 28 Apl | Newmarket | Knockroe | Jockey Club Stks | 3,155 | 12 | Maj V McCalmont | P Nelson | 4/1 |
| 4 May | Chester | Brambleberry (USA) | | 700 | 7 | Mrs C W Engelhard | R Houghton | 13/8 |
| 9 May | Windsor | The Go-Between | | 276 | 5 | Mrs D Heimann | J Hindley | 9/4 |
| 10 May | York | Red Mask | Spring Cup | 2,640 | 7 | W Maskell | A Kerr | 3/1F |
| 11 May | York | Knockroe | Yorkshire Cup | 3,572 | 14 | Maj V McCalmont | P Nelson | 10/11 |
| 17 May | Goodwood | Starch Reduced | | 542 | 5 | A Spence | A Pitt | 3/1 |
| 26 May | Kempton | Mr Bojangles | | 560 | 5 | E Lal | K Payne | 11/10 |
| 26 May | Kempton | Mallard | | 613 | 11 | Mrs C W Engelhard | J Tree | 13/8F |
| 27 May | Haydock | Flambeau | Wills Embassy Stks | 911 | 5 | Sir K Butt | B Hobbs | 4/7F |
| 27 May | Haydock | Roy Bridge | Cecil Frail | 3,316 | 8 | Maj Gen Sir R Feilden | J Oxley | 9/4F |
| 27 May | Haydock | Avon Valley | | 986 | 5 | J Stallard | B W Hills | 13/8F |
| 27 May | Haydock | Swinging Junior | Garswood | 1,030 | 6 | O/trainer | N Angus | 3/1F |
| 29 May | Sandown | Shoolerville(USA) | Temple | 2,217 | 5 | Mrs J F C Bryce | F Armstrong | 13/8 |

(I) = Ireland (USA) = America

| Date | Race Course | Horse | Race | Value £ | Dist Fur | Owner | Trainer | S/P |
|---|---|---|---|---|---|---|---|---|
| 31 May | Yarmouth | Claudius | | 672 | 5 | Capt J Macdonald-Buchanan | J Oxley | 2/9F |
| 31 May | Yarmouth | Grey Autumn | | 574 | 6 | C P Goulandris | F Armstrong | 6/4 |
| 31 May | Yarmouth | Meiawa King | | 305 | 5 | R Morloka | J Oxley | 6/4 |
| 31 May | Yarmouth | Trumpet Dance | | 276 | 10 | S Joel | J Hindley | 11/4F |
| 3 June | Kempton | The Go-Between | Wills Castella | 1,268 | 5 | Mrs D Heimann | J Hindley | 11/2F |
| 7 June | Epsom | Roberto(USA) | The Derby | 53,735 | 12 | J Galbreath | M V O'Brien(I) | 3/1F |
| 8 June | Epsom | Finmoss | | 872 | 10 | R Porter | A Kerr | 4/1 |
| 9 June | Epsom | Red Power | | 780 | 8 | O/trainer | J E Sutcliffe | 5/2 |
| 19 June | Windsor | Finmoss | | 587 | 11 | R Porter | A Kerr | 11/8F |
| 19 June | Windsor | Spanish Princess | | 587 | 8 | Mrs R Mason | R Mason | 4/1F |
| 20 June | Royal Ascot | Sparkler | Queen Anne | 3,236 | 8 | Mrs M Mehl-Mulhens | F Armstrong | 9/4 |
| 21 June | Royal Ascot | Calve | Coronation Stks | 9,239 | 8 | Lord Granard | P Prendergast(I) | 12/1 |
| 27 June | Salisbury | Wigged(USA) | | 345 | 6 | J H Whitney | J Tree | 9/4F |
| 27 June | Brighton | Golden Passenger | | 722 | 8 | L Naylor | R Sturdy | 7/4 |
| 4 July | Newmarket | Red Mask | Bunbury Cup | 3,273 | 7 | W Maskell | A Kerr | 10/3F |
| 8 July | Sandown | Bright Fire | Benson & Hedges Anniv | 2,258 | 8 | H Blagrave | P Nelson | 8/1 |
| 10 July | Pontefract | Brambleberry (USA) | | 594 | 10 | Mrs C W Engelhard | R Houghton | 9/4 |
| 11 July | Kempton | Birdie | | 567 | 5 | B Shine | B Swift | 10/3 |
| 19 July | Yarmouth | Perambulate | | 315 | 10 | Capt J Macdonald-Buchanan | J Oxley | EvF |
| 21 July | Ascot | Hamadan | Cranborne Chase | 672 | 10 | J Thursby | S Clayton | 4/6F |
| 22 July | Ascot | Fiery Diplomat (USA) | Princess Margaret | 1,992 | 6 | Mrs R Gallagher | M Fogarty(I) | 13/8 |
| 26 July | Goodwood | Cloonach | | 991 | 6 | A Boyd-Rochfort | H Cecil | 5/2 |
| 27 July | Goodwood | Harvest Sun | Foxhall | 1,013 | 6 | D Robinson | P Davey | 10/3 |
| 28 July | Goodwood | Red Power | | 965 | 10 | R Chinn | J E Sutcliffe | 11/8F |
| 29 July | Goodwood | China Silk | | 933 | 8 | W Tsui | P Supple | 15/8F |
| 2 Aug | Brighton | Facetious Lady* | | 455 | 5 | Mrs M Hall | R Hannon | 7/2 |
| 2 Aug | Brighton | Sillins Pride | | 525 | 6 | F Allison | R Sturdy | 4/5F |
| 3 Aug | Yarmouth | Abernethy | | 266 | 6 | O/trainer | J Hindley | EvF |
| 3 Aug | Yarmouth | Janus | | 527 | 14 | J Weston-Evans | B Hobbs | 1/2F |
| 3 Aug | Yarmouth | King Concorde | | 587 | 6 | C Hindley | J Hindley | 5/6F |
| 3 Aug | Yarmouth | Tactless | | 301 | 10 | Lord Fairhaven | B Hobbs | 5/4F |
| 5 Aug | Newmarket | Gold of the Day | | 813 | 6 | O/trainer | T Molony | 15/8 |
| 5 Aug | Newmarket | Reading Room | | 679 | 6 | Mrs C W Engelhard | R Houghton | 3/1 |
| 5 Aug | Newmarket | Single Spur | | 584 | 8 | Lord Porchester | J Clayton | 7/1 |
| 7 Aug | Newcastle | Some Hand | Northumberland Sprint Trophy | 3,202 | 6 | Mrs M Haggas | J Hindley | 5/2F |
| 9 Aug | Salisbury | Coupon | | 334 | ? | C Loyd | R Houghton | 2/1 |
| 11 Aug | Newbury | Home Guard | | 2,949 | 7 | Mrs C W Engelhard | M V O'Brien (I) | 6/4 |
| 14 Aug | Leicester | Mary Connor | | 276 | 8 | C A B St George | J Hindley | 11/8 |
| 14 Aug | Leicester | Guard of Honour | | 587 | 6 | H J Joel | T Walsh | 11/10 |
| 16 Aug | York | Our Mirage | Great Voltigeur | 4,191 | 12 | N Cohen | B W Hills | 7/4 |
| 17 Aug | York | Golden Passenger | Great Yorkshire | 1,404 | 9 | L Naylor | R Sturdy | 3/1 |
| 17 Aug | York | Carrot Top | Galtres | 1,848 | 5 | J Whitney | J Tree | 4/1 |
| 17 Aug | York | The Go-Between | City of York Nursery Hcp | 1,226 | 5 | Mrs D Heimann | J Hindley | 2/1 |
| 18 Aug | Lingfield | Hamadan | | 830 | 10 | J Thursby | J Clayton | 15/8 |
| 26 Aug | Windsor | Windflower | | 323 | 10 | Lord Porchester | J Clayton | 11/8F |
| 28 Aug | Epsom | Rozel Star | | 647 | 6 | T Robinson | S Ingham | 2/1 |
| 29 Aug | Epsom | Cut and Thrust | | 587 | 8 | R McEnery | G Pritchard-Gordon | 2/1 |
| 30 Aug | York | Cavo Doro | | 883 | 7 | Capt M D Lemos | F Armstrong | 5/4F |
| 30 Aug | York | The Go-Between | Garrowby | 1,039 | 5 | Mrs D Heimann | J Hindley | 8/13F |
| 30 Aug | York | Raffle Hymn | | 746 | 16 | J H Whitney | J Tree | 6/4F |

* Dead Heat (I) = Ireland (USA) = America

| Date | Race Course | Horse | Race | Value £ | Dist Fur | Owner | Trainer | S/P |
|---|---|---|---|---|---|---|---|---|
| 1 Sept | Chester | Lime | | 580 | 5 | J Kahiyame | R Houghton | 4/5F |
| 1 Sept | Chester | Cote d'Azur | | 747 | 12 | L Freedman | N Murless | 5/4F |
| 2 Sept | Kempton | Shamsan | Volvo | 2,098 | 11 | J King | H B T Jones | 5/4F |
| 8 Sept | Doncaster | Red Power | | 984 | 10 | R Chinn | R Houghton | 4/5F |
| 9 Sept | Doncaster | Boucher(USA) | St Leger | 35,708 | 14 | O Phipps | M V O'Brien(I) | 3/1 |
| 9 Sept | Doncaster | Marble Arch (USA) | Norfolk | 6,717 | 5 | N B Hunt | T Curtin(I) | 5/6F |
| 9 Sept | Doncaster | Hickleton | Rufford Abbey | 1,702 | 18 | W Ward | B W Hills | 4/6F |
| 11 Sept | Goodwood | Wenceslas(F) | Valdoe | 1,780 | 10 | Mrs C W Engelhard | M V O'Brien(I) | 10/11F |
| 11 Sept | Yarmouth | Little Manny | | 301 | 6 | C Gaventa | N Callaghan | 11/12 |
| 12 Sept | Yarmouth | Swirl | | 562 | 14 | Mrs J A de Rothschild | J Clayton | 1/3F |
| 19 Sept | Lingfield | True Song | | 539 | 10 | J H Whitney | J Tree | 9/4F |
| 19 Sept | Lingfield | Franwin | | 847 | 16 | G Green | A Davison | 11/4 |
| 21 Sept | Ascot | Knockroe | Cumberland Lodge | 3,031 | 10 | Maj V McCalmont | P Nelson | 4/1 |
| 22 Sept | Ascot | Goosie | Rosemary | 1,030 | 8 | J Phillips | M V O'Brien(I) | EvF |
| 22 Sept | Ascot | Home Guard | Diadem | 3,815 | 6 | Mrs C W Engelhard | M V O'Brien(I) | 6/1 |
| 23 Sept | Ascot | Grasse(USA) | Cunard | 2,545 | 6 | J A Mulcahy | M V O'Brien(I) | 15/8F |
| 29 Sept | Haydock | Mr Difficult (USA) | Altrincham Pl. | 1,035 | 5 | P Marriott | R Houghton | 7/1 |
| 30 Sept | Newmarket | Salira | Buckenham | 1,459 | 6 | C A B St George | H Cecil | 5/1 |
| 6 Oct | Ascot | Sea Pigeon (USA) | Duke of Edinburgh | 2,890 | 6 | J H Whitney | J Tree | 9/2 |
| 12 Oct | Newmarket | Irvine | Jockey Club Cup | 3,162 | 16 | C A B St George | H Cecil | 3/1 |
| 13 Oct | Newmarket | Abergwaun | Challenge | 2,856 | 6 | C A B St George | M V O'Brien(I) | 2/1F |
| 22 Oct | Doncaster | Noble Decree(USA) | Observer Gold Cup | 24,623 | 8 | N B Hunt | B van Cutsem | 8/1 |
| 4 Nov | Haydock | Abergwaun | Vernons' Sprint Cup | 6,666 | 6 | C A B St George | M V O'Brien(I) | 11/10F |

1972: 103 wins; 68 2nds; 75 3rds; 464 rides

| Date | Race Course | Horse | Race | Value £ | Dist Fur | Owner | Trainer | S/P |
|---|---|---|---|---|---|---|---|---|
| 1973 | | | | | | | | |
| 26 Mar | Leicester | Abernoon | Humber M Stks | 1,292 | 8 | A Weston | R Sturdy | 13/8F |
| 26 Mar | Leicester | King's Cloth | | 276 | 6 | R Davis | N Callaghan | 10/11F |
| 2 April | Nottingham | Sidewalk | | 276 | 8 | R Galpin | R Boss | 4/1 |
| 2 April | Nottingham | James Young | | 276 | 8 | C A B St George | H Cecil | 6/4F |
| 7 April | Ascot | After Burner | | 679 | 8 | R Teskill | J Hindley | 2/1F |
| 11 Apl | Newmarket | Golden Master | | 690 | 7 | G Biggs | S Ingham | 7/4F |
| 12 Apl | Newmarket | James Young | Brandon Hcp | 1,035 | 8 | C A B St George | H Cecil | 5/2F |
| 25 Apl | Epsom | Raffles Lady | | 584 | 5 | B Snead | S Ingham | 11/8F |
| 25 Apl | Epsom | Natsun | Warren | 1,586 | 12 | N Cohen | B W Hills | 11/4F |
| 26 Apl | Epsom | Mystic Circle | Princess Elizabeth | 4,167 | 8 | T F Blackwell | B Hobbs | 2/1F |
| 2 May | Ascot | Blonville | Golden Hind | 1,320 | 8 | Mrs H O H Frelinghuysen | F Maxwell | 13/2 |
| 2 May | Ascot | Hackadate(F) | Paradise | 1,840 | 16 | Z Yoshida | R Houghton | 11/8F |
| 4 May | Newmarket | Quill's Prince | | 993 | 7 | W Gooch | B W Hills | 8/1 |
| 8 May | Chester | Rozel Queen | | 902 | 5 | T Robinson | S Ingham | 4/6F |
| 8 May | Chester | Bandstand | | 696 | 10 | J H Whitney | J Tree | 4/1 |
| 9 May | Chester | High Wire | | 549 | 5 | B Firestone | R Houghton | 7/2 |
| 9 May | Chester | Wrekinianne | | 904 | 7 | O/trainer | F Maxwell | 13/8F |
| 9 May | Chester | Decimo | | 716 | 7 | Lady Iveagh | P Prendergast (I) | 13/8F |
| 17 May | York | Trackers Highway | | 912 | 5 | E Akins | R Mason | 12/1 |
| 21 May | Windsor | Kingly Street | | 276 | 5 | Mrs I Tooth | R Houghton | 10/3 |
| 22 May | Nottingham | Star Chief | | 276 | 5 | S Joel | J Hindley | 4/5F |
| 25 May | Newbury | Hackadate(F) | Aston Park | 1,662 | 13 | Z Yoshida | R Houghton | 6/5F |
| 25 May | Newbury | Mandera | Enborne Heath | 1,794 | 10 | Mrs C W Engelhard | J Tree | 8/1 |
| 26 May | Newbury | Sparkler | Lockinge | 8,147 | 8 | Mrs M Mehl-Mulhens | R Armstrong | 7/2 |
| 26 May | Newbury | Raffles Lady | | 563 | 5 | B Sneed | S Ingham | 8/13F |

(I) = Ireland (F) = France (USA) = America

| Date | Race Course | Horse | Race | Value £ | Dist Fur | Owner | Trainer | S/P |
|---|---|---|---|---|---|---|---|---|
| 28 May | Redcar | De Mada | | 464 | 16 | S Joel | H Cottrill | 5/4F |
| 29 May | Sandown | Dragonera Palace | | 690 | 5 | Mrs B Stein | B W Hills | 8/15F |
| 7 June | Epsom | Roberto(USA) | Coronation Cup | 11,571 | 12 | J Galbreath | M V O'Brien(I) | 4/9F |
| 7 June | Epsom | Laurentian Hills | | 669 | 10 | Mrs J F C Bryce | R Armstrong | 3/1 |
| 8 June | Epsom | Slipperty | Acorn | 1,811 | 5 | E Holland-Martin | R Houghton | 15/8F |
| 9 June | Epsom | Workboy | Cherkley | 3,903 | 5 | Mrs L Brotherton | M W Easterby | 7/2F |
| 14 June | Newbury | Blue Star | | 835 | 6 | J H Whitney | B W Hills | 5/4F |
| 18 June | Windsor | James Young | | 623 | 10 | C A B St George | H Cecil | 11/10F |
| 19 June | Royal Ascot | Gift Card | Prince of Wales | 9,132 | 10 | M Batthyany | W Hern | 7/2 |
| 19 June | Royal Ascot | Thatch(USA) | St James's Palace | 11,068 | 8 | J A Mulcahy | M V O'Brien(I) | EvF |
| 22 June | Royal Ascot | Abergwaun | King's Stand | 9,796 | 5 | C A B St George | M V O'Brien(I) | 7/4F |
| 23 June | Royal Ascot | Laurentian Hills | Churchill | 1,896 | 12 | Mrs J F C Bryce | R Armstrong | 7/4F |
| 23 June | Ascot | Blessed Rock | Erroll | 1,330 | 5 | Mrs E Povret | J Hindley | 4/6F |
| 25 June | Brighton | Mountain Girl (USA) | | 521 | 12 | R P Scully | R Armstrong | 8/11F |
| 25 June | Brighton | Latin Melody | | 794 | 6 | H Demetriou | R Armstrong | |
| 29 June | Doncaster | Quill's Prince | Chesterfield Hcp | 1,017 | 8 | W Gooch | B W Hills | 4/5F |
| 29 June | Doncaster | Gerard Street | | 483 | 6 | K Hsu | B W Hills | 1/2F |
| 29 June | Lingfield | Habitation | | 690 | 5 | Mrs G Johnson Houghton | R Houghton | 8/11F |
| 29 June | Lingfield | Silver Doctor | | 507 | 12 | Lt Col R Verdin | R Houghton | 2/9F |
| 2 July | Windsor | Manwari | | 392 | 10 | A McCall | R Houghton | 4/5F |
| 3 July | Newmarket | Majordomo | | 690 | 7 | Count C Seilern | J Clayton | 7/2 |
| 4 July | Newmarket | Dragonara Palace | July Stks | 7,860 | 6 | Mrs B Stein | B W Hills | 1/2F |
| 5 July | Newmarket | Thatch(USA) | July Cup | 5,725 | 6 | J A Mulcahy | M V O'Brien(I) | 4/5F |
| 9 July | Pontefract | Miss Gruckles | | 276 | 5 | M Howard | B W Hills | 4/6F |
| 11 July | Kempton | Abertywi | | 768 | 7 | Mrs D Jones | M Stoute | 4/1 |
| 11 July | Kempton | Maniwari(USA) | | 759 | 12 | A McCall | R Houghton | 5/4 |
| 12 July | Doncaster | Mr Light | | 483 | 8 | Mrs A Paus | W O'Gorman | 10/1 |
| 14 July | York | Twilight Boy | | 817 | 14 | J Taylor | E Carr | 2/1 |
| 14 July | York | Pass a Glance | Courage | 1,811 | 7 | Mrs R Sutton | T Darling | 7/4F |
| 14 July | York | Dragonara Palace | Friargate | 1,053 | 5 | Mrs B Stein | B W Hills | 4/9F |
| 14 July | York | Palace of Medina | | 898 | 7 | Mrs A Hindley | J Hindley | 4/9F |
| 16 July | Ayr | Winning Hand | | 564 | 8 | Mrs M Haggas | J Hindley | 8/11F |
| 17 July | Ayr | Gerard Street | Knockjarder | 1,129 | 7 | K Hsu | B W Hills | 2/5F |
| 17 July | Ayr | Edwards Hill | | 542 | 5 | Mrs B Thomson | B W Hills | 4/6F |
| 18 July | Yarmouth | Wrong Direction | | 690 | 8 | R F Scully | R Armstrong | 11/4 |
| 19 July | Nottingham | Forcett | | 272 | 8 | Mrs G Swinbank | W A Stephenson | 11/10 |
| 19 July | Nottingham | Pirate Way | | 665 | 8 | R Ellis | R Vibert | 7/1 |
| 19 July | Nottingham | Shinto | | 345 | 13 | A Parke | D Nichols | 9/2 |
| 27 July | Ascot | Blessed Rock | Hyperion | 1,980 | 6 | Mrs E Pouret | J Hindley | 1/8F |
| 28 July | Ascot | Loyal Manzer | Blacknest | 1,114 | 8 | K Gulrajani | C Brittain | 3/1F |
| 31 July | Goodwood | Trackers Highway | New Ham | 2,076 | 6 | E Adkins | R Mason | 11/2 |
| 1 Aug | Goodwood | Dragonara Palace | Richmond | 8,750 | 6 | Mrs B Stein | B W Hills | 4/9F |
| 1 Aug | Goodwood | Thatch(USA) | Sussex | 14,559 | 8 | J A Mulcahy | M V O'Brien(I) | 4/5F |
| 3 Aug | Goodwood | Evvia | Sussex M | 1,100 | 6 | R More O'Ferrall | H Wragg | 3/1F |
| 4 Aug | Goodwood | Cheveley Princess | Nassau | 6,244 | 10 | R B Moller | H Wragg | 15/2 |
| 4 Aug | Windsor | De Musset | | 582 | 11 | Lady Hothfield | J Clayton | 10/11F |
| 9 Aug | Yarmouth | Raynham | | 690 | 10 | H Demetriou | R Armstrong | 3/1 |
| 10 Aug | Newmarket | Rouser | | 690 | 7 | Mrs J A de Rothschild | J Clayton | 9/2 |
| 10 Aug | Newmarket | Plunger | | 767 | 12 | Duchess of Norfolk | J Dunlop | 2/1 |
| 11 Aug | Redcar | Royal Prerogative | Wm Hill Gold Cup | 9,085 | 8 | Duchess of Norfolk | Denys Smith | 13/8 |
| 11 Aug | Redcar | Buffins | | 513 | 12 | R B Moller | H Wragg | 5/2 |
| 14 Aug | Newcastle | River Doon | | 483 | 6 | D Richardson | W A Stephenson | 13/8F |
| 14 Aug | Newcastle | Blessed Rock | Seaton Delavel | 5,097 | 5 | Mrs E Pouret | J Hindley | 2/5F |

(I) = Ireland (USA) = America

| Date | Race Course | Horse | Race | Value £ | Dist Fur | Owner | Trainer | S/P |
|---|---|---|---|---|---|---|---|---|
| 14 Aug | Newcastle | Hurrah | | 1,084 | 16 | R B Moller | H Wragg | 15/8F |
| 17 Aug | Newbury | Street Light | St Hugh's | 1,287 | 5 | Lord Harrington | J Hindley | 1/2F |
| 17 Aug | Newbury | Blonville(USA) | Stratton | 1,024 | 7 | Mrs H O H Frelinghuysen | J Maxwell | 13/2 |
| 22 Aug | York | Gerard Street | Knavesmire | 1,328 | 7 | R Hsu | B W Hills | 9/4F |
| 24 Aug | Haydock | Argentan | Beresford | 1,091 | 10 | R B Moller | H Wragg | 6/4F |
| 24 Aug | Newmarket | Ambuscade | | 518 | 12 | Lord Porchester | J Clayton | 4/6F |
| 25 Aug | Goodwood | Lapis | | 694 | 6 | O/trainer | B W Hills | 8/11F |
| 27 Aug | Newcastle | Clouds | | 658 | 9 | Mrs J Burk Hardt | Denys Smith | 11/4 |
| 30 Aug | Haydock | Pot Pourri | Colomele Ashton | 1,339 | 12 | Lord Howard de Walden | E Weymes | 11/8F |
| 6 Sept | York | Press Luncheon | | 929 | 6 | Mrs J Mullion | R Armstrong | 5/4F |
| 6 Sept | York | Ata Chief Scout | | 984 | 14 | Count C Seilern | J Clayton | 6/4F |
| 10 Sept | Windsor | Ragstone | | 370 | 11 | Duke of Norfolk | J Dunlop | 1/4F |
| 10 Sept | Windsor | Silk and Satin | | 674 | 6 | Mrs J F C Bryce | P Davey | 4/5F |
| 15 Sept | Doncaster | Gentle Thoughts | Flying Childers | 9,326 | 5 | O/trainer | T G Curtin(I) | EvF |
| 15 Sept | Doncaster | Reformed Character | Clumber | 1,005 | 12 | L Holliday | Denys Smith | 9/4 |
| 15 Sept | Doncaster | Cumbernauld | | 1,676 | 18 | R Muddle | H Price | 9/4F |
| 17 Sept | Goodwood | Humble Pickings(USA) | | 555 | 8 | R F Scully | R Armstrong | 13/2 |
| 17 Sept | Goodwood | Press Luncheon | | 663 | 6 | Mrs J R Mullion | R Armstrong | 8/15F |
| 17 Sept | Goodwood | Silver Tiger(USA) | | 1,028 | 5 | J Edwards | J Dunlop | 11/4F |
| 19 Sept | Ayr | Royal Prerogative | Ladbroke Hcp | 3,188 | 8 | L Holliday | Denys Smith | 10/3 |
| 20 Sept | Ayr | Tom Noddy | Ayrshire Hcp | 3,025 | 11 | Mrs L Brotherton | L Shedden | 2/1F |
| 20 Sept | Ayr | Reformed Character | Kelburn | 1,110 | 13 | L Holliday | Denys Smith | 3/1 |
| 21 Sept | Ayr | Nevermore | | 746 | 6 | W Stirling | J Dunlop | 13/8F |
| 21 Sept | Ayr | Ragstone | Arran | 1,136 | 15 | Duke of Norfolk | J Dunlop | 4/7F |
| 27 Sept | Ascot | Scottish Rifle | Cumberland Lodge | 3,127 | 10 | A J Struthers | J Dunlop | 4/11F |
| 28 Sept | Ascot | Escorial | Green Shield | 2,236 | 8 | | I Balding | 7/4F |
| 2 Oct | Nottingham | Colonel Nelson | | 345 | 8 | C A B St George | H Cecil | 13/8F |
| 2 Oct | Nottingham | Ovation II | | 345 | 8 | Mrs M Hammond | R Armstrong | 15/8F |
| 3 Oct | Newmarket | Bas Bleu | Phantom House | 1,442 | 6 | H Morriss | H Wragg | 7/2F |
| 3 Oct | Newmarket | Rouser | Rowley Mile Hcp | 1,035 | 12 | Mrs J A de Rothschild | J Clayton | 5/1 |
| 4 Oct | Newmarket | Ragstone | | 1,109 | 12 | Duke of Norfolk | J Dunlop | 3/1 |
| 5 Oct | Haydock | Court Melody | | 535 | 8 | B Wigham | J Sutcliffe Jnr | 6/4F |
| 5 Oct | Haydock | Irvine | Knutsford | 1,015 | 10 | C A B St George | H Cecil | 2/9F |
| 6 Oct | Newmarket | Cheveley Princess | Sun Chariot | 6,666 | 10 | R B Moller | H Wragg | 6/1 |
| 7 Oct | Ascot | Helmsdale | Duke of Edinburgh | 2,780 | 16 | H Wills | R Houghton | 7/1 |
| 13 Oct | Ascot | Mandera(USA) | Princess Royal | 2,658 | 12 | Mrs C Engelhard | J Tree | 4/1 |
| 13 Oct | Ascot | Kew Gardens | Sandwich | 1,758 | 7 | P Mellon | I Balding | 13/2 |
| 15 Oct | Warwick | My Brief | | 414 | 10 | J Edwards | J Dunlop | 5/6F |
| 15 Oct | Warwick | Relka | | 207 | 8 | R R Guest | R Armstrong | 7/4F |
| 15 Oct | Warwick | Feliciano | | 414 | 10 | C A B St George | H Cecil | 6/4F |
| 15 Oct | Warwick | Bright Bird | | 207 | 8 | Mrs I Lewin | R Armstrong | 11/4F |
| 16 Oct | Warwick | Hay Bridge | | 207 | 7 | M Wrigley | P Beasley | 9/4F |
| 16 Oct | Warwick | Grey Mouse | | 207 | 5 | Mrs J F C Bryce | R Armstrong | 1/2F |
| 18 Oct | Newmarket | Abide with Me | | 690 | 8 | Y Yamatoto | G Barling | 5/2F |
| 19 Oct | Newmarket | Cellini(USA) | Dewhurst | 26,847 | 7 | C A B St George | M V O'Brien(I) | 40/85F |
| 20 Oct | Newmarket | Go Go Gunner | Snailwell M | 1,038 | 6 | A Ball | I Walker | 6/4F |
| 23 Oct | Sandown | Imperial Crown | | 1,061 | 14 | K Gulrajani | C Brittain | 7/4F |
| 27 Oct | Doncaster | Apalachee | Observer Gold Cup | 30,050 | 8 | J A Mulcahy | M V O'Brien(I) | EvF |
| 2 Nov | Haydock | Tsu Chou | | 501 | 7 | Lady Rothermere | I Balding | 5/2F |
| 2 Nov | Haydock | Elegant Tern | | 1,061 | 8 | P Mellon | I Balding | 8/13F |
| 2 Nov | Haydock | Tin Lid | | 1,031 | 8 | B Jenks | J Johnson | 10/1 |

1973: 129 wins; 80 2nds; 58 3rds; 483 rides

(I) = Ireland (USA) = America

| Date | Race Course | Horse | Race | Value £ | Dist Fur | Owner | Trainer | S/P |
|---|---|---|---|---|---|---|---|---|
| 1974 | | | | | | | | |
| 29 Mar | Liverpool | Funny Man | Spring Cup | 1,651 | 10 | Mrs J F C Bryce | R Armstrong | 7/2 |
| 2 Apl | Nottingham | Duke of Marmalade | | 345 | 10 | Mrs J F C Bryce | R Armstrong | 15/8F |
| 3 Apl | Folkestone | Hot Abbot | | 274 | 6 | R Clark | R Sturdy | 3/1F |
| 3 Apl | Folkestone | Wanlockhead | | 1,143 | 8 | Mrs J R Mullion | R Armstrong | 10/3 |
| 17 Apl | Newmarket | Plum Preserves (USA) | | 596 | 5 | T Willis | R Armstrong | 6/4F |
| 20 Apl | Newbury | Coup de Feu | Newbury Spring Cup | 2,586 | 8 | F Sasse | F Sasse | 7/1 |
| 20 Apl | Newbury | Freefoot | John Porter | 5,179 | 12 | R B Moller | H Wragg | 13/2 |
| 23 Apl | Epsom | Streak | | 601 | 5 | B Myers | J E Sutcliffe | 11/10F |
| 24 Apl | Epsom | Pass a Glance(USA) | | 1,271 | 8 | Mrs R Sutton | H Cecil | 8/11 |
| 30 Apl | Brighton | Colonel Nelson | Hethersett | 1,981 | 12 | C A B St George | H Cecil | 1/2F |
| 2 May | Newmarket | Lady Icarus | | 1,035 | 8 | M Javett | H Cecil | 11/2 |
| 3 May | Newmarket | Silky(USA) | | 690 | 5 | R B Moller | H Wragg | 13/8F |
| 3 May | Newmarket | Relay Race | Jockey Club Stks | 4,120 | 12 | Sir R Macdonald-Buchanan | H Cecil | 4/5F |
| 3 May | Newmarket | Arisaig† | The Whip | 100 | 16 | Sir R Macdonald-Buchanan | H Cecil | |
| 8 May | Chester | Kangetsu | | 517 | 5 | J Kashiyama | R Houghton | 4/7F |
| 9 May | Chester | Averof | Dee | 3,616 | 10 | Capt M D Lemos | C Brittain | 13/2 |
| 9 May | Chester | Manwari(USA) | | 949 | 12 | A McCall | R Houghton | 7/2 |
| 10 May | Lingfield | Paul Alison | | 414 | 5 | A David | A J Pitt | 9/4F |
| 10 May | Leicester | Soccer | | 690 | 10 | H Demetriou | R Armstrong | 13/8F |
| 15 May | York | Ginnie's Pet | FPA Gold Cup | 4,110 | 6 | J Jackson | J E Sutcliffe | 6/1 |
| 15 May | York | Escorial | | 2,928 | 10½ | The Queen | I Balding | 4/5F |
| 17 May | Newbury | Furioso | Sandleford Priory | 1,643 | 10 | R B Moller | H Wragg | 11/2 |
| 17 May | Newbury | Arthurian(USA) | | 554 | 11 | Mrs J Hanes | H Cecil | 4/5F |
| 17 May | Newbury | Madrisa(USA) | | 584 | 5 | Lord Vestey | F Maxwell | 7/4F |
| 17 May | Newbury | Peter Prompt (USA) | | 554 | 11 | Mrs J Hanes | H Cecil | 11/8F |
| 21 May | Nottingham | Firemiss | | 397 | 5 | R Spencer | F Carr | 11/10F |
| 24 May | Kempton | Kingshott | | 414 | 5 | Mrs M Hall | N Callaghan | 6/1 |
| 25 May | Haydock | Lady Rowley | | 1,450 | 5 | G Cooke | N Callaghan | 8/11F |
| 27 May | Sandown | Rustic Lad | | 766 | 7 | Lady B Ness | J Hindley | 11/2 |
| 29 May | Yarmouth | Noble Emperor (USA) | | 314 | 5 | K Maharaj | H Cecil | 7/1 |
| 29 May | Yarmouth | Dashing Hussar | | 356 | 5 | Mrs P Winstone | H Cecil | 8/15F |
| 29 May | Yarmouth | Peter Pan(USA) | | 276 | 10 | Mrs J Hanes | H Cecil | 10/11F |
| 5 June | Epsom | Averof | Diomed | 7,393 | 8 | Capt M D Lemos | C Brittain | 11/10F |
| 6 June | Epsom | Rustic Lad | | 874 | 7 | P Evans | J Hindley | 8/11F |
| 8 June | Epsom | Child of Grace | | 851 | 6 | E Montgomery | M Connolly | 6/5F |
| 19 June | Royal Ascot | Lisadell | Coronation Cup | 9,909 | 8 | J A Mulcahy | M V O'Brien(I) | 7/2 |
| 20 June | Royal Ascot | Saritamer | Cork and Orrery | 14,288 | 6 | C A B St George | M V O'Brien(I) | 11/1 |
| 21 June | Royal Ascot | Ginnie's Pet | Wokingham | 3,856 | 6 | J Sutcliffe | J E Sutcliffe | 7/1 |
| 21 June | Royal Ascot | Relay Race | Hardwicke | 11,491 | 12 | Sir R Macdonald-Buchanan | H Cecil | 10/1F |
| 22 June | Ascot | Tom Cribb | Halifax | 1,429 | 16 | late Lord Rosebery | B Hobbs | 7/2 |
| 22 June | Ascot | Arthurian(USA) | Churchill | 1,834 | 12 | Mrs J Hanes | H Cecil | 2/1F |
| 1 July | Nottingham | Lord Henham | Home Ales | 1,729 | 6 | A Smith | N Callaghan | 13/2 |
| 1 July | Nottingham | Silk and Satin | | 690 | 8 | J F C Bryce | R Armstrong | 7/2 |
| 4 July | Brighton | Remodel | | 1,158 | 10 | Lord Howard de Walden | H Cecil | 6/1 |
| 4 July | Brighton | Olympic Casino | | 712 | 8 | H Demetriou | C Brittain | 6/4F |
| 6 July | Sandown | Windy Glen | Star Stks | 2,512 | 5 | J Brown | D K Weld(I) | 11/2 |
| 6 July | Sandown | General Vole | | 1,226 | 8 | Mrs P Aldridge | R Jarvis | 11/8F |
| 8 July | Windsor | One Night Stand | | 669 | 11 | P Richards | H Cecil | 5/1 |

† Walkover (I) = Ireland (USA) = America

| Date | Race Course | Horse | Race | Value £ | Dist Fur | Owner | Trainer | S/P |
|---|---|---|---|---|---|---|---|---|
| 8 July | Windsor | Dashing Hussar | | 587 | 6 | Mrs P Winstone | H Cecil | 6/1 |
| 8 July | Windsor | Nyssa | | 404 | 10 | Lord Howard de Walden | H Cecil | 15/8F |
| 9 July | Newmarket | Roussalka | Cherry Hinton | 6,673 | 6 | N Phillips | H Cecil | 2/1F |
| 9 July | Newmarket | Mon Parnes | Hamilton | 1,541 | 6 | H Demetriou | R Armstrong | 5/1 |
| 10 July | Newmarket | Pitskelly | Bunbury Cup | 2,536 | 7 | D Robinson | M Jarvis | 6/1 |
| 10 July | Newmarket | Fool's Mate | | 1,173 | 14 | Lord Howard de Walden | H Cecil | EvF |
| 10 July | Newmarket | Helmsdale | | 1,058 | 7 | H Wills | R Houghton | 17/2 |
| 10 July | Newmarket | Indian Question (USA) | | 690 | 6 | S Joel | H Cecil | 6/4F |
| 11 July | Newmarket | Green Belt* | | 440 | 6 | Lord Zetland | H Wragg | 11/8F |
| 11 July | Newmarket | Saritimer(USA) | July Cup | 7,819 | 6 | C A B St George | M V O'Brien(I) | 11/4 |
| 12 July | Leicester | Calaba | | 757 | 10 | Lord Fairhaven | A M Kerr | 7/2F |
| 13 July | York | Lady Rowley | Courage | 1,741 | 6 | G Cooke | N Callaghan | 5/4F |
| 13 July | York | Trackers Highway | Harp Lagar Hcp | 1,823 | 8 | E Adkins | R Mason | 4/1 |
| 15 July | Leicester | Remodel | | 276 | 10 | Lord Howard de Walden | H Cecil | 8/11F |
| 16 July | Leicester | The Baker | | 606 | 10 | A Wiseman | D Gandolfo | 6/5F |
| 16 July | Leicester | Midsummer Lad | | 276 | 12 | Mrs L Davies | B Hanbury | 15/2 |
| 17 July | Kempton | Peter Prompt(USA) | | 621 | 10 | Mrs J Hanes | H Cecil | 8/11F |
| 17 July | Kempton | Multiple | | 977 | 7 | Mrs D Thompson | A Pitt | 10/3F |
| 19 July | Newbury | Sarasota Star(USA) | | 1,280 | 6 | Mrs K Leonard | D K Weld | 3/1 |
| 20 July | Newmarket | Pot Luck | | 1,457 | 12 | Mrs J F C Bryce | R Armstrong | 4/6F |
| 20 July | Newmarket | Indian Question (USA) | | 912 | 7 | S Joel | H Cecil | 5/4F |
| 22 July | Windsor | Melody Time | | 382 | 10 | J Rowles | R Houghton | 10/3 |
| 23 July | Pontefract | One Night Star | Darley Brewery Hcp | 1,805 | 10 | P Richards | H Cecil | 7/4F |
| 23 July | Pontefract | Lauretta | | 631 | 12 | R B Moller | H Wragg | 1/4F |
| 23 July | Pontefract | Kwang Su | | 595 | 10 | F O Ferrall | H B T Jones | 4/6F |
| 24 July | Sandown | Imperial Crown | Cosmopolitan | 1,621 | 14 | K Gulrajani | R Akehurst | 3/1F |
| 25 July | Sandown | Headin' Home | | 690 | 8 | Mrs B Firestone | R Houghton | 9/2 |
| 26 July | Ascot | Radical | | 1,338 | 10 | L Holliday | Denys Smith | 10/11F |
| 27 July | Ascot | Olympic Casino | | 1,416 | 8 | H Demetriou | C Brittain | 2/1F |
| 27 July | Ascot | Roussalka | | 1,922 | 6 | N Phillips | H Cecil | 4/9F |
| 27 July | Ascot | Dahlia(USA) | King George VI and Queen Elizabeth | 81,240 | 12 | N B Hunt | M Zilber(F) | 15/8F |
| 27 July | Ascot | Cumbernauld | | 1,383 | 22 | R Muddle | H Price | 17/2 |
| 29 July | Windsor | Indian Question (USA) | | 587 | 6 | S Joel | H Cecil | 3/10 |
| 30 July | Goodwood | Lady Rowley | Molecomb | 3,517 | 5 | G Cooke | N Callaghan | 4/5F |
| 30 July | Goodwood | Calaba | Warren Stks | 1,632 | 12 | Lord Fairhaven | A Kerr | 11/10F |
| 30 July | Goodwood | General Vale | | 1,333 | 8 | Mrs R Aldridge | R Jarvis | 11/8F |
| 31 July | Goodwood | Abide with Me | | 1,310 | 14 | Y Yamamoto | M Stoute | 7/2 |
| 1 Aug | Goodwood | Great Brother | | 1,142 | 6 | Capt M D Lemos | R Armstrong | 7/4F |
| 1 Aug | Goodwood | Proverb | Goodwood Cup | 5,132 | 21 | Lt Col J Chandos-Pole | B W Hills | 4/8F |
| 1 Aug | Goodwood | Silk and Satin | | 1,293 | 7 | J F C Bryce | R Armstrong | 5/6F |
| 2 Aug | Goodwood | Peter Prompt(USA) | | 1,232 | 10 | Mrs J Hanes | H Cecil | 6/4F |
| 3 Aug | Goodwood | Panomark | Rous Memorial | 1,956 | 6 | R Clifford Turner | P Nelson | 4/6F |
| 7 Aug | Doncaster | Final Call | West Riding Hcp | 1,623 | 8 | G Alton | B Hanbury | 9/4F |
| 8 Aug | Yarmouth | Lot One | | 279 | 8 | Miss M McGowan | B Hanbury | 10/3 |
| 7 Aug | Doncaster | Final Call | West Riding Hcp | 1,623 | 8 | G Alton | B Hanbury | 9/4F |

* Dead Heat (I) = Ireland (F) = France (USA) = America

| Date | Race Course | Horse | Race | Value £ | Dist Fur | Owner | Trainer | S/P |
|---|---|---|---|---|---|---|---|---|
| 9 Aug | Newmarket | Duke of Marmalade (USA) | | 978 | 12 | J F C Bryce | R Armstrong | 1/6F |
| 8 Aug | Yarmouth | The Old Pretender | | 690 | 6 | B Armstrong | R Armstrong | 11/10F |
| 9 Aug | Newmarket | Enchanting | | 483 | 10 | G Reed | S Hall | 11/4F |
| 9 Aug | Newmarket | Silk and Satin | Tapestry | 1,331 | 8 | J F C Bryce | R Armstrong | 8/11F |
| 9 Aug | Newmarket | Limpopo | | 690 | 6 | Lord Howard de Walden | H Cecil | 11/4F |
| 12 Aug | Windsor | Coming About | | 276 | 5 | Mrs J Mullen | R Armstrong | 11/10F |
| 12 Aug | Windsor | Minigold | | 308 | 10 | Mrs G Davison | A Davison | 5/2F |
| 12 Aug | Windsor | Jenny Driver | | 681 | 6 | Mrs R MacLeod | R Armstrong | 9/4F |
| 12 Aug | Windsor | Noblero(F) | | 307 | 10 | A Richards | D Hanley | 8/11F |
| 10 Aug | Newmarket | Reformed Character | Junior Trust Hcp | 1,623 | 12 | L Holliday | Denys Smith | 13/8F |
| 20 Aug | York | Tanzor(USA) | Acomb | 2,255 | 6 | J Wakefield | C Brittain | 6/4F |
| 20 Aug | York | Dahlia(USA) | Benson & Hedges Cup | 39,531 | 10 | N B Hunt | M Zilber(F) | 8/15F |
| 21 Aug | York | Peter Culter | Rous | 2,136 | 5 | D Robinson | P Davey | 9/2 |
| 21 Aug | York | Phoenix Hall (USA) | Convivial | 2,985 | 6 | R Tikkoo | D K Weld(I) | 11/2 |
| 21 Aug | York | Calaba | Falmouth | 1,816 | 10 | Lord Fairhaven | A Kerr | 7/4F |
| 21 Aug | York | Green Belt | Knavesmire Hcp | 1,581 | 6 | Sir P Oppenheimer | H Wragg | 7/4F |
| 22 Aug | York | Pot Luck | Melrose | 2,168 | 14 | Mrs J F C Bryce | R Armstrong | 85/40 |
| 22 Aug | York | Steel Heart | Gimcrack | 19,303 | 6 | R Tikkoo | D K Weld(I) | 17/2 |
| 23 Aug | Newmarket | Magnum Force | | 690 | 5 | Mrs K Weihtag | R Armstrong | 8/15F |
| 24 Aug | Chepstow | Hail the Pirates(USA) | Chesterfield Cup | 2,640 | 10 | D Galbreath | M V O'Brien(I) | 7/4F |
| 26 Aug | Epsom | Marcela | | 1,246 | 6 | J F C Bryce | R Armstrong | 8/11F |
| 27 Aug | Epsom | Bombshell | | 522 | 8 | Mrs B Firestone | R Houghton | 10/3 |
| 28 Aug | Yarmouth | Ruling Class | | 276 | 5 | B Samuel | J Hindley | 5/4F |
| 2 Sept | Windsor | Never Return (USA) | | 341 | 10 | Mrs T Hardin | R Armstrong | 4/7F |
| 7 Sept | Sandown | Ahdeek(USA) | Pepsi Stks | 2,693 | 7 | R Guest | R Armstrong | 4/1F |
| 7 Sept | Doncaster | Calaba | | 385 | 10 | Lord Fairhaven | A Kerr | 11/4F |
| 9 Sept | Windsor | Never Return (USA) | | 276 | 10 | Mrs T Hardin | R Armstrong | 1/6F |
| 12 Sept | Doncaster | Pee Mai | Town Moor Hcp | 2,388 | 10 | G Barber-Lomax | A Goodwill | 11/4F |
| 12 Sept | Doncaster | One Night Stand | | 1,366 | 12 | F Richards | H Cecil | 5/1 |
| 13 Sept | Doncaster | Laurentian Hills (USA) | | 1,263 | 12 | Mrs J F C Bryce | R Armstrong | 5/2 |
| 13 Sept | Doncaster | Pleasure Lane(USA) | | 1,279 | 6 | Mrs L Schwitzer Jnr | R Armstrong | 11/2 |
| 14 Sept | Doncaster | Hot Spark | Flying Childers | 9,621 | 5 | R Tikkoo | D K Weld(I) | 9/2 |
| 20 Sept | Ayr | Howells | | 682 | 6 | R Sangster | B W Hills | 13/8F |
| 25 Sept | Lingfield | Never Return (USA) | | 786 | 12 | Mrs T Hardin | R Armstrong | 5/4F |
| 26 Sept | Ascot | Saritimer | Diadem | 3,842 | 6 | C A B St George | M V O'Brien(I) | 1/10F |
| 3 Oct | Newmarket | Joking Apart | | 690 | 6 | The Queen | I Balding | 11/1 |
| 3 Oct | Newmarket | Seminar | | 1,173 | 5 | R Sangster | B W Hills | 7/1 |
| 3 Oct | Newmarket | Steel Heart | Middle Park | 25,319 | 6 | R Tikkoo | D K Weld(I) | 10/11F |
| 11 Oct | Ascot | Klairvimy | | 1,416 | 10 | Mrs B Allen-Jones | D K Weld(I) | 4/1 |
| 18 Oct | Newmarket | Duke of Marmalade (USA) | | 1,266 | 12 | Mrs J F C Bryce | R Armstrong | 10/1 |
| 19 Oct | Newmarket | Giagometti | Champion | 36,106 | 10 | C A B St George | H Price | 4/1F |
| 21 Oct | Leicester | Bernicia | | 276 | 5 | Miss J Sebag-Montefiore | B Hobbs | EvF |
| 22 Oct | Sandown | Creetown | | 483 | 5 | V Cooper | P Nelson | 9/4F |

(I) = Ireland (F) = France (USA) = America

| Date | Race Course | Horse | Race | Value £ | Dist Fur | Owner | Trainer | S/P |
|---|---|---|---|---|---|---|---|---|
| 22 Oct | Sandown | Sky Messenger | | 871 | 8 | L Holliday | Denys Smith | 5/2F |
| 26 Oct | Doncaster | Willy Willy | | 870 | 6 | Dr C Kuhlmann | B McCormick | 9/2 |
| 31 Oct | Newmarket | Fastacre | Potter Trophy | 1,725 | 6 | V Advani | A Breasley | 11/8F |
| 1 Nov | Newmarket | Top Secret | | 909 | 8 | Sqn Ldr R Millsom | P Robinson | 7/4F |
| 4 Nov | Lingfield | Romper | | 759 | 7 | Dr J Hobby | R Houghton | 4/5F |
| 5 Nov | Leicester | Run Tell Run(USA) | | 690 | 5 | J Edwards | J Dunlop | 2/1 |
| 12 Nov | Haydock | Unicorn's Fancy | | 577 | 7 | W McDonald | P Cole | 5/4F |
| 12 Nov | Haydock | Sailing Ship | | 828 | 8 | J R Mullion | R Armstrong | 8/1 |

1974: 143 wins; 90 2nds; 75 3rds; 585 rides

| Date | Race Course | Horse | Race | Value £ | Dist Fur | Owner | Trainer | S/P |
|---|---|---|---|---|---|---|---|---|
| 1975 | | | | | | | | |
| 29 Mar | Kempton | Creetown | Queen Elizabeth | 1,232 | 6 | V Cooper | P Nelson | 10/11F |
| 31 Mar | Kempton | Bay Express | | 1,129 | 5 | P Cooper | P Nelson | 11/8 |
| 15 Apl | Newmarket | Genesis | | 690 | 7 | Mrs G Johnson Houghton | R Houghton | 5/1 |
| 17 Apl | Newmarket | Brave Panther | | 507 | 5 | R Tikkoo | B Hanbury | 9/2 |
| 17 Apl | Newmarket | Rose Bowl | Nell Gwyn | 3,213 | 7 | Mrs C W Engelhard | R Houghton | 7/4F |
| 17 Apl | Newmarket | Shantallah | | 690 | 12 | R More O'Ferrall | H Wragg | 9/4F |
| 18 Apl | Newbury | Tampa | | 684 | 5 | B McCormack | P Cole | 5/2F |
| 19 Apl | Newbury | Mark Anthony | Greenham | 6,422 | 7 | Capt M D Lemos | C Brittain | 11/2 |
| 19 Apl | Newbury | Rebec | | 698 | 8 | Lord Howard de Walden | H Cecil | 4/5F |
| 22 Apl | Epsom | Alanrod | | 621 | 5 | D Crawford | S Ingham | 1/3F |
| 23 Apl | Epsom | Hey Presto | | 577 | 5 | H J Joel | S Ingham | 5/6F |
| 24 Apl | Epsom | Asdic | | 1,183 | 12 | Maj Gen D'Avigdor-Goldsmit | S Ingham | 11/8F |
| 25 Apl | Sandown | Prince of Egypt | | 743 | 8 | J H Whitney | J Tree | 7/2F |
| 26 Apl | Sandown | Never Return(USA) | Westbury | 3,645 | 10 | Mrs T Hardin | R Armstrong | 9/4 |
| 28 Apl | Brighton | Hey Presto | | 462 | 5 | H J Joel | S Ingham | 2/7F |
| 30 Apl | Ascot | Night in Town | Paradise | 1,784 | 16 | B Firestone | I Balding | 4/1 |
| 1 May | Newmarket | African Winner | | 690 | 5 | Mrs T Wade | C Brittain | 11/8F |
| 2 May | Newmarket | Fool's Mate† | The Whip | | 16 | Lord Howard de Walden | H Cecil | |
| 3 May | Newmarket | Mimika | | 844 | 5 | Mrs M D Lemos | C Brittain | 3/1F |
| 9 May | Chester | Amere Mare | | 633 | 5 | M Johnson | I Johnson | 7/2F |
| 9 May | Lingfield | Divine King | | | 6 | G Hendry | R Hannon | 7/1 |
| 10 May | Lingfield | Juliette Marny | Oaks Trial | 3,649 | 12 | J Morrison | J Tree | 6/4F |
| 10 May | Lingfield | Brave Panther | | 1,240 | 5 | R Tikkoo | B Hanbury | 6/5F |
| 12 May | Windsor | Midsummer Lap | | 714 | 11 | Mrs L Davies | B Hanbury | 5/2F |
| 12 May | Windsor | African Winner | | 483 | 5 | Mrs T Wade | C Brittain | 95/40 |
| 14 May | York | Rodado | Fitzwilliam | 1,852 | 16 | Lord Howard de Walden | E Weymes | 4/5F |
| 14 May | York | Bold Sage | | 1,352 | 5 | R Tikkoo | B Hanbury | 11/4F |
| 15 May | York | Steel Heart | Duke of York | 3,882 | 6 | R Tikkoo | D K Weld(I) | 15/8F |
| 19 May | Windsor | Brave Panther | | 690 | 5 | R Tikkoo | B Hanbury | 1/4F |
| 20 May | Goodwood | Hunza Dancer | | 701 | 10 | R Tikkoo | A Breasley | 5/4F |
| 22 May | Goodwood | Royfern* | | 491 | 5 | A Kennedy | A Breasley | 85/40F |
| 23 May | Kempton | Chaplin | | 573 | 6 | Mrs J Cook | D K Weld(I) | 85/40F |
| 27 May | Sandown | Galway Boy | | 690 | 5 | J R Mullion | I Balding | 11/2 |
| 28 May | Yarmouth | Vanua(USA) | | 345 | 10 | Mrs K Kerybut | H B T Jones | 5/1 |
| 31 May | Kempton | John Cherry | Harpers & Queen | 2,484 | 16 | J H Whitney | J Tree | 5/1 |
| 31 May | Kempton | Midsummer Lad | | 918 | 11 | Mrs L Davies | B Hanbury | 11/8F |
| 3 June | Epsom | Hey Presto | | 1,516 | 5 | H J Joel | S Ingham | 9/2 |
| 3 June | Epsom | Juliette Marny | The Oaks | 44,958 | 12 | J Morrison | J Tree | 12/1 |
| 3 June | Epsom | Dial-a-lad(USA) | | 873 | 8 | C Stein | B W Hills | 10/11F |
| 11 June | Newbury | African Winner | | 1,664 | 15 | Mrs T Wade | C Brittain | 5/4F |

* Dead Heat † Walkover (I) = Ireland (USA) = America

| Date | Race Course | Horse | Race | Value £ | Dist Fur | Owner | Trainer | S/P |
|---|---|---|---|---|---|---|---|---|
| 13 June | Sandown | Captain's Table | | 483 | 8 | J H Whitney | J Tree | 10/3F |
| 14 June | Sandown | Marchant(USA) | | 1,348 | 11 | C A B St George | H Cecil | 9/4F |
| 17 June | Royal Ascot | Galway Bay(F) | Coventry | 6,576 | 6 | J R Mullion | I Balding | 2/1F |
| 17 June | Royal Ascot | Galina(USA) | Ribblesdale | 10,017 | 12 | S Fraser | M V O'Brien(I) | 7/1 |
| 18 June | Royal Ascot | Gay Fandango | Jersey | 3,770 | 7 | A Clore | M V O'Brien(I) | 11/10F |
| 18 June | Royal Ascot | Roussalka | Coronation | 9,923 | 8 | N Phillips | H Cecil | 9/1 |
| 18 June | Royal Ascot | Blood Royal (USA) | Queen's Vase | 4,753 | 16 | Mrs G Getty II | M V O'Brien (I) | 11/2 |
| 19 June | Royal Ascot | Fauraki | Norfolk | 5,866 | 5 | Mrs M A O'Toole | M O'Toole(I) | 6/1 |
| 19 June | Royal Ascot | Sagaro | Gold Cup | 19,079 | 20 | G A Oldham | F Boutin(F) | 7/4F |
| 20 June | Royal Ascot | Boone's Cabin | Wokingham | 3,502 | 6 | R Sangster | M V O'Brien (I) | 6/1 |
| 21 June | Ascot | Guillaume Tell(USA) | Churchill | 2,044 | 12 | Mrs W Haefner | M V O'Brien (I) | 4/11F |
| 27 June | Lingfield | Hayloft(F) | | 414 | 5 | J Rowles | R Houghton | 11/8 |
| 30 June | Windsor | Silage | | 692 | 10 | J Rowles | R Houghton | 15/2 |
| 30 June | Nottingham | Dame Foolish | | 345 | 5 | Lord Howard de Walden | H Cecil | 5/4F |
| 30 June | Nottingham | Court Circus | | 345 | 10 | R Muddle | B Hanbury | 6/4F |
| 1 July | Warwick | Heraclius(F) | | 40 | 7 | C A B St George | H Cecil | 8/13F |
| 3 July | Yarmouth | Ticklish(F) | | 403 | 10 | P Arnold | H Cecil | 8/11F |
| 4 July | Sandown | Orina | | 1,035 | 7 | P Bull | B W Hills | 7/4F |
| 5 July | Sandown | Spanish Warrior | Timeform M Pl | 2,265 | 8 | R Wallace | K Ivory | 10/1 |
| 7 July | Windsor | Midsummer Lad | | 892 | 11 | Mrs L Davies | B Hanbury | 5/4F |
| 9 July | Nottingham | Albrighton | | 1,236 | 14 | Sir R Macdonald-Buchanan | H Cecil | 11/4 |
| 12 July | York | Castaway | | 1,130 | 12 | R B Moller | H Wragg | 13/2 |
| 16 July | Kempton | Ticklish(F) | | 690 | 12 | P Arnold | H Cecil | 2/7F |
| 17 July | Nottingham | Sally Downes (USA) | | 345 | 13 | R Sangster | H Cecil | 4/5F |
| 17 July | Nottingham | Cappuccilli | | 345 | 6 | C A B St George | H Cecil | 11/8F |
| 23 July | Sandown | Slim Jim | | 885 | 10 | P Roberts | I Balding | 11/2 |
| 25 July | Ascot | Galway Bay(F) | Hyperion | 1,780 | 6 | J Mullion | I Balding | 4/9F |
| 25 July | Ascot | Sir Daniel(USA) | | 1,272 | 16 | J Mulcahy | M V O'Brien (I) | 11/10F |
| 29 July | Goodwood | Hayloft | Molecomb | 4,656 | 5 | J Rowles | R Houghton | 3/1 |
| 29 July | Goodwood | Beauvallon(F) | | 1,652 | 12 | T Wada | M V O'Brien (I) | 4/9F |
| 31 July | Goodwood | Girandole | Goodwood Cup | 5,688 | 21 | J Hattersley | M Stoute | 7/2 |
| 31 July | Goodwood | Guillaume Tell (USA) | Gordon | 4,934 | 12 | Mrs W Haefner | M V O'Brien (I) | 11/8F |
| 2 Aug | Goodwood | Hail the Pirates | PTS Laurel | 8,640 | 10 | D Galbreath | M V O'Brien (I) | 9/2F |
| 2 Aug | Goodwood | Roussalka | Nassau | 10,720 | 10 | N Phillips | H Cecil | 9/4 |
| 2 Aug | Goodwood | Amadou | | 1,266 | 6 | W Reynolds | B Hanbury | 5/4F |
| 12 Aug | Nottingham | Long Love | | 374 | 10 | Dr C Labrecciosa | B Hanbury | EvF |
| 18 Aug | Windsor | Ginger | | 483 | 5 | B McCormack | P Cole | 10/3F |
| 18 Aug | Windsor | Great Idea | | 690 | 6 | S Joel | H Cecil | 5/4F |
| 19 Aug | York | Dahlia(USA) | Benson & Hedges Cup | 39,397 | 10 | N B Hunt | M Zilber(F) | 7/2 |
| 22 Aug | Goodwood | Cappucilli | | 1,821 | 7 | Mrs C A B St George | H Cecil | 15/2 |
| 22 Aug | Newmarket | Jujube | | 518 | 12 | Lord Howard de Walden | H Cecil | 8/13F |
| 22 Aug | Newmarket | Queen Anne | | 690 | 6 | Lord Carnarvon | P Nelson | 8/15F |
| 29 Aug | Sandown | Pave the Way | | 925 | 8 | Mrs N Mountain | J Winter | 5/1 |
| 1 Sept | Windsor | Floral Royal(USA) | | 483 | 6 | late Mrs K Weihtag | R Armstrong | 4/6F |
| 3 Sept | York | Leonello | | 1,205 | 16 | C Elliott | C Brittain | 9/2 |
| 4 Sept | York | Ca Marche | | 1,131 | 14 | J H Whitney | J Tree | 1/2F |

(I) = Ireland (F) = France (USA) = America

| Date | Race Course | Horse | Race | Value £ | Dist Fur | Owner | Trainer | S/P |
|---|---|---|---|---|---|---|---|---|
| 4 Sept | York | Peaceful(USA) | | 1,333 | 12 | J H Whitney | J Tree | 4/1 |
| 10 Sept | Doncaster | Quiet Fling (USA) | Fitzwilliam | 1,685 | 12 | J H Whitney | J Tree | 3/1F |
| 11 Sept | Doncaster | Gunner B | | 308 | 6 | Mrs P Barratt | G Toft | 11/2 |
| 13 Sept | Doncaster | Calaba | Gt Yorkshire | 1,702 | 14 | Lord Fairhaven | D Morley | 9/4F |
| 17 Sept | Yarmouth | Take Your Place(USA) | | 690 | 7 | Count d'Alessio | H Cecil | 4/5F |
| 17 Sept | Yarmouth | Strabo | | 483 | 6 | Sir M Sobell | W Hern | 5/4F |
| 18 Sept | Yarmouth | Konafa(Can) | | 485 | 7 | L Gatto-Roissard | H Cecil | 2/5F |
| 22 Sept | Leicester | Baroncroft | | 690 | 12 | Mrs S Crowe | A Breasley | 5/1F |
| 24 Sept | Lingfield | Laurentian Hills(USA) | | 690 | 12 | Mrs J F C Bryce | R Armstrong | 8/13F |
| 25 Sept | Ascot | Spring Time* | | 2,925 | 6 | J Mulcahy | M V O'Brien(I) | 9/4F |
| 25 Sept | Ascot | Calaba | Cumberland Lodge | 4,800 | 12 | Lord Fairhaven | D Morley | 11/2 |
| 25 Sept | Ascot | John Cherry | Gordon Carter Hcp | 1,173 | 16 | J H Whitney | J Tree | 15/8F |
| 26 Sept | Ascot | Loh | Vidal Sassoon | 2,705 | 7 | Mrs D Goldstein | R Akehurst | 4/1 |
| 27 Sept | Ascot | Sir Wimborne (USA) | Royal Lodge | 7,397 | 8 | Mrs A Manning | M V O'Brien(I) | 4/6F |
| 27 Sept | Ascot | Sarania | Blue Seal | 1,395 | 6 | Cmdr H Grenfell | J Tree | 11/2 |
| 4 Oct | Newmarket | Ca Marche | | 1,086 | 16 | J H Whitney | J Tree | 11/4F |
| 4 Oct | Newmarket | Fluellen | | 1,185 | 7 | Sir P Oppenheimer | H Wragg | 10/3 |
| 8 Oct | York | Vice Squad(USA) | | 1,173 | 16 | J H Whitney | J Tree | 7/1 |
| 9 Oct | York | Sarania | | 1,553 | 6 | Cmdr H Grenfell | J Tree | 2/1F |
| 10 Oct | Ascot | Calaba | | 1,363 | 10 | Lord Fairhaven | D Morley | 6/5F |
| 16 Oct | Newmarket | Blood Royal (USA) | Jockey Club Cup | 4,901 | 16 | Mrs G Getty II | M V O'Brien(I) | 11/10 |
| 17 Oct | Newmarket | Baroncroft | | 1,200 | 12 | Mrs S Crowe | A Breasley | 10/3 |
| 17 Oct | Newmarket | Brilliantine (USA) | | 1,205 | 10 | J H Whitney | J Tree | 3/1 |
| 18 Oct | Newmarket | Doctor Wall | | 1,023 | 6 | J Morrison | J Tree | 4/1F |
| 21 Oct | Leicester | Subaltern | | 435 | 10 | P Cane | C Dingwall | 8/1 |
| 21 Oct | Leicester | Ramdien | | 690 | 6 | Miss M Sheriffe | J Tree | 4/5F |
| 23 Oct | Newbury | Flash Back | | 1,028 | 5 | Mrs G Davison | A Davison | 2/1F |

1975: 113 wins; 88 2nds; 62 3rds; 525 rides

| Date | Race Course | Horse | Race | Value £ | Dist Fur | Owner | Trainer | S/P |
|---|---|---|---|---|---|---|---|---|
| 1976 | | | | | | | | |
| 6 Apl | Newmarket | Charley's Revenge | | 845 | 5 | A Zuiderenf | R Armstrong | 13/8F |
| 6 Apl | Newmarket | Malinowski | Ladbroke Craven | 3,923 | 8 | C A B St George | M V O'Brien(I) | 8/15F |
| 6 Apl | Newmarket | La Bombola | | 937 | 7 | S Vanian | R Boss | 10/1 |
| 10 Apl | Newbury | Quiet Fling(USA) | John Porter | 8,626 | 12 | J H Whitney | J Tree | 5/11 |
| 13 Apl | Nottingham | Il Padrone | | 695 | 10 | M Davis | J Sutcliffe | EvF |
| 20 Apl | Epsom | Trasi's Son | | 1,407 | 10 | J Hickman | M Tate | 14/1 |
| 22 Apl | Epsom | Ahdeek(USA) | | 1,539 | 12 | P Guest | R Armstrong | 15/8 |
| 22 Apl | Epsom | Mad Carew | | 992 | 8 | H J Joel | S Ingham | 3/1 |
| 1 May | Ascot | Marco Ricci | Paradise | 3,068 | 16 | C A B St George | B W Hills | 7/1 |
| 5 May | Chester | John Cherry | Chester Cup | 6,294 | 18 | J H Whitney | J Tree | 7/2 |
| 12 May | York | Jumping Hill | Hambleton | 1,991 | 8 | G Pope Jnr | N Murless | 9/4F |
| 13 May | York | Bruni | Yorkshire Cup | 8,525 | 14 | C A B St George | H Price | 7/4F |
| 14 May | Goodwood | Easy Landing | | 930 | 5 | J H Whitney | J Tree | 6/4F |
| 19 May | Goodwood | General Ironside | Predominate | 3,149 | 12 | G Weston | H Cecil | 11/2 |
| 21 May | Kempton | Mr Nice Guy | | 1,024 | 5 | Mrs F Todd | E Reavey | 2/1 |
| 22 May | Kempton | Ahdeek(USA) | | 1,977 | 12 | R R Guest | R Armstrong | 8/11F |
| 22 May | Kempton | Step Ahead(USA) | | 1,548 | 7 | Mrs D Anderson | P Cole | 4/1 |
| 31 May | Sandown | Anne's Pretender | | 7,065 | 10 | Sir C Clore | H Price | 2/1F |
| 31 May | Sandown | Rhodomantade | Yellow Paces | 4,633 | 8 | J Carrington | P Makin | 6/1 |
| 2 June | Epsom | Empery(USA) | The Derby | 111,825 | 12 | N B Hunt | M Zilber(F) | 2/6 |
| 2 June | Epsom | Mr Nice Guy | Woodcote | 2,590 | 6 | Mrs F Todd | E Reavey | 13/4F |
| 3 June | Epsom | Quiet Fling(USA) | Coronation Cup | 21,420 | 12 | J H Whitney | J Tree | 5/2F |
| 5 June | Epsom | Sweet Lad | | 1,355 | 8 | J Peyton Jones | B W Hills | 8/15F |

* Dead Heat (I) = Ireland (F) = France (USA) = America (Can) = Canada

| Date | Race Course | Horse | Race | Value £ | Dist Fur | Owner | Trainer | S/P |
|---|---|---|---|---|---|---|---|---|
| 9 June | Newbury | Silken Way | | 1,822 | 10 | M Sobell | W Hern | 11/7F |
| 12 June | York | Intermission | | 1,380 | 8 | J H Whitney | J Tree | 8/13F |
| 12 June | York | Bright Finish (USA) | | 1,380 | 10½ | J H Whitney | J Tree | 15/2 |
| 16 June | Royal Ascot | Jumping Hill | Royal Hunt Cup | 9,263 | 8 | G A Pope | N Murless | 6/1F |
| 16 June | Royal Ascot | General Ironside | Queen's Vase | 6,514 | 16 | G Weston | A Cecil | 11/8F |
| 17 June | Royal Ascot | Sagaro | Gold Cup | 19,179 | 20 | G Oldham | F Boutin(F) | 8/15F |
| 19 June | Ascot | Albrighton | | 2,033 | 16 | Sir R Macdonald-Buchanan | A Cecil | 11/10F |
| 25 June | Lingfield | Paddington | | 798 | 8 | L Freedman | N Murless | 6/1 |
| 2 July | Sandown | Bee Splendid | | 690 | 5 | A Mullings | S Ingham | 7/2 |
| 2 July | Sandown | Miss Pinkie | | 1,035 | 7 | H J Joel | N Murless | 4/6F |
| 2 July | Sandown | Fools Rush In | | 1,035 | 10 | Mrs J F C Bryce | R Armstrong | 11/8F |
| 5 July | Windsor | Kyriakos | | 694 | 10 | Mrs I Antoni | A Pitt | 9/4 |
| 6 July | Newmarket | May Beck | Hamilton Hcp | 1,813 | 6 | Mrs N Murless | N Murless | 6/4F |
| 8 July | Newmarket | J O Tobin | Fulbourn Memorial | 1,973 | 6 | G Pope Jnr | N Murless | 6/4F |
| 8 July | Newmarket | Paddington | | 1.590 | 7 | L Freedman | N Murless | 4/6F |
| 10 July | York | Miss Pinkie | Courage | 3,251 | 6 | H J Joel | N Murless | 4/5F |
| 10 July | York | Rory's Rocket | Fishergate | 2,519 | 6 | O/trainer | J Dunlop | 5/1 |
| 22 July | Sandown | Piney Ridge | National | 6,706 | 5 | M Throsby | M Kauntze | 7/4F |
| 22 July | Sandown | Lucky Shot | | 954 | 14 | H J Joel | S Ingham | 15/8F |
| 24 July | Sandown | Mossberry | | 1,293 | 8 | H J Joel | N Murless | 7/2F |
| 24 July | Ascot | Al Stanza(USA) | Princess Margaret | 3,256 | 6 | K Weihtag | R Armstrong | 3/1F |
| 27 July | Goodwood | Fool's Mate | Trundle Hcp | 1,942 | 12 | Lord Howard de Walden | H Cecil | 11/8F |
| 28 July | Goodwood | J O Tobin | Richmond | 14,124 | 6 | G Pope Jnr | N Murless | 8/11F |
| 30 July | Newmarket | Bariole | | 562 | 12 | Mrs L Schwitzer Jnr | R Armstrong | 7/2F |
| 30 July | Newmarket | Bright Finish | | 1238 | 12 | J H Whitney | J Tree | 8/13F |
| 30 July | Newmarket | Tiger Trail | | 1,165 | 8 | H J Joel | N Murless | 11/8F |
| 31 July | Goodwood | Paddington | Rous Memorial | 3,460 | 6 | L Freedman | N Murless | 7/2 |
| 31 July | Goodwood | Fool's Mate | PTS Laurel | 7,839 | 10 | Lord Howard de Walden | H Cecil | 5/1 |
| 31 July | Goodwood | Roussalka | Nassau | 13,092 | 10 | N Phillips | H Cecil | 15/8F |
| 3 Aug | Brighton | Cake Popper | | 958 | 6 | Mrs N Murless | N Murless | 10/11F |
| 3 Aug | Brighton | Kallissima | | 1,167 | 8 | S Vanian | R Boss | 1/2F |
| 3 Aug | Brighton | Lord David | | 1,019 | 10 | W Skinner | N Marshall | 4/11F |
| 3 Aug | Brighton | Peranka | | 972 | 5 | C Allen | N Marshall | 13/8F |
| 16 Aug | Windsor | Jin Jang(F) | | 882 | 10 | S Vanian | R Boss | 11/4 |
| 17 Aug | York | Padroug(USA) | Acomb | 3,916 | 6 | Mrs W Haefner | M V O'Brien(I) | 11/8F |
| 19 Aug | York | Haveroid | Prince of Wales's Stks | 3,842 | 5 | T W Newton | N Adam | 7/1 |
| 21 Aug | Kempton | Peranka | | 1,612 | 5 | C Allen | W Marshall | 13/8F |
| 21 Aug | Kempton | Filipachi | | 948 | 7 | J St George | B Hanbury | 12/1 |
| 31 Aug | Kempton | Tiger Trail | | 1,682 | 10 | H J Joel | N Murless | 6/4F |
| 1 Sept | York | Royal Plume | Sancton | 2,400 | 8 | H J Joel | N Murless | 2/1F |
| 1 Sept | York | Forty Winks | Cuseburn Nursery Hcp | 1,777 | 6 | W Clarke | D Thom | 4/5F |
| 1 Sept | York | Sandford Lady | Playboy Bookmakers | 3,149 | 5 | C Offey | H Price | 7/2F |
| 1 Sept | York | Sauceboat | Strensall | 2,397 | 8 | J Hornung | N Murless | 4/6F |
| 8 Sept | Doncaster | Ivory Girl | Fitzwilliam | 1,752 | | C A B St George | H Cecil | 9/2 |
| 8 Sept | Doncaster | J O Tobin | Laurent Perrier Champagne | 10,194 | 7 | G Pope Jnr | N Murless | 4/9F |
| 8 Sept | Doncaster | Brave Lass | Bradgate Park | 1,864 | 6 | H J Joel | T Waugh | 4/5F |
| 9 Sept | Doncaster | Royal Plume | Vernons Organisation | 1,725 | 8 | H J Joel | N Murless | 5/2F |

(I) = Ireland (F) = France (USA) = America

| Date | Race Course | Horse | Race | Value £ | Dist Fur | Owner | Trainer | S/P |
|---|---|---|---|---|---|---|---|---|
| 13 Sept | Goodwood | Claironcita | | 862 | 12 | B Holland-Martin | R Houghton | 5/1 |
| 13 Sept | Goodwood | Cake Popper | | 1,444 | 7 | Mrs N Murless | N Murless | 9/2 |
| 17 Sept | Newbury | Ad Libra(USA) | | 1,151 | 8 | Mrs J Rogers | R Houghton | 9/4F |
| 23 Sept | Ascot | Bruni | Cumberland Lodge | 5,967 | 12 | C A B St George | H Price | 4/7F |
| 23 Sept | Ascot | Brave Lass | | 1,205 | 5 | H J Joel | T Waugh | 1/2F |
| 24 Sept | Ascot | Royal Plume | SGB | 2,863 | 7 | H J Joel | N Murless | 9/2F |
| 24 Sept | Ascot | Intermission | Taylor Woodrow Charity | 6,211 | 8 | J H Whitney | J Tree | 7/2 |
| 24 Sept | Ascot | Miss Pinkie | Argos Star Fillies' Mile | 5,608 | 8 | H J Joel | N Murless | 5/1 |
| 29 Sept | Newmarket | Durtal | Wm Hill Cheveley Park | 34,428 | 6 | R Sangster | B W Hills | 5/1 |
| 30 Sept | Newmarket | Rheola | Alington Memorial | 1,730 | 6 | Lady Scott | W Wightman | 3/1F |
| 7 Oct | York | Bright Finish | Middlethorpe | 2,006 | 14 | J H Whitney | M Stoute | 1/4F |
| 14 Oct | Newmarket | Bright Finish | Jockey Club Cup | 9,035 | 16 | J H Whitney | M Stoute | 2/1F |
| 15 Oct | Newmarket | The Minstrel (Can) | Wm Hill Dewhurst | 37,195 | 7 | R Sangster | M V O'Brien(I) | 6/5F |
| 16 Oct | Newmarket | John Cherry | Cesarewitch | 9,849 | 18 | J H Whitney | J Tree | 13/2 |
| 19 Oct | Sandown | Elizabethan | | 841 | 8 | H J Joel | N Murless | 7/4F |
| 2 Nov | Lingfield | Tinsley Green | | 657 | 5 | Lt Col Sir J Hornung | N Murless | 7/4F |

1976: 87 wins; 68 2nds; 51 3rds; 402 rides

| Date | Race Course | Horse | Race | Value £ | Dist Fur | Owner | Trainer | S/P |
|---|---|---|---|---|---|---|---|---|
| 1977 | | | | | | | | |
| 2 Apr | Ascot | The Minstrel (Can) | 2000 Gn Trial | 5,299 | 7 | R Sangster | M V O'Brien(I) | 4/5F |
| 14 Apl | Newmarket | Golden Libra | | 1,217 | 5 | Mrs D Solomon | R Hannon | 13/8F |
| 15 Apl | Newbury | Japsilk | | 1,215 | 16 | G Deards | R Hannon | 5/2F |
| 15 Apl | Newbury | Durtal | Fred Darling | 5,271 | 7 | R Sangster | B W Hills | 8/13F |
| 16 Apl | Newbury | Decent Fellow | John Porter | 10,677 | 12 | Brig Gen W Gilbride | G Balding | 4/1 |
| 19 Apl | Epsom | Toco Tommy | | 876 | 5 | Dr S Bennett | R Hannon | 5/1 |
| 19 Apl | Epsom | Be My Guest (USA) | Ladbroke Blue Riband Trial | 6,024 | 8 | Mrs A Manning | M V O'Brien(I) | 9/4 |
| 21 Apl | Epsom | Lady Mere | Princess Elizabeth | 5933 | 8 | R Sangster | B W Hills | 7/4F |
| 26 Apl | Newmarket | Emboss | | 1,230 | 5 | R Galpin | R Boss | 5/2 |
| 23 Apl | Sandown | Artaius | Classic Trial | 5,117 | 10 | Mrs G Getty II | M V O'Brien(I) | EvF |
| 30 Apl | Newbury | Golden Libra | Garter | 2,183 | 5 | Mrs D Solomon | R Hannon | 6/1 |
| 3 May | Chester | Slim Jim | Ladbroke Chester Hcp | 2,309 | 10 | P Roberts | I Balding | 9/2 |
| 3 May | Chester | Hot Grove | Chester Vase | 7,570 | 12 | Lord Leverhulme | R Houghton | 10/3 |
| 3 May | Chester | All Hope(F) | | 1,573 | 7 | D Robinson | M Jarvis | 5/1 |
| 4 May | Chester | Pak Lok | | 1,014 | 7 | W Sulke | R Houghton | 9/2 |
| 10 May | York | Amaranda(USA) | | 1,875 | 5 | R Moller | H Wragg | 9/2 |
| 12 May | York | Bright Finish | Yorkshire Cup | 12,124 | 14 | J H Whitney | J Tree | 10/3F |
| 16 May | York | Degas | | 759 | 5 | R Overall | F Maxwell | 5/6F |
| 16 May | Windsor | Fire Parcel | | 900 | 5 | R Cooney | R Hannon | 10/1F |
| 20 May | Kempton | Emboss | | 1,293 | 5 | R Galpin | R Boss | 8/15F |
| 21 May | Kempton | Muster Lane | | 950 | 6 | Mrs R Hutchinson | H B T Jones | 4/1 |
| 21 May | Kempton | Lord Helpus | Silver Jubilee | 7,733 | 10 | M Standen | B W Hills | 11/2 |
| 24 May | Salisbury | Lady Be Quick | | 954 | 5 | Duke of Marlborough | J Tree | 9/4F |
| 1 June | Epsom | Fire Angel | Great Surrey | 3,054 | 5 | R Cooney | R Hannon | 13/8F |
| 1 June | Epsom | The Minstrel (Can) | The Derby | 107,530 | 12 | R Sangster | M V O'Brien(I) | 5/1 |
| 4 June | Epsom | Elland Road | | 1,270 | 8 | M Cussins | R Armstrong | 1/2F |
| 11 June | York | Elland Road | Daniel Prenn | 2,415 | 10 | M Cussins | R Armstrong | 5/6F |
| 14 June | Royal Ascot | Solinus | Coventry | 15,386 | 6 | D Schwartz | M V O'Brien(I) | 7/4F |
| 15 June | Royal Ascot | Amaranda(USA) | Queen Mary | 13,046 | 5 | R B Moller | H Wragg | 4/6F |
| 16 June | Royal Ascot | Emboss | Norfolk | 8,500 | 5 | T Saud | R Boss | 11/4 |
| 16 June | Royal Ascot | Sagaro | Gold Cup | 17,837 | 20 | G A Oldham | F Boutin(F) | 9/4 |

(I) = Ireland (F) = France (USA) = America (Can) = Canada

| Date | Race Course | Horse | Race | Value £ | Dist Fur | Owner | Trainer | S/P |
|---|---|---|---|---|---|---|---|---|
| 17 June | Royal Ascot | Meneval(USA) | Hardwicke | 13,525 | 12 | Mrs G Getty II | M V O'Brien(I) | 2/1F |
| 17 June | Royal Ascot | Oldswalk(USA) | King's Stand | 19,592 | 5 | R Sangster | M V O'Brien(I) | 4/6F |
| 17 June | Royal Ascot | John Cherry | Queen Alexandra | 4,292 | 22 | M Ritzenberg | H B T Jones | 4/6F |
| 18 June | Ascot | Transworld(USA) | Churchill | 2,616 | 12 | S Fraser | M V O'Brien(I) | 6/5F |
| 22 June | Salisbury | Persian Bold | | 1,054 | 6 | R Vahabzadeh | A Ingham | 5/6F |
| 24 June | Lingfield | Hill Station | | 1,272 | 16 | D Wollard | M Bolton | 5/2F |
| 2 July | Sandown | Petty Purse | Star | 3,043 | 5 | E Holland-Martin | R Houghton | 10/11F |
| 2 July | Sandown | Artaius | Joe Coral Eclipse Stks | 37,792 | 10 | Mrs G Getty II | M V O'Brien(I) | 9/2 |
| 2 July | Sandown | Rhodomantade | Victoria Hcp | 2,120 | 7 | J Carrington | P Makin | 7/1 |
| 5 July | Newmarket | Turkish Treasure (USA) | Cherry Hinton | 13,485 | 6 | R Sangster | M V O'Brien(I) | 2/5F |
| 5 July | Newmarket | Lord Helpus | Princess of Wales | 12,438 | 12 | M Standen | B W Hills | 5/1 |
| 5 July | Newmarket | Hawkins | Chesterfields | 2,506 | 5 | R Galpin | R Boss | 10/11F |
| 7 July | Newmarket | Fast Colour | Fulbourn | 2,150 | 6 | Mrs H B T Jones | H B T Jones | 4/1 |
| 8 July | York | Champagne Willie | Monkgate | 2,227 | 8 | Mrs B Dash | N Callaghan | 4/7F |
| 8 July | York | Aythorpe | Black Duck | 2,515 | 6 | D Cock | N Callaghan | 7/4 |
| 9 July | York | Misalliance | | 1,696 | 12 | J H Whitney | J Tree | 10/3 |
| 12 July | Kempton | Persian Bold | | 1,545 | 6 | R Vahabzadeh | A Ingham | 4/5F |
| 12 July | Kempton | Lucky Mickmoosh | | 1,266 | 12 | Mrs E Harrison | J L Winter | 10/11 |
| 12 July | Kempton | Orange Squash | | 1,136 | 8 | J Haverhais | B Hanbury | 9/2 |
| 20 July | Sandown | Iliad | | 1,343 | 7 | A Macdonald-Buchanan | J Tree | 7/4F |
| 21 July | Sandown | Gypsy Castle* | | 616 | 5 | D Prenn | J L Winter | 9/4F |
| 22 July | Ascot | Sir Raymond | | 2,511 | 10 | Mrs A Manning | M V O'Brien(I) | 11/10F |
| 22 July | Ascot | Tardot | Hyperion | 3,126 | 6 | R Sangster | M V O'Brien(I) | 8/11F |
| 23 July | Ascot | The Minstrel (Can) | King George VI and Queen Elizabeth Diamond | 88,355 | 12 | R Sangster | M V O'Brien(I) | 7/4F |
| 23 July | Ascot | Valuation | Brown Jack | 2,934 | 16 | The Queen | W Hern | 7/2 |
| 27 July | Goodwood | Persian Bold | Richmond | 16,936 | 6 | R Vahabzadeh | A Ingham | 4/6F |
| 27 July | Goodwood | Artaius | Sussex | 31,409 | 8 | Mrs G Getty II | M V O'Brien(I) | 6/4F |
| 28 July | Goodwood | Captain's Wings | | 1,755 | 8 | M House | R Boss | 9/2 |
| 29 July | Newmarket | Greenhill God | | 1,676 | 6 | Sir C Clore | M Stoute | 13/8F |
| 29 July | Goodwood | Hillbrow | | 2077 | 6 | Mrs L Buswell | R Armstrong | 8/1 |
| 29 July | Goodwood | Ad Libra | Extel | 8,623 | 10 | Mrs J Rogers | R Houghton | 4/1F |
| 5 Aug | Lingfield | Girl of Shiraz | | 885 | 12 | P Milani | R Houghton | |
| 5 Aug | Lingfield | Belle-et-Vite | | 975 | 6 | W French | P Mitchell | 6/1 |
| 12 Aug | Newbury | Amaranda | St Hugh's | 4,479 | 5 | R B Moller | H Wragg | 4/9F |
| 12 Aug | Newbury | Court Barons | | 1,143 | 6 | R B Moller | H Wragg | 6/4F |
| 13 Aug | Newbury | Valinsky | Geoffrey Freer | 12,688 | 13 | Sir C Clore | M V O'Brien(I) | 8/13F |
| 13 Aug | Newbury | English Harbour | | 1,366 | 7 | The Queen | I Balding | 9/2 |
| 16 Aug | Epsom | Epsom Imp | Harewood | 2,557 | 5 | Mrs O Negus-Fancey | D Kent | 2/1F |
| 17 Aug | York | Negative Response | Rous S | 2,863 | 5 | Miss M Sheriffe | J Tree | 5/4F |
| 17 Aug | York | Alleged | Great Voltigeur | 17,757 | 12 | R J Fluor | M V O'Brien(I) | 5/2 |
| 18 Aug | York | Galleto | Galtres | 3,085 | 12 | J Mulcahy | M V O'Brien (I) | 11/1 |
| 25 Aug | Haydock | Cladagh | Restoration | 1,668 | 10 | R More O'Ferrall | H Wragg | 1/2F |
| 26 Aug | Newmarket | Girl of Shiraz | | 1,072 | 12 | P Milani | R Houghton | 12/1 |
| 27 Aug | Goodwood | Be My Guest (USA) | Waterford Crystal Mile | 17,013 | 8 | Mrs A Manning | M V O'Brien(I) | 6/4F |
| 29 Aug | Epsom | Master Craftsman | | 825 | 6 | Mrs A Campbell Harris | R Houghton | 5/4F |
| 29 Aug | Epsom | Peruchio | | 1,601 | 10 | T Morris | R Akehurst | 5/1 |
| 31 Aug | York | Cladagh | Silver Jubilee Trophy | 5,767 | 10½ | R More O'Ferrall | H Wragg | 5/2F |

*Dead Heat (I) = Ireland (USA) = America (Can) = Canada

| Date | Race Course | Horse | Race | Value £ | Dist Fur | Owner | Trainer | S/P |
|---|---|---|---|---|---|---|---|---|
| 1 Sept | York | Cherry Hinton | Tadcaster | 3,189 | 6 | R B Moller | H Wragg | 6/4F |
| 5 Sept | Windsor | Home Run | | 951 | 6 | Capt N Peto | J Tree | 7/2 |
| 5 Sept | Windsor | Aytidee | | 605 | 10 | P Gratsos | D Ringer | 9/4F |
| 13 Sept | Yarmouth | First Joker | | 658 | 10 | Mrs L Schwitzer | R Armstrong | 6/1 |
| 13 Sept | Yarmouth | Hugo di Tours | | 707 | 6 | Mrs E Palmier | L Cumani | 11/10F |
| 14 Sept | Yarmouth | Crown Major | | 550 | 7 | B Grove | M Bolton | 5/2F |
| 23 Sept | Ascot | Cherry Hinton | Argos Star | 6,725 | 8 | R B Moller | H Wragg | 11/10F |
| 23 Sept | Ascot | Home Run | Phillips Electrical | 6212 | 7 | Capt N Peto | J Tree | 11/4 |
| 26 Sept | Goodwood | John Cherry | Stonewall | 2,966 | 19 | M Ritzenburg | H B T Jones | 5/4F |
| 26 Sept | Goodwood | Overlock | | 952 | 10 | R B Moller | H Wragg | 11/2 |
| 1 Oct | Newmarket | Goblin | Westley | 2337 | 7 | W M Douglas-Home | W Wightman | 9/4F |
| 5 Oct | Lingfield | Heir Presumptive | | 1,006 | 6 | Lord Leverhulme | R Houghton | 11/8F |
| 5 Oct | Lingfield | Wager Ballot | | 1,037 | 7 | Mrs B Firestone | R Houghton | 11/2 |
| 6 Oct | Lingfield | Double Form | Burr | 2,805 | 7 | Baroness H Thyssen | R Houghton | 2/1F |
| 6 Oct | Lingfield | Hillbrow | | 1,013 | 7 | Mrs L Boswell | R Armstrong | 8/1 |
| 7 Oct | Ascott | Matinale | | 1,428 | 16 | Mrs O Thurston | D Kent | 7/1 |
| 8 Oct | Ascot | Yamadori | Brocas | 2,624 | 8 | J Kashiyama | R Houghton | 5/1 |
| 14 Oct | Newmarket | Try My Best | Wm Hill Dewhurst | 39,936 | 7 | R Sangster | M V O'Brien(I) | 4/1F |
| 18 Oct | Sandown | Overlook | Leatherhead | 1,116 | 10 | R B Moller | H Wragg | 2/1F |
| 19 Oct | Sandown | Heir Presumptive | | 1,240 | 7 | Lord Leverhulme | R Houghton | 7/4F |
| 19 Oct | Sandown | Hallodri | | 1,257 | 14 | Count C Seilern | J Hindley | 4/1 |
| 20 Oct | Newbury | Persian Bold* | Horris Hill | 7,581 | 7 | R Vahabzadeh | A Ingham | 9/2 |
| 28 Oct | Newmarket | Empty Jest | | 1,274 | 14 | D Adams | W Elsey | 9/2 |
| 1 Nov | Leicester | Makar-March | | 701 | 5 | S Cohen | T Gosling | 6/5F |
| 1 Nov | Leicester | Can Run | | 1,266 | 7 | J Rose | D Gandolfo | 3/1F |

1977: 103 wins; 82 2nds; 62 3rds; 512 rides

| Date | Race Course | Horse | Race | Value £ | Dist Fur | Owner | Trainer | S/P |
|---|---|---|---|---|---|---|---|---|
| 1978 | | | | | | | | |
| 30 Mar | Teesside | Miss Mops | | 697 | 5 | R Ogle | P Rohan | 2/1F |
| 30 Mar | Teesside | Wallop | | 778 | 10 | Lord Harrington | M Jarvis | 4/5F |
| 4 Apl | Haydock | Salbob | | 1,017 | 5 | B B Jones (Bangor) Ltd | P Rohan | 6/5F |
| 4 Apl | Haydock | Manor Farm Boy | Field Marshal | 3,716 | 5 | Manor Farm Dairies (Haverhill Ltd) | W O'Gorman | 4/6F |
| 6 Apl | Doncaster | Manor Farm Boy | | 1,900 | 6 | Manor Farm Dairies (Haverhill Ltd) | W O'Gorman | 8/13F |
| 15 Apl | Newbury | Yamadora | Newbury Spring Cup | 4,916 | 8 | J Kashiyama | R Houghton | 11/4F |
| 18 Apl | Newmarket | Gold Prospector | | 2,071 | 6 | C Driver | R Armstrong | 6/1 |
| 18 Apl | Newmarket | Spanish Armada | | 1,921 | 14 | R Wheatley Ltd | W Marshall | 2/1F |
| 19 Apl | Newmarket | Crest of Gold | | 1,270 | 5 | T Tek Tan | W O'Gorman | 3/1 |
| 20 Apl | Newmarket | House Guard | | 2,379 | 7 | Kalifa Sasi | R Armstrong | 3/1F |
| 26 Apl | Epsom | Cry No More | Great Surrey Hcp | 2,406 | 6 | W Lusty | W Marshall | 10/3F |
| 9 May | Chester | Overlook | Ladbroke Chester Hcp | 2,473 | 10 | R B Moller | H Wragg | 9/2 |
| 9 May | Chester | Yamadori | Earl of Chester Hcp | 2,159 | 7 | J Kashiyama | R Houghton | 11/4F |
| 10 May | Chester | Singador | | 1,077 | 5 | Mrs H Attwood | P Rohan | 9/4 |
| 10 May | Chester | Royal Emblem | | 1,657 | 7 | R B Moller | H Wragg | 9/4F |
| 11 May | Chester | Heir Presumptive | Dee Stakes | 7,196 | 10 | Lord Leverhulme | R Houghton | 9/2 |
| 16 May | York | House Guard | Sinnington Hcp | 2,658 | 7 | Kalifa Sasi | R Armstrong | 2/1F |
| 16 May | York | Ceilidh | | 2,456 | 8 | Lady Murless | Denys Smith | 8/1 |
| 19 May | Newbury | Hurakan | | 1,266 | 11 | Lady Beaverbrook | M Jarvis | 9/1 |
| 19 May | Newbury | Casino Royale | | 2,301 | 7 | J Pearce | Doug Smith | 7/2 |
| 20 May | Newmarket | Double Form | Great Eastern Hcp | 3,921 | 6 | Baroness H Thyssen | R Houghton | 9/4F |
| 20 May | Newmarket | Intercraft Boy | | 1,674 | 5 | Intercraft | W Marshall | 11/2 |
| 23 May | Goodwood | Bogey Man | | 1,730 | 8 | G Greenwood | W Marshall | 11/2 |
| 24 May | Goodwood | Elland Road | | 1,515 | 10 | M Cussins | R Armstrong | 11/2 |
| 26 May | Haydock | Prince Titian | | 1,627 | 8 | Mrs W Sulke | R Houghton | 5/1 |

* Dead Heat (I) = Ireland

| Date | Race Course | Horse | Race | Value £ | Dist Fur | Owner | Trainer | S/P |
|---|---|---|---|---|---|---|---|---|
| 29 May | Sandown | Elland Road | Whitsun Cup | 3,635 | 8 | M Cussins | R Armstrong | 4/1 |
| 2 June | Kempton | Catechism | | 1,214 | 11 | S Keswick | J Tree | 5/2F |
| 3 June | Kempton | Pollerton | Tote Golden Jubilee | 3,616 | 11 | Mrs R Vereker | H B T Jones | 7/2 |
| 2 June | Kempton | Winter Wind | | 1,639 | 5 | C Driver | R Armstrong | 7/4F |
| 12 June | Lingfield | Swinging Sam | | 2,768 | 6 | S Hsu | R Armstrong | 5/4 |
| 12 June | Lingfield | Jubilee Lord | | 1,016 | 12 | G Leeven | R Houghton | 7/1 |
| 13 June | Lingfield | Galka | | 1,450 | 5 | Baroness H Thyssen | R Houghton | 15/8F |
| 13 June | Lingfield | Attivo | | 1,209 | 16 | P O'Sullevan | P Mitchell | 6/5F |
| 16 June | York | Kandos(USA) | | 2,201 | 16 | U Wijewardene | R Armstrong | 11/2 |
| 17 June | York | Plektrudis | | 2,070 | 8 | Mrs E Palmier | L Cumani | 7/2 |
| 20 June | Royal Ascot | Jaazeiro | St James's Palace | 14,977 | 8 | R Sangster | M V O'Brien(I) | 5/2 |
| 21 June | Royal Ascot | Billion | Bessborough | 6,503 | 12 | N B Hunt | J Dunlop | 13/2 |
| 23 June | Royal Ascot | Solinus | Kings Stand | 22,400 | 5 | D Schwarz | M V O'Brien(I) | 4/6F |
| 24 June | Ascot | Noble Quillo (USA) | Churchill | 4,090 | 12 | Mrs W Haefner | M V O'Brien(I) | 9/4F |
| 24 June | Ascot | Imperial Fling | | 2,988 | 5 | G Strawbridge | H B T Jones | 13/8F |
| 29 June | Salisbury | Escape Me Never | | 983 | 8 | Lavinia Duchess of Norfolk | J Dunlop | 6/4F |
| 30 June | Lingfield | Rheinbloom | | 953 | 12 | Mrs E Longton | J Tree | 7/4 |
| 30 June | Lingfield | Attivo | | 1,707 | 16 | P O'Sullevan | P Mitchell | 15/8F |
| 30 June | Lingfield | Bonnie Isle | | 1,102 | 6 | A Struthers | J Dunlop | 11/10F |
| 4 July | Yarmouth | Lorelene (F) | | 1,259 | 10 | L Gatto-Roissard | L Cumani | 13/8F |
| 5 July | Yarmouth | Crest of Gold | | 1,173 | 5 | T Tek Tan | W O'Gorman | 8/11F |
| 7 July | Sandown | Go Total | | 1,973 | 5 | Hendon Central Garage | R Boss | 4/5F |
| 7 July | Sandown | Bogey Man | | 2,776 | 8 | G Greenwood | W Marshall | 9/1 |
| 8 July | Sandown | Tribal Warrior | | 2,944 | 5 | M House | R Boss | 8/11F |
| 10 July | Windsor | Just Married | | 921 | 5 | Mrs E Longton | J Tree | 8/13F |
| 10 July | Windsor | General Atty | | 1,233 | 5 | U Wijewardene | R Armstrong | EvF |
| 11 July | Newmarket | Pollerton | Princess of Wales | 16,068 | 12 | Mrs R Vereker | H B T Jones | 7/1 |
| 13 July | Newmarket | Solinus | William Hill July Cup | 23,225 | 6 | D Schwarz | M V O'Brien(I) | 4/7F |
| 17 July | Windsor | General Atty | | 1,185 | 6 | U Wijewardene | R Armstrong | 8/15F |
| 19 July | Sandown | Solimena | | 1,783 | 7 | C A B St George | H Cecil | 2/1 |
| 19 July | Sandown | Celebrated | | 2,511 | 10 | N B Hunt | J Dunlop | 9/4 |
| 26 July | Goodwood | Jaazeiro(USA) | Sussex | 34,610 | 8 | R Sangster | M V O'Brien(I) | 8/13F |
| 29 July | Goodwood | Valour(USA) | Warren | 3,007 | 12 | G Ward | R Houghton | 4/6F |
| 5 Aug | Lingfield | Arapahos | Gatwick Hcp | 5,560 | 16 | R Sangster | B W Hills | 10/11F |
| 9 Aug | Yarmouth | Le Solentaire | | 1,335 | 7 | Sheikh Mohammed | R Houghton | 2/1F |
| 10 Aug | Yarmouth | Chalumeau | | 971 | 7 | Mrs D Coker | W Hastings-Bass | 5/4F |
| 14 Aug | Leicester | Wolveriana | | 1,197 | 8 | Col Sir D Clague | J Winter | 9/4F |
| 19 Aug | Kempton | Swiss Maid | Twickenham | 6,921 | 7 | M Fine | P Kelleway | 15/2 |
| 21 Aug | Windsor | Nusantara | | 1,023 | 6 | F Crouch | R Armstrong | 8/13F |
| 22 Aug | York | Hawaiian Sound | Benson & Hedges Gold Cup | 49,206 | 10½ | R Sangster | B W Hills | 2/1F |
| 23 Aug | York | Jeroboam | Convivial | 3,756 | 6 | L Lilley | H Wragg | 10/3 |
| 24 Aug | York | Solinus | Wm Hill Sprint | 18,640 | 5 | D Schwartz | M V O'Brien(I) | 1/2F |
| 24 Aug | York | Spence Bay | City of York | 3,137 | 7 | Mrs R McGrath | S McGrath(I) | 9/2 |
| 28 Aug | Ripon | Hedingham Lad | | 1,721 | 5 | G Tanner | W O'Gorman | 4/1 |
| 28 Aug | Ripon | Great Monza | | 1,016 | 12 | A Chin Chong | A Hide | 4/1 |
| 8 Sept | Lingfield | Miss Mirage | | 859 | 12 | I Thoday | R Armstrong | 7/4F |
| 8 Sept | Lingfield | Merci | | 1,255 | 6 | E Sign | W O'Gorman | 4/1 |
| 11 Sept | Windsor | Hedingham Lad | | 1,182 | 5 | G Tanner | W O'Gorman | 5/4F |
| 11 Sept | Windsor | Hailane | | 1,119 | 6 | L A H Ames Builders | R Hannon | 8/11F |
| 11 Sept | Windsor | Kerry Bold | | 815 | 10 | Mrs A Banks | M McCourt | 3/1 |
| 13 Sept | Doncaster | Epsom Imp | Scarbrough | 3,028 | 5 | Mrs O Negus-Fancey | J Holt | 2/1 |
| 13 Sept | Doncaster | Son Fils | Fitzwilliam | 2,544 | 10 | Mrs B Davis | R Hannon | 9/4F |
| 14 Sept | Doncaster | Tribal Call | | 1,836 | 5 | Y Tanmoto | P Metcalfe | 5/1F |

(I) = Ireland (F) = France (USA) = America

| Date | Race Course | Horse | Race | Value £ | Dist Fur | Owner | Trainer | S/P |
|---|---|---|---|---|---|---|---|---|
| 21 Sept | Yarmouth | Spring in the Air | | 860 | 7 | G Guetta | L Cumani | 8/13F |
| 21 Sept | Yarmouth | Do Be Daring | | 1,184 | 7 | L Gatto-Roissard | L Cumani | 8/13F |
| 21 Sept | Yarmouth | Eludiana | | 1,027 | 10 | Mrs E Palmieri | L Cumani | 4/7F |
| 28 Sept | Newmarket | Hutton Girl | | 2,397 | 10 | Mrs B Shack | P Kelleway | 4/5F |
| 2 Oct | Goodwood | Billion | Stonehill | 3,603 | 9 | N B Hunt | J Dunlop | 1/2F |
| 2 Oct | Goodwood | House Guard | | 1,965 | 7 | Kalifa Sasi | R Armstrong | 5/1 |
| 4 Oct | Newmarket | Baptism | Dry Cane Nursery Hcp | 2,827 | 6 | J H Whitney | J Tree | 15/2 |
| 5 Oct | Newmarket | Junius(USA) | Middle Park | 29,930 | 6 | S Fraser | M V O'Brien(I) | 7/1 |
| 7 Oct | Newmarket | Swiss Maid | Sun Chariot | 13,428 | 10 | M Fine | P Kelleway | 5/1 |
| 19 Oct | Newmarket | Jeroboam | Birdcage Nursery Hcp | 2,836 | 6 | J Lilley | H Wragg | 7/4F |
| 20 Oct | Newmarket | Baptism | Tattersalls Nursery Hcp | 3,027 | 7 | J H Whitney | J Tree | EvF |
| 25 Oct | Sandown | Silver Bay | | 1,027 | 8 | Mrs J Mullion | R Armstrong | 10/11F |
| 25 Oct | Sandown | House Guard | Moor Lane Hcp | 2,506 | 7 | Kalifa Sasi | R Armstrong | 5/1 |
| 25 Oct | Sandown | Peerless Prince | | 1,704 | 10 | A Reynolds | P Kelleway | 13/2 |
| 3 Nov | Haydock | Silver Lord | | 1,772 | 7 | C Brittain | C Brittain | 5/1 |
| 4 Nov | Newmarket | The Martyr | | 937 | 6 | L Tory | V Cross | 11/2F |
| 4 Nov | Newmarket | Balacho | | 1,272 | 10 | J Woodman | S Woodman | 6/4F |
| 4 Nov | Newmarket | Catechism(USA) | | 1,640 | 12 | S Keswick | J Tree | 6/1 |
| 7 Nov | Lingfield | Pluval | | 921 | 5 | Mrs J Drake | W Hastings-Bass | 4/9F |

1978: 97 wins; 78 2nds; 61 3rds; 485 rides

| Date | Race Course | Horse | Race | Value £ | Dist Fur | Owner | Trainer | S/P |
|---|---|---|---|---|---|---|---|---|
| 1979 | | | | | | | | |
| 16 Apl | Kempton | Young Man | | 2,569 | 12 | M Fine | P Kelleway | 6/4F |
| 26 Apl | Epsom | Titauri | | 2,124 | 5 | Mrs M Kendall | P V Doyle(I) | 9/4 |
| 27 Apl | Sandown | Shere Beauty | | 1,417 | 5 | Mrs J Nicolaides | P Kelleway | 4/6F |
| 9 May | Chester | Record Lightning | | 1,981 | 7 | K Marcell | P Kelleway | 11/8F |
| 14 May | Windsor | Charming Native | | 896 | 5 | K Abdulla | J Tree | 5/1 |
| 16 May | York | Marzook | | 2,187 | 16 | K Abdulla | J Tree | 10/11F |
| 17 May | York | Thatching | Duke of York | 10,792 | 6 | R Sangster | M V O'Brien(I) | 7/2 |
| 17 May | York | Buz Kashi | | 2,557 | 8 | A Oppenheimer | H Wragg | 12/1 |
| 18 May | Newmarket | Rollahead | | 2,088 | 5 | R McAlpine | J Hindley | 5/6F |
| 18 May | Newmarket | House Guard | | 2,813 | 7 | Kalifa Sasi | R Armstrong | 85/40F |
| 19 May | Newbury | Known Fact | | 1,545 | 5 | K Abdulla | J Tree | 6/4F |
| 19 May | Newbury | Rhyme Royal | | 2,616 | 11 | The Queen | R Hern | 11/8F |
| 22 May | Goodwood | Baltic | | 1,383 | 12 | R Hollingsworth | R Hern | 9/4F |
| 28 May | Sandown | Brian's Venture | Whitsun Cup | 3,863 | 8 | R Lalemont | R Hannon | 13/2 |
| 28 May | Sandown | Marzook | | 2,040 | 14 | K Abdulla | J Tree | 5/2 |
| 1 June | Kempton | Spartan Call | | 1,318 | 7 | H Weavers | R Armstrong | 8/1 |
| 5 June | Salisbury | Abeer | | 1,492 | 5 | K Abdulla | J Tree | 9/4F |
| 8 June | Epsom | Braconda | | 2,637 | 5 | F J Crouch | R Armstrong | 3/8F |
| 11 June | Lingfield | Loyal Manacle | | 2,637 | 5 | Y Bin Saud | R Boss | 3/1 |
| 12 June | Yarmouth | Minigold | | 638 | 8 | Mrs G Davison | A Davison | 7/1 |
| 13 June | Newbury | Claerwen | | 1,784 | 5 | Lady Murless | J Tree | 11/2 |
| 15 June | York | Charming Native (USA) | | 4,071 | 6 | K Abdulla | J Tree | 11/4 |
| 15 June | York | Brian's Venture‡ | | 3,178 | 7 | R Lelemont | R Hannon | 8/1 |
| 16 June | York | Choice | | 1,725 | 5 | O/trainer | D Thom | |
| 16 June | York | The Shrew | Michael Sobell Hcp | 2,560 | 8 | Lady Halifax | J Dunlop | 4/1 |
| 16 June | York | Stetchworth | Michael Sobell Hcp | 3,840 | 14 | R B Moller | H Wragg | 4/1 |
| 19 June | Royal Ascot | Baptism | Queen Anne | 10,830 | 8 | J H Whitney | J Tree | 6/1 |
| 19 June | Royal Ascot | Crimson Beau | Prince of Wales | 17,170 | 10 | H Spearing | P Cole | 17/2 |
| 21 June | Royal Ascot | Thatching | Cork & Orrery | 10,864 | 6 | R Sangster | M V O'Brien(I) | 6/1 |

‡ On objection (I) = Ireland (USA) = America

| Date | Race Course | Horse | Race | Value £ | Dist Fur | Owner | Trainer | S/P |
|---|---|---|---|---|---|---|---|---|
| 21 June | Royal Ascot | Le Moss | Gold Cup | 27,060 | 10 | Count d'Alessio | H Cecil | 7/4F |
| 21 June | Royal Ascot | Starway | Chesham | 7,187 | 6 | Mrs L Glaser | P Kelleway | 9/4F |
| 21 June | Royal Ascot | Sea Chimes | King George V | 6,212 | 12 | J Thursby | J Dunlop | 3/1F |
| 27 June | Salisbury | Columnist | | 1,283 | 6 | J H Whitney | J Tree | 10/3 |
| 27 June | Salisbury | Alnasr Ashamali | | 1,080 | 10 | E Alkhalifa | R Boss | 11/4F |
| 2 July | Windsor | Charming Native | | 1,465 | 6 | K Abdulla | J Tree | 2/5F |
| 7 July | Sandown | Given | | 2,406 | 16 | Susan Hadida Ltd | P Kelleway | 3/1 |
| 11 July | Newmarket | Strathspey | Duchess of Montrose Hcp | 3,817 | 7 | Mrs R Chaplin | I Balding | 5/6F |
| 12 July | Newmarket | Thatching | July Cup | 26,885 | 6 | R Sangster | M V O'Brien(I) | 2/1F |
| 14 July | York | Nusantara | Fishergate | 3,137 | 6 | F Crouch | R Armstrong | 3/1 |
| 14 July | York | State Trooper | | 2,712 | 7 | R Prettie | B Hanbury | 8/1 |
| 19 July | Kempton | House Guard | | 1,758 | 8 | Kalifa Sasi | R Armstrong | 5/2 |
| 25 July | Sandown | Moore's Concerto | | 1,853 | 7 | Moores Furnishings | R Armstrong | 12/1 |
| 25 July | Sandown | House Guard | | 2,586 | 8 | Kalifa Sasi | R Armstrong | 3/1F |
| 28 July | Ascot | Abington | Granville | 4,084 | 6 | R Moller | H Wragg | 10/11F |
| 30 July | Newcastle | Jeroboam | Beeswing | 12,170 | 7 | J A C Lilley | H Wragg | 4/5F |
| 31 July | Goodwood | Strathspey | | 2,998 | 7 | Mrs R Chaplin | I Balding | 13/8F |
| 3 Aug | Newmarket | House Guard | | 1,853 | 8 | Kalifa Sasi | R Armstrong | 5/4F |
| 13 Aug | Newcastle | Valeriga | Northumberland Sprint | 10,006 | 6 | Count d'Alessio | L Cumani | 9/4F |
| 22 Aug | York | Harlyn | | 2,666 | 5 | M Hambley | P Rohan | 9/4F |
| 22 Aug | York | Noble Saint | Great Voltigeur | 20,900 | 12 | R R Guest | R Armstrong | 8/13F |
| 22 Aug | York | Beggars Bridge | Falmouth | 3,293 | 10½ | T Smith | D Laing | 11/2 |
| 22 Aug | York | Moore's Song | Convivial | 4,584 | 6 | Moores Furnishings | R Armstrong | 11/4F |
| 27 Aug | Newcastle | Beldale Conflict | | 1,881 | 7 | Beldale Homes Ltd | M Jarvis | 5/4 |
| 29 Aug | Yarmouth | Nusantara | | 1,671 | 6 | F Crouch | R Armstrong | 5/1 |
| 30 Aug | Yarmouth | Jazz King | | 1,331 | 7 | J Carmichael | R Armstrong | 5/2F |
| 30 Aug | Yarmouth | Repeat Performance | | 832 | 5 | J Carmichael | R Armstrong | 5/4F |
| 31 Aug | Sandown | Bonnie Isle | Atalanta | 3,059 | 8 | A Struthers | J Dunlop | 11/8 |
| 24 Sept | Leicester | Good Prospector | | 1,948 | 6 | C Driver | R Armstrong | 11/1 |
| 27 Sept | Ascot | Absalom | Diadem | 9,536 | 6 | Mrs C Alington | R Jarvis | 9/4F |
| 28 Sept | Ascot | Swinging Sam* | Wm Hill Trophy | 2,128 | 5 | S Hsu | R Armstrong | 7/4 |
| 28 Sept | Ascot | Cragador | Morston | 3,286 | 5 | Sir P Oppenheimer | H Wragg | 7/2 |
| 29 Sept | Ascot | House Guard | Cavendish Cape | 9,169 | 7 | Kalifa Sasi | R Armstrong | 7/2F |
| 1 Oct | Newbury | Billion(USA) | Stonehill Hcp | 3,713 | 16 | N B Hunt | J Dunlop | 9/4 |
| 2 Oct | Nottingham | Hot Case | | 1,202 | 6 | Mrs H Heinz | J Dunlop | EvF |
| 2 Oct | Nottingham | Sipapa | | 1,197 | 6 | M Mutawa | J Dunlop | 7/4F |
| 6 Oct | Newmarket | Topsy | Sun Chariot | 15,972 | 10 | R B Moller | H Wragg | 7/2F |
| 11 Oct | York | Absalom | Playboy | 5,689 | 6 | Mrs C Alington | R Jarvis | 1/2F |
| 14 Oct | Newmarket | Renovate | Bloodstock & General | 4,071 | 5 | M Taylor | J Hardy | |
| 19 Oct | Newmarket | Monteverdi | Dewhurst | 36,050 | 7 | R Sangster | M V O'Brien(I) | |
| 20 Oct | Sandown | Night Alert(USA) | Houghton | 5,064 | 7 | R Sangster | M V O'Brien(I) | 10/11F |
| 24 Oct | Sandown | Anna Batic | | 1,450 | 5 | E Alkhalifa | R Armstrong | 9/11F |
| 24 Oct | Sandown | Ringgit | | 2,264 | 8 | U Wijewardene | R Armstrong | 10/3F |
| 27 Oct | Doncaster | Moorestyle | | 1,718 | 5 | Moores Furnishings | R Armstrong | 6/13F |
| 27 Oct | Doncaster | Beaureef Boy | | 2,662 | 14 | D Prenn | J Dunlop | 15/1 |
| 2 Nov | Newmarket | Intercraft | | 1,760 | 7 | Intercraft | P Cole | 11/8F |
| 2 Nov | Newmarket | Blues Swinger | | 2,043 | 6 | Wheatley Leisure | W Marshall | 7/1 |
| 10 Nov | Doncaster | Susarma(USA) | Poppy Hcp | 4,006 | 5 | R Tikkoo | A E Breasley | 10/1 |

1979: 77 wins; 54 2nds; 40 3rds; 403 rides

| 1980 | | | | | | | | |
|---|---|---|---|---|---|---|---|---|
| 24 Mar | Leicester | Baron Blakeney | | 1,303 | 10 | Wheatley Leisure Ltd | W Marshall | 11/8F |
| 31 Mar | Nottingham | Tallishire Abode | | 945 | 5 | Tallishire Ltd | G Toft | 7/2 |

* Dead Heat (I) = Ireland (USA) = America

| Date | Race Course | Horse | Race | Value £ | Dist Fur | Owner | Trainer | S/P |
|---|---|---|---|---|---|---|---|---|
| 1 Apl | Kempton | Broad Principle | Playboy Bookmakers | 3,189 | 10 | L Holliday | M Stoute | 10/3 |
| 15 Apl | Newmarket | Loralane | | 2,617 | 7 | Sir P Oppenheimer | H Wragg | 12/1 |
| 16 Apl | Newmarket | Moorestyle | Newmarket Tote Free Hcp | 13,142 | 7 | Moores Furnishings | R Armstrong | 6/1 |
| 16 Apl | Newmarket | Gypsy Dancer (F) | Ladbroke Abernant Stks | 4,339 | 6 | R Griggs & Co Ltd | W O'Gorman | 9/2 |
| 18 Apl | Newbury | Saviour | | 2,589 | 11 | J Morrison | J Tree | 9/2 |
| 18 Apl | Newbury | Millingsdale Lillie | Fred Darling | 8,396 | 7 | R Sangster | C R Nelson | 5/2F |
| 23 Apl | Epsom | Son Fils | | 2,825 | 12 | Mrs B Davis | R Hannon | 5/4F |
| 24 Apl | Epsom | Bay Street | Princess Elizabeth | 10,202 | 8 | Oceanic Ltd | R Houghton | 11/4 |
| 24 Apl | Epsom | Susarma(USA) | | 2,721 | 5 | R Tikkoo | A E Breasley | 9/2F |
| 8 Apl | Warwick | Double High | | 745 | 10 | R Clifford Turner | M Stoute | 11/10F |
| 25 Apl | Sandown | Ringgit | Sandown Cup | 3,739 | 10 | U Wijewardene | R Armstrong | 7/4F |
| 26 Apl | Sandown | Carry on Again | | 1,940 | 5 | L Asu | R Armstrong | 2/1F |
| 26 Apl | Sandown | Gregorian(USA) | Westbury | 11,890 | 10 | D Schwartz | M V O'Brien(I) | 11/4 |
| 26 Apl | Sandown | African Song | | 1,875 | 5 | G Kaye | P Kelleway | 13/8F |
| 30 Apl | Ascot | Dukedom | White Rose | 9,297 | 10 | The Queen | I Balding | 11/4 |
| 2 May | Newmarket | Bold Image | Ely | 3,381 | 6 | D Prenn | J Winter | 9/2 |
| 3 May | Newmarket | Valbriga | Palace House | 12,490 | 5 | Count d'Alessio | L Cumani | 9/2 |
| 3 May | Newmarket | Shining Finish | | 2,826 | 12 | J Whitney | J Tree | 9/2 |
| 5 May | Doncaster | Sea Chimes | Sporting Chronicle Spring Hcp | 9,092 | 10 | J Thursby | J Dunlop | 4/5F |
| 5 May | Doncaster | Te Kenawa(USA) | | 1,759 | 8 | C A B St George | H Cecil | 2/7F |
| 7 May | Chester | Double High | | 2,001 | 12 | R Clifford Turner | M Stoute | 4/5F |
| 14 May | York | House Guard | Hambleton | 8,491 | 8 | K Hsu | R Armstrong | 2/1F |
| 15 May | York | Moorestyle | Norwest Holst Trophy | 8,861 | 7 | Moores Furnishings | R Armstrong | 2/1F |
| 15 May | York | Noble Saint(USA) | Yorkshire Cup | 16,672 | 14 | R R Guest | R Armstrong | 10/1 |
| 16 May | Newmarket | Silley's Knight | | 2,758 | 7 | Dr M Solomon | M Stoute | 4/1 |
| 26 May | Sandown | Gregorian(USA) | Brigadier Gerard | 14,111 | 10 | D Schwarz | M V O'Brien(I) | 4/6F |
| 26 May | Sandown | Imperial Ace | Whitsun Cup | 3,882 | 8 | Sir G White | M Stoute | 11/2 |
| 26 May | Sandown | Enchantment | | 2,197 | 7 | K Abdulla | J Tree | 7/4F |
| 29 May | Brighton | Varuna | | 1,792 | 7 | R Tikkoo | A E Breasley | 3/1 |
| 31 May | Kempton | Ringgit | UBM Motors Hcp | 3,095 | 10 | U Wijewardene | R Armstrong | 13/8F |
| 31 May | Kempton | Dalsaan(USA) | Heron | 3,152 | 7 | Aga Khan | M Stoute | 10/11F |
| 4 June | Epsom | Hard Green | Diomed | 14,105 | 8 | Sir G White | M Stoute | 9/4 |
| 4 June | Epsom | Intercraft Boy | Bookmakers Cup | 4,415 | 7 | C Sparrowhawk | A Pitt | 10/3F |
| 5 June | Epsom | Sea Chimes | Coronation Cup | 38,500 | 12 | J Thursby | J Dunlop | 5/4 |
| 5 June | Epsom | Poldhu | Staff Ingham | 3,795 | 6 | Sq Ldr R Milsom | M Jarvis | 8/11F |
| 6 June | Epsom | Susarma(USA) | Canada House Centenary Sprint | 3,980 | 5 | R Tikkoo | A Breasley | 10/3F |
| 6 June | Epsom | Halyudh | Northern Dancer | 6,794 | 12 | R Tikkoo | A Breasley | 13/8F |
| 7 June | Epsom | Grand Conde(F) | Abbots Hill Hcp | 3,674 | 8 | R Tikkoo | A Breasley | 9/4F |
| 7 June | Epsom | Davenport Boy | NMT Hcp | 3,785 | 6 | E Davenport | A Pitt | 5/6F |
| 9 June | Lingfield | Karamita | | 1,489 | 10 | Aga Khan | M Stoute | 5/4F |
| 10 June | Yarmouth | Ringgit | | 1,991 | 10 | U Wijewardene | R Armstrong | 9/4 |
| 14 June | York | Hide the Key | | 2,560 | 8 | P Mellon | I Balding | 10/11F |
| 14 June | York | Moore's Miracle | | 2,560 | 6 | Moores Furnishings | R Armstrong | 5/2F |
| 18 June | Royal Ascot | Hard Fought | Jersey | 12,992 | 7 | L Holliday | M Stoute | 15/8F |
| 21 June | Ascot | Pellegrini | Fenwolf | 3,215 | 6 | C A B St George | H Price | 9/4 |
| 25 June | Salisbury | Summer Soldier | | 1,194 | 8 | J H Whitney | J Tree | 5/4F |
| 2 July | Yarmouth | Spring is Grey | | 1,019 | 8 | Fittocks Stud | L Cumani | 1/2F |
| 4 July | Sandown | Hunston | Shatin | 3,043 | 7 | T Blackwell | B Hobbs | 8/11F |
| 4 July | Sandown | Beggars Bridge | Hong Kong Hcp | 7,269 | 10 | T Smith | D Laing | 12/1 |
| 5 July | Sandown | Schiller | | 1,833 | 7 | C A B St George | H Price | 5/2 |
| 5 July | Sandown | Popsi's Joy | | 2,607 | 16 | V Lawson | M Haynes | 7/4F |
| 8 July | Newmarket | Marwell | Chesterfield | 3,811 | 5 | E Loder | M Stoute | 11/10F |

(I) = Ireland (F) = France (USA) = America

| Date | Race Course | Horse | Race | Value £ | Dist Fur | Owner | Trainer | S/P |
|---|---|---|---|---|---|---|---|---|
| 10 July | Newmarket | Friendly Falcon | | 2,159 | 7 | J Winspear | P Rohan | 2/1F |
| 10 July | Newmarket | Moorestyle | Wm Hill July Cup | 33,296 | 6 | Moores Furnishings | F Armstrong | 3/1F |
| 11 July | York | State Trooper | | 2,515 | 9 | R Prettie | B Hanbury | 9/4F |
| 12 July | York | Chateau Dancer | John Courage | 4,064 | 6 | R West | C Thornton | 5/4F |
| 15 July | Leicester | Rabdan | | 1,750 | 7 | E Alkhalifa | R Armstrong | 20/21F |
| 15 July | Leicester | Princess Matilda | | 1,208 | 7 | Mrs G Weston | R Houghton | 4/1 |
| 18 July | Newbury | Karamata | | 2,148 | 10 | Aga Khan | M Stoute | 10/3F |
| 23 July | Sandown | Sandon Buoy | | 1,786 | 5 | W Holder | R Armstrong | 2/1F |
| 23 July | Sandown | Windsor Boy | | 2,393 | 5 | K C B MacKenzie | A R Turnell | 11/4 |
| 24 July | Sandown | Popsi's Joy | | 2,485 | 14 | N Morley Lawson | M Haynes | 5/4F |
| 24 July | Sandown | Mattaboy | Star | 4,675 | 5 | R Tikkoo | R Armstrong | 4/5F |
| 25 July | Ascot | Beggars Bridge | | 2,978 | 12 | T Stratton Smith | D Laing | 2/1F |
| 26 July | Ascot | New Years Day(USA) | Granville | 3,941 | 6 | D Rowland | P Cole | 3/1 |
| 28 July | Windsor | Zoro | | 1,507 | 11 | Mrs M Watt | G Balding | 11/2 |
| 29 July | Goodwood | Marwell | Molecomb | 10,270 | 5 | E Loder | M Stoute | 4/6F |
| 30 July | Goodwood | Hanu | Singleton Hcp | 3,048 | 5 | R Tikkoo | A Breasley | 9/4F |
| 31 July | Goodwood | Valeriga | King George | 12,768 | 5 | Count d'Alessio | L Cumani | 9/2 |
| 1 Aug | Goodwood | Fine Honey | Findon | 2,582 | 5 | K Abdulla | J Tree | 4/6F |
| 2 Aug | Goodwood | Astonished | Surplice | 3,277 | 8 | Sir R McAlpine | J Dunlop | 9/2 |
| 6 Aug | Yarmouth | Miss Raffles | | 1,565 | 7 | Ian Price | P Haslam | 9/4F |
| 7 Aug | Yarmouth | Sainera(USA) | | 1,187 | 7 | L Salice | L Cumani | 6/4F |
| 7 Aug | Yarmouth | Mississippi Shuffle | | 1,662 | 6 | S Stanhope | P Cole | 6/4F |
| 7 Aug | Yarmouth | Sashka | | 956 | 10 | Aga Khan | M Stoute | 2/5F |
| 8 Aug | Newmarket | Sideline | | 1,352 | 7 | O/trainer | P Rohan | 13/8F |
| 8 Aug | Newmarket | Golden Gayle | | 2,683 | 12 | Mrs D Williams | P Rohan | 9/2 |
| 9 Aug | Redcar | Sunion(Ger) | | 2,628 | 7 | Baroness Oppenheim | M Stoute | EvF |
| 9 Aug | Redcar | Crispin | | 1,635 | 12 | M Arnold | J Dunlop | 3/1 |
| 11 Aug | Windsor | Mementa Mia | | 1,389 | 6 | C Armstrong | C Nelson | 7/4F |
| 12 Aug | Nottingham | Cavalry Twill | | 1,035 | 6 | Mrs J Phillips | M Stoute | EvF |
| 12 Aug | Nottingham | Chincoteague | | 1,323 | 16 | Mrs C Brudenell-Bruce | M Stoute | 7/2 |
| 12 Aug | Nottingham | Green Haze | | 1,033 | 6 | Sir G White | M Stoute | 5/4F |
| 13 Aug | Salisbury | Sanu | | 1,452 | 5 | R Tikkoo | A Breasley | 4/1 |
| 18 Aug | Windsor | Cavalry Twill | | 1,518 | 6 | Mrs I Phillips | M Stoute | 13/8F |
| 18 Aug | Windsor | Astonished | | 1,304 | 10 | Sir R McAlpine | J Dunlop | 8/15F |
| 19 Aug | York | Shoot a Line | Yorkshire Oaks | 33,092 | 12 | R A Budgett | W Hern | 13/8 |
| 20 Aug | York | Kitty Hawk | Lowther | 8,504 | 6 | Lord Porchester | W Hern | 10/11F |
| 20 Aug | York | Prince Bee | Great Volticeur | 23,400 | 12 | Sir M Sobell | W Hern | 4/6F |
| 20 Aug | York | Beggars Bridge | Falmouth | 3,674 | 10½ | T Smith | D Laing | 2/1F |
| 21 Aug | York | Marwell | Prince of Wales | 5,078 | 5 | E Loder | M Stoute | 4/9F |
| 21 Aug | York | Deadly Serious(USA) | Galtres | 4,480 | 12 | The Queen | W Hern | 7/2 |
| 22 Aug | Goodwood | Our Home | | 1,886 | 8 | P Phillips | M Stoute | 1/5F |
| 23 Aug | Goodwood | Sanu | | 1,749 | 5 | R Tikkoo | A Breasley | 13/2 |
| 25 Aug | Newcastle | Mott the Hoople | | 2,842 | 6 | S Dinsmore | P Haslam | 7/4F |
| 25 Aug | Newcastle | Faiz | | 1,289 | 6 | N Shuaib | J Dunlop | 4/7F |
| 26 Aug | Epsom | Queen's Equerry | | 1,685 | 8 | R Green | W Wightman | 5/2F |
| 26 Aug | Epsom | Cavalry Twill | | 1,730 | 7 | Mrs J Phillips | M Stoute | 1/5F |
| 27 Aug | Yarmouth | Salty Susie | | 979 | 10 | S Hanson | M Stoute | 4/6F |
| 28 Aug | Yarmouth | Daphnes Favour | | 701 | 5 | Mrs P Cole | P Cole | EvF |
| 28 Aug | Yarmouth | Tower Joy | | 1,278 | 7 | F Fairioli | L Cumani | 10/11F |
| 28 Aug | Yarmouth | Lacework(USA) | | 1,067 | 5 | R Sangster | M Stoute | 2/1 |
| 29 Aug | Sandown | Sanu | | 2,246 | 5 | R Tikkoo | A Breasley | EvF |
| 29 Aug | Sandown | Fernaro | | 2,611 | 7 | Mrs R Henriques | R Hannon | 5/2F |
| 30 Aug | Sandown | Popsi's Joy | | 2,911 | 14 | V Morley Lawson | M Haynes | 11/8F |
| 3 Sept | York | Stanislavski | Garrowby Stks | 8,263 | 10½ | C A B St George | H Price | 7/2F |
| 5 Sept | Kempton | Lord Raffles | | 1,413 | 8 | W Ponsonby | W Musson | 9/2F |
| 5 Sept | Kempton | Rasa Penang | | 2,931 | 7 | U Wijiwardene | R Armstrong | 14/1 |
| 5 Sept | Kempton | Rabdan | | 2,488 | 7 | E Alkhalifa | R Armstrong | 4/1 |

(USA) = America (Ger) = Germany

| Date | Race Course | Horse | Race | Value £ | Dist Fur | Owner | Trainer | S/P |
|---|---|---|---|---|---|---|---|---|
| 6 Sept | Haydock | Moorestyle | Vernons Sprint Cup | 29,560 | 6 | Moores Furnishings | R Armstrong | 8/13F |
| 6 Sept | Haydock | Pellegrini(USA) | Lytham | 4,135 | 8 | C A B St George | H Price | 6/4F |
| 6 Sept | Haydock | Greyburn | | 2,425 | 7 | A Robinson | W Haigh | 6/1 |
| 9 Sept | Pontefract | Cavalry Twill | | 1,551 | 5 | Mrs I Phillips | M Stoute | 4/7F |
| 17 Sept | Yarmouth | Spark of Life | | 1,157 | 6 | R Clifford-Turner | M Stoute | 4/7F |
| 17 Sept | Yarmouth | Sones(USA) | | 1,157 | 6 | C A B St George | H Cecil | 1/2F |
| 19 Sept | Newbury | Shergar | | 2,560 | 8 | Aga Khan | M Stoute | 11/8F |
| 22 Sept | Leicester | Moment of Weakness | | 769 | 10 | W Ponsonby | P Cole | 5/2F |
| 22 Sept | Leicester | Allagretta | | 1,266 | 8 | Aga Khan | M Stoute | 7/2 |
| 23 Sept | Leicester | I-Ching | | 745 | 8 | F Steeples | D Laing | 7/2F |
| 29 Sept | Goodwood | Kalaglow | | 3,086 | 8 | J Vanner | G Harwood | 1/3F |
| 30 Sept | Goodwood | Native Prospector | | 2,074 | 8 | Concorde BA | A Breasley | 3/1F |
| 30 Sept | Goodwood | Herons Hollow | | 2,666 | 8 | A Solomons | G Harwood | 11/4F |
| 1 Oct | Newmarket | Marwell | Wm Hill Cheveley Pk | 31,518 | 6 | E Loder | M Stoute | 4/9F |
| 2 Oct | Newmarket | Mattaboy | Middle Park | 33,198 | 6 | R Tikkoo | R Armstrong | 7/1 |
| 3 Oct | Lingfield | Palleor | | 2,449 | 10 | Dr C Vittadini | L Cumani | 9/4F |
| 3 Oct | Lingfield | Belloc | | 2,230 | 7 | C A B St George | H Price | 4/5F |
| 4 Oct | Newmarket | Snow | Sun Chariot Cup | 16,646 | 10 | M Fraser | K Prendergast (I) | 5/6F |
| 4 Oct | Newmarket | Ardross | Jockey Club | 13,948 | 16 | late P J Prendergast | K Prendergast (I) | 9/4F |
| 8 Oct | York | Franciscus | | 2,746 | 12 | J Mullion | R Armstrong | EvF |
| 8 Oct | York | Jims Tricks | | 2,771 | 9 | R Stigwood | D Laing | 10/1 |
| 9 Oct | Lingfield | Sea Aura | | 2,348 | 6 | K Stroud | G Pritchard-Gordon | 3/1 |
| 9 Oct | Lingfield | Lautrec | | 1,264 | 7 | C A B St George | H Price | 11/8F |
| 10 Oct | Ascot | Our Home | | 3,002 | 8 | P Phillips | M Stoute | 2/1F |
| 11 Oct | Ascot | Karamita | | 10,841 | 12 | Aga Khan | M Stoute | 15/8F |
| 11 Oct | Ascot | Shining Finish | | 2,950 | 12 | V Stein | J Tree | 7/4F |
| 13 Oct | Pontefract | Perlesse | | 1,527 | 6 | Sir H Moore | M Stoute | 6/1 |
| 14 Oct | Warwick | Sandra's Secret | | 1,107 | 5 | J Dooler | R Whitaker | 7/1 |
| 16 Oct | Newmarket | Steeple Bell | Fordham Hcp | 3,683 | 7 | Mrs C Brudenell-Bruce | M Stoute | 9/1 |
| 16 Oct | Newmarket | Spark of Life | Somerville Tattersall | 6,420 | 7 | R Clifford-Turner | M Stoute | 10/11F |
| 16 Oct | Newmarket | Moorestyle | Biscuit Conduit Challenge | 12,742 | 7 | Moores Furnishings | R Armstrong | 2/5F |
| 16 Oct | Newmarket | Riberetto | | 2,863 | 8 | D McIntyre | R Boss | 4/1 |
| 16 Oct | Newmarket | Main Reef† | Newmarket Challenge Cup | | 16 | H J Joel | H Cecil | |
| 18 Oct | Newmarket | Popsi's Joy | Tote Cesarewitch | 26,677 | 18 | V Lawson | M Haynes | 10/1 |
| 18 Oct | Newmarket | Shark Song | | 2,796 | 6 | R Tikkoo | J Hindley | 10/11F |
| 20 Oct | Leicester | Button Top | | 917 | 7 | O/trainer | N Callaghan | 5/4F |
| 21 Oct | Sandown | Brauching | | 2,679 | 8 | W Gredley | C Brittain | 10/1 |
| 24 Oct | Doncaster | Oratavo | | 2,105 | 8 | A Gretton | J Sutcliffe | 7/4F |
| 25 Oct | Doncaster | Shark Song | | 2,536 | 5 | R Tikkoo | J Hindley | 4/7F |
| 27 Oct | Nottingham | Spin of a Coin | | 997 | 10 | K Higson | H Price | 1/2F |
| 27 Oct | Nottingham | Withy Copse | | 2,108 | 13 | Mrs H Renshaw | M Stoute | 9/2F |
| 28 Oct | Nottingham | Marking Time | | 1,125 | 5 | R Gilbert | B Hanbury | 13/8F |
| 31 Oct | Newmarket | Popsi's Joy | | 2,344 | 14 | V Lawson | M Haynes | 9/4F |
| 1 Nov | Newmarket | Princess Pageant | | 2,152 | 12 | M Oakshott | B W Hills | 7/2F |
| 4 Nov | Leicester | Belloc | | 1,543 | 7 | C A B St George | H Price | 1/2F |

1980: 156 wins; 96 2nds; 65 3rds; 635 rides

† Walkover (I) = Ireland (USA) = America

| Date | Race Course | Horse | Race | Value £ | Dist Fur | Owner | Trainer | S/P |
|---|---|---|---|---|---|---|---|---|
| 1981 | | | | | | | | |
| 31 Mar | Leicester | Beeleigh | | 948 | 7 | D Cock | N Callaghan | 13/8F |
| 31 Mar | Leicester | Belloc | | 1,956 | 8 | C A B St George | H Price | 10/11F |
| 31 Mar | Leicester | Daring Dame | | 868 | 8 | M Kirkby | P Cole | 5/2F |
| 10 Apl | Newbury | Brave Hussar | | 2,830 | 11 | O/trainer | G Hunter | 9/2 |
| 11 Apl | Newbury | Belmont Bay | Playboy B'makers Newbury Spring Cup | 9,216 | 8 | D Wildenstein | H Cecil | 11/1 |
| 13 Apl | Wolver'ton | BA Poundstretcher | | 828 | 5 | J Williams | R Hannon | 14/1 |
| 13 Apl | Wolver'ton | Prince Sandro | | 1,870 | 11 | Mrs W Sulke | R Houghton | 5/1 |
| 13 Apl | Wolver'ton | Canaille | | 985 | 8 | D Wildenstein | H Cecil | 7/4F |
| 15 Apl | Newmarket | Rabdan | Ladbroke Abernant | 5,280 | 6 | E Alkhalifa | R Armstrong | 6/1 |
| 16 Apl | Newmarket | Long Legend (USA) | | 2,519 | 6 | D Wildenstein | H Cecil | 13/8 |
| 16 Apl | Newmarket | Fairy Footsteps | Ladbroke Nell Gwyn | 9,637 | 7 | H J Joel | H Cecil | 4/6F |
| 16 Apl | Newmarket | Ackermann(USA) | | 2,859 | 7 | C A B St George | H Cecil | 6/5F |
| 20 Apl | Nottingham | Barwin(USA) | | 897 | 6 | late H Barker | H Cecil | 6/5F |
| 20 Apl | Nottingham | Paul's Ivory | | 897 | 5 | B Samialsingh | J Sutcliffe | 3/1 |
| 22 Apl | Epsom | Denmore | Otis Elevator | 4,378 | 6 | Maj T Adam | C Nelson | 4/1F |
| 23 Apl | Epsom | Petroleuse | Princess Elizabeth | 11,072 | 8 | D Wildenstein | H Cecil | 5/2F |
| 30 Apl | Newmarket | Fairy Footsteps | 1000 Guineas | 52,180 | 8 | H J Joel | H Cecil | 6/4F |
| 30 Apl | Newmarket | Popsi's Joy | | 2,986 | 16 | N M Lawson | M Haynes | 5/6F |
| 1 May | Newmarket | Celestial City | | 2,691 | 5 | Capt J Macdonald-Buchanan | H Cecil | 8/1 |
| 1 May | Newmarket | Algardi(USA) | | 2,599 | 5 | C A B St George | H Cecil | 6/4F |
| 1 May | Newmarket | Button Top | Burwell Hcp | 4,181 | 7 | A Morton | N Callaghan | 4/1F |
| 1 May | Newmarket | Sacrilege† | The Whip | | | H J Joel | H Cecil | |
| 4 May | Kempton | Brave Hussar | | 2,523 | 12 | H J Joel | H Cecil | 3/1 |
| 5 May | Chester | Jester | | 2,502 | 5 | P H Marsh | P Rohan | 8/13F |
| 5 May | Chester | Sacrilege | Laskys Hi-Fi | 4,025 | 10 | H J Joel | H Cecil | 5/12F |
| 7 May | Chester | Kirtling | Dee | 9,441 | 10 | E Moller | H Wragg | 3/1 |
| 7 May | Chester | Gearys for Strip | | 2,435 | 5 | H Geary Steels | Denys Smith | 11/2 |
| 7 May | Chester | Beeleigh | Laskys Video | 4,006 | 7 | D Cock | N Callaghan | 8/13F |
| 9 May | Lingfield | State Trooper | | 2,656 | 10 | A Prettie | B Hanbury | 13/8F |
| 14 May | York | Celestial City | | 3,028 | 5 | Capt J Macdonald-Buchanan | H Cecil | 2/1 |
| 14 May | York | Ardross | Yorkshire Cup | 19,536 | 14 | C A B St George | H Cecil | 2/1 |
| 15 May | Newbury | Strigida | Sir Charles Clore Memorial Tote | 7,656 | 10 | Lord Howard de Walden | H Cecil | 7/1 |
| 16 May | Newbury | Belmont Bay | Lockinge | 21,460 | 8 | D Wildenstein | H Cecil | 11/10F |
| 27 May | Brighton | Steel Pass | | 2,645 | 6 | R Tikkoo | G Hunter | 11/1 |
| 29 May | Kempton | Decorative | | 1,875 | 11 | Mrs N Fenton | D Kent | 10/11F |
| 3 June | Epsom | Rabdan | Playboy Bookmakers | 4,365 | 7 | E Alkalifa | R Armstrong | EvF |
| 4 June | Epsom | Algardi(USA) | Staff Ingham | 4,557 | 6 | C A B St George | H Cecil | EvF |
| 5 June | Epsom | Cavallerizzo | Uplands Park | 2,658 | 5 | D Thorne | G Balding | 16/1 |
| 6 June | Epsom | Celestial City | Acorn | 5,371 | 5 | Capt J Macdonald-Buchanan | H Cecil | 13/8F |
| 6 June | Epsom | Blue Wind | Oaks | 74,568 | 12 | Mrs B Firestone | D K Weld(I) | 3/2F |
| 8 June | Leicester | Rose Music | | 1,336 | 7 | J F C Bryce | R Armstrong | 7/2 |
| 8 June | Leicester | Custer(USA) | | 1,761 | 6 | Count d'Alessio | H Cecil | EvF |
| 10 June | Yarmouth | Lavender Dance | | 1,168 | 5 | S Hornung | H Cecil | 1/3F |
| 13 June | Sandown | State Trooper | | 3,132 | 8 | A Prettie | B Hanbury | 10/3 |
| 13 June | Sandown | Aperitivo | Trafalgar Hcp | 4,744 | 10 | Mrs J Spencer | R Armstrong | 5/2 |
| 13 June | Sandown | Thahul(USA) | | 1,875 | 14 | Sheikh Mohammed | R Houghton | 7/1 |
| 16 June | Royal Ascot | Belmont Bay | Queen Anne | 12,909 | 8 | D Wildenstein | H Cecil | 4/1 |

† Walkover (I) = Ireland (USA) = America

| Date | Race Course | Horse | Race | Value £ | Dist Fur | Owner | Trainer | S/P |
|---|---|---|---|---|---|---|---|---|
| 16 June | Royal Ascot | Strigida | Ribblesdale | 18,920 | 12 | Lord Howard de Walden | H Cecil | 5/1 |
| 17 June | Royal Ascot | Raja Penang | Jersey | 15,220 | 7 | U Wijewardene | R Armstrong | 11/1 |
| 18 June | Royal Ascot | Ardross | Gold Cup | 39,013 | 20 | C A B St George | H Cecil | 3/10F |
| 18 June | Royal Ascot | Cajun | Chesham | 8,512 | 6 | J Stone | H Cecil | 10/11F |
| 20 June | Warwick | Home on the Range | | 2,590 | 12 | L Freedman | H Cecil | 10/11F |
| 20 June | Ascot | Admiral's Princess | Erroll | 4,045 | 5 | W Ponsonby | P Cole | 5/1 |
| 22 June | Pontefract | Canaille | | 3,329 | 8 | D Wildenstein | H Cecil | EvF |
| 25 June | Salisbury | Burnbeck | | 1,496 | 5 | Mrs N Sampson | P Cole | 10/11F |
| 26 June | Doncaster | Padalco | | 1,035 | 6 | T Hillman | H Cecil | 4/9F |
| 29 June | Nottingham | Bright Wire | | 897 | 6 | C Sparrowhawk | A Jarvis | 2/1 |
| 30 June | Yarmouth | Lady be Mine (USA) | | 1,130 | 8 | P Burrell | H Cecil | EvF |
| 30 June | Yarmouth | Long Legend | | 2,068 | 6 | D Wildenstein | H Cecil | 8/13F |
| 1 July | Yarmouth | Military Band | | 998 | 14 | H J Joel | H Cecil | 2/7F |
| 1 July | Yarmouth | Pagapas Bay | | 1,500 | 5 | P Saville | A Jarvis | 13/8F |
| 3 July | Sandown | Clare Island | | 3,833 | 7 | Snailwell Stud | H Cecil | 5/4F |
| 3 July | Sandown | Ponchelli* | | 2,918 | 5 | A Donaldson | R Armstrong | 11/2 |
| 4 July | Nottingham | Tomaschek | | 897 | 13 | C A B St George | H Cecil | 1/4F |
| 4 July | Sandown | Santella Man | | 2,826 | 7 | R Taiano | G Harwood | 11/10F |
| 4 July | Sandown | Miss Mirabelle | | 3,090 | 7 | Lord Walpole | M Jarvis | 7/2F |
| 7 July | Newmarket | Treboro(USA) | | 3,250 | 7 | A Ward | G Harwood | 4/6F |
| 7 July | Newmarket | Light Cavalry | Princess of Wales | 20,966 | 12 | H J Joel | H Cecil | 11/4F |
| 7 July | Newmarket | Custer(USA) | Chesterfield | 4,025 | 5 | Count d'Alessio | H Cecil | 11/4 |
| 7 July | Newmarket | Steel Pass | Hamilton Hcp | 3,999 | 6 | R Tikkoo | G Hunter | 11/2 |
| 8 July | Newmarket | Padalco | Bernard van Cutsem | 4,696 | 7 | T Hillman | H Cecil | 8/11F |
| 10 July | York | Reside | | 2,662 | 9 | H Craig | E Carter | 9/4F |
| 10 July | Chester | Mac's Delight | | 2,553 | 12 | T Macdonald | D Smith | 3/1F |
| 10 July | Chester | Lady of Cornwall | | 1,278 | 10 | R Sangster | B W Hills | 7/4 |
| 11 July | York | State Trooper | | 3,505 | 8 | A Prettie | B Hanbury | 3/1 |
| 13 July | Windsor | Paterno | | 2,085 | 8 | Mrs C Smith | R Armstrong | 11/4 |
| 14 July | Leicester | Hab Dancer | | 1,962 | 7 | R Tikkoo | R Armstrong | 6/5F |
| 15 July | Kempton | Special Pleasure | | 1,379 | 5 | J McNamee Sullivan | R Armstrong | 11/8F |
| 16 July | Kempton | Bracadale | | 1,746 | 6 | F J Crouch | R Armstrong | 4/1 |
| 17 July | Newbury | Macmillion | | 2,897 | 7 | T McCarthy | Mrs B Waring | 9/2 |
| 18 July | Nottingham | Baltimore Belle | | 912 | 6 | A Boyd-Rochfort | H Cecil | 5/4F |
| 22 July | Yarmouth | Alma Ata | | 1,238 | 14 | Mrs D Zurcher | L Cumani | 4/1 |
| 22 July | Yarmouth | Custer(USA) | | 1,688 | 7 | Count d'Alessio | H Cecil | 2/13F |
| 23 July | Sandown | Hula Ruler(USA) | | 2,876 | 7 | Mrs D Zurcher | L Cumani | 3/1F |
| 24 July | Ascot | Crimson Royale | Cranbourn Chase | 3,850 | 10 | L Walker | P Cole | 11/2 |
| 28 July | Goodwood | Prowess Prince (USA) | Molecombe | 11,624 | 5 | S Lieni | E Eldin | 4/5F |
| 30 July | Goodwood | Ardross | Goodwood Cup | 20,995 | 21 | C A B St George | H Cecil | 2/9F |
| 31 July | Newmarket | Bracadale | | 3,251 | 6 | S Crouch | R Armstrong | 10/11F |
| 31 July | Newmarket | Young Daniel | | 2,668 | 7 | F Wicks | R Armstrong | 6/4F |
| 1 Aug | Windsor | Custer(USA) | | 1,923 | 6 | Count d'Alessio | H Cecil | 1/7F |
| 1 Aug | Goodwood | The Dinmont | Rous | 4,885 | 6 | W Benson | J Dunlop | 9/2 |
| 1 Aug | Goodwood | End of War | | 3,184 | 12 | J Whitney | J Tree | 7/1 |
| 5 Aug | Yarmouth | Al Nasr | | 873 | 14 | H Al-Maktoum | J Dunlop | 2/7F |
| 6 Aug | Yarmouth | Hula Ruler (USA) | | 1.296 | 7 | D Zurcher | L Cumani | 4/7F |
| 6 Aug | Yarmouth | Tomaschek† (USA) | | 2,280 | 14 | C A B St George | H Cecil | |
| 8 Aug | Newmarket | Baltimore Belle | | 3,960 | 7 | A Boyd-Rochfort | H Cecil | 7/2 |
| 10 Aug | Newcastle | Ackermann(USA) | Northumberland Sprint | 9,975 | 6 | C A B St George | H Cecil | 11/10F |
| 11 Aug | Nottingham | Al Hasa | | 897 | 6 | P Burrell | H Cecil | 6/1 |

* Dead Heat † Walkover (USA) = America

| Date | Race Course | Horse | Race | Value £ | Dist Fur | Owner | Trainer | S/P |
|---|---|---|---|---|---|---|---|---|
| 11 Aug | Newcastle | Hot Fire | | 1,858 | 12 | N Nuttall | J Fitzgerald | 11/4 |
| 11 Aug | Newcastle | Praetorian Guard | | 2,656 | 8 | C Attwood | Denys Smith | 2/1 |
| 15 Aug | Newbury | Ardross | Geoffrey Freer | 24,430 | 13 | C A B St George | H Cecil | 10/11F |
| 15 Aug | Newbury | Custer | Washington Singer | 4,487 | 6 | Count d'Alessio | H Cecil | 10/11F |
| 15 Aug | Newbury | Ponchielli | | 2,599 | 5 | A Donaldson | R Armstrong | 4/1 |
| 18 Aug | York | Height of Fashion | Acomb | 6,536 | 7 | The Queen | W Hern | 7/2 |
| 19 Aug | York | Donegal Prince | Lonsdale | 7,536 | 16 | J McGonagle | P Kelleway | 4/5F |
| 20 Aug | York | Silver Season | Rose of York | 7,343 | 8 | M Hassan | C Brittain | 6/1 |
| 21 Aug | Kempton | Bedford(USA) | | 2,253 | 11 | J Moseley | I Balding | 13/8F |
| 21 Aug | Kempton | Faiz | | 3,454 | 7 | N Shauib | J Dunlop | 6/4F |
| 21 Aug | Kempton | Vocalist | Atalanta | 4,862 | 8 | G Greenwood | F Durr | 2/1 |
| 22 Aug | Kempton | Critique(USA) | | 1,688 | 8 | G Vanian | H Cecil | 4/6F |
| 22 Aug | Kempton | Montekin | | 3,090 | 7 | P Winfield | J Dunlop | 4/6F |
| 24 Aug | Windsor | Minne Love | | 787 | 6 | J Stafford | C Nelson | 11/2 |
| 24 Aug | Windsor | Lavender Dance | | 2,800 | 5 | S Hornung | H Cecil | 4/9F |
| 25 Aug | Yarmouth | Nioulargo | | 1,517 | 7 | Mrs A Reid | R Armstrong | 5/4F |
| 25 Aug | Yarmouth | Tomaschek(USA) | | 1,730 | 14 | C A B St George | H Cecil | 2/5F |
| 26 Aug | Yarmouth | Par Pak | | 655 | 5 | N Parker | J Czerpak | 8/11F |
| 26 Aug | Yarmouth | Young Daniel | | 2,138 | 8 | F Wicks | R Armstrong | 9/2 |
| 26 Aug | Yarmouth | Acclaimed | | 911 | 14 | D Wildenstein | H Cecil | 11/4 |
| 27 Aug | Brighton | Hostess | | 2,021 | 7 | J North | H Cecil | 5/2F |
| 27 Aug | Brighton | Rose Music | | 2,620 | 7 | J F C Bryce | R Armstrong | 9/4F |
| 27 Aug | Brighton | Dark Monarch | | 1,299 | 10 | Dexham Ltd | J Dunlop | 4/11F |
| 28 Aug | Goodwood | Valentinian | | 3,142 | 12 | Lord Scarbrough | W Hern | 6/4F |
| 28 Aug | Goodwood | Northern Chance | | 2,708 | 8 | Lady Clague | J Winter | 3/1F |
| 29 Aug | Goodwood | Gambler's Dream | August Hcp | 5,726 | 6 | Sporting Club | D Wilson | 2/1F |
| 4 Sept | Kempton | Hyjill | | 1,459 | 8 | J Willie | J Fitzgerald | 4/1F |
| 5 Sept | Kempton | Home on the Range | Sean Graham | 7,765 | 10 | L Freedman | H Cecil | 2/5F |
| 5 Sept | Kempton | Harp Strings(F) | Geoffrey Hamlyn | 4,668 | 8 | The Queen | I Balding | 4/1 |
| 7 Sept | Nottingham | Match Winner | | 897 | 6 | D Wildenstein | H Cecil | 4/7F |
| 7 Sept | Nottingham | Critique(USA) | Kiveton | 1,250 | 10 | G Vanian | H Cecil | 1/5F |
| 10 Sept | Doncaster | Kitty Hawk | Park Steel | 13,266 | 7 | R Sangster | W Hern | 11/8F |
| 10 Sept | Doncaster | Lobkowiez | | 3,407 | 8 | Mrs C Eliot | C Brittain | 6/1 |
| 10 Sept | Doncaster | Sally Rose | | 3,194 | 10 | Sir M Sobell | W Hern | 9/2 |
| 11 Sept | Doncaster | Valentinian | | 3,200 | 12 | Lord Scarbrough | W Hern | 2/1 |
| 11 Sept | Doncaster | Mirabeau | | 2,070 | 6 | J Lilley | H Wragg | 9/2 |
| 15 Sept | Yarmouth | Gauleiter(USA) | | 1,093 | 14 | D Wildenstein | H Cecil | 1/2F |
| 15 Sept | Yarmouth | Nioulargo | Jack Leader | 4,301 | 7 | Mrs A Reid | R Armstrong | EvF |
| 15 Sept | Yarmouth | Think Ahead | | 1,825 | 6 | N Wachman | H B T Jones | 9/4F |
| 16 Sept | Yarmouth | Vascan(USA) | | 1,056 | 8 | P Burrell | H Cecil | 1/3F |
| 16 Sept | Yarmouth | Military Band(F) | | 2,578 | 14 | H J Joel | H Cecil | 4/7F |
| 16 Sept | Yarmouth | Match Winner (F) | | 1,718 | 7 | D Wildenstein | H Cecil | 9/11F |
| 16 Sept | Yarmouth | Celestial Dancer | | 1,296 | 6 | J Phillips | A Hide | 4/1F |
| 16 Sept | Yarmouth | Knave of Trumps | | 1,296 | 6 | Mrs D Butler | H Cecil | 5/4F |
| 17 Sept | Yarmouth | Tomaschek(USA) | | 2,481 | 18 | C A B St George | H Cecil | 6/4F |
| 18 Sept | Newbury | Long Legend (USA) | | 2,540 | 5 | D Wildenstein | H Cecil | 5/2F |
| 18 Sept | Newbury | Candide | | 2,327 | 7 | Lord Porchester | W Hern | 9/2 |
| 22 Sept | Leicester | Adonis Rex | | 1,222 | 7 | C A B St George | H Cecil | 8/13F |
| 22 Sept | Leicester | Airspin | | 1,149 | 7 | D Mort | H Price | 5/4F |
| 22 Sept | Leicester | Liberated | | 2,740 | 10 | Lavinia Duchess of Norfolk | R Baker | 2/1F |
| 22 Sept | Leicester | Northleigh | | 1,103 | 7 | Duke of Marlborough | J Dunlop | EvF |
| 24 Sept | Ascot | Moorestyle | Diadem | 12,650 | 6 | Moores Furnishings | R Armstrong | EvF |
| 24 Sept | Ascot | Critique | Cumberland Lodge | 12,326 | 12 | G Vanian | H Cecil | 11/2 |
| 25 Sept | Ascot | General Anders | Mornington | 4,140 | 7 | R Creery | W Hern | 9/2 |
| 25 Sept | Ascot | Hampton Bay | | 3,152 | 5 | P Schmidt | R Armstrong | 3/8F |
| 26 Sept | Ascot | To-Agori-Mou | Queen Elizabeth II | 16,292 | 8 | Mrs A Muinos | G Harwood | 5/4F |

(F) = France (USA) = America

| Date | Race Course | Horse | Race | Value £ | Dist Fur | Owner | Trainer | S/P |
|---|---|---|---|---|---|---|---|---|
| 26 Sept | Ascot | Dancing Rocks | Blue Seal | 4,939 | 6 | Sir P Oppenheimer | H Wragg | 6/5F |
| 28 Sept | Goodwood | Jalmond(USA) | | 3,325 | 8 | Sheikh Mohammed | J Dunlop | 4/5F |
| 28 Sept | Goodwood | Belmont Bay | Harroways | 6,399 | 7 | D Wildenstein | H Cecil | 10/11F |
| 29 Sept | Nottingham | Dish Dash | | 897 | 6 | J F C Bryce | R Armstrong | 4/7F |
| 29 Sept | Nottingham | Dewanadance (USA) | | 897 | 6 | Count d'Alessio | H Cecil | 2/7F |
| 30 Sept | Newmarket | Nioulargo | | 4,636 | 8 | Mrs A Reid | R Armstrong | 9/4F |
| 1 Oct | Newmarket | Casun | Wm Hill Middle Park | 42,862 | 6 | J Stone | H Cecil | 20/1 |
| 1 Oct | Newmarket | I'm Hot(USA) | | 2,918 | 6 | M Fustok | M Albina | 13/2 |
| 3 Oct | Newmarket | Home on the Range | Sun Chariot | 17,974 | 10 | L Freedman | H Cecil | 2/1F |
| 3 Oct | Newmarket | Simply Great | | 3,078 | 7 | D Wildenstein | H Cecil | EvF |
| 8 Oct | York | Cracking Form | | 2,955 | 8 | S S Niarchos | P Walwyn | 11/2 |
| 10 Oct | Ascot | Paradis Terrestre (USA) | Hyperion | 5,080 | 7 | D Wildenstein | H Cecil | 3/1F |
| 10 Oct | Ascot | Maryland Cookie | Bovis Hcp | 6,295 | 5 | Food Brokers Ltd | J Bethell | 11/2 |
| 15 Oct | Newmarket | Capricorn Line | | 3,902 | 14 | R Allan | L Cumani | 2/1F |
| 15 Oct | Newmarket | Moorestyle | Bisquit Cognac Challenge | 16,084 | 7 | Moores Furnishings | R Armstrong | 8/15F |
| 15 Oct | Newmarket | Welsh Chanter† (USA) | Newmarket Challenge Cup | | 16 | H J Joel | H Cecil | |
| 17 Oct | Newmarket | Ivano | Houghton | 7,304 | 7 | Count d'Alessio | H Cecil | 6/1 |
| 19 Oct | Leicester | Tants | | 1,149 | 7 | Mrs H Phillips | H Cecil | 4/7F |
| 19 Oct | Leicester | Knave of Trumps | | 2,586 | 6 | Mrs D Butler | H Cecil | 4/7F |
| 19 Oct | Leicester | Clymene | | 1,172 | 7 | N Phillips | H Cecil | 6/1 |
| 23 Oct | Doncaster | Rushmoor | | 3,090 | 10 | The Queen | W Hern | 13/2 |
| 24 Oct | Doncaster | Rollrights | | 6,425 | 10 | Mrs M Lequime | J Dunlop | 11/8F |
| 26 Oct | Nottingham | On Show | | 897 | 10 | Sir P Oppenheimer | H Wragg | 4/5F |
| 26 Oct | Nottingham | Never So Lucky | | 1,713 | 6 | Lady Harrison | G Harwood | 6/1F |
| 30 Oct | Newmarket | Chalon | | 3,640 | 7 | M Riordan | H Cecil | 7/4F |

1981: 179 wins; 113 2nds; 87 3rds; 703 rides

| Date | Race Course | Horse | Race | Value £ | Dist Fur | Owner | Trainer | S/P |
|---|---|---|---|---|---|---|---|---|
| 1982 | | | | | | | | |
| 30 Mar | Leicester | Century City | | 1,434 | 7 | I Allan | L Cumani | 2/1F |
| 10 Apl | Kempton | Rare Gift | Easter | 5,238 | 8 | C A B St George | J Sutcliffe | 10/1 |
| 13 Apl | Newmarket | Victory House | | 3,334 | 6 | L Freedman | H Cecil | 3/1 |
| 13 Apl | Newmarket | Military Band (F) | | 2,955 | 14 | H J Joel | H Cecil | EvF |
| 14 Apl | Newmarket | Match Winner (F) | Tote European Free Hcp | 21,934 | 7 | D Wildenstein | H Cecil | 9/4F |
| 15 Apl | Newmarket | Chalon | Ladbrookes Nell Gwyn | 12,539 | 7 | M Riordan | H Cecil | 8/1 |
| 15 Apl | Newmarket | Ivano(Can) | | 6,576 | 9 | Count d'Alessio | H Cecil | 10/11F |
| 17 Apl | Newbury | Cajun | Clerical Medical Greenham | 14,840 | 7 | J Stone | H Cecil | 7/2 |
| 17 Apl | Newbury | Mr Fluorocarbon | | 3,149 | 8 | J McAllister | H Cecil | EvF |
| 19 Apl | Wolver'ton | First Phase(USA) | | 1,429 | 7 | V Manoukain | G Hunter | 4/1 |
| 20 Apl | Epsom | Gavo | | 1,895 | 7 | G Shack | P Kelleway | 4/5F |
| 22 Apl | Epsom | Dream Again | | 2,103 | 5 | A Duffield | A Jarvis | 6/4F |
| 22 Apl | Epsom | Clare Isle | Princess Elizabeth | 14,680 | 8 | Snailwell Stud | H Cecil | 11/4 |
| 23 Apl | Sandown | Aperitivo(USA) | Sunley Sandown Cup | 5,654 | 10 | Mrs J Spencer | R Armstrong | 5/1 |
| 23 Apl | Sandown | Vadrouille | | 3,036 | 10 | D Wildenstein | H Cecil | EvF |
| 27 Apl | Nottingham | The Dice Man (USA) | | 897 | 10 | C A B St George | H Cecil | 4/6F |
| 27 Apl | Nottingham | Francesco | | 1,189 | 13 | Count d'Alessio | H Cecil | 1/2F |
| 29 Apl | Newmarket | Mr Fluorocarbon | Heathorn | 8,012 | 10 | J McAlister | H Cecil | 4/5F |
| 30 Apl | Newmarket | Songroid | | 2,666 | 5 | D Miller | A Jarvis | 7/2 |

†Walkover (F) = France (USA) = America (Can) = Canada

| Date | Race Course | Horse | Race | Value £ | Dist Fur | Owner | Trainer | S/P |
|---|---|---|---|---|---|---|---|---|
| 30 Apl | Newmarket | Sing Softly | | 7,850 | 10 | H J Joel | H Cecil | 6/1 |
| 30 Apl | Newmarket | Ardross | Jockey Club | 18,050 | 12 | C A B St George | H Cecil | EvF |
| 1 May | Newmarket | Chalon | Ward Hill | 8,038 | 7 | M Riordan | H Cecil | 8/15F |
| 3 May | Doncaster | Lafontaine (USA) | Sporting Chronicle Spring Hcp | 8,962 | 10 | Mrs J Bigg | C Brittain | 11/8F |
| 6 May | Chester | In Motion | | 2,029 | 5 | Mrs P Doyle | P Doyle(I) | 9/2 |
| 6 May | Chester | Ivano(Can) | Dee | 12,120 | 10 | Count d'Alessio | H Cecil | 8/11F |
| 7 May | Lingfield | Tants | Bookmakers Oaks Trial | 15,745 | 12 | Mrs H Cecil | H Cecil | 7/2 |
| 10 May | Windsor | Ridgefield | | 1,574 | 11 | R Doughty | D Thom | 15/2F |
| 12 May | York | Bal Royal | | 3,454 | 5 | D Wildenstein | H Cecil | 15/8F |
| 12 May | York | Simply Great(F) | Mecca Dante | 49,584 | 10 | D Wildenstein | H Cecil | 11/10F |
| 12 May | York | Hostess | | 3,064 | 8 | Mrs W Nehorai | H Cecil | 3/1F |
| 13 May | York | Right Dancer | | 3,022 | 5 | N Mardell | P Kelleway | 13/8F |
| 13 May | York | Ardross | Yorkshire Cup | 21,650 | 14 | C A B St George | H Cecil | 2/5F |
| 13 May | York | Padalco | | 2,641 | 8 | T Hillman | H Cecil | 7/4F |
| 14 May | Newmarket | Steel Charger | | 3,616 | 5 | D McIntyre | R Boss | 7/4F |
| 14 May | Newmarket | Concorde Hero (USA) | | 2,737 | 5 | Mrs E Milbury | H Cecil | 1/5F |
| 17 May | Windsor | Knave of Trumps† | | 3,476 | 10 | Mrs D Buckner | H Cecil | |
| 17 May | Windsor | County Broker | | 1,368 | 5 | E. Rawlinson | A Jarvis | 11/10 |
| 17 May | Windsor | Hippo Disco | | 1,371 | 11 | Mrs D Haynes | M Stoute | 7/2 |
| 19 May | Yarmouth | Dream Again | | 2,519 | 5 | A Duffield | A Jarvis | 7/4 |
| 21 May | Brighton | Lavender Gray | | 2,490 | 8 | J Porter | J Winter | 13/8F |
| 21 May | Brighton | Curve the Wind | | 1,825 | 6 | Elisha Holdings | P Haslam | EvF |
| 22 May | Kempton | Aberfield | | 2,166 | 11 | G Kaye | P Kelleway | 9/2 |
| 24 May | Kempton | Concorde Hero | | 3,470 | 6 | Mrs E Milbury | H Cecil | 1/5F |
| 24 May | Kempton | Chalon | International Fillies | 6,070 | 8 | M Riordan | H Cecil | 4/11F |
| 31 May | Leicester | Video King | | 4,090 | 8 | Mrs E Maloney | C Brittain | 8/11F |
| 31 May | Doncaster | Alchise(USA) | | 1,035 | 6 | S Bowle | H Cecil | 11/10F |
| 1 June | Sandown | Ardross | | 16,422 | 16 | C A B St George | H Cecil | 2/7F |
| 3 June | Epsom | Prince Keymo | | 4,526 | 6 | R Emmitt | R Armstrong | 3/10F |
| 4 June | Epsom | Steel Charger | | 3,765 | 5 | D McIntyre | R Boss | 5/1 |
| 5 June | Epsom | Curve the Wind | | 2,586 | 7 | Elisha Holdings | P Haslam | 9/4 |
| 8 June | Yarmouth | Fire Thatch | | 1,182 | 5 | Count d'Alessio | H Cecil | 2/7F |
| 8 June | Yarmouth | Compound | | 713 | 8 | Miss S Baldwin | Mrs N Kennedy | 7/1 |
| 8 June | Yarmouth | Dollymixture Boy | | 2,435 | 10 | A Baker (Hyde) Ltd | R Armstrong | 8/13F |
| 9 June | Yarmouth | Key Wind | | 892 | 5 | N Mitchell | A Jarvis | 6/4F |
| 9 June | Yarmouth | Francesco | | 2,199 | 14 | Count d'Alessio | H Cecil | N/B |
| 10 June | Newbury | Bright Crocus (USA) | Kingsclere | 5,410 | 6 | Mrs B Walters | H Cecil | 4/9F |
| 14 June | Windsor | Brown Shadow | | 1,413 | 6 | P Donoghue | M Pipe | 15/8F |
| 15 June | Royal Ascot | Mr Fluorocarbon | Queen Annes | 14,776 | 8 | J McAlister | H Cecil | 3/1F |
| 16 June | Royal Ascot | Chalon | Coronation | 26,667 | 8 | M Riordan | H Cecil | 9/11F |
| 16 June | Royal Ascot | Evson | Queen's Vase | 15,520 | 16 | Capt M D Lemos | C Brittain | 16/1 |
| 18 June | Royal Ascot | Critique | Hardwicke | 23,027 | 12 | G Vanian | H Cecil | 7/2 |
| 18 June | Royal Ascot | Ardross | Gold Cup | 42,649 | 20 | C A B St George | H Cecil | 1/5F |
| 18 June | Royal Ascot | Right Dancer | Chesham | 8,655 | 6 | N Mandell | P Kelleway | 6/4F |
| 19 June | Ascot | Lyphmas | Churchill | 4,822 | 12 | C A B St George | H Cecil | 11/2 |
| 19 June | Ascot | Gormanstown Prince | Erroll | 4,729 | 5 | M Heaslip | M Cunningham (I) | 4/1 |
| 21 June | Pontefract | Winter Grace(USA) | | 2,236 | 8 | Mrs J Hanes | H Cecil | 11/10F |
| 25 June | Newcastle | King's Forest | | 1,819 | 7 | Lt Col M Frieze | H Wragg | 10/3 |
| 25 June | Newmarket | Alchise(USA) | | 1,951 | 7 | S Bowie | H Cecil | 8/13F |
| 26 June | Newmarket | Bright Crocus(USA) | Dance in Time | 4,051 | 6 | Miss B Walters | H Cecil | 1/2F |
| 30 June | Yarmouth | Willy James | | 1,238 | 5 | J How | R Armstrong | 11/10F |

†Walkover (I) = Ireland (F) = France (USA) = America (Can) = Canada

| Date | Race Course | Horse | Race | Value £ | Dist Fur | Owner | Trainer | S/P |
|---|---|---|---|---|---|---|---|---|
| 2 July | Sandown | Lafontaine | Royal Hong Kong JC Trophy | 7,677 | 10 | Mrs J Bigg | C Brittain | 5/1F |
| 3 July | Haydock | Alchise | Cock of the North | 11,041 | 7 | S Bowie | H Cecil | 3/1 |
| 3 July | Haydock | Blue Emanuelle | Sporting Chronicle Hcp | 6,572 | 7 | Roldvale Ltd | N Callaghan | 7/2 |
| 3 July | Haydock | Sing Softly | Lancashire Oaks | 21,270 | 12 | Mrs P Harris | H Cecil | 5/4F |
| 5 July | Windsor | Sabre Dance | Garfield | 897 | 10 | Lord Howard de Walden | H Cecil | 4/9F |
| 6 July | Newmarket | Paterno | Ward Hill Bunbury Cup | 9,474 | 7 | Mrs C P Smith | R Armstrong | 6/1 |
| 6 July | Newmarket | Fire Thatch | Chesterfield | 4,073 | 6 | C Weight | D Laing | 6/1 |
| 7 July | Newmarket | Chalon | Child | 16,620 | 8 | M Riordan | H Cecil | 8/15F |
| 7 July | Newmarket | Miramar Reef | | 3,750 | 10 | Mrs A Richards | C Brittain | 8/1 |
| 9 July | York | Gallant Special (USA) | | 3,999 | 6 | W Hawn | R Armstrong | 1/5F |
| 9 July | York | Padalco | | 3,106 | 8 | T Hillman | H Cecil | 5/6F |
| 9 July | Chester | Lakenheath | | 2,406 | 12 | O/trainer | H Wragg | 9/4F |
| 9 July | Chester | Amenity | | 1,671 | 10 | D Wildenstein | H Cecil | 15/2F |
| 9 July | Chester | Special Pleasure | | 2,427 | 5 | J McNamee Sullivan | R Armstrong | 5/4F |
| 10 July | York | Leadenhall Lad | | 3,397 | 6 | P J Meredew | R Boss | 5/2 |
| 12 July | Windsor | Snatch and Run (USA) | | 897 | 5 | A J Kelly | M Jarvis | 2/1 |
| 12 July | Windsor | Tirawa(USA) | | 1,341 | 11 | T Tek Tam | M Jarvis | 9/4F |
| 12 July | Windsor | Sabre Dance | | 897 | 10 | Lord Howard de Walden | H Cecil | 6/4F |
| 15 July | Yarmouth | John French | | 1,335 | 7 | C A B St George | H Cecil | 1/3F |
| 15 July | Yarmouth | Five Jacks | | 853 | 6 | Mrs B Dash | N Callaghan | 4/9F |
| 15 July | Yarmouth | That's My Son | | 1,347 | 8 | Capt M D Lemos | C Brittain | 8/13F |
| 17 July | Newmarket | Salieri(USA) | | 3,069 | 6 | C A B St George | H Cecil | 11/10F |
| 17 July | Newmarket | On Stage | Limekilns | 4,064 | 7 | A Foustok | W O'Gorman | 1/6F |
| 17 July | Nottingham | Cavaradossi(USA) | | 1,453 | 13 | C A B St George | H Cecil | 4/11F |
| 17 July | Nottingham | Lady Justice | | 2,236 | 10 | D McIntyre | R Boss | 9/2 |
| 17 July | Nottingham | Return to Paris | | 897 | 6 | Mrs B Firestone | H Cecil | 3/1 |
| 19 July | Windsor | Sinister Smile(USA) | | 897 | 5 | S Medall | H Cecil | 11/10F |
| 21 July | Sandown | Beldale Concorde (USA) | | 2,754 | 7 | A Kelly | M Jarvis | 2/1F |
| 22 July | Sandown | That's My Son | | 3,415 | 7 | Capt M D Lemos | C Brittain | 4/9F |
| 26 July | Newcastle | Blue Emanuelle | Harry Peacock Challenge Cup | 5,697 | 7 | Roldvale Ltd | N Callaghan | 2/1F |
| 26 July | Newcastle | Rollfast | | 1,738 | 12 | M Lequime | J Dunlop | 5/2F |
| 26 July | Nottingham | Valiancy | | 897 | 10 | T Holland-Martin | H Cecil | 8/15F |
| 26 July | Nottingham | Sparkling Sin | | 1,616 | 8 | Mrs P Brown | R Boss | 11/10F |
| 26 July | Nottingham | Magnetic Field | | 897 | 6 | M Foustok | H Cecil | 5/4F |
| 27 July | Goodwood | Chalon | | 8,701 | 7 | M Riordan | H Cecil | 2/11F |
| 28 July | Goodwood | Gallant Special | Richmond | 24,688 | 6 | W Hawn | R Armstrong | 4/6F |
| 29 July | Goodwood | Balanchine | Darnley Hcp | 7,460 | 12 | Mrs I Phillips | M Stoute | 5/2 |
| 29 July | Goodwood | Tina's Pet | King George | 16,460 | 5 | Cheveley Park Stud | G Huffer | 8/1 |
| 30 July | Goodwood | Dunbeath(USA) | Foxhall Memorial | 5,517 | 7 | M Riordan | H Cecil | 10/11F |
| 31 July | Goodwood | Salieri | Rous Memorial Trident | 5,663 | 6 | C A B St George | H Cecil | N/B |
| 31 July | Goodwood | Criterion | Chesterfield Cup | 8,116 | 10 | A Bodie | G Harwood | 7/1 |
| 31 July | Windsor | Sabre Dance | | 897 | 10 | Lord Howard de Walden | H Cecil | 4/6F |
| 31 July | Nottingham | Mennea | | 3,869 | 8 | C A B St George | H Price | 4/6F |
| 4 Aug | Yarmouth | Steel Kid(USA) | | 1,260 | 14 | R Tikkoo | R Armstrong | 1/3F |
| 5 Aug | Yarmouth | Compound | | 682 | 8 | Miss P Baldwin | Mrs N Kennedy | 11/4 |
| 6 Aug | Newmarket | The Fort | | 3,519 | 7 | Mrs H Phillips | H Cecil | 4/1 |
| 6 Aug | Newmarket | John French | Richmond | 4,077 | 7 | C A B St George | H Cecil | 3/1 |

(USA) = America

| Date | Race Course | Horse | Race | Value £ | Dist Fur | Owner | Trainer | S/P |
|---|---|---|---|---|---|---|---|---|
| 7 Aug | Newmarket | Diesis | | 3,153 | 6 | Lord Howard de Walden | H Cecil | 4/7F |
| 9 Aug | Newcastle | Bancario | | 2,110 | 8 | Lord Howard de Walden | H Price | 7/4 |
| 10 Aug | Nottingham | Now and Again | | 897 | 6 | K Al Sabah | H Cecil | 8/13F |
| 12 Aug | Salisbury | Shadan | | 2,106 | 6 | F Emami | P Haslam | 3/1 |
| 12 Aug | Salisbury | That's My Son | | 1,469 | 8 | Capt M D Lemos | C Brittain | 8/13F |
| 14 Aug | Newbury | Ardross | Geoffrey Freer | 23,890 | 13 | C A B St George | H Cecil | 1/3F |
| 14 Aug | Newbury | Balanchine | ATS Trophy | 5,244 | 12 | Mrs I Phillips | M Stoute | 11/10F |
| 16 Aug | Windsor | Return to Paris | | 897 | 6 | Mrs B Firestone | H Cecil | 8/11F |
| 16 Aug | Leicester | Lakenheath (USA) | | 2,071 | 12 | O/trainer | H Wragg | 1/2F |
| 16 Aug | Leicester | Linda's Fantasy | | 2,313 | 6 | J Bray | R Armstrong | 2/5F |
| 17 Aug | York | Awaash(Can) | Yorkshire Oaks | 40,564 | 12 | Sheikh Mohammed | J Dunlop | 4/1 |
| 18 Aug | York | Capricorn Line | Lonsdale | 7,017 | 16 | I Allen | L Cumani | 3/1 |
| 19 Aug | York | Mirabeau | City of York | 5,277 | 7 | J Lilley | H Wragg | 2/1F |
| 21 Aug | Sandown | Mennea(USA) | | 3,074 | 8 | C A B St George | H Price | 15/8F |
| 21 Aug | Sandown | The Fort | Intercraft Solario | 10,727 | 7 | Mrs H Phillips | H Cecil | 2/1F |
| 21 Aug | Sandown | Voracity | | 1,931 | 11 | Lord Derby | J Winter | EvF |
| 24 Aug | Yarmouth | Polished Silver | | 1,545 | 7 | M Foustok | H Cecil | 2/7F |
| 25 Aug | Yarmouth | Super Sox | | 1,545 | 7 | C Duke | A Jarvis | 2/7F |
| 27 Aug | Goodwood | Sidab | | 3,726 | 5 | O Zawawi | W Musson | 9/4 |
| 27 Aug | Goodwood | Sa-Vegas | Wm Hill Hcp | 4,620 | 12 | E Landi | J Dunlop | 13/8F |
| 27 Aug | Goodwood | Play Our Song | | 3,609 | 5 | S Vanian | J Dunlop | 11/2 |
| 30 Aug | Newcastle | Roman Beach | Ladbroke N/H | 4,279 | 7 | R Canham | M Tompkins | 7/2 |
| 1 Sept | York | Now and Again | Gilbey Championship | 7,126 | 7 | K Al Sabah | H Cecil | 8/13F |
| 2 Sept | York | Dunbeath | | 3,620 | 7 | M Riordan | H Cecil | 4/9F |
| 3 Sept | Kempton | Grand Maître | | 2,470 | 11 | D Wildenstein | H Cecil | 7/1 |
| 4 Sept | Kempton | Critique | September | 13,136 | 11 | G Vanian | H Cecil | 8/11F |
| 4 Sept | Kempton | Mennea | Geoffrey Hamlyn | 4,721 | 8 | C A B St George | H Price | 13/8F |
| 4 Sept | Kempton | Polished Silver | Chertsey Lock | 4,857 | 7 | M Foustok | H Cecil | 4/6F |
| 8 Sept | Doncaster | Cock Robin | Ribero | 4,708 | 7 | Mrs V Hue-Williams | M Stoute | 10/11F |
| 8 Sept | Doncaster | Karadar | Esal Bookmakers | 18,601 | 14 | Aga Khan | M Stoute | 11/12 |
| 8 Sept | Doncaster | Linda's Fantasy | Rous National Hunt | 4,376 | 6 | J Bray | R Armstrong | 7/1 |
| 9 Sept | Doncaster | Ardross | Doncaster Cup | 19,195 | 18 | C A B St George | H Cecil | 2/9F |
| 9 Sept | Doncaster | Vorvados | Portland Hcp | 8,051 | 5 | Miss F Gallichan | M Haynes | 6/1 |
| 9 Sept | Doncaster | Bright Crocus(USA) | May Hill | 15,600 | 8 | Mrs B Walters | H Cecil | 6/1 |
| 10 Sept | Goodwood | Mr Fluorocarbon | | 3,480 | 8 | J McAlister | H Cecil | N/B |
| 10 Sept | Goodwood | Ghaiya(USA) | | 3,579 | 8 | Sheikh Mohammed | J Dunlop | 11/10F |
| 14 Sept | Yarmouth | Lucky Ivor | | 1,290 | 14 | O Phipps | J Dunlop | 9/4F |
| 15 Sept | Yarmouth | Compound | | 732 | 7 | Miss S Baldwin | Mrs N Kennedy | 7/2 |
| 16 Sept | Yarmouth | Lord Protector | | 1,524 | 7 | B Kirkorian | H Cecil | 1/2F |
| 17 Sept | Newbury | Special Pleasure | | 2,857 | 5 | J Sullivan | R Armstrong | 6/1 |
| 17 Sept | Newbury | Polished Silver | Haynes, Hanson & Clark | 4,187 | 8 | M Foustok | H Cecil | 5/6F |
| 18 Sept | Newbury | Wiki Wiki Wheels | Champagne | 6,372 | 5 | P Savill | C R Nelson | 13/8 |
| 18 Sept | Newbury | Salieri (USA) | Mill Reef | 20,325 | 6 | C A B St George | H Cecil | 11/4 |
| 18 Sept | Newbury | Misguided | | 2,943 | 5 | T Holland-Martin | H Cecil | 11/4 |
| 21 Sept | Lingfield | Ultimate Price | | 1,431 | 7 | R G Brennan | B Hanbury | 5/1 |
| 21 Sept | Lingfield | Coquito's Friend | | 1,431 | 6 | A Alvarado | B Hanbury | 8/11F |
| 25 Sept | Ascot | Dunbeath (USA) | Royal Lodge | 31,102 | 8 | M Riordan | H Cecil | 5/2F |
| 28 Sept | Goodwood | Misguided | | 3,015 | 6 | T Holland-Martin | H Cecil | 5/4F |
| 28 Sept | Goodwood | The Fort | | 3,356 | 7 | Mrs H Phillips | H Cecil | 5/6F |
| 29 Sept | Newmarket | Johnny Nobody | Rowley Mile National Hunt | 5,049 | 8 | J Bergin | A Jarvis | 10/1 |
| 30 Sept | Newmarket | What Lake | | 3,574 | 6 | J Rafsky | B Hanbury | 9/4F |

(USA) = America (Can) = Canada

| Date | Race Course | Horse | Race | Value £ | Dist Fur | Owner | Trainer | S/P |
|---|---|---|---|---|---|---|---|---|
| 30 Sept | Newmarket | Diesis | Wm Hill Middle Park | 39,268 | 6 | Lord Howard de Walden | H Cecil | 10/11F |
| 1 Oct | Newmarket | Tolomeo | Westley M | 4,432 | 7 | Count d'Alessio | L Cumani | 4/6F |
| 1 Oct | Newmarket | Polished Silver | Somerville Tattersall | 9,692 | 7 | M Fustock | H Cecil | 13/8 |
| 5 Oct | Brighton | Elite Syncopation (USA) | | 1,368 | 6 | Mrs W Taylor | H Cecil | 4/5F |
| 6 Oct | York | Blue Nantucket | | 3,630 | 6 | Mrs C Dibble | D Thom | 6/1 |
| 6 Oct | York | John French | | 3,355 | 7 | C A B St George | H Cecil | 7/4F |
| 7 Oct | Lingfield | Cavaradossi(USA) | | 2,557 | 12 | C A B St George | H Cecil | 2/7F |
| 11 Oct | Pontefract | Plegdon Green | | 769 | 10 | A J Smith | N Callaghan | 9/4F |
| 11 Oct | Pontefract | Reves Celestes(USA) | | 2,666 | 8 | A Clore | B W Hills | 5/2F |
| 11 Oct | Pontefract | Misguided | | 2,043 | 6 | T Holland-Martin | H Cecil | 4/11F |
| 14 Oct | Newmarket | Oula Owl | | 3,886 | 8 | Mrs A Brucker | L Cumani | 3/1F |
| 14 Oct | Newmarket | Holy Spark | | 3,860 | 8 | J Leek | G Harwood | 20/1 |
| 15 Oct | Newmarket | Vorvados | Phantom House Hcp | 5,134 | 6 | Miss F Gallichan | M Haynes | 7/1 |
| 15 Oct | Newmarket | Diesis | Wm Hill Dewhurst | 46,228 | 7 | Lord Howard de Walden | H Cecil | 2/1 |
| 15 Oct | Newmarket | Sheer Grit | | 3,999 | 12 | Capt M D Lemos | C Brittain | 7/1 |
| 19 Oct | Leicester | Herodote(USA) | | 1,526 | 7 | D Wildenstein | H Cecil | 10/11F |
| 23 Oct | Doncaster | Dunbeath(USA) | Wm Hill Futurity | 50,842 | 8 | M Riordan | H Cecil | 4/7F |
| 26 Oct | Nottingham | Holy Spark | | 2,581 | 8 | J Leek | G Harwood | 1/2F |
| 8 Oct | Ascot | Vadrouille(USA) | Marlborough House | 4,503 | 8 | D Wildenstein | H Cecil | 10/3 |
| 30 Oct | Newmarket | John French | Jonnie's The Bookmakers Zetland | 8,324 | 10 | C A B St George | H Cecil | EvF |

1982: 188 wins; 87 2nds; 94 3rds; 698 rides

| Date | Race Course | Horse | Race | Value £ | Dist Fur | Owner | Trainer | S/P |
|---|---|---|---|---|---|---|---|---|
| 1983 | | | | | | | | |
| 3 Apl | Doncaster | Vorvados | Cammidge Trophy | 7,683 | 6 | Miss F Galligham | M Haynes | 17/2 |
| 9 Apl | Salisbury | Pusey Street | | 1,833 | 6 | S S Niarchos | G Harwood | 13/8F |
| 9 Apl | Salisbury | Shanley's Style | | 1,689 | 10 | Mrs C Orme | Mrs C J Reavey | 13/8F |
| 9 Apl | Salisbury | Gaelic Jewel | | 1,788 | 8 | J Neville | R Holder | 3/1F |
| 13 Apl | Newmarket | Ivano(Can) | Earl of Sefton | 14,710 | 9 | Count d'Alessio | H Cecil | 7/1 |
| 16 Apl | Newbury | Solva | | 1,651 | 5 | D Garfield | Mrs C J Reavey | 6/4 |
| 16 Apl | Newbury | Adonijah | | 3,313 | 8 | Mrs F Allen | H Cecil | 7/4F |
| 23 Apl | Newbury | Ivano(Can) | | 17,000 | 10 | Count d'Alessio | H Cecil | 4/6F |
| 23 Apl | Newbury | Conrad Hilton | | 2,236 | 5 | E Alkhalifa | H Cecil | 5/4F |
| 28 Apl | Newmarket | Rex Lake | | 2,834 | 5 | Mrs M Burrell | H Cecil | 13/8 |
| 28 Apl | Newmarket | Popsi's Joy | | 3,889 | 16 | V Lawson | M Haynes | 11/4F |
| 29 Apl | Newmarket | Be My Valentine | | 2,582 | 5 | A Chatila | H Cecil | 4/7F |
| 30 Apl | Newmarket | Precocious | | 3,579 | 5 | Lord Tavistock | H Cecil | 6/4F |
| 2 May | Kempton | Star of Ireland | | 2,670 | 7 | H Pink | A Jarvis | 7/4F |
| 7 May | Lingfield | Tulsa Flyer | | 3,869 | 10 | Tulsa Holdings Ltd | J Bethell | 6/1 |
| 7 May | Lingfield | Adonijan | | 2,315 | 10 | Mrs F Allen | H Cecil | 4/7F |
| 10 May | York | Malvern Beauty | | 3,444 | 10½ | H J Joel | H Cecil | 11/12 |
| 12 May | York | Vorvados | Duke of York | 18,050 | 6 | Miss F Galligham | M Haynes | 11/1 |
| 14 May | Newbury | Pusey Street | | 4,932 | 6 | O/trainer | J R Bosley | 6/4F |
| 14 May | Newbury | Ore | | 3,928 | 13 | O Zawawi | W Musson | 5/12 |
| 16 May | Wolver'ton | Caius | | 828 | 5 | Count d'Alessio | H Cecil | 8/15F |
| 16 May | Wolver'ton | Norfolk Realm | | 1,467 | 7 | Mrs D Goldstein | P Makin | 7/1 |
| 16 May | Wolver'ton | Honeybeta | | 1,035 | 9 | L Freedman | H Cecil | 4/6F |
| 18 May | Goodwood | Corn Street | | 2,355 | 8 | M Wilkins | J R Bosley | 3/1F |
| 19 May | Goodwood | Magdalena(USA) | | 3,393 | 7 | D Wildenstein | H Cecil | 9/4F |
| 23 May | Kempton | Tulsa Flyer | | 2,632 | 10 | Tulsa Holdings Ltd | J Bethell | 9/4F |

(USA) = America (Can) = Canada

| Date | Race Course | Horse | Race | Value £ | Dist Fur | Owner | Trainer | S/P |
|---|---|---|---|---|---|---|---|---|
| 31 May | Sandown | Ore | Henry II | 5,880 | 16 | O Zawawi | W Musson | 5/4F |
| 31 May | Sandown | Precocious | National 2-y-o | 4,568 | 5 | Lord Tavistock | H Cecil | 2/5F |
| 30 May | Sandown | Fearless Lad | Temple | 18,650 | 5 | G Soulsby | R D Peacock | 5/4F |
| 1 June | Epsom | Teenosa(USA) | The Derby | 165,080 | 12 | E B Moller | G Wragg | 11/2F |
| 2 June | Epsom | Be My Native | Coronation Cup | 42,338 | 12 | K Hsu | R Armstrong | 8/1 |
| 7 June | Yarmouth | Defecting Dancer | | 1,301 | 5 | Sheikh Mohammed | H Cecil | 2/7F |
| 8 June | Newbury | Follow Me Follow | | 3,124 | 5 | Sheikh Ali Abu Khamsin | J Winter | 3/1 |
| 10 June | Sandown | Miramar Reef | | 3,350 | 10 | Mrs A Richards | C Brittain | 8/1 |
| 10 June | Sandown | Never So Bold | | 2,931 | 7 | E Kessly | R Armstrong | 9/4 |
| 13 June | Windsor | Son of Kandy(USA) | | 890 | 5 | A Bingley | D Elsworth | 6/4F |
| 16 June | Royal Ascot | Precocious | Norfolk | 8,184 | 5 | Lord Tavistock | H Cecil | 4/11F |
| 17 June | Royal Ascot | Defecting Dancer | Windsor Castle | 8,662 | 5 | Sheikh Mohammed | H Cecil | 6/4F |
| 18 June | Ascot | Vacarme (USA) | Erroll | 6,263 | 6 | D Wildenstein | H Cecil | 5/4F |
| 20 June | Ascot | Pontchartrain | | 2,385 | 8 | J Stone | H Cecil | 5/2F |
| 21 June | Pontefract | Caius | | 2,421 | 6 | Count d'Alessio | H Cecil | 2/9F |
| 27 June | Nottingham | Mark of Respect | | 1,560 | 10 | Capt J Durham-Matthews | R Armstrong | 8/1 |
| 29 June | Yarmouth | All is Forgotten | | 1,668 | 5 | Miss I Norman | D Thom | 6/5F |
| 29 June | Yarmouth | Easy Air | | 1,984 | 6 | M Robinson | R Armstrong | 9/2 |
| 29 June | Yarmouth | Trojan Fen | | 1,724 | 7 | S S Niarchos | H Cecil | 8/11F |
| 4 July | Windsor | Countess Concorde (USA) | | 690 | 6 | Mrs R Rogers | B Hanbury | 11/10F |
| 5 July | Newmarket | Mummy's Pleasure | Ward Hill Bunbury Cup | 10,503 | 7 | A Cull | P Haslam | 9/1 |
| 5 July | Newmarket | Defective Dancer | Chesterfield | 4,283 | 5 | Sheikh Mohammed | H Cecil | 2/9F |
| 7 July | Newmarket | Chicago Bid | Fulbourn Memorial | 4,198 | 6 | C Wacker III | R Armstrong | 11/1 |
| 8 July | York | Miss Import | Lin Pac | 4,526 | 5 | Miss I M Raine | T D Barron | 15/2 |
| 8 July | Newmarket | Lord Protector (USA) | | 2,632 | 8 | B Kirkorian | H Cecil | 6/4F |
| 9 July | Ayr | Sabre Dance | Land of Burns | 9,269 | 10 | Lord Howard de Walden | H Cecil | 8/11F |
| 11 July | Leicester | Lady Fish | | 2,102 | 8 | Mrs E M Burke | B Hanbury | 2/1F |
| 11 July | Leicester | Bour Bonnan(USA) | | 828 | 7 | S S Niarchos | H Cecil | 3/10F |
| 12 July | Leicester | St Terramar | | 1,752 | 5 | N Sarif | D C Jermy | 3/1F |
| 12 July | Leicester | Lady Moon | | 1,035 | 12 | H J Joel | H Cecil | 13/8F |
| 12 July | Leicester | Tai Fu Kwai | | 2,080 | 10 | N Howley | C N Williams | 10/3F |
| 12 July | Leicester | Pig Tail | | 1,035 | 7 | D Wildenstein | H Cecil | 4/11F |
| 14 July | Yarmouth | Millbow | | 1,350 | 7 | S S Niarchos | H Cecil | 2/5F |
| 14 July | Yarmouth | Shantung Lace | | 650 | 6 | R Green | G Blum | 6/1 |
| 15 July | Newbury | Crown Godiva | | 2,278 | 8 | R Sangster | B W Hills | 2/1F |
| 15 July | Newbury | Well Covered | | 3,498 | 7 | H J Joel | R Hannon | 10/3 |
| 16 July | Nottingham | Steel Kid | | 1,857 | 10 | R N Tikkoo | R Armstrong | 10/3 |
| 16 July | Nottingham | Jameston | | 1,251 | 6 | Mrs A Read | R Armstrong | EvF |
| 16 July | Nottingham | Prickle | | 690 | 6 | P D Player | H Cecil | 7/4F |
| 16 July | Newbury | Trojan Fen | Donnington Castle | 4,815 | 7 | S S Niarchos | H Cecil | 4/9F |
| 16 July | Newbury | Adonijah | | 913 | 10 | K Abdulla | H Cecil | 8/11F |
| 18 July | Wolver'ton | Honeybeta | | 3,298 | 18 | L Freedman | H Cecil | 3/8F |
| 20 July | Sandown | Dunant | | 1,752 | 5 | W J Greedley | C Brittain | 2/1F |
| 20 July | Yarmouth | Fai La Bella | | 1,685 | 10 | Fittock's Stud | L Cumani | 13/8F |
| 21 July | Sandown | Sunoak | | 2,404 | 8 | J A Haverhals | G Harwood | 16/1 |
| 22 July | Ascot | Miss Import | Rous Memorial | 5,444 | 5 | Mrs I M Raine | T D Barron | 4/1 |
| 22 July | Ascot | Harvard | Sandwich | 5,035 | 7 | P J Meredew | R Boss | 12/1 |
| 23 July | Ascot | Desirable | Princess Margaret | 5,435 | 6 | Mrs J M Corbett | B W Hills | 4/7F |

(USA) = America

| Date | Race Course | Horse | Race | Value £ | Dist Fur | Owner | Trainer | S/P |
|---|---|---|---|---|---|---|---|---|
| 23 July | Ascot | Keen | Granville | 5,735 | 6 | Lord Howard de Walden | H Cecil | 3/1 |
| 25 July | Nottingham | Danseur de Corde(USA) | | 690 | 10 | D Wildenstein | H Cecil | 4/7F |
| 26 July | Goodwood | Precocious | Molecomb | 13,228 | 5 | Lord Tavistock | H Cecil | 3/10F |
| 26 July | Goodwood | John French | Gordon | 18,688 | 12 | C A B St George | H Cecil | 4/11 |
| 26 July | Goodwood | Magnetic Field | Charlton Hcp | 4,828 | 8 | M Fustok | H Cecil | 14/1 |
| 28 July | Goodwood | Trojan Fen | Lanson Champagne | 9,505 | 7 | S S Niarchos | H Cecil | 4/11F |
| 29 July | Newmarket | All Is Forgiven | Lavenham | 4,207 | 6 | Mrs I Norman | D T Thom | 6/1 |
| 30 July | Windsor | Laurencin(USA) | | 690 | 6 | C A B St George | H Cecil | 4/7F |
| 3 Aug | Yarmouth | Honeybeta | | 2,473 | 10 | L Freedman | H Cecil | 9/4 |
| 4 Aug | Yarmouth | Nasr | | 1,366 | 6 | Y Nasib | N Callaghan | 1/2F |
| 11 Aug | Salisbury | Magnetic Field | | 1,583 | 8 | M Fustok | H Cecil | 4/11F |
| 12 Aug | Newbury | Salieri(USA) | Hungerford | 15,284 | 7 | C A B St George | H Cecil | 7/2 |
| 12 Aug | Newbury | Trojan Fen | Washington Singer | 5,490 | 7 | S S Niarchos | H Cecil | 8/15F |
| 13 Aug | Newbury | Be My Valentine* | | 3,484 | 5 | D Harris | H Cecil | 9/2 |
| 15 Aug | Leicester | Coquito's Star | | 1,940 | 6 | A Alvardo | B Hanbury | 7/2F |
| 16 Aug | York | Adonijah | High Line | 26,119 | 10 | K Abdulla | H Cecil | 2/5F |
| 17 Aug | York | Jupiter Island | Tote Ebor | 27,652 | 14 | S M Threadwell | C Brittain | 9/1 |
| 17 Aug | York | Prickle | Lowther | 15,832 | 6 | P D Player | H Cecil | 11/4F |
| 18 Aug | York | Precocious | Gimcrack | 41,181 | 6 | Lord Tavistock | H Cecil | 8/11F |
| 18 Aug | York | Hymettus | | 1,789 | 12 | Lord Halifax | J Dunlop | 6/1 |
| 19 Aug | Sandown | Dunant | | 2,124 | 5 | W J Gredley | C Brittain | 5/4F |
| 20 Aug | Ripon | Monongelia | | 2,847 | 9 | T F Brennan | H Cecil | 2/1F |
| 20 Aug | Ripon | Who Knows the Game | | 1,486 | 5 | J E Abbey | B McMahon | 7/2F |
| 22 Aug | Windsor | Anton Pillar (USA) | | 690 | 5 | C A B St George | H Cecil | 1/4F |
| 23 Aug | Yarmouth | El Hakam(USA) | | 1,035 | 7 | Sheikh Mohammed | H Cecil | 2/5F |
| 27 Aug | Windsor | Sky Jump | | 963 | 8 | O/trainer | B Swift | 7/2 |
| 27 Aug | Goodwood | Valerio(USA) | | 2,218 | 7 | B N Hamoud | L Cumani | 6/5F |
| 29 Aug | Epsom | Aulait | | 1,822 | 7 | R Sangster | B W Hills | 7/2 |
| 29 Aug | Epsom | Kalamont | | 2,427 | 12 | Mrs V Hue-Williams | J Dunlop | 9/4F |
| 29 Aug | Epsom | Tetron Bay | | 3,100 | 8 | R J Shannon | R Hannon | 7/2 |
| 29 Aug | Epsom | Jameelapi | | 1,853 | 6 | M Al Maktoum | H Cecil | 3/10F |
| 30 Aug | Epsom | Cutting Wind | | 1,928 | 7 | Mrs P Meynet | B Hanbury | 5/1 |
| 2 Sept | Kempton | Lady Moon | | 2,292 | 11 | H J Joel | H Cecil | 5/2F |
| 2 Sept | Kempton | Defecting Dancer | Bonus Print Sirenia | 7,625 | 6 | Sheikh Mohammed | H Cecil | 4/7F |
| 3 Sept | Kempton | Sedra | Intercraft | 7,146 | 10 | M Alqatum | J Dunlop | 11/4JF |
| 3 Sept | Kempton | Tetron Bay | Geoffrey Hamlyn | 4,006 | 8 | R J Shannon | R Hannon | 9/4 |
| 5 Sept | Windsor | View | | 1,348 | 6 | R J McAulay | B Hanbury | 9/4 |
| 9 Sept | Doncaster | Hedaka | | 3,200 | 8 | O/trainer | I S Walker | 9/4F |
| 13 Sept | Yarmouth | Valerio | | 2,561 | 8 | B N Hamoud | L Cumani | 5/1 |
| 13 Sept | Yarmouth | Jinny Beaumont | | 1,463 | 11 | L Freedman | H Cecil | 6/4F |
| 14 Sept | Yarmouth | Legend of France | | 828 | 8 | D Wildenstein | H Cecil | 7/4F |
| 15 Sept | Yarmouth | Van Dyck Brown | | 1,035 | 7 | H Demetriou | H Cecil | 9/4F |
| 16 Sept | Yarmouth | Millside | | 1,035 | 8 | S S Niarchos | H Cecil | 1/2F |
| 16 Sept | Yarmouth | Video King | | 2,124 | 7 | Mrs G E Maloney | C Brittain | 6/4F |
| 16 Sept | Yarmouth | Elect(USA) | | 2,085 | 10 | J Clement | L Cumani | 11/8F |
| 17 Sept | Newbury | Jupiter Island | Coral Autumn | 9,819 | 13 | S M Threadwell | C Brittain | 4/1F |
| 17 Sept | Newbury | Vacarme(USA) | Mill Reef | 20,473 | 6 | D Wildenstein | H Cecil | 2/7F |
| 19 Sept | Leicester | Senane | | 1,035 | 8 | Mrs D Butter | H Cecil | 11/8F |
| 20 Sept | Leicester | Master Wit(USA) | | 1,035 | 7 | S S Niarchos | H Cecil | 4/1 |
| 22 Sept | Ascot | Salieri(USA) | Diadem | 14,728 | 6 | C A B St George | H Cecil | 9/4F |
| 23 Sept | Ascot | Alpine Springs | Kensington Palace | 5,162 | 5 | K Hsu | R Armstrong | 8/13F |
| 24 Sept | Ascot | Cutting Wind | Golden Gates | 5,917 | 6 | Mrs P Meynet | B Hanbury | 6/1 |
| 27 Sept | Nottingham | Que Marido(USA) | | 690 | 6 | Sheikh Mohammed | H Cecil | 8/3F |

* Dead Heat (USA) = America

| Date | Race Course | Horse | Race | Value £ | Dist Fur | Owner | Trainer | S/P |
|---|---|---|---|---|---|---|---|---|
| 27 Sept | Nottingham | Westview(F) | | 2,654 | 13 | L Freedman | H Cecil | 5/1F |
| 29 Sept | Newmarket | Jupiter Island | Southfield | 4,713 | 12 | S M Threadwell | C Brittain | 15/8F |
| 30 Sept | Newmarket | Chelkov(F) | | 4,390 | 7 | W R Hawn | R Armstrong | 1/2 |
| 30 Sept | Newmarket | Alleging(USA) | Westley | 4,490 | 7 | Elisha Holdings | H Cecil | 10/1 |
| 4 Oct | Brighton | Innamarta(USA) | | 1,473 | 6 | Dr J K Robbins | H Cecil | 4/5F |
| 7 Oct | Sandown | Lion City | | 12,135 | 8 | C Machos | E Eldin | 5/2F |
| 8 Oct | Ascot | Tetron Bay | BRCAS | 5,599 | 8 | R J Shannon | R Hannon | 8/1 |
| 11 Oct | Warwick | Welsh Warrior | | 1,293 | 8 | H J Joel | H Cecil | 13/8F |
| 13 Oct | Newmarket | Salieri(USA) | Bisquit Cognac Challenge | 21,320 | 7 | C A B St George | H Cecil | 13/8F |
| 15 Oct | Newmarket | Condrillae (USA) | Houghton | 9,351 | 7 | P Burrell | R J R Williams | 13/8F |
| 17 Oct | Leicester | Ophrys | | 1,035 | 7 | A C Hall | H Cecil | 1/13F |
| 17 Oct | Leicester | Innamorato(USA) | | 2,477 | 6 | D J K Robbins | H Cecil | 4/11F |
| 17 Oct | Doncaster | El Jazzi | | 1,035 | 7 | Prince F Khaled | H Cecil | 4/7F |
| 18 Oct | Leicester | Bold Patriarch (Can) | | 1,035 | 7 | P Winfield | J L Dunlop | 8/15F |
| 20 Oct | Newbury | Cremets | | 2,784 | 6 | R G Percival | J L Dunlop | 6/4F |
| 22 Oct | Doncaster | Bastille | | 3,200 | 7 | Lavinia Duchess of Norfolk | J L Dunlop | 5/1 |
| 22 Oct | Doncaster | Athenia(USA) | | 2,139 | 6 | D Lane | H Cecil | 8/11F |
| 25 Oct | Nottingham | Alleging(USA) | | 3,376 | 8 | Elisha Holdings | H Cecil | 2/1F |
| 29 Oct | Newmarket | Travel Away | | 2,964 | 7 | R A Patrick | B Hanbury | 10/1 |
| 31 Oct | Leicester | Tender Moon | | 1,035 | 6 | S T Wong | B Hanbury | 3/1F |
| 31 Oct | Leicester | Swift Return | | 1,035 | 6 | G S Beccle | J R Winter | 11/8F |
| 1 Nov | Leicester | Sam M(USA) | | 828 | 8 | Sheikh Mohammed | J L Dunlop | 6/4F |
| 4 Nov | Doncaster | Singing Sailor | | 1,870 | 5 | Introgroup Holdings | R Hannon | 9/4F |

1983: 150 wins; 109 2nds; 64 3rds; 641 rides

| Date | Race Course | Horse | Race | Value £ | Dist Fur | Owner | Trainer | S/P |
|---|---|---|---|---|---|---|---|---|
| 1984 | | | | | | | | |
| 13 Apl | Newbury | Spicy Story | | 2,715 | 11 | P Mellon | I Balding | 5/1 |
| 17 Apl | Newmarket | Prince of Peace | | 4,259 | 14 | Sheikh Mohammed | H Cecil | 11/2F |
| 18 Apl | Newmarket | Baynoun | | 2,966 | 12 | Aga Khan | R Houghton | 11/1 |
| 19 Apl | Newmarket | Trojan Fen | Gerry Feilden Memorial | 7,778 | 9 | S S Niarchos | H Cecil | 7/4F |
| 21 Apl | Kempton | Keen | Bonus Print Easter | 7,532 | 8 | Lord Howard de Walden | H Cecil | 8/13F |
| 28 Apl | Sandown | Old Bailey | | 2,674 | 5 | Mrs C B Thompson | G Harwood | 1/2F |
| 28 Apl | Sandown | Caliph | | 2,670 | 5 | V J Avani | R Simpson | 6/1 |
| 30 Apl | Warwick | Thalberg‡ | | 906 | 5 | Swinton Holdings | M J Hinchcliffe | 7/4F |
| 30 Apl | Warwick | Double Celt | | 1,339 | 8 | L Freedman | H Cecil | 3/1F |
| 3 May | Newmarket | Prince of Peace | | 4,549 | 16 | Sheikh Mohammed | H Cecil | 11/8F |
| 4 May | Newmarket | Sandy Island | Pretty Polly | 8,927 | 10 | Lord Howard de Walden | H Cecil | 15/8F |
| 18 May | Newbury | Circus Plume | Sir Charles Clore | 8,467 | 10 | Sir R McAlpine | J L Dunlop | 15/2 |
| 19 May | Newbury | Jupiter Island | | 3,947 | 13 | S M Threadwell | C Brittain | 10/11F |
| 19 May | Newbury | Soldier Ant | | 3,980 | 11 | A J Richards | C Brittain | 7/1 |
| 19 May | Newbury | Face Facts | | 2,784 | 11 | Lady Howard de Walden | H Cecil | 4/6F |
| 21 May | Yarmouth | Jolly Business | | 826 | 5 | Mrs V J Lewis | A P Ingham | 6/4F |
| 21 May | Yarmouth | Going Broke | | 1,760 | 12 | J G O'Neil | D J C Murray-Smith | 2/1F |
| 21 May | Yarmouth | Tocave | | 1,044 | 7 | M Al Maktoum | H Cecil | 4/11F |
| 21 May | Yarmouth | Llinos | | 1,300 | 8 | J E Lloyd | J Winter | 6/4F |
| 22 May | Goodwood | Really Honest | | 3,553 | 8 | C A B St George | B Hanbury | 9/4F |
| 23 May | Goodwood | Single Love | | 2,343 | 5 | Dr C Labrecciosa | B Hanbury | 9/4 |
| 24 May | Goodwood | Miss Beaulieu | Lupe | 8,558 | 10 | J L C Pearse | G Wragg | 4/1 |
| 26 May | Haydock | Double Celt | | 3,110 | 10 | L Freedman | H Cecil | 4/1 |
| 26 May | Haydock | Prince of Peace | | 897 | 16 | Sheikh Mohammed | H Cecil | 8/11F |

‡On objection (F) = France (USA) = America (Can) = Canada

| Date | Race Course | Horse | Race | Value £ | Dist Fur | Owner | Trainer | S/P |
|---|---|---|---|---|---|---|---|---|
| 26 May | Haydock | Standing Orders | | 1,755 | 5 | R J McAuley | B Hanbury | 10/11F |
| 28 May | Sandown | Adonijah | Brigadier Gerard | 18,675 | 10 | K Abdulla | H Cecil | EvF |
| 28 May | Goodwood | Van Dyck Brown | | 3,022 | 14 | H Demetriou | H Cecil | 7/1 |
| 30 May | Brighton | Maziara | | 880 | 8 | G A Chagoury | A P Ingham | 2/1F |
| 2 June | Newmarket | Sharp Romance (USA) | | 918 | 5 | Sheikh Rashid Al Khalifa | P Kelleway | 11/8F |
| 4 June | Folkestone | Tocave | | 613 | 6 | M Al Maktoum | H Cecil | 1/4F |
| 4 June | Folkestone | Art Edict | | 829 | 12 | S S Niarchos | H Cecil | 6/5F |
| 6 June | Epsom | Adonijah | | 19,260 | 8 | K Abdulla | H Cecil | 4/5F |
| 7 June | Epsom | Braka(USA) | | 4,534 | 12 | C A B St George | H Cecil | 3/1F |
| 8 June | Epsom | Prince of Peace | | 10,965 | 12 | Sheikh Mohammed | H Cecil | 3/1F |
| 9 June | Epsom | Circus Plume | Gold Seal Oaks | 122,040 | 12 | Sir R McAlpine | J Dunlop | 4/1 |
| 11 June | Leicester | Kip | | 2,262 | 6 | Mrs A Hollest | D Thom | 9/2 |
| 11 June | Leicester | Athenia(USA) | | 1,616 | 7 | D Lane | H Cecil | 4/5F |
| 12 June | Yarmouth | Rothco | | 1,137 | 14 | C A B St George | O J Douieb | 4/1 |
| 15 June | York | Indian Flower | | 3,271 | 5 | K Bethel | R Boss | 10/11F |
| 16 June | York | One Way Street | Vernons | 8,714 | 8 | L Freedman | H Cecil | 10/1 |
| 19 June | Royal Ascot | Trojan Fen | Queen Anne | 28,896 | 8 | S S Niarchos | H Cecil | 9/4 |
| 21 June | Royal Ascot | Magic Mirror | Norfolk | 14,278 | 5 | S S Niarchos | M V O'Brien(I) | 11/8 |
| 23 June | Ascot | The Miller(F) | Churchill | 6,482 | 12 | S S Niarchos | M V O'Brien(I) | 11/8F |
| 25 June | Wolver'ton | Call of the Wild | | 718 | 5 | Count d'Alessio | H Cecil | EvF |
| 25 June | Wolver'ton | One Way Street | | 1,460 | 9 | L Freedman | H Cecil | 2/5F |
| 25 June | Wolver'ton | Viceroy Lad | | 2,690 | 8 | O/trainer | R Hannon | 9/2 |
| 28 June | Salisbury | Viceroy Lad | | 2,456 | 8 | F S Broom | R Hannon | 9/4F |
| 30 June | Newmarket | Fatah Flare (USA) | | 4,513 | 6 | Sheikh Mohammed | H Cecil | 4/5F |
| 4 July | Yarmouth | Pacific Mail (USA) | | 1,704 | 7 | Sheikh Mohammed | H Cecil | 5/4F |
| 5 July | Brighton | Induit(Can) | | 822 | 6 | Swinton Holdings | B W Hills | 5/1 |
| 5 July | Brighton | Bassett Boy | | 2,892 | 12 | J Ross | R Armstrong | 13/8F |
| 6 July | Yarmouth | Siderell | | 926 | 6 | Sheikh Mohammed | H Cecil | 1/2F |
| 7 July | Haydock | Sandy Island | Lancashire Oaks | 24,992 | 12 | Lord Howard de Walden | H Cecil | 5/6F |
| 10 July | Newmarket | Troy Fair | | 3,944 | 7 | Sir M Sobell | W R Hern | 13/2 |
| 10 July | Newmarket | Head for Heights | Princess of Wales | 27,518 | 12 | Sheikh Mohammed | W R Hern | 10/3F |
| 11 July | Newmarket | Pacific Mail (USA) | | 4,776 | 7 | Sheikh Mohammed | H Cecil | 9/4F |
| 12 July | Newmarket | Rusty Law | | 4,131 | 6 | S S Niarchos | H Cecil | 15/8F |
| 14 July | Lingfield | Doulab(USA) | Williams de Broe | 5,384 | 6 | M Al Maktoum | H B T Jones | EvF |
| 14 July | Lingfield | Condrillac | Marley Roof Tiles | 12,213 | 7 | P Burrell | H Cecil | 7/4F |
| 17 July | Ayr | Mr Jay-zee | | 3,993 | 6 | J Swirn | N Callaghan | 8/10F |
| 17 July | Leicester | Homo Sapien | | 3,319 | 6 | S S Niarchos | H Cecil | 8/15F |
| 18 July | Kempton | North Queen | | 3,463 | 7 | Elisha Holdings | G Lewis | 4/1F |
| 19 July | Yarmouth | Lanfranco | | 826 | 7 | C A B St George | H Cecil | 1/4F |
| 19 July | Yarmouth | Taimisha | | 640 | 6 | Swinton Holdings | M J Hinchcliffe | 5/1 |
| 24 July | Pontefract | Call of the Wild | | 2,215 | 5 | Count d'Alessio | H Cecil | 8/11F |
| 25 July | Yarmouth | Nigel's Girl | | 633 | 5 | V Coomaraswamy | P Haslam | 1/2F |
| 28 July | Ascot | Teenoso(USA) | King George and Queen Elizabeth Diamond | 141,247 | 12 | E B Moller | G Wragg | 13/2 |
| 31 July | Goodwood | Commanche Run | Gordon | 19,566 | 12 | I Allan | L Cumani | 7/2 |
| 2 Aug | Goodwood | Anitas Prince | King George | 16,416 | 5 | Mrs A Quinn | R Lister | 2/1F |
| 4 Aug | Newmarket | Lanfranco | Exeter | 5,198 | 7 | C A B St George | H Cecil | 1/5F |
| 4 Aug | Newmarket | Hadeer | Colman's of Norwich National Hunt | 8,376 | 6 | M Al Maktoum | M Stoute | EvF |
| 6 Aug | Wolver'ton | Rusty Law | | 1,130 | 7 | S S Niarchos | H Cecil | 4/9F |
| 1 Sept | Sandown | Oh So Sharp | Solario | 11,283 | 7 | Sheikh Mohammed | H Cecil | 6/4F |
| 7 Sept | Kempton | One Way Street | Twickenham | 7,322 | 10 | L Freedman | H Cecil | 7/4 |

(I) = Ireland (F) = France (USA) = America (Can) = Canada

| Date | Race Course | Horse | Race | Value £ | Dist Fur | Owner | Trainer | S/P |
|---|---|---|---|---|---|---|---|---|
| 10 Sept | Windsor | Record Gift | | 1,561 | 5 | S T Wong | B Hanbury | 8/1 |
| 10 Sept | Windsor | Alleging(USA) | | 3,980 | 10 | Elisha Holdings | H Cecil | 5/4 |
| 10 Sept | Windsor | Tamino | | 762 | 11 | Lord Howard de Walden | H Cecil | 10/11F |
| 12 Sept | Windsor | Prince Reymo | Scarbrough | 9,052 | 5 | R L Emmitt | R Armstrong | 9/2 |
| 13 Sept | Doncaster | Ever Genial | May Hill | 18,063 | 8 | L Freedman | H Cecil | 10/11F |
| 14 Sept | Doncaster | Braka(USA) | | 3,200 | 12 | C A B St George | H Cecil | 7/2 |
| 15 Sept | Doncaster | Commanche Run | Holsten Pils St Leger | 110,700 | 14 | I Allan | L Cumani | 7/4F |
| 17 Sept | Goodwood | Bobo Ema | | 3,183 | 6 | C A B St George | P Kelleway | 5/1 |
| 18 Sept | Yarmouth | Field Conquerer | | 1,120 | 14 | M Fustok | H Cecil | 9/2 |
| 18 Sept | Yarmouth | That's Your Lot | Jack Leader Memorial | 6,054 | 7 | L Freedman | H Cecil | 7/1 |
| 19 Sept | Yarmouth | Make Strides (USA) | | 2,402 | 6 | Sheikh Mohammed | H Cecil | 13/8F |
| 20 Sept | Yarmouth | Dawn Star | | 1,296 | 10 | Windflower Overseas Holdings | J Dunlop | 6/4F |
| 22 Sept | Newbury | Miss Saint-Cloud | Peter Hastings | 7,830 | 10 | J L C Pearce | M Stoute | 10/3 |
| 24 Sept | Leicester | Master Wit(USA) | | 3,107 | 10 | S S Niarchos | H Cecil | 4/1F |
| 24 Sept | Sandown | Tom Boat | | 3,649 | 7 | J F C Bryce | R Armstrong | 10/1 |
| 27 Sept | Ascot | Prince Crow (USA) | Gordon Carter Hcp | 5,444 | 16 | Sir G White | M Stoute | 3/1F |
| 27 Sept | Ascot | Oh So Sharp | Hoover Mile | 21,498 | 8 | Sheikh Mohammed | H Cecil | 6/5F |
| 12 Oct | Ascot | Capricorn Belle | Marlborough House | 6,284 | 8 | I Allan | L Cumani | 6/4F |
| 13 Oct | Ascot | One Way Street | Princess Royal | 14,728 | 12 | L Freedman | H Cecil | 10/1 |
| 15 Oct | Sandown | Concorde Affair(USA) | | 2,964 | 8 | Mrs T Scheumann | H Cecil | 4/1 |
| 22 Oct | Leicester | Mary Davies | | 1,145 | 7 | C A B St George | H Cecil | 8/1 |
| 27 Oct | Doncaster | Roman Beach | Bedford Trucks Trophy | 5,120 | 8 | R C Graham | W Musson | 5/1 |
| 27 Oct | Doncaster | Lanfranco | Wm Hill Futurity | 41,798 | 8 | C A B St George | H Cecil | 10/3 |
| 6 Nov | Leicester | Lysander | | 1,477 | 8 | Lord Howard de Walden | H Cecil | 4/6F |
| 13 Nov | Newmarket | Jamesmead | | 2,627 | 12 | L Becker | D Elsworth | 7/2F |
| 1984: 100 wins; 79 2nds; 72 3rds; 491 rides | | | | | | | | |
| 1985 | | | | | | | | |
| 19 Apl | Newbury | Great Northern | | 3,204 | 8 | A J Struthers | J Dunlop | 8/11 |
| 20 Apl | Newbury | Bairn(USA) | Clerical Medical Greenham | 19,998 | 7 | Sheikh Mohammed | L Cumani | 11/10F |
| 4 May | Newmarket | Shadeed(USA) | General Accident 2000 gns | 94,689 | 8 | M Al Maktoum | M Stoute | 4/5F |
| 6 May | Kempton | Highland Image | | 2,721 | 7 | Mrs A Reid | R W Armstrong | 7/1 |
| 14 May | York | New Edition | | 3,505 | 5 | R J McAuley | B Hanbury | 2/5F |
| Match (with J Francome) Walton Hall Duel of Champions | | | | | | | | |
| 18 May | Warwick | The Liquidator | | | 14 | R Wheatley | M C Pipe | 1/2F |
| 27 May | Sandown | Commanche Run | Brigadier Gerard | 6,168 | 10 | I Allan | L Cumani | 11/10F |
| 1 June | Newmarket | Perkin Warbeck (USA) | | 908 | 8 | Sheikh Mohammed | L Cumani | 13/8F |
| 15 June | York | Top Ruler | Duchess of Kent | 5,790 | 6 | G Tong | R Armstrong | 7/4F |
| 18 June | Royal Ascot | Bairn(USA) | St James's Palace | 31,138 | 8 | Sheikh Mohammed | L Cumani | 6/4F |
| 21 June | Royal Ascot | Jupiter Island | Hardwicke | 28,006 | 12 | Marquess of Tavistock | C Brittain | 85/40 |
| 21 June | Royal Ascot | Never So Bold | King's Stand | 44,060 | 5 | E D Kessly | R Armstrong | 4/1 |
| 28 June | Doncaster | Khaki Nartak | | 1,053 | 7 | R Tikkoo | B Hanbury | 13/8F |

(USA) = America

| Date | Race Course | Horse | Race | Value £ | Dist Fur | Owner | Trainer | S/P |
|---|---|---|---|---|---|---|---|---|
| 28 June | Doncaster | Perkin Warbeck (USA) | | 920 | 8 | Sheikh Mohammed | L Cumani | 1/5F |
| 6 July | Doncaster | Black Hunter | | 4,006 | 11 | Sheikh Mohammed | M Stoute | 6/4F |
| 20 Aug | York | Commanche Run | Benson and Hedges Gold Cup | 93,600 | 10 | I Allan | L Cumani | 5/1 |
| 6 Sept | Kempton | Bambolona | Bonus Print Sirenia | 7,727 | 6 | D O McIntyre | R Sheather | 25/1 |
| 11 Sept | Doncaster | Eastern Mystic | Unipart Hcp | 18,455 | 14 | Maj R W Harden | L Cumani | 12/1 |
| 11 Sept | Doncaster | Storm Warning | Scarbrough | 9,505 | 5 | K H Fischer | W Hastings-Bass | 2/1 |
| 11 Sept | Doncaster | I Want To Be (USA) | Park Hill | 21,360 | 14 | Sheikh Mohammed | J Dunlop | 6/5F |
| 12 Sept | Doncaster | Midway Lady (USA) | May Hill | 15,423 | 8 | H H Ranier | B Hanbury | 11/2 |
| 14 Sept | Doncaster | Green Desert (USA) | Brian Swift Flying Childers | 15,702 | 5 | M Al Maktoum | M Stoute | EvF |
| 14 Sept | Doncaster | MacArthurs Head | Battle of Britain | 15,401 | 8 | A J Struthers | J Dunlop | 13/2 |
| 14 Sept | Doncaster | Perkin Warbeck (USA) | Holst Diat Pils Final | 10,791 | 10 | Sheikh Mohammed | L Cumani | 6/5F |
| 20 Sept | Ayr | Vienna Belle (USA) | | 1,571 | 7 | Mrs R S Rittenberry | J Dunlop | 11/8F |
| 21 Sept | Newbury | Eastern Mystic | | 1,026 | 13 | Maj R W Harden | L Cumani | 11/2 |
| 21 Sept | Newbury | Cyrano de Bergerac | | 4,006 | 5 | J L C Pearce | W Hastings-Bass | 11/2F |
| 27 Sept | Ascot | Fish'n Chips | Geranium Hcp | 7,921 | 10 | Dr M Boffa | L Cumani | 7/4F |
| 3 Oct | Newmarket | Cyrano de Bergerac | Bloodstock and General Insurance Nursery Hcp | 5,881 | 5 | J L C Pearce | W Hastings-Bass | 2/1F |
| 3 Oct | Newmarket | Perkin Warbeck (USA) | Choke Jade | 19,292 | 12 | Sheikh Mohammed | L Cumani | 2/1 |
| 4 Oct | Newmarket | Illumineux | | 4,191 | 7 | M Al Maktoum | M H Albina | 5/1 |
| 17 Oct | Newmarket | Cyrano de Bergerac | A R Dennis Nursery Hcp | 5,290 | 6 | J L C Pearce | W Hastings-Bass | 13/8F |
| 19 Oct | Newmarket | Tralthee(USA) | Chevington Stud Rockfel | 12,271 | 7 | A Clore | L Cumani | 9/1 |
| 29 Oct | Nottingham | Full Choke | Willington | 1,389 | 18 | Lady Macdonald-Buchanan | J Dunlop | 15/8F |

1985: 34 wins; 32 2nds; 30 3rds; 257 rides

Total British Wins on the Flat 4,349

(USA) = America

# Lester Piggott – Hurdle Wins

| Date | Race Course | Horse | Race | Value £ | Dist Mile | Owner | Trainer | S/P |
|---|---|---|---|---|---|---|---|---|
| 1953/4 | | | | | | | | |
| 26 Dec | Wincanton | Eldoret | Dartmouth Hcp Hurdle | 170 | 2m7f | T G Johnson | W Payne | EvF |
| 24 Feb | Ludlow | Strokes | Clee Selling Hurdle | 186 | 2 | J E Sutcliffe | K Piggott | 4/5F |
| 24 Feb | Ludlow | Deux Points | Stokesay Stayers Hurdle | 170 | 3 | H K Jones | K Piggott | 3/1F |
| 1 Mar | Worcester | Carola Pride | Astwood Hurdle | 136 | 2 | A W MacNamara | K Piggott | 15/8 |
| 2 Mar | Cheltenham | Mull Sack | Birdlip Selling Hurdle | 462 | 2 | J E Sutcliffe | K Piggott | 10/1 |
| 6 Mar | Hurst Park | Prince Charlemagne | Triumph Hurdle (4-yr-olds) | 1,370 | 2 | L Lipton | T H Carey | 11/4 |
| 8 Mar | Wolver'ton | Carola Pride | Gorsebrook National Hunt Hurdle (Novice Hurdle) | 204 | 2 | A W MacNamara | K Piggott | 8/13F |
| 10 Mar | Windsor | Deux Points | Waterloo Long Distance Hurdle | 170 | 3 | H K Jones | K Piggott | 4/1 |
| 10 Mar | Newbury | Stranger | Hants (Maiden) Hurdle II | 204 | 2 | Lady Baron | W Payne | 5/2JF |

1953/4: 9 wins; 3 2nds; 4 3rds; 25 rides

| Date | Race Course | Horse | Race | Value £ | Dist Mile | Owner | Trainer | S/P |
|---|---|---|---|---|---|---|---|---|
| 1954/5 | | | | | | | | |
| 28 Dec | Wolver'ton | Dessin | Walsall Hcp Hurdle | 170 | 2 | H J Barlow | F Hudson | 3/1F |

1954/5: 1 win; 2 2nds; 3 3rds; 15 rides

| Date | Race Course | Horse | Race | Value £ | Dist Mile | Owner | Trainer | S/P |
|---|---|---|---|---|---|---|---|---|
| 1956/7 | | | | | | | | |
| 29 Nov | Kempton | Royal Task | Barnes Selling Hurdle | 286 | 2 | O/trainer | K Piggott | 9/4F |
| 12 Dec | Sandown | Royal Task | Winter Selling Hurdle | 186 | 2 | O/trainer | K Piggott | 4/6F |
| 12 Dec | Sandown | Rich Bloom | December Juvenile Hurdle (3-yr-olds) | 204 | 2 | C W Bell | W Nightingall | 13/8F |
| 12 Jan | Newbury | Royal Task | Faringdon Hurdle | 272 | 2½ | P B Raymond | K Piggott | 5/1 |
| 9 Feb | Hurst Park | Ocean King | Weir Selling Hurdle | 186 | 2 | P B Raymond | K Piggott | 13/8 |
| 27 Feb | Windsor | Ocean King | Waterloo Long Distance Hurdle | 204 | 3 | P B Raymond | K Piggott | 7/4F |

1956/7: 6 wins; 1 2nd; 9 rides

| Date | Race Course | Horse | Race | Value £ | Dist Mile | Owner | Trainer | S/P |
|---|---|---|---|---|---|---|---|---|
| 1957/8 | | | | | | | | |
| 17 Jan | Sandown | Royal Task | Winter Selling Hurdle | 284 | 2 | P B Raymond | K Piggott | 4/9F |
| 12 Feb | Newbury | Wild Knave | Compton National Hunt Hurdle (Novice Hurdle) | 204 | 2 | E Sturman | B Marshall | 5/2F |

1957/8: 2 wins; 3 rides

| Date | Race Course | Horse | Race | Value £ | Dist Mile | Owner | Trainer | S/P |
|---|---|---|---|---|---|---|---|---|
| 1958/9 | | | | | | | | |
| 6 Feb | Windsor | Royal Task | Cobham Selling Hurdle | 186 | 2 | P B Raymond | K Piggott | 8/13F |
| 13 Feb | Sandown | Jive | Spring Selling Hurdle (4-yr-olds) | 284 | 2 | C Steuart | K Piggott | 6/4F |

1958/9: 2 wins; 2 rides

Total British Wins over Hurdles 20

# Lester Piggott – Overseas Wins

Although the totals of overseas wins are accurate, only the major races have been listed.

| Major wins | Race Course | Year | Horse | Number of wins |
|---|---|---|---|---|
| ARGENTINA | | | | 2 |
| AUSTRALIA | | | | 19 |
| International Riders Stks | Brisbane | 1969 | Duchesne | |
| Morphetville Schweppes Oaks | Adelaide | 1985 | Centaurea | |
| AUSTRIA | | | | 0 |
| BAHREIN | | | | 2 |
| BELGIUM | | | | 4 |
| Gran International D'Ostende | Ostend | 1958 | Orsini | |
| Bruxelles Ex Grand Prix | Brussels | 1958 | Orsini | |
| Criterium D'Ostende | Ostend | | | |
| BRAZIL | | | | 1 |
| CANADA | | | | 1 |
| Woodbine International | Woodbine, Toronto | | Dahlia | |
| Rothmans | | | | |
| DENMARK | | | | 2 |
| Scandinavian Open Championship | Klampenborg | 1977 | Trainers Seat | |
| | Klampenborg | 1978 | Pollerton | |
| FRANCE | | | | 352 |
| Pr' d'Essai des Pouliches | Longchamp | 1964 | Rajput Princess | |
| Pr Robert Papin | Maisons-Laffitte | 1965 | Kashmir II | |
| Pr Vermeille | Longchamp | 1965 | Aunt Edith | |
| Grand Critorium | Longchamp | 1967 | Sir Ivor | |
| Pr Gladiateur | Longchamp | 1967 | Alciglide | |
| Pr Maurice de Gheest | Longchamp | 1968 | Mountain Call | |
| Pr Maurice de Nieuil | Saint-Cloud | 1969 | Copsale | |
| Pr de Reux | Deauville | 1969 | Copsale | |
| Poule d'Essai Longchamp 2000 and 1000 | Longchamp | 1969 | Copsale | |
| Pr Diane | Chantilly | 1969 | Copsale | |
| Pr de Jockey Club | Chantilly | 1969 | Copsale | |
| Pr Royal-Oak | Longchamp | 1969 | Copsale | |
| Pr Quincey | Deauville | 1969 | Habitat | |
| Pr Henri Foy | Longchamp | 1969 | Park Top | |

| Major wins | Race Course | Year | Horse | Number of wins |
|---|---|---|---|---|
| Cape de Maisons-Laffitte | Maisons-Laffitte | 1969 | Karabas | |
| Pr de l'Abbaye de Longchamp | Longchamp | 1969 | Tower Walk | |
| Pr du Moulin de Longchamp | Longchamp | 1969 | Habitat | |
| Criterium des Pouliches | Longchamp | 1969 | Vela | |
| Grand Criterium | Longchamp | 1969 | Breton | |
| Pr du Conseil Municipal | Longchamp | 1969 | Karabas | |
| Pr de Pomone | Deauville | 1970 | Santa Tina | |
| Coup de Longchamp | Longchamp | 1970 | Park Top | |
| Pr du Royaumont | Chantilly | 1970 | Santa Tina | |
| Gran Pr du Paris | Longchamp | 1970 | Roll of Honour | |
| Pr Robert Papin | Maisons-Laffitte | 1970 | My Swallow | |
| Pr Kergurlay | Deauville | 1970 | Reindeer | |
| Pr de la Côte Normande | Deauville | 1970 | Gold Rod | |
| Pr Morny | Deauville | 1970 | My Swallow | |
| Pr Quincey | Deauville | 1970 | Lorenzaccio | |
| Pr de la Nonette | Longchamp | 1970 | Popkins | |
| Pr Henri Foy | Longchamp | 1970 | Lorenzaccio | |
| Pr de la Salamandre | Longchamp | 1970 | My Swallow | |
| Pr Henry Delamarre | Longchamp | 1970 | Golden Monad | |
| Pr de l'Abbaye de Longchamp | Longchamp | 1970 | Balidar | |
| Pr du Moulin | Longchamp | 1970 | Gold Rod | |
| Grand Criterium | Longchamp | 1970 | My Swallow | |
| Pr de la Salamandre | Longchamp | 1971 | Our Mirage | |
| Pr Royallieu | Longchamp | 1971 | Example | |
| Pr Mesidor | Saint-Cloud | 1971 | Joshua | |
| Pr Lupin | Longchamp | 1972 | Hard to Beat | |
| Pr Maurice de Gheest | Deauville | 1972 | Abergwaun | |
| Pr de la Côte Normandie | Deauville | 1972 | Jolly Me | |
| Pr du Jockey Club | Chantilly | 1972 | Hard to Beat | |
| Pr Meautry | Deauville | 1972 | Some Hand | |
| Pr Niel | Deauville | 1972 | Hard to Beat | |
| Pr Henry Delamarre | Longchamp | 1972 | Roulton | |
| Pr la Force | Longchamp | 1973 | White Spade | |
| Pr Nouailles | Longchamp | 1973 | Eddystone | |
| Pr Morny | Deauville | 1973 | Nonoalco | |
| Pr Salamandre | Longchamp | 1973 | Nonoalco | |
| Pr de Seine et Oise | Maisons-Laffitte | 1973 | Abergwaun | |
| Pr de l'Arc de Triomphe | Longchamp | 1973 | Rheingold | |
| Pr du Moulin de Longchamp | Longchamp | 1973 | Sparkler | |
| Pr de l'Esperante | Longchamp | 1974 | Sagaro | |
| Pr Jacques le Marois | Deauville | 1974 | Nonoalco | |
| Pr de la Grotto | Longchamp | 1975 | Nobiliary(USA) | |
| Pr de Chemin de Fer | Chantilly | 1975 | Son of Silver | |
| Pr du Petit Coubrit | Longchamp | 1975 | Realty(USA) | |
| Pr de Saint-Georges | Longchamp | 1975 | Flirting Around | |
| Pr St-Alary | Longchamp | 1975 | Nobiliary(USA) | |
| Jean Prat | Chantilly | 1975 | Speedy Dakota(USA) | |
| La Coupe | Maisons-Laffitte | 1975 | Son of Silver | |
| La Coupe | St Cloud | 1975 | Beauvallon(F) | |
| Pr Niel | Longchamp | 1976 | Youth | |
| Pr de l'Arc de Triomphe | Longchamp | 1977 and 1978 | Alleged | |
| Pr Gladiateur | Longchamp | 1977 and 1978 | John Cherry | |
| Pr Ganay | Longchamp | 1978 | Trillion(USA) | |
| Pr Dollar | Longchamp | 1978 | Trillion(USA) | |
| Jean Prat | Chantilly | 1978 | Dom Racine | |
| Pr Henri Foy | Longchamp | 1978 | Trillion(USA) | |
| Pr Dollar | Longchamp | 1979 | Trillion(USA) | |
| Pr d'Astarte | Deauville | 1979 | Topsy | |

| Major wins | Race Course | Year | Horse | Number of wins |
|---|---|---|---|---|
| Pr de l'Opera | Longchamp | 1979 | Producer | |
| Gr Pr de Deauville | Deauville | 1980 | Glencrum(Can) | |
| Pr de Diane de Revlon | Chantilly | 1980 | Mrs Penny | |
| Pr de l'Abbaye de Longchamp | Longchamp | 1980 | Moorestyle | |
| Pr de la Forêt | Longchamp | 1980 | Moorestyle | |
| Pr Greffulhe | Longchamp | 1981 | The Wonder | |
| French Oaks | Chantilly | 1981 | Madam Gay | |
| Pr Maurice de Geest | Deauville | 1981 | Moorestyle | |
| Pr Marcel Boussac | Maisons-Laffitte | 1981 | Play it Safe | |
| Pr de la Fort | Maisons-Laffitte | 1981 | Moorestyle | |
| Pr Royal Oak | Maisons-Laffitte | 1981 | Ardross | |
| Pr Noailles | Longchamp | 1982 | Persepolis | |
| French 1000 Gns | Longchamp | 1982 | River Lady | |
| Pr Lupin | Longchamp | 1982 | Persepolis | |
| Pr de la Cascade | Longchamp | 1983 | Treizième(USA) | |
| A la Force | Longchamp | 1983 | White Spade | |
| Pr de la Jonchere | Longchamp | 1983 | Aragon | |
| Pr de la Grotte | Longchamp | 1984 | Treizième(USA) | |
| Pr de Royaumont | Chantilly | 1985 | Galla Placida | |
| Pr de Diane | Chantilly | 1985 | Lypharita | |
| GERMANY | | | | 27 |
| German Derby | Hamburg | 1958 | Orsini | |
| Munich Gr Pr der Spielbank | Munich | 1972 | Sparkler | |
| Gettingen – Reonen | Baden-Baden | 1974 | Ace of Aces(USA) | |
| 4 races on Aracari | Dusseldorf and Baden-Baden | 1978 | Aracari | |
| Preis von Europa | Cologne | 1978 | Esprit du Nord | |
| Gettingen – Reonen | Baden-Baden | 1985 | Hot Rodder(USA) | |
| GREECE | | | | 11 |
| HOLLAND | | | | 0 |
| HONG KONG | | | | 29 |
| Invitation Cup | Happy Valley | 1977 | | |
| INDIA | | | | 8 |
| Calcutta Derby | Calcutta | 1968 | Fair Haven | |
| IRELAND | | | | 176 |
| Irish Sweeps Derby | Curragh | 1965 | Meadow Court | |
| Irish Sweeps Derby | Curragh | 1967 | Ribocco | |
| Irish St Leger | Curragh | 1967 | Dan Kano | |
| Royal Ulster Harp Lager Derby | Down Royal | 1967 | Dan Kano | |
| Irish Sweeps Derby | Curragh | 1968 | Ribero | |
| Irish 2000 Gns | Curragh | 1970 | Decies | |
| Irish Oaks | Curragh | 1970 | Santa Tina | |
| Gladness | Curragh | 1971 | Minsky | |
| The Tetrarch | Curragh | 1971 | Minsky | |
| 1000 Gns | Curragh | 1971 | Favoletta | |
| Pretty Polly | Curragh | 1971 | Mariel | |
| Carling Blue Label | Leopardstown | 1971 | Mariel | |
| Carling Blue Label | Phoenix Park | 1973 | Thatch(USA) | |
| Ballymoss | Curragh | 1973 | Cavo Doro | |
| The Tetrarch | Curragh | 1973 | Dapper(USA) | |
| Royal Whip | Curragh | 1973 | Cavo Doro | |
| Player-Wills | Leopardstown | 1973 | Hail the Pirates | |
| Player-Wills | Curragh | 1973 | Hail the Pirates | |
| Angelsey | Curragh | 1973 | Saritimer | |
| Angelsey | Curragh | 1973 | Cellini | |

| Major wins | Race Course | Year | Horse | Number of wins |
|---|---|---|---|---|
| Beresford | Curragh | 1973 | Saritimer | |
| The Tetrarch | Curragh | 1974 | Cellini | |
| Gladness | Curragh | 1974 | Apalachee | |
| Vauxhall | Phoenix Park | 1974 | Cellini | |
| Vauxhall | Curragh | 1974 | Lisadell | |
| Nijinsky | Leopardstown | 1974 | Hail the Pirates | |
| Blandford | Curragh | 1974 | Richard Grenville | |
| Guinness Oaks | Curragh | 1975 | Juliette Marny | |
| Railway | Curragh | 1975 | Niebo(USA) | |
| Blandford | Curragh | 1975 | King Pellinore | |
| Angelsey | Curragh | 1975 | Niebo(USA) | |
| National | Curragh | 1975 | Sir Wimborne | |
| Irish St Leger | Curragh | 1975 | Caucasus(USA) | |
| Mulcahy | Phoenix Park | 1976 | I've a Bee | |
| Bally Sax | Curragh | 1976 | Meneval(USA) | |
| Nijinsky | Leopardstown | 1976 | Meneval(USA) | |
| Gallinule | Curragh | 1976 | Meneval(USA) | |
| Railway | Curragh | 1976 | Brahms(USA) | |
| Diamond | Curragh | 1976 | Nier(USA) | |
| Irish St Leger | Curragh | 1976 | Meneval(USA) | |
| Ashford Castle | Curragh | 1976 | Padroug(USA) | |
| Ashford Castle | Leopardstown | 1976 | Malacate(USA) | |
| Larkspur | Leopardstown | 1976 | The Minstrel | |
| Gallinule | Curragh | 1977 | Alleged | |
| Irish Sweeps Derby | Curragh | 1977 | The Minstrel | |
| Irish Cambridgeshire | Curragh | 1977 | Poachers Moon | |
| Airlie Coolmore Sprint Champ | Curragh | 1977 | Godswalk(USA) | |
| Irish 2000 Gns | Curragh | 1978 | Jazzeiro | |
| Vauxhall | Phoenix Park | 1978 | Try My Best | |
| Royal Whip | Curragh | 1978 | Alleged | |
| Gallinule | Curragh | 1978 | Inkermann | |
| Probationers | Curragh | 1978 | Miami Springs | |
| Park | Phoenix Park | 1978 | Solar(USA) | |
| Whitehall | Phoenix Park | 1978 | Stradivarius | |
| Gilltown Stud | Curragh | 1978 | Kalamaika | |
| Liam Flood Autumn | Curragh | 1978 | Aristocracy | |
| Airlie-Coolmore | Curragh | 1978 | Solinus | |
| Airlie-Coolmore | Leopardstown | 1978 | Inkermann(USA) | |
| Athasi | Curragh | 1979 | Godetia | |
| Greenlands | Curragh | 1979 | Golden Thatch | |
| Goff's Irish 1000 Gns | Curragh | 1979 | Godetia | |
| Pretty Polly | Curragh | 1979 | Godetia | |
| Greenlands | Curragh | 1979 | Golden Thatch(USA) | |
| Gladness | Curragh | 1980 | Night Alert | |
| Gallinule | Curragh | 1980 | Gonzales | |
| Gallinule | Curragh | 1980 | Calandra | |
| July Scurry | Curragh | 1980 | Miss Pudoe | |
| Irish Sweeps Derby | Curragh | 1981 | Shergar | |
| Magyn TV | Curragh | 1983 | Hegemany | |
| Tattersalls Rogers Gold Cup | Curragh | 1985 | Elegant Air | |
| Gallinule | Curragh | 1985 | Lord Duke | |
| Phoenix Champion | Phoenix Park | 1985 | Commanche Run | |
| | | | | |
| ITALY | | | | 36 |
| Gr Pr de Jockey Club Milan | Milan | 1958 | Nagami | |
| Gr Pr de Jockey Club Milan | Milan | 1965 | Atilla | |
| Gr Pr de Milan | Milan | 1966 | Marco Visconti | |
| Italian Derby | Milan | 1969 | Bonconte di Monte Feltro | |
| Pr Roma | Rome | 1972 | Irvine | |
| Italian Derby | Rome | 1973 | Cerreto | |
| Pr Presidente della Republica | Rome | 1973 | Moulton | |
| Pr Chilfura | Milan | 1979 | Absalom | |

| Major wins | Race Course | Year | Horse | Number of wins |
|---|---|---|---|---|
| Pr Roma | Rome | 1979 | Noble Saint | |
| Gran Premio de Milano | Milan | 1981 | Kirtling | |
| Pr Ribot | Rome | 1981 | Vargas Llosa | |
| Gr Pr de Jockey Club | Milan | 1983 | Awaasif(USA) | |
| Emanuele Filiberto | Milan | 1984 | Awaasif(USA) | |
| Italian Derby | Rome | 1984 | Welnor | |
| Chiuscira | Rome | 1984 | Capricorn Belle | |
| Pr Roma | Rome | 1985 | Old Country | |
| JAMAICA | | | | 11 |
| JAPAN | | | | 0 |
| JERSEY | | | | 2 |
| KENYA | | | | 1 |
| MALAYSIA | | | | 30 |
| Ritz Club Gold Trophy | Kuala Lumpur | 1983 | Ontario | |
| NEW ZEALAND | | | | 7 |
| NORWAY | | | | 7 |
| Oslo Cup | Övrevoll | 1958 | Orsini | |
| PUERTO RICO | | | | 0 |
| RHODESIA | | | | 3 |
| SINGAPORE | | | | 45 |
| Queen Elizabeth Cup | Bukit Timah | 1972 | Jumbo Jet | |
| Lion City Cup | Bukit Timah | 1976 | Blue Star | |
| Lion City Cup | Bukit Timah | 1977 | Blue Star | |
| Lion City Cup | Bukit Timah | 1978 | Gentle Jim | |
| Tunku Gold Cup | Bukit Timah | 1979 | Dragon Command | |
| Singapore Derby | Bukit Timah | 1979 | Saas Fee | |
| SOUTH AFRICA | | | | 19 |
| SPAIN | | | | 5 |
| SWEDEN | | | | 7 |
| Swedish Derby | Täby | 1958 | Flying Friendship | |
| Jocky Championship | Täby | 1979 | Flying Friendship | |
| Swedish St Leger | Täby | 1980 | Kansas | |
| SWITZERLAND | | | | 0 |
| TRINIDAD | | | | 1 |
| USA | | | | 12 |
| Washington International | Laurel | 1968 | Sir Ivor | |
| Washington International | Laurel | 1969 | Karabas | |
| Washington International | Laurel | 1980 | Argument(F) | |
| VENEZUELA | | | | 0 |

Minimum Total Overseas Wins 822

| | |
|---|---|
| British Flat Race Wins | 4,349 |
| British Hurdles Wins | 20 |
| Minimum Total Overseas Wins | 822 |
| Minimum Total | 5,191 |

# Index

# Index

The names of horses are set in *italic*